The Essential Reference for the

Database Engine Used in

Microsoft Windows® 95

Applications and

Programming

Environments

# Microsoft®
# Jet
# Database Engine
# Programmer's Guide

PUBLISHED BY
Microsoft Press
A Division of Microsoft Corporation
One Microsoft Way
Redmond, Washington 98052-6399

Library of Congress Cataloging-in-Publication Data
Microsoft Jet database engine programmer's guide / Microsoft Press.
     p.  cm.
   Includes index.
   ISBN 1-55615-877-7
   1. Database management.  2. Microsoft Jet.  I. Haught, Dan.
II. Ferguson, Jim.  III. Microsoft Press.
QA76.9.D3M573    1995
005.75'65--dc20                          95-39132
                                          CIP

Printed and bound in the United States of America.

1 2 3 4 5 6 7 8 9  MLML  0 9 8 7 6 5

Distributed to the book trade in Canada by Macmillan of Canada, a division of Canada Publishing
Corporation.

A CIP catalogue record for this book is available from the British Library.

**Acquisitions Editor:** Casey D. Doyle
**Project Editor:** Brenda L. Matteson

# Contents

# Foreword

Welcome to the *Microsoft Jet Database Engine Programmer's Guide*. If you're a database developer who wants to know more about what's really going on behind the scenes within the Microsoft® Jet database engine and Data Access Objects (DAO), this guide was created for you: It's designed to help you get the most out of Microsoft Jet. From speaking with many database developers at conferences and trade shows, holding beta forums, and corresponding through e-mail, I know that many of you are hungry for information that goes beyond the initial how-to material.

When I was trying to convince my teammates here in the Data Access and Retrieval Technologies (DART) group that this guide would be worth our time and energy, one of my most persuasive arguments was that so few people are using all of Microsoft Jet's cool functionality: features such as heterogeneous updatable joins, nested stored queries, multiple transparent data formats, advanced SQL syntax (UNION and sub-SELECT queries), and the new client/server controls. These features are often overlooked—even by advanced developers who've been designing database applications for years.

If you already know Microsoft Jet but want technical information about features new to Microsoft Jet 3.0, this guide gives you the low down: information on the new data replication capabilities, details on how to use DAO from C++ (including header files and sample programs on the CD-ROM), and the nitty-gritty on all the new Microsoft Jet Registry settings. There's even a BNF description of the Microsoft Jet SQL syntax and a list of all errors that Microsoft Jet can produce (also in a database on the CD-ROM). You also get:

- Internal information previously known only by the software developers who write Microsoft Jet.

- Tips from the testers who've each written more code using Microsoft Jet than most development teams write in a lifetime.

- Expanded information that was left out of product documentation because it was "too technical."

- Insights from people like me who designed Microsoft Jet and DAO.

- Common pitfalls, traps, and useful techniques from the talented product support engineers who take your phone calls.

- Tables and appendixes that assemble technical errata into a useful form.

Ideally, the entire DART team—writers, developers, designers, product support engineers, and testers—would have written this guide, with each person focusing on his or her specialty. The result would be a compendium of all possible Microsoft Jet knowledge. But if everyone on the team were writing, we wouldn't be shipping any new products!

Fortunately, we solved this dilemma. We wrote a superior guide *and* created some powerful new software. How? We were lucky to enlist two prominent Microsoft Jet users to work in collaboration with the DART team. I have no idea how Dan Haught decrypted our tortured and jumbled e-mail messages explaining the intricacies of Microsoft Jet, nor why Jim Ferguson chose to take on the task of demystifying SQL statement execution. However, their real-world experience with using Microsoft Jet and DAO tempered the raw technical information the team provided, producing a stronger, more relevant guide.

But even with Dan's and Jim's expert help, this guide would not exist if it weren't for the hundred-odd folk that comprise the DART team. They took time out of their already overloaded schedules to bring this information to you. Why? So you could make even better use of the tools DART labors to create for you. As I'm sure you can appreciate, we like to see our work used, and used well. Study this guide, play with the examples, write some code, run some queries. I know that you'll produce faster, smaller, and more robust database applications, and maybe even have some fun in the process!

Cheers,

Michael Mee
DAO Program Manager

# Acknowledgments

This guide was possible only through the combined efforts of a large number of people at Microsoft and in the database developer community.

The authors would like to thank the managers of the Data Access and Retrieval Technologies (DART) group at Microsoft, especially Theresa Daly and Dennis Comfort for their support of the guide's concept and for allocating the necessary resources. We would also like to thank Mike Mee and Maya Opavska for conceiving of the idea for the guide and for their close guidance of the guide's design and contents. Maya was especially instrumental in moving the guide from an idea to a reality by recruiting the authors, gathering resources, and negotiating publication with Microsoft Press.

Several people outside of the DART group provided both moral and logistical support, and we are indebted to them. We would like to thank Casey Doyle at Microsoft Press for believing in the guide's importance and in DART's ability to make it happen. We thank Brenda Matteson for guiding us through the high standards and production processes of Microsoft Press. We would also like to thank Frida Kumar and Claudia Mazzie-Ballheim for providing encouragement and resources in the early stages of the guide, and Robin Lyle for organizing the complexities of the project into a coherent timetable of milestones.

Throughout the writing and production of the guide, we asked many different types of professionals to review and comment on the material. These people included those who developed portions of the Microsoft Jet database engine, who develop products that incorporate the engine, and who use the engine on a daily basis. We are especially indebted to the core technical contributors who allowed us to include portions of the white papers and other documents they have written and who took time to carefully check the technical explanations we drafted. These core contributors include Neil Black, Evan Callahan, Kevin Collins, Greg Ellison, Steve Hecht, John McCullough, Michael Mee, Maya Opavska, Bruce Schatzman, Peter Tucker, and Jim Wilson. You can read about these people in "About the Technical Contributors."

We would also like to thank a large number of reviewers who provided us with comments, suggestions, technical corrections, and supplementary information: Mahbubul Alam Ali, Trudy Anthony-Hoppe, Kam Foo Aw, Mary Bacon, Raj Batra, Marc Beck, Ryan Beegle, MariEsther Burnham, David Cameron, Beth Chapman, Vince Curley, Curtis Deems, Peter Diemert, Phillip Durr, Nigel Ellis, Robert Fifer, Phillip Garding, Naveen Garg, Arman Gharib, Goetz Graefe, Brad

Hammond, Jim Hance, Kimberly Harms, Mark Johnson, Emily Kruglick, Tamra Myers, Sylvia Moestl, Charu Narayanan, Richard Patterson, Michael Pizzo, Balaji Rathakrishnan, Monte Slichter, Gordon Smith, Ron Pihlgren, Tony Poll, Terence Richards, Lynn Shanklin, Michael Shulman, George Snelling, Murali Venkatrao, Lee Woods, and Tom Woods.

In the final stages of writing, we asked five respected developers to serve as external reviewers and help us identify areas that still needed improvement. We would like to thank Ken Getz, Michael Gunderloy, Michael Kaplan, Stan Leszynski, and Michael Liczbanski for their expert opinion and guidance.

A team of three editors, an artist, a code tester, and an indexer made sure that what you are about to read is understandable and that it works. Our special thanks to Nicole Fischer, Pam Turner, and Diana Boyle for long hours of editing, to Steven Fulgham for translating our rough sketches into finished art, to Jerry Flynn for testing the 100+ code examples, to Sam Dawson for his work indexing the entire guide, and to Ken Lassesen for his map of the DAO hierarchy. We'd also like to thank Pamela Anderson-Zaki, Martha White, and Cristina Chapman for their assistance in the design of the companion CD-ROM and for converting our files into online form, and Mike McKay, who helped us obtain the hardware and software tools required to produce the guide.

Warm thanks go to Peter Bateman, who, in addition to writing a chapter, pulled the project together, surprised us with his resourcefulness and patience, and managed to remember those details that everyone else forgot.

We save our final and most heartfelt thanks for Melissa Shaw, who solved the myriad technical production problems for the printed guide as well as for the companion CD-ROM. Melissa's skills made the guide take the final form that you see.


Sincerely,


The Authors

# About the Authors

**Dan Haught** handles product development for FMS, Inc. in Vienna, Virginia. He's been developing database applications and tools on a variety of platforms for more than ten years and developing database tools for Microsoft Access for the last three years. Dan is a contributing editor to *Access Advisor* magazine and has written extensively on Microsoft Access. He is a co-author of *Microsoft Access 2.0 How-To* from the Waite Group Press and writes database articles for a variety of journals. Dan has also written documentation for Microsoft Access and has been a featured speaker at Microsoft's Tech Ed conferences.

**Jim Ferguson** is a custom database developer for FMS, Inc. in Vienna, Virginia. He has been working with Microsoft Access and Visual Basic® since those products were first released, and was awarded the Microsoft MVP (Most Valuable Professional) award for his work on the CompuServe® MSBASIC and MSACCESS forums.

**Peter Bateman** is a database developer for Digital Information Services in Seattle, Washington. Over the last 12 years, he has built custom database applications for education research, real estate management, trade show and convention management, child protective services, and international conference management. In addition to his other responsibilities, Peter is a technical writer in the Data Access and Retrieval Technologies User Education group at Microsoft and currently manages the *Microsoft Jet Database Engine Programmer's Guide*.

**Mark Bukovec** is a programmer writer in the Data Access and Retrieval Technologies User Education group at Microsoft. Mark is currently the documentation lead for the upcoming OLE DB SDK. He has previously worked on the Microsoft Open Database Connectivity (ODBC) and DAO SDKs. Prior to joining DART, Mark was an editor for Visual C++™ and Win32 SDK documentation.

**Joel Gilman** is the lead writer for Microsoft Jet and DAO documentation in the DART User Education group at Microsoft. He began writing for Microsoft Jet and DAO with Microsoft Access 2.0. Prior to that, he was a member of the original team that created Microsoft Omega, the Microsoft Windows® database management system that became Microsoft Access. He's also worked on Visual Basic 4.0, Microsoft C 5.0, and the OS/2® Presentation Manager®.

**Jim Gordon** is a programmer writer in the Data Access and Retrieval Technologies User Education group at Microsoft. Jim worked as a computing consultant and instructor at North Carolina State University and the Institute for Academic Technology until 1990, when he left academia and started writing technical documentation. His work includes documentation for DaVinci eMAIL, Paradox® for DOS, Paradox for Windows, Paradox SQL Link, the Essbase™ Multidimensional Analysis System, TGV MultiNet, and Microsoft Access. Jim currently works on the OLE DB Software Development Kit.

**Jim Van de Erve** is a programmer writer in the Data Access and Retrieval Technologies User Education group at Microsoft. His responsibilities include documentation for Microsoft ODBC and Desktop Database Drivers. He has 15 years of experience as a technical writer in the computer, electronics, telecommunications, and aerospace industries.

# About the Technical Contributors

**Neil Black** is a program manager in the Data Access and Retrieval Technologies group at Microsoft. He's currently the lead program manager for the Microsoft Jet query engine. Neil began his Microsoft career more than six years ago as a tester for Microsoft Omega. He has also been program manager for the ODBC Desktop Database Drivers versions 2.*x* and 3.*x*.

**Evan Callahan** owns Callahan Software Solutions, a database consulting firm specializing in Microsoft Access. He worked for Microsoft from 1989 to 1995, where he created documentation, online Help, and sample applications for Microsoft Access and Visual Basic. Evan has also delivered training in Microsoft Access and spoken at Microsoft Tech Ed and other conferences.

**Kevin Collins** is a program manager in the Data Access and Retrieval Technologies group at Microsoft. He works on performance-related issues for the Microsoft Jet database engine used in Microsoft Access and Visual Basic. Prior to Microsoft, Kevin worked at Microrim® and contributed to performance improvements for the R:BASE® database engine.

**Gregory Ellison** is a senior technical writer for the Visual Basic group at Microsoft, where he is currently responsible for data access and client/server documentation. Before joining Microsoft in 1993, Gregory was documentation manager for Borland® C++. He's been a software developer and technical writer since 1972.

**Steve Hecht** is currently a software design engineer in the Interactive Television group at Microsoft. Steve started at Microsoft in 1989 and was a member of the Microsoft Jet database engine development team for four years. He also worked on the development of the Upsizer and Table Analyzer wizards in Microsoft Access for Windows 95.

**Emily Kruglick** is a software test engineer in the Data Access and Retrieval Technologies group at Microsoft. She tests the Data Access Objects used by Microsoft Access and Visual Basic, focusing on client/server implementations. Before coming to Microsoft she was a computer consultant specializing in client/server application development.

**Maya Opavska** is the user education manager for the Data Access and Retrieval Technologies User Education group at Microsoft. Maya's been documenting software products since 1981, primarily as technical writer for network software, OS software, and databases. She started at Microsoft on the SQL Server team, where she specialized in configuration and troubleshooting documents.

**John McCullough** is a C++ programmer for Avatar Consulting who worked on the DAO SDK included in Visual C++ 4.0. He holds a BA in electrical engineering and an MS in software engineering from Seattle University.

**Michael Mee** is a program manager in the Data Access and Retrieval Technologies group at Microsoft. Michael designs and coordinates the Data Access Objects used by Microsoft Access, Visual Basic, Visual C++ and other Microsoft products. While at Microsoft, he's worked on programmability in Microsoft Access 1.*x*, and has designed parts of FoxPro® 2.5, including its support for DDE and OLE. His Microsoft experience builds on several years as a software engineer in the database industry, a BS in applied mathematics, and an honors degree in computer science.

**Bruce Schatzman** is a computer industry consultant with 15 years of experience in application design and development. Bruce is president of BDS Consulting in Mercer Island, Washington, which provides custom application design and programming services to clients throughout the United States. BDS Consulting specializes in database design and implementation using Microsoft Access, and application development with Visual Basic and Visual C++.

**Dave Sell** is a program manager in the Data Access and Retrieval Technologies group at Microsoft. He is involved with the Microsoft Jet database engine used in Microsoft Access and Visual Basic and works on the Installable ISAMs. Prior to Microsoft, Dave worked for Autodesk®, Inc. as a development manager on the Generic CADD product lines. Dave has also worked for Microrim as a lead development engineer.

**Keith Toussaint** is a program manager in the Data Access and Retrieval Technologies group at Microsoft. He is involved in the design and development of next-generation Microsoft Jet technology. Keith holds a BSEE and has over 14 years of experience in many aspects of the software industry.

**Peter Tucker** is a test lead in the Data Access and Retrieval Technologies group at Microsoft. He has been test lead for the Data Access Objects programming interface to Microsoft Jet since DAO 1.1. Peter's also written and executed multiuser tests on Microsoft Jet and helped ship versions of Microsoft Access and Visual Basic.

# Preface

Since its introduction in 1992, the Microsoft Jet database engine has been in a unique position. Because Microsoft Jet is not a stand-alone product—you cannot buy it at your local software retailer—most developers who use it have learned about its functionality in a second-hand fashion from the documentation included in Microsoft Access or Visual Basic. Previously, no one has written a guide that fully describes Microsoft Jet on its own terms. This is that guide.

The *Microsoft Jet Database Engine Programmer's Guide* is the definitive reference for all users of Microsoft Jet, from developers programming in applications such as Microsoft Access and Microsoft Excel, to those working in a dedicated programming environment such as Visual Basic or Visual C++. This guide offers comprehensive coverage of all aspects of Microsoft Jet, including the structure of the engine, the services it provides, and complete examples showing how to use its functionality in your development projects.

## Who This Guide Is For

Because many applications use Microsoft Jet, this guide is directed toward a large audience of developers and programmers. If you are leafing through this guide, chances are you already have at least a rough idea of what Microsoft Jet is and where it is used. As of this writing, the following applications use various versions of Microsoft Jet.

| Application | Microsoft Jet version |
| --- | --- |
| Microsoft Access 1.0 | 1.0 |
| Microsoft Access 1.1 | 1.1 |
| Microsoft Access 2.0 | 2.0 and 2.5 |
| Microsoft Access for Windows 95 | 3.0 |
| Visual Basic 3.0 | 1.1 (or 2.0 using the Visual Basic compatibility layer) |
| Visual Basic 4.0 (16-bit) | 2.5 |
| Visual Basic 4.0 (32-bit) | 3.0 |
| Microsoft Excel | 3.0 |
| Microsoft Project 4.0 and Microsoft Project for Windows 95 | 2.0 |
| Microsoft Foundation Classes (MFC) | 3.0 |

Although this guide will be most helpful if you are primarily developing database applications in Microsoft Access, Visual Basic, or Visual C++, it also provides invaluable information for users of Microsoft Excel and other Microsoft Office applications.

## What This Guide Covers

This guide covers Microsoft Jet 3.0. All examples throughout this guide are compatible with this version. Special notes are placed throughout that describe differences between version 3.0 and earlier versions.

## What You Should Already Know

This guide is written to enhance your existing database knowledge with information specific to Microsoft Jet. It's assumed you're comfortable with programming in a procedural language, are familiar with the concepts of relational databases and queries, and know something of Structured Query Language (SQL). Although the code examples are given in Visual Basic for Applications (VBA), they can be easily ported to other languages, such as C++.

## How To Use This Guide

The *Microsoft Jet Database Engine Programmer's Guide* contains all the information necessary to use Microsoft Jet in your development efforts. Whether you use Microsoft Access, Visual Basic, or any other environment that hosts Microsoft Jet, you will learn the details of this complex and powerful system.

The guide is divided into thirteen chapters, with four appendixes. Although much of the topic matter is not linear in nature, careful attention has been paid to the order of the chapters. Information presented in later chapters builds on material in previous chapters. Feel free to skip to specific chapters, but you should read this introduction, and Chapter 1, "An Overview of Microsoft Jet," as a prerequisite for later chapters.

Each chapter follows the same basic structure. An introduction summarizes the topic matter to be covered and includes a brief outline of the chapter contents. The main body of the chapter is then presented. Each chapter, where applicable, ends with an optimizations section that describes how to improve performance in the areas covered in the chapter.

The following section outlines each of the chapters.

### Chapter 1    An Overview of Microsoft Jet

This chapter introduces you to Microsoft Jet with a brief history of its development. It then covers the structure of Microsoft Jet, the components used, the services provided, and the layout of the database file.

### Chapter 2    Introducing Data Access Objects

Data Access Objects (DAO) provide a powerful framework for calling Microsoft Jet functions from your programming code. Coverage includes the DAO hierarchy, a description of each of the object types, a primer on using DAO in your applications, and examples of the most common types of DAO routines.

### Chapter 3    Data Definition and Integrity

Microsoft Jet provides powerful facilities for defining data and maintaining data integrity. It provides two interfaces for data definition, DAO and SQL, and offers a rich array of data integrity tools. This chapter shows you how to create tables, fields, and other data objects with both DAO and SQL. You also learn how to set up validation rules and referential integrity constraints.

### Chapter 4    Queries

Microsoft Jet has one of the most powerful query processors available in a desktop database. This chapter is the complete reference to the query services that Microsoft Jet provides. An overview of the query engine explains the query processor and the operations it performs. You learn about the different types of queries, and how to create and save queries.

### Chapter 5    Working with Records and Fields

Manipulating data is the most fundamental operation in a database. For Microsoft Jet, the DAO layer provides programmable data manipulation with the **Recordset** and **Field** objects. This chapter provides a comprehensive look at the properties and methods of the **Recordset** object, along with several of the data-manipulation properties and methods of the **Field** object.

### Chapter 6    Creating Multiuser Applications

Microsoft Jet provides services for database applications shared among multiple users. This chapter explores strategies for controlling multiuser access to data by locking and handling resource contention. It discusses how an application can handle locking conflicts in a multiuser environment. The engine is also discussed in terms of file-server versus client/server architecture.

### Chapter 7    Database Replication

Introduced with Microsoft Jet 3.0, database replication provides powerful distributed computing capabilities. Using database replication, programmers and database administrators can reproduce a database so that two or more users can simultaneously work on their own replica of the database. Once created, the replicas can be located on different computers, in different offices, or even in different countries, and the replicas remain synchronized with one another. This chapter describes the major uses for—and components of—database replication, how to program replication into your applications, and important issues affecting the synchronization of data updates and design changes.

### Chapter 8    Accessing External Data

One great strength of Microsoft Jet is its ability to seamlessly connect to data in foreign formats. This chapter shows you how to use Microsoft Jet to connect to other desktop databases such as FoxPro, dBASE®, and Paradox, to spreadsheets such as Microsoft Excel and Lotus® 1-2-3®, and to character-delimited and fixed-length text files. You will learn how to link to each external data source with which Microsoft Jet can connect, and how to directly open data sources. Performance guidelines are also provided.

### Chapter 9    Developing Client/Server Applications

Client/server computing has become the accepted way of upsizing database applications. This chapter introduces you to the concepts of client/server development using Microsoft Jet. The relationship between Microsoft Jet and the Open Database Connectivity (ODBC) standard is discussed, and examples are given for connecting to Microsoft SQL Server as a back-end database. This chapter also discusses techniques for creating client/server applications and offers tips for optimizing performance.

### Chapter 10    Managing Security

Microsoft Jet provides a sophisticated security environment that controls access to object definitions and data. This chapter discusses the Microsoft Jet security model and how to implement it successfully. A discussion of workgroups and permissions explains the model, and complete code examples for programmatically creating and maintaining security settings augment the text.

### Chapter 11    DAO C++ Classes

This chapter describes how to programmatically access Microsoft Jet using the DAO C++ classes, also known as dbDAO. The dbDAO classes expose the same Data Access Objects and functionality as Visual Basic, and use similar syntax. By handling such tasks as managing object instance lifetime, these classes make programming in C++ as convenient as programming in Visual Basic.

### Chapter 12    OBDC Desktop Database Drivers

Open Database Connectivity (ODBC) drivers are used by ODBC-enabled applications to access data created in any of a variety of database management systems (DBMSs). The Microsoft ODBC Desktop Database Drivers use the Microsoft Jet database engine to access data in six desktop DBMSs. This chapter discusses the architecture of the drivers (and their use of the Microsoft Jet engine), Microsoft Jet features exposed by the drivers, implementation details, and performance considerations.

### Chapter 13    Performance

This chapter covers database repair and compaction, along with an in-depth technical discussion of how Microsoft Jet 3.0 has been optimized for performance. Information on unsupported tuning functions rounds out the chapter.

### Appendix A    Specifications

This appendix lists the specifications of Microsoft Jet data types, showing table and field types, query types, and data limits.

### Appendix B    SQL Reference

Using Backus-Naur Form (BNF), this appendix provides a syntactical description of the Microsoft Jet implementation of SQL.

### Appendix C    Registry Settings

This appendix describes each of the settings that Microsoft Jet 3.0 installs into the Windows Registry.

### Appendix D    Error Reference

This appendix lists the error number, error message, and class of each Microsoft Jet error.

# Typographic Conventions

This guide provides comprehensive examples for many of the topics discussed. The following typographic conventions are used:

| Example of convention | Description |
| --- | --- |
| **Sub, If, ChDir, Print, Time$, RecordsAffected, Recordset** | Words in bold with initial letter capitalized indicate language-specific keywords with special meaning to Visual Basic for Applications. Objects, methods, statements, functions, and properties appear in bold with initial letter capitalized. Concatenated names may contain other capital letters. |
| *expr, path* | In text, italic letters are used for defined terms, usually the first time they occur in the guide. Italics are also used occasionally for emphasis. In syntax, italics indicate placeholders for information you supply. |
| [*expressionlist*] | In syntax, items in square brackets are optional. |

| Example of convention | Description (*cont'd*) |
|---|---|
| {While\|Until} | In syntax, braces and a vertical bar indicate a choice between two or more items. You must also choose one of the items unless all of the items also are enclosed in square brackets. |
| `Function fRetRecords () As Integer`<br>`  Dim rstCust As Recordset` | A monospaced font indicates code. |
| `Syntax Error` | A monospaced font in text indicates error messages. |
| `Set rstCust = dbCurrent. _`<br>`OpenRecordset ("Customers", _`<br>`dbOpenDynaset)` | The line-continuation character (_) indicates that code continued from one line to the next in the guide should be typed as one line in the editor. |
| ALT+F1, ENTER | Small capital letters are used for the names of keys and key sequences, such as ENTER and CTRL+R. A plus sign (+) between key names indicates a combination of keys. |

# Code Examples and Programming Style

This guide contains numerous code examples that you can type to experiment with the concepts covered. Unless otherwise noted, the code is compatible with Visual Basic for Applications as it is implemented in Visual Basic 4.0 and Microsoft Access for Windows 95.

For more information on naming conventions, see "Leszynski Naming Conventions for Microsoft Jet" on the companion CD-ROM.

This guide uses the following conventions in the sample code:

- Reserved words appear with an initial letter capitalized; concatenated words may contain other capital letters. Constants appear in mixed case:

```
If rstCustomerList.RecordCount = 0 Then strText = "Empty"
Public Const dbOpenRecordset = 2
```

- In full procedures, all variables are declared locally or are listed with an initialization procedure that declares global variables. All code has been tested with the VBA Option Explicit setting to ensure that there are no un-initialized variables.

- An apostrophe (') introduces a comment:

```
' This is a comment.
Dim intNew As Integer  ' This is also a comment.
```

- Control-flow blocks and statements in **Sub** and **Function** procedures are indented:

```
Sub MyCode ()
    Dim intX As Integer
    If intX > 0 Then
        intP = intQ
    End If
End Sub
```

- Naming conventions are used to make it easier to identify objects and variables in the code examples. The popular Stan Leszynski Naming Convention for prefix notation is used. The following tables list some of the conventions.

### Naming Conventions for Database Objects and Variables

| Object | Prefix | Example |
|---|---|---|
| Container | con | conForms |
| Database | dbs | dbsCustomers |
| Document | doc | docReport |
| Dynaset | dyn | dynOrders |
| Error | err | errCurrent |
| Field | fld | fldLastName |
| Group | gru | gruUsers |
| Index | idx | idxPrimaryKey |
| Parameter | prm | prmBeginDate |
| Property | prp | prpValue |
| QueryDef | qdf | qdfShowCustomers |
| Recordset | rst | rstCustomers |
| Relation | rel | rel!OrdersItems |
| Snapshot | snp | snpReadOnly |
| Table | tbl | tblOrders |
| TableDef | tdf | tdfCustomers |
| User | usr | usrMary |
| Workspace | wrk | wrkPrimary |

**Naming Conventions for Visual Basic Variables**

| Data type | Prefix | Example |
|---|---|---|
| Byte | byt | bytAttributes |
| Currency | cur | curDollars |
| Date | dte | dteToday |
| Double | dbl | dblPi |
| Boolean | f | fInitialized |
| Integer | int | intCount |
| Long | lng | lngAttributes |
| Single | sng | sngDays |
| String | str | strLastName |
| Type (user-defined) | typ | typePartRecord |
| Variant | var | varTemp |

# Using the Companion CD-ROM

Inside the back cover of this guide you can find the companion CD-ROM for the *Microsoft Jet Database Engine Programmer's Guide*. The CD-ROM contains an online version of this guide, online versions of all the code examples in this guide, the DAO Software Development Kit, seven white papers giving additional information about the Microsoft Jet database engine, several important utilities, and the source code for the Microsoft Access Security Wizard.

## Online Version of the *Programmer's Guide*

The entire contents of the *Microsoft Jet Database Engine Programmer's Guide* have been converted into an online form similar to books found on the Microsoft Developer's Network CD-ROM. You can install the online version of the guide by going to the JETBOOK folder on the CD-ROM and double-clicking the file SETUP.EXE. After the online version has been installed on your hard disk, you can start the guide by clicking the Microsoft Jet icon in your Microsoft Jet folder or program group. The online version of the guide has a number of navigation features to help you find specific information.

## Code Examples

This guide contains over 100 code examples that show how to correctly use the Microsoft Jet database engine. To help you learn about these features and incorporate them into your applications, the companion CD-ROM contains an electronic version of each code example used in the printed guide. All of the code examples for Microsoft Access for Windows 95 are stored as modules in a Microsoft Access database (.MDB file). All of the code examples for Visual Basic 4.0 are stored as modules (.BAS file) in a Visual Basic project (.VBP file).

The code examples are stored in the SAMPLES folder on the companion CD-ROM. In the SAMPLES folder you can find a separate folder for chapters 2 through 10 and Chapter 13. Each chapter folder contains two more folders: The ACCESS folder contains the code example for Microsoft Access and the VB40 folder contains the code examples for Visual Basic. For example, you can find the Microsoft Access code examples for Chapter 2 in \SAMPLES\CHAP02\ACCESS\CH02.MDB. All of the code examples are designed to be executed from your hard disk. Use the Windows Explorer or File Manager to copy the complete directory structure to the root directory of your C drive. For more information on specific file names or additional requirements for the code example in each chapter, see the introduction in that chapter.

## The DAO Software Development Kit

The DAO Software Development Kit (SDK) includes the dbDAO C++ library for accessing DAO functions from your Visual C++ code. You can find the SDK in the DAOSDK folder on the companion CD-ROM.

The dbDAO classes expose the full functionality of all DAO objects, methods, and properties. They were designed to be the smallest possible wrapper on top of the DAO OLE Automation interfaces while still providing Basic-like syntax from C++. At approximately 150K, these classes provide full collection support, dynamic allocation and deallocation, reference counting, and support for bulk fetches directly into your data structures.

## White Papers

Microsoft staff and contractors have prepared a number of white papers that describe specific aspects of Microsoft Jet and the applications that use it. The following white papers and Help file pertaining to version 3.0 of the Microsoft Jet database engine are included on the companion CD-ROM in the PAPERS folder (the file names are indicated in parentheses):

- Collins, Kevin. "Understanding Jet Locking." (JETLOCK.DOC)
- Collins, Kevin. "Jet 3.0 Performance Overview." (V3PERF.DOC)
- Leszynski, Stan, "The Leszynski Naming Conventions for Microsoft Jet." (LNC95JET.HLP)
- Mee, Michael. "Advanced Client-Server Issues." (AC303.DOC)
- Mee, Michael. "Advanced Data Access Objects (DAO) for Client Server." (AC301.DOC)
- Mee, Michael. "Client-Server Applications Using Data Access Objects." (AC305.DOC)
- Mee, Michael. "Forty-Two Ways to Make DAO Faster—Programming to DAO Using Microsoft Access." (AC307.DOC)

> **Note**  The information contained in these white papers represents the current view of Microsoft Corporation on the issues discussed as of the date of publication. Because Microsoft must respond to changing market conditions, the statements in these papers should not be interpreted as commitments on the part of Microsoft, and Microsoft cannot guarantee the accuracy of any information presented after the date of publication.

## Utilities

The companion CD-ROM contains several helpful utilities for understanding database locking. The utilities in the UTILITIES folder on the companion CD-ROM are explained in the white paper, "Understanding Jet Locking."

### Security Wizard

For more information about the Security Wizard, see Chapter 10, "Managing Security."

The Microsoft Access Security Wizard makes it easy to secure a Microsoft Access application using Microsoft Jet security services. The source code for the Security Wizard in Microsoft Access for Windows 95 is provided on the companion CD-ROM in \SAMPLES\CHAP10\WZSECURE.MDA.

# Using the Companion DAO Hierarchy Map

Inside the back cover of this guide you can also find a map showing the hierarchy of DAO objects, properties, and methods. The map is a valuable learning tool and presents the complete family of objects in a single diagram. You may find that posting the map on a wall near your workstation provides a faster reference tool than using online Help to look up the properties and methods available for a particular object.

C H A P T E R   1

# An Overview of Microsoft Jet

In November of 1992, Microsoft released its first desktop database product for Windows, Microsoft Access 1.0. This product was singular in its ability to provide database functionality to a broad spectrum of Windows users—from complete beginners to seasoned developers—and quickly became the top-selling Windows database. Powerful form and report engines accompanied by wizards helped Microsoft Access redefine the balance between ease of use and power. But hidden behind this new user interface was a piece of software every bit as powerful: the Microsoft Jet database engine.

While Microsoft Jet was envisioned by its developers as an application-independent database engine, due to its close integration with Microsoft Access, it was initially viewed as just a component of Microsoft Access. It was not until some time later, with the release of Visual Basic 3.0, that it became clear Microsoft Jet is an engine that can be used in more than one product. As it has evolved, Microsoft Jet has been incorporated into a variety of products, from Microsoft Excel to Visual C++.

**Contents**

## A Brief History of Microsoft Jet

Microsoft Jet is a mature product that has grown into a powerful relational database engine. The development of Microsoft Jet, which began in 1988, has been an evolutionary process that continues to this day. What follows is a brief history of that evolution.

## Early Development

Designed for the original Omega product (an early prototype Windows database designed by Microsoft), Microsoft Jet was initially intended to be a single-user engine. Even though it was a distant relative of the database engine used in the Microsoft Professional Development System (PDS), four years before its initial release the Microsoft Jet code was barely recognizable as derivative.

An early version of Microsoft Jet shipped with the WinLogin program, before Microsoft Access 1.0. WinLogin was a utility shipped for Microsoft Windows for Workgroups that managed user names, file locations, and other administrative data. Intended as a stopgap until Microsoft Systems Management Server shipped, WinLogin was not widely used.

There is some debate over the origins of the name "Jet engine." Some claim that "Jet" is an acronym for "Joint Engine Technology," but other Microsoft Jet insiders dismiss this, saying the name is simply a play on words. Microsoft Jet was originally chosen as the code name for the engine development effort and was never intended to be used outside Microsoft.

## Microsoft Jet 1.0

When it made its debut in November 1992 with the release of Microsoft Access 1.0, Microsoft Jet 1.0 introduced breakthrough technology for the desktop database market. Microsoft Jet 1.0 was a relational database engine providing not only the standard DBMS functionality such as data definition, data manipulation, querying, security, and maintenance, but also technology that had not yet been seen in desktop databases. These features included updatable views, query on query capabilities, and seamless access to heterogeneous data.

Described by its development team as "a significant engine hidden behind an easy user interface," Microsoft Jet 1.0 raised the bar in terms of database features. But it also lacked programmatic control over database objects. The engine provided a few methods for accessing table and query structures, but did not have a cohesive model for programmatic control over object structures and data manipulation.

## Microsoft Jet 1.1

The quick acceptance of Microsoft Access 1.0 surprised even Microsoft. In a very short period of time, over one million copies had been sold. This meant that one million copies of the Microsoft Jet database engine had entered the workplace. It quickly became clear that new features and solutions were needed. These goals were accomplished in Microsoft Jet 1.1, introduced in May 1993 with Microsoft Access 1.1 and Visual Basic 3.0.

Various improvements were made in Microsoft Jet 1.1 to provide greater connectivity between Microsoft Jet and Open Database Connectivity (ODBC) databases. This included a new Oracle® ODBC driver, the introduction of a connection manager (known internally as "ConMan") that provides services for sharing and caching connections, and general improvements in the ability to work with any ODBC driver. This version also saw the addition of the MSysConf table. This table, which resides on the server, was added so that database administrators could prevent the saving of password and user ID information in an attached ODBC table.

Additionally, the maximum size of a database file was increased from 128 megabytes to approximately 1.1 gigabytes. Microsoft also added support for attaching to Microsoft FoxPro tables, and some new collating sequences for international users.

Microsoft Jet 1.1 includes version 1.1 of the Data Access Objects (DAO) interface. This revision of DAO added the Data Definition Language (DDL) capabilities that were missing from DAO 1.0. These benefits were available in Visual Basic 3.0, but not in Microsoft Access 1.1.

# Microsoft Jet 2.0

Introduced in April 1994 with Microsoft Access 2.0, Microsoft Jet 2.0 offers major enhancements over previous versions. Key areas of improvement include enforced referential integrity and data validation at the engine level, optimized query performance (using Rushmore technology gained in the FoxPro merger), increased conformance to ANSI-standard SQL syntax rules, support for UNION, sub-SELECT, and data-definition queries, and a full programming interface to Microsoft Jet using DAO 2.0.

Microsoft Jet 2.0 also introduced support for cascading updates and deletions, remote transaction management allowing transactions to be "sent" to servers that support them, SQL pass-through queries, and new MSysConf settings controlling how often and how many data fetches are made against ODBC data sources. Additionally, support was added for remote index joins, and new initialization file settings for debugging and tuning data operations.

Referential integrity improvements were added to the engine late in the development cycle. There was some internal debate as to whether it would be prudent to develop this functionality at such a late stage (work began only six months before Microsoft Access 2.0 shipped). As a compromise, work proceeded on referential integrity, but a mechanism was put in place to pull it from the product if it proved to be destabilizing for the engine as a whole. A small group of Microsoft Jet developers was able to pull off what some thought impossible: Cascading updates and deletes made it into Microsoft Jet 2.0 on schedule.

Although Microsoft Jet 1.0 was revolutionary in the desktop database arena for its inclusion of updatable joins, many complex rules governed when a query was updatable. Basically, the rule was that you could update either side of a one-to-one join, the many side of a one-to-many join, but neither side of a many-to-many join. In version 2.0 the updatability rules were changed such that you could update the one side of a one-to-many query. This includes the ability to take advantage of the engine's new cascading update and delete functionality.

Data Access Objects in Microsoft Jet 2.0 were greatly enhanced to provide a complete hierarchical model of collections, objects, properties, and methods. This hierarchy provides the developer with almost complete access to the engine's underlying services, including support for data definition and manipulation, workspace and transaction management, and programmatic access to security. The DAO library that shipped with Microsoft Jet 2.0 contains the first vestiges of OLE Automation. As some users have discovered, the DAO2016.DLL file can be browsed with a type library browser such as the one in Microsoft Excel 5.0 (**Tools** menu, **References** command). However, it is not usable unless Microsoft Access is running. The Data Outline control that shipped with the Microsoft Access Developer's Toolkit made some use of these new interfaces. They were, however, added mainly in anticipation of future DAO releases.

With all the new features in Microsoft Jet 2.0, it was apparent that some mechanism would have to be created to allow users of Visual Basic 3.0 to take advantage of them. The Visual Basic compatibility layer arose as a classic example of compromise between conflicting constraints. The necessity of changing the data format to provide features like table-level validation and referential integrity, when combined with the Microsoft Access 2.0 decision to require users to convert their databases from 1.*x* format, meant that something had to be done for users of Visual Basic 3.0. The easy solution for the Microsoft Jet development team would have been a new version of Visual Basic. However, the Visual Basic team was still recovering from two releases in six months, and an immediate new version was not an option for them. From much negotiation and hard technical analysis, the Visual Basic compatibility layer was born. It was decided that in the future, Microsoft Access and Visual Basic would share engine revisions.

# Microsoft Jet 2.5

Introduced in October 1994 with the Microsoft Access 2.0 Service Pack, Microsoft Jet 2.5 was an interim release designed to achieve two goals: to minimize the incidence of databases being incorrectly marked as corrupt, and to add support for the new ODBC Desktop Database Drivers.

Probably the biggest feature of Microsoft Jet 2.5 was that it contained the first 32-bit release of the engine. Many minor features were added to support the ODBC Desktop Database Drivers. The previous version of the drivers included only the bottom layer of Microsoft Jet, which allows reading and writing of database files. With the new drivers, support was added to include all of the Microsoft Jet query engine, so some changes were necessary to provide enhanced compatibility with the much simpler query engine that had been developed for version 1.0.

Another change modified when the commit byte values were changed. Microsoft Jet 2.0 had a delay period before the commit byte status changed from a flag indicating that data was being written to disk to a flag indicating that the database for that user was in a normal state. There were some instances in which a user could normally close the database without setting his or her flag back to a normal state. Microsoft Jet 2.5 changed this behavior by immediately changing the flag back to a normal state after a write to the database was completed. In this way, performance is not impacted.

Version 2.5 was the first release following an internal reorganization that placed the ODBC and Microsoft Jet groups under common management. One of the immediate gains, was, of course, having the full Microsoft Jet database engine available with the Desktop Database Drivers. Another of the gains for Microsoft Jet was the addition of the Text and Microsoft Excel data formats as true formats rather than formats just for import and export.

Finally, internal changes were made to support a new expression service provided by Visual Basic for Applications (VBA) for use with the Desktop Database Drivers (VBA2[32].DLL). The requirement that Microsoft Jet continue to run with Microsoft Access made for some interesting internal architecture problems resulting from trying to cope with multiple simultaneous users running Microsoft Jet.

## Microsoft Jet 3.0

Introduced in the fall of 1995, Microsoft Jet 3.0 offers new features and improved performance. The most important aspect of this upgrade is its full 32-bit implementation for use in environments such as Microsoft Windows 95 and Microsoft Windows NT™.

Many changes were made to the database format and the way the engine handles data, with the goal of making most operations substantially faster. Among these changes was the implementation of multithreading: By default, Microsoft Jet 3.0 uses three threads to perform read-ahead and write-behind operations and for cache management.

To meet the increase in workgroup applications, Microsoft Jet 3.0 introduced replication capabilities. These capabilities allow developers to create replicable databases that can be used in different locations. Microsoft Jet can synchronize these replicas and keep data current.

# The Structure of the Microsoft Jet Database Engine

Microsoft Jet provides a variety of database management services, including data definition, data manipulation, data integrity, and access control. This section introduces each of these services and explains which components are responsible for the actual work.

## Services Provided

According to classic database texts, there are six basic functions that a database management system (DBMS) should provide. This section introduces these functions and shows how Microsoft Jet accomplishes each. The six basic functions of a DBMS are:

- Data definition and integrity: Data definition is the ability to create and modify structures for holding data, such as tables and fields. Integrity is the ability to make sure rules that prevent data corruption due to invalid entries or operations are applied to data operations.
- Data storage: the ability to store data in the file system.
- Data manipulation: the ability to add new data, modify or delete existing data.
- Data retrieval: the ability to retrieve data from the system.
- Security: the ability to control users' access to the data thereby protecting the data against unauthorized use.
- Data sharing: the ability to share data in a multiuser environment.

## Data Definition

For more information on data definition, see Chapter 3, "Data Definition and Integrity."

Probably the first operations you perform with a DBMS are the creation and definition of objects that will hold your data. With Microsoft Jet, you can create and modify the following types of objects.

### Databases

All Microsoft Jet objects are contained in a single file known as a database file. This file contains both the object definitions and the data contained in Microsoft Jet tables.

### Tables

Microsoft Jet provides a great deal of flexibility in using tables. Tables can contain data in a native Microsoft Jet format, or they can represent links to data stored in a variety of other data sources such as Microsoft Excel or FoxPro, or ODBC data sources such as Microsoft SQL Server.

### Fields

A variety of field data types are available, including **Text**, **Number**, **Currency**, and **Memo**. Tables can contain up to 255 fields. Microsoft Jet supports both variable-length and fixed-length fields. For example, if a variable-length text field is created, only the amount of text stored in that field is actually stored in the database file; extra space is not wasted to pad out the field to its maximum size.

### Indexes

Microsoft Jet allows both primary and secondary indexes that can be based on one or more fields. You can create indexes using both DAO and SQL.

### Relations

In a Microsoft Jet database, relations define how data in multiple tables is related. With Microsoft Jet, you can define relations between fields and enforce referential integrity with cascading updates and deletes.

## Queries

You can create and save a variety of query types using Microsoft Jet. Retrieval queries that return data are supported, as are a variety of action queries such as update and append.

## Users and Groups

To implement security, Microsoft Jet uses a form of workgroup security that defines users and groups. **User** and **Group** objects represent specific users who are authorized to use Microsoft Jet, and groups of related users.

## Application-Specific Objects

Applications that use Microsoft Jet can store their own objects in the database. These objects are maintained through a **Containers** collection. For example, Microsoft Access takes advantage of **Container** objects to store its forms, reports, macros, and modules.

# Data Storage

Microsoft Jet uses a form of data storage known as the Indexed Sequential Access Method (ISAM). The Microsoft Jet ISAM implementation has the following characteristics:

- Records can be ordered by the use of an index, such as a primary key.

- Variable-length records are the standard method of storage.

- Data is stored and managed in 2K *pages*, similar to those in Microsoft SQL Server.

Microsoft Jet implements a page-based system. Data stored in the database is structured as a set of pages, each containing one or more records. A record cannot span more than a single page; **Memo** and **OLE Object** fields can, however, be stored in pages separate from the rest of the record. Each record occupies only as much space as needed to store its data, so each record within the same table may not necessarily be the same length. Variable-length encoding is used.

## Data Manipulation and Retrieval

Microsoft Jet provides a powerful query engine that supports data retrieval and manipulation using Structured Query Language (SQL). You can also use DAO to programmatically access data in tables.

Using the data manipulation services of Microsoft Jet, you can add, modify, and delete records in tables. This can be accomplished through action queries or directly through DAO using **Recordset** objects. Microsoft Jet uses an advanced *keyset* model for representing data. Updatable queries, heterogeneous joins, and queries on queries are supported.

## Security

For more information on Microsoft Jet security, see Chapter 10, "Managing Security."

Microsoft Jet provides a sophisticated security model with which you can define your application's users and groups, and set specific permissions for each object in the database for these users and groups.

## Data Sharing

When used in a file-server network, Microsoft Jet provides data-sharing services that enable multiple users to access and change a shared database. Microsoft Jet locks data in the 2K pages mentioned earlier. When a database resides on a file server, Microsoft Jet uses the underlying network operating system's locking primitives to lock pages when a table record is being modified.

Microsoft Jet supports two types of locking. *Pessimistic* locking locks the page containing the record being edited as soon as the editing begins. The page is unlocked when editing is completed or abandoned. No two users can edit the same record at the same time. *Optimistic* locking locks the page containing the edited record only when the editing is committed. In this scenario, two users can edit the same record at the same time, but a trappable run-time error occurs when the values are posted.

To coordinate locking in a multiuser environment, Microsoft Jet uses a locking information file (known by its .LDB extension) that is stored in the same directory as the database itself. Each user who opens the database has an entry in this file. This list of users is used to determine which records in a database are locked and who has them locked, to prevent possible file contention errors, and to avoid data corruption while the database is being accessed by multiple users. If it does not already exist, the .LDB file is created when you open a database for shared access.

## Maintenance Functions

For more information on maintenance functions, see Chapter 13, "Performance."

All databases require periodic maintenance. Microsoft Jet provides compaction, repair, and conversion functionality to make the day-to-day task of administering your databases manageable.

As a database file is used, it can become fragmented as objects and records are created and deleted. Periodic defragmentation reduces the amount of wasted space in the file and can enhance performance. Microsoft Jet provides a **CompactDatabase** method that compacts the database file and reclaims wasted space.

If databases are not closed properly (as the result of workstation failure, for example), they can become corrupted. Microsoft Jet provides repair functionality that scans the database file for inconsistencies and attempts to repair them.

With Microsoft Jet, you can create workgroups to define users, groups, and passwords in a secure environment. This function is supplied in a stand-alone executable called Workgroup Administrator (WRKGADM.EXE), which ships with Microsoft Access.

# Application Independence

Although Microsoft Jet was introduced with Microsoft Access 1.0, it quickly was adopted as the database engine for other applications, including Visual Basic 3.0, Microsoft Word 6.0, and Microsoft Excel 5.0. As these applications began to share Microsoft Jet, it became clear that the engine would have to be application independent.

Although Microsoft Jet does not recognize any application-specific objects, through application-defined properties applications that use Microsoft Jet can dynamically add application-specific information to the **Engine** objects.

# Compatibility Among Versions

With each new version of Microsoft Jet, enhancements in functionality and changes to the structure of the database file cause problems with backward compatibility. Wherever possible, efforts have been made to ensure an easy migration path between versions. However, incompatibilities do exist. The following table illustrates how database files and objects can be used with different versions of Microsoft Jet.

|  |  | Microsoft Jet version | | | | |
|---|---|---|---|---|---|---|
|  |  | **1.0** | **1.1** | **2.0** | **2.5** | **3.0** |
| .MDB version | 1.0 | Y | Y | Y | Y | Y |
|  | 1.1 | N | Y | Y | Y | Y |
|  | 2.0 | N | N | Y | Y | Y |
|  | 3.0 | N | N | N | N | Y |

A "Y" indicates that the database can be used without conversion; "N" indicates that the database cannot be used or converted.

From DAO code, you can open databases created with the version of Microsoft Jet running the DAO code, and those created with any previous version. For example, if you're running DAO code using version 3.0 of the DAO DLLs, you can open version 1.0, 1.1, 2.0, 2.5, and 3.0 databases. If you are using version 2.0 of the DAO DLLs, you can open version 1.0, 1.1, 2.0 and 2.5 databases, but not 3.0 databases. Note that Microsoft Access can only open databases through its user interface that were created with that version of Microsoft Access. Of course, you can *link* tables from any previous version of a database file.

# Microsoft Jet Components

To provide database management services, Microsoft Jet uses a variety of components, each designed to perform a specific group of functions. These components, implemented primarily as dynamic-link libraries (DLLs), constitute the engine as a whole. This section outlines each of the main DLLs and shows the services that each provides.

The following diagram represents an overview of how the various Microsoft Jet components fit together.

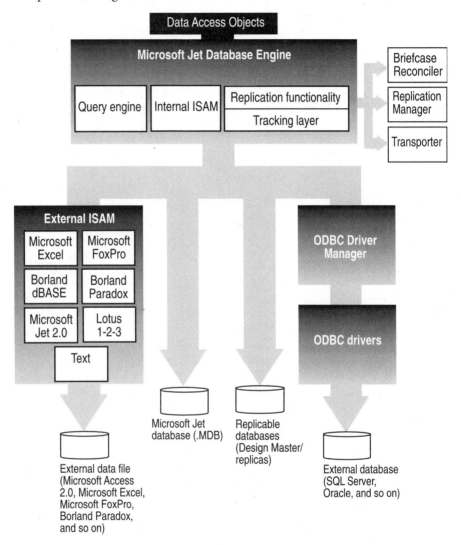

**Figure 1.1   The structure of Microsoft Jet**

## Microsoft Jet ISAM Components

The Microsoft Jet ISAM is responsible for storing data in the database file. It is also responsible for providing query and access control (security) services. The following table describes components that provide these ISAM services.

| Component | Description |
| --- | --- |
| MSJT3032.DLL | Contains the main engine functionality, including the Microsoft Jet engine that is responsible for data storage, the query engine, and security routines. It handles all data storage and retrieval from the native ISAM and all querying against native and non-native data. |
| MSJINT32.DLL | Contains all localized Microsoft Jet strings. Because Microsoft Jet is translated or *localized* for many different countries, it employs the practice of keeping its language-specific strings in a separate library. |
| MSJTER32.DLL | Contains Microsoft Jet error services. Moving strings and error messages to a separate DLL allows easier maintenance of the various components. |

## External ISAM Components

Microsoft Jet provides the capability to access non-native, or *external*, data such as Microsoft FoxPro, Lotus 1-2-3, and Borland dBASE and Paradox. The process of retrieving and storing non-native data is handled by the following external ISAM components (also known as installable ISAMs).

| Component | Description |
| --- | --- |
| MSXL3032.DLL | Provides access to Microsoft Excel worksheets and workbooks created by versions 3.0, 4.0, 5.0, and 7.0. Microsoft Jet 2.5 introduced access to Microsoft Excel data but it was not until Microsoft Access for Windows 95 and Visual Basic 4.0 that this functionality surfaced to Microsoft Jet users. |
| MSRD2X32.DLL | Provides access to Microsoft Jet 1.*x* and 2.0 databases. The storage engine and format were completely revised with Microsoft Jet 3.0. Given the large number of structural changes, Microsoft Jet 3.0 treats version 2.0 databases as external ISAMs. |
| MSLT3032.DLL | Provides access to Lotus 1-2-3 worksheets created by versions 1.*x*, 2.*x*, 3.*x*, and 4.*x*. |
| MSPX3032.DLL | Provides access to Borland Paradox tables from versions 3.5, 4.0, 4.5, and 5.0. |
| MSXB3032.DLL | Provides access to XBase files including Borland dBASE versions III, IV, and V and Microsoft FoxPro versions 2.0, 2.5, 2.6, and 3.0. |

| Component | Description (*cont'd*) |
|---|---|
| MSTX3032.DLL | Provides the services required for accessing Text files. Using Microsoft Jet, you can either link (*attach* in version 2.0 parlance) or directly open Text files, which can be stored in either fixed-width or delimited format. The procedures for retrieving the data in Text files are similar to those used to access data in other external data sources. Generally, the ability to access Text files is provided so you can import existing Text files into your Microsoft Jet database, or export Microsoft Jet or other attached database tables to Text files. |

## Replication Components

Microsoft Jet 3.0 introduced database replication as a service. With replication, it is possible to create and maintain replicas of databases at multiple sites and synchronize these databases at regular intervals. The following table describes components that provide the replication services.

| Component | Description |
|---|---|
| MSWNG300.DLL | Provides the main replication services, including creation of replicable databases and replica reconciliation. |
| MSJTRCLR.DLL | Provides reconciliation services for the Microsoft Windows 95 Briefcase component. |
| MSJTTR.EXE | Physically moves data among systems. |
| REPLMAN.EXE | Provides a user interface for various replication services. This component currently ships with the Microsoft Access Developer's Toolkit. |
| MSAJETFS.DLL | Interfaces the transported databases to the file system. |
| MSJRMI30.DLL and MSJRCI30.DLL | Provides international resources and localized strings for the replication components. |

## Visual Basic for Applications (VBA) Interface Components

Although VBA is not a component of Microsoft Jet, it works as an *expression evaluator* to evaluate various functions that appear in SQL statements and to do arithmetic. The Microsoft Jet expression service takes an expression and builds a tree out of it. Elements of this tree are then passed to VBA for evaluation.

Various VBA components are used to provide this functionality to Microsoft Jet. VBAJET32.DLL is used to start VBA. When Microsoft Jet is running in a stand-alone environment (not being run by a host application such as Microsoft Access), the VBA run-time component, VBAR2132.DLL, is used. However, if a host application such as Microsoft Access for Windows 95 or Visual Basic 4.0 is running, then VBA2132.DLL is used. The following table describes VBA interface components.

| Component | Description |
|---|---|
| VBAJET32.DLL | Initializes the VBA expression service for Microsoft Jet. |
| VBAEN232.OLB | Contains international resources and localized strings for the VBA components. |
| VBAR2132.DLL | A run-time version of the VBA expression services. |

## Notable VBA Interactions

Prior to version 2.5, Microsoft Jet made calls to the Basic interpreter built into Microsoft Access and Visual Basic to get its expression evaluation functionality. In current versions, Microsoft Jet uses VBA. This dichotomy leads to some interesting interactions between Microsoft Jet and VBA.

For example, if you are using the ODBC Desktop Database Drivers (which use Microsoft Jet 2.5), you are using the 1994 version of VBA for expression services. At the same time, you may be running Microsoft Access 2.0, which uses Microsoft Jet 2.0, which in turn calls the Access Basic interpreter (MSABC200.DLL) for expression services. Finally, if you call Microsoft Jet 2.5 from Microsoft Excel (possible, although not supported), you are using the 1993 version of VBA to run DAO and the 1994 version of VBA to supply expression services to the engine.

It is also worthwhile to note the order in which you load engine hosts, such as Microsoft Access and Microsoft Excel. For example, if you first load the ODBC Desktop Database Drivers, Microsoft Jet uses the VBA run-time DLL (VBAR232.DLL). If you subsequently load Microsoft Access, then the instance of Microsoft Jet loaded by Microsoft Access uses the full VBA DLL (VBA232.DLL). If, on the other hand, you load Microsoft Access first, and then the ODBC Desktop Database Drivers, both instances of Microsoft Jet use the VBA232.DLL because the engine's VBA initialization DLL sees that VBA232.DLL is already in memory and uses it. If you want to reduce the memory footprint of Microsoft Jet, load Microsoft Access first, and then other applications or drivers that use the engine.

## DAO Interface Components

For more information on DAO's use of type libraries and its OLE capabilities, see Chapter 2, "Introducing Data Access Objects."

As mentioned earlier, DAO is the programming interface to Microsoft Jet. The following table describes the components that provide DAO services.

| Component | Description |
| --- | --- |
| DAO3032.DLL | The DAO library, containing the object layer interface to the engine. This file contains both the DAO DLL and the type library. |
| DAO2532.TLB | This file provides access to the obsolete DAO **Snapshot**, **Table**, and **Dynaset** objects and other obsolete methods. It's used only for code in Microsoft Access 1.1 and earlier and Visual Basic 3.0 and earlier. |

## Driver Management Components

Microsoft Jet can access data through the ODBC standard. While the Microsoft Jet components contain no intrinsic ODBC services, they do call the standard ODBC Driver Manager. The ODBC32.DLL dispatches calls to ODBC drivers for processing. This file is not a Microsoft Jet component.

# Structure of the Database File

The database file used by Microsoft Jet is interesting in that all database objects are stored in a single file in the file system. This file is given the .MDB extension by default, so it is often referred to as the .MDB file, though it can have any extension. During early development, Microsoft Jet developers debated the virtues and drawbacks of the single-file approach. The benefits were obvious: easy object management because all objects could be moved as a single unit, long object names (up to 64 characters), and control over where the individual database objects would be located.

Given that the database file contains a variety of objects, its format is quite complex. This section does not attempt to document this file format; rather, it points out some of the characteristics of this file.

## Types of Pages

For more information on pages, see Chapter 6, "Creating Multiuser Applications," and Chapter 13, "Performance."

All the information stored in a database file is organized into 2K pages. There are a variety of page types used to store data.

### Database Header Page

The first page in every database is the database header page (DBH). It stores 256 commit bytes that track user operations in a multiuser environment. There is no set order for subsequent pages.

### Index Pages

These pages store indexes, including "root" pages and "leaf" pages. Microsoft Jet 3.0 introduced an entirely new layout format for compressing index data that results in a substantial reduction in storage size and a significant reduction in the time needed to create indexes that are highly duplicated. When the database is compacted, Microsoft Jet 3.0 copies the records from the source table into the destination table in primary key order.

### Long Value Pages

Long value pages store two types of data. The first is **Memo** data that has flowed over from data pages. The second type includes all other binary data types, such as **OLE Object** fields. In Microsoft Jet 2.0, these pages are all stored in one hidden table. This results in contention issues when multiple users are accessing Microsoft Jet. In Microsoft Jet 3.0, long values of a particular column are stored with other long values of the same column. This helps reduce multiuser contention when using long values from different columns. Additionally, long value pages now have two distinct types: Fixed-length long value pages are used internally for special database scenarios; variable-length long value pages are used for non-internal data.

### System Table Pages

These pages contain the system tables MSysObjects, MSysACES, and MSysQueries. These system tables are discussed in the following section.

## System Tables

In system tables, Microsoft Jet stores information about each of the objects. These tables are much like the tables you create in a database—with a few exceptions. First, they are identified internally as system objects so that you can differentiate your tables from system tables. Secondly, some tables are inherently read-only. Microsoft Jet prevents you from updating the contents of some system tables to avoid breaches in security. The following table describes each of the system tables.

**Warning**  The existence and structure of system tables are subject to change in every revision of Microsoft Jet. When their format changes or they disappear, applications that use system tables may no longer work. System tables are documented here solely for the purpose of giving you a better understanding of how Microsoft Jet works internally.

| System table | Description |
|---|---|
| MSysObjects | Stores additional information about objects in the database, including tables and queries. The ID field in this table is used to link objects to other system tables. This table extends the application-independent nature of Microsoft Jet by including binary fields that allow the host application (such as Microsoft Access) to store information on application-specific objects such as forms, reports, and module code. |
| MSysQueries | Stores information about the queries stored in the database. This includes information about the type of query, the tables and fields used, criteria, sorting, and parameters. |
| MSysACES | Stores permission information for each object for each user. As you will see in Chapter 10, "Managing Security," Microsoft Jet implements security using a workgroup model. In this model, users are assigned access to specific objects through permissions settings. |
| MSysRelationships | Stores information about each of the relationships in the database, including information on the tables and fields used in the relationship. |

**Microsoft Access Users**  Microsoft Access defines its own additional system tables to store application-specific information. These include MSysModules and MSysToolbars. When you create a Microsoft Jet database using Microsoft Access, these system tables are automatically created.

# Engine Configuration

For more information on the Windows Registry, see Appendix C, "Registry Settings."

Versions of Microsoft Jet prior to 3.0 store configuration information in an initialization file that follows the Microsoft Windows .INI file standard. (The one exception to this is version 2.5, which stores the location of the installable ISAM DLL in the system registry.) Microsoft Jet 3.0 uses the Windows 95 Registry exclusively. The Registry is a structured file used in Windows 95 to store information about the system's configuration, including software components like Microsoft Jet.

CHAPTER 2

# Introducing Data Access Objects

This guide provides information on two key aspects of Microsoft Jet: how the engine works and how to access the engine's functionality through your program. The latter topic is the focus of this chapter. As a developer, you probably want to use the same type of engine capabilities that are supplied to the user interface in Microsoft Access, or to the **Data** control in Visual Basic. This access is provided in the form of Data Access Objects (DAO). DAO, the programming interface to Microsoft Jet, provides a framework for directly accessing and manipulating database objects.

DAO was designed with the Visual Basic and Access Basic programmer in mind. Its hierarchy model and syntax closely match the constructs introduced in Visual Basic and later in VBA. Additionally, with the dbDAO library, the C++ programmer can also use similar syntax.

**Contents**

For information on copying the code examples from the companion CD-ROM to your hard disk drive, see "Using the Companion CD-ROM" in the Preface.

### Using CH02.MDB and CHAP02.VBP

If you copied the samples from the companion CD-ROM, you can find the code examples for Microsoft Access in C:\SAMPLES\CHAP02\ ACCESS\CH02.MDB. The corresponding code examples for Visual Basic are in C:\SAMPLES\CHAP02\VB40\CHAP02.VBP.

To run any of the code examples in this chapter, open the .MDB file in Microsoft Access or open the .VBP file in Microsoft Visual Basic 4.0. You can use the examples to help you understand the concepts discussed in the chapter—or you can modify them and use them in your own applications.

# Hello DAO

"Hello World" is the first code example in the now-classic book, *The C Programming Language,* by Brian Kernighan and Dennis Ritchie. The following examples show you how to perform a simple task with DAO using Hello World. But instead of printing a string variable to the screen, our version searches for a value in a table and retrieves a message for display.

Let's assume that you have a table with one field that contains possible greetings. This Greeting field is also indexed as the table's primary key and looks something like this:

**Greeting**

Hi

Howdy

Bonjour

Hello world!

Buenos dias

Following is a possible subroutine to retrieve this greeting:

```
Sub FindData()
    Dim dbsHello As DATABASE
    Dim rstGreetings As Recordset

    Set dbsHello = OpenDatabase("C:\Samples\Chap02\Hello.mdb")

    Set rstGreetings = dbsHello.OpenRecordset _
        ("tblGreetings", dbOpenTable)
```

```
    rstGreetings.Index = "PrimaryKey"
    rstGreetings.Seek "=", "Hello World!"

    If Not rstGreetings.NoMatch Then
        MsgBox rstGreetings!Greeting
    Else
        MsgBox "Could not find the greeting!"
    End If

    rstGreetings.Close
    dbsHello.Close
End Sub
```

Here what's happening with the code:

1. First, two object variables called dbHello and rstGreetings are declared. These are used to point to the actual objects involved.

2. The **Set** statement is used to assign the dbHello variable to an actual Microsoft Jet database called Hello.MDB located in the root directory of drive C:. This is accomplished with the **OpenDatabase** method.

3. The **Set** statement is used again, this time to assign the rstGreetings variable to a table called tblGreetings. This is done using the **OpenRecordset** method. Because the method is used after the dbHello variable, the code is telling DAO to look in the Hello.MDB database for the table.

4. Next, DAO is told which index to use to search the table. This is done by setting the **Index** property of the rstGreetings object.

5. The **Seek** method is called to find the record where the primary key is equal to the string "Hello World!"

6. Next, the **NoMatch** property is checked to see if a match was found. If a match was found, the value of the Greeting field is displayed. If not, an error message is displayed.

The end result is a program that displays the message "Hello World!" The key concepts you should come away with are:

- DAO is hierarchical. Opening the Greetings table under the database variable tells DAO where to find the table.

- Methods initiate actions. Methods are used to open a database and table, and to find a record.

- Properties define characteristics. The value of the **Index** property is set to tell DAO how to search on it.

As you progress through the rest of this chapter, you'll see how all these elements work together to form a cohesive model that gives you flexible access to the objects in your database.

# A Brief History of DAO

From its genesis in Visual Basic 2.0, DAO has evolved from a limited set of simple objects to a robust tool that can access nearly all Microsoft Jet functionality. The following table shows the evolution of DAO.

| Interface | Host version | Major capabilities |
|---|---|---|
| Not named | Visual Basic 2.0 | Limited data access through ODBC. Forward-only data access. |
| DAO 1.0 | Microsoft Access 1.0 | Interface to table and query structures, objects to represent tables, dynasets, and snapshots with a limited number of properties. |
| Data Access Objects 1.0 | Visual Basic 3.0 | Added **TableDef**, **QueryDef**, and **Field** objects to programmatically expose structures. |
| Data Access Objects 2.0 | Microsoft Access 2.0 | First vestiges of OLE Automation, full programmatic access to almost all Microsoft Jet functionality. Full object model with robust set of objects and properties. |
| Data Access Objects 2.5 | ODBC Desktop Database Drivers | Created for both 16- and 32-bit platforms. Designed for use with ODBC Desktop Database Drivers 2.0. Only the 16-bit version has been shipped (for use with the 16-bit version of Visual Basic 4.0). |
| Data Access Objects 3.0 | Microsoft Access for Windows 95, Visual Basic 4.0 (32-bit), Microsoft Excel 7.0, Visual C ++ | Enhanced to support a stand-alone interface for any compatible host. |

# The Data Access Objects

DAO is implemented as a hierarchy of collections and objects. All tables, fields, indexes, queries, and so on, are represented by objects organized into collections. Each object has a set of properties that define its characteristics and one or more methods that you use to perform various operations on objects. This section introduces each collection and provides information about the objects it contains.

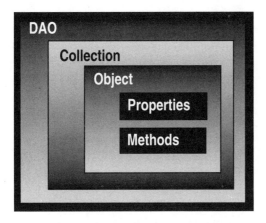

**Figure 2.1    Collections, objects, properties, and methods**

In the DAO hierarchy, all objects branch out from a single object that represents the Microsoft Jet database engine. Figure 2.2 shows each of the collections that branch off the **DBEngine** object.

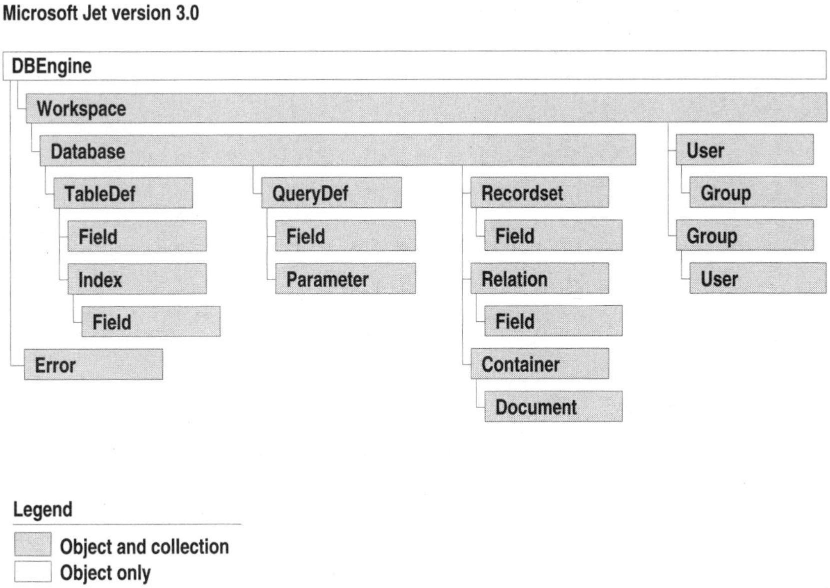

**Microsoft Jet version 3.0**

```
DBEngine
  Workspace
    Database                                  User
      TableDef        QueryDef      Recordset   Group
        Field           Field         Field     Group
        Index           Parameter     Relation  User
          Field                         Field
      Error                           Container
                                        Document
```

**Legend**
▢ Object and collection
▢ Object only

**Figure 2.2    The Data Access Object hierarchy**

## DBEngine

The **DBEngine** object represents the Microsoft Jet database engine. As the top-level object, it contains and controls all other objects in the hierarchy of Data Access Objects. This object doesn't have an associated collection.

**Note** Prior to version 3.0, Microsoft Jet was limited to ten instances on any particular system: You could execute up to ten applications that simultaneously used the engine. With version 3.0, you can run as many processes (executions of the engine, other applications, and so on) as your system resources allow. Additionally, within each process, you can have up to 64 instances of the engine. For example, you could create 64 private **DBEngine** objects within an application.

## Errors

For a list of errors returned by Microsoft Jet, see Appendix D, "Error Reference."

As you perform operations using DAO, errors may occur. Each error is stored as an **Error** object in the **Errors** collection. You can use this information to determine what caused the error, and perhaps display meaningful error messages to your application's users.

It's important to note that as each DAO error occurs, the **Errors** collection is cleared of previous errors, and the new **Error** object is placed in the **Errors** collection. There can be several related **Error** objects in the collection caused by a single operation.

DAO operations that don't generate an error have no effect on the **Errors** collection.

## Workspaces

A **Workspace** object exists for each active session of the engine. A session delineates a sequence of operations performed by the database engine. A session begins when a user logs on and ends when the user logs off. All operations during a session form one transaction scope and are subject to permissions determined by the logon user name and password. Think of the **Workspace** object as providing a user/password security "space" and a transaction "space" within which a specific user operates. The **Workspaces** collection contains all **Workspace** objects defined by the currently running Microsoft Jet.

The ability to programmatically create multiple workspaces is mainly of interest when you have to log on to Microsoft Jet as another user. Also, because each **Workspace** maintains its transactions independent of other workspaces, managing multiple workspaces can be useful when you have to manage multiple sets of independent transactions.

When you start Microsoft Jet, what happens with workspaces depends on whether or not you have security enabled. If you don't have security enabled, Microsoft Jet automatically creates the default **Workspace**, DBEngine.Workspaces(0). The settings of the **Name** and **UserName** properties of the default **Workspace** are "#Default Workspace#" and "Admin," respectively.

If you want to use security, you can set the **SystemDB** property to the System.MDW, set the **DefaultUserName** property, and set the **DefaultPassword** property. When you use the **OpenDatabase** method without specifying a **Workspace** object, a default **DBEngine.Workspaces** object is created using these defaults.

## Users

For more information on workgroup databases and security, see Chapter 10, "Managing Security."

Microsoft Jet provides security services with which you can protect objects in the database from unwanted access. The security model relies on users and groups defined in a workgroup database. The **Users** collection contains all **User** objects for a workspace. A **User** object defines a user account as it exists in the **Workspace** object's workgroup database. Each **User** object also has a **Groups** collection, that contains a **Group** object representing each group to which the user belongs.

## Groups

As with the **Users** collection, the **Groups** collection is used by Microsoft Jet in its security model to control access to objects. The **Groups** collection contains all **Group** objects. A **Group** object defines a group of users as it exists in the **Workspace** object's workgroup database. Each **Group** object also has a **Users** collection that contains a **User** object for each of the users in the group.

## Databases

In DAO, a **Database** object represents a currently open database. This can be a native Microsoft Jet database file or an external database. You can have multiple databases open at a time, even databases of different types. The **Databases** collection contains all **Database** objects for a workspace.

---

**Microsoft Access and Visual Basic Users**   In Microsoft Access 2.0 and earlier, a number of databases are automatically opened when you open your database through the Microsoft Access interface. These include the various wizard and utility libraries that Microsoft Access uses to perform its own functions. When you open a database through the user interface by clicking **Open Database** on the **File** menu, Microsoft Access uses DAO to assign this database to the first ordinal position in the **Databases** collection, Databases(0). The other databases that Microsoft Access opens are used internally by Microsoft Access and are not part of the **Databases** collection.

In Microsoft Access for Windows 95, library databases are identified by VBA references, but are not actually loaded until needed.

Microsoft Access also assigns the default **Workspace** object, Workspaces(0), to the user currently logged on.

In Visual Basic, no databases are open in a workspace until you explicitly open them—unless you use the **Data** control, which automatically opens the appropriate database for you when the form containing the data control is loaded.

## TableDefs

The **TableDef** object represents a table that is saved in the database. This includes tables in the current database, as well as linked tables (known as *attached* tables in previous versions of Microsoft Jet). It is important to note that **TableDef** objects do not represent data stored in the table—they represent the structure of the table. The **TableDefs** collection contains all **TableDef** objects for a database.

## QueryDefs

The **QueryDef** object represents a saved query in the database and maintains information on the query's properties including its SQL representation. The **QueryDefs** collection contains all **QueryDef** objects for a database.

## Fields

**Field** objects define a specific field (or *column* in relational parlance). **TableDef**, **QueryDef**, **Index**, **Relation**, and **Recordset** objects all contain **Fields** collections. The following table explains the **Field** object's representation for each object type that can contain a **Fields** collection.

| Collection | Description |
| --- | --- |
| TableDefs | Defines the fields in a table, but does not contain data. |
| QueryDefs | Defines the fields in a query, but does not contain data. |
| Indexes | Defines the characteristics of the fields that make up an index in the context of the information the index must maintain about the field. |
| Relations | Defines the characteristics of the fields that make up a relation in the context of the information the relation must maintain about the field. |
| Recordsets | Defines the fields that exist in the tables or queries that the **Recordset** is based on. Contains data in the field's **Value** property. |

## Parameters

For more information on formal and implicit parameters, see Chapter 4, "Queries."

With Microsoft Jet queries, you can define formal *parameters*. These parameters represent unknown values that must be supplied by the user running the query or the program executing the query. A query's formal parameters are represented by **Parameter** objects in the **Parameters** collection of the QueryDef. This collection is particularly useful when you execute a QueryDef in code and have to plug values into the parameters.

## Recordsets

The **Recordset** object is somewhat different from other Data Access Objects shown so far in that it exists only while your code or application is running. A **Recordset** object represents, in memory, a set of records from one or more tables. **Recordset** objects are one of the most powerful constructs in Microsoft Jet because they enable you to programmatically access not only native Microsoft Jet tables, but any tables from ISAM data sources such as Microsoft FoxPro, or ODBC data sources such as Microsoft SQL Server. In addition, **Recordset** objects can be based on queries that join multiple tables from heterogeneous data sources.

For more information on **Recordset** objects, see Chapter 5, "Working with Records and Fields."

The **Recordsets** collection contains all **Recordset** objects open in the current **Database** object. Again, note that a **Recordset** is an object that you explicitly open through code. For example, in Microsoft Access, when you are viewing a table through the interface, this table is not a **Recordset** object. Microsoft Jet internally sets a recordset to access the data, but this recordset is not part of the **Recordsets** collection.

## Relations

Microsoft Jet provides powerful relational and referential integrity abilities through its use of relations. A **Relation** object represents a relationship between columns in two or more tables. The **Relations** collection contains all **Relation** objects for a given **Database** object.

## Containers

One of the important requirements of the engine is that it must retain application independence: The engine is not specifically tied to any one host application. However, Microsoft Jet does provide a generic collection and object type so that an application can store its objects in the database. This generic object is known as a container. The **Containers** collection holds all container objects for a **Database** object.

As an example, Microsoft Access relies on Microsoft Jet to store its application-specific objects such as forms, reports, macros, and modules. Microsoft Jet keeps track of these foreign objects through the **Containers** collection. Microsoft Jet treats these objects as binary streams of data: It is the **Container** object that enables Microsoft Jet to store application-specific objects without violating its application independence. You can set security to control access to containers.

## Documents

The **Document** object represents a specific object in the **Documents** collection. In the **Containers** example in the previous paragraph, it was noted that Microsoft Access uses the **Containers** collection to organize its own objects. The **Document** object stores a specific instance of an application-specific object. For example, when Microsoft Access creates a database, it creates a variety of container objects, one each to store forms, reports, macros, and modules. As the Microsoft Access user creates forms, the forms are stored as individual **Document** objects in the

**Forms** container added to the database by Microsoft Access. You can set security to control access to a document.

## Properties

Every Data Access Object has a **Properties** collection. A **Property** object contains information on the characteristics of an object. You can read property values to get information about an object's characteristics or write to a property to define an object's characteristics. You can also define your own properties.

# DAO Basics

Now that you're familiar with object types represented in DAO, it's time to move on to the basics of using DAO. This section shows you how to work with DAO objects and collections, how to refer to objects, and how to represent objects using object variables.

# Objects and Collections

As you've seen from the discussion of the DAO hierarchy, the concept of objects and collections is very important. Most object types have collections that contain each of that type's members. For example, the **TableDefs** collection represents a set of all table objects in the database, and it contains all individual **TableDef** objects.

You usually refer to an object through its collection hierarchy. That is, you specify the hierarchical path that points to the object you want to refer to. In general, you start with the **DBEngine** object and work your way through the hierarchy:

DBEngine.*ParentCollection.ChildCollection!Name*

There are four syntactical forms used to refer to an object in a collection:

- *Collection!name,* or *Collection![name]* if the object *name* contains non-standard characters such as spaces
- *Collection("name")*
- *Collection(string)* where *string* is an expression or variable containing the name of the object
- *Collection(index)* where *index* is the object's position within the collection

Using the first form, the *Collection!name* or *Collection![Name]* syntax, you can directly refer to an object by its name. This form is more compact and can make long object references more readable than the other forms. For example, compare the following two references:

```
TableDefs("Customers").Indexes("PrimaryKey").Fields("LastName")
```

versus

```
TableDefs!Customers.Indexes!PrimaryKey.Fields!LastName
```

With the second form, the *Collection("name")* syntax, you can refer to an object using a string expression. The following two examples are equivalent:

```
TableDefs("Customers")
TableDefs("Cust" &  "omers")
```

Using the third form, the *Collection(string)* syntax, you can refer to an object using a variable:

```
Dim strName As String
strName = "Customers"

TableDefs(strName)
```

With the fourth form, the *Collection(index)* syntax, you can refer to an object according to its position in a collection. The primary use of this form is to iterate through a collection's members in a program loop. For example:

```
' Show the first ten TableDef names.
For intX = 0 To 9
    Debug.Print Workspaces(0).Databases(0).TableDefs(intX).Name
Next intX
```

Indexes on DAO collections are always zero-based. This means that the first element in the collection is zero. This is important to note because you're probably used to working with one-based indexes, where the first element is one.

It's important to note that an object's position within a collection isn't fixed. It can change as objects are added to and removed from the collection. You shouldn't refer to objects by way of their position within a collection except within a loop, as shown previously.

## Using Bang (!) and Dot (.) Syntax

In DAO syntax, you separate parts of your object references using either the bang (!) character or the dot (.) character. When to use bang and when to use dot depends on the context of its use. In general:

- Use the dot to refer to a member or property that is created and maintained by Microsoft Jet.
- Use the bang to refer to a member or property that you create.

For example, to refer to a TableDef's **Name** property (a property created and maintained by Microsoft Jet), use the dot operator:

```
TableDefs("Customers").Name
```

However, to refer to a **TableDef** field (a member you create), use the bang operator.

In DAO 2.0, you could use the bang and dot separators to refer to members of default DAO collections. In DAO 3.0, the use of the dot separator is supported only on the **Fields** collection of **Recordset**, dynaset, table, and snapshot objects. For all others, only the bang is supported.

```
TableDefs("Customers").Fields!LastName
```

## Determining the Boundaries of Collections

The previous example, which lists the first 10 **TableDef** names, is hardly a robust piece of code. It assumes that there are at least 10 tables in the database and has no provision for showing all table names. To work effectively with collections, it's important to understand how collections are ordered and how to determine their boundaries.

To determine the boundaries of a collection, use the **Count** property of the collection. The value of this property reflects the number of objects in the collection. For example, if a collection's **Count** property returns 5, then there are five objects in that collection. DAO collections, however, are *zero-based*: The collection starts at 0, with the first object in the collection occupying slot 0. This requires your code to subtract one from the **Count** property when comparing it to the current index position of the collection. For example, the following code illustrates how to print the names of all the tables in the database:

```
For intX = 0 to Workspaces(0).Databases(0).TableDefs.Count - 1
    Debug.Print Workspaces(0).Databases(0).TableDefs(intX).Name
Next intX
```

You can see how this example subtracts one from the **Count** property to make sure the comparison works.

You can avoid these problems in your VBA programs by using the **For Each** structure instead of a **For...Next** loop. The following code accomplishes the same task, but without requiring you to handle collection boundaries:

```
For Each tbl In Workspaces(0).Databases(0).TableDefs
    Debug.Print tbl.Name
Next tbl
```

When an object is deleted, the count for its collection is decremented. Therefore, loops that cycle through and delete objects should not use the starting collection count as an upper bound.

## Default Collections

Almost all of the Data Access Objects have default collections. With these default collections, you can use a more compact form for referencing in your code. For example, the default collection of the **Workspace** object is the **Databases** collection. Using normal syntax, you refer to a database like this:

```
DBEngine.Workspaces(0).Databases(0)
```

Using the default collection of the **Workspace** object, you could shorten this line to:

```
DBEngine.Workspaces(0)
```

Also, given that the default collection of the **DBEngine** object is the **Workspaces** collection, you could further shorten the example to:

```
DBEngine(0)
```

The following table lists the default collections available in DAO:

| Object | Default collection |
| --- | --- |
| DBEngine | Workspaces |
| Workspace | Databases |
| User | Groups |
| Group | Users |
| Database | TableDefs |
| Recordset | Fields |
| TableDef | Fields |
| QueryDef | Parameters |

| Object | Default collection (*cont'd*) |
|---|---|
| Index | Fields |
| Relation | Fields |
| Container | Documents |

## Setting and Using Object Variables

As you start working with DAO, you will realize that your code can become quite cumbersome as you continually refer to objects by their position in the DAO hierarchy. For example, consider the following code, which shows the names of all the fields in the Customers table:

```
Function ShowFieldNames()
    Dim intX As Integer

    For intX = 0 To DBEngine(0)(0).TableDefs("Customers"). _
        Fields.Count - 1
        Debug.Print DBEngine(0)(0).TableDefs("Customers"). _
            Fields(intX).Name
    Next intX
End Function
```

This type of coding presents two problems. The first is that you must type and maintain long code lines that refer to objects. The second is that your application's performance may suffer as each long reference is parsed and resolved. The solution to these problems lies in *object variables*.

Object variables are a special type of variable supported by VBA. Using object variables you can set a reference to an object once, and then refer to the object variable instead of making an explicit reference through the DAO hierarchy. Each object type in DAO has a corresponding object variable type. For example, the **Workspace** object has a corresponding workspace object variable, the **Database** object has a corresponding database object variable, and so on.

To use an object variable, you first declare the variable type and then use the **Set** statement to assign an object to it. The general form is:

**Dim** *VarName* **As** *ObjectVariable*
**Set** *VarName=SomeDataAccessObject*

By using object variables, you could shorten the previous example to:

```
Function BetterShowFieldNames()
    Dim intX As Integer
    Dim tblCustomers As TableDef

    Set tblCustomers = DBEngine(0)(0).TableDefs("Customers")
```

```
      For intX = 0 To tblCustomers.Fields.Count - 1
          Debug.Print tblCustomers.Fields(intX).Name
      Next intX
End Function
```

From this example it's clear that object variables enable a coding style that reduces the number of direct object references. This results in code that is easier to read and maintain. Additionally, because Microsoft Jet has to resolve the reference to the Customers table only once, it should run marginally faster.

It's important to note that object variables differ from regular variables in that they have no intrinsic value. They point to an object, not a value. In other words, an object variable points to an object's representation in memory. All object variables that are assigned to an object point to the same object.

## Closing Object Variables

Four of the Data Access Objects are considered *temporary* objects. That is, they exist only in memory and are never saved as part of the database file. These objects are **Workspace**, **Database**, **QueryDef**, and **Recordset** objects.

---

**Note**  **QueryDef** objects are not generally temporary objects. As mentioned earlier, a **QueryDef** object represents a saved query in the database. However, unlike other permanent objects, if a QueryDef is created using DAO, the QueryDef can be used without first appending it to the **QueryDefs** collection.

Another slight exception is the **Database** object. Although it's a temporary object, it does refer to the database file on disk, which is permanent.

---

Because these objects exist in memory, you generally want to close them when your code no longer needs them. DAO defines a **Close** method used to close these temporary objects.

### Closing Workspaces

Prior to Microsoft Jet 2.0, you couldn't close a **Workspace** object that contained any open **Database** objects. In version 3.0, if you close a **Workspace**, Microsoft Jet closes all the **Workspace** object's **Database** objects and rolls back any pending transactions.

In Microsoft Access, a *default workspace*, Workspaces(0), is automatically created when you open a database through the user interface. Attempts to close this default **Workspace** are ignored.

### Closing Databases

If you open a database with the **OpenDatabase** method, you should close it when you are done. There is an important exception to this rule: Do not close the DBEngine(0)(0) database unless you want to de-reference all other active database variables pointing to DBEngine(0)(0). (A simple way to handle this exception in Microsoft Access is to refer to the current database through the CurrentDB function.)

When you assign a database variable to DBEngine(0)(0), the variable simply references an existing internal pointer to the database object. When you close that database variable, *all* references, whether local or not, are closed. Consider the following two procedures:

```
Sub OpenOne()
    Dim dbs As DATABASE, dbsOne As DATABASE

    Set dbs = OpenDatabase("C:\Samples\Chap02\NwindJet.mdb")

    ' NOTE: If this code is executing in a Microsoft Access
    ' module, the following expression should be:
    ' Set dbsOne = DBEngine.Workspaces(0).Databases(0)(1)
    Set dbsOne = DBEngine.(0)(0)

    Call OpenTwo
    Debug.Print dbsOne.Name
End Sub


Sub OpenTwo()
    Dim dbsTwo As DATABASE

    ' NOTE: If this code is executing in a Microsoft Access
    ' module, the following expression should be:
    ' Set dbsOne = DBEngine.Workspaces(0).Databases(0)(1)
    Set dbsTwo = DBEngine.Workspaces(0).Databases(0)(0)

    dbsTwo.Close
End Sub
```

When you run the OpenOne procedure, you would expect it to open a pointer to the database, call the OpenTwo procedure, and then print the **Name** property of the **Database** object. As it turns out, OpenOne fails with a run-time error when it tries to access the **Name** property of the **dbOne** object. This is because the OpenTwo procedure has closed the internal pointer to the database, and therefore, all database variables set using DBEngine(0)(0) are now invalid.

Closing a **Database** object also affects any open DAO 1.*x* **Dynaset** or **Recordset** objects that have pending edits. The close behavior depends on the version of DAO you are using, and is represented in the following table.

| DAO version | Explicitly closing a dynaset's database | Implicitly closing a dynaset's database | Explicitly closing a Recordset's database | Implicitly closing a Recordset's database |
|---|---|---|---|---|
| 1.*x* (Microsoft Access) | Dynaset stays open | Dynaset stays open | NA | NA |
| 1.*x* (Visual Basic) | Causes an error | Dynaset stays open | NA | NA |
| 2.*x* | Dynaset stays open | Dynaset stays open | Causes an error | Recordset is closed |
| 3.0 | NA | NA | Recordset is closed | Recordset stays open |

For example, in DAO 3.0, if you explicitly close a **Database** object (using the **Close** method) and that database contains a **Recordset** with pending edits or uncommitted transactions, the edits are canceled, the transactions are rolled back, and the **Recordset** is closed. If you implicitly close a **Database** object (by exiting a procedure that has the **Database** object as a local object variable) the database's **Recordset** objects are left open.

### Closing QueryDefs

DAO allows you to have temporary **QueryDef** objects that you can actually use in code. For example, you could create a temporary **QueryDef** object in your code by naming it "". You can then execute the QueryDef, and discard it after you have the results you need. However, this functionality does not extend to other data-definition objects such as TableDefs. This behavior is particularly useful with parameterized and pass-through queries. Because such queries are often temporary in nature, the behavior of temporary **QueryDef** objects is well suited to creating and running pass-through queries.

# DAO Properties

Objects and collections have little value if there is no way to interrogate and manipulate the characteristics of those objects. Objects in DAO all have *properties* that define their characteristics. Property values can be retrieved to allow you to see the characteristics of an object, and changed to allow you to change the characteristics of an object.

Properties are represented by **Property** objects. **Property** objects themselves contain properties. Each **Property** object has the following properties:

| Property | Description | Data type |
|---|---|---|
| Name | Name of the property | Text |
| Value | Value of the property | Variant |
| Type | Data type of the property | Integer constant |
| Inherited | Identifies the property as inherited from another object. For example, a recordset **Field** property inherited from a TableDef field. | Boolean |

## Types of Properties

Microsoft Jet identifies two types of properties. *Built-in* properties are those automatically created and maintained by Microsoft Jet. For example, when you create a **TableDef** object, Microsoft Jet automatically creates a set of properties for the table, including **Name** and **Connect**.

*User-defined* properties are those you create and add to an object. For example, you might want each field in your table to store a description that explains what the field is for. By adding a user-defined property called **Description** to the field object's **Properties** collection, you can store and retrieve this information.

For more information about creating replicable databases, see Chapter 7, "Database Replication."

### Replication Properties

When you create a replicable database, Microsoft Jet automatically adds new properties to tables, indexes, and application-specific objects in the **Containers** collection. These properties are used by the engine to determine whether or not objects are replicable.

## The Properties Collection

Each Data Access Object has an associated **Properties** collection. This collection contains a **Property** object that identifies each characteristic or attribute that the object exposes to DAO. Like other collections, you can iterate through the collection and refer to specific elements. You refer to properties and **Properties** collections using the same syntax as in other DAO collections:

- Properties!*PropertyName* or Properties![*PropertyName*], if the property name contains non-standard characters such as a space
- Properties("*PropertyName*")
- Properties(*expression*) where *expression* is a string expression or variable
- Properties(*index*) where *index* is the property's position within the collection

For example, to refer to the **Type** property of the LastName field in the Customers table, you could use any of the following:

```
TableDefs!Customers.Fields!LastName.Properties!Type
TableDefs("Customers").Fields("LastName").Properties("Type")
TableDefs("Customers").Fields("LastName").Properties(strType)
TableDefs("Customers").Fields("LastName").Properties!Type
TableDefs("Customers").Fields("LastName").Properties(3)
```

In the third line of this example, a string variable, strType, is set to the value of "Type".

Also note that in the last line, the code assumes that the **Type** property is always going to be in the fourth position in the **Properties** collection of the **Property** object. As mentioned earlier in the "Objects and Collections" section, you should not rely on an object's position within its collection. The only time you would refer to a property by its index is when you are iterating through the **Properties** collection to retrieve or write values.

## Read-Only Properties

When you programmatically create an object, you set its properties to define its characteristics. You then append the object to its collection to make it a permanent part of the database. However, some properties become read-only after the property's parent is appended. For example, after you append a new TableDef and its **Field** objects to its collection, some of its properties become read-only. To change these properties, you must delete the object and re-create it.

## Setting Bitwise Properties

Some properties store bitwise values. To correctly store and retrieve values for these properties, you must use bitwise operators. For example, the **Attributes** property of a **TableDef** object defines certain characteristics such as how the table is linked. To set this property for a new **TableDef** object, you would use the following line of code:

```
tblMyNew.Attributes = dbAttachExclusive OR dbAttachSavePWD
```

You can use the AND operator to retrieve bitwise values, and the AND NOT operator to clear them.

**Microsoft Access Users**  When you create an object through DAO using Microsoft Jet, only the standard built-in properties are created in the new object's **Properties** collection. However, when Microsoft Access creates a Microsoft Jet object, it might add several user-defined properties to objects. These properties are a special case of user-defined properties known as *application-defined* properties. For example, when you use Microsoft Access to create a table, and type a value in the Description field, it automatically adds a new property to the **TableDef** object to represent the Description.

Many Microsoft Access developers are confused by the fact that Microsoft Access does not automatically add these application-defined properties to new objects. When you create a new table through the user interface in Microsoft Access, the **Description** and **Format** properties are not created unless you type a value in the Description and Format fields. This can cause a problem, because when you try to read the value of these properties on a table where they have not been specified, a run-time error occurs. The technique for avoiding this problem, and for writing more robust property-retrieval code in general, is to trap for errors when looking at **Property** objects. For more information, see the "Retrieving Properties" section later in this chapter. In general, for properties not created by Microsoft Access through the interface, you can add them by using the user interface, or by programmatically creating the property and appending it to the appropriate object's **Properties** collection.

This behavior is also of interest to non-Microsoft Access users who might open a database created by Microsoft Access and wonder where these properties have come from, or for developers whose code may be affected if a user unexpectedly opens the database using Microsoft Access, causing more properties to be added.

# DAO Methods

*Methods* are procedures that act on objects. Most Data Access Objects have associated methods you can use to interact with them in useful ways. Methods are similar to procedures that you create in your code, with the important distinction that methods are explicitly tied to an object, whereas your procedures can generally be called independently.

Like a procedure, a method can return a value or return nothing. The general form for using methods is:

*object.method* $[[() \text{ arglist } ()]]$

If the method returns a value, use the assignment operator:

*variable=object.method*

If the method doesn't return a value, omit the assignment operator.

# Using DAO

So far, this chapter has dealt with DAO in an abstract fashion, describing its syntax and architecture. In this section, those ideas are put to work.

Note that this section introduces the creation and manipulation of objects. It does not fully cover all of the DAO operations you may want to perform. For complete information see the following chapters.

| For information on | See |
| --- | --- |
| Using data definition objects (databases, tables, fields, and so on) | Chapter 3, "Data Definition and Integrity" |
| **Recordset** objects representing actual data | Chapter 5, "Working with Records and Fields" |
| Setting multiuser properties | Chapter 6, "Creating Multiuser Applications" |
| Using groups, users, and permissions for access control | Chapter 10, "Managing Security" |

# Creating Database Objects

The first operation you are likely to perform using DAO involves data definition: creating objects, assigning characteristics through properties, and interrogating the structures of existing objects.

Creating an object is a two-step process. First you create the object and define its characteristics, and then you append the object to its collection. The process of appending an object to a collection makes it a permanent or *persistent* part of the database. Additionally, if the object you're creating contains child objects, you first create the parent object, then create and append the child object, and finally, append the parent object to its collection.

---

**Note**   Unlike other Data Access Objects, **Workspace** objects can be created and then appended to the **Workspaces** collection, but they do not become a permanent part of the database. When you exit Microsoft Jet, any workspaces in use are destroyed. It is important to remember that a **Workspace** is only a "space" used to identify a specific user and transaction sequence. **Recordset** objects work in the same way.

Also, when you create a new **Database** object using the **CreateDatabase** method, it automatically becomes a persistent object on the drive where it is created. You do not have to append it to the **Databases** collection to make it persistent.

---

For more information, see Chapter 8, "Accessing External Data."

You can also "create" tables that are links to tables in other databases. These links are actually pointers to tables that exist outside the current database. And because Microsoft Jet supports a variety of external data sources, you are not limited to linking to Microsoft Jet databases.

## Creating Your Own Properties

Earlier in this chapter, you were introduced to the concept of user-defined properties. Microsoft Jet objects are extensible through DAO using these properties, which allow you to store and retrieve your own information with an object. The next example opens an existing table and adds a property called **DateLastModified** to each field. You could then use this property to store the date when the field's structure was last changed:

```
Sub AddNewProp()
    Dim dbsContacts As DATABASE
    Dim tblCustomers As TableDef
    Dim fldTmp As Field
    Dim prpNew As Property

    Set dbsContacts = OpenDatabase("C:\Samples\Chap02\Contacts.mdb")
    Set tblCustomers = dbsContacts.TableDefs("Customers")

    For Each fldTmp In tblCustomers.Fields
        Set prpNew = fldTmp.CreateProperty("DateLastModified")
        prpNew.Type = dbText
        prpNew.Value = Now
        fldTmp.Properties.Append prpNew
    Next fldTmp
    dbsContacts.Close
End Sub
```

Of course, simply adding a property does not automatically update and maintain it. In the previous example, the **DateLastModified** property would be added to the **Field** object, but that's the extent of what the code does. Your application must programmatically update the value of this property when appropriate.

For more information, see Chapter 10, "Managing Security."

## Adding Groups and Users

Microsoft Jet implements security through users, groups, and permissions settings on specific objects. You can use DAO to programmatically create users and groups, and to assign permissions to objects.

# Using the Error Object

The **Errors** collection contains **Error** objects that represent Microsoft Jet errors that have occurred. You can use these objects to determine if errors have occurred, and to try to work around them. The following example attempts to open a database that doesn't exist, and then displays the errors that result:

```
Sub ShowErrors()
    Dim dbsNotThere As DATABASE
    Dim intX As Integer
    Dim errTmp As Error
```

```
    ' Disable VBA error handling
    On Error Resume Next

    ' Try to open a nonexistent database
    Set dbsNotThere = OpenDatabase("XYZ123.456")

    ' Renable VBA error handling
    On Error GoTo 0

    ' Look at the errors generated
    For Each errTmp In DBEngine.Errors
        Debug.Print errTmp.Description
        Debug.Print errTmp.Number
        Debug.Print errTmp.Source
    Next errTmp
End Sub
```

The **Error** object is unlike the error variables and functions that you are used to with VBA in that more than one error can be generated by a single operation. Also, objects in the **Errors** collection are appended in a manner different from the other DAO collections. The most detailed errors are placed at the end of the collection, and the most general errors are placed at the beginning.

The set of **Error** objects in the **Errors** collection describes one error. The first **Error** object is the lowest-level error, the second the next-highest level, and so on. For example, if an ODBC error occurs while trying to open a **Recordset** object, the last **Error** object contains the DAO error indicating that the object couldn't be opened. The first **Error** object contains the lowest-level ODBC error. Subsequent errors contain the ODBC errors returned by the various layers of ODBC. In this case, the Driver Manager, and possibly the driver itself, returns separate **Error** objects.

# Interrogating Existing Database Objects

Now that you have seen how to create objects, it's time to explore another side of data definition using DAO: looking at existing objects and determining their structures. The key concept in retrieving structures is that of iterating through collections. For example, you iterate through the **TableDefs** collection to find all the tables, and then iterate through a specific **TableDef** object's **Fields** collection to find information about the table's fields.

### Refreshing Collections

A key aspect of interrogating collections is the concept of *refreshing* collections. As objects are appended to and deleted from collections, DAO generally keeps track of the collection. However, there are situations where DAO does not know the current state of a collection. This occurs when:

- Users are modifying a shared database's object in a multiuser environment.

- SQL statements alter structures (for example, "DROP TABLE Customers").

- Changes are made through a host program's user interface. Note that this is not the case for applications that use DAO directly, such as Visual Basic and Microsoft Excel.

If you want to make sure that you're looking at the most up-to-date version of a collection, you should refresh the collection. This is done using the **Refresh** method of the collection. The general syntax for the **Refresh** method is:

*Collection*.**Refresh**

where *collection* is the name of the collection you want to refresh. For example, if your code needs a complete list of **TableDef** objects in the database, you might want to refresh the collection before using it. You can accomplish this with the following line of code:

```
dbCurrent.TableDefs.Refresh
```

where dbCurrent is a pointer to the database.

Use the **Refresh** method only when necessary, because it may take time to refill the collection.

## Listing the Objects in a Database

This first thing you'll want to do is get a list of Data Access Objects in the current database. The following example displays all **TableDef**, **QueryDef**, **Relation**, and **Container** objects in the Contacts database:

```
Sub ShowInventory()
    Dim dbsContacts As DATABASE
    Dim tblDef As TableDef
    Dim qryDef As QueryDef
    Dim relDef As Relation
    Dim conDef As Container

    Set dbsContacts = OpenDatabase _
        ("C:\Samples\Chap02\Contacts.mdb")

    Debug.Print "TableDefs"
    For Each tblDef In dbsContacts.TableDefs
        Debug.Print "  " & tblDef.Name
    Next tblDef

    Debug.Print "QueryDefs"
    For Each qryDef In dbsContacts.QueryDefs
        Debug.Print "  " & qryDef.Name
    Next qryDef

    Debug.Print "Relations"
    For Each relDef In dbsContacts.Relations
        Debug.Print "  " & relDef.Name
    Next relDef

    Debug.Print "Containers"
    For Each conDef In dbsContacts.Containers
        Debug.Print "  " & conDef.Name
    Next conDef
    dbsContacts.Close
End Sub
```

## Retrieving Properties

To identify the properties associated with an object, you write code to iterate through the object's **Properties** collection, retrieving the information you want. Some special cases in referencing properties might be problematic:

- Some properties are not readable. The **Password** property of the **User** object is a good example. You can set the value of the property through code, but you cannot retrieve the value. (If you could, it would be an obvious hole in the Microsoft Jet security model.)

- Certain properties that you are explicitly looking for might not exist. This is common when you're expecting a certain user-defined or application-defined property to exist and it doesn't. For example, if you're using Microsoft Access, you may have code that retrieves the **Description** property of a **TableDef** object. However, unless you explicitly add a description to the table through the Microsoft Access user interface or through DAO code, this user-defined property does not exist, and a run-time error occurs when the code executes.

The following example code displays each of the properties of each **User** object in the current **Workspace**. It uses VBA error handling to work around errors that might occur by using the **On Error Resume Next** statement. After it has tried to retrieve the property value, it checks to see if an error has occurred, and if so, checks the specific error number. If the error was anticipated, as in the case of trying to retrieve a write-only property (error 3251), error text is printed. If the error was not anticipated, it is asserted using the error command:

```
Sub ShowUserProps()
    Dim usrDef As User
    Dim prpDef As Property
    Dim varPropertyValue As Variant

    For Each usrDef In Workspaces(0).Users
        For Each prpDef In usrDef.Properties
            ' Disable VBA error handling
            On Error Resume Next
            varPropertyValue = prpDef.Value
            ' See if an error occurred
        Select Case Err
            Case 3251 ' Feature not available error
                Debug.Print prpDef.Name & ": <error: " _
                        & Error$ & ">"
            Case 0     ' No error
                Debug.Print prpDef.Name & ":" & varPropertyValue
            Case Else ' Unanticipated error
                Error Err
        End Select
            ' Re-enable VBA error handling
        On Error GoTo 0
        Next prpDef
    Next usrDef
End Sub
```

## Getting a Table Structure

The previous two examples are rolled into the following example, which displays all of the property and field information for all tables in the database. It does this by calling a function that generically handles the retrieving of property values. As each **Property** object is encountered in the DescribeTable procedure, it is passed to the GetProp procedure, which checks and formats it:

```
Function GetProp(prpDef As Property) As String
    Dim strTmp As String
    Dim varPropertyValue As Variant

    ' Put the property name in a temporary string.
    strTmp = "Property:" & prpDef.Name

    ' Disable VBA error handling.
    On Error Resume Next

    ' Attempt to retrieve the property value.
    varPropertyValue = prpDef.Value

    ' Check for an error.
    If Err <> 0 Then
        varPropertyValue = "Error: " & Error$
    End If
    ' Re-enable VBA error handling
    On Error GoTo 0

    ' Concatenate the string.
    GetProp = strTmp & " Value:" & varPropertyValue
End Function
```

# Modifying Existing Database Objects

For complete information on modifying database objects, see Chapter 3, "Data Definition and Integrity."

Another key point of DAO's use is the ability to modify the structure of existing objects. Wherever it is possible, you can use DAO to modify an object's structure. However, there are things that you cannot programmatically alter using DAO. For example, you cannot use DAO to change a **TableDef Field** object's **Type** property. Because this would change the data type of the field and require a conversion of existing data in the table, you must delete the field object and then re-create it, specifying the new data type.

# Manipulating Data

Finally, to round out the discussion of using DAO, you'll learn about one of its most important uses: data manipulation. In DAO, the **Recordset** object is the primary object for interacting with data stored in the database. **Recordset** objects are extremely powerful because they provide a great deal of flexibility in working with data.

**Recordset** objects are different from most other Data Access Objects in that they exist only as temporary objects. Even though the method is called **OpenRecordset**, you don't actually *open* existing **Recordset** objects; you create new ones. After you close a **Recordset** object, it no longer exists.

To create a **Recordset**, you use the **OpenRecordset** method based on a **Database** object. The general syntax is:

**Set** *variable* = *database*.**OpenRecordset**(*source*[, *type*[, *options*]])

where *variable* is the **Recordset** variable to assign to the **Recordset**, *database* is the database variable pointing to the database where you want to open the **Recordset**, *source* is the source of the data, *type* is a numeric constant denoting the type of **Recordset** to open, and *options* specifies various options to be applied to the **Recordset**.

There are three types of **Recordset** objects:

- Table-type **Recordset**. A representation in code of a table in the current database that you can use to retrieve, add, change, or delete records.
- Dynaset-type **Recordset**. The result of a query that can have updatable records. A dynaset is a dynamic set of records that you can use to add, change, or delete records from an underlying database table or tables. A dynaset can contain fields from one or more tables in a database.
- Snapshot-type **Recordset**. A static copy of a set of records that you can use to find data or generate reports. A snapshot can contain fields from one or more tables in a database, but it can't be updated.

You can open **Recordset** objects:

- Directly on tables in the database.
- On tables in other databases.
- On tables linked to external data sources such as ODBC or ISAM.
- On queries.
- Based on SQL strings that you dynamically create in code.

You can also use a variety of options when creating a **Recordset**. You can specify:

- That other users can't modify or add records in the table or tables you are accessing.
- That other users can't view records (table-type **Recordset** only).
- That your view of the database is read-only.
- That you can append only new records (dynaset-type **Recordset** only).
- That inconsistent updates are allowed (dynaset-type **Recordset** only).
- That only consistent updates are allowed (dynaset-type **Recordset** only).
- That the **Recordset** is a forward-scrolling snapshot.

# New Features In Version 3.0

Numerous changes have been made to DAO with version 3.0. If you are already using Microsoft Jet, you will probably migrate your application to make use of the new functionality in the engine. This section outlines the major changes made to DAO in version 3.0. For complete information, use this section in conjunction with DAO online Help.

## Accessing DAO

DAO is now enhanced to be callable as an OLE Automation in-process server: Any licensed program that can call an OLE server can access DAO functionality. Unlike a regular DLL that exposes calls but no details about them, an OLE Automation server contains a *type library* that describes every object, method, and property, and so forth, in the DLL. An OLE Automation client, such as Visual Basic or Microsoft Excel, can read this type library and make the appropriate calls to the DLL.

Microsoft Access, which relies on Microsoft Jet for its database functionality, has calls to Microsoft Jet written into its internal code, and does not generally call the DAO DLL except when VBA code in an Microsoft Access database calls DAO. In other words, when you display a table through the Microsoft Access user interface, Microsoft Access calls Microsoft Jet directly through hard-coded routines. When you open a table using VBA, Microsoft Access hands the request to the DAO component.

## DBEngine Object

The **INIPath** property is now set to the path to the Windows Registry, because .INI files are no longer used by Microsoft Jet. You should use the **SystemDB** property of the **Database** object to point to the workgroup information file you want to use. The **SystemDB** property sets or returns the path for the current location of the system database file.

## Workspace Object

You can now assign a password to a database. You can specify the password to open a password-protected database in a workspace using the Source argument (also known as the Connect string).

## Database Object

For more information, see Chapter 7, "Database Replication."

Replication adds new properties to database objects: **Replicable**, **DefaultPartner**, **ReplicaID**, and **DesignMasterID**. Note that only **ReplicaID** and **DesignMasterID** exist on every database, whether it's replicable or not, and the **Replicable** property exists only if the user creates and appends it. If a database is made replicable (by appending the **Replicable** property), then the additional properties **DefaultPartner** and **LastUpdated** are created by Microsoft Jet.

With the new **Synchronize** method, you can synchronize the current database (through replication) with a replica database. The new **MakeReplica** method creates a new replica based on the current replicable database.

To support the new database password functionality, a new method, **NewPassword**, enables you to assign a new password to the database.

The behavior of the **Database** object's **Close** method has changed in the way it closes any pending **Recordset** changes. For more information, see the "Closing Object Variables" section earlier in this chapter.

## Recordset Object

You can now retrieve rows from a **Recordset** into an array using the new **GetRows** method.

The previously undocumented **AbsolutePosition** property is now supported and documented, and **PercentPosition** now supports **TableDef** objects without indexes.

## TableDef Object

For Replication, the **Replicable, KeepLocal,** and **ConflictTable** properties have been added.

## Container Object

Supports the new **AllPermissions** property, discussed under **Document** object.

## Document Object

Supports the new **AllPermissions** property, which differs from the existing **Permissions** property in that it returns all permissions for an object, including group permissions.

The ability to add and delete properties to the **Document** object is also new to version 3.0.

## All Objects

You can specify a version 3.0–only DAO type library that removes support for obsolete objects, methods, and properties. For more information, see the following section, "Compatibility Issues."

## Licensing Issues

Microsoft Jet is a technology that Microsoft sells and includes as part of its products as a feature. When you create an application using Microsoft Jet, certain restrictions apply to how you can distribute it. For the vast majority of applications, this is not a problem, but some examples may help:

- If users of your application already have Microsoft Office (or Visual C++, Visual Basic, Microsoft Excel, or Microsoft Access) installed on their machines, then your application has no restrictions. The users already have a full license for DAO by virtue of owning those Microsoft applications.

- If users of your application do not have any of these Microsoft applications, then they can use Microsoft Jet only in conjunction with your application. This is the default behavior, and it's enforced by various protection mechanisms.

- If your product is intended to be used by other developers who will then create their own product (Product B), this is okay as long as their product does not require Microsoft Jet. If Product B requires Microsoft Jet, it must rely on the Microsoft Jet already on the users' machines (for example, Product B must require users to install Microsoft Office). Alternatively, your product must require the use of Visual Basic, Microsoft Access, or Visual C++ in the process of building Product B, so that Product B already has the right to redistribute Microsoft Jet.

This last example may make more sense if you think of it this way: Microsoft wants to ensure that you don't compete directly with Microsoft Jet by creating a clone of Microsoft Jet that you then sell to developers who can in turn give it to other people.

Again, see the license agreement that came with your product if you have any doubts about licensing.

# Compatibility Issues

As with any new version of software, you should be aware of compatibility issues when converting existing applications to Microsoft Jet 3.0.

## The DAO 3.0 Type Library

As DAO has evolved, new objects, methods, and properties have been introduced that render their prior equivalents obsolete. To enhance performance and decrease memory usage, future versions of Microsoft Jet will eliminate support for these obsolete constructs. In order to ease the conversion of applications that use the older objects, methods, and properties, the DAO3032.DLL file contains dual type libraries. These type libraries define the properties and methods that DAO can use.

The DAO 2.5 type library is backward compatible with previous versions of Microsoft Jet and supports all previous objects, methods, and properties. Use this type library if you want existing DAO code to work with Microsoft Jet 3.0 without conversion.

The DAO 3.0 type library removes support for obsolete objects, methods, and properties. Because they are not supported, use of these constructs while the DAO 3.0 type library is in use causes compile errors in your code. The benefit of this behavior is that it allows you to verify that your programs use the latest DAO features by quickly identifying code that uses outdated methods and properties.

In Microsoft Access for Windows 95, Visual Basic 4.0, Microsoft Excel 7.0, and Microsoft Project 7.0, the **Tools** menu contains a **References** command when you are in a code module. Clicking this command gives you a list of the OLE Automation servers that are available. Two versions of DAO are now available: the DAO 2.5/3.0 Compatibility Library and DAO 3.0 Object Library.

By clicking DAO 3.0 Object Library and then recompiling, you can identify any obsolete DAO code with compiler errors that place you at the appropriate line.

---

**Microsoft Access Users**   When you create a new database, the DAO 3.0 Object Library is automatically selected. This ensures that all new DAO code you create uses the new objects. Note that you can't use both libraries at once.

---

The following table details the differences between the two DAO type libraries.

| Excluded in DAO 3.0 | What to use instead |
| --- | --- |
| All CreateDynaset methods | **OpenRecordset** |
| All CreateSnapshot methods | **OpenRecordset** |
| All ListFields methods | **Fields** collections |
| All ListIndexes methods | **Indexes** collection |
| DBEngine.FreeLocks | Idle |
| DBEngine.SetDefaultWorkspace | DefaultUser/Password |
| DBEngine.SetDataAccessOption | IniPath |
| Database.BeginTrans | Workspace.BeginTrans |
| Database.CommitTrans | Workspace.CommitTrans |
| Database.Rollback | Workspace.Rollback |
| Database.CreateDynaset | **OpenRecordset** |
| Database.CreateSnapshot | **OpenRecordset** |
| Database.DeleteQuerydef | Delete |
| Database.ExecuteSQL | Execute |
| Database.ListFields | **Fields** collection |
| Database.ListTables | **TableDefs** collection |

| Excluded in DAO 3.0 | What to use instead (*cont'd*) |
|---|---|
| Database.OpenQuerydef | **QueryDefs** collection |
| Database.OpenTable | **OpenRecordset** |
| Querydef.CreateDynaset | **OpenRecordset** |
| Querydef.CreateSnapshot | **OpenRecordset** |
| Querydef.ListParameters | **Parameters** collection |
| Snapshot | **Recordset** object |
| Dynaset | **Recordset** object |
| Table | **Recordset** object |

As you can see in the table, DBEngine.Freelocks has been replaced with Idle. You may have used Idle with FreeLocks, but with Microsoft Jet 3.0, read locks are persistent as long as you have currency on a row. Locks are removed when currency is no longer on the row.

However, Idle affects how remote ODBC connections check to see if they can be closed down. If a connection is not in a transaction, Idle is the timeout seconds value, and no pending results are pending for any statement, an attempt will be made to close an ODBC connection.

FreeLocks is valid if the Microsoft Jet 2.5 or 3.0 DAO type library is loaded, even though it has no functionality against a Microsoft Jet 3.0 database. FreeLocks will generate an error message if the DAO 3.0 type library is loaded.

# Optimizing DAO

When using DAO, you can apply specific techniques to your code to improve its performance. In the scope of this introductory chapter, only optimizations that are intrinsic to the operation of DAO as a programming interface are covered. Each chapter (where appropriate) in this guide contains an optimizations section that may contain further DAO optimizations. Use the following table to find other DAO optimizations.

| To optimize | See |
|---|---|
| Accessing local data | Chapter 5, "Working with Records and Fields" |
| Accessing external ISAM data | Chapter 8, "Accessing External Data" |
| Accessing ODBC data | Chapter 9, "Developing Client/Server Applications" |
| Multiuser environments | Chapter 6, "Creating Multiuser Applications" |

# Caveats

Few absolutes exist in the area of performance optimization. While a technique may work well in one piece of code, it may slow down other code. As with any optimization tips, use the following techniques judiciously. Try them on your code, and be sure to verify that they actually improve performance. Additionally, by concentrating on the 10% of your code that is executed most frequently, you will achieve better results than spending an inordinate amount of time tuning code that is rarely used.

Finally, the techniques shown in this chapter relate to using DAO in a generic sense. Usually, the most important optimizations involve your data, and reading and writing data to the true bottleneck in your system: the disk. As a general rule, you should concentrate 95% of your optimization efforts on disk I/O–related code, and 5% on the type of optimizations shown here.

## Cache TableDef and Field Property Collection References

Some properties of **TableDef** and **Field** objects can be time-consuming to retrieve. User-defined properties that can be accessed only by way of the **Properties** collection fall into this category. Rather than referencing such properties directly in a loop, it is more efficient to assign them to an object variable before entering the loop, and then use the object variable instead of a property reference. In the following example, SlowProc reads a property value each time the loop is iterated. FastProc shows you how to make this faster:

```
Sub SlowProc()
    Dim intCount As Integer

    For intCount = 0 To 100
        Debug.Print DBEngine(0)(0).TableDefs!Customers.Properties!Name
    Next intCount
End Sub

Sub FastProc()
    Dim tblCustomers As TableDef
    Dim intCount As Integer
    Dim prp As Property

    Set tblCustomers = DBEngine(0)(0).TableDefs!Customers
    Set prp = tblCustomers.Properties!Name

    For intCount = 0 To 100
        Debug.Print prp.Value
    Next intCount
End Sub
```

## In Loops, Use Field Objects Instead of Direct Field References

To speed up iterative (looping) processes through large numbers of rows using DAO, declare all field references explicitly. The following is an example of VBA code that can be improved by using direct **Field** references:

```
While Not rstOrd.EOF
    rstOrd.Edit
    rstOrd.Fields!Price = rstOrd!Qty * rstOrd!UnitCost
    rstOrd.Update
    rstOrd.MoveNext
Wend
```

In this example, the field variable "lookup" (where VBA equates variable names with database fields) for the field variables Price, Qty, and UnitCost is performed in the same While loop where the calculations are performed. In this configuration, both calculations and lookups must be performed inside the While loop, which is not an efficient design. This is how the changes might look:

```
Dim fldPrice As Field
Dim fldQty as Field
Dim fldUnitCost As Field

Set fldPrice = rstOrd!Price
Set fldQty = rstOrd!Qty
Set fldUnitCost = rstOrd!UnitCose

While rstOrd.EOF
    rstOrd.Edit
    fldPrice = fldQty * fldUnitCost
    rstOrd.Update
    rstOrd.MoveNext
Wend
```

This tip is especially true for users accessing DAO from Microsoft Excel. This optimization could be further improved by using an Update query to accomplish the same task. Also, the performance differences of this technique will be marginal for a small number of records.

## Take Advantage of Default Collections

Most Data Access Objects have several collections. One of these collections is the default collection for that object and allows an abbreviated syntax. For example:

```
dbEngine.Workspaces(0).Databases(0)
```

can be shortened to

```
dbEngine(0)(0)
```

This shorter syntax is also slightly faster. Before rushing in and changing all your code, however, you might want to consider whether the loss in readability is worth the marginal increase in speed. This may be something to consider only when trying to squeeze the last drop of performance out of a loop. Even then, the previous tip suggests a potentially more effective way of doing this.

## Replace Old ListTables Code With Collection-Based Code

Microsoft Access 1.*x* shipped with some List methods that have better equivalents in Visual Basic 3.0 and Microsoft Access 2.0. In addition to the syntax being shorter, using the new syntax is often quicker.

## Avoid Refreshing Collections

You learned earlier that you can use the **Refresh** method to get an up-to-date view of a collection and its objects. This is particularly useful in multiuser environments. Unfortunately, this method is a time-consuming operation relative to most other DAO operations and should be used sparingly.

CHAPTER 3

# Data Definition and Integrity

This chapter discusses how to create, delete, and maintain TableDefs, QueryDefs, relations, and referential integrity with the Microsoft Jet database engine.

As discussed in Chapter 2, "Introducing Data Access Objects," Microsoft Jet stores its objects, and information about objects, using a hierarchical system of containers. A database contains TableDefs, which further contain Fields, which in turn have Properties, and so on. Data Access Objects map those objects onto a programming interface you can control through VBA.

You can create tables and set up relationships among those tables entirely through the native Microsoft Jet DAO interface. Using DAO gives you a great deal of flexibility and control over how your database objects are created. With DAO, you write Visual Basic code to create a new object, assign values to that object's properties to specify data type, length, validation rule, and so on, and then append that object to a collection within the database's object hierarchy.

Many people are familiar with the industry-standard SQL language and its Data Definition Language (DDL) subset. Most of the features of Microsoft Jet that can be manipulated through DAO can also be controlled with SQL DDL commands. This chapter shows both methods and points out differences.

### Contents

For information on copying the code examples from the companion CD-ROM to your hard disk drive, see "Using the Companion CD-ROM" in the Preface.

### Using CH03.MDB and CHAP03.VBP

If you copied the samples from the companion CD-ROM, you can find the code examples for Microsoft Access in C:\SAMPLES\CHAP03\ ACCESS\CH03.MDB. The corresponding code examples for Visual Basic are in C:\SAMPLES\CHAP03\VB40\CHAP03.VBP.

To run any of the code examples in this chapter, open the .MDB file in Microsoft Access or open the .VBP file in Microsoft Visual Basic 4.0. You can use the examples to help you understand the concepts discussed in the chapter—or you can modify them and use them in your own applications.

# Creating a Database

As a developer, you are probably familiar with creating a new Microsoft Jet database file either interactively through the Microsoft Access user interface, or through the Data Manager utility that ships with Visual Basic. You can also create a new database file programmatically. Perhaps your Visual Basic application is designed to build a new database when the application is first installed, or perhaps your application must create an archive or export database.

The following creates a new database using VBA:

```
Dim dbNew As Database
Set dbNew = CreateDatabase("C:\Samples\Ch03\New Database.mdb", _
    dbLangGeneral, dbVersion30)
```

This code uses the **CreateDatabase** method on a **Workspace** object to build a new, empty database. The arguments to **CreateDatabase** specify the name, location, language, and version of the new database.

# The Database Owner

For information on using Microsoft Jet security, see Chapter 10, "Managing Security."

In the previous example, the **CreateDatabase** method is used on the default **Workspace**. The effect of using the default **Workspace** depends on which host application is running the Visual Basic code. For example, in Microsoft Access for Windows 95, the default **Workspace** is identical to the one used to sign on to the application database that is executing the code. The new database's owner is the user who executes the **CreateDatabase** command.

In Visual Basic 4.0, the default **Workspace** consists of the Admin user and the **Workspace** named "#DefaultWorkspace#." Because the user doesn't log on to the database independently of the code executed by Visual Basic, there is no user **Workspace** for Visual Basic to inherit as there is with Microsoft Access.

As an alternative to using the default **Workspace**, you can explicitly open a **Workspace**, and then create the new database using that **Workspace**:

```
Sub CreateSecuredDatabase()
    Dim wspSecured As Workspace
    Dim dbNew As Database

    DBEngine.IniPath = _
        "HKEY_LOCAL_MACHINE\Software\Microsoft\MyApp\3.0\KeyFolder"

    Set wspSecured = _
        DBEngine.CreateWorkspace("SecuredWS", "Admin", "")
    Set dbsNew = _
        wspSecured.CreateDatabase("C:\Samples\Chap03\Secdb.MDB", _
        dbLangGeneral, dbVersion30)
End Sub
```

Microsoft Jet security requires that the creator of the database build the new database while logged on to the appropriate secured **Workspace**. The owner of the database can be specified *only* when the database is first created.

A new database can be created programmatically only with DAO; there is no SQL DDL method to create a new database. A database, however, cannot be deleted programmatically through DAO. If you want to delete a database programmatically, use the VBA **Kill** statement to remove the file at the file-system level of the operating system.

## Microsoft Jet vs. Other Data Source Types

To Microsoft Jet, a "database" has different meanings depending on the source of the data. While a Microsoft Jet database is physically represented on disk as an .MDB file, the database for other data sources is just a logical construction. For example, a dBASE or FoxPro database is nothing more than a directory on a hard disk that contains one or more .DBF or .CDX files, or both. You must still "open" the database by creating a **Database** object, but the database is not a physical object.

You don't have to use the **CreateDatabase** method if you intend to build non-Jet database files. It's possible to create new dBASE or FoxPro tables with Microsoft Jet, as shown later in this chapter and in subsequent chapters.

## Creating and Modifying Tables

In Chapter 2, you were introduced to the concept of using DAO to add a new TableDef to a database by appending **Fields** into the **Fields** collection of a **TableDef** object, and then appending that TableDef to the **TableDefs** collection of the database. In the same way, you can add field-level and table-level validation rules, or specify indexes and inter-table relationships entirely through DAO code or SQL DDL statements.

When you use the Microsoft Access user interface to add fields to a table design datasheet or specify validation rules and default values in a property cell, Microsoft Access is using DAO behind the scenes to tell the underlying Microsoft Jet database engine how to build or modify your tables.

Anything that a user can do through the Microsoft Access user interface can be done within your own code. In some cases, properties and capabilities of Microsoft Jet available to you as a DAO programmer are not available through Microsoft Access. For example, through DAO you can specify fixed-length text fields for your tables. Microsoft Access specifies only variable-length fields.

# Creating Tables Using SQL Data Definition Language

Even the most basic TableDef in a Microsoft Jet database must contain at least one field. It's not necessary to specify a primary key, validation rules, or any of the other optional properties such as **Description** or **DefaultValue**. The table is nothing without its fields.

Using SQL DDL statements, the simplest statement you can use to create a new table in a database is as follows:

```
CREATE TABLE MYTABLE (MYFIELD TEXT);
```

The CREATE TABLE statement creates a table called MYTABLE with one field called MYFIELD. MYFIELD is built as a variable-length text field with a maximum length of 255 characters. The field is not required, and may contain **Nulls**. It's not indexed.

## Communicating with Microsoft Jet Using SQL DDL

You can pass SQL DDL statements to Microsoft Jet in a variety of ways.

Microsoft Access provides the RunSQL action and the **DoCmd** object. Using RunSQL, you can execute an SQL statement that acts on the current database. For example, the CREATE TABLE statement could be executed from a RunSQL macro action as follows:

```
Sub MakeTableMYTABLE()
    DoCmd.RunSQL "CREATE TABLE MYTABLE (MYFIELD TEXT);"
End Sub
```

There is no equivalent for the **DoCmd** object in other Microsoft Jet host languages such as Visual Basic 4.0 or Microsoft Excel 7.0. In Visual Basic 4.0 and Microsoft Access for Windows 95, you can use the **Execute** method on a **Database** object declared in code:

```
Private Sub cmdCreateTable_Click()
    Dim dbs As Database
    Set dbs = OpenDatabase("C:\Samples\Chap03\New Database.mdb")
```

```
        dbs.Execute "CREATE TABLE MYTABLE (MYFIELD TEXT);"
        dbs.Close
End Sub
```

Finally, you can create a Microsoft Jet QueryDef that contains the previous SQL statement, and then execute that QueryDef in code. Assuming that you had saved the query under the name qryMakeTableMYTABLE, you could execute it in the following way:

```
Sub ExecuteCreateTableQuery()
    Dim dbs As DATABASE, qdf As QueryDef

    Set dbs = .OpenDatabase ("C:\Samples\Chap03\New Database")
    Set qdf = dbs.QueryDefs("qryMakeTableMYTABLE")

    qdf.Execute
    dbs.Close
End Sub
```

For a complete discussion on using Microsoft Jet **QueryDef** objects, see Chapter 4, "Queries."

For information on creating QueryDefs, see the "Microsoft Jet QueryDef Objects" section later in this chapter.

For the remainder of this chapter, SQL DDL examples are given with the actual text of the SQL statement only. Remember, however, that to actually communicate your SQL statements to Microsoft Jet, you must execute the DDL statement using one of the previously described code techniques.

# Creating Tables Using DAO

The DAO equivalent for the SQL DDL statement shown previously is as follows:

```
Sub CreateTable_MYTABLE_WithDAO()
    Dim dbs As DATABASE
    Dim tdfMYTABLE As TableDef
    Dim fldMYFIELD As Field

    Set dbs = OpenDatabase ("C:\Samples\Chap03\New Database")
    Set tdfMYTABLE = dbs.CreateTableDef("MYTABLE")
    Set fldMYFIELD = tdfMYTABLE.CreateField("MYFIELD", dbText)

    tdfMYTABLE.Fields.Append fldMYFIELD
    dbs.TableDefs.Append tdfMYTABLE
    dbs.Close
End Sub
```

The DAO method and the SQL DDL method create identical tables. Which method you use depends on the style of programming with which you are most comfortable.

The DAO techniques used to create and modify tables are similar to the way Microsoft Jet uses hierarchical collections in other contexts. For example, you can append a field to the **Fields** collection using DAO in ways very similar to those used to add a user-defined property to a form document in a Microsoft Access application. In addition, certain types of database properties can be set only through the Microsoft Access user interface, or through DAO in code.

# Specifying Field Properties

The previous examples show a simple case of building a table with a single field using default property values. You usually specify many additional properties and override certain default values.

This example, using DAO, creates a table with four fields, specifying various non-default values for the fields ID, Name, Response, and Class:

```
Sub CreateMarketingSurvey()
    Dim dbs As DATABASE
    Dim tdf As TableDef
    Dim fldID As Field
    Dim fldName As Field
    Dim fldResponse As Field
    Dim fldClass As Field

    Set dbs = OpenDatabase ("C:\Samples\Chap03\New Database")
    Set tdf = dbs.CreateTableDef("Marketing Survey")
    Set fldID = tdf.CreateField("ID", dbInteger)
    fldID.Required = True

    Set fldName = tdf.CreateField("Name", dbText)
    fldName.Required = True
    fldName.Size = 40
    fldName.AllowZeroLength = True
    fldName.DefaultValue = "Unknown"

    Set fldResponse = tdf.CreateField("Response", dbMemo)
    Set fldClass = tdf.CreateField("Class", dbText, 10)
    fldClass.Required = True
    fldClass.ValidationRule = "in('A','B','X')"
    fldClass.ValidationText = "Enter one of A, B, or X"

    tdf.Fields.Append fldID
    tdf.Fields.Append fldName
    tdf.Fields.Append fldResponse
    tdf.Fields.Append fldClass
    dbs.TableDefs.Append tdf
    dbs.Close
End Sub
```

Using SQL DDL statements, you can specify only the field names and data types. Microsoft Jet 3.0 doesn't support such ANSI SQL constructs as field-level CHECK or DEFAULT clauses. You cannot use SQL DDL to fill in the **ValidationRule** and **DefaultValue** properties of a field, for example. The closest you can come to re-creating the previous table using only SQL DDL statements is:

```
CREATE TABLE [Marketing Survey]
   (ID SHORT,
   Name TEXT (40),
   Response MEMO,
   Class TEXT (10));
```

## Built-In vs. Application-Defined Properties

The **ValidationRule** property, along with other properties such as **Size**, **Required**, and **DefaultValue**, are known as built-in properties.

In addition to these built-in properties, you can specify a variety of other application-defined properties. For example, when you build a table using the Microsoft Access user interface, it's common to add a **Caption** property or a **Description** property:

```
Dim dbs As database
Dim tdf As TableDef

Dim fldID As Field

Set dbs = DBEngine(0)(0)
Set tdf = dbs.CreateTableDef("Marketing Survey")
Set fldID = tdf.CreateField("ID", dbInteger)
fldID.Required = True
fldID.Description = "Survey Identification Number" '<<<Error here

tdf.Fields.Append fldID

dbs.TableDefs.Append tdf
```

Unfortunately, this code will not execute as written. There is no built-in **Description** property for a field object in a Microsoft Jet table. This property is meaningful only to Microsoft Access. It's set by Microsoft Access whenever the user enters a field description in a table's Design view, though it's not created by default. If you want Microsoft Access to recognize a **Description** property for fields you create through DAO, you have to manually add the property to the **Properties** collection of the field:

```
Sub CreateMarketingSurveyWithDescription()
    Dim dbs As DATABASE
    Dim tdf As TableDef
    Dim prp As Property
    Dim fldID As Field

    Set dbs = OpenDatabase("C:\Samples\Chap03\New Database.mdb")
    Set tdf = dbs.CreateTableDef("Marketing Survey With Description")

    Set fldID = tdf.CreateField("ID", dbInteger)
    fldID.Required = True

    tdf.Fields.Append fldID
    dbs.TableDefs.Append tdf

    Set prp = fldID.CreateProperty("Description", _
        dbText, "Survey Identification Number")

    fldID.Properties.Append prp
    dbs.Close
End Sub
```

## Field-Level Validation

A field-level validation rule is enforced directly by Microsoft Jet: It doesn't matter whether you attempt to update the field through Microsoft Access, a custom Visual Basic program, or an ODBC call from a third-party program such as PowerBuilder.

The validation rule must be an expression that evaluates either to **True** or **False**. If the validation rule doesn't evaluate to **True**, then an error is raised, and the contents of the **ValidationText** property of the field are made available to the calling program.

How this message is conveyed to the user depends on the context of the calling program. For example, if the user attempts to enter an invalid value into the Microsoft Access Datasheet view of a table, then Microsoft Access beeps, displays the validation text in a message box, and waits for the user to respond. If the validation rule is violated by a Visual Basic or Microsoft Excel VBA code routine, then a trappable run-time error occurs.

Because Microsoft Jet is independent from host applications, the validation rule may not refer to features that are available from a specific application. You cannot use a custom function in the validation rule expression. Nor can you make reference to objects in the user environment, such as to Microsoft Access forms or controls.

It may seem reasonable to have a validation rule expression such as the following:

```
between 10 and MyUpperLimit()
```

However, even if you were to define a function called MyUpperLimit within a Microsoft Access module or within your Visual Basic code, the validation rule expression would still not be valid.

## Table-Level Validation

You might want to create a validation rule for a particular field that depends on the values of one or more of the other fields in the table. You can create a table-level validation rule to compare one field to another.

Suppose you want to specify a rule for a Marketing Survey table that requires that all surveys using the name TestAccount have a Class value of X. You cannot validate the Name field without knowing the value of the Class field, and vice versa. Only when a row is either updated or inserted is all the information available to evaluate the rule.

The validation rule should create an expression that can be evaluated as either **True** or **False**. If the expression evaluates to **True**, then the update is allowed. If the expression doesn't evaluate to **True**, then Microsoft Jet creates a trappable run-time error.

The following example uses DAO to add a table-level validation rule:

```
Sub AddTableLevelValidationRule()
    Dim dbs As DATABASE
    Dim tdf As TableDef
    Dim strValRule As String

    Set dbs = OpenDatabase("C:\Samples\Chap03\New Database.mdb")
    Set tdf = dbs.TableDefs("Marketing Survey")

    If Len(tdf.ValidationRule) Then
        MsgBox "Validation rule already exists."
    Else
        strValRule = "iif(Name = 'TestAccount' and " & _
            "Class <> 'X',false,true)"
        tdf.ValidationRule = strValRule
    End If
    dbs.Close
End Sub
```

Notice that you can test the properties as well as set them from DAO code. The previous example checks to make sure no current table-level validation rule exists before adding the new one.

Because table-level validation rules cannot be evaluated until all of the fields in a new row are populated, the validation rule is not checked until just before the new row is inserted into the table, or just before the existing row is updated.

The validation rule in the previous example makes use of the built-in **IIf** (ImmediateIf) function. While you cannot use your own custom functions within a validation rule, you can make use of a wide variety of built-in functions, including date functions and string manipulation functions such as **InStr**, **Len**, and **Mid**.

# Modifying Existing Tables

When you want to make structural changes to existing tables, you use the same techniques used to create the table. In SQL DDL, you use the appropriate ALTER TABLE statement to modify a table, or the DROP TABLE statement to delete it. In DAO, you either append or delete a field from the **Fields** collection of a TableDef, or delete the TableDef from the **TableDefs** collection of the database.

## Structural Changes Using SQL DDL

Starting with SQL DDL, you can remove a table from the database with the following statement:

```
DROP TABLE MYTABLE;
```

Note that this action is subject to all the security restrictions and referential integrity constraints that have been established on the database. If the table is part of one or more relationships that have been defined in the database, you will not be able to drop the table until you have first dropped the relationship. For more information, see the "Creating and Modifying Relations Using DAO" section later in this chapter.

Similarly, you can add or remove a column from an existing table:

```
ALTER TABLE MYTABLE ADD COLUMN NEWCOLUMN TEXT (20);
```

–Or–

```
ALTER TABLE MYTABLE DROP COLUMN NEWCOLUMN;
```

When you use SQL DDL statements, you have no control over the order in which new columns are added to a table. Columns are inserted at the beginning of the list of columns when using an ALTER TABLE ADD COLUMN statement. Additional ALTER TABLE ADD COLUMN statements from the original CREATE TABLE statement are placed before the existing columns and alphabetized by column name for the remaining columns that are added. For example:

```
CREATE TABLE DDLTest (A CHAR (10))
```

yields the column A in the first column slot.

```
ALTER TABLE ADD COLUMN G CHAR(10)
```

yields the column G in the first column slot and A in the second slot.

```
ALTER TABLE ADD COLUMN F CHAR(10)
```

yields the column F in the first column, G in the second slot, and A in the third slot.

You can't alter the data type of a column once it's created, or change its name. The only way to convert an existing column from one data type to another is to add a new column, run an update query to populate the column with values from the original column, and then drop the original column. The same limitation applies to changes made through DAO; you can change a column's name through DAO, but not its data type.

## Structural Changes Using DAO

In the discussion on creating tables, you learned that using DAO to make table modifications gives you much more flexibility than using SQL DDL statements.

Deleting a table using DAO requires you to delete the TableDef from the database's collection of **TableDef** objects:

```
Sub DeleteTableDefMyTable()
    Dim dbs As DATABASE

    Set dbs = OpenDatabase("C:\Samples\Chap03\New Database.mdb")

    dbs.TableDefs.Delete "MYTABLE"
    dbs.Close
End Sub
```

The following code creates the new column, specifies a default value, and specifies that the column is the second column in the table (ordinal position of one, with numbering beginning at zero):

```
Sub AddColumnToMarketingSurvey()
    Dim dbs As DATABASE
    Dim tdf As TableDef
    Dim fld As Field

    Set dbs = OpenDatabase("C:\Samples\Chap03\New Database.mdb")
    Set tdf = dbs.TableDefs("Marketing Survey")
    Set fld = tdf.CreateField("FollowupSent", dbBoolean)
    fld.DefaultValue = False
    fld.OrdinalPosition = 1

    tdf.Fields.Append fld
    dbs.Close
End Sub
```

The equivalent code to drop a field from a table is:

```
Sub DropColumnFromMarketingSurvey()
    Dim dbs As DATABASE
    Dim tdf As TableDef

    Set dbs = OpenDatabase("C:\Samples\Chap03\New Database.mdb")
    Set tdf = dbs.TableDefs("Marketing Survey")

    tdf.Fields.Delete "FollowupSent"
    dbs.Close
End Sub
```

## Altering Field and Table Properties Using DAO

You can modify certain field and table properties after the table is created. See the "Table-Level Validation" section earlier in this chapter for an example of adding a table-level validation rule to an existing table.

Unlike SQL DDL, which gives you no way to change a field's name, you can use DAO to change the **Field** object's **Name** property:

```
Sub ChangeColumnName()
    Dim dbs As DATABASE
    Dim tdf As TableDef

    Set dbs = OpenDatabase("C:\Samples\Chap03\New Database.mdb")
    Set tdf = dbs.TableDefs("Marketing Survey")

    tdf.Fields("Name").Name = "CustomerName"
    dbs.Close
End Sub
```

Other properties, however, cannot be changed. For example, the following code fails because you cannot change the **Type** property of a field once it has been created:

```
Set tdf = db.tabledefs("Marketing Survey")
tdf.fields("FollowupSent").Type = dbInteger  '<<< Error here
```

# Linking Tables from External Sources

For more information on working with external data types, see Chapter 8, "Accessing External Data."

With Microsoft Jet, you can work in a variety of external formats in addition to the native Microsoft Jet .MDB database. You can also open tables in other Microsoft Jet .MDB files without connecting them to the local database. It's possible to work with these external data sources directly—by opening table-type **Recordset** objects in code, for example.

The most flexible way to work with external data sources is to *link,* or attach, tables to the local database. The linked tables appear in the **TableDefs** collection of the database, and you can freely query and update them as if they were local tables.

For example, it's common in Microsoft Access applications to place all table objects in one database located centrally on a network server, and place the remaining application-specific objects, such as forms, reports, and modules, in a separate database that resides on the user's machine. Although the user's database doesn't contain any tables, there are links back to the original database. The application can look and act as if the linked tables were local.

This section describes how you can programmatically link to external tables using DAO to add the linked tables to the local **TableDefs** collection of your database.

## Adding a TableDef That References an External Table

When you add to a database a TableDef that is a reference to an external table, you must specify several additional items:

- The type and location of the external table
- The name of the table as it exists in its original location
- Whether or not you want to provide an alias for the table when using it in the local database

The following example links to the Customers table in the NWINDJET.MDB Microsoft Jet database:

```
Sub LinkToCustomersInNWIND()
    Dim dbs As DATABASE
    Dim tdf As TableDef

    Set dbs = OpenDatabase("C:\Samples\Chap03\New Database.mdb")
    Set tdf = dbs.CreateTableDef("Linked Customers")

    tdf.SourceTableName = "Customers"
    tdf.Connect = ";DATABASE=C:\Samples\Chap03\NwindJet.mdb"
    dbs.TableDefs.Append tdf
End Sub
```

Depending on the type of database you are linking to, the actual contents of the **Connect** property of the new TableDef will change. The **Connect** property in this example begins with:

```
;DATABASE=
```

Notice that nothing precedes the semicolon. This is the default value used when attaching to Microsoft Jet–format databases. If you are linking to a table in another format, such as Microsoft FoxPro, you must specify the name of the installable ISAM driver that Microsoft Jet should use:

```
FoxPro 2.0;DATABASE=C:\Access\Samples
```

The connection to an external ODBC source might require even more information:

```
ODBC;DSN=POWERDB;UID=sa;APP=My Application; _
    WSID=FastMachine;DATABASE=POWERDB;TABLE=dbo.PRODUCT
```

# Creating and Modifying Table Indexes

For information on how Microsoft Jet uses indexes for efficient data retrieval, see Chapter 4, "Queries."

So far, only tables that contain one or more fields have been built and assigned properties. For your tables to be truly useful, however, they must provide indexes for quickly finding and ordering particular records. Without indexes, it's necessary to search through each record in the table to find any given value.

A special form of index, the unique index, provides an additional data validation check. If you designate one field or combination of fields as a unique index, then Microsoft Jet stores only one occurrence of that particular value or combination of values in your table. The unique index also serves to uniquely identify each row in the table.

This section assumes you know which types of indexes you need, and explains how to build and modify them.

# Creating and Deleting Indexes Using SQL DDL

You can designate one or more indexes on a table either at the time the table is built, or after the fact.

## Adding Unique Indexes With SQL DDL

Using DDL SQL statements, you can specify a CONSTRAINT clause to add a unique index at the time the table is created:

```
CREATE TABLE Parking_Tickets
    (Ticket_ID INTEGER CONSTRAINT PrimaryKey PRIMARY KEY,
    Violator_Name TEXT (30),
    Violation_Type TEXT (10));
```

This DDL statement creates a unique index for the Ticket_ID field, and gives it the name "PrimaryKey." Although the primary key could have been given any name, PrimaryKey is a good choice, because that is the name Microsoft Access assigns by default when you create a primary key for a table in Design view.

## Adding Non-Unique Indexes With SQL DDL

You cannot use CREATE TABLE to add a non-unique index. To add a non-unique index to an existing table, you can use the CREATE INDEX statement:

```
CREATE INDEX IX_Violation_Type
    ON Parking_Tickets (Violation_Type)
    WITH DISALLOW NULL;
```

Because the index is not specified as unique, any number of rows within the Parking_Tickets table can have the same Violation_Type value. After the IX_Violation_Type index is created, searches for records involving the Violation_Type column are noticeably faster. The example uses the optional WITH DISALLOW NULL clause, which prohibits NULL entries in the indexed field.

An index can consist of combinations of more than one field:

```
CREATE TABLE Order_Item
    (OrderID INTEGER,
    LineItem INTEGER,
    ProductType TEXT (10),
    ProductCode TEXT (20),
    CONSTRAINT PrimaryKey PRIMARY KEY
    (OrderID, LineItem));
```

and

```
CREATE INDEX IX_ProdTypeCode
    ON Order_Item (ProductType, ProductCode);
```

## Deleting Indexes With SQL DDL

You can delete an index from a table with the DROP INDEX statement:

```
DROP INDEX IX_Violation_Type ON Parking_Tickets;
```

Note that it may or may not be possible to delete an index at any given time, depending on the inter-table relationships you've defined. To set up referential integrity between two tables, the linking fields must be indexed. For more information on setting up table relationships and their effect on indexes, see the "Referential Integrity and Relationships" section later in this chapter.

# Creating and Deleting Indexes Using DAO

For information on the various types of **Recordset** objects and how to use them, see Chapter 5, "Working with Records and Fields."

As you may recall from the discussion in Chapter 2, "Introducing Data Access Objects," a **TableDef** object can have one or more **Index** objects in its **Indexes** collection. Each **Index** object is in turn made up of one or more **Field** objects in its **Fields** collection.

Don't confuse the **Fields** collection of the **TableDef** object itself with the **Fields** collection of any given **Index**. All of the **Fields** in an **Index** object's **Fields** collection must also be **Fields** in the **Fields** collection of the TableDef itself, but each **Index** has its own **Fields** collection. These collections exist as a hierarchy of objects and collections.

Unlike some database systems, such as Microsoft FoxPro, with Microsoft Jet you cannot create an index on an expression, such as a subset of a field or a calculated field.

It's common to designate one field, or combination of fields, as the primary key of a table at the time it's created. The following example creates a unique index for the CustID field and names it PK_CustID:

```
Sub BuildTableWithUniqueIndex()
    Dim dbs As DATABASE
    Dim tdf As TableDef
    Dim fldCustID As Field
    Dim fldCustID_PK As Field
    Dim fldCustName As Field
    Dim idxPK As Index

    Set dbs = OpenDatabase("C:\Samples\Chap03\New Database.mdb")
    Set tdf = dbs.CreateTableDef("Customer")

    Set fldCustID = tdf.CreateField("CustID", dbText, 20)
    tdf.Fields.Append fldCustID

    Set fldCustName = tdf.CreateField("CustName", dbText, 30)
    tdf.Fields.Append fldCustName

    Set idxPK = tdf.CREATEINDEX("PK_CustID")

    Set fldCustID_PK = idxPK.CreateField("CustID")
    idxPK.Fields.Append fldCustID_PK
    idxPK.PRIMARY = True

    tdf.Indexes.Append idxPK
    dbs.TableDefs.Append tdf
    dbs.Close
End Sub
```

The name PK_CustID is used for the primary key of this table simply to show that any legal Microsoft Jet name can be used. However, this index might confuse a user of Microsoft Access who opens the table and expects to see the name "PrimaryKey" as the name of the primary key.

In most cases, the actual names used for the indexes are not significant. However, if you are opening table-type **Recordset** objects in code and want to specify the **Index** property of the **Recordset**, you must know and specify the actual index name.

You can delete an index from a table by using the **Delete** method of a **TableDef** object:

```
Sub DropCustomerPrimaryKey()
    Dim dbs As DATABASE
    Dim td As TableDef

    Set dbs = OpenDatabase("C:\Samples\Chap03\New Database.mdb")
    Set td = dbs.TableDefs("Customer")

    td.Indexes.Delete "PK_CustID"
    dbs.Close
End Sub
```

# Index Properties

An **Index** object can have one or more combinations of several property settings that influence its behavior. For example, the **Unique** property may be set, which ensures that only one record with a particular value (or combination of values, if the index consists of multiple fields) can exist. You can set the **Primary** property to **True** to designate the index as the primary key of the table.

Because a Primary Key is by definition a unique index, you might wonder what the difference is between the **Primary** property and the **Unique** property.

The main difference is that none of the fields that make up the primary key of a table can be **Null**. This restriction doesn't apply to an index with the **Unique** property. In addition to the **Unique** property of an index, you can specify that IgnoreNulls = **True**, and the **Null** values are not added to the index, so that a **Seek** for **Null** always fails. The following code creates a unique index for SSN, which forces all non-null values to be unique, but allows **Nulls** when the SSN is not known:

```
Sub CreateIndexWithIgnoreNulls()
    Dim dbs As DATABASE
    Dim tdf As TableDef
    Dim idx As Index
    Dim fld As Field

    Set dbs = OpenDatabase("C:\Samples\Chap03\NwindJet.mdb")

    dbs.TableDefs.Refresh

    Set tdf = dbs.TableDefs("Employees")
    Set idx = tdf.CREATEINDEX("IX_SSN")

    Set fld = idx.CreateField("SSN")
    idx.Fields.Append fld
    idx.UNIQUE = True
    idx.IgnoreNulls = True
```

```
                    tdf.Indexes.Append idx
                    dbs.Close
          End Sub
```

# Indexes and ODBC Views

For information on the updatability of external data sources, see Chapter 8, "Accessing External Data."

Earlier in this chapter, linking tables from external data sources such as Microsoft FoxPro or Microsoft SQL Server to a Microsoft Jet database file was discussed. A new TableDef was appended to the **TableDefs** collection of the database, and the original source of the table in the **Connect** property of the TableDef was specified.

In addition to linking to tables in external databases, you can also link to views in SQL data sources such as Microsoft SQL Server or Oracle. A view is a named SQL SELECT statement executed on the server that joins one or more tables, and selects one or more columns.

Normally, a linked view is not updatable even if it's based on an updatable table. For a linked table to be updatable, it must contain a Primary Key or a unique index.

When you link to a view rather than to a table, there is no index available and Microsoft Jet doesn't have enough information to treat the view as updatable. You can create a pseudo-index for the TableDef of the linked view to tell Microsoft Jet which of the columns in the linked view comprise the Primary Key or unique index in the table underlying the view. The index exists within the Microsoft Jet database only. Nothing is created on the server.

Assume there is a view named TPX_PRODUCT in a Microsoft SQL Server database with the following SQL statement:

```
create view TPX_PRODUCT as
    select * from PRODUCT where PRODFAMILY = 'TPX'
```

The following code links to a view on the server and then creates an **Index** on the view to make it updatable:

```
Dim dbs As database
Dim tdf As tabledef

Set dbs = DBEngine(0)(0)
dbs.tabledefs.Refresh

Set tdf = dbs.createtabledef("TPX_PRODUCT_LINK")

tdf.SourceTableName = "TPX_PRODUCT"
tdf.connect = "ODBC;DSN=POWERDB;UID=sa;APP=My Application;" & _
    "WSID=FastMachine;DATABASE=POWERDB"
```

```
dbs.tabledefs.append tdf

dbs.execute "CREATE UNIQUE INDEX PrimaryKey " & _
    "ON TPX_PRODUCT_LINK (PRODCODE)"
```

The newly linked view, TPX_PRODUCT, can now be updated as though it were a normal table.

# Creating Tables and Indexes in Installable ISAM Databases

As noted earlier, for database data sources other than Microsoft Jet, such as Microsoft FoxPro or Borland's dBASE, a "database" is simply a directory that contains a number of table files: There is no need to create a physical database for these data sources.

You can use DAO to create new tables, fields, and indexes on these external databases. You cannot, however, store **QueryDef** objects in any database type other than the native Microsoft Jet .MDB file.

The methods used to create objects in external database formats are the same, for the most part, as those used to create Microsoft Jet objects. The following example builds a new table called DBCUST.DBF in the C:\FOXPRO directory, and adds an index file called CUSTID.CDX to the CUSTID field:

```
Sub CreateFoxProTable()
    Dim dbs As DATABASE
    Dim tdf As TableDef
    Dim fldCustID As Field
    Dim fldCustName As Field
    Dim fldCustAddress As Field
    Dim fldCustCity As Field
    Dim fldCustState As Field
    Dim fldCustZip As Field
    Dim idxCustID As Index
    Dim fldCustIDIX As Field

    Set dbs = OpenDatabase("C:\Foxpro", _
        False, False, "FoxPro 2.5;")
    Set tdf = dbs.CreateTableDef("DBCUST")
    Set fldCustID = tdf.CreateField("CUSTID", dbText, 10)
    Set fldCustName = tdf.CreateField("NAME", dbText, 30)
    Set fldCustAddress = tdf.CreateField("ADDRESS", dbText, 30)
    Set fldCustCity = tdf.CreateField("CITY", dbText, 30)
    Set fldCustState = tdf.CreateField("STATE", dbText, 10)
    Set fldCustZip = tdf.CreateField("ZIP", dbText, 30)

    tdf.Fields.Append fldCustID
    tdf.Fields.Append fldCustName
    tdf.Fields.Append fldCustAddress
```

```
                      tdf.Fields.Append fldCustCity
                      tdf.Fields.Append fldCustState
                      tdf.Fields.Append fldCustZip

                      Set idxCustID = tdf.CREATEINDEX("CUSTID")
                      Set fldCustIDIX = idxCustID.CreateField("CUSTID")

                      idxCustID.Fields.Append fldCustIDIX
                      idxCustID.UNIQUE = True

                      tdf.Indexes.Append idxCustID
                      dbs.TableDefs.Append tdf
                      dbs.Close
                  End Sub
```

# Microsoft Jet QueryDef Objects

As its name implies, a **QueryDef** object is the definition of a query, either saved permanently in a Microsoft Jet database, or created as a temporary object in memory. A QueryDef doesn't contain any data or perform any action; it's simply the set of instructions Microsoft Jet uses to select information or perform an action, such as the deletion or insertion of rows in a database table.

Not everything that can be stored in a QueryDef is what is usually thought of as a "query." In addition to SQL SELECT statements, which select, join, and order information from one or more tables, a QueryDef can contain an SQL DELETE, INSERT, or CREATE TABLE statement.

Some **QueryDef** objects return their results in the form of a set of rows: These perform similarly to what are known as *views* in other relational database systems. You can create an SQL statement and save it as a permanent QueryDef in the database, and then use that QueryDef as if it were an actual table. You can join it to another table or QueryDef, and even update it.

Other QueryDefs can perform an action, such as an SQL DELETE statement, or modify the database structure, such as the CREATE TABLE statements used throughout this chapter. A special form of QueryDef, known as a *pass-through* query, is used to communicate directly with a back-end ODBC database such as Microsoft SQL Server or Oracle. The contents of these pass-through QueryDefs are not evaluated by Microsoft Jet, but are simply passed through to the back-end database, which then interprets the text contained in the **SQL** property of the QueryDef.

For a full discussion of how to use the various forms of QueryDef, see Chapter 4, "Queries."

This section covers how to create and manipulate QueryDefs in a database.

Note that QueryDefs can be created only in a native Microsoft Jet database. They cannot be stored in a FoxPro or SQL Server database, for example.

There is no SQL DDL method that can be used to create permanent **QueryDef** objects. All QueryDefs must be created either interactively, through a product such as Microsoft Access, or programmatically.

# Creating a Permanent QueryDef

In its most basic form, creating a new permanent QueryDef amounts to little more than naming the object and assigning an SQL text string that contains the function the QueryDef is to perform.

The following code creates a QueryDef called "qryJuneOrders":

```
Sub CreateqryJuneOrders()
    Dim dbs As DATABASE
    Dim qdf As QueryDef
    Dim strSQL As String

    Set dbs = OpenDatabase("C:\Samples\Chap03\NwindJet.mdb")
    Set qdf = dbs.CreateQueryDef("qryJuneOrders")

    strSQL = "SELECT DISTINCTROW Orders.EmployeeID, " & _
        "Sum(([UnitPrice]*[Quantity])-[Discount]) AS ExtendedPrice " & _
        "FROM Orders INNER JOIN [Order Details] ON " & _
        "Orders.OrderID = [Order Details].OrderID " & _
        "WHERE (((Orders.OrderDate) & _
        "Between #6/1/94# And #6/30/94#)) " & _
        "GROUP BY Orders.EmployeeID;"

    qdf.SQL = strSQL
End Sub
```

Notice that unlike with other collections, such as **Properties**, **Fields**, or **Indexes**, it's not necessary to explicitly append the QueryDef onto the **QueryDefs** collection of the database. Simply assigning the name and the SQL property immediately creates the QueryDef.

You can immediately use this new QueryDef in your application. You can create a **Recordset** object from it, join it to another query or table, base a report on it, and so on.

## Setting and Retrieving QueryDef Properties

When you create the new QueryDef and assign an SQL string to the **SQL** property, Microsoft Jet automatically supplies several other properties that describe the QueryDef—what type of action it performs, when it was created, whether or not it returns rows, and so on.

Most of these properties cannot be set in code. They are derived from the actual contents of the **SQL** property of the QueryDef. For example, the **Type** property is a QueryDef attribute that may be one of dbQSelect, dbQCrosstab, dbQMakeTable, and so on, depending on the function of the **SQL** property of the QueryDef. DateCreated and LastUpdated are maintained by the system when the query is first created or when it's modified.

The **ReturnsRecords** property is always created when you add a new QueryDef to the database, but it has meaning only in the context of an SQL pass-through query. If you are creating a pass-through QueryDef, you should specify whether or not the query performs an action (such as DELETE or INSERT), or whether it returns its result as a set of records. Microsoft Access uses this setting to determine whether or not to create a datasheet to display the results of the pass-through query when the query is executed interactively. It's also used to indicate whether the QueryDef can be used in an SQL SELECT statement to join to another table or QueryDef.

Recall from our discussion in Chapter 2, "Introducing Data Access Objects," that a **QueryDef** object can be both a permanent object stored in the database and an object created and executed within code. Certain properties, such as **RecordsAffected**, have a value only after the QueryDef is executed. For example, the following code creates a permanent QueryDef that deletes rows from the Customer table, and then executes the QueryDef. After the QueryDef executes, the **RecordsAffected** property contains the number of rows that were deleted:

```
Sub CreateAndExecuteDeleteQuery()
    Dim dbs As DATABASE
    Dim qdfNew As QueryDef

    Set dbs = OpenDatabase("C:\Samples\Chap03\NwindJet.mdb")
    Set qdfNew = dbs.CreateQueryDef("qryDeleteInactiveCustomers")

    qdfNew.SQL = "delete * from [Customer] where [Active] = false;"
    qdfNew.Execute

    MsgBox "Number of Customers deleted: " & qdfNew.RecordsAffected
    dbs.Close
End Sub
```

In this example, the actual permanent QueryDef is called qryDeleteInactiveCustomers, and qdfNew is the object variable that points to that QueryDef. You refer to properties of permanent **QueryDef** objects by creating an object variable on those objects, and then testing or setting those properties on the object variable. When this code executes, qdfNew disappears when the variable goes out of scope, but the permanent QueryDef, qryDeleteInactiveCustomers, remains.

## QueryDef Property Collections

For information on
using permanent
QueryDefs, including
how to supply
parameter values
programmatically, see
Chapter 4, "Queries."

In addition to the properties that pertain directly to an individual QueryDef, such as **SQL** or **ReturnsRecords**, a QueryDef can in turn contain other object collections. For example, a SELECT query has a **Fields** collection that identifies each field in the result set. The **Parameters** collection identifies the formal parameters. The following example creates a new parameter query and itemizes the **Fields** and **Parameters** collections of the new QueryDef:

```
Sub CreateCustSearchParameterQuery()
    Dim dbs As DATABASE
    Dim qdfNew As QueryDef
    Dim strSQL As String
    Dim prmTmp As Parameter
    Dim fldTmp As Field

    Set dbs = OpenDatabase("C:\Samples\Chap03\NwindJet.mdb")
    strSQL = "PARAMETERS [Enter Start of Customer Name] Text, " & _
        "[Enter the City] Text; " & _
        "SELECT DISTINCTROW Customer.* " & _
        "FROM Customer WHERE " & _
        "(((Customer.CustName) Like " & _
        "[Enter Start of Customer Name] & '*') " & _
        "AND ((Customer.City)=[Enter the City]));"

    Set qdfNew = dbs.CreateQueryDef("qryCustSearch")

    qdfNew.SQL = strSQL

    For Each prmTmp In qdfNew.PARAMETERS
        Debug.Print "Parameter: " & prmTmp.Name
    Next prmTmp

    For Each fldTmp In qdfNew.Fields
        Debug.Print "Field: " & fldTmp.Name
    Next fldTmp
    dbs.Close
End Sub
```

This code displays the two parameters, [Enter Start of Customer Name] and [Enter the City], in the debug window. It then displays each field that will be output by the query.

Unlike a **TableDef** object, in which you have to explicitly append each **Field** to the **Fields** collection, the **Fields** and **Parameters** collections for **QueryDef** objects are automatically derived by Microsoft Jet based on the contents of the **SQL** property of the QueryDef.

### Deleting QueryDefs

You can delete a permanent QueryDef simply by using the **Delete** method on a **Database** object:

```
Sub DeleteqryJuneOrders()
    Dim dbs As DATABASE

    Set dbs = OpenDatabase("C:\Samples\Chap03\NwindJet.mdb")

    dbs.QueryDefs.Delete "qryJuneOrders"
    dbs.Close
End Sub
```

# Temporary QueryDefs

It's not always necessary to create a permanent **QueryDef** object to execute an SQL statement, or to create a **Recordset** object in code. For example, you can pass an SQL string directly to the **Execute** method of a **Database** object to delete or insert rows in a table:

```
Sub DeleteInactiveCustomers()
    Dim dbs As DATABASE

    Set dbs = OpenDatabase("C:\Samples\Chap03\NwindJet.mdb")

    dbs.Execute "delete * from [Customer] where [Active] = false"
    dbs.Close
End Sub
```

Microsoft Jet automatically parses the **SQL** statement and creates a temporary QueryDef in the database, executes the temporary QueryDef, and then deletes the QueryDef.

The advantage to this method, from the programmer's standpoint, is that you avoid adding many permanent **QueryDef** objects to the database. The code becomes more readable, because you don't have to refer to an external tool such as Microsoft Access to find out what the QueryDef is supposed to accomplish.

You cannot, however, take advantage of certain properties of permanent QueryDefs, such as the **RecordsAffected** property. In addition, there is a slight performance hit taken each time the QueryDef is created and deleted; it must be parsed and "compiled" into its internal storage format each time this code is executed. A permanent QueryDef is parsed and compiled once, when it's first created, so subsequent executions can begin more quickly. Also, because the temporary QueryDef is not named, it cannot be used in a SELECT statement to join to another table or QueryDef.

It's possible for the user to create a **QueryDef** object that is not permanently saved in the database. You might want to do this, for example, if you are building up a SELECT query on the fly in code based on user input. After the temporary QueryDef is executed, it's no longer used, so there is no need to permanently save it in the database. This way, you don't need to create uniquely named **QueryDef** objects in a multiuser database.

To create a temporary QueryDef, you simply supply a zero-length string ("") as its name when you create it in code:

```
Sub CreateTempQuerydefDropTblImport()
    Dim dbs As DATABASE
    Dim qdfTemp As QueryDef

    Set dbs = OpenDatabase("C:\Samples\Chap03\NwindJet.mdb")
    Set qdfTemp = dbs.CreateQueryDef("", "drop table tblImport")

    qdfTemp.Execute
    dbs.Close
End Sub
```

A common case in which it would be to your advantage to create a temporary QueryDef is when you have to execute it repeatedly, but it's not needed on a permanent basis. The following example creates a temporary parameter QueryDef that repeatedly builds a **Recordset** until the user enters "Exit":

```
Sub CreateAndExecuteCustSearch()
    Dim dbs As DATABASE
    Dim qdfTemp As QueryDef
    Dim rst As Recordset
    Dim strCust As String

    Set dbs = OpenDatabase("C:\Samples\Chap03\NwindJet.mdb")
    Set qdfTemp = dbs.CreateQueryDef("")

    qdfTemp.SQL = "select count(*) as RecCount from Orders " & _
        "where [CustomerID] = [Which CustomerID] "

    Do While strCust <> "Exit"
        strCust = InputBox("Which Customer?")
        If strCust <> "Exit" Then
            qdfTemp![Which Customer] = strCust
            Set rst = qdfTemp.OpenRecordset()
        MsgBox "Orders for Customer " & strCust & ": " & rst!RecCount
        End If
    Loop
    dbs.Close
End Sub
```

If the action specified by the QueryDef is going to be performed only once, then there is little need to create a temporary QueryDef. You could simply pass the **SQL** statement directly on to the **Execute** method of a **Database** object, for example, or use the SQL SELECT statement directly as the argument to an **OpenRecordset** method:

```
Sub CountCustomers()
    Dim dbs As DATABASE
    Dim rst As Recordset

    Set dbs = OpenDatabase("C:\Samples\Chap03\NwindJet.mdb")
    Set rst = dbs.OpenRecordset("select count(*) As RecCount " & _
        "from Customer")

    MsgBox "Customer count: " & rst!RecCount
    dbs.Close
End Sub
```

# Referential Integrity and Relationships

So far, individual table objects have been looked at in isolation. TableDefs have been added to a database, and **Fields** added to those tables. **Indexes** have been added to speed searching, and **QueryDef** objects created.

With Microsoft Jet, you can specify a variety of inter-table rules that define how tables relate to one another. By creating **Relation** objects in your database, you can ensure that the data in your tables remains logically consistent. You can, for example, make sure that no orders are taken for nonexistent customers. You can prevent someone from deleting an employee record if there are corresponding entries in a tasks table.

The rules that govern these types of relations between tables are known as *referential integrity* constraints.

In addition to merely flagging as errors attempts to violate referential integrity, with Microsoft Jet, you can specify what action should be taken if the attempt occurs. For example, using cascading deletes, your application could automatically delete all of the related task's entries when you delete an employee. Cascading updates can be used to change foreign key values in related tables when the primary key of a master table is changed.

After you establish the referential integrity rules governing the relationships among the tables in your database, the burden of enforcing these rules is removed from your application code. You don't have to check explicitly for conditions that would violate referential integrity. Microsoft Jet informs you when a violation attempt occurs.

Thus, whether your database program is updated by a user browsing the tables directly from within Microsoft Access, or by an ODBC call from a custom third-party application, the logical consistency of the data in your tables is preserved.

# Foreign Key Constraints in SQL DDL

In the section of this chapter dealing with indexes, one form of the CONSTRAINT clause used in the SQL DDL language was discussed. In those examples, CONSTRAINT was used to create single-field or multifield indexes for a table, either at the time the table was created (with CREATE TABLE) or after the fact (with ALTER TABLE).

Another use of the CONSTRAINT clause is to create a relationship (or reference) from a foreign key of one table to the primary key of another table. With this constraint in place, it's impossible to enter a value in the foreign key of a table that doesn't already exist as the primary key of the master table.

In the following example, two indexes are created. The first is the primary key **Index** on TaskID, and the second is a foreign key index on the EmployeeID field:

```
CREATE TABLE TASKS
    (TaskID INTEGER CONSTRAINT PrimaryKey PRIMARY KEY,
    EmployeeID INTEGER
    CONSTRAINT FK_EmployeeID REFERENCES Employees
        (EmployeeID),
    DeptID TEXT (10),
    TaskCompleted DateTime);
```

Examining the **Indexes** collection of the newly created TASKS **TableDef** object, it's apparent that two new indexes are created by this statement, PrimaryKey and FK_EmployeeID:

```
Sub CountCustomers()
    Dim dbs As DATABASE
    Dim rst As Recordset

    Set dbs = OpenDatabase("C:\Samples\Chap03\NwindJet.mdb")
    Set rst = dbs.OpenRecordset("select count(*) As RecCount " & _
        "from Customer")

    MsgBox "Customer count: " & rst!RecCount
    dbs.Close
End Sub
```

In addition to the index, a new **Relation** object is created in the database. If you recall from the discussion in Chapter 2, a database contains a **Relations** collection, which stores information about all the inter-table relationships defined for your database. Each **Relation** contains several properties, such as **Table** and **ForeignTable**, which identify the tables that participate in the relation. Each **Relation** object in turn contains a **Fields** collection, which identifies the **Fields** that make up the **Relation**. In the previous example, there is only one field in the **Relation**: EmployeeID.

The following code displays information about the newly created FK_EmployeeID Relation:

```
Sub DisplayEmployeeRelations()
    Dim dbs As DATABASE
    Dim relTmp As Relation
    Dim prpTmp As Property
    Dim fldTmp As Field

    Set dbs = OpenDatabase("C:\Samples\Chap03\NwindJet.mdb")
    Set relTmp = dbs.Relations!FK_EmployeeID

    For Each prpTmp In relTmp.Properties
        Debug.Print prpTmp.Name & ": " & prpTmp
    Next prpTmp

    For Each fldTmp In relTmp.Fields
        Debug.Print "Field: " & fldTmp.Name
    Next fldTmp
    dbs.Close
End Sub
```

The results displayed in the debug window are:

```
Name: FK_EmployeeID
Table: Employee
ForeignTable: TASKS
Attributes: 0
Field: EmployeeID
```

Notice that creating the **Relation** called "FK_EmployeeID" also creates an index with the same name. To create a relation between two tables, the field or fields that define the **Relation** must be indexed. If the index doesn't already exist, Microsoft Jet creates it.

You can create a relation for an existing table by using the ALTER TABLE statement. First create a new table called DEPARTMENTS that will serve as a master table for the DeptID field in TASKS:

```
CREATE TABLE DEPARTMENT
    (DeptID TEXT (10) CONSTRAINT PrimaryKey PRIMARY KEY,
    Description TEXT (50) );
```

Then create a new relation between the TASKS table and the DEPARTMENT table:

```
ALTER TABLE TASKS
    ADD CONSTRAINT FK_DeptID
    FOREIGN KEY (DeptID) REFERENCES DEPARTMENT (DeptID);
```

The debug output for this new relation is:

```
Name: FK_DeptID
Table: DEPARTMENT
ForeignTable: TASKS
Attributes: 0
Field: DeptID
```

Setting a referential integrity foreign key constraint is the only form of relationship that can be established through SQL DDL. To set other **Relation** types, such as cascading updates or cascading deletes, you must create the **Relation** through DAO.

# Creating and Modifying Relations Using DAO

**Relations** can be created using DAO in much the same way you would create an **Index** object or a **TableDef** object. You append a new **Relation** onto the **Relations** collection of the database after first appending one or more **Fields** to the **Fields** collection of the new **Relation**. In addition, you can set the appropriate **Attributes** property for the **Relation** to specify that the **Relation** enforce cascading updates or cascading deletes.

Assume the following tables already exist in the database:

```
EMPLOYEE
   EmployeeID      Primary Key
   SSN
   EmpName
   DeptID


DEPARTMENT
   DeptID          Primary Key
   Description


TASKS
   TaskID          Primary Key
   EmployeeID
   DeptID
   TaskCompleted


DEPARTMENT_WORKERS
   EmployeeID      Primary Key Field 1
   DeptID          Primary Key Field 2
```

Starting with the EMPLOYEE table, you can create a referential integrity relationship between the DeptID field of the EMPLOYEE table and the primary key of the DEPARTMENT table:

```
Sub CreateRelationDepartmentToEmployee()
    Dim dbs As DATABASE
    Dim relNew As Relation
    Dim fldDeptID As Field

    Set dbs = OpenDatabase("C:\Samples\Chap03\NwindJet.mdb")

    Set relNew = dbs.CreateRelation("FK_DeptID")
    relNew.TABLE = "DEPARTMENT"
    relNew.ForeignTable = "EMPLOYEE"
    relNew.Attributes = dbRelationDeleteCascade

    Set fldDeptID = relNew.CreateField("DeptID")
    fldDeptID.ForeignName = "DeptID"

    relNew.Fields.Append fldDeptID
    dbs.Relations.Append relNew
    dbs.Close
End Sub
```

This code first creates a new **Relation** object by using the **CreateRelation** method of the **Database** object. It sets various properties of this **Relation** object. "Table" specifies the "one" table in the one-to-many relationship; "ForeignTable" specifies the "many" table. Setting these two properties ensures that no DeptID value will be entered into the EMPLOYEE table that doesn't already exist in the DEPARTMENT table.

An additional property, **Attributes**, is set to the built-in constant value dbRelationDeleteCascade. This attribute specifies that cascading deletes should be performed when a record is deleted from the DEPARTMENT table. If a DEPARTMENT record is deleted, then all records in the EMPLOYEE table that have a DeptID matching the deleted DEPARTMENT record are also deleted.

Attributes can be combined by adding the various constant values. For example, the following code specifies an optional left join between DEPARTMENT and EMPLOYEES:

```
relNew.Attributes = dbRelationLeft + _
                    dbRelationUnique + _
                    dbRelationDontEnforce
```

**Microsoft Access Users**  Designating a relation attribute as "left" or "right" has no effect on referential integrity. It's used in Microsoft Access just to show the type of join that's created by default when the tables are added to a new query in Design view.

As with the SQL DDL example shown earlier in this chapter, creating a **Relation** involving a table creates an index if one doesn't already exist. In this case, a new index, FK_DeptID, is created with the same name as the new **Relation**.

It's possible to create a **Relation** that is made up of more than one field. In your database, you might want to make sure that the combination of EmployeeID and DeptID on the TASKS table matches a combination of the same two fields on the DEPARTMENT_WORKERS table. The following code example creates the new **Relation** by appending the fields DeptID and EmployeeID to the **Fields** collection of the new **Relation**:

```
Sub CreateMultifieldRelation()
    Dim dbs As DATABASE
    Dim relNew As Relation
    Dim fldDeptID As Field
    Dim fldEmployeeID As Field

    Set dbs = OpenDatabase("C:\Samples\Chap03\NwindJet.mdb")

    Set relNew = dbs.CreateRelation("Rel_EmployeeID_DeptID")
    relNew.TABLE = "DEPARTMENT_WORKERS"
    relNew.ForeignTable = "TASKS"
    relNew.Attributes = dbRelationUnique + dbRelationDontEnforce

    Set fldDeptID = relNew.CreateField("DeptID")
    fldDeptID.ForeignName = "DeptID"

    Set fldEmployeeID = relNew.CreateField("EmployeeID")
    fldEmployeeID.ForeignName = "EmployeeID"

    relNew.Fields.Append fldDeptID
    relNew.Fields.Append fldEmployeeID
    dbs.Relations.Append relNew
    dbs.Close
End Sub
```

# Other Relation Types

So far, **Relations** created between two permanent tables that exist in the same database have been discussed. With Microsoft Jet, you can create relations between tables and QueryDefs, or between tables in the local database and tables in external databases.

For example, assume you had created a permanent QueryDef called "qryDepartment_A_Employees" with the following SQL SELECT statement:

```
SELECT DISTINCTROW EMPLOYEE.*
    FROM EMPLOYEE
    WHERE (((EMPLOYEE.DeptID)="A"));
```

You might want to create a relationship between this QueryDef and a table called DEPT_A_ASSIGNMENTS. The following code creates this relationship:

```
Sub CreateRelationBetweenTableAndQuery()
    Dim dbs As DATABASE
    Dim relNew As Relation
    Dim fldEmployeeID As Field

    Set dbs = OpenDatabase("C:\Samples\Chap03\NwindJet.mdb")

    Set relNew = dbs.CreateRelation("Rel_DeptA")
    relNew.TABLE = "qryDepartment_A_Employees"
    relNew.ForeignTable = "DEPT_A_ASSIGNMENTS"
    relNew.Attributes = dbRelationUnique + dbRelationDontEnforce

    Set fldEmployeeID = relNew.CreateField("EmployeeID")
    fldEmployeeID.ForeignName = "EmployeeID"

    relNew.Fields.Append fldEmployeeID
    dbs.Relations.Append relNew
    dbs.Close
End Sub
```

It's not possible to create a cascading update or cascading delete relationship between a table and QueryDef. Nor is it possible to enforce referential integrity between a table and a query. Enforced relations are valid only on tables.

The primary benefit of creating a relation such as this is for documentation purposes and for interactive use with a product such as Microsoft Access. Microsoft Access can make certain assumptions about the relationships between your tables if you have defined these non-enforceable relations. For instance, if you were to add both the DEPT_A_ASSIGNMENTS table and the qryDepartment_A_Employees QueryDef to a new query design screen, Microsoft Access would automatically draw in the "join line" between the table and the query.

Just as you can create a relation between a table and a local table, you can also create a relation between a local table and a linked table. In this case, the **Attributes** property of the **Relation** would include the value **dbRelationInherited**.

CHAPTER 4

# Queries

The Microsoft Jet database engine is often linked in the public mind with Microsoft Access, because it was with this product that the Microsoft Jet engine first appeared. Microsoft Access is often thought of as a simple user-oriented database management system: It includes numerous ease-of-use features such as wizards and graphical object builders. Underneath the surface, however, Microsoft Jet incorporates some very sophisticated query and optimization techniques.

The Microsoft Jet database engine boasts capabilities that are unmatched by other desktop databases in its class. These features include updatable views, heterogeneous joins, and the ability to work seamlessly with a wide variety of industry-standard database formats.

The Microsoft Jet query engine is designed to accept user requests for information or action in the form of Structured Query Language (SQL) statements. Microsoft Jet parses, analyzes, and optimizes these queries, and either returns the resulting information in the form of a **Recordset** or performs the requested action.

Although Microsoft Jet borrows many query techniques from client/server relational database management systems such as Microsoft SQL Server, it remains a file-server database. All queries are processed on individual workstations running copies of a Microsoft Jet host application such as Microsoft Access or Visual Basic. Microsoft Jet does not act as a back-end server that processes data requests independent of the application as with Microsoft SQL Server. The exception to this is in the case of queries that refer to tables stored in ODBC data sources such as Oracle or SQL Server. In these cases, Microsoft Jet off-loads as much of the query work as possible onto the back-end server.

To understand how Microsoft Jet parses, optimizes, and processes your query requests, it's important to understand the distinction between a client/server database management system and a file-server system.

Understanding how the Microsoft Jet query engine works will give you a head start in designing your application to take advantage of Jet's unique strengths and features.

**Contents**

For information on copying the code examples from the companion CD-ROM to your hard disk drive, see "Using the Companion CD-ROM" in the Preface.

### Using CH04.MDB and CHAP04.VBP

If you copied the samples from the companion CD-ROM, you can find the code examples for Microsoft Access in C:\SAMPLES\CHAP04\ ACCESS\CH04.MDB. The corresponding code examples for Visual Basic are in C:\SAMPLES\CHAP04\VB40\CHAP04.VBP.

To run any of the code examples in this chapter, open the .MDB file in Microsoft Access or open the .VBP file in Microsoft Visual Basic 4.0. You can use the examples to help you understand the concepts discussed in the chapter—or you can modify them and use them in your own applications.

# Getting Answers to Your Questions

Microsoft Jet uses a variation on the industry-standard SQL language. You form your requests for information through writing SQL queries or by building the query interactively through a tool such as the query design (or QBE) grid in Microsoft Access.

It's not the intention of this chapter to provide a tutorial on SQL. Instead, focus is on the unique features of the Microsoft Jet implementation of SQL, and how Microsoft Jet turns SQL statements into the answers you want.

# Communicating with Microsoft Jet

For information on creating **QueryDef** objects, see Chapter 3, "Data Definition and Integrity."

For information on how to create **Recordset** objects based on these SQL statements, see Chapter 5, "Working with Records and Fields."

For a full discussion of how **QueryDef** objects are created and stored in a Microsoft Jet database file, see Chapter 3, "Data Definition and Integrity."

Your SQL queries can be saved as permanent QueryDefs in the database or created, analyzed, and executed on an ad-hoc basis.

The saved QueryDef is a particularly important object in a Microsoft Jet database. It's a convenient way to store and reuse commonly asked database questions. After you have analyzed your business problem and created a query that answers that question, you can save the "question" as a permanent query. From then on, you can ask the question again just by rerunning the query.

Each time you prepare a request for information, either by sending an SQL statement as an argument to the **OpenRecordset** method of a **Database** object or by saving a **QueryDef** object in your database, Microsoft Jet runs through a complex series of analysis and optimization steps. When you create a permanent **QueryDef** object, Microsoft Jet performs a parsing phase (reading and interpreting your SQL statements) and an optimization phase (turning that SQL statement into a plan for the most efficient way to retrieve your answer). When you create a permanent **QueryDef** object, these steps are performed once. You can then simply execute the saved QueryDef either to retrieve the answer you need, or to perform the action you requested. For a full discussion on how Microsoft Jet interprets and executes your queries, see "Query Optimization" later in this chapter.

The QueryDef is also important because it can be used, for the most part, as if it were a table in your database. You can prepare a complex, multitable join that brings together data from a variety of sources and then summarizes and analyzes that data. But because the query is saved as a permanent QueryDef, that complexity can be hidden from your application. You only have to know the name of the QueryDef and its function in order to use it. Depending on the type of query created, the query can be *updatable:* Any changes made to the **Recordset** built from the QueryDef are automatically reflected in the underlying tables.

The examples in this chapter present only the text of the SQL statements that illustrate various Microsoft Jet query features under discussion. To execute these queries, you must save them as permanent **QueryDef** objects, or execute them in VBA code.

# Selecting Columns From a Single Table

For more information, see Chapter 10, "Managing Security."

As other variations of the SQL language, the Microsoft Jet SQL language uses the SELECT statement to retrieve one or more columns from a given table. You may be familiar with the SQL statements generated by the Microsoft Access query design grid. Following is a simple example that selects all columns from the Customers table for those customers living in Madrid:

```
SELECT DISTINCTROW Customers.*
FROM Customers
WHERE (((Customers.City)="Madrid"));
```

If you're familiar with other dialects of SQL, at least a couple features in this example will stand out for you, such as the DISTINCTROW statement, or the use of double quotation marks to enclose string literals.

Because DISTINCTROW is a qualifier used to make sure that entire duplicate rows are omitted from multitable joins, it has no effect on this particular query. Unlike most other SQL databases, Microsoft Jet allows query results to be updated. DISTINCTROW is required to ensure updatability of multitable joins in which columns are not output from all tables. It can be omitted if there is no need to update the data returned by the query.

Some SQL dialects require you to enclose text literals within single quotation marks, whereas this example uses double quotation marks. (Microsoft Jet can accept literals quoted with single quotation marks as well.)

Here is another example generated by Microsoft Access, which selects particular columns rather than all columns:

```
SELECT DISTINCTROW
   Products.ProductID,
   Products.ProductName,
   Products.UnitsInStock,
   UnitPrice*UnitsInStock AS InventoryValue
FROM Products;
```

Note that when Microsoft Access creates this query it automatically qualifies each column reference with its base-table name. Microsoft Jet accepts a wide variety of table and column identifiers, including names with spaces and other punctuation. If an identifier contains any non-standard characters, then it must be enclosed within square brackets.

Microsoft Jet is very flexible in its interpretation of SQL text strings. The previous query would work just as well if it were rewritten in a style slightly more familiar to experienced SQL users:

```
SELECT
   P.ProductID,
   P.ProductName,
   P.UnitsInStock,
   P.UnitPrice*P.UnitsInStock AS InventoryValue
FROM Products P;
```

This example uses the alias "P" to refer to the Products table and qualifies references to columns with that alias name. Although Microsoft Jet allows this familiar syntax, queries built with the Microsoft Access query design grid add the AS reserved word in front of the alias name:

```
SELECT
   P.ProductID,
   P.UnitsInStock
FROM Products AS P;
```

# Restricting, Ordering, and Summarizing

In most cases, you want to do more than just list all items in a single table, or even all items in selected columns in that table. You want to narrow your selection to a manageable subset, and you want to see the result in a certain sequence. It's often helpful to have the query engine summarize and analyze your data.

## The WHERE Clause

For more information on SQL syntax, see Appendix B, "SQL Reference."

You use the familiar WHERE clause to restrict selection of rows to those matching your criteria. The WHERE clause evaluates each row in the set of input records and decides whether or not the expression contained in the WHERE clause evaluates to TRUE. If it does, the record is selected. If not, the record is omitted from the result set.

While it's beyond the scope of this chapter to give a complete tutorial on SQL, the following representative examples point out some of the unique features of the Microsoft Jet version of SQL.

### Selecting Matching Values

```
SELECT DISTINCTROW Products.* FROM Products
WHERE Products.CategoryID=2;
```

For each row in Products where the CategoryID column is equal to the literal value 2, the row is selected.

### Selecting Using Partial String Matching

```
SELECT DISTINCTROW Products.* FROM Products
WHERE Products.ProductName Like 'CH*';
```

Microsoft Jet uses different partial match characters with the **Like** operator than most SQL dialects. The asterisk (*) character matches zero or more characters and is equivalent to the percent (%) character in ANSI SQL. The other Microsoft Jet partial match characters are the question mark (?), which matches any character in a single column, and the number sign (#), which matches any digit in a single column.

### Selecting Boolean Values

```
SELECT DISTINCTROW Products.* FROM Products
WHERE (((Products.Discontinued)=True));
```

Microsoft Jet stores Boolean values as either $-1$ or 0. The constant value TRUE is equal to $-1$; FALSE is equal to 0. You can substitute YES for TRUE and NO for FALSE within the text of the SQL statement. Note, however, that if you refer to Boolean recordset values within your VBA code, you must use the values $-1$ for True and 0 for False, because YES and NO will not be recognized there.

### Selecting Using Date Literals and the Between...And Operator

```
SELECT DISTINCTROW Orders.* FROM Orders
WHERE (((Orders.OrderDate) Between #3/1/94# And #6/30/94#));
```

The convention Microsoft Jet uses to search for DATETIME values is to enclose literal search values in number signs (#). The literal can either include the date only, as in this example, or can be fully qualified with the date and time:

```
...WHERE (Orders.OrderDate>#5/24/94 12:45:25 PM#);
```

Note that this date literal must always be expressed in MM/DD/YY order. To avoid the ambiguity of the meaning of stored queries, Microsoft Jet does not follow the international date format settings specified in the user's Control Panel.

### Selecting Using the IN Clause and a Value List

```
SELECT DISTINCTROW Orders.* FROM Orders
WHERE (((Orders.ShipCity) In ("London","Madrid","Rome")));
```

The previous code selects a single value in the underlying table against a list of literal values. The IN clause can be combined with NOT:

```
...WHERE (Orders.ShipVia Not In (1,3));
```

### Combining More Than One Expression

```
SELECT DISTINCTROW Orders.* FROM Orders
WHERE (((Orders.OrderDate)>#6/1/94#) AND ((Orders.ShipVia)=2));
```

A WHERE clause can consist of more than one **Sub** procedure that combines various AND and OR clauses. The truth of the entire WHERE clause is evaluated using standard rules of Boolean logic. You can use parentheses with the **Sub** procedure to ensure the order of evaluation. Note, however, that the absence or presence of parentheses does not affect the order in which joins are performed: Parentheses affect only the order in which Boolean expressions are evaluated.

### Selecting Unique Values

```
SELECT DISTINCT Employees.Title
FROM Employees;
```

Although not related to the WHERE clause, you can use the DISTINCT predicate of the SELECT clause to limit output rows to specific unique combinations of output fields. In the previous example, one occurrence of each unique Title used in the Employees table is retrieved. If the output contains more than one field, then only rows unique across all selected fields are output, as in the following example:

```
SELECT DISTINCT
  Employees.Title,
  Employees.TitleOfCourtesy
FROM Employees;
```

### Selecting Using Nested Subqueries

```
SELECT DISTINCTROW Orders.* FROM Orders
WHERE (((Orders.CustomerID) In
(SELECT CustomerID from Customers where City = 'London')));
```

This example matches each CustomerID value in Orders against a list that is created by selecting the CustomerIDs of all Customers whose City is London. Although this is a standard SQL query, and legal in Microsoft Jet SQL, this particular search might be executed more efficiently by directly joining the Orders table to the Customers table.

### Selecting Using Correlated Subqueries

```
SELECT
  T1.LastName,
  T1.FirstName,
  T1.Title,
  T1.Salary
FROM Employees AS T1
WHERE T1.Salary>=
  (SELECT avg(Salary)
   FROM Employees
   WHERE Employees.Title = T1.Title)
ORDER BY T1.Title;
```

A correlated subquery is evaluated once for each row processed by the outer query. In this example, the Salary field of each input row in the Employees table (here given the "alias" name T1) is compared to the results of an inner query. The inner query uses the value in the outer Title field as a selection criterion. Because the Title field in the outer Employees table can change for each row processed, the inner subquery must be re-executed for each row of the outer table that is processed.

In addition to the features shown in the previous examples, Microsoft Jet supports a variety of other predicates for subqueries including EXISTS, ANY, and ALL.

## Ordering the Result Set

Microsoft SQL uses the ORDER BY clause to present the selected rows in the order you designate:

```
SELECT DISTINCTROW Orders.* FROM Orders
ORDER BY Orders.ShippedDate DESC, Orders.ShipVia;
```

In this example, rows are retrieved in descending order by ShippedDate. All rows that match a given date are further ordered by the ShipVia column in ascending order. Although it's legal to use the ASC reserved word with an ORDER BY clause, it's not required. If ASC is omitted, the default ascending order is used.

If an ORDER BY clause is used in combination with a WHERE clause, it follows the WHERE clause:

```
SELECT DISTINCTROW Orders.* FROM Orders
WHERE (((Orders.OrderDate)=#6/12/94#))
ORDER BY Orders.EmployeeID;
```

The ORDER BY clause can contain an expression as well as a column in the underlying table, as in this example:

```
SELECT DISTINCTROW
  Orders.OrderID,
  Orders.RequiredDate,
  IIf(ShipCountry='USA',RequiredDate+5,RequiredDate+10)
    AS PastDueDate
FROM Orders
ORDER BY
  IIf(ShipCountry='USA',RequiredDate+5,RequiredDate+10);
```

It's also possible to specify the sort columns by their column positions rather than by their names, as in the following example:

```
SELECT DISTINCTROW
  Employees.EmployeeID,
  Employees.LastName,
  Employees.FirstName
FROM Employees
ORDER BY 3, 1;
```

This orders the query output on the third and first output columns. In this case, the sort columns would be the FirstName and EmployeeID columns. One case in which this feature can be useful is with UNION queries, which are discussed later in this chapter.

## Summing and Analyzing

For information on how to optimize queries used with ODBC data sources, see Chapter 8, "Accessing External Data."

Microsoft Jet supports the standard SQL aggregate functions COUNT, SUM, AVG, MAX, and MIN to perform table-level or group-level totaling:

```
SELECT DISTINCTROW
  Count(Products.UnitPrice) AS CountOfUnitPrice,
  Sum(Products.UnitPrice) AS SumOfUnitPrice,
  Avg(Products.UnitPrice) AS AvgOfUnitPrice,
  Min(Products.UnitPrice) AS MinOfUnitPrice,
  Max(Products.UnitPrice) AS MaxOfUnitPrice
FROM Products;
```

This query retrieves a single row that collects statistics on all Products in the table. It can be combined with a WHERE clause:

```
SELECT DISTINCTROW
  Count(Products.UnitPrice) AS CountOfUnitPrice,
  Avg(Products.UnitPrice) AS AvgOfUnitPrice
FROM Products
WHERE Products.SupplierID=6;
```

If no rows match the selection criteria, the output is still produced: The value of any COUNT aggregate columns is zero; the value of the other aggregate types is NULL.

You use the SQL function COUNT (*columnname*) to tally occurrences of non-NULL values in a specified column. A special form of COUNT is COUNT(*), which simply counts the number of rows. As discussed in the section "The Microsoft Jet Query Engine Optimizer" later in this chapter, COUNT(*) should be used whenever possible, because this expression can sometimes be executed much more quickly by using the Microsoft Jet Rushmore query-optimization technology.

The argument to these aggregate functions can be an expression as well as a column name, as in the following example:

```
SELECT DISTINCTROW Max(UnitPrice*Quantity) AS MaxExtPrice
FROM [Order Details];
```

In addition to these standard aggregate functions, Microsoft Jet supports SQL aggregates **First** and **Last**, which retrieve the first and last values of the set of rows, and the **StDev**, **StDevP**, **Var**, and **VarP** statistical and financial functions. Note that because the **StDev**, **StDevP**, **Var**, and **VarP** functions are Microsoft Jet–specific, they are not likely to be supported on any other client/server database management system, and so will have to be evaluated locally.

## Aggregate Values and GROUP BY

Aggregate values can be calculated at levels other than for the entire table. The SQL GROUP BY clause is used to create one output row per each group of unique values, and optionally, to produce summary values for selected columns. GROUP BY used alone simply creates an output row that specifies the unique values:

```
SELECT DISTINCTROW
  Products.CategoryID,
  Products.SupplierID
FROM Products
GROUP BY
  Products.CategoryID,
  Products.SupplierID;
```

This query simply lists the unique combinations of CategoryID and SupplierID, and produces the same results as:

```
SELECT DISTINCT
  Products.CategoryID,
  Products.SupplierID
FROM Products;
```

As in other SQL dialects, any output columns in a GROUP BY query must be either part of an aggregate or be in the GROUP BY clause.

When an aggregate function is combined with a GROUP BY clause, one row of output is produced for each unique value in the GROUP BY clause. The aggregate totals are accumulated and output for each row, and then reset for the next group, as in this example, which finds the oldest birth date for each Title value in the Employees table:

```
SELECT DISTINCTROW
  Employees.Title,
  Min(Employees.BirthDate) AS MinOfBirthDate
FROM Employees
GROUP BY Employees.Title;
```

If you want, you can sort the output of the GROUP BY query by adding an ORDER BY clause, as in this example, which finds the most recently hired employee in each Region:

```
SELECT DISTINCTROW
  Employees.Country,
  Max(Employees.HireDate) AS MaxOfHireDate
FROM Employees
GROUP BY Employees.Country
ORDER BY Max(Employees.HireDate) DESC;
```

## Applying Selection After Grouping with HAVING

You use the HAVING clause to apply selection after data aggregation has been performed. Rows are selected and summarized, and then only those meeting the conditions specified in the HAVING clause are displayed:

```
SELECT DISTINCTROW
   Products.CategoryID,
   Sum(Products.UnitsInStock) AS SumOfUnitsInStock
FROM Products
GROUP BY Products.CategoryID
HAVING Sum(Products.UnitsInStock)>400;
```

The HAVING clause determines which groups created by the GROUP BY clause are returned in the query output.

# Joining Tables

The real power of a relational database system is evident when you combine results from one table with those from another. Microsoft Jet is flexible in the type and format of the SQL statements used to create the relational join. In addition to joins in which the linking criteria is specified in the WHERE clause, Microsoft Jet SQL can use the JOIN clause to specify inner, left, and right outer joins, as well as non-equi-joins, in which the linking criterion is not a match in values between two tables, but a generic conditional expression that evaluates to TRUE. Microsoft Jet also supports the UNION statement, which concatenates the results of two or more SELECT statements.

## Joins Specified in the WHERE clause

With Microsoft Jet, you can create relational joins in SQL by specifying the linking condition in the WHERE clause:

```
SELECT
   Products.ProductID,
   Products.ProductName,
   Categories.CategoryID,
   Categories.CategoryName
FROM Categories, Products
WHERE Products.CategoryID = Categories.CategoryID;
```

This query selects two fields each from Products and Categories, selecting rows from each table where the CategoryID field in Products matches the CategoryID field in Categories.

## The INNER JOIN

The SQL query produced by the query design grid in Microsoft Access uses the INNER JOIN clause to join two tables. Here is the same query as produced by Microsoft Access:

```
SELECT DISTINCTROW
   Products.ProductID,
   Products.ProductName,
   Categories.CategoryID,
   Categories.CategoryName
FROM Categories
INNER JOIN Products
ON Categories.CategoryID = Products.CategoryID;
```

The INNER JOIN names the linking criterion used to find matches between the two tables. This is the preferred format for specifying joins with Microsoft Jet, for two reasons. First, this format makes the join criteria explicit, rather than inferring it from the condition in the WHERE clause. Second, Microsoft Jet requires the use of this format in order for the results of this join to be updatable.

For a full discussion of query updatability, see Chapter 5, "Working with Records and Fields."

Many people also prefer this format because it's self-documenting, unlike the implicit join specified in the WHERE clause. The WHERE clause is then reserved for selection criteria, rather than doing dual-duty as a join specifier:

```
SELECT DISTINCTROW
   Products.ProductID,
   Products.ProductName,
   Categories.CategoryID,
   Categories.CategoryName
FROM Categories INNER JOIN Products
ON Categories.CategoryID = Products.CategoryID
WHERE Products.CategoryID In (1,3);
```

A join can specify more than one linking condition:

```
SELECT DISTINCTROW
   PreferredVendors.ProductID,
   PreferredVendors.SupplierID,
   Products.CategoryID,
   Products.ProductName
FROM PreferredVendors
INNER JOIN Products
ON    (PreferredVendors.SupplierID = Products.SupplierID)
   AND (PreferredVendors.ProductID = Products.ProductID);
```

Complex join conditions can be specified. The following example joins six tables:

```
SELECT DISTINCTROW
  Orders.OrderID,
  Employees.EmployeeID,
  Customers.CompanyName,
  [Order Details].ProductID,
  Products.ProductName,
  Categories.CategoryName
FROM
  Categories INNER JOIN
   (Products INNER JOIN
    (Employees INNER JOIN
     (Customers INNER JOIN
      (Orders INNER JOIN [Order Details]
       ON Orders.OrderID = [Order Details].OrderID)
      ON Customers.CustomerID = Orders.CustomerID)
     ON Employees.EmployeeID = Orders.EmployeeID)
    ON Products.ProductID = [Order Details].ProductID)
   ON Categories.CategoryID = Products.CategoryID;
```

## The Left and Right Outer Join

The INNER JOIN clause only retrieves rows in which there is a match in both tables. In some cases, you might want to retrieve the values from one table even when there are no matching values in the other joined table. For example, you might have to accept a batch of Orders records in which the EmployeeID is unknown for one reason or another. You want to create a join from Orders to Employees, but you don't want to exclude Orders from the result set simply because there is no corresponding Employee record.

When you specify a left or right outer join, Microsoft Jet retrieves all rows from one table even though there are no matches in the other table:

```
SELECT DISTINCTROW
  Orders.*,
  Employees.LastName
FROM Employees
RIGHT OUTER JOIN Orders ON Employees.EmployeeID = Orders.EmployeeID;
```

Note that the word "OUTER" is optional in Microsoft Jet SQL syntax, as a left or right join implies an outer join. In this example, all rows from Orders are retrieved even if the EmployeeID column in Orders does not find any matches in the Employees table.

Whether the join is considered a left or a right join is determined from the point of view of the tables listed in the join clause. There is no effect on efficiency, or in the actual rows returned. This previous query could be rewritten as follows, and the same rows would be returned:

```
SELECT DISTINCTROW
  Employees.LastName,
  Orders.*
FROM Orders
LEFT JOIN Employees ON Orders.EmployeeID = Employees.EmployeeID;
```

Microsoft Jet treats a right join as if it were a left join with the tables reversed.

## Outer Joins and NULL

Microsoft Jet returns the special value NULL in all columns for the rows in the "outer" table in which no match is found. You can take advantage of this feature by testing for the presence of NULL in the outer table. For example, assume you have a special table called TemporaryEmployees, and you want to find all Orders entries taken by Employees who were not listed in this table.

One way would be to create a nested sub-SELECT query:

```
SELECT DISTINCTROW Orders.*
FROM Orders
WHERE (Orders.EmployeeID Not In
  (Select EmployeeID from TemporaryEmployees));
```

This query creates a list of EmployeeIDs in the TemporaryEmployees table, and then checks each entry in Orders to make sure that it's *not* in this list.

Another way to achieve the same result makes use of the fact that non-matching rows are NULL. The following example creates a left join between Orders and TemporaryEmployees, and then tests for a NULL value in the EmployeeID field in TemporaryEmployees. EmployeeID is the primary key of the TemporaryEmployees table, and cannot normally be NULL. Therefore, the presence of a NULL in the result set of the left join implies that there is no join between Orders and TemporaryEmployees, which is the condition that should be detected:

```
SELECT DISTINCTROW
  Orders.*
FROM Orders
LEFT JOIN TemporaryEmployees
ON Orders.EmployeeID = TemporaryEmployees.EmployeeID
WHERE TemporaryEmployees.EmployeeID Is Null;
```

## Self-Joins

It's possible to create a join between a table and a second instance of the same table. A common example is an Employees table in which the ReportsTo field contains EmployeeID values found in the Employees table itself.

The following example joins the Employees table to itself. The ReportsTo field in the first instance of the Employees table is linked to the EmployeeID field in the second instance. The second instance of the Employees table is given the alias "Supervisors":

```
SELECT DISTINCTROW
  Employees.EmployeeID,
  Employees.LastName,
  Supervisors.FirstName & " " & Supervisors.LastName AS SupervisorName
FROM Employees
INNER JOIN Employees AS Supervisors
ON Employees.ReportsTo = Supervisors.EmployeeID;
```

In this example, a calculated column called SupervisorName is created. Note the use of the & concatenation operator, which is used to combine the output of the FirstName and LastName fields in the Supervisors table.

Because an inner join was specified, if the value in the ReportsTo field of any given row is not also found in the Employees table, then the row is not selected. If you want to select the row even when the self-join does not find a match, you can specify a left join as in the earlier examples in this chapter.

The following revised query specifies a left join. The calculated SupervisorName column has been revised to anticipate that certain rows may have a NULL value in the ReportsTo field (perhaps indicating that the employee is a supervisor, and does not report to another Employee in the Employees table). The calculated column returns the specified value "No Supervisor" for those rows in which the ReportsTo column is NULL:

```
SELECT DISTINCTROW
  Employees.EmployeeID,
  Employees.LastName,
  IIf(IsNull(Employees.ReportsTo),
    "No Supervisor",
    Supervisors.FirstName & " " & Supervisors.LastName)
    AS SupervisorName
FROM Employees
LEFT JOIN Employees AS Supervisors
ON Employees.ReportsTo = Supervisors.EmployeeID;
```

**Note**  This query uses the **IIf** (Immediate If) function in the calculated expression, which creates the column "SupervisorName." This is one of many built-in functions understood by Microsoft Jet. Other functions you can use include string manipulation functions and date functions. While these functions can be extremely useful, they should be used with care. Because they are not available on all back-end database systems, they must be evaluated locally by the Microsoft Jet engine running on the user's computer. If calculated columns using these functions are part of the selection criteria, then this forces a table scan (serial read) of all rows in the result set, so that the condition can be evaluated locally. Consider creating calculated items in the form or report to display the query results rather than adding a calculated column directly to the query itself.

## Joining Tables and QueryDefs

In addition to joins based on permanent tables, Microsoft Jet supports joins between tables and saved QueryDefs, or even between two QueryDefs. Queries can be based on other queries, which can further be based on other queries, and so on. Microsoft Jet automatically resolves all references to queries and tables.

It has been shown that Microsoft Jet **QueryDef** objects can be treated, for the most part, as if they were tables in the database. A QueryDef performs the function of an SQL View. **QueryDef** and **TableDef** objects occupy the same "name space" within a Microsoft Jet database. You cannot have a TableDef and a QueryDef with the same name, for example. Generally, wherever you might use a base table, you can use a query based on that table instead.

Suppose you want to find the percentage of your total sales of certain products that were generated by particular customers. One way to do this is to create a query that totals orders by customer and product:

```
SELECT DISTINCTROW
  Orders.CustomerID,
  [Order Details].ProductID,
  Sum((UnitPrice*Quantity)-Discount) AS ExtPrice
FROM Orders
INNER JOIN [Order Details]
ON Orders.OrderID = [Order Details].OrderID
GROUP BY Orders.CustomerID, [Order Details].ProductID;
```

Save this query as a permanent QueryDef in the database with the name
qryCustomerOrderTotalsByProduct. You can now treat this query as if it were a
table. The sample output it produces might be:

| Customer | Product | ExtPrice |
|---|---|---|
| Alfreds Futterkiste | Aniseed Syrup | $ 60.00 |
| Alfreds Futterkiste | Grandma's Boysenberry Spread | $399.95 |
| Alfreds Futterkiste | Rössle Sauerkraut | $774.95 |
| Alfreds Futterkiste | Chartreuse verte | $377.75 |
| Alfreds Futterkiste | Spegesild | $ 23.75 |

Now you have to find the order totals for each ProductID. Create a permanent
QueryDef called qryOrderTotalsByProduct with the following SQL statement:

```
SELECT DISTINCTROW
   [Order Details].ProductID,
   Sum((UnitPrice*Quantity)-Discount) AS ExtPrice
FROM Orders
INNER JOIN [Order Details]
ON Orders.OrderID = [Order Details].OrderID
GROUP BY [Order Details].ProductID;
```

Part of the output produced by this query might be:

| Product | ExtPrice |
|---|---|
| Chai | $14,274.65 |
| Chang | $18,554.70 |
| Aniseed Syrup | $ 3,079.80 |
| Chef Anton's Cajun Seasoning | $ 9,423.30 |
| Chef Anton's Gumbo Mix | $ 5,800.40 |

Now you can create a third QueryDef called
qryCustomerOrderPercentOfTotalByProduct, which joins
qryOrderTotalsByProduct with qryCustomerOrderTotalsByProduct:

```
SELECT DISTINCTROW
   qryCustomerOrderTotalsByProduct.CustomerID,
   qryCustomerOrderTotalsByProduct.ProductID,
   qryCustomerOrderTotalsByProduct.ExtPrice AS CustTot,
   qryOrderTotalsByProduct.ExtPrice AS ProdTot,
   Format(CustTot/ProdTot,"#.###") AS PercentOfTot
FROM qryOrderTotalsByProduct
INNER JOIN qryCustomerOrderTotalsByProduct
ON qryOrderTotalsByProduct.ProductID =
   qryCustomerOrderTotalsByProduct.ProductID;
```

Part of the output from this query might be:

| Customer | Product | CustTot | ProdTot | PercentOfTot |
|---|---|---|---|---|
| Alfreds Futterkiste | Aniseed Syrup | $ 60.00 | $ 3,079.80 | .019 |
| Alfreds Futterkiste | Grandma's Boysenberry Spread | $399.95 | $ 7,344.63 | .054 |
| Alfreds Futterkiste | Rössle Sauerkraut | $774.95 | $26,864.35 | .029 |
| Alfreds Futterkiste | Chartreuse verte | $377.75 | $13,148.80 | .029 |
| Alfreds Futterkiste | Spegesild | $ 23.75 | $ 6,142.28 | .004 |

Finally, you can join from this third QueryDef back into the Customers and Products table to pick up the CompanyName and ProductName fields:

```
SELECT DISTINCTROW
   qryCustomerOrderPercentOfTotalByProduct.*,
   Products.ProductName,
   Customers.CompanyName
FROM
   (qryCustomerOrderPercentOfTotalByProduct
      INNER JOIN Customers
      ON qryCustomerOrderPercentOfTotalByProduct.CustomerID =
         Customers.CustomerID)
   INNER JOIN Products
   ON qryCustomerOrderPercentOfTotalByProduct.ProductID =
      Products.ProductID;
```

## Non-equi-joins

So far, our join conditions have been based on matching values in selected columns in two or more tables. However, with Microsoft Jet you can also create join conditions based on tests other than equality. You can join based on a range of acceptable values, for example.

Suppose you have a table called PerformanceGrade with the following values.

| PerformanceGradeKey | LowRange | HighRange |
|---|---|---|
| 0 | $ 0.00 | $ 100,000.00 |
| 1 | $100,000.01 | $ 200,000.00 |
| 2 | $200,000.01 | $ 300,000.00 |
| 3 | $300,000.01 | $ 400,000.00 |
| 4 | $400,000.01 | $9,999,999.99 |

You want to assign a PerformanceGradeKey value to Employee Sales. Employees with sales between 0 and $100,000 receive a 0, those with sales between $100,000.01 and $200,000 receive a 1, and so on.

The first step is to create a QueryDef that sums up the sales by Employee. Call this QueryDef qryEmployeeSales:

```
SELECT DISTINCTROW
  Orders.EmployeeID,
  Sum((UnitPrice*Quantity)-Discount) AS ExtPrice
FROM Orders
INNER JOIN [Order Details]
ON Orders.OrderID = [Order Details].OrderID
GROUP BY Orders.EmployeeID;
```

Sample output from this query might be:

| Employee | ExtPrice |
| --- | --- |
| Davolio, Nancy | $202,126.72 |
| Fuller, Andrew | $177,738.71 |
| Leverling, Janet | $213,035.35 |
| Peacock, Margaret | $250,161.70 |
| Buchanan, Steven | $ 75,559.95 |
| Suyama, Michael | $ 78,188.95 |
| King, Robert | $141,283.04 |
| Callahan, Laura | $133,286.43 |
| Dodsworth, Anne | $ 82,956.70 |

Now this saved QueryDef has to be joined to the PerformanceGrade table. The grade assigned is determined by the high and low ranges, and the actual sales of the Employee. Here is the SQL statement that produces the desired result:

```
SELECT DISTINCTROW
  qryEmployeeSales.EmployeeID,
  qryEmployeeSales.ExtPrice,
  PerformanceGrade.PerformanceGradeKey
FROM qryEmployeeSales, PerformanceGrade
WHERE (qryEmployeeSales.ExtPrice between PerformanceGrade.LowRange
      and PerformanceGrade.HighRange)
ORDER BY PerformanceGrade.PerformanceGradeKey;
```

As you can see from the sample output shown, Microsoft Jet is able to link values from the qryEmployeeSales query to the PerformanceGrade table even though neither table has common columns or shares common values. The join is based entirely on a condition specified in the WHERE clause.

| Employee | ExtPrice | PerformanceGradeKey |
|---|---|---|
| Dodsworth, Anne | $ 82,956.70 | 0 |
| Suyama, Michael | $ 78,188.95 | 0 |
| Buchanan, Steven | $ 75,559.95 | 0 |
| Callahan, Laura | $133,286.43 | 1 |
| King, Robert | $141,283.04 | 1 |
| Fuller, Andrew | $177,738.71 | 1 |
| Peacock, Margaret | $250,161.70 | 2 |
| Leverling, Janet | $213,035.35 | 2 |
| Davolio, Nancy | $202,126.72 | 2 |

Be aware that Microsoft Jet cannot perform its normal optimization techniques on non-equi-join queries.

## UNION Queries

You often have to treat the results of one or more queries, or the contents of one or more tables, as if they were in the same table. You might want to create a list of names and addresses that combines entries from both the Customers and the Suppliers table. Microsoft Jet supports the special UNION operator, which combines the results of two or more SELECT queries.

For example, the combined Customer and Supplier list could be created with the following query:

```
SELECT
  Customers.CompanyName,
  Customers.Address,
  Customers.City,
  Customers.Region,
  Customers.PostalCode
FROM Customers
UNION
SELECT
  Suppliers.CompanyName,
  Suppliers.Address,
  Suppliers.City,
  Suppliers.Region,
  Suppliers.PostalCode
FROM Suppliers;
```

The individual SELECT queries are combined by the UNION statement. Each SELECT statement can be as complex as necessary, and can include multitable joins. Each SELECT statement can also use GROUP BY to sum values. An optional ORDER BY clause can be added after the last SELECT statement to order the values of the results returned by all of the individual SELECT statements.

The number of the columns in each SELECT statement must match, but the names of the columns can differ. The data types of the matching columns don't have to match exactly. For example, an integer column can be united with a floating point column.

When referring to the output of the entire UNION query, the column names for the *first* SELECT statement are used.

Usually, Microsoft Jet hides rows that contain entirely duplicated data in a UNION query. If you want to include duplicated rows in the output, use the UNION ALL clause instead of UNION.

If you're joining two tables or queries that have identical structure, you can use a special form of the UNION statement with which you can specify the tables you want to combine, rather than listing the columns you want to select. For example, instead of listing the columns as in the earlier example that combined values from Customers and Suppliers, you could create one query called qryCustomerNameAndAddress:

```
SELECT DISTINCTROW
   Customers.CompanyName,
   Customers.Address,
   Customers.City,
   Customers.Region,
   Customers.PostalCode
FROM Customers;
```

and another called qrySupplierNameAndAddress:

```
SELECT DISTINCTROW
   Suppliers.CompanyName,
   Suppliers.Address,
   Suppliers.City,
   Suppliers.Region,
   Suppliers.PostalCode
FROM Suppliers;
```

The following UNION query combines the two queries without explicitly specifying the names of the columns:

```
TABLE qrySupplierNameAndAddress
UNION
TABLE qryCustomerNameAndAddress;
```

There are some limitations when using Memo and OLE fields in the output of a UNION query. You cannot explicitly include memo fields in the output SELECT statement of a UNION query. The following query results in an error:

```
SELECT Table1.Memo1
FROM Table1
UNION
SELECT Table2.Memo2
FROM Table2;
```

If it's sufficient for your purposes to include only the first 255 characters of the Memo field in the output, one alternative is to select an expression based on the Memo field:

```
SELECT left(Table1.Memo1,255) as FirstPartOfMemo
FROM Table1
UNION SELECT left(Table2.Memo2,255) as FirstPartOfMemo
FROM Table2;
```

Results of a UNION query are never updatable.

# Other Query Features

Microsoft Jet includes several other unique features that solve common problems. You can perform spreadsheet-like cross-tabulations, or filter large amounts of data based on the desired top number or percentage of values. With the flexible Parameter query, you can create and test a query once, but supply variable parameter input at run time.

## Parameter Queries

With Microsoft Jet, you can specify one or more QueryDef parameters. The parameters are used to accept input values at run time from the host program, and merge this user-input data with an existing **QueryDef** object. Parameters are commonly used to supply selection criteria, but they can also be used to specify terms in an expression.

You declare parameters with the PARAMETERS declaration, which specifies the names and data types of the parameters. The following example takes an EmployeeID value as a parameter, which returns values for only the selected employee, and another parameter whose value will be multiplied with the Employee's current salary, to calculate the proposed new salary. The first parameter, "prmEmployeeIDSelect," is used as part of the selection criteria; the second parameter, "prmSalaryIncreaseFactor," is used as part of an expression:

```
PARAMETERS
  prmEmployeeIDSelect Long,
  prmSalaryIncreaseFactor Single;
```

```
SELECT DISTINCTROW
  Employees.LastName,
  Employees.FirstName,
  Employees.Salary,
  Employees.Salary*prmSalaryIncreaseFactor AS NewSalary
FROM Employees
WHERE Employees.EmployeeID=prmEmployeeIDSelect;
```

How does your program supply the parameter values? If you're working with
Microsoft Access, you may be familiar with the way it prompts the user to supply
missing parameter values.

This behavior is not built into Microsoft Jet, however. It's a function performed
by Microsoft Access, and then only when the parameter query is executed
through the user interface. Microsoft Access prompts the user for parameter
values for forms and reports based on parameter queries, or when a datasheet is
opened on a parameter query.

If you want to supply parameter values to a QueryDef that's being executed
programmatically, you have to do so explicitly, as in the following example.
Assume that you have saved the parameter query shown previously as a
permanent QueryDef named "qryProposedEmployeeSalaryIncrease."

```
Function SupplyParameterValue(lngEmpID As Long, sngIncFact As Single)
  Dim db As Database
  Dim qd As QueryDef
  Dim rs As Recordset

  Set db = DBEngine(0)(0)
  Set qd = db.QueryDefs("qryProposedEmployeeSalaryIncrease")

  qd!prmEmployeeIDSelect = lngEmpID
  qd!prmSalaryIncreaseFactor = sngIncFact

  Set rs = qd.OpenRecordset()
  If rs.RecordCount <> 0 Then
    MsgBox "The proposed new salary is: " & rs!NewSalary
  End If

End Function
```

This example uses the ! (bang) operator to specify the names of the parameters
explicitly. Alternatively, the parameters could be supplied using the following
format:

```
qd.Parameters("prmEmployeeIDSelect") = lngEmpID
qd.Parameters("prmSalaryIncreaseFactor") = sngIncFact
```

Both methods assume that you know the names of the parameters at the time your program is written. One way to avoid the need to explicitly specify parameters is to iterate through all the parameters in the **Parameters** collection of the QueryDef and prompt the user for values, thus emulating to a certain extent the behavior in Microsoft Access:

```
Function PromptForParms()
  Dim db As Database
  Dim qd As QueryDef
  Dim rs As Recordset
  Dim prm As Parameter

  Set db = DBEngine(0)(0)
  Set qd = db.QueryDefs("qryProposedEmployeeSalaryIncrease")

  For Each prm In qd.Parameters
    qd.Parameters(prm.Name) = _
      InputBox("Enter Parameter: " & prm.Name)
  Next prm

  Set rs = qd.OpenRecordset()
  If rs.RecordCount <> 0 Then
    MsgBox "The proposed new salary is: " & rs!NewSalary
  End If

End Function
```

Although Microsoft Jet includes the PARAMETERS clause in order for you to name and type your QueryDef parameters explicitly, it actually treats any unrecognized term as a parameter. If you make a spelling error on a column name, for example, Microsoft Jet treats the misspelled column name as a parameter. If you don't supply the parameter value in your program, a trappable run-time error is generated.

It's a good idea to get into the habit of specifying the names and data types of your parameters rather than relying on the Microsoft Jet implicit parameter behavior.

For a discussion of various database object collections, including **QueryDefs** and **Parameters**, see Chapter 3, "Data Definition and Integrity."

## TOP N and TOP N PERCENT Clauses

Although you can use the WHERE and HAVING clauses to filter the selection of records, sometimes this is not sufficient. For example, you might want to select all rows where the State is CA, but only see the Orders for the top ten Customers. Microsoft Jet provides TOP N and TOP N PERCENT clauses to limit the presentation of rows *after* they're selected.

## TOP N Clause

You can specify that only a specific number of rows be returned to your program by using the TOP N clause:

```
SELECT DISTINCTROW TOP 5
  Employees.EmployeeID,
  Employees.Salary
FROM Employees
ORDER BY Employees.Salary;
```

The TOP criteria is applied after the rows are selected. TOP doesn't necessarily imply "higher" or "more." It actually might better be thought of as the "first 'N' rows of" the result set. For example, the previous query actually produces a list of employees with the *lowest* salary, not the highest, because the rows are sorted in ascending order by Salary. If you want to find the employees with the highest salary, sort the rows in descending order based on salary:

```
SELECT DISTINCTROW TOP 5
  Employees.EmployeeID,
  Employees.Salary
FROM Employees
ORDER BY Employees.Salary DESC;
```

If more than one row ties for the Nth value, then all of the tied values are displayed. If the fifth, sixth, and seventh highest salaries were the same, then the previous query would retrieve seven rows, not five.

Note that the selection of rows is based on the *entire* output set, even if the query uses the GROUP BY clause to aggregate like values. It's not possible, for example, to retrieve the "top 5 rows within each group," or the "top 10 salesmen within each region."

## TOP N PERCENT Clause

TOP N PERCENT works much the same as the TOP N query, except the number of rows returned is not fixed. A selected percentage of the rows are retrieved:

```
SELECT DISTINCTROW TOP 10 PERCENT
  Products.UnitsInStock,
  Products.ProductID,
  Products.ProductName
FROM Products
ORDER BY Products.UnitsInStock DESC , Products.ProductName;
```

This query retrieves the 10 percent of Products with the highest UnitsInStock value.

**Note**  Be cautious with the use of the TOP N PERCENT feature if you're working with a back-end server such as Microsoft SQL Server. Because most servers don't natively support this feature, the output of this query must be evaluated on the local machine. It's possible that a large number of rows will need to be returned from the server in order for Microsoft Jet to determine which rows to select.

## Crosstab Queries

A crosstab query summarizes tabular data and places it into a columnar format. Like values can be counted, summed, averaged, and so on, and compared to other values.

Suppose you want to know the average salary paid for various employee classifications in different countries. One way to do this is to create a standard SELECT query that uses the GROUP BY clause for Country and Title, and sums on Salary:

```
SELECT Employees.Country,
Employees.Title,
Avg(Employees.Salary) AS AvgOfSalary
FROM Employees
GROUP BY Employees.Country, Employees.Title;
```

This query results in the following table.

| Country | Title | AvgOfSalary |
|---------|-------|-------------|
| UK | Sales Manager | $59,600.00 |
| UK | Sales Representative | $47,500.00 |
| USA | Inside Sales Coordinator | $39,000.00 |
| USA | Sales Representative | $48,960.00 |
| USA | Vice President, Sales | $85,000.00 |

It's difficult, however, to make certain kinds of comparisons. The Country information is repeated for each row, and in order to compare the average salary for various Titles across countries, you must match numbers that are physically distant from one another on the page. You might easily overlook the fact that no Advertising Specialist is listed for the USA.

A crosstab query solves this problem by organizing the data so that the summarized information is placed in contiguous columns across the page. The following crosstab query produces the same information as the first query, but in a much more readable format:

```
TRANSFORM Avg(Employees.Salary) AS AvgOfSalary
SELECT Employees.Title
FROM Employees
GROUP BY Employees.Title
PIVOT Employees.Country;
```

The contents of the Country field become column headings. The Title field (specified in the SELECT clause) becomes the row heading and the value that is summarized in the Salary field.

| Title | UK | USA |
|---|---|---|
| Inside Sales Coordinator | | $39,000.00 |
| Sales Manager | $59,600.00 | |
| Sales Representative | $47,500.00 | $48,960.00 |
| Vice President, Sales | | $85,000.00 |

Microsoft Jet includes extensions to the standard SQL language to support crosstab operations:

- TRANSFORM. Specifies that the query is a crosstab query. The first statement following the TRANSFORM statement must be an aggregate function such as AVG, SUM, MIN, MAX, or COUNT, which summarizes the selected data.

- PIVOT. Specifies the field or expression used to create the column headings in the query's result set.

By default, Microsoft Jet presents the summarized columns in alphabetical order from left to right. Missing values are returned as NULL. In the previous example, because no Advertising Specialist employees exist in the USA, there is no salary to average. The value in the USA column for Advertising Specialist is NULL.

Column headings are based on the actual values contained in the column specified by the PIVOT statement. If values are missing, no column is created. For example, if your company has offices in Germany, but no Employees were selected whose Country was Germany, then there would be no empty column created for Germany.

You can force Microsoft Jet to create columns in an order other than alphabetical and force the creation of columns even if there is no data for that column value, by using the optional IN clause with the PIVOT clause. Our crosstab query could be revised as follows:

```
TRANSFORM Avg(Employees.Salary) AS AvgOfSalary
SELECT Employees.Title
FROM Employees
GROUP BY Employees.Title
PIVOT Employees.Country In ("UK","Germany","France","USA");
```

This query results in the following table.

| Title | UK | Germany | France | USA |
|---|---|---|---|---|
| Inside Sales Coordinator | | | | $39,000.00 |
| Sales Manager | $59,600.00 | | | |
| Sales Representative | $47,500.00 | | | $48,960.00 |
| Vice President, Sales | | | | $85,000.00 |

The target of the SELECT statement used to create the column headings can be an expression as well as an actual column name. A common use of this feature is to create groupings that don't exist in the actual data. You could group all Orders into Month groupings with a technique such as the following:

```
TRANSFORM Count(*)
SELECT Orders.EmployeeID
FROM Orders
GROUP BY Orders.EmployeeID
PIVOT Format(OrderDate,"mmm");
```

This query results in the following table.

| Employee | Apr | Aug | Dec | Feb |
|---|---|---|---|---|
| Davolio, Nancy | 9 | 8 | 17 | 12 |
| Fuller, Andrew | 19 | 4 | 12 | 5 |
| Leverling, Janet | 13 | 6 | 13 | 14 |

The column headings in this query are created with the **Format** function, which turns the OrderDate into a three-letter month abbreviation. All orders within a given month (even if they were placed in different years) are summarized together.

Because the IN clause with the PIVOT statement was not used, the months are displayed alphabetically. A more complete query, which combines a WHERE clause to limit the selection to Orders within a given year, is:

```
TRANSFORM Count(*)
SELECT Orders.EmployeeID
FROM Orders
WHERE (((Orders.OrderDate) Between #1/1/94# And #12/31/94#))
GROUP BY Orders.EmployeeID
PIVOT Format(OrderDate,"mmm") In
("Jan","Feb","Mar","Apr","May","Jun","Jul","Aug","Sep","Oct","Nov","Dec"
);
```

The following table shows a portion of the result of this query.

| Employee | Jan | Feb | Mar | Apr |
|---|---|---|---|---|
| Davolio, Nancy | 1 | 2 | 5 | 3 |
| Fuller, Andrew | 3 | 2 | 3 | 3 |
| Leverling, Janet | 9 | 7 | 5 | 3 |

# Updating Your Data with Queries

This section describes the rules governing query updatability. You can use the dynamic selecting and sorting capabilities of the query engine for more than just static searches: After a result set is retrieved, the data can also be updated through a program such as Microsoft Access, or a custom Visual Basic program.

Chapter 5, "Working with Records and Fields," discusses the various types of **Recordset** objects that can be built from Microsoft Jet queries, and how those **Recordset** objects can be manipulated through Visual Basic.

## Single-Table Query Updatability

A query based on a single table can select some or all records, and some or all columns, from that table. In the simplest case, the query returns all rows and all columns:

```
SELECT * FROM Customers;
```

Every row retrieved, and every column in every row, is accessible and subject to change (except calculated columns based on expressions). Every row can be deleted and new rows inserted.

If you were to use Microsoft Access to open a datasheet based on this query, you would be able to freely browse forward and backward, making any changes you want (subject to security restrictions, validation rules, and referential integrity requirements). Any changes made to the **Recordset** created by this QueryDef would automatically be reflected in the underlying table.

A query can also select and sort rows from the original table and remain updatable:

```
SELECT *
FROM Customers
WHERE (((Customers.ContactTitle)="Owner"))
ORDER BY Customers.CompanyName;
```

An updatable single-table query like this can be useful in a data entry situation in which you would like to present the rows to the user in a certain order, or hide certain rows based on the selection criteria.

One thing to be aware of, however, is that Microsoft Jet does not prevent the user from adding a new row through a QueryDef that would not have met the original selection criteria. For example, the previous query selects only rows in which the ContactTitle is "Owner." The user could add a new row and specify a value other than "Owner" as the ContactTitle, in which case the user would add a row that the query, if subsequently rerun, would no longer select. It's up to your application to enforce insert restrictions such as this.

## Single-Table Query Updatability Restrictions

A query can select specific columns rather than selecting all columns with the asterisk (*) character:

```
SELECT
  Customers.ContactName,
  Customers.ContactTitle,
  Customers.Address,
  Customers.City,
  Customers.Region,
  Customers.PostalCode
FROM Customers;
```

This can be a useful technique to hide certain columns from users, while still allowing them access to the information they need. The columns made available through a query like this are fully updatable. It may, however, be impossible to *add* a new row through this query, either because the fields not included in the output are specified as "required" at the table level, or because the primary key or foreign keys cannot be created with default values.

Another restriction is on non-native tables, such as those created using Borland's Paradox. Microsoft Jet requires that a primary key be defined for Paradox tables. Btrieve® and xBase data sources don't require a unique index, but ODBC tables do. On Microsoft SQL Server, a table may be updatable if it has a timestamp column, even if it does not have a unique index. Any queries based on tables lacking a unique index are not updatable.

# Multitable Query Updatability

In addition to allowing updates to single-table queries, Microsoft Jet supports updatable multitable joins. This is extremely useful, because it enables you to combine data from the main table with lookup information from other tables (a many-to-one join), or to join a master table with a related detail table (a one-to-many join) and still have an updatable result set.

## Many-to-One Joins

This example joins the Products table (the focus of the query) with the Suppliers table, which provides lookup information, including the Supplier CompanyName and City:

```
SELECT DISTINCTROW
   Products.*,
   Suppliers.CompanyName,
   Suppliers.City
FROM Suppliers INNER JOIN Products
ON Suppliers.SupplierID = Products.SupplierID;
```

The user can change data in any column from the Products table, including the SupplierID that links the Products table to the Suppliers table. If you change the value of the linking field through a datasheet or a form in a Microsoft Access application, you will also see that the corresponding "lookup" information from the "one" table is automatically retrieved and redisplayed. This technique is known as *row fix-up* or *AutoLookup*.

Although the focus of this many-to-one query is the Products table, it's also possible (though perhaps not desirable) to change the values in columns retrieved from the lookup table, such as the CompanyName or City field in Suppliers. The user may attempt to alter the CompanyName value on one row of the **Recordset** created from this query, under the impression that the change will affect only the current row. However, because the value is actually stored back in the Suppliers lookup table, the value is changed for *every* row in the **Recordset**.

## One-To-Many Joins

There is no real logical difference between a "many-to-one" join, as described previously, and a "one-to-many" join, except from the point of view of the user. A one-to-many join is sometimes referred to as a master–detail relationship. A single row in the "one" or "master" table is related to one or more rows in the "many" or "detail" table. Updatable multitable joins are especially useful with these types of one-to-many relationships.

The following query joins the Orders table to the Order Details table in a classic one-to-many relationship:

```
SELECT DISTINCTROW
  Orders.*,
  [Order Details].*
FROM Orders INNER JOIN [Order Details]
ON Orders.OrderID = [Order Details].OrderID;
```

Columns in the Orders table focus on the order itself: the Customer who placed the order, the Employee who took the order, the date the order was taken, and so on. Columns derived from the Order Details table specify the actual items that were ordered: the Product ID and pricing details. Just as with the many-to-one example shown previously, changes to columns from the "one" table on any given row are automatically made for all other rows based on the same value in the "one" table. For example, if the user changes the Customer ID field, which is drawn from the "master" Orders table, on any given row, the change is automatically reflected in all other rows for this same Order.

Updatable multitable joins are not limited to a single-level hierarchy. For example, the following query links from Employees to Orders to Order Details:

```
SELECT DISTINCTROW
  Employees.EmployeeID,
  Employees.LastName,
  Orders.OrderID,
  Orders.OrderDate,
  [Order Details].ProductID
FROM (Employees INNER JOIN Orders
    ON Employees.EmployeeID = Orders.EmployeeID)
  INNER JOIN [Order Details]
    ON Orders.OrderID = [Order Details].OrderID;
```

Columns from all three of these joined tables are updatable in the resulting **Recordset**.

## Inserting Rows Into a Multitable Query

When inserting a row into a **Recordset** based on a multitable join, rows can be added to one, several, or all of the tables included in the join. It's easy to see that rows from the "many" side of the join are simply appended to the "many" table as needed. Rows from the "one" side of the join can be added as well, as long as they don't violate referential integrity constraints.

The following query joins the SalesReps (many) table to the Division (one) table:

```
SELECT DISTINCTROW
  SalesReps.EmployeeID,
  SalesReps.LastName,
  SalesReps.FirstName,
```

```
  SalesReps.DivID,
  Division.DivID,
  Division.Description
FROM SalesReps INNER JOIN Division
ON SalesReps.DivID = Division.DivID;
```

If, while adding a new SalesReps entry, the user specifies a DivID value that is already present in the Division table, then only the Products row is added. Row fix-up occurs; values from the corresponding Division record are retrieved.

It's possible to add a new DivID value to the SalesRep table and have that new value automatically added to the Division table if the primary key from the "one" table is included in the join, as in the previous example.

In general, values for all required fields, and for the field or fields making up the primary key, must be supplied when inserting a new row into a recordset based on a query. The exception to this rule is for Counter fields (also known as "AutoNumber"). You must not supply an explicit value for AutoNumber fields. The value for AutoNumber fields is automatically assigned by Microsoft Jet.

## Updatable One-to-Many Outer Joins

As discussed earlier in this chapter, an outer join selects all rows from one table in a multitable join, while only selecting rows with matching values from another table. For rows in which there is no match in one table, artificial NULL column values are supplied. Microsoft Jet allows you to "fill in the blanks" in these artificial NULL rows.

Consider the following outer join and its result:

```
SELECT
  Customers.CustomerName,
  Customers.CustomerID,
  Orders.CustomerID,
  Orders.OrderID
FROM Customers LEFT JOIN Orders
ON Customers.CustomerID = Orders.CustomerID;
```

| Cust.CustName | Cust.CustID | Orders.CustID | Orders.OrderID |
|---|---|---|---|
| Johnson | 1000 | 1000 | 1 |
| Johnson | 1000 | 1000 | 2 |
| Smith | 1001 | 1001 | 3 |
| Smith | 1001 | 1001 | 4 |
| Blair | 1002 | 1002 | 5 |
| Anderson | 1003 | | |

In this example, the Cust table is outer joined with the Orders table to show all customers regardless of whether or not they have placed an order. Customer "Anderson" (with CustID 1003) has not placed an order. The "fill in the blank with key propagation" rule states that the user can add an order for this customer by filling in the Orders.OrderID field (and any other Order information except OrderID). The value in Cust.CustID is automatically propagated into Orders.CustID. In this update scenario, the child key (Orders.CustID) is read-only. The act of "filling in the blank" locks the new Order row to Customer 1003.

## Multitable Query Updatability Restrictions

To be fully updatable, a query must meet several requirements.

You must specify an explicit inner or outer join between the tables. Joins created implicitly in the WHERE clause of the SELECT statement are not updatable. For example, the following join is not updatable:

```
SELECT
  Products.ProductID,
  Products.ProductName,
  Categories.CategoryID,
  Categories.CategoryName
FROM Categories, Products
WHERE Products.CategoryID = Categories.CategoryID;
```

Summary (GROUP BY), UNION, DISTINCT, and crosstab queries are never updatable. Queries joined to one or more summary queries are not updatable, even if you don't attempt to modify fields from an otherwise updatable table. However, a query may be updatable if it refers to a summary query in a sub-SELECT statement, as in the following example:

```
SELECT DISTINCTROW Orders.*
FROM Orders
WHERE (((Orders.Freight)>
  (SELECT DISTINCTROW Avg(Orders.Freight) AS AvgOfFreight
  FROM Orders;))));
```

Columns from the Orders table are updatable.

To be able to insert new rows into a table in any query, all primary key columns must be present.

While updating a single query row, changes to certain fields may render certain other fields non-updatable until the row edit is either saved or canceled. As soon as the user edits data on the "one" side of a query, then the join key on the "many" side can no longer be modified. Usually, the "many" side join key is updatable. However, because data on the "one" side was modified first, this column is temporarily rendered unmodifiable because row fix-up would discard changes to the "one" side data. As soon as the change to the "one" side of the query is committed or canceled, the "many" side join key becomes updatable again.

A change to a multitable query must not create "orphaned" records. You can change the join key in the "many" table to a value already present in the "one" table, but you cannot specify a nonexistent value, except in the case of outer joins.

# Data Manipulation Language SQL Statements

So far, only selecting, sorting, and summarizing data using various forms of the SQL SELECT clause has been covered. Microsoft Jet also uses SQL to perform modifications to its databases. You can insert new rows, delete from existing rows, and update values in existing rows using syntax that is quite similar to that used with the SELECT statement.

Data manipulation queries can either be created as permanent **QueryDef** objects in the database, or executed directly in Visual Basic code by using the **Execute** method of a database object variable. In many of the examples that follow, only the actual SQL statements that make up the QueryDef are shown—but keep in mind that the code must be executed by creating a **QueryDef** object that contains those SQL statements.

The single-table and multitable query updatability rules for **Recordsets** created from SQL SELECT statements that were discussed in the previous section also apply to updates done with the Data Manipulation Language (DML) statements discussed in this section.

## The UPDATE Query

You can use the UPDATE query to specify a set of rows from one or more tables and assign new values to one or more columns in that result set. The new value can be either a literal value assigned to each row to be updated, or an expression that uses existing values as part of the new value.

The following example updates the Salary field for all Sales Managers:

```
UPDATE Employees
SET Employees.Salary = 50000
WHERE Employees.Title="Sales Manager";
```

Every Employees record that meets the selection criterion is assigned the same value of 50,000.

The next example applies a formula that increases the employees' salaries by 10 percent for all employees who are *not* Sales Managers:

```
UPDATE Employees
SET Employees.Salary = Employees.Salary*1.1
WHERE Employees.Title<>"Sales Manager";
```

The Salary value of each row in the result set produced by applying the WHERE clause is multiplied by the constant value 1.1 and stored back into the same Salary field.

### Multitable UPDATE Queries

In addition to simple single-table updates, with Microsoft Jet you can create an UPDATE query that is the result of a multitable join. The following example joins the Orders and Order Details tables. It uses a selection criterion from the Orders table, but updates values in the Order Details table:

```
UPDATE Orders INNER JOIN [Order Details]
ON Orders.OrderID = [Order Details].OrderID
SET [Order Details].Discount = 0.25
WHERE Orders.CustomerID="FRANS";
```

In this case, the fields in the table on the "many" side of a one-to-many relationship are being updated. Fields on the "one" side of the join can also be updated, with certain limitations:

```
UPDATE Orders INNER JOIN [Order Details]
ON Orders.OrderID = [Order Details].OrderID
SET [Order Details].Discount = 0.25,
    Orders.OrderDate = #6/16/95#
WHERE Orders.CustomerID="FRANS";
```

You cannot create a multitable UPDATE query if one of the tables in the join is a summary query—a query that uses the GROUP BY clause, for example.

## The DELETE Query

The DELETE query uses the same join and selection syntax as the SELECT and UPDATE query forms, but instead of retrieving rows or updating the retrieved rows, it deletes the selected rows from the table or tables in the query. The simplest case deletes, from a single table, rows that match a selection criterion:

```
DELETE *
FROM Suppliers
WHERE (Suppliers.VendorRating<0);
```

### Multitable DELETE Queries

A DELETE query can also be based on a multitable join, as in the UPDATE query example shown previously.

This sample query joins the Categories table to the Products table, and deletes Products that match the selection criterion specified on the Categories table:

```
DELETE Products.*
FROM Categories INNER JOIN Products
ON Categories.CategoryID = Products.CategoryID
WHERE (((Categories.CategoryName)="Junk Food"));
```

## The INSERT INTO Query

You can insert new rows into an existing table using an INSERT query. In the simplest case, literal values are assigned to a single row that is inserted into the table:

```
INSERT INTO PerformanceGrade
  ( PerformanceGradeKey, LowRange, HighRange )
VALUES (5, 500000.01, 600000);
```

### INSERT...VALUES

The INSERT query lists the table to which the row will be added, the fields that will be populated with new values, and a corresponding VALUES clause with the literal values that will be assigned to those fields. The number and data types of the Fields list and the Values list must match.

It's not necessary to specify every field in the table. Any fields not specified are filled with the DefaultValue specified in the field properties for that particular field. However, all required fields must be assigned, including those fields participating in indexes or as part of the primary key.

However, an INSERT query cannot violate any referential integrity or ValidationRule clauses established at either the field level or the table level. If the **Required** property is set to TRUE on a particular field, for example, and you don't assign a value for this field, then a trappable run-time error is generated when you attempt to execute the INSERT query.

Similarly, if a referential integrity rule that requires a matching value in a foreign key field has been established, and that value does not exist in the related table, then the INSERT query will fail.

### INSERT...SELECT

An alternative form of this statement (and one likely to be created if you generate this query in Microsoft Access) is:

```
INSERT INTO PerformanceGrade
  ( PerformanceGradeKey, LowRange, HighRange )
SELECT 5 AS Expr1, 500000.01 AS Expr2, 600000 AS Expr3;
```

Rather than using the customary VALUES clause to assign field values, this form of the INSERT statement takes its values from another SELECT clause. In this particular case, because the inner SELECT statement doesn't contain a FROM clause, a single row is inserted into the new table, using the calculated columns Expr1, Expr2, and Expr3 as the source items.

When the source SELECT statement does have a FROM clause, then all rows retrieved by the SELECT statement are inserted into the first table:

```
INSERT INTO Employees
( EmployeeID,
  LastName,
  FirstName,
  Title,
  TitleOfCourtesy,
  BirthDate,
  HireDate,
  Address,
  City,
  Region,
  PostalCode,
  Country,
  HomePhone,
  Extension,
  Photo,
  Notes,
  ReportsTo )
SELECT
  TemporaryEmployees.EmployeeID,
  TemporaryEmployees.LastName,
  TemporaryEmployees.FirstName,
  TemporaryEmployees.Title,
  TemporaryEmployees.TitleOfCourtesy,
  TemporaryEmployees.BirthDate,
  TemporaryEmployees.HireDate,
  TemporaryEmployees.Address,
  TemporaryEmployees.City,
  TemporaryEmployees.Region,
  TemporaryEmployees.PostalCode,
  TemporaryEmployees.Country,
  TemporaryEmployees.HomePhone,
  TemporaryEmployees.Extension,
  TemporaryEmployees.Photo,
  TemporaryEmployees.Notes,
  TemporaryEmployees.ReportsTo
FROM TemporaryEmployees
WHERE (((TemporaryEmployees.Title)="New Hire"));
```

Instead of itemizing the columns in the source and target tables, you can use the shorthand form of this statement:

```
INSERT INTO Employees
SELECT TemporaryEmployees.*
FROM TemporaryEmployees
WHERE (((TemporaryEmployees.Title)="New Hire"));
```

This format requires that the column names in the source and the target tables match.

### The Make-Table Query (SELECT...INTO)

With the SELECT...INTO statement, you can simultaneously select columns from one or more tables and create a new table with the result of that selection. The following table selects rows from the Products table, in which the Discontinued field is set to TRUE, builds a new table called DiscontinuedProducts, and appends the selected rows into the new table:

```
SELECT Products.*
INTO DiscontinuedProducts
FROM Products
WHERE (((Products.Discontinued)=True));
```

If the table specified with the INTO clause already exists, then a trappable run-time error occurs.

Only the names and the data types of the original columns are created in the new table. None of the **DefaultValue**, **ValidationRule**, **Caption** properties, and so on, are transferred. The new table is built with no indexes and no referential integrity constraints.

An alternative to this approach would be to create the empty table, either through DAO methods or by creating a SELECT INTO query that returns no rows. Then create any indexes you want using SQL ALTER TABLE statements or by using the DAO methods discussed in Chapter 3. Finally, populate the new table with an append query—using INSERT...SELECT rather than SELECT INTO. It might also be useful to defer creating the indexes until after the table is populated, which will speed up the insert operation.

# Other Query Types

For information on setting **QueryDef** properties through DAO Code, see Chapter 3, "Data Definition and Integrity."
For more information on ODBC, see Chapter 12, "ODBC Desktop Database Drivers."

Microsoft Jet supports two other query types: The data definition language query alters the structure of a Microsoft Jet database, and the pass-through query communicates with back-end ODBC database management systems.

### Data Definition Language Queries

You use DDL queries to modify the structure of a Microsoft Jet database. They can be used to build and delete tables, to add and drop fields and indexes from those tables, and to create referential integrity relationships between two tables.

This is an example of a DDL QueryDef that creates a new table with three fields, and builds a primary key index on the AUTO_ID field:

```
CREATE TABLE AUTOS
(AUTO_ID TEXT (10) CONSTRAINT PrimaryKey PRIMARY KEY,
 MAKE TEXT(20),
 MODEL TEXT(20))
```

## Pass-Through Queries

For specific types of and uses for Microsoft Jet DDL queries, see Chapter 3, "Data Definition and Integrity."

Microsoft Jet is designed to work transparently, for the most part, with a wide variety of data sources, whether they're native Microsoft Jet databases, installable ISAM data sources such as Microsoft FoxPro or Borland's Paradox, or ODBC data sources such as Microsoft SQL Server. Microsoft Jet supports the concept of linked tables—tables that physically reside in an external database, but are treated as though they're local. When you design a SELECT or UPDATE query, you generally don't have to worry about whether the tables in the query are native Microsoft Jet tables or are in another data format.

Many data sources have no native SQL interface. Microsoft Jet translates your SQL statement into direct data manipulation functions that are specific to that data source. Other data sources, such as Microsoft SQL Server, support the use of SQL by definition, although the dialect of SQL can differ radically from one database management system to another. Even when you create an SQL statement and save it in a **QueryDef** object, Microsoft Jet transforms the "native" Jet SQL statement into a format that you might barely recognize.

Occasionally, you might want to get Microsoft Jet out of the way and directly communicate with your back-end SQL database system. You can use a pass-through query to send any arbitrary SQL statement to your server. Microsoft Jet does no translation or error checking of any kind: It simply passes the text of the pass-through query on to the back-end server for processing.

A pass-through QueryDef is one whose **Connect** property contains the string "ODBC;". The **Type** property of a pass-through QueryDef should be set to the VBA constant dbQSQLPassthrough.

Your SQL statement must conform to the rules of the server you're using. For example, while Microsoft Jet uses the asterisk (*) character with the **Like** operator, Microsoft SQL Server uses the ANSI-standard percent (%) character:

```
SELECT * FROM PRODUCT WHERE PRODCODE LIKE 'B%'
```

This query acts like a normal SELECT query. It returns rows and can be used to create a **Recordset** object, but is not updatable.

If this pass-through query is saved as a permanent QueryDef, it can even be used to join to other tables or queries. For example, if this pass-through query is saved as "qryB_PRODUCT," it could be used to build another query:

```
SELECT
  qryB_PRODUCT.PRODCODE,
  qryB_PRODUCT.PRODNAME,
  BOOKINGPRODUCT.CPUID,
  BOOKINGPRODUCT.BOOKINGID
FROM qryB_PRODUCT INNER JOIN BOOKINGPRODUCT
ON qryB_PRODUCT.PRODCODE = BOOKINGPRODUCT.PRODUCTCODE;
```

In this example, the pass-through query is executed on the server, which retrieves all rows from the Product table where the Prodcode column begins with a "B." The result of this query is joined with a local BookingProduct table, and the result is created transparently.

Anything that the back-end server can interpret can be successfully used in a pass-through query. This includes DDL statements that create and drop tables, or DELETE and INSERT DML statements that don't return rows but instead act directly on the back-end server database.

The contents of a pass-through query don't even have to be an SQL statement. You can execute stored procedures, as in the following example:

```
sp_who
```

This code returns statistics on current users of the back-end database. Because this stored procedure happens to return rows, the pass-through query that executes it can be used to create a **Recordset**. For example, if this were saved as a pass-through **QueryDef** object called "qrySPT_who," it could be used in another query:

```
SELECT DISTINCTROW qrySPT_who.*
FROM qrySPT_who
WHERE (((qrySPT_who.status)='sleeping'));
```

You can supply parameters to a stored procedure by concatenating the value of the parameter with a call to the stored procedure.

# Microsoft Jet Query Engine Overview

The Microsoft Jet database engine contains a sophisticated query processor that is responsible for query execution. There is, however, much more to the query engine than just a query processor. The query engine also contains a sophisticated query optimizer that takes any given query as its input and determines the fastest join strategy for executing that query.

A query may be internally "rearranged" to yield a more optimized join strategy, but this is all done without intervention from the user. The goal of the query engine is to take any query, no matter how poorly structured, and execute that query in an efficient manner.

Be aware, however, that given two equivalent queries, the simpler one is usually optimized better. The number one rule for performance is to use simple SQL constructs and good database design.

# Query Engine Components

The query engine has eight major components:

- Parser/Binder. The parser/binder parses the SQL statement that defines a query and binds the names referenced in the query to columns in the underlying tables. The parser/binder first checks the query for proper syntax. If there are any syntactical problems with the query, an error is returned. Next, the parser/binder converts the SQL string into the internal query-object definition format in which queries are stored.

- Folder. The folder moves expressions "up" the query tree. The top of the query tree, or root, is the final result set. By moving expressions to the top of the tree, the expressions don't have to be computed against records that may be discarded. Although it may have a beneficial effect on performance, the goal of folding is to enable updatable views, not to increase performance.

- Splitter. The splitter splits conglomerate **QueryDef** objects into their discrete components. The conglomerate query objects are then removed from the tree. This operation is performed on the query tree starting from the leaves and moving in reverse order up to the root.

- Flattener. The flattener takes the output of the splitter and combines joins, ORDER BY clauses, and WHERE clauses as much as possible.

- Optimizer. The optimizer is one of the most complex components of the query engine. It uses statistics to determine the most efficient way to execute a query. The optimizer in the Microsoft Jet database engine is a cost-based optimizer. This means the optimizer assigns a cost to each task and then chooses the least expensive list of tasks to perform that will generate the desired result set. The longer a task takes to perform, the more costly or expensive it's.

The algorithms that the optimizer uses are dependent on the accuracy of the statistics provided by the underlying engine. For example, the statistics that some ODBC drivers return are not accurate. This may cause the optimizer to choose a less than optimal execution plan. However, if the whole query is sent to the ODBC server for processing (the usual case), then the optimizer's execution plan is irrelevant.

In the native Microsoft Jet database engine, statistics can become out-of-date over time. Statistics become out-of-date if transactions are performed and then rolled back, or if your machine is turned off before the database is closed. The problem in the latter situation occurs because the statistics are cached in memory, and shutting off the machine without closing the database does not allow the statistics to be written out to disk.

To update the statistics in a Microsoft Jet database, you must compact the database. Compaction of the database may also speed up queries, because the process writes all of the data in a table in contiguous pages. This makes scanning sequential pages much faster than when the database is fragmented.

- Remote Post-Processor. The remote post-processor determines how much of a query can be sent to an ODBC back-end for processing by the server. The goal is to send as much of the query as possible to the server for processing. The remote post-processor walks through the query tree from the bottom up, marking subtrees that can be sent to the server. As subtrees are found, they are marked as "remoteable." Finally, SQL strings are generated for the remote queries.

- Post-Processor. The post processor takes the query graph in its current compiled form and moves it to a new, cleaner, smaller data-execution structure.

- Join Processor. The join processor is the component responsible for executing the compiled query. It uses the join strategy that was chosen by the optimizer to return the desired result set.

# Join Strategies

Microsoft Jet can choose from five join strategies. Each of these join strategies serves a particular purpose, and ranges in complexity from a "brute force" table scan to more complex execution plans. The five join strategies are nested iteration, index, lookup, merge, and index-merge.

## Nested Iteration Join

The nested iteration join is a "brute force" method and is used only as a last-ditch attempt at performing a join. A nested iteration is performed only when the tables contain few records and, most probably, no useful indexes.

### Algorithm for Performing a Nested Iteration Join

1. Pair each record in the outer table with a record in the inner table.

2. Check each pair to make sure it meets the join restrictions.

   If a record matches the restriction, it's kept for the result set; otherwise, it's discarded.

Following is an example of a nested iteration join:

```
SELECT DISTINCTROW
  Categories.CategoryName,
  Products.ProductName,
  Categories.Description,
  Categories.Picture,
  Products.ProductID,
  Products.QuantityPerUnit,
  Products.UnitPrice, Products.Discontinued
FROM Categories INNER JOIN Products
ON Categories.CategoryID = Products.CategoryID
WHERE Products.Discontinued=No
ORDER BY Categories.CategoryName, Products.ProductName;
```

## Index Join

Microsoft Jet chooses an index join when the inner table has an index over the joined column. The index join tends to be used when the outer table is small or data does not have to be retrieved from the inner table. Microsoft Jet might also use an Index join if the outer table is small or highly restricted. Index joins are often used for dynasets.

### Algorithm for Performing an Index Join

1. Retrieve a value from the outer table.

2. Make a key for the inner table.

3. Search on the inner table to find matches, based on the key retrieved in step 2.

4. Check the remaining restrictions for each match.

Following is an example of an index join:

```
SELECT DISTINCTROW
  Products.ProductID,
  Orders.OrderDate,
  Sum(CLng([Order Details].UnitPrice*Quantity*(1-Discount)*100))/100 AS
ProductAmount
FROM Orders
  INNER JOIN (Products
    INNER JOIN [Order Details]
      ON Products.ProductID = [Order Details].ProductID)
    ON Orders.OrderID = [Order Details].OrderID
GROUP BY Products.ProductID, Orders.OrderDate;
```

## Lookup Join

A lookup join is very similar to an index join: The only difference is that the lookup join performs a projection and sort as part of the index creation on the inner table before performing the join. Projection reduces the set of columns in the inner relation and, therefore, reduces its size. A lookup join is often used for static queries and ordered dynaset-type **Recordset** objects.

### Algorithm for Performing a Lookup Join

1. Create a sorted and indexed temporary table, projecting out the necessary columns from the inner table.

2. Retrieve a value from the outer table.

3. Make a key for the inner table.

4. Search on the temporary table to find matches, based on the key retrieved in step 3.

5. Check the remaining restrictions for each match.

## Merge Join

Merge joins tend to be performed when the inputs are large. Merge joins also tend to be used in cases when ordering the output of a join can save resorting.

## Index-Merge Join

An index-merge join may be used when each input is a table in native Microsoft Jet database format. Each input must have an index over its join column, and at least one of the indexes must not allow nulls if there is more than one join column.

### Algorithm for Performing an Index-Merge Join

1.  For the current outer record, advance the inner cursor until the outer key is greater than or equal to the inner key.

2.  If equal, return record.

3.  If greater, advance the outer input one record.

4.  Move backward the number of matches for the previous key on the inner input if the outer input reference is not unique and matches the current inner input.

Following is an example of an index-merge join:

```
SELECT DISTINCTROW
  [Order Details].OrderID,
  Products.ProductName,
  [Order Details].ProductID,
  [Order Details].UnitPrice
FROM Products INNER JOIN [Order Details]
ON Products.ProductID = [Order Details].ProductID;
```

# Query Optimization

This section discusses the techniques for maximizing database performance using the Microsoft Jet database engine. It covers the Microsoft Jet query engine and how it optimizes queries, as well as how to avoid common pitfalls in query design that can lead to performance degradation. Finally, specific optimization techniques for dealing with data from ODBC data sources are covered.

Queries are the heart of a Microsoft Jet database. Because the purpose of most database applications is to retrieve the data stored in the database, **QueryDef** objects are usually used more than any other object in a database. Queries are used more frequently in Microsoft Jet–based applications than in other database products due to powerful query functionality, such as query updatability, *hybrid* queries (queries combining from more than one data source), and *stacked* queries (queries that use other queries as input).

# The Microsoft Jet Query Engine Optimizer

As previously mentioned, the optimizer uses statistics on the tables in the query to determine which join strategy to use. This section looks closer into the statistics that are used, as well as how the joins themselves affect join strategy selection.

## Optimizer Statistics

The optimizer uses two sets of statistics when determining a join strategy on the base tables and on non-base table inputs such as other **QueryDef** objects.

For base table inputs, the optimizer looks at:

- The number of records in the base table. The number of records gives the optimizer information as to how large the tables are, which affects which join strategy to use.

- The number of data pages in the base table. The more data pages that need to be read from disk, the more costly the query is.

- The location of the table. Is the table in a local ISAM format or is it from an ODBC database? Each distinct ODBC server is given a number. This helps the optimizer and remote post-processor do their work.

- The indexes on the table. When looking at indexes, the optimizer is concerned with:

  - Selectivity. If a particular index returns only three unique values out of 100,000, it's considered highly selective. A unique index is the most highly selective index available, because every value is distinct. It's always best to use highly selective indexes.

  - Number of index pages. As with data pages, the more index pages that must be read from disk, the more costly the query is.

  - Whether nulls are allowed in the index. Nulls in an index may rule out the usage of an index-merge join.

  - Whether duplicates are allowed in the index. Duplicates in an index affect its selectivity.

For non-base table inputs, the optimizer looks at:

- Record counts. As with base tables, the number of records in the input query affects the join strategy chosen.

- Input costs. Because the input is another query, the cost of executing that query must be factored into the total cost.

**Note** The record count and input costs are estimates.

- Location of inputs. Each distinct ODBC server is given a number. This helps the remote post-processor do its work.

- Record ordering. An ordered input may be a candidate for a lookup join.

## Choosing Join Combinations

Using the statistics described, the optimizer chooses a join strategy. Because Microsoft Jet uses a cost-based optimizer, each possible join combination is looked at to determine which will yield the least costly query execution.

In choosing a join combination, the optimizer first selects a base table access strategy. The optimizer then stores the estimated number of records returned and a cost—how expensive it is to read the table. The optimizer then generates all combinations of pairs of tables and determines the cost of each join strategy. Finally, the optimizer adds tables to the joins and continues to calculate statistics until the cheapest strategy for the entire query is found.

## Choosing a Base-Table Access Plan

Three methods are available for accessing a base table:

- Table scan. This is generally the slowest access to a table's data, because every data page must be read. Using a table scan, single-table restrictions are checked for each row in the table, but no base-table page is read from disk more than once.

- Index range. Using an index range, a table is opened with a particular index that is over one of the single-table restrictions. Records in the index are then checked against remaining restrictions; however, a base-table page may be read from disk more than once.

- Rushmore restriction. A Rushmore restriction is used when there are restrictions on multiple-indexed columns. By using multiple indexes to solve the query, the number of base-table pages that need to be read from disk is minimized. For more information, see the following section.

# Rushmore Query Optimization

One of the most powerful ways to execute queries is to take advantage of Rushmore query optimization.

## What Is Rushmore?

Simply put, Rushmore query optimization uses indexes efficiently to quickly find a set of records. Rushmore query optimization is used on queries involving multiple column, indexed restrictions. Index Intersection alone is the most straightforward and obvious Rushmore feature, but Rushmore encompasses several other ideas, such as Index Union. COUNT(*) queries can also be elegantly handled by Rushmore.

# Operations That Can Use Rushmore

## Index Intersection

Solving a query using Index Intersection involves scanning multiple indexes for records matching a criteria such as:

*column1* = *<expression>* AND *column2* = *<expression>*

As described in the previous section, Rushmore uses the indexes on both columns to find the bookmarks of matching records for each clause in the predicate. The resulting bookmarks from each of the indexes are intersected to find the records that match both criteria.

For example, consider a table containing demographic information about all of the people in New York City. The table contains information regarding age, height, weight, hair color, and eye color. Suppose a query is written to find all of the people with blonde hair and blue eyes:

hair_color = blonde AND eye_color = blue

Assuming indexes have been created on the hair_color and eye_color columns, this query would be solved using Rushmore Index Intersection. The index on hair_color is used to find all of the blondes, and then the index on eye_color is used to find all of the blue-eyed people. The results of each index search are then intersected to find all of the people with both characteristics.

## Index Union

Solving a query with Index Union involves scanning multiple indexes for records matching a criteria such as:

*column1* = *<expression>* OR *column2* = *<expression>*

Again, Rushmore uses the indexes on both columns to find the matching records. The resulting records from each of the indexes are then united to find the records with either one criterion or the other.

For example, again consider the table containing demographic information about all of the people in New York City. Suppose a query is written to find all of the people with black hair or green eyes. The criteria would look like:

hair_color = "black" OR eye_color = "green"

This query would be solved using Rushmore Index Union. The index on hair_color is used to find all of the black-haired people, and then the index on eye_color is used to find all of the green-eyed people. The result of each index search is then united to find all of the people with either characteristic.

# Common Pitfalls to Avoid

Many common mistakes can cause unnecessary bottlenecks when executing queries. Following is a list of these common mistakes and what to do to correct them.

- Expressions in query output. Often users place expressions, such as an **IIf**, on an output column of a query. This can cause optimization problems if this query is used as the input to another query. For example, consider the following two queries:

```
Q1: SELECT IIF(MyColumn="H","Hello", "Goodbye") AS X FROM MyTable;

Q2: SELECT * FROM Q1 WHERE X="HELLO";
```

Because Microsoft Jet cannot optimize the **IIf**, it cannot optimize Q2. Sometimes expressions get buried so far down in a query tree that you don't even realize they're there. If expressions are necessary in the output, try to place the expression in a control on a form or report.

The more optimal way to write this query would be:

```
Q1: SELECT *FROM MyTable WHERE MyColumn = "H";
```

- GROUP BY on too many columns. When creating a "totals" query, use the GROUP BY clause on as few columns as necessary to achieve the query's goal. The more columns in the GROUP BY, the longer the query takes to execute. Be sure that you're not including extraneous columns.

- GROUP BY in same query as a join. If possible, place a GROUP BY clause on a table and then join it to another table—rather than joining the two tables and doing the GROUP BY in the same query as the join. For example, instead of this query:

```
' Q1:
SELECT
     Orders.CompanyID,
     Count(Orders.OrderID) AS CountOfOrderID
    FROM Customers INNER JOIN Orders
    ON Customers.CustomerID = Orders.CustomerID
    GROUP BY Orders.CompanyName;
```

you might benefit by using two separate queries as follows:

```
' Q1:
SELECT
     Customers.CompanyID
    FROM Customers
    GROUP BY Customers.CompanyID;
```

```
' Q2:
SELECT
     Orders.CustomerID,
     Count(Orders.OrderID) AS CountOfOrderID
   FROM Query1 INNER JOIN Orders
   ON Query1.CustomerID = Orders.CustomerID
   GROUP BY Orders.CustomerID;
```

- Missing indexes on join columns. When joining tables, always try to index the fields on both sides of a join. This can speed query execution by allowing more sophisticated join strategies such as the index and index-merge joins. The use of indexes also provides better statistics. For more information, see the "Join Strategies" section earlier in this chapter.

- Under-indexing fields. "When in doubt, index!" If the database is used solely for DSS types of applications, then you should place an index on all columns that have a fairly high uniqueness and are used in a join or restriction. With the use of Rushmore query optimization, Microsoft Jet can take advantage of multiple indexes on a single table. This makes indexing many columns quite advantageous. However, please keep in mind that adding indexes to columns directly affects both performance and concurrency when doing any DML-type statement.

- Using COUNT(*ColumnName*) instead of COUNT(*). When you have to determine the number of records, you should use COUNT(*) rather than COUNT(*ColumnName*). This is because there are Rushmore optimizations that allow COUNT(*) to be executed much faster than COUNT(*ColumnName*).

# Optimizing Access to ODBC Data Sources

You can use several techniques to improve the speed of access to ODBC data. The following guidelines improve performance when dealing with data from an ODBC data source:

- Restrict the amount of data you request from the server. Don't ask for more data than you need. Use queries to select only the fields and rows needed.

- Use only the functionality that you need. Snapshot-type **Recordset** objects are less powerful than dynaset-type **Recordset** objects, but may be faster against servers.

- Use attached or linked tables to access server data. Don't use "direct" server access; that is, don't open remote databases and execute queries against them; attach tables and use the attachments, or use pass-through queries.

- Use list boxes and combo boxes wisely. Be cautious when creating Microsoft Access forms with many list boxes, combo boxes, subforms, and controls containing totals. Each of these controls requires a separate query. Against local data, performance may be adequate due to data caching and in-memory query processing. Against remote data, each query must be sent to the server and a response returned, resulting in an unacceptably long delay when opening the form.

- Avoid large combo boxes. Presenting a combo box of hundreds or even thousands of choices based on a local table may yield reasonable response time, especially if you define an appropriate index on the local table. Against a remote table, such a combo box, response is sluggish, and server and network resources can be drained as the data to fill the list is fetched.

- Use **Find** only on smaller **Recordset** objects. Microsoft Jet optimizes the **FindFirst** and **FindNext** methods to work well against local recordsets of almost any size and remote recordsets of reasonable size. When working with large remote recordsets (thousands of records), you should use a filter or query and be careful to use restrictions that your server can process.

- Make sure queries are sent to the server for processing. The most important factor in query performance against remote data is making sure your server executes as much of the query as possible. Microsoft Jet attempts to send the entire query to your server, but locally evaluates (on your computer) any query clauses and expressions that are not supported by servers generally (for example, Microsoft Jet–specific functionality), or by your server in particular.

## Generally Unsupported Functionality

Functionality not supported by servers in general includes:

- Operations that cannot be expressed in a single SQL statement. This can occur when you use a query as an input to another query, or your query's FROM clause contains a totals query or DISTINCT query. Often, you can rearrange your queries to calculate totals or DISTINCT queries after all other operations.

- Operations that are Microsoft Jet–specific extensions to SQL, such as crosstab queries, TOP queries, and reports with multiple levels of grouping and totals. Simple crosstab queries can be sent to the server.

- Expressions that contain Microsoft Access–specific operators or functions. The Microsoft Access financial functions and statistical aggregates often have no server equivalents.

- User-defined Visual Basic functions that take remote columns as arguments. These functions don't exist on the server, but they must process remote column data.

- Mixing textual and numeric data types in operators or UNION query outputs. Most servers lack the Microsoft Access data type leniency. Use explicit conversion functions where needed.

- Heterogeneous joins between local tables and remote tables, or between remote tables in different ODBC data sources.

- Non-remoteable expressions. A *non-remoteable* expression is one that cannot be evaluated by your server. Non-remoteable output expressions (those in the SELECT clause) don't force local evaluation of your query unless they occur in a totals query, a DISTINCT query, or a UNION query. Non-remoteable expressions in other clauses (WHERE, ORDER BY, GROUP BY, HAVING, and so on) force at least part of your query to be evaluated locally.

## Optionally Supported Functionality

Servers differ in some areas of functionality. When you attach a remote table, Microsoft Jet asks the ODBC driver for capability information about these areas. If supported by the driver and the server, Microsoft Jet sends these operations to the server for processing; if not, Microsoft Jet performs the operations locally. These areas include, but are not limited to:

- Outer joins.

    **Note**  Microsoft Jet does not send multiple outer joins to a server, although many inner joins can accompany a single outer join.

- Numeric, String, and Date/Time functions, such as **Log**, **Mid$**, **DatePart**, and so on.

- Conversion functions, such as **CInt**, **CStr**, **CDate**, and so on.

CHAPTER 5

# Working with Records and Fields

The Microsoft Jet database engine supports a rich set of DAO features for organizing, sorting, searching, updating, adding, and deleting data. The **Recordset** object alone provides 22 methods and 25 properties that give you a great deal of control over records in a database. With the **Recordset** object's **Fields** collection and a number of **Field** object properties and methods, you can manipulate data at the field level. This chapter describes in detail how to manipulate records and fields using the data access **Recordset** and **Field** objects.

**Contents**

For information on copying the code examples from the companion CD-ROM to your hard disk drive, see "Using the Companion CD-ROM" in the Preface.

## Using CH05.MDB and CHAP05.VBP

If you copied the samples from the companion CD-ROM, you can find the code examples for Microsoft Access in C:\SAMPLES\CHAP05\ACCESS\CH05.MDB. The corresponding code examples for Visual Basic are in C:\SAMPLES\CHAP05\VB40\CHAP05.VBP.

To run any of the code examples in this chapter, open the .MDB file in Microsoft Access or open the .VBP file in Microsoft Visual Basic 4.0. You can use the examples to help you understand the concepts discussed in the chapter—or you can modify them and use them in your own applications.

# Using Recordset Objects

You use **Recordset** objects to manipulate the data in a database. The three types of **Recordset** objects—table, dynaset, and snapshot—differ from each other in significant ways:

- A table-type **Recordset** object refers to either a local table in the current database, or to a linked table in an external database created with Microsoft Access or Microsoft Jet. When you create a table-type **Recordset**, the database engine opens the actual table, and your subsequent data manipulations operate directly on base-table data. A table-type **Recordset** can be opened against only one table; it cannot be opened against a join or union query.

- One of the biggest advantages of this type is that it can be indexed, using an index created for the underlying table. This allows much faster sorting and filtering than is possible with the other types. To locate specific records, use the **Seek** method, which is faster than the Find methods.

- A dynaset-type **Recordset** object refers to either local or linked tables, or to the result of a query. It's actually a set of references to records in one or more tables. With a dynaset, you can extract and update data from more than one table, including linked tables from other databases. Heterogeneous joins are a unique feature of dynasets—they enable you to use updatable join queries against tables in different types of databases.

- One of the main benefits of this type is that a dynaset and its underlying tables update each other: Changes made to records in the dynaset are also made in the underlying table, and changes made by other users to data in the underlying tables while the dynaset is open are reflected in the dynaset. The dynaset is the most flexible and powerful type of **Recordset**, although queries and other manipulations may not execute as fast as with a table-type **Recordset**.

- A snapshot-type **Recordset** object contains a fixed copy of the data as it exists at the time the snapshot is created. A snapshot can't be updated.

- The main advantage of a snapshot is that it creates less processing overhead than the other types, so it may execute queries and return data faster, especially when working with Open Database Connectivity (ODBC) data sources. When you need to make only a single pass through the records, you can create a forward-scrolling snapshot that executes even faster. Note that for .MDB files, LongBinary and Memo fields are represented in a snapshot by pointers, rather than the actual data.

Figure 5.1 illustrates the difference between how data is stored in a snapshot and how it's stored in a dynaset. The snapshot stores a copy of the entire record (except for Memo and OLE Object fields). The dynaset stores just the primary key for each record, copying the full record only when it's needed for editing or display purposes.

**Snapshot**                                                                    **Dynaset**

Primary Key                                    Primary Key

All records are fetched                                          Records are fetched
                                                                 only as needed

| Part # | Vendor | Price | Availability | | Part # | | Part # | Vendor | Price | Availability |
|--------|--------|-------|--------------|---|--------|---|--------|--------|-------|--------------|
| 101 | Acme Standard Widget | $99.00 | 7/1 | | 101 | → | 101 | Acme Standard Widget | $99.00 | 7/1 |
| 102 | Acme Deluxe Widget | $139.00 | Now | | 102 | → | 102 | Acme Deluxe Widget | $139.00 | Now |
| 201 | Spacely Small Sprocket | $29.95 | Now | | 201 | → | 201 | Spacely Small Sprocket | $29.95 | Now |
| 202 | Spacely Large Sprocket | $59.99 | 8/15 | | 202 | → | 202 | Spacely Large Sprocket | $59.99 | 8/15 |
| 301 | Cogswell Small Cog | $75.00 | 12/10 | | 301 | → | 301 | Cogswell Small Cog | $75.00 | 12/10 |
| 302 | Cogswell Super Cog | $99.00 | Now | | 302 | → | 302 | Cogswell Super Cog | $99.00 | Now |

**Figure 5.1    The difference between records stored in dynaset- and snapshot-type Recordset objects.**

The type of **Recordset** you use depends on what you want to do and whether you want to change or simply view the data. For example, if you must sort the data or work with indexes, use a table. Because they are indexed, table-type **Recordset** objects also provide the fastest way to locate data. If you want to be able to update a set of records selected by a query, use a dynaset. If the table-type is unavailable in a specific situation and you only need to scan through a set of records, using a forward-scrolling snapshot may improve performance.

All other things being equal, using a table-type **Recordset** object, if that type is available, almost always results in the best performance.

**Note**  In this chapter, the terms table, snapshot, and dynaset are often used for the sake of simplicity. Keep in mind, however, that these are all types of **Recordset** objects. For example, the term dynaset refers to a dynaset-type **Recordset** object.

# Creating a Recordset Variable

The **OpenRecordset** method is the basic method of creating a **Recordset** object variable. To use it, you first declare a variable of type **Recordset**, and then set the variable to the object returned by the **OpenRecordset** method.

The **OpenRecordset** method is available from **Database**, **TableDef**, **QueryDef** and existing **Recordset** objects. The syntax of the **OpenRecordset** method for **Database** objects is:

Set *variable* = *database*.**OpenRecordset** (*source* [, *type* [, *options*]])

The syntax of the **OpenRecordset** method for all other types of objects is:

Set *variable* = *object*.**OpenRecordset** ([*type* [, *options*]])

The *variable* argument is the name of the new **Recordset** object.

The *database* argument is the name of an open **Database** object from which you're creating the new **Recordset** object.

Then *object* argument is a **TableDef**, **QueryDef**, or existing **Recordset** object from which you're creating the new **Recordset** object. Microsoft Jet uses the *source* argument only for **Recordset** objects created from **Database** objects.

The *source* argument is an existing **TableDef** or **QueryDef** object in the database or a valid row-returning SQL query or statement. For **TableDef**, **QueryDef**, and **Recordset** objects, the object itself is automatically used as the *source*.

The *type* argument is an intrinsic constant that specifies the kind of **Recordset** you want to create. The available *type* constants are:

- **dbOpenTable**
- **dbOpenDynaset**
- **dbOpenSnapshot**

If you don't specify the *type* argument, Microsoft Jet selects the most functional type available, depending on the data source.

## OpenRecordset Options

With the *options* argument of the **OpenRecordset** method, you can specify a number of other features for a **Recordset** object, using the following constants:

- **dbAppendOnly**   With this option, you can only append new records to the **Recordset**; you cannot edit or delete existing records. This is useful in applications that collect and archive data (dynaset only).

- **dbSeeChanges**   If another user changes data in a record on which this **Recordset** has invoked the **Edit** method, but before it has invoked the **Update** method, a run-time error will occur. This is useful in applications where multiple users have simultaneous read/write access to the same data (dynaset and table only).

- **dbDenyWrite**   When used on a dynaset or snapshot, this option prevents other users from adding or modifying records, although they can still read data. When used on a table, no other user can open any type of **Recordset** from an underlying table.

- **dbDenyRead**   Prevents other users from reading data in the table (table only).

- **dbReadOnly**   Prevents your Recordset from modifying data. This is useful where the Recordset will be used to display data in a form that otherwise allows data entry.

- **dbForwardOnly**   Creates a forward-scrolling snapshot. Note that **Recordset** objects created with this option cannot be cloned and only supports the **Move** and **MoveNext** methods to move directly through the records (snapshot only).

- **dbSQLPassThrough**   Where the *source* argument is an SQL statement, use this option to pass the SQL statement to an ODBC database for processing. If used with a dynaset, data is not updatable (dynaset and snapshot only).

- **dbConsistent**   (Default) Only consistent updates are allowed (dynaset only).

- **dbInconsistent**   Inconsistent updates are allowed. Opposite of **dbConsistent** (dynaset only).

For more information on inconsistent updates, see the "Inconsistent Updates" sidebar.

## Creating a Recordset from a Table

The method you use to create a **Recordset** object from a base table depends on whether the table is local to the current database or is a linked table in another database. The following discussion explains the differences and provides examples for each type of base table.

### From a Table in a Local Microsoft Jet Database

The following example uses the **OpenRecordset** method to create a table-type **Recordset** object for a table in the current database:

```
Dim dbsCurrent As Database, rstCustomer As Recordset

Set dbsCurrent = OpenDatabase("C:\Samples\Chap05\NwindJet.mdb")
Set rstCustomer = dbsCurrent.OpenRecordset("Customer")
```

Note that you don't need to use the **dbOpenTable** constant to create a table-type **Recordset**. If you omit the type constant, Microsoft Jet chooses the highest-functionality **Recordset** type available, depending on the object the **Recordset** is created in, and the data source. Because the table type is available when you open a **Recordset** from a local table, Microsoft Jet uses it.

### From a Linked Table in a Different Database Format

For more information on connecting to data in external databases, see Chapter 8, "Accessing External Data."

The next example creates a dynaset-type **Recordset** object for a linked Paradox 3.*x* table. Because the table type is not available when you open a **Recordset** from a linked table in a non-Jet database, Microsoft Jet selects the next most efficient type, opening a dynaset-type **Recordset**.

```
Dim dbsCurrent As Database
Dim tdfNonJetLinked As TableDef, rstTableData As Recordset
```

```
' Get current database.
Set dbsCurrent = OpenDatabase("C:\Samples\Chap05\NwindJet.mdb")
Set tdfNonJetLinked = dbsCurrent.CreateTableDef("PDXAuthor")

' Connect to Paradox table Author in database C:\PDX\Publish.
tdfNonJetLinked.Connect = "Paradox 3.X;DATABASE=C:\PDX\Publish"
tdfNonJetLinked.SourceTableName = "Author"

' Attach table.
dbsCurrent.TableDefs.Append tdfNonJetLinked

' Create a dynaset-type Recordset for the table.
Set rstTableData = tdfNonJetLinked.OpenRecordset()
```

You can also open a Paradox table directly by first opening the Paradox database.

For more information on improving performance by directly opening an attached table, see Chapter 3, "Data Definition and Integrity."

## Using an Index on a Table-Type Recordset

You can order records in a table-type **Recordset** object by setting its **Index** property. Any **Index** object in the **Indexes** collection of the **Recordset** object's underlying table can be specified in the **Index** property.

The following example illustrates a table-type **Recordset** based on the Customers table, using an existing index called City:

```
Dim dbsCurrent As Database, rstTableData As Recordset

Set dbsCurrent = OpenDatabase("C:\Samples\Chap05\NwindJet.mdb")
Set rstTableData = dbsCurrent.OpenRecordset("Customers", dbOpenTable)

rstTableData.MoveFirst                  ' Move to first record.
MsgBox rstTableData!CompanyName         ' First record with no index set.
rstTableData.Index = "City"             ' Select City index.
rstTableData.MoveFirst                  ' Move to first record.
MsgBox rstTableData!CompanyName
```

You must set the **Index** property before using the **Seek** method. If you set the **Index** property to an index that doesn't exist, a trappable run-time error occurs. If you want to sort records according to an index that doesn't exist, either create the index first, or create a dynaset- or snapshot-type **Recordset** using a query that returns records in a specified order.

## Creating a Recordset from a Query

You can also create a **Recordset** object based on a stored select query. In the following example, Customer List is an existing select query stored in the current database:

```
Dim dbsCurrent As Database, rstCustomers As Recordset

Set dbsCurrent = OpenDatabase("C:\Samples\Chap05\NwindJet.mdb")
Set rstCustomers = dbsCurrent.OpenRecordset("Customer List")
```

For more information
on SQL statements,
see Chapter 4,
"Queries," and
Appendix B, "SQL
Reference."

If a suitable select query doesn't already exist, the **OpenRecordset** method also accepts an SQL string instead of the name of a query. The previous example can be rewritten as follows:

```
Dim dbsCurrent As Database, rstCustomers As Recordset
Dim strQuerySQL As String

Set dbsCurrent = OpenDatabase("C:\Samples\Chap05\NwindJet.mdb")
strQuerySQL = "SELECT * FROM Customers ORDER BY CustomerID;"
Set rstCustomers = dbsCurrent.OpenRecordset(strQuerySQL)
```

The disadvantage of this approach is that the query string must be compiled each time it's executed, whereas the stored query is compiled the first time it's saved, which usually results in slightly better performance.

---

**Note**   When you create a **Recordset** object using an SQL string or a stored query, your code doesn't continue running until the query returns the first row in the **Recordset**. Consider displaying a message in the status bar while the query is running.

---

## Default Recordset Types

Because Microsoft Jet automatically chooses the default **Recordset** type depending on the data source and how the **Recordset** is opened, you don't need to specify a **Recordset** type. However, you can force a different type by specifying a *type* argument in the **OpenRecordset** method.

The following list describes the available types and the default type, depending on how you open the **Recordset** object:

- **OpenRecordset** method from a **Database** object:

  ```
  Set rstNew = dbsCurrent.OpenRecordset("Data Source")
  ```

  If `Data Source` is a base table local to the database, all three types are available, and the default type is table. If `Data Source` is anything else, only dynaset and snapshot are available, and dynaset is the default.

- **OpenRecordset** method from a **TableDef** object:

  ```
  Set rstNew = tdfTableData.OpenRecordset
  ```

  If `tdfTableData` refers to a table in a Microsoft Jet database or to an ISAM database opened directly, then all three types are available and table is the default type. If `tdfTableData` is in an ODBC database or is a linked table in an external database, only dynaset and snapshot are available and dynaset is the default.

- **OpenRecordset** method from a **QueryDef** object:

```
Set rstNew = qdfQueryData.OpenRecordset
```

Only dynaset and snapshot are available, and the default is dynaset.

- **OpenRecordset** method from an existing **Recordset** object:

```
Set rstNew = rstExisting.OpenRecordset
```

Only dynaset and snapshot are available. The default is the type of `rstExisting`.

---

**Microsoft Access Users**   To create a **Recordset** object based on a Microsoft Access form, you can use the **RecordsetClone** property of the form. This creates a dynaset-type **Recordset** that refers to the same underlying query or data as the form. If a form is based on a query, for example, referring to the **RecordsetClone** property is the equivalent of creating a dynaset with the same query. You can use the **RecordsetClone** property when you want to apply a method that can't be used with forms, such as the **FindFirst** method. The **RecordsetClone** property provides access to all the methods and properties that you can use with a dynaset. The syntax for the **RecordsetClone** property is:

**Set** rstNewRecordset = *form*.**RecordsetClone**

The *form* argument is the name of a Microsoft Access form. The following example shows how to assign a **Recordset** object to the records in the Orders form.

```
Dim rstOrders As Recordset
Set rstOrders = Forms!Orders.RecordsetClone
```

This code always creates the type of **Recordset** being cloned (the type of **Recordset** on which the *form* is based); no other types are available.

---

**Visual Basic Users**   You can create a **Recordset** object from a **Data** control by setting a new **Recordset** object equal to the value of the control's **Recordset** property. For more information, see the *Microsoft Visual Basic Programmer's Guide*.

---

## Sorting and Filtering Records

Unless you open a table-type **Recordset** object and set its **Index** property, you can't be sure records will appear in any specific order. Most of the time, however, you want to retrieve records in order. For example, you may want to view invoices arranged by increasing invoice number or retrieve employee records in the alphabetic order of their last names.

To sort non-table **Recordset** data, use an SQL ORDER BY clause in the original query that constructs the **Recordset**, whether that clause is contained in a **QueryDef** object, a stored query in a database, or in an SQL string passed to the **OpenRecordset** method.

With any type of **Recordset**, use an SQL WHERE clause in the original query to filter data (to restrict the result set to records that meet some criteria).

The following example opens a dynaset-type **Recordset** object, and uses an SQL statement to retrieve, filter, and sort records, using the WHERE and ORDER BY clauses:

```
Dim dbsCurrent As Database, rstManagers As Recordset

Set dbsCurrent = OpenDatabase("C:\Samples\Chap05\NwindJet.mdb")
Set rstManagers = dbsCurrent.OpenRecordset("SELECT FirstName, " & _
    "LastName FROM Employees WHERE Title = 'Manager' " & _
    "ORDER BY LastName")
```

One drawback of an SQL query executed in an OpenRecordset method is that it has to be recompiled every time you run it. If this query is to be used frequently, you can improve performance by creating a stored query using the same SQL statement, and then opening a **Recordset** object against the query, as shown in the following example:

```
Dim dbsCurrent As Database, rstManagers As Recordset

Set dbsCurrent = OpenDatabase("C:\Samples\Chap05\NwindJet.mdb")
Set rstManagers = dbsCurrent.OpenRecordset("Managers")
```

For even greater flexibility and control at run time, you can use query parameters to determine the sort order and filter criteria. This is discussed in greater detail in the "Using Parameter Queries" section later in this chapter.

## Re-creating a Query from a Recordset

A **Recordset** object opened from a **QueryDef** object can also be used as a template to re-create the **QueryDef** object, using the **CopyQueryDef** method. This is useful in situations where a **Recordset** variable created from a **QueryDef** is passed to a function, and the function must re-create the SQL equivalent of the query and possibly modify it.

## Modifying a Query from a Recordset

You can use the **Requery** method on a dynaset- or snapshot-type **Recordset** when you want to re-execute the underlying query after changing a parameter. This is more convenient than opening a new **Recordset** and executes faster.

The following example opens a **Recordset** from an existing query, uses the **CopyQueryDef** method to extract the equivalent SQL string, prompts the user to add an additional WHERE clause to the query, and finally re-executes the query using the **Requery** method:

```
Sub AddQueryFilter(rstQuery As Recordset)
    Dim qdfNew As QueryDef
    Dim strNewFilter As String, strQuery As String

    Set qdfNew = rstQuery.CopyQueryDef

    ' Hint: try WHERE LastName LIKE 'D*'
    strNewFilter = InputBox("Enter new constraint")

    ' Strip colon, CR & LF from end of string.
    strQuery = Left(qdfNew.SQL, Len(qdfNew.SQL) - 3)
    ' Reassemble new query string with added constraint.
    qdfNew.SQL = strQuery & " AND " & strNewFilter & ";"
    ' Requery recordset.
    rstQuery.Requery qdfNew
    ' Populate recordset fully.
    rstQuery.MoveLast
    ' "Lastname LIKE 'D*'" Should return 2.
    MsgBox "Number returned = " & rstQuery.RecordCount
End Sub
```

**Note**  To execute the **Requery** method, the **Recordset** object's **Restartable** property must be **True**. The **Restartable** property is always **True** when the **Recordset** is created from a query other than a crosstab query against tables in a Microsoft Jet database. SQL pass-through queries are not restartable. Queries against attached tables in another database format may or may not be restartable. To determine whether a **Recordset** can re-execute its query, check the **Restartable** property.

## The Sort and Filter Properties

Another approach to sorting and filtering recordsets is to set the **Sort** and **Filter** properties on an existing **Recordset**, and then open a new **Recordset** from the existing one. However, this is usually much slower than just including the sort and filter criteria in the original query or changing the query parameters and re-executing it with the **Requery** method. The **Sort** and **Filter** properties are useful when you want to allow a user to sort or restrict a result set, but the original data source is unavailable for a new query—for example, when a **Recordset** object variable is passed to a function, and the function must reorder records or restrict the records in the set. With this approach, performance is likely to be slow if more than 100 records are in the **Recordset**. Using the **CopyQueryDef** method described in the previous section is preferable.

# Moving Through a Recordset

A **Recordset** object usually has a *current position*, usually at a record. When you refer to the fields in a **Recordset**, you obtain values from the record at the current position, which is known as the *current record*. However, the current position can also be immediately before the first record in a **Recordset** or immediately after the last record. In certain circumstances, the current position is undefined.

You can use the Move methods to loop through the records in a **Recordset**:

- The **MoveFirst** method moves to the first record.
- The **MoveLast** method moves to the last record.
- The **MoveNext** method moves to the next record.
- The **MovePrevious** method moves to the previous record.
- The **Move** [0] method moves forward or backward a specified number of records.

The following example changes the job title of all sales representatives in a table called Employees. After opening the table, the code sets the index, which makes it necessary to use the **MoveFirst** method to locate the first record. For each record satisfying the title condition, the example changes the title and saves the change with the **Update** method. It uses the **MoveNext** method to move to the next record.

```
Dim dbsCurrent As Database, rstEmployees As Recordset

Set dbsCurrent = OpenDatabase("C:\Samples\Chap05\NwindJet.mdb")
Set rstEmployees = dbsCurrent.OpenRecordset("Employees", dbOpenTable)

rstEmployees.Index = "LastName"                 ' Set current index.
rstEmployees.MoveFirst                          ' Locate first record.
Do Until rstEmployees.EOF                       ' Begin loop.
    If rstEmployees!Title = "Sales Representative" Then
        rstEmployees.Edit                       ' Enable editing.
        rstEmployees!Title = "Account Executive" ' Change title.
        rstEmployees.Update                     ' Save changes.
    End If
    rstEmployees.MoveNext                        ' Locate next record.
Loop                                        ' End of loop.
rstEmployees.Close                              ' Close table.
```

---

**Visual Basic Users**   You can use the **Data** control to browse and display records in a **Recordset** object and to edit data in records as they are displayed. For more information on the **Data** control, see the *Microsoft Visual Basic Programmer's Guide.*

---

# Detecting the Limits of a Recordset

In a **Recordset**, if you try to move too far in one direction, a run-time error occurs. For example, if you try to use the **MoveNext** method when you're already at the end of the **Recordset**, a trappable error occurs. For this reason, it's helpful to know the limits of the **Recordset** object.

The **BOF** property indicates whether the current position is at the beginning of the **Recordset**. If **BOF** is **True**, the current position is before the first record in the **Recordset**. The **BOF** property is also **True** if there are no records in the **Recordset** when it's opened. Similarly, the **EOF** property is **True** if the current position is after the last record in the **Recordset** or if there are no records.

The following example shows you how to use the **BOF** and **EOF** properties to detect the beginning and end of a **Recordset**. This code fragment creates a table-type **Recordset** based on the Orders table from the current database. It moves through the records, first from the beginning of the **Recordset** to the end, and then from the end of the **Recordset** to the beginning.

```
Dim dbsCurrent As Database, rstOrders As Recordset

Set dbsCurrent = OpenDatabase("C:\Samples\Chap05\NwindJet.mdb")
Set rstOrders = dbsCurrent.OpenRecordset("Orders", dbOpenTable)

Do Until rstOrders.EOF                ' Until end of table.
    ...                               ' Work with data.
    rstOrders.MoveNext                ' Move to next record.
Loop
rstOrders.MoveLast                    ' Move to last record.
Do Until rstOrders.BOF                ' Until beginning of file.
    ...                               ' Work with data.
    rstOrders.MovePrevious            ' Move to previous record.
Loop
rstOrders.Close                       ' Close Recordset.
```

Note that there's no current record immediately following the first loop. The **BOF** and **EOF** properties both have the following characteristics:

- If the **Recordset** contains no records when you open it, both **BOF** and **EOF** are **True**.

- When **BOF** and **EOF** are **True**, they remain **True** until you move to an existing record, at which time the value of **BOF** and **EOF** becomes **False**.

- When **BOF** or **EOF** is **False**, and the only record in a **Recordset** is deleted, the property remains **False** until you attempt to move to another record, at which time both **BOF** and **EOF** become **True**.

- At the moment you create or open a **Recordset** that contains at least one record, the first record is the current record, and both **BOF** and **EOF** are **False**.

- If the first record is the current record when you use the **MovePrevious** method, **BOF** is set to **True**. If you use **MovePrevious** while **BOF** is **True**, a run-time error occurs. When this happens, **BOF** remains **True** and there is no current record.

- Similarly, moving past the last record in the **Recordset** changes the value of the **EOF** property to **True**. If you use the **MoveNext** method while **EOF** is **True**, a run-time error occurs. When this happens, **EOF** remains **True** and there is no current record.

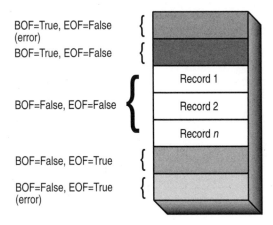

**Figure 5.2    Relationship between the current record position and the BOF and EOF properties.**

# Counting the Number of Records in a Recordset

You may want to know the number of records in a **Recordset** object. For example, you may want to create a form that shows how many records are in each of the tables in a database. Or you may want to change the appearance of a form or report based on the number of records it includes.

The **RecordCount** property contains the number of records accessed in a specified **Recordset**. A **Recordset** with no records has a **RecordCount** value of 0.

**Note**  The **RecordCount** value equals the number of records actually accessed. For example, when you first create a dynaset or snapshot, you have accessed (or "visited") only one record. If you check the **RecordCount** property immediately after creating the dynaset or snapshot (assuming it has at least one record), the value is 1. To visit all the records, use the **MoveLast** method immediately after opening the **Recordset**, then use **MoveFirst** to return to the first record. This is not done automatically, because it may be slow, especially for large result sets.

Opening a table-type **Recordset** object effectively visits all of the records in the underlying table, and **RecordCount** totals the number of records in the table as soon as the **Recordset** is opened. Aborted transactions may make the **RecordCount** value out of date in some multiuser situations. Compacting the database restores the table's record count to the correct value.

The following example creates a dynaset-type **Recordset** (because it's based on an SQL statement) from the Employees table, and then determines the number of records in the **Recordset**:

```
Dim dbsCurrent As Database, rstEmployees As Recordset, lngTotal As Long

Set dbsCurrent = OpenDatabase("C:\Samples\Chap05\NwindJet.mdb")
Set rstEmployees = dbsCurrent.OpenRecordset("SELECT LastName, " _
    & "FirstName FROM Employees")
rstEmployees.MoveLast
lngTotal = rstEmployees.RecordCount
```

As records in a dynaset-type **Recordset** are deleted by your application, the value of the **RecordCount** property decreases. However, in a multiuser environment, records deleted by other users aren't reflected in the value of **RecordCount** until the current record is positioned on a deleted record. At that time, the setting of the **RecordCount** property decreases by one. Using the **Requery** method on a **Recordset**, followed by the **MoveLast** method, sets the **RecordCount** property to the current total number of records in the **Recordset**.

A snapshot-type **Recordset** is static and its **RecordCount** value doesn't change when you add or delete records in the snapshot's underlying table.

# Finding the Current Position in a Recordset

In some situations, you need to determine how far through a **Recordset** you have moved the current record position, and perhaps indicate the current record position to a user. For example, you may want to indicate the current position on a dial, meter, or similar type of control. Two properties are available to indicate the current position: the **AbsolutePosition** property and the **PercentPosition** property.

The **AbsolutePosition** property value is the position of the current record relative to 0. However, don't think of this property as a record number; if the current record is undefined, **AbsolutePosition** returns −1. Further, there is no guarantee that records will appear in the same order every time the **Recordset** is accessed.

The **PercentPosition** property shows the current position expressed as a percentage of the total number of records indicated by the **RecordCount** property. Because the **RecordCount** property does not reflect the total number of records in the **Recordset** until the **Recordset** has been fully populated, the **PercentPosition** property only reflects the current record position as a percentage of the number of records that have been accessed since the **Recordset** was opened. To make sure that the **PercentPosition** property reflects the current record position relative to the entire **Recordset**, use the **MoveLast** and **MoveFirst** methods immediately after opening the **Recordset**: This fully populates the **Recordset** before you attempt to use the **PercentPosition** property. If you have a large result set, you may not want to use **MoveLast** because it may take a long time.

---

**Caution**   The **PercentPosition** property is only an approximation and shouldn't be used as a critical parameter. This property is best suited for driving an indicator, such as a "percent complete" control, or a similar indicator that marks a user's progress while moving though a set of records.

---

The following example opens a **Recordset** on a table called Employees and fully populates it. The program then lists the content of each field of each record in the table, numbering the records as they are printed. When half the records have been printed, a message indicates that the user is more than halfway through the table.

```
Dim dbsCurrent As Database, rstEmployees As Recordset

Set dbsCurrent = OpenDatabase("C:\Samples\Chap05\NwindJet.mdb")
Set rstEmployees = dbsCurrent.OpenRecordset("Employees", dbOpenDynaset)

rstEmployees.MoveLast      ' The Recordset is now fully populated.
rstEmployees.MoveFirst
While rstEmployees.EOF = False
    Debug.Print "Record No. " & rstEmployees.AbsolutePosition
    Debug.Print rstEmployees!LastName
    Debug.Print rstEmployees!FirstName
    If rstEmployees.PercentPosition > 50.0 Then
        Debug.Print "More than half way!"
    EndIf
    rstEmployees.MoveNext
Wend
rstEmployees.Close
dbsCurrent.Close
```

# Finding a Specific Record

The previous section, "Moving Through a Recordset," explores ways you can use the Move methods—**MoveFirst**, **MoveLast**, **MovePrevious**, and **MoveNext**—to loop through a **Recordset**. In most cases, however, it's more efficient to search for a specific record.

For example, you may want to find a particular employee based on an employee number, or you may want to find all of the detail records that belong to a specific order. In these cases, looping through all of the employee or order detail records could be time consuming. Instead, you can use the **Seek** method to locate records with table-type **Recordset** objects, and the Find methods with dynaset- and snapshot-type **Recordset** objects.

## Finding a Record in a Table-Type Recordset

You use the **Seek** method to locate a record in a table-type **Recordset**. To locate a record in a dynaset or snapshot, use one of the Find methods described in the next section. When you use the **Seek** method to locate a record, Microsoft Jet uses the table's current index, as defined by the **Index** property.

The syntax for the **Seek** method is:

*table*.**Seek** *comparison, key1, key2 ...*

The *table* argument is a table-type **Recordset** object you're searching through. The **Seek** method accepts a number of arguments, the first of which is *comparison*, a string that determines the kind of comparison being performed. The following table lists the comparison strings you can use with the **Seek** method.

| Comparison string | Description |
| --- | --- |
| "=" | Equal to the specified key values |
| ">=" | Greater than or equal to the specified key values |
| ">" | Greater than the specified key values |
| "<=" | Less than or equal to the specified key values |
| "<" | Less than the specified key values |

The *keyn* arguments are a series of one or more values that correspond to the field or fields that make up the current index of the **Recordset**. Microsoft Jet compares these values to values in the corresponding fields of the **Recordset** object's records.

The following example opens a table-type **Recordset** called Products, and uses the **Seek** method to locate the first record containing a value of 1 in the SupplierID field (which is a non-unique index field). It changes 1 to 2 and saves the change with the **Update** method. Subsequent passes through the loop locate the next record that satisfies the condition.

```
Dim dbsCurrent As Database, rstProducts As Recordset

Set dbsCurrent = OpenDatabase("C:\Samples\Chap05\NwindJet.mdb")
Set rstProducts = dbsCurrent.OpenRecordset("Products", dbOpenTable)
rstProducts.Index = "SupplierID"          ' Define current index.
rstProducts.Seek "=", 1                   ' Seek record.
Do Until rstProducts.NoMatch              ' Until no record is found.
    rstProducts.Edit                      ' Enable editing.
    rstProducts("SupplierID") = 2         ' Change SupplierID.
    rstProducts.Update                    ' Save changes.
    rstProducts.Seek "=", 1               ' Seek next record.
Loop                                 ' End of loop.
rstProducts.Close                         ' Close Recordset.
```

If you use the **Seek** method on a table-type **Recordset** object without first setting the current index, a run-time error occurs.

The next example illustrates how you can create a function that uses the **Seek** method to locate a record using a multiple-field index.

```
Function GetFirstPrice(ByVal lngOrderID As Long, _
    ByVal lngProductID As Long) As Variant
    Dim dbsCurrent As Database, rstOrderDetail As Recordset

    Set dbsCurrent = OpenDatabase("C:\Samples\Chap05\NwindJet.mdb")
    Set rstOrderDetail = dbsCurrent.OpenRecordset("Order Details", _
        dbOpenTable)

    rstOrderDetail.Index = "PrimaryKey"
    rstOrderDetail.Seek "=", lngOrderID, lngProductID

    If rstOrderDetail.NoMatch Then
        GetFirstPrice = Null
        MsgBox "Couldn't find order detail record."
    Else
        GetFirstPrice = rstOrderDetail!UnitPrice
    End If

    rstOrderDetail.Close
    dbsCurrent.Close
End Function
```

In this example, the table's primary key consists of two fields, OrderID and ProductID. When you call the **GetFirstPrice** function with a valid (existing) combination of OrderID and ProductID field values, the function returns the unit price from the found record. If the combination of field values you want can't be found in the table, the function returns **Null**.

If the current index is a multiple-field index, trailing key values can be omitted and are treated as **Null**. That is, you can leave off any number of key values from the end of a **Seek** method's *key* argument, but not from the beginning or the middle. However, if you don't specify all values in the index, you can use only the ">" or "<" comparison operator with the **Seek** method.

# Finding a Record in a Dynaset- or Snapshot-Type Recordset

You can use the following methods to locate a record in a dynaset- or snapshot-type **Recordset**. (To locate a record in a table-type **Recordset**, use the **Seek** method, which is described in the previous section.) Microsoft Jet supports four Find methods:

- The **FindFirst** method finds the first record satisfying the specified criteria.
- The **FindLast** method finds the last record satisfying the specified criteria.
- The **FindNext** method finds the next record satisfying the specified criteria.
- The **FindPrevious** method finds the previous record satisfying the specified criteria.

When you use the Find methods, you specify the search criteria, typically an expression equating a field name with a specific value.

The following example looks up phone numbers in an Employees table:

```
Sub Tel_Lookup()
    Dim dbsNorthwind As DATABASE, rstEmployees As Recordset
    Dim strName As String, strCriteria As String, strNumber As String
    Dim strQuery As String, intResponse As Integer

    Set dbsNorthwind = OpenDatabase("C:\Samples\Chap05\NwindJet.mdb")
    strQuery = "SELECT DISTINCTROW Employees.LastName, " & _
        "Employees.HomePhone FROM Employees"
    Set rstEmployees = dbsNorthwind.OpenRecordset(strQuery, _
        dbOpenSnapshot)

    strName = InputBox("Search for : ")
    strCriteria = "Employees.LastName = '" & strName & "'"
    rstEmployees.FindFirst strCriteria

    Do
    intResponse = MsgBox("The number for " & strName & " is " & _
            rstEmployees!HomePhone & ". Search again?", vbYesNo)
        If intResponse = vbYes Then
            strName = InputBox("Search for last name: ")
            strCriteria = "LastName = '" & strName & "'"
            rstEmployees.FindFirst strCriteria
        End If
    Loop While intResponse = vbYes
End Sub
```

You can locate the matching records in reverse order by finding the last occurrence with the **FindLast** method and then using the **FindPrevious** method instead of the **FindNext** method.

Microsoft Jet sets the **NoMatch** property to **True** whenever a Find method fails and the current record position is undefined. There may be a current record, but you have no way to tell which one. If you want to be able to return to the previous current record following a failed Find method, use a bookmark (as described in the following section).

**NoMatch** is **False** whenever the operation succeeds. In this case, the current record position is the record found by one of the Find methods.

For information on creating a temporary table, see Chapter 3, "Data Definition and Integrity."

The following example illustrates how you can use the **FindNext** method to find all records that contain **Null** in the Phone field in a table called Customers. It then prompts the user to enter a phone number for the customer:

```
Dim dbsCurrent As Database, rstCustomers As Recordset
Dim strCriterion As String, strNumber As String

Set dbsCurrent = OpenDatabase("C:\Samples\Chap05\NwindJet.mdb")
Set rstCustomers = dbsCurrent.OpenRecordset("Customers", dbOpenDynaset)
strCriterion = "Phone Is Null"

rstCustomers.FindFirst strCriterion
Do Until rstCustomers.NoMatch
    strNumber = InputBox(rstCustomers!CompanyName & _
        " is missing a phone number.")
    rstCustomers.Edit
    rstCustomers!Phone = strNumber
    rstCustomers.Update
    rstCustomers.FindNext strCriterion
Loop
```

If you need to frequently search records in a dynaset, you may find it easier to create a temporary indexed table and use the **Seek** method instead.

## Marking Record Position with Bookmarks

A bookmark is a system-generated **Byte** array that uniquely identifies each record. The **Bookmark** property of a **Recordset** object changes each time you move to a new record. To identify a record, move to that record and then assign the value of the **Bookmark** property to a variable of type **Variant**. To return to the record, set the **Bookmark** property to the value of the variable.

The following example illustrates how you can use a bookmark to save the current record position and then quickly return to that record position if a Find or **Seek** method fails. A bookmark is useful, because if the method fails, the current record position is undefined.

```
Dim dbsCurrent As Database, rstCustomers As Recordset
Dim varOrigin As Variant

Set dbsCurrent = OpenDatabase("C:\Samples\Chap05\NwindJet.mdb")
Set rstCustomers = dbsCurrent.OpenRecordset("Customers", dbOpenTable)

rstCustomers.Index = "CompanyName"
...                                     ' Move to other records.
varOrigin = rstCustomers.Bookmark
rstCustomers.Seek ">=", "Z"
If rstCustomers.NoMatch Then
    MsgBox "Can't find a company name starting with 'Z'."
    rstCustomers.Bookmark = varOrigin
End If
rstCustomers.Close
dbsCurrent.Close
```

In this example, saving the **Bookmark** property and then resetting the **Bookmark** property to its previous value when the **Seek** method fails makes the previously current record current again.

The **LastModified** property of the **Recordset** object provides a good illustration of how to use a bookmark. The **LastModified** property is the bookmark of the last record in the **Recordset** to be added or modified. To use it, set the **Bookmark** property equal to the **LastModified** property as follows:

```
rstCustomers.Bookmark = rstCustomer.LastModified
```

This moves the current record position to the last record that was added or modified, something that's particularly useful when adding new records, because by default the current record after adding a new record is the record you were on *before* using **AddNew**. With **LastModified**, you can move to the newly added record if that's what your application expects.

## Bookmark Scope

When you close a **Recordset**, any bookmarks you saved become invalid. You can't use a bookmark from one **Recordset** in another **Recordset**, even if both **Recordset** objects are based on the same underlying table or query. However, you can use a bookmark on the duplicate (clone) of a **Recordset**, as shown in the following example:

```
Dim dbsCurrent As Database
Dim rstOriginal As Recordset, rstDuplicate As Recordset
Dim strPlaceholder As String
```

```
Set dbsCurrent = OpenDatabase("C:\Samples\Chap05\NwindJet.mdb")
' Create first Recordset.
Set rstOriginal = dbsCurrent.OpenRecordset("Orders", dbOpenDynaset)

strPlaceholder = rstOriginal.Bookmark     ' Save current record position.
Set rstDuplicate = rstOriginal.Clone()    ' Create duplicate Recordset.
rstDuplicate.Bookmark = strPlaceholder    ' Go to same record.
```

**Microsoft Access Users**  You can also use the **Bookmark** property on the **Recordset** underlying a form. With this property, your code can mark which record is currently displayed on the form, and then change the record being displayed. For example, on a form containing employee information, you may want a button that a user can click to show the record for an employee's supervisor. The following example illustrates the event procedure you would use for the button's Click event:

```
Sub cmdShowSuper_Click ()
    Dim frmEmployees As Form, rstEmployees As Recordset
    Dim strOrigin As String, strEmployee As String, strSuper As String

    Set frmEmployees = Screen.ActiveForm
    Set rstEmployees = frmEmployees.RecordsetClone    ' Open Recordset.

    strOrigin = frmEmployees.Bookmark
    strEmployee = frmEmployees!FirstName & " " & frmEmployees!LastName
    rstEmployees.FindFirst "EmployeeID = " & frmEmployees!ReportsTo
    If rstEmployees.NoMatch Then
        MsgBox "Couldn't find " & strEmployee & "'s supervisor."
    Else
        frmEmployees.Bookmark = rstEmployees.Bookmark
        strSuper = frmEmployees!FirstName & " " & frmEmployees!LastName
        MsgBox strEmployee & "'s supervisor is " & strSuper
        frmEmployees.Bookmark = strOrigin
    End If
    rstEmployees.Close
End Sub
```

## Why Use Bookmarks Instead of Record Numbers?

If you have used another database or programming environment, you may be accustomed to referring to record numbers. For example, you may have written code that opens a text file and thereafter refers to specific records by their relative position in the file. The first record in the file would be record 1, the second would be record 2, and so on.

In Microsoft Jet databases, your view of records (a **Recordset**) is usually a subset of the records in one or more tables. Because the actual number of records in a **Recordset** can change at any time, especially in a multiuser environment, there's no absolute record number you can always use to refer to a particular record. The **AbsolutePosition** property is not the same as a record number, because this property changes if a lower-numbered record is deleted.

Furthermore, records returned in a **Recordset** object appear in no particular order, unless the **Recordset** was created with a query that includes an ORDER BY clause, or is a table-type **Recordset** with an **Index**. Record numbers would usually be meaningless in a **Recordset** object.

Instead of record numbers, Microsoft Jet provides bookmarks to uniquely identify a particular record. A given record retains its unique bookmark for the life of the **Recordset**.

For more information about **GetRowsEx**, see Chapter 11, "DAO C++ Classes."

**Visual C++ Users** Bookmarks are especially useful in conjunction with the DAO SDK **GetRowsEx** function. If you choose dbBindBookmark as one of the fields to be bound, it will retrieve a bookmark as a pseudo-field. This enables you to combine the speed and convenience of **GetRowsEx** with easy updating.

For example, you could have retrieved code to fill a list box that looks something like:

```
// Structure for DoGetRowsEx
typedef struct
    {
    LONG        lEmpId;
    LPVOID      lpbm;
    TCHAR       *lpstrLastName;
    TCHAR       strFirstName[20];
    } EMP, *LPEMP ;
```

```
// Employee table binding
DAORSETBINDING   Bindings[] =
{
//Index Type     Column     Type          Offset
    Size
{dbBindIndexINT, EMP_ID,    dbBindI4,        offsetof(EMP,lEmpId),
    sizeof(LONG)},
{dbBindIndexINT, NULL,      dbBindBookmark, offsetof(EMP,lpbm),
    sizeof(LPVOID)},
{dbBindIndexINT, EMP_LNAME, dbBindLPSTRING,
    offsetof(EMP,lpstrLastName),sizeof(TCHAR *)},
{dbBindIndexINT, EMP_FNAME, dbBindSTRING,   offsetof(EMP,strFirstName),
    sizeof(TCHAR) * 20}
};

// Perform C++ GetRowsEx against the Employee table.
void CDlg::DoGetRowsEx()
{
    LPEMP         pEmpRows = new EMP[MAX_EMP_REC];
    CString       strLBRow;
    TCHAR         szId[16];
    LONG          lNumRecords;
    LONG          lCount;
    LONG          cbBuf = ( MAX_EMP_REC * sizeof(TCHAR) * 15 ); // Allow
average of 15 chars/name.
    LPVOID        pvBuf = new LPVOID[cbBuf];
    //Perform GetRows on Employee table.
    //This GetRows uses a specific C++ structure.
    lNumRecords = m_rs.GetRowsEx(pEmpRows, sizeof(EMP),
                                 &Bindings[0], sizeof(Bindings) /
sizeof(DAORSETBINDING),
                                 pvBuf, cbBuf,
                                 MAX_EMP_REC); //Arbitrarily get
MAX_EMP_REC rows.

//Step through the returned rows.
    for (lCount = 0; lCount < lNumRecords; lCount++)
        {
        strLBRow.Empty();
        wsprintf(szId, _T("%d,  "), pEmpRows[lCount].lEmpId);
        strLBRow += szId;
        strLBRow += pEmpRows[lCount].lpstrLastName;
        strLBRow += _T(", ");
        strLBRow += (LPCTSTR) pEmpRows[lCount].strFirstName;
        //Put the bookmark in the global array.
        m_rgbm[lCount] = CdbBookmark((LPSAFEARRAY)pEmpRows[lCount].lpbm
);
```

```
                            // Put a pointer to it in the ItemData for the list box entry.
                            m_lstEmps.SetItemData( m_lstEmps.AddString(strLBRow),
                                                   (DWORD)&m_rgbm[lCount] );
                        }
                    delete [] pEmpRows;
                    delete [] pvBuf;
                }
```

For a complete sample program, see the Visual C++ project file in the \DAOSDK30\ SAMPLES\ GETROWS folder of the DAO SDK installation.

This could be combined with selection code that moves the current record as follows:

```
void CDlg::OnSelchangeListEmployees()
{
    // Cast the dword held in ItemData back into a pointer to a
    // bookmark. The actual bookmarks are being held in m_rgbm
    // and will automatically deallocate the system safe arrays and
    // destruct on CDlg destruction.
    CdbBookmark *pbm = (CdbBookmark
*)m_lstEmps.GetItemData(m_lstEmps.GetCurSel());
    m_rs.SetBookmark( *pbm );
    m_strMoreInfo.Format(
        _T("Notes:  %s\n"),
        (LPCTSTR)( m_rs[15].GetValue().bstrVal ) );
    UpdateData( FALSE );
}
```

## Which Recordset Objects Support Bookmarks?

Dynasets based on certain linked tables, such as Paradox tables that have no primary key, do not support bookmarks, nor do snapshots opened with the **dbForwardOnly** option.

You can determine whether a given **Recordset** object supports bookmarks by checking the value of the **Bookmarkable** property, as in the following example:

```
If rstLinkedTable.Bookmarkable Then
    MsgBox "The underlying table supports bookmarks."
Else
    MsgBox "The underlying table doesn't support bookmarks."
End If
```

If you try to use bookmarks on a **Recordset** that doesn't support bookmarks, a run-time error occurs.

# Changing Data

After you've created a table- or dynaset-type **Recordset** object, you can change, delete, or add new records. You can't change, delete, or add records to a snapshot-type **Recordset** object. This section presents the methods and procedures for changing data in table- and dynaset-type **Recordset** objects.

# Using Parameter Queries

In many situations, you'll want a user or another program to provide parameters to your stored queries and **Recordset** objects. Microsoft Jet provides the means to do this. You first create a stored query, specifying which parameters are to be provided by the end user. When you open a **Recordset** against one of these queries, the application opens a dialog box that prompts the user to enter a value, such as the criteria for a WHERE clause or the field on which to sort the selected records.

The following example uses Visual Basic code to create a new parameter query called Seniority that returns the last name of each employee hired after a certain date. Before running the query, the program calls the **InputBox** function to prompt the user for a threshold date. The names are then shown in the Debug window, starting with the most recent hire.

```
Sub Param_Query ()
    Dim dbsCurrent As Database, rstEmployees As Recordset
    Dim qdfEmployees As QueryDef
    Dim strSQLQuery As String, strHireDate As String

    Set dbsCurrent = OpenDatabase("C:\Samples\Chap05\NwindJet.mdb")
    strSQLQuery = "PARAMETERS BeginningDate DateTime; " & _
        "SELECT LastName FROM Employees " & _
        "WHERE HireDate >= BeginningDate " & _
        "ORDER BY HireDate DESC;"
    Set qdfEmployees = dbsCurrent.CreateQueryDef("Seniority", _
        strSQLQuery)
    strHireDate = InputBox("Enter the earliest hire date")
    qdfEmployees.Parameters("BeginningDate") = strHireDate

Set rstEmployees = qdfEmployees.OpenRecordset()
    rstEmployees.MoveFirst
    While rstEmployees.EOF = False
        Debug.Print rstEmployees!LastName
        rstEmployees.MoveNext
    Wend
End Sub
```

Most of the database maintenance tasks described in the rest of this chapter can be accomplished using stored parameter queries.

# Making Bulk Changes

Many of the changes you may otherwise perform in a loop can be done more efficiently with an update or delete query:

```
Dim dbsCurrent As Database, qdfChangeTitles As QueryDef

Set dbsCurrent = OpenDatabase("C:\Samples\Chap05\NwindJet.mdb")
Set qdfChangeTitles = dbsCurrent.CreateQueryDef("")

qdfChangeTitles.SQL = "UPDATE DISTINCTROW Employees " & _
    "SET Employees!Title = 'Account Executive' " & _
    "WHERE Employees!Title = 'Sales Representative';"
qdfChangeTitles.Execute dbFailOnError              ' Invoke query.
```

Of course, the entire SQL string in this example can be replaced with a stored parameter query, in which case the program would prompt the user for parameter values. The following example shows how the previous example might be rewritten as a stored parameter query:

```
Dim dbsCurrent As Database, qdfChangeTitles As QueryDef
Dim strSQLUpdate As String, strOld As String, strNew As String

Set dbsCurrent = OpenDatabase("C:\Samples\Chap05\NwindJet.mdb")

strSQLUpdate = "PARAMETERS [Old Title] Text, [New Title] Text; " & _
    "UPDATE DISTINCTROW Employees " & _
    "SET Employees!Title = [New Title] " & _
    "WHERE Employees!Title = [Old Title]; "

' Create the QueryDef object.
Set qdfChangeTitles = dbsCurrent.CreateQueryDef("", strSQLUpdate)
strOld = InputBox("Enter old job title") ' Prompt for old title.
strNew = InputBox("Enter new job title") ' Prompt for new title.
qdfChangeTitles.Parameters("Old Title") = strOld     ' Set parameters.
qdfChangeTitles.Parameters("New Title") = strNew
qdfChangeTitles.Execute                              ' Invoke query.
```

You'll also find that a delete query is more efficient than code that loops through records looking for records to delete, especially with Microsoft Jet 3.0 databases.

# Modifying an Existing Record

Changing an existing record in a **Recordset** object is a four-step process:

1. Go to the record you want to change.

2. Use the **Edit** method to prepare the current record for editing.

3. Make the necessary changes to the record.

4. Use the **Update** method to save the changes to the current record.

The following example illustrates how to change the job titles for all sales representatives in a table called Employees:

```
Set dbsCurrent = OpenDatabase("C:\Samples\Chap05\NwindJet.mdb")
Set rstEmployees = dbsCurrent.OpenRecordset("Employees")

rstEmployees.MoveFirst
Do Until rstEmployees.EOF
    If rstEmployees!Title = "Sales Representative" Then
        rstEmployees.Edit
        rstEmployees!Title = "Account Executive"
        rstEmployees.Update
    End If
    rstEmployees.MoveNext
Loop
rstEmployees.Close
dbsCurrent.Close
```

If you don't use the **Edit** method before you try to change a value in the current record, a run-time error occurs.

For more information on consistent and inconsistent updates, see Chapter 4, "Queries."

## Inconsistent Updates

Dynaset-type **Recordset** objects can be based on a multiple-table query, with the query often implementing a one-to-many relationship. For example, suppose you want to create a multiple-table query that combines fields from the Orders and Order Details tables. Generally speaking, you can't change values in the Orders table because it's on the "one" side of the relationship. Depending on your application, however, you may want to be able to make changes to the Orders table. To make it possible to freely change the values on the "one" side of a one-to-many relationship, use the **dbInconsistent** constant of the **OpenRecordset** method to create an *inconsistent* dynaset.

```
Set rstTotalSales = dbsCurrent.OpenRecordset("Sales Totals",, _
    dbInconsistent)
```

When you update an inconsistent dynaset, you can easily destroy the relational integrity of the data in the dynaset. You must take care to understand how the data is related across the one-to-many relationship and update the values on both sides in a way that preserves data integrity.

The **dbInconsistent** constant is available only for dynaset-type **Recordset** objects. It's ignored for table- and snapshot-types, but no compile or run-time error is returned if **dbInconsistent** is used with those types of **Recordset** objects.

Even with an inconsistent **Recordset**, some fields may not be updatable. For example, you can't change the value of an AutoNumber field, and a **Recordset** based on certain linked tables may not be updatable.

---

**Important**  If you change the current record and then move to another record or close the **Recordset** without first using the **Update** method, your changes are lost without warning. For example, omitting the **Update** method from the preceding example results in no changes being made to the Employees table.

---

You can also terminate the **Edit** method and any pending transactions without saving changes using the **CancelUpdate** method. While you can terminate the **Edit** method just by moving off the current record, this is not practical when the current record is the first or last record in the **Recordset**, or is a new record. It's therefore generally simpler to use the **CancelUpdate** method.

# Deleting an Existing Record

You can delete an existing record in a table- or dynaset-type **Recordset** using the **Delete** method. You can't delete records from a snapshot-type **Recordset**. The following example deletes all the records for trainees in a table called Employees:

```
Dim dbsCurrent As Database, rstEmployees As Recordset

Set dbsCurrent = OpenDatabase("C:\Samples\Chap05\NwindJet.mdb")
Set rstEmployees = dbsCurrent.OpenRecordset("Employees")

rstEmployees.MoveFirst
Do Until rstEmployees.EOF
    If rstEmployees!Title = "Trainee" Then
        rstEmployees.Delete
    End If
    rstEmployees.MoveNext
Loop
rstEmployees.Close
dbsCurrent.Close
```

When you use the **Delete** method, Microsoft Jet immediately deletes the current record without any warning or prompting. Deleting a record doesn't automatically cause the next record to become the current record; to move to the next record you must use the **MoveNext** method. Keep in mind, however, that after you've moved off the deleted record, you cannot move back to it.

If you try to access a record after deleting it on a table-type **Recordset**, you'll get error 3167, "Record is Deleted." On a dynaset you'll get error 3021, "No Current Record."

If you have a **Recordset** clone positioned at the deleted record and try to read its value, you'll get error 3167 regardless of the type of **Recordset**. Trying to use a bookmark to move to a deleted record will also result in error 3167.

# Adding a New Record

Adding a new record to a dynaset- or table-type **Recordset** is a three-step process:

1. Use the **AddNew** method to prepare a new record for editing.
2. Assign values to each of the record's fields.
3. Use the **Update** method to save the new record.

The following example adds a new record to a table called Shippers:

```
Dim dbsCurrent As Database, rstShippers As Recordset

Set dbsCurrent = OpenDatabase("C:\Samples\Chap05\NwindJet.mdb")
Set rstShippers = dbsCurrent.OpenRecordset("Shippers")
```

```
rstShippers.AddNew
rstShippers!CompanyName = "Global Parcel Service"
...                                ' Set remaining fields.
rstShippers.Update
rstShippers.Close
dbsCurrent.Close
```

When you use the **AddNew** method, Microsoft Jet prepares a new, blank record and makes it the current record. When you use the **Update** method to save the new record, the record that was current before you used the **AddNew** method becomes the current record again. The new record's position in the **Recordset** depends on whether you added the record to a dynaset- or a table-type **Recordset**.

If you add a record to a dynaset-type **Recordset**, the new record appears at the end of the **Recordset**, no matter how the **Recordset** is sorted. To force the new record to appear in its properly sorted position, you can use the **Requery** method or re-create the **Recordset** object.

If you add a record to a table-type **Recordset**, the record appears positioned according to the current index, or at the end of the table if there is no primary key and no current index. Because Microsoft Jet 3.0 allows multiple users to create new records on a table simultaneously, your record may not appear right at the end of the **Recordset** as it did in previous versions of Microsoft Jet. Be sure to use the **LastModified** property rather than **MoveLast** to move to the record you just added.

---

**Important**  If you use the **AddNew** method to add a new record, then move to another record or close the **Recordset** without first using the **Update** method, your changes are lost without warning. For example, omitting the **Update** method from the preceding example results in no changes being made to the Shippers table.

---

For more information on caching ODBC data, see Chapter 9, "Developing Client/Server Applications."

## Caching ODBC Data with a Recordset

You can use the dynaset-type **Recordset** to create a local cache for ODBC data. This lets you fetch records in batches instead of one at a time as each record is requested, and makes much better use of your server connection, improving performance.

The **CacheSize** and **CacheStart** properties establish the size and starting offset (expressed as a Bookmark) for the cache. For example, you may set **CacheSize** to 100 records. Then, using the **FillCache** method, you can fetch sufficient records to fill the cache.

## Tracking Recordset Changes

You may need to determine when the underlying table of a table-type **Recordset** was created, or the last time it was modified. The **DateCreated** and **LastUpdated** properties, respectively, give you this information. Both properties return the date stamp applied to the table by the machine on which the table resided at the time it was stamped.

# Microsoft Jet Transactions

Defined as a "logical unit of work," a transaction is one of the features common to most database management systems. By wrapping multiple database operations into a single unit, transactions offer the developer the ability to enforce data integrity by making sure multiple operations can be treated by the engine as an "all or nothing" proposition, thereby never allowing the database to end up in an inconsistent state.

The most common example of transaction processing involves a bank's automated teller machine. The processes of dispensing cash and then debiting the user's account are considered a logical unit of work and are wrapped in a transaction: The cash is not dispensed unless the system is also able to debit the account. By using a transaction, the entire operation either succeeds or fails. This maintains the consistent state of the ATM database.

Transactions can be defined by what are known as the ACID properties. The following attributes of transactions make up the ACID acronym:

- **Atomic** denotes that transactions are all-or-nothing operations. Each operation wrapped in a transaction must be successful for all operations to be committed.

- **Consistent** denotes that a transaction enables data operations to transform the database from one consistent state to another, even though at any point during the transaction the database may be inconsistent.

- **Isolated** denotes that all transactions are "invisible" to other transactions. That is, no transaction can see another transaction's updates to the database until the transaction is committed.

- **Durable** denotes that after a transaction commits, its updates survive—even if there is a subsequent system crash.

For information on transaction usage and behavior using ODBC data sources, see Chapter 9, "Developing Client/Server Applications."

With file-server databases such as Microsoft Jet, the concept of durability becomes somewhat complicated. There are currently no file-server based database engines that can fully support this criterion of true transactions. For example, a database connected to a file server cannot be expected to fully support the durability rule if the file-server crashes before a transaction has had time to commit its changes. If you require true transaction support with respect to durability, you should investigate the use of a client/server architecture.

---

**Note**  The behavior of transactions with Microsoft Jet databases differs from the behavior of ODBC data sources such as Microsoft SQL Server.

---

# Using Transactions in Your Applications

Microsoft Jet supports transactions through the **BeginTrans**, **CommitTrans** and **Rollback** methods of the **Workspace** object. The basic syntax is shown in the following table.

| Method | Operation |
| --- | --- |
| *workspace.***BeginTrans** | Begins the transaction. |
| *workspace.***Rollback** | Cancels the transaction. |
| *workspace.***CommitTrans** | Posts the transaction, writing its updates to the permanent database objects. |

The following example changes the job title of all sales representatives in the Employees table of the SALES.MDB database. After the **BeginTrans** method starts a transaction that isolates all of the changes made to the Employees table, the **CommitTrans** method saves the changes. Notice that you can use the **Rollback** method to undo changes that you saved with the **Update** method:

```
Sub ChangeTitle()
    Dim dbsSales As DATABASE
    Dim rstEmp As Recordset
    Dim wspCurrent As Workspace

    Set wspCurrent = DBEngine.Workspaces(0)
    Set dbsSales = OpenDatabase("C:\Samples\Chap05\NwindJet.mdb")
    Set rstEmp = dbsSales.OpenRecordset("Employees", dbOpenTable)

    wspCurrent.BeginTrans

    Do Until rstEmp.EOF
        If rstEmp!Title = "Sales Representative" Then
        rstEmp.Edit
            rstEmp!Title = "Sales Associate"
            rstEmp.UPDATE
        End If
        rstEmp.MoveNext
    Loop
```

```
          If MsgBox("Save all changes?", vbQuestion + vbYesNo) = vbYes Then
          wspCurrent.CommitTrans
          Else
              wspCurrent.Rollback
          End If
          rstEmp.Close
          dbsSales.Close
      End Sub
```

It's important to note that because transactions are scoped to the **Workspace** object, transactions are global to the workspace, not to a specific database or recordset. If you perform operations on more than one database or recordset within a workspace transaction, the **Commit** and **Rollback** methods affect all the objects changed within that workspace during the transaction.

# Managing Transactions

Microsoft Jet uses sophisticated algorithms to enhance transaction performance, reliability, and usability. This section discusses topics related to how the engine manages transactions.

## The Temporary Database

Almost all database transaction systems work their magic by storing intermediate changes in a temporary log file instead of writing them directly to the database. Microsoft Jet uses a similar mechanism in that it buffers all transaction activity to a temporary database. When the transaction is committed, the contents of the temporary database are merged into the real database. If you issue a **Rollback** method to cancel the transaction, the engine frees the pages in the temporary database.

Microsoft Jet does not create the temporary database until it has to. It uses whatever cache memory is available to store changes to data. After the cache is exhausted, the engine creates the temporary database and starts to write changes there.

Microsoft Jet creates the temporary directory specified by the TEMP environment variable of the workstation. If the available disk space for the temporary database is exhausted during a transaction, a trappable run-time error occurs. Your code should check for this error (number 2004) and react accordingly. If you attempt to commit the transaction after this error occurs, the engine will commit an indeterminate number of changes, possibly leaving the database in an inconsistent state. You should usually roll back the transaction when this error occurs to ensure a consistent database state.

Although the temporary database is a Microsoft Jet database, it's used internally by the engine only. It cannot be opened from other applications. After a transaction is complete, the engine frees the pages in the temporary database.

**Note** Prior to version 2.0, Microsoft Jet only supported transactions of 4 MB or less. That is, only transactions that involved logging of 4 MB or less of data would work. Since version 2.0, transaction size has been limited only by the amount of physical space on the disk drive holding the temporary database.

## Nesting Transactions

You can have up to five levels of transactions active at any one time by nesting combinations of **BeginTrans** and **CommitTrans** or **Rollback.** If you nest transactions you must make sure you commit or roll back the current transaction before trying to commit or roll back a transaction at a higher level of nesting.

If you want to have additional levels of nesting, or want to have transactions with overlapping, non-nested scopes, you can open additional **Workspace** objects and manage other transactions within those new workspaces.

## When a Transaction is Rolled Back by the Engine

If you close a database variable, any uncommitted transactions that were within the scope of that database variable are automatically rolled back. Microsoft Jet never automatically commits any transactions you have started. This behavior is also true of the **Workspace** object. If you close a **Workspace** object, any transactions within the scope of the workspace are rolled back. You should be aware of this behavior when you write your code. Never assume that the engine is going to commit your transaction for you.

## Transactions on External Data Sources

Transactions are not supported on external non-Jet data sources, with the exception of ODBC data. For example, if your database has linked FoxPro or dBASE tables, any transactions on those objects are ignored. This means that the transaction will not fail or generate a run-time error, but it won't actually do anything, either.

You may recall from Chapter 1 that Microsoft Jet 2.0 databases are opened by Microsoft Jet 3.0 as external ISAM databases. However, unlike the other non-native external data sources, the engine does support transactions on Microsoft Jet 2.0 databases.

You can check the value of the **Transactions** property on **Database** and **Recordset** objects to determine whether or not the object supports transactions. A value of **True** indicates that the object does support transactions, and a value of **False** indicates that the object does not support transactions.

# Transactions and Performance

In versions 1.*x* and 2.*x* of Microsoft Jet, it was generally recommended that you use transactions as a performance enhancement. In almost every case, wrapping DAO updates in a transaction would be much faster because the transaction forced the engine to buffer changes in the cache rather than writing them directly to disk. Various performance enhancements have been made in Microsoft Jet 3.0 to remove the need to use transactions for performance reasons.

For more information on Microsoft Jet 3.0 performance enhancements, see Chapter 13, "Performance." For complete information on Registry settings used by Microsoft Jet, see Appendix D, "Registry Settings."

Microsoft Jet 3.0 provides automatic, internal transactions for all DAO add, update, and delete operations. In most situations, this automatic support provides your application with the best possible performance. However, there may be situations where you want to fine-tune the engine's internal transaction behavior. You can do this by creating and modifying various settings in the Registry.

The default settings used by Microsoft Jet for controlling transactions are generally the best available for general-purpose application design. You may find yourself tuning these settings to enable the engine to better handle your data.

## The Engine's Two Modes

Microsoft Jet has two modes of operation when it comes to transaction processing: synchronous and asynchronous. Synchronous processing was the only mode available in version 2.*x* of the engine.

**Synchronous processing** allows nothing else to occur until the current operation is completed. This is the model that Microsoft Jet 2.*x* follows.

**Asynchronous processing** involves the engine queuing up a series of changes to the database. For example, several recordset **Update** methods could be grouped together. At some point, these updates are written to disk and the engine begins grouping new changes. The updates occur when one the following happens:

- A specified period of time passes from the first stored change (controlled by the ExclusiveAsyncDelay and SharedAsyncDelay Registry settings).

- Internal memory set aside for this (as defined by the MaxBufferSize Registry setting) is exceeded.

To better understand these modes, consider the following DAO code:

```
Set rst = dbs.OpenRecordset("SELECT * FROM Customer")
While Not rst.EOF
    rst.Edit
    '......
    rst.Update
    rst.Movenext
Wend
```

With synchronous processing, Microsoft Jet would not continue the loop until the `rst.update` completed successfully.

With asynchronous processing, Microsoft Jet would immediately process the `rst.Update` method, and while it was using a thread to do the work, would continue on another thread to process the `rst.MoveNext` operation

Microsoft Jet places temporary files according to paths specified by the TEMP environment variable. The behavior is the same for Windows 95 and Windows NT.

# Extracting Data from a Record

After you've located a particular record or records, you may want to extract data to use in your application instead of modifying the underlying source table.

A single field of a record can be copied to a variable of the appropriate data type. The following example extracts three fields from each record in a **Recordset** object:

```
Dim dbsCurrent As Database, rstEmployees As Recordset
Dim strFirstName As String, strLastName As String, strTitle As String

Set dbsCurrent = OpenDatabase("C:\Samples\Chap05\NwindJet.mdb")
Set rstEmployees = dbsCurrent.OpenRecordset("Employees")

rstEmployees.MoveFirst
strFirstName = rstEmployees!FirstName
strLastName = rstEmployees!LastName
strTitle = rstEmployees!Title
```

# Copying Entire Records to an Array

To copy one or more entire records, you can create a two-dimensional array and copy records one at a time. You increment the first subscript for each field and the second subscript for each record.

A fast way to do this is with the **GetRows** method. The **GetRows** method returns a two-dimensional array. The first subscript identifies the field and the second identifies the row number, as follows:

```
varRecords(intField, intRecord)
```

The following example uses an SQL statement to retrieve three fields from a table called Employees into a **Recordset** object. It then uses the **GetRows** method to retrieve the first three records of the **Recordset**, and stores the selected records in a two-dimensional array. Each record is then printed, one field at a time, using the two array indexes to select specific fields and records.

To clearly illustrate how the array indexes are used, the following example uses a separate statement to identify and print each field of each record. In practice, it would be more reliable to use two loops, one nested in the other, and to provide integer variables for the indexes that step through both dimensions of the array.

```
Sub GetRows_Test()
    Dim dbsCurrent As DATABASE
    Dim rstEmployees As Recordset
    Dim varRecords As Variant
    Dim intNumReturned As Integer, intNumColumns As Integer
    Dim intColumn As Integer, intRow As Integer

    Set dbsCurrent = OpenDatabase("C:\Samples\Chap05\NwindJet.mdb")
    Set rstEmployees = dbsCurrent.OpenRecordset("SELECT FirstName, " & _
        "LastName, Title FROM Employees", dbOpenSnapshot)

    varRecords = rstEmployees.GetRows(3)
    intNumReturned = UBound(varRecords, 2) + 1
    intNumColumns = UBound(varRecords, 1) + 1

    For intRow = 0 To intNumReturned - 1
        For intColumn = 0 To intNumColumns - 1
            Debug.Print varRecords(intColumn, intRow)
        Next intColumn
    Next intRow
End Sub
```

You can use subsequent calls to the **GetRows** method if more records are available. Because the array is filled as soon as you call the **GetRows** method, you can see why this approach is much faster than using assignment statements to copy one field at a time.

Notice also that you don't have to dimension the **Variant** as an array, because this is done automatically when the **GetRows** method returns records. This enables you to use fixed-length array dimensions without knowing how many records or fields will be returned, instead of using variable-length dimensions that take up more memory.

If you're trying to fetch all the rows using multiple **GetRows** calls, use the **EOF** property to be sure that you're at the end of the **Recordset**. **GetRows** returns fewer than the number requested at the end of the **Recordset** or if it cannot fetch a row in the range requested. For example, if the fifth record cannot be retrieved in a group of ten records that you're trying to fetch, **GetRows** returns four records and leaves the current record position on the record that caused a problem—and does not generate a run-time error. This situation may occur if a record in a dynaset was deleted by another user. If fewer records were returned than the number requested and you're not at EOF, you will need to read each field in the current record to determine what error **GetRows** encountered.

Because **GetRows** always returns all the fields in the **Recordset**, you may want to create a query that returns just the fields you need. This is especially important for Memo and LongBinary fields.

---

**Microsoft Excel Users**  You can import the contents of a **Recordset** object into a range on a Microsoft Excel worksheet with the **CopyFromRecordset** method. This method begins to copy at the current row of the result set; when the transfer is completed, the **Recordset** object pointer is positioned just past the last row, or at EOF. For more information, see the Microsoft Excel *Microsoft Visual Basic Programmer's Guide*.

---

# Using Field Objects

The default collection of a **Recordset** object is its **Fields** collection. This collection includes a single **Field** object corresponding to each field (or column) in the **Recordset**. Each **Field** object has a set of properties uniquely identifying the field name, data type, and so on, as well as the value of the field in the current record.

# Referencing Field Objects

A **Field** object can be identified by its **Name** property, which corresponds to the column name in the table from which the data in the field was fetched. Because the **Fields** collection is the default collection of a **Recordset** object, you can use either of the following syntax forms:

```
rstEmployees.Fields("LastName")
rstEmployees!LastName
```

Within the **Fields** collection, each **Field** object can also be identified by its index:

```
rstEmployees.Fields(0)
```

The index enables you to walk through the collection in a loop, replacing the index with a variable that is incremented with each pass through the loop. Object numbers in the collection are zero-based, so the first **Field** is number 0, the second is 1, and so on. The field order is determined by the underlying table. Fields are usually numbered in the order fetched when the **Recordset** is opened. One drawback to this approach is that you can't be certain which field will be referenced, because the underlying table structure may change, fields may be added or deleted, and so on.

The **Field** object also provides two properties that indicate its position relative to the other fields in the collection—the **OrdinalPosition** property and the **CollectionIndex** property. These properties are closely related, yet subtly different. **CollectionIndex** is a read-only number that indicates the **Field** object's absolute position within the collection as determined by the collection population. The **OrdinalPosition** property, in contrast, is a read-write property that you can set to any positive integer to change the field order when data is displayed in a form or copied to an array or a Microsoft Excel worksheet, and so on. **OrdinalPosition** usually corresponds to the field's **CollectionIndex**.

When you write a loop to walk through the **Fields** collection, the loop counter always identifies fields in the same sequence, which corresponds to **CollectionIndex**, regardless of the **OrdinalPosition** value.

---

**Caution**  The **CollectionIndex** property is not exposed to DAO users through the Object Browser. Although **CollectionIndex** is available, its use is discouraged because at the present time Microsoft is not committed to maintaining it in future versions of DAO. Consequently, this feature is not tested to the same reliability level as other DAO features, and assistance on its use is not available through Microsoft Product Support Services.

---

**Microsoft Excel Users**  You can also copy individual fields from a **Recordset** to a **ListBox**, using the **ListBox** control's **AddItem** method. For more information, see the Microsoft Excel *Microsoft Visual Basic Programmer's Guide.*

---

# Field Data Types

A **Field** object has a **Type** property that can be set to one of the following 12 DAO data types.

| Type property setting | Data type |
| --- | --- |
| dbBoolean | Boolean |
| dbByte | Byte |
| dbInteger | Integer |
| dbLong | Long |
| dbCurrency | Currency |
| dbSingle | Single |
| dbDouble | Double |
| dbDate | Date/Time |
| dbText | Text |
| dbLongBinary | OLE Object (Long Binary) |
| dbMemo | Memo |
| dbGUID | GUID (Replication ID) |

For a **Field** object on a **Recordset**, the **Type** property is read-only. However, you must be aware of the **Field** type when copying data to or from a field in code or a type mismatch error may occur. For example, you cannot copy text data to an integer field.

For more information on equivalent DAO data types, see Appendix B, "SQL Reference."

The **Type** property of a **Field** on a **Recordset** is determined by the underlying table from which the record was fetched. If you created the table and its fields using DAO DDL statements, you can easily determine the source table's data type. However, if you're fetching data from tables created with Microsoft Jet SQL DDL statements or through the Microsoft Access user interface, the data type specified when creating the table may not match one of the 12 DAO data types.

---

**Note**   The **GUID** type is used to store a Globally Unique Identifier, a unique string of digits that identifies OLE objects, Microsoft SQL Server remote procedure calls, and other entities that need a unique reference identification. The GUID type is also used in Microsoft Jet database applications to identify a replica, such as the **Database** object's **ReplicaID** property.

---

## Large Value Fields

OLE Object and Memo fields are collectively referred to as "large value" fields because they are typically much larger than fields of other data types. A record containing one or more large value fields usually exceeds the 2K size limit of a record. When this happens, each large value field is represented in the record by a pointer, which references one or more separate 2K memory pages on which the data is actually stored.

When you query tables containing large value fields, don't include those fields in the field list unless you need them, because returning large value fields takes time.

A snapshot-type **Recordset** opened against large value fields in an .MDB file does not actually contain that data. Instead, the snapshot maintains references to the data in the original tables, the same way a dynaset references all data.

### Handling Large Value Data

Sometimes you'll need to read or copy data from a large value field where you don't have sufficient memory to copy the entire field in a single statement. You instead have to break up the data into smaller units, or "chunks," that will fit available memory. The **FieldSize** method tells you how large the field is, measured in bytes. Then you can use the **GetChunk** method to copy a specific number of bytes to a buffer, and use the **AppendChunk** method to copy the buffer to the final location. You then continue using **GetChunk** and **AppendChunk** until the entire field is copied.

# Reading and Writing Data

When you read and write data to a field, you're actually reading or setting the **Value** property of a **Field** object. The **Value** property is the default property of a **Field**, so you can use either of the following syntax:

```
rstEmployees!LastName.Value = strName
rstEmployees!LastName = strName
```

## Write Permission

The tables underlying a **Recordset** object may not permit you to modify data, even though the **Recordset** is of type dynaset or table, which are normally updatable. Check the **Updatable** property of the **Recordset** to determine whether its data can be changed. If the property is **True**, the **Recordset** can be updated.

Individual fields within an updatable Recordset may not be updatable, and attempting to write to these fields generates a run-time error. To determine whether a given field is updatable, check the **DataUpdatable** property of the corresponding **Field** object in the **Fields** collection of the **Recordset**.

In the following example, a **Recordset** object variable is passed to a function that first determines whether the **Recordset** is updatable. If it is, the function counts how many **Field** objects are updatable and returns the total. It also prints the **Name** property of each **Field** object that is not updatable. If all the fields are updatable, the function returns −1. If the entire **Recordset** is not updatable, the function returns 0.

```
Function UpdateTest(rstUnknown As Recordset) As Integer
    Dim intCount As Integer, intX As Integer
    Dim fldUnknown As Field

    intCount = 0

    If rstUnknown.Updatable Then
        For intX = 0 To rstUnknown.Fields.Count - 1
            Set fldUnknown = rstUnknown.Fields(intX)
            If fldUnknown.DataUpdatable Then
                intCount = intCount + 1
            Else
                Debug.Print fldUnknown.Name
            End If
        Next intX
        If intCount = rstUnknown.Fields.Count Then
            UpdateTest = -1
        Else
            UpdateTest = intCount
        End If
```

```
        Else
            UpdateTest = 0
        End If
End Function
```

## Constraints

For more information
on how to set these
properties on the
**Field** objects of a
**TableDef** object, or by
using SQL DDL
statements, see
Chapter 3, "Data
Definition and
Integrity."

Any single field can impose a number of constraints on data in that field when
records are added or updated. These constraints are defined by a handful of
properties. The **AllowZeroLength** property on a Text or Memo field indicates
whether or not the field will accept a zero-length string. The **Required** property
indicates whether or not some value must be entered in the field, or if it instead
can accept a **Null**. For a **Field** object on a **Recordset**, these properties are read-
only; their state is determined by the underlying table.

### Field-Level Data Validation

Validation is the process of determining whether data entered into a field's **Value**
property is within an acceptable range. A **Field** object on a **Recordset** may have
the **ValidationRule** and **ValidationText** properties set. **ValidationRule** is simply a
criteria expression, similar to the criteria of an SQL WHERE clause, without the
WHERE keyword. The **ValidationText** property is a string that's displayed in an
error alert by Microsoft Access, or by the **Data** control in Visual Basic if you
attempt to enter data in the field that is outside the limits of the **ValidationRule**
property. If you're coding from DAO directly, then you can use the
**ValidationText** for a message you want to display to the user.

For more information
on setting table-level
validation properties,
see Chapter 3, "Data
Definition and
Integrity."

**Note**  The **ValidationRule** and **ValidationText** properties also exist at the
**Recordset** level. These are read-only properties, reflecting the table-level
validation scheme established on the base table from which the current record is
fetched.

A **Field** object on a **Recordset** also features the **ValidateOnSet** property. When
set to **True**, validation is checked as soon as the field's **Value** property is set. If set
to **False**, validation is checked only when the completed record is updated. The
default value is **False**. For example, if you're adding data to a record containing a
large Memo or OLE Object field with a **ValidationRule**, you should determine
whether the new data violates the validation rule before attempting to write the
data (you should write the data when the field value is set, not when the entire
record is written to disk) so you don't waste time attempting to write an invalid
record to disk. If you do so, set the **ValidateOnSet** property to **True**.

# Tracing the Origin of Dynaset Fields

A dynaset-type **Recordset** can include records from more than one source table. Also, within a single record, fields from different tables can be joined into new records. Sometimes it's useful to know the table from which a field originated. The **SourceTable** property of a **Field** object returns the name of the base table from which the field's current data was fetched.

Within a query, a field can be renamed for display purposes. For example, in an SQL SELECT query, the AS operator in the select field list can create an alias for one of the returned fields. In a **Recordset** based on an SQL query, a field that has been aliased is represented by a **Field** object whose **Name** property reflects the alias, not the original field name. To find out the original field name, check the **Field** object's **SourceField** property.

CHAPTER 6

# Creating Multiuser Applications

For more information on using Microsoft Jet in a client/server configuration, see Chapter 9, "Developing Client/Server Applications."

Microsoft Jet supports the network environment with a variety of services designed to make your life as a developer easier. Microsoft Jet 3.0 boasts improved multiuser performance and increased concurrency.

To implement multiuser applications that run smoothly using Microsoft Jet, you should be familiar with the engine's multiuser model. Moving an existing single-user application to a multiuser environment is not always a simple port, and you should plan ahead and address several issues. A multiuser application should be designed as such from the ground up, with the database engine's functionality in mind. This chapter guides you through these issues and shows you how to effectively use Microsoft Jet to manage resources and minimize contention for data and objects. This chapter covers the use of Microsoft Jet in a file-server configuration.

**Contents**

For information on copying the code examples from the companion CD-ROM to your hard disk drive, see "Using the Companion CD-ROM" in the Preface.

## Using CH06.MDB and CHAP06.VBP

If you copied the samples from the companion CD-ROM, you can find the code examples for Microsoft Access in C:\SAMPLES\CHAP06\ ACCESS\CH06.MDB. The corresponding code examples for Visual Basic are in C:\SAMPLES\CHAP06\VB40\CHAP06.VBP.

To run any of the code examples in this chapter, open the .MDB file in Microsoft Access or open the .VBP file in Microsoft Visual Basic 4.0. You can use the examples to help you understand the concepts discussed in the chapter—or you can modify them and use them in your own applications.

# File-Server vs. Client/Server

When discussing Microsoft Jet multiuser database systems, it's important to note the differences in available technology. A multiuser database system, as implemented on personal computers, generally falls into one of two categories: a file-server system or a client/server system.

In a file-server configuration, no intelligent process is active at the server level. All intelligence resides on the individual workstation. When your application needs data, it's the workstation software's responsibility to determine which files should be read and how to directly access the network drive. Because all data in the database file must be sent from the server to the workstation, network traffic is increased—see Figure 6.1.

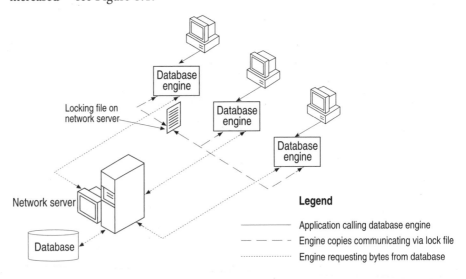

Figure 6.1    A typical file-server configuration

A multiuser database system within a file-server environment is made up of:

- A database that resides on a network file server running an operating system such as Microsoft Windows NT Server or Novell® NetWare®.
- One or more users accessing the database from a workstation's application software.

In a client/server configuration, the server is responsible for intelligently servicing requests for data. The workstation does not request data at the file level but sends a high-level request to the server to execute a specific query and return its results. The primary advantage to this technique is that network traffic is reduced, because only the result set of the query is returned to the workstation, as shown in Figure 6.2.

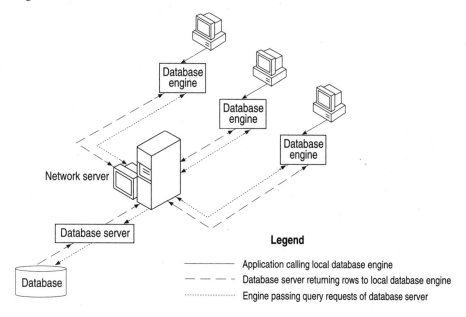

**Figure 6.2   A typical client/server configuration**

A client/server configuration is typified by:

- A back-end database residing on the server controlled and maintained by the server software, such as Microsoft SQL Server.
- One or more users running a local application that requests data from the server through an interface such as the Microsoft Open Database Connectivity (ODBC) standard.

# The Microsoft Jet Multiuser Model

In a file-server environment, a multiuser database system using Microsoft Jet consists of the following components:

- One or more database files residing on the network server
- A locking information file (.LDB) for each database
- A workgroup database, residing either centrally on the network server, or on each user's workstation
- A copy of Microsoft Jet running on the local workstation

The following diagram illustrates how these components are related.

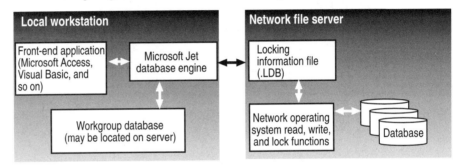

**Figure 6.3    The Microsoft Jet multiuser model**

# The Locking Information File

When a database is opened in shared mode, it's necessary to address concurrency issues. This is done through a locking information file.

You can delete a locking information file only when no users have its related database file (.MDB) open. If you move a database file to a new location, it's not necessary to move the .LDB file. For more information on the locking information file, see the "Microsoft Jet Locking Architecture" section later in this chapter.

# The Workgroup Database

For more information on workgroup databases, see Chapter 10, "Managing Security."

In addition to the locking information file, there is the workgroup database file (also known as SYSTEM.MDA in Microsoft Access 2.0 or SYSTEM.MDW in Microsoft Access for Windows 95). Although this file is primarily used to store security information about users and groups, its location in multiuser environments is important. This file is a Microsoft Jet database that stores user, group, and password information, as well as information on various options the user has set. This component can be placed on the local workstation or shared on a network drive. However, if it's stored locally, you must take the steps necessary to update it when security settings change.

**Microsoft Access Users**   Microsoft Access uses the workgroup database to store various options that the user can set. It also stores the most recently used (MRU) list of databases opened. If you want your application's users to have their own MRU lists, you should store the workgroup database on their local drives.

# Workstation Locking

If a database resides on a workstation's local disk, Microsoft Jet requires the availability of some form of operating-system locking. This is typically handled by the SHARE.EXE program that ships with MS-DOS, the VSHARE driver that ships with Microsoft Windows for Workgroups, or the network services built into Microsoft Windows 95 and Windows NT.

# Multiuser Settings

For more information on Registry settings, see Appendix C, "Registry Settings."

You can use a variety of settings to control how Microsoft Jet behaves in a multiuser environment. Settings are stored in the Windows Registry and can be changed using the Registry Editor (REGEDIT.EXE for Windows 95 or REGEDT32.EXE for Windows NT). The settings in the Registry affect the additional settings that Microsoft Access provides (described in the following note.)

**Microsoft Access Users**   In Microsoft Access 2.0 and 7.0, you can set a number of options that control how Microsoft Access interacts with Microsoft Jet in a multiuser environment. The following settings are available, either through the **Options** command on the **Tools** menu, or programmatically through the **Application** object's **SetOption** method.

If you have applications other than Microsoft Access that use Microsoft Jet for database access, you may want to modify engine settings by directly updating the Registry. The benefit to this approach is that you're making settings directly to Microsoft Jet. These settings are then used by all applications that use the engine.

**Default Open Mode** specifies how the database is to be opened if no explicit options are specified. If the database is to be used in a multiuser environment, set this option to Shared.

**Default Record Locking** specifies how rows are to be locked when they are edited within the context of a Microsoft Access form. The three settings correspond to locking modes that Microsoft Jet defines. No Locks corresponds to *optimistic* locking, Edited Record corresponds to *pessimistic* locking, and All Records corresponds to *recordset* locking.

**Number of Update Retries** specifies how many times Microsoft Access retries saving a locked page.

**Update Retry Interval** specifies the number of milliseconds Microsoft Access waits before retrying saving a locked page.

**ODBC Refresh Interval** specifies how often (in seconds) Microsoft Access refreshes a form with data changes from ODBC data sources.

**Refresh Interval** specifies how often (in seconds) Microsoft Access refreshes a form with data changes from native Microsoft Jet data sources. It should be noted that this setting overrides the PageTimeout setting for Microsoft Jet in the Registry. Microsoft Access is the only Microsoft application that can override this setting.

# File-Server Networks Supported

Microsoft Jet supports most file-server and peer-to-peer networks that work on personal computers. The following networks have been tested with Microsoft Jet and are supported:

- Banyan® VINES® 5.52
- DECnet™ 4.1
- LANtastic® 5.0
- Novell NetWare 3.*x* and 4.*x*
- OS/2 LAN Manager®, 2.1 and 2.2

Although Microsoft Jet supports these networks equally, it's important to note that the performance of peer-to-peer networks is not generally up to the requirements of a multiuser database system. Most successful applications that perform database access are implemented on dedicated file-server network operating systems.

# Managing Shared Databases

To effectively use Microsoft Jet in multiuser applications, you must understand how to work with the database file. Because this file contains not only the data, but also structural objects such as queries, controlling its use and location is very important. Your application should be designed to balance the need for centralized administration with the performance benefits gained by moving parts of your application to the local level.

# Location of Components

Because network file access is typically slower than local disk access, you might want to improve performance by storing some of your application's components on the local workstation. You have a great deal of flexibility with most network operating systems for controlling where various components of your multiuser application reside. For this discussion, components are grouped into two categories:

- *Static* components are the parts of your application that don't change often. The dynamic link libraries (.DLL) and executable files (.EXE) that make up the host program calling Microsoft Jet—such as Visual Basic, Microsoft Access, and Microsoft Excel—are examples of static components. Components in your application, such as forms, reports, and program code, are also static components.

- *Active* components are the files that contain the actual data that your application's users access in a multiuser environment. These can include Microsoft Jet databases, external databases such as Microsoft FoxPro database files, or ODBC databases stored on database servers.

Because static components don't change often, they are ideal candidates for workstation storage. In this scenario, you install the Microsoft Jet components and the host application on the local workstation along with your application's static objects. Active components, such as your application's data files, are stored on the network server. Using this scenario, you optimize performance but have to worry about updating objects on local workstations when the application's design changes.

In situations where user workstations don't have sufficient disk space, or you would like greater control over modification of static components, static components can be stored on the network. This has the obvious effect of increasing network traffic and reducing application performance, but it minimizes administrative issues.

## Self-Updating Applications

You should bear in mind that administrative concerns arise as you move components to the workstation level. For example, when you need to modify a static object in your application, such as a table's structure or a program's code, you must have mechanisms in place for updating all affected components on each individual workstation.

This problem can be somewhat minimized by building intelligence into your application that checks for latest versions upon startup. For example, your application's startup code can check the modification dates of static objects in the local database and compare them to dates in a central database located on the server. Whenever a newer date is found on a server object, the code automatically imports the latest version of the object, keeping the local database up-to-date.

For more information on replication, see Chapter 7, "Database Replication."

You can also leverage the replication features in Microsoft Jet 3.0 to keep objects synchronized. For example, you can create replicas of the database and store them at the workstation level. In this scenario, engine replication takes care of the details of synchronizing objects.

# The Two-Database Approach

When developing multiuser applications with Microsoft Jet, you may find it helpful to split your objects into two databases. This approach offers many advantages. These two databases are known as the *application* database and the *data* database.

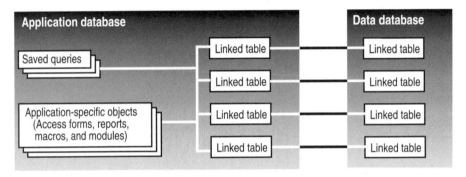

**Figure 6.4    The two-database approach**

The application database has two basic characteristics. First, it contains nondata objects such as saved queries. If you're a Microsoft Access user, it also contains your forms, reports, macros, and modules. Second, it serves as an area for managing temporary objects. Most multiuser applications perform some type of data access that is temporary in nature: creating tables with transient data, for example.

The data database contains the tables that hold your application's data. This database is accessed by your application through links in the application database.

For more information on linking tables, see Chapter 8, "Accessing External Data."

The advantages of the two-database approach become obvious in multiuser environments. By storing the application database on the user's workstation, there is no contention for temporary objects, as your application doesn't have to worry about creating a temporary table that may conflict with another user. Secondly, by storing application-specific objects that are typically static in nature at the local level, the amount of network traffic that occurs while your application runs is minimized.

# Microsoft Jet Locking Architecture

Locking is one of the more complex issues you face when developing multiuser applications. This section describes the Microsoft Jet locking behavior, providing information on how Microsoft Jet versions 2.*x* and 3.0 work in multiuser settings.

## Layout of the Locking Information File

For more information on Microsoft Jet locking, see the white paper "Understanding Jet Locking" on the companion CD-ROM. You can find it in the Papers folder under JETLOCK.DOC.

The locking information file, identified by its .LDB extension, plays a crucial role in Microsoft Jet's multiuser scheme. This file stores computer and security names and places extended byte range locks from Microsoft Jet. One locking information file is created for every Microsoft Jet database file that is opened in shared mode. The file always retains the same name as the database that was opened. For example, NWIND.MDB has an associated locking information file called NWIND.LDB. If the locking information file doesn't exist when the database is opened, Microsoft Jet creates it.

Microsoft Jet retrieves the computer name by making a request to the operating system. Windows for Workgroups stores the computer name in the Network section of the SYSTEM.INI file. To modify the computer name in Windows 95 or Windows NT, just go to the Control Panel and click the Network icon. From there, the computer name can be changed. The security name is determined by passing a value to the **Workspace** object. The default security name is Admin.

Extended byte range locks are placed outside of the physical boundaries of a file —no data is physically locked. An example of an extended byte range lock is a lock placed at 10 million hex for a file that has a physical size of only 64 bytes: A lock is virtually placed at a location that does not exist on the hard disk. Extended byte range locks are used because they're not limited by the size of the physical file, thus allowing for locking algorithms that would not otherwise be possible. Also, placing locks inside a data file prevents other users from reading that data. For example, in the earlier versions of dBASE, a user could place a lock on a record located in the data file, preventing everyone else from reading that data.

The physical structure of the locking information file can best be thought of as an array of up to 255 elements. Each element contains 64 bytes and represents a user. The first 32 bytes contain the computer name of the user and the second 32 bytes contain the user's logon name. This name is the machine name supplied by the operating system (Microsoft Windows 95 or Microsoft Windows NT). The physical size of the locking information file never exceeds 16320 bytes. This is because the maximum number of concurrent Microsoft Jet users is 255 (255 * 64 = 16320). Each element in the array is used by Microsoft Jet to determine which users are holding locks on data.

**Note** Unlike Microsoft Jet 2.*x*, version 3.0 automatically deletes the locking information file when the last user closes the database. This is done to alleviate replicated database issues and to allow for performance gains in determining which users have locks open. However, this automatic deletion cannot occur if the user doesn't have sufficient operating system or network operating system rights to delete the file, or the database is in a compromised state.

# The Database Header Page

To use the values discussed in this section, view the LDBVIEW.EXE utility in the \UTILITIES\ LDBVIEW FOLDER on the companion CD-ROM, and read "Understanding Jet Locking," also on the CD-ROM. You can find it in the Papers folder under JETLOCK.DOC.

The database header page (DBH) is the first page of data in every Microsoft Jet database. Remember that a page is defined as 2K (or 2048 bytes) of data. The DBH is primarily used to store *commit* byte(s) for each of the 255 possible users connected to the database. A commit byte (or pair of bytes in Microsoft Jet 3.0) is a value used by the database engine to determine the state of the database.

Microsoft Jet version 2.*x* uses 256 bytes to store the commit byte starting at 700 hex and continuing to the end of the page at 800 hex. Microsoft Jet 3.0 uses 512 bytes that use 2 bytes per user starting at 600 hex. The first byte (version 2.*x*) or the first 2 bytes (version 3.0) are used only when the database is open in exclusive mode, and the remaining 255 bytes (version 2.0) or 510 bytes (version 3.0) are used when the database is open in shared mode.

Commit bytes in Microsoft Jet 2.0 databases have only two valid values, 00 and FF. The 00 value indicates a neutral state and the FF value indicates that the engine is in the process of physically writing data to the disk. If the database has an FF value and no corresponding user lock, then a user interrupted the process of writing to disk. New users attempting to open the database receive the message `Database is corrupt or is not a database file` and will be forced to repair the database before opening it.

**Note** Microsoft Jet 2.0 allowed situations in which the database could be closed with a value of FF, thus preventing other users from opening the database without repairing it first. This was fixed in Microsoft Jet 2.5.

Commit bytes in Microsoft Jet 2.5 databases have five valid values ranging from 00 to 04. This range of values provides more information on what users were doing if the database were left in a compromised state. As with Microsoft Jet 2.0, the database is in a suspect state if there is a nonzero value without a corresponding user lock. A value of 01 indicates that a user accessed a corrupted page in the database. The value 02 is not used. A value of 03 indicates that the database is being repaired. A value of 04 indicates that the user is in the process of committing a transaction to disk.

Commit bytes in Microsoft Jet 3.0 can have many different values, thus their size has been increased to 2 bytes. Values of 00 00 indicate that the user is in the process of committing a transaction to disk, and values of 01 00 indicate that a user has accessed a corrupted page. Thus, if a value of 00 00 is present without a corresponding user lock, or if a value of 01 00 is present, the user will not be able to open the database without first repairing it. Additional values in the 600-800 hex range are used by Microsoft Jet for performance tracking.

# Microsoft Jet Locks

Microsoft Jet uses two categories of locks: shared locks and exclusive locks. These locks are used by Microsoft Jet and should not be confused with the types of locks that you apply to data in your application through VBA code. Each extended byte range lock (with the exception of user locks) represents a page in the .MDB file. However, no data is physically locked in the .MDB file.

A shared lock occupies only 1 byte and never conflicts with another shared lock. Shared locks are typically used to allow more than one person to read data from a file at the same time.

Exclusive locks span between 256 and 512 bytes and, by their nature, always conflict with other shared and exclusive locks. The exclusive lock always locks the first 256 bytes of the extended byte range lock to prevent any shared locks from being set and to determine if any shared locks exist. In addition, extended locks lock enough additional bytes to determine which user is holding the lock. For example, when a user wants to open a table in deny-read mode, Microsoft Jet tries to place an exclusive lock. This exclusive lock would be prevented if another user had a shared lock on the table. If the exclusive lock succeeded, it would prevent other users from obtaining a shared lock.

Microsoft Jet uses seven types of locks:

- User locks
- Write locks
- Read locks
- Commit locks (version 2.*x* only)
- Table-read locks
- Table-write locks
- Table deny-write locks

Using the extended byte range locks discussed earlier, these seven types are organized into six virtual regions of the locking information file in version 2.*x*, and five virtual regions in version 3.0. These regions are used by Microsoft Jet to place extended byte range locks that range from 10000001 to 6FF800FF hex. These locks are present only when users have the database open in shared or read-only mode.

The names of these locks were assigned by Microsoft Jet development and don't necessarily have the same meanings in other database products.

## User Locks

User locks are used for modifying the commit byte values in the Database Header Page (DBH), for writing the computer and user names in the correct location in the locking information file, and for retrieving the computer and user names of users with conflicting locks. A user lock is obtained when the user opens the database and is persistent for as long as a user has the database open. (Persistence in this context indicates the duration of the lock, or how long the lock is held.) Only one user lock exists for each connected user; however, multiple instances of Microsoft Jet on the same computer create an additional user lock per instance.

User locks are always in the range of 10000001 hex through 100000FF hex and occupy only 1 byte.

## Write Locks

Write locks prevent users from changing data while another user is modifying data. A write lock is typically placed on data, index, or long value pages. (Long value pages are a type of data page that contains ANSI SQL data types of CHARACTER, VARYING, BIT, or BIT VARYING. These data types are known as **Memo** or **OLE Object** fields in Microsoft Access and Visual Basic.) The persistence of write locks is directly related to the duration of a transaction. All SQL DML statements have implicit transactions placed around them. Therefore, an UPDATE statement holds persistent write locks until the entire update is committed. The persistence of write locks is also determined by the type of locking chosen for recordset navigation and form editing (in Microsoft Access), and the presence of explicit transactions.

Write locks are in the range of 20000000 hex through 2FF80FF hex. They always span between 256 and 512 bytes, and therefore are always exclusive locks.

## Read Locks (Version 2.*x*)

You use read locks, a type of shared lock, primarily for the immediate recycling of index pages and for ensuring that index pages in the engine's cache are up-to-date. This type of lock is placed on long value pages and index pages. It's used to prevent an index page from being recycled while that page is being referenced in the Microsoft Jet cache and to provide an integral view of the index.

Read locks are placed in the range of 30000000 to 3FF800FF hex. They occupy only 1 byte.

Read locks in version 2.*x* are perhaps the most troublesome locks to deal with because they can cause locking conflicts that are not obvious to the developer or user. The persistence of read locks is determined by:

For more information on Microsoft Jet configuration settings, see Appendix C, "Registry Settings."

- The LockedPageTimeout Registry setting, specified in tenths of a second. This setting determines the amount of time the engine retains locks before releasing them. By increasing the LockedPageTimeout setting, read locks are retained for a longer period of time, which reduces the need for Microsoft Jet to reread data pages into the cache. The LockedPageTimeout is set in the ISAM section of the .INI file for Microsoft Jet 2.*x*, or in the Windows Registry (Jet 2.*x*\ISAM) for Microsoft Jet 3.0.

- The **DBEngine.Idle DBFreeLocks** statement or **Freelocks** statement. However, these statements don't always free all read locks when inside a transaction.

Read locks are typically placed when an index or long value page is read and placed in the Microsoft Jet cache. An example would be performing an SQL UPDATE statement on a table that has a primary key.

### Read Locks (Version 3.0)

The primary purpose of read locks in Microsoft Jet 3.0 is to allow multiple users to read long value pages, simultaneously preventing others from writing to those pages. Microsoft Jet 3.0 has reduced the number of read locks placed on index pages, which directly results in greater concurrency and performance. Read locks placed on index pages are now placed only when referential integrity is being enforced. Unlike version 2.*x*, the persistence of read locks in version 3.0 is determined by the currency of the row. Thus, a read lock on a long value page remains until the user leaves that row. An exception to this is when a long value page contains data from more than one row of data. In this case, the engine releases the lock on that page. An example of this situation is when several rows' worth of memo data are placed in one long value page.

Microsoft Jet 3.0 read locks are placed in the same range as write locks. They are differentiated from write locks in that they are shared locks and occupy only 1 byte.

For more information on the DAO 2.5/3.0 compatibility type library, see Chapter 2, "Introducing Data Access Objects."

**Important**   Read locks are persistent in Microsoft Jet 3.0 until the user loses currency on the row. Microsoft Jet 2.*x* leaves read locks until they time out or until the user issues a **DBEngine.Idle DBFreeLocks** or **FreeLocks** statement. These statements no longer have functionality regarding the removal of read locks in version 3.0. The **FreeLocks** statement is also no longer supported unless the user references the DAO 2.5/3.0 compatibility type library.

## Commit Locks

Commit locks are present only in Microsoft Jet 2.*x*. They are similar to read locks, except that they are always exclusive locks. These locks are also placed in the 30001A01 to 3FF800FF hex range. They are placed when index pages or long value pages are being written to the database file, and they conflict only with read locks. Read locks are typically placed on index pages whenever an index page is placed in the engine's cache. Index pages reference many data pages, so you can understand why many users experience locking conflicts even when they know other users are not editing data on the same page.

One of the best ways to prevent these conflicts is to judiciously use the **Idle** method with the *DB_FreeLocks* argument or the **FreeLocks** statement.

Commit locks do not exist in Microsoft Jet 3.0 because the range for read locks has been moved into the same range as write locks, thus eliminating the need for this type of lock.

## Table-Read Locks

Table-read locks are used to control placing a table in deny-read mode, which prevents other users from reading data from the table. Unlike the previous types of locks, table-read locks and the rest of the table-type locks are placed only on a special type of page called a Table Header Page (TBH). There is one TBH page for each table in the database, and each TBH contains statistics about the table, such as row count, next counter value, field data types, and index types.

Table-read locks are placed in the 40000000 to 4FF800FF hex range and can be placed as shared locks or exclusive locks.

When a table is opened, a shared table-read lock is placed. Deny-Read mode is set when a **Recordset** object is opened through DAO with the dbDenyRead option. Microsoft Access also places a shared table-read lock on a table when a Microsoft Access form accesses the table with the "All Records" type of locking (on the Advanced Options tab in Microsoft Access for Windows 95). If the exclusive table-read lock can be obtained, then no other users who have the table open with a shared table-read lock exist. The exclusive table-read lock prevents other users from acquiring shared locks when they try to open a table. The table-read locks are persistent until the user closes the table.

## Table-Write Locks

Table-write locks are used in conjunction with table deny-write locks and are placed in the 50000000 to 5FF800FF hex range. These shared locks are persistent whenever a table is opened in a state that allows writing.

### Table Deny-Write Locks

These locks are used in conjunction with table-write locks and are explicitly set when opening a table in deny-write mode. These locks are placed in the 60000000 to 6FF800FF hex range and have a persistent shared lock while a table is open in deny-write mode. An exclusive lock is placed, but not held, to determine which other users have the table opened in deny-write mode.

## Summary of Lock Behavior

This table summarizes when the locks are set, what is locked, what the lock prevents, and how long the lock is held.

| Lock name | What sets the lock | What is locked | What the lock prevents | Persistence of the lock | Shared or exclusive | Byte range examples |
|---|---|---|---|---|---|---|
| User | User opens a database | NA | Nothing | Until user closes the database | NA | 10000001–10000001 |
| Write | Insert, update, or delete | All available pages | Updates or deletes to data and sometimes inserts to a table | Controlled by locking mode set by user or the duration of a transaction | Exclusive | 2000A601–2000A701 |
| Read (version 2.x) | Reads on long value or index pages | Long value, index, or table header pages | Updates or deletes to long value or index pages | Controlled by LockedPage-Timeout configuration setting or DBEn-gine.Idle dbFreelocks | Shared | 30001E01–30001E01 |
| Read (version 3.0) | Reads on certain long value or index pages when referential integrity is being enforced | Long value, index, or directory pages | Updates or deletes to long value or index pages | Until a read or a transaction is complete or the user moves to a new row | Shared | 20063801–20063801 |
| Commit (version 2.x only) | Writes to long value or index pages | Long value or index pages | Prevents reads when data is being written to disk | Held until data is written to disk | Exclusive | 30001A01–30001B01 |

| Lock name | What sets the lock | What is locked | What the lock prevents | Persistence of the lock | Shared or exclusive | Byte range examples (*cont'd*) |
|---|---|---|---|---|---|---|
| Table-read | Shared lock is obtained when table is opened. Exclusive lock is obtained when default locking on a Microsoft Access form is set to All Records or a recordset is opened through DAO using the dbDenyRead option. | Table Header Page | Prevents exclusive read lock from being set | As long as the table is kept open by the user | Both | 4000C801– 4000C801 |
| Table-write | Shared lock is obtained when a table is opened; exclusive lock is obtained when default locking on a Microsoft Access form is set to All Records or a **Recordset** is opened through DAO using the dbDenyRead option. | Table Header Page | Prevents exclusive write lock from being set; doesn't prevent table deny-write lock | As long as the table is kept open by the user | Both | 5000C801– 5000C801 |
| Table deny-write | Can be set only through DAO | Table Header Page | Prevents all writes to the table | As long as the table is kept open by the user | Both | 6000C801– 6000C801 |

## The User Lock Algorithm

All Microsoft Jet multiuser locking operations revolve around the placement of a user lock. As stated previously, user locks are placed in the 10 million hex range and occupy only 1 byte. When Microsoft Jet opens a database in shared mode, the following activities occur before a user lock is placed.

First, Microsoft Jet checks to see if the database engine is in a suspect or read-only state. This is done by examining the DBH page and seeing what bytes have a corresponding nonzero value. If the first byte (version 2.*x*) or the first 2 bytes (version 3.0) contain a nonzero value, or the remaining 255 bytes (version 2.*x*) or 510 bytes (version 3.0) have a nonzero value and don't have a corresponding user lock, Microsoft Jet forces the user to repair the database. When opening a database in shared mode, there is never a need to check for a user lock on the first byte because it's used only when a database is opened exclusively. A corresponding user lock would be a lock that shares the same offset in the 10 million hex range as the offset from the first byte in the DBH page. Thus, a non-zero commit byte at 701 hex (version 2.*x*) or 602–603 hex (version 3.0) would need to have a user lock at 10000001 for the database to be opened without being considered suspect.

Second, the engine opens the locking information file, or creates one if it doesn't exist. It tries to place a lock at 10000001 hex. If Microsoft Jet is successful in obtaining this lock, it writes the computer and user name to the first 64 bytes of the file. If this lock cannot be acquired, the engine continues moving 1 byte farther in the file until a lock can be obtained. After the user lock is acquired, the engine writes the computer name and user name at the corresponding location in the file. For example, a user lock at 10000040 hex would write an entry at 4096 bytes in the physical part of the .LBD file.

Some users may experience delays in opening a database that already has many users connected. This is mainly due to network drivers that are not optimized. An example of this is a situation where a user is running a Microsoft Windows NT 3.5 client connected to a Novell NetWare server. If a user is trying to open the database and 30 other users are currently connected, it can take more than 30 seconds to perform the user lock algorithm. Microsoft Windows NT 3.51 has a modified NetWare requester driver that decreases the wait to approximately two seconds.

# Handling Conflicts

When working in a single-user environment, your application doesn't encounter conflicting requests for resources. Because only one user is concurrently accessing data, you can reasonably assume that the needed data will always be exclusively available. However, after you move into a multiuser environment, the only reasonable assumption is that conflicts will occur among users accessing data. Microsoft Jet manages these conflicts through the locking services it provides to the application. By locking data, your application ensures that only one user can simultaneously access it at a given time.

# Locking Modes

To understand locking, you must be familiar with the levels at which you can "lock" data. With Microsoft Jet, you can lock data at three different levels that vary from the most restrictive to the least restrictive.

- Exclusive mode prevents all other users from using the database. This is the most restrictive mode.

- Recordset locking locks a **Recordset** object's underlying tables with either table-read locks, table-write locks, or both.

- Page locking locks the 2048 byte (2K) page where the data being edited resides. This is the least restrictive mode.

To determine the level at which to lock objects in your application, you must decide the level of concurrency needed. For example, if you want the objects to be available as often as possible, a high-concurrency strategy would dictate that you use page locking, the least restrictive level. However, if your application requires guaranteed access to most or all of the data in the database, you may opt for exclusive mode. This ensures that your application has the database exclusively.

Note that the three levels are not mutually exclusive. Many multiuser applications employ all three levels at various times. For example, in an order entry system, page locking may be used to control locks on the Orders table to enable the highest concurrency among order takers. **Recordset** locking may be used at the end of the day to lock a summary table to update it with summary data. Finally, exclusive mode can be used nightly to compact the database.

# Using Exclusive Mode

As previously mentioned, exclusive mode is the most restrictive way you can open a database: It prevents all other users from opening the database. This is generally useful for administrative or bulk changes to the database, such as repair or compact operations, or when making structural changes to the database's schema.

When you access a database in a single-user environment, you typically open it in exclusive mode. This may provide better performance because Microsoft Jet doesn't have to lock and unlock objects or refresh its cache. When you deploy your application in a multiuser environment, exclusive mode is no longer an option; you must open the database in shared mode.

▶ **To open a database in exclusive mode**

1. Dimension a database variable using the **Dim** statement.

2. Use the **OpenDatabase** method to open the database you want, specifying a value of **True** for the **Exclusive** property.

3. Close the database object when finished to allow it to be accessed by other users.

The following code opens a database exclusively and checks for errors to determine if the operation was successful:

```
Sub OpenDatabaseExclusive()
    Dim dbsOrdEntry As Database
    Dim errCurrent As Error

    ' Try to open the database exclusively.
    On Error Resume Next
    Set dbsOrdEntry = _
        OpenDatabase("C:\Samples\Chap06\OrdEntry.mdb", True)
    If Err <> 0 Then
        ' If errors occurred, display them.
        For Each errCurrent In DBEngine.Errors
            Debug.Print errCurrent.Description
        Next
    Else
        ' No errors: You have exclusive access.
        Debug.Print "Opened Database Exclusive"
    End If
    dbsOrdEntry.Close
End Sub
```

For more information on setting permissions, see Chapter 10, "Managing Security."

You may want to prevent your application's users from opening a shared database in exclusive mode. This is particularly true if your users use applications such as Microsoft Access that allow databases to be opened exclusively through the user interface. You can accomplish this by using Microsoft Jet security. By setting a user's Open Exclusive permission to **No** on a database, you prevent that user from opening the database in exclusive mode. Note that you probably want to allow administrative users the option of opening the database exclusively.

One of the critical aspects of coding for locks is the handling of errors. In Microsoft Jet, you don't check to see if a lock can be applied before doing it. Instead, you try the operation and check to see if it succeeded: This approach makes it unnecessary for Microsoft Jet to supply a large number of status functions that must be invoked before attempting an operation.

The typical approach to locking is a four-step process:

1. Disable VBA error handling.

2. Attempt the operation.

3. Check to see if an error occurred. If so, handle the error based on the error number.

4. Re-enable VBA error handling.

This approach works well because you don't have to anticipate every possible error before attempting to place a lock; you handle the error only if it occurs. When writing multiuser code, you should generally handle the error by displaying some type of informational message to the user and optionally allowing the user to retry the operation.

In the OpenDatabaseExclusive procedure shown earlier in this section, you can see this technique in action.

# Using Read-Only Mode

Read-only mode is a modified form of shared mode. When you open a database in read-only mode, you cannot change objects in the database—data and structural information included. This mode, however, does not prevent other users from changing data and should not be confused with opening the file in read-only mode from an operating system level. You could modify the previous example to open the database in exclusive, read-only mode by changing the arguments to the **OpenDatabase** method as follows:

```
Set dbsOrdEntry = OpenDatabase("OrdEntry.mdb", True, True)
```

To open a database in shared, read-only mode, use the following code:

```
Set dbsCust = OpenDatabase("Customers.mdb", False, True)
```

---

**Note** Opening a database in read-only mode does not prevent shared table-type locks or read locks; therefore, opening a database in read-only mode does not prevent locking conflicts.

---

# Using Recordset Locking

Recordset locking enables you to control how the **Recordset** object's underlying tables are locked. You can specify read-only or write-only access, or both. Note that recordset locking applies only to table- and dynaset-type **Recordset** objects. Page locking doesn't apply to snapshot-type **Recordset** objects, because these are inherently read-only objects. However, shared table-read and shared table-write locks are placed by Microsoft Jet.

## Opening the Database in Shared Mode

If you want to implement recordset locking, you must open your database in shared mode. This is the typical mode for opening databases in multiuser environments. When a database is opened in shared mode, multiple users can simultaneously access the database and Microsoft Jet handles conflicts between users.

▶ **To open a database in shared mode**

1. Dimension a database variable using the **Dim** statement.

2. Use the **OpenDatabase** method to open the database, specifying a value of **False** for the **Exclusive** property.

The following code opens a database in shared mode:

```
Sub OpenDatabaseShared()
    Dim dbsOrdEntry As Database
    Dim errCurrent As Error

    ' Try to open the database shared.
    On Error Resume Next
    Set dbsOrdEntry = OpenDatabase _
        ("C:\Samples\Chap06\OrdEntry.mdb", False)
    If Err <> 0 Then
        ' Errors occurred: Display them.
        For Each errCurrent In DBEngine.Errors
            Debug.Print errCurrent.Description
        Next
    Else
        ' No errors: The database is in shared mode.
        Debug.Print "Opened Database in Shared Mode"
    End If
    dbsOrdEntry.Close
End Sub
```

## Opening the Recordset

After you open the database in shared mode, you can implement **Recordset** locking by specifying various options in the *options* argument of the **OpenRecordset** method. You can combine options to more completely describe the type of locking you want to employ.

▶ **To open a Recordset with locking enabled**

For more information on opening a recordset, see the "OpenRecordset Options" section in Chapter 5, "Working with Records and Fields."

1. Open the **Recordset** object's database in shared mode.

2. Determine the locking mode to use.

3. Open the **Recordset** using the **OpenRecordset** method and set the *options* argument equal to the locking mode you want.

4. Close the **Recordset** object when you're finished with it to release any recordset-level locks.

For example, the following code opens the Orders table exclusively by combining the dbDenyWrite and the dbDenyRead option constants. For the duration of the procedure, no other users can access this table:

```
Sub OpenTableExclusive()
    Dim dbsOrdEntry As Database
    Dim rstOrders As Recordset
    Dim errCurrent As Error

    ' Open the database in shared mode.
    Set dbsOrdEntry = OpenDatabase _
        ("C:\Samples\Chap06\Ordentry.mdb", False)

    ' Open the Orders table exclusively.
    On Error Resume Next
    Set rstOrders = dbsOrdEntry.OpenRecordset _
        ("Orders", dbOpenTable, dbDenyRead + dbDenyWrite)

    If Err <> 0 Then
        ' Errors occurred: Display them.
        For Each errCurrent In DBEngine.Errors
            Debug.Print errCurrent.Description
        Next
    Else
        ' No errors: The table is ours exclusively.
        Debug.Print "Opened Orders Table Exclusive"
    End If

    rstOrders.Close
    dbsOrdEntry.Close
End Sub
```

**Note**  If you open a **Recordset** object without specifying any value for the *options* argument, Microsoft Jet uses page locking by default: The **Recordset** is opened in shared mode; it does not lock other users out of its data, and locks only the data being edited in the current page.

## Checking for Errors when Opening Recordsets

As with opening databases exclusively, setting locks on recordsets can cause errors if the lock fails. Using the four-step process described earlier, you can handle recordset locking problems with a generic procedure that takes into account the most common multiuser errors.

The most common error in locking recordsets occurs when another user has the recordset open in a way that prevents you from obtaining the lock you want. This is identified as error 3262. The following table explains this error.

| Error code and text | Cause and suggested response |
|---|---|
| **3262** Couldn't lock *<object> <objectname>*; currently in use by user *<username>* on machine *<machinename>*. | Occurs when you attempt to use the **OpenRecordset** method based on an object that cannot be locked. This is usually another user who has the same table or tables locked in a way that prevents your lock.<br><br>Wait a short interval and retry the operation. |

# Using Page Locking

This level of locking causes only the page containing the row currently being edited to be locked. You may recall from Chapter 1, "An Overview of Microsoft Jet," Microsoft Jet accesses and locks data in pages of 2048 bytes. When you use page locking, which is the default locking level for **Recordset** objects, other users can read data from the locked page, but cannot change it. You control page locking by specifying the locking mode. In the parts of your application that lock data at the page level, you must determine which locking mode you're going to use. The locking mode determines how Microsoft Jet actually locks the data. Two modes of page locking are available: pessimistic locking and optimistic locking.

## Pessimistic Locking

Using pessimistic locking, the engine locks the page that contains the row being edited as soon as the **Edit** method is issued, and doesn't release the lock until the changes to the row are explicitly posted or canceled. Pessimistic locking is the default locking mode for recordsets.

For more information, see Chapter 5, "Working with Records and Fields."

**Note** Explicit transactions change the behavior regarding when a lock is released.

The primary advantage of pessimistic locking is that after you have obtained a lock, you know that you will not encounter any locking conflicts as long as the row is locked. Additionally, pessimistic locking is the only way to guarantee that your application reads the most current data, because one user can't change a row after another has begun editing it.

The disadvantage of pessimistic locking is that the entire page containing the row is locked for the duration of the procedure that has edited and locked the row. If you're giving users access to data through a user interface, there is also the problem of a user starting an edit on a row, locking it, and leaving the computer for a period of time. This causes not only the row the user is editing to be locked, but possibly other records that reside within the locked page.

The following code gives an example of how to implement pessimistic locking:

```
Sub LockPessimistic()
    Dim dbsOrdEntry As Database
    Dim rstOrders As Recordset
    Dim errCurrent As Error
    Dim fEdit As Boolean

    On Error GoTo 0
    ' Open the database in shared mode.
    Set dbsOrdEntry = OpenDatabase _
        ("C:\Samples\Chap06\Ordentry.mdb", False)

    ' Open the Orders table in shared mode.
    Set rstOrders = dbsOrdEntry.OpenRecordset("Orders", dbOpenDynaset)

    ' Set the multiuser options for the recordset.
    With rstOrders
        ' Setting LockEdits to True tells Jet to use
        ' pessimistic locking.
        .LockEdits = True
        .FindFirst "[OrderID]=10565"

        ' Try to edit the row. This causes a lock attempt.
        fEdit = True
        Do While True
            On Error Resume Next
            .Edit
            ' If lock fails, allow user to retry.
            If Err <> 0 Then
                If MsgBox("Cannot edit: " & Error$ & " Try again?", _
                    vbYesNo + vbQuestion) <> vbYes Then
                    fEdit = False
                    Exit Do
                End If
            Else
                Exit Do
            End If
        Loop

        ' If row was locked, make changes and post.
        If fEdit Then
            ![ShipName] = "New2 Address"
            .Update
```

```
        Else
            ' Cancel the edit.
            .CancelUpdate
        End If
    End With


    rstOrders.Close
    dbsOrdEntry.Close
End Sub
```

## Optimistic Locking

With optimistic locking, the engine locks the page only when you try to post the row changes using the **Update** method. Because the lock is applied only when your application attempts to post changes, the time the lock is in place is minimized; this is optimistic locking's main advantage.

The disadvantage of optimistic locking is that when a user begins to edit a row, you can't be sure that the update will succeed. An update that relies on optimistic locking fails if another user changes a row that the first user is editing. Imagine a scenario where users Mike and Maya are editing the same row. Using optimistic locking, Mike starts editing the Acme customer row. Because Mike's optimistically locked row is not actually locked, there is nothing to prevent Maya from attempting to edit the same row. Maya starts editing the same Acme row. Unfortunately, Maya has no idea that Mike is already editing the row, and also does not have the most up-to-date view of the data. When Mike attempts to save his changes, he receives an error because Maya is also editing the row.

▶   **To use optimistic locking in your code**

1. Open a table- or dynaset-type **Recordset** on the data you want to edit.

2. Move to the row you're interested in.

3. Enable optimistic locking by setting the **LockEdits** property of the **Recordset** to **False**.

4. Use the **Edit** method to allow edits to the row (the row is not yet locked).

5. Make changes to the row.

6. Post the row changes using the **Update** method (this attempts to lock the row).

7. Check to see if the **Update** method succeeded. If it didn't, try again.

The following code gives an example of how to implement optimistic locking:

```
Sub LockOptimistic()
    Dim dbsOrdEntry As Database
    Dim rstOrders As Recordset
    Dim errCurrent As Error
```

```
On Error GoTo 0
' Open the database in shared mode.
Set dbsOrdEntry = OpenDatabase _
    ("C:\Samples\Chap06\Ordentry.mdb", False)

' Open the Orders table in shared mode.
Set rstOrders = dbsOrdEntry.OpenRecordset("Orders", dbOpenDynaset)

' Set the multiuser options for the recordset.
With rstOrders
    ' Setting LockEdits to False tells Jet to use
    ' optimistic locking.
    .LockEdits = False
    .FindFirst "[OrderID]=10565"
    .Edit
    ![ShipName] = "New3 Address"

    ' Check for errors when trying to post the row.
    Do While True
        On Error Resume Next
        .Update
        If Err <> 0 Then
            If MsgBox("Cannot post: " & Error$ & " Try again?", _
                vbYesNo + vbQuestion) <> vbYes Then
                ' Cancel the edit.
                .CancelUpdate
                Exit Do
            End If
        Else
            Exit Do
        End If
    Loop
End With

rstOrders.Close
dbsOrdEntry.Close
End Sub
```

It's important to note that optimistic locking turns into pessimistic locking when transactions are used. Because a transaction holds a write lock until the transaction is committed, a pessimistic locking mode occurs even though the **LockEdits** property may have been set to **False**. Also, it's possible for the **Update** method to fail in optimistic locking. Just because a write lock has not been placed by an **Edit** method, it does not mean that a write lock is not being placed by the **Update** method. In other words, one user could have a **Recordset** open with pessimistic locking and cause the other user to fail when updating the same data in optimistic mode.

## Checking for Errors with Page Locking

For more information on Microsoft Jet error codes, see Appendix D, "Error Reference."

When using page locks, before proceeding, your code must check to see if the attempted lock succeeded. As with the previous examples, use the four-step process of disabling error handling, attempting the operation that will initiate a lock, checking for errors, and finally, re-enabling error handling.

Most of the page-locking multiuser errors your code encounters will be one of the following three. These aren't the only errors, just the most commons ones.

| Error code and text | Cause and suggested response |
| --- | --- |
| 3186  Couldn't save; currently locked by user *<name>* on machine *<name>*. | This error occurs when a user attempts to update a page that contains a read lock placed by another user. |
| | To handle this error, wait for a short interval, and then try to save the row again. Optionally, you can inform users of the problem and allow them to indicate whether or not they want to retry the operation. |
| 3197  Data has changed; operation stopped. | This error occurs when you use the **Edit** method or the **Update** method and another user has changed the current row since you opened the **Recordset** or last read data from the row. |
| | If this error occurs when you use the **Edit** method, you may want to refresh the user's view of the data with the current data and then attempt the **Edit** method a second time. |
| | If this error occurs when you use the **Update** method, you're using optimistic locking and the row has changed since you used the **Edit** method. Inform the user that someone else has changed the data. You may want to display the current data and give the user the choice of whether to overwrite the other user's changes or cancel edits. |
| 3260  Couldn't update; currently locked by user *<name>* on machine *<name>*. | This error occurs when you use the **Edit** method and the page containing the current row is locked, and when you use the **AddNew** method or the **Update** method. |
| | This error also occurs when you use the **Update** method to save a row on a locked page. This situation can occur when a user is trying to save a new row or when you're using optimistic locking and another user locks the page. |
| | To handle this error, wait for a short interval, and then try to save the row again. Optionally, you can inform users of the problem and allow them to indicate whether or not they want to retry the operation. |

In the previous LockPessimistic procedure, the code checked to see if an error occurred and reacted regardless of the type of error. This example can be made more versatile by actually checking the error that occurs and responding to it. The following function modifies the LockPessimistic procedure to include better error handling:

```
Sub EditARecord()
    Dim dbsOrdEntry As Database
    Dim rstOrders As Recordset
    Dim errCurrent As Error
    Dim fEdit As Boolean
    Dim intLockCount As Integer
    Dim intRndCount As Integer
    Dim intChoice As Integer
    Dim intX As Integer

    On Error GoTo 0
    ' Open the database in shared mode.
    Set dbsOrdEntry = OpenDatabase _
        ("C:\Samples\Chap06\Ordentry.mdb", False)

    ' Open the Orders table in shared mode.
    Set rstOrders = dbsOrdEntry.OpenRecordset("Orders", dbOpenDynaset)

    ' Set the multiuser options for the recordset.
    With rstOrders
        ' Setting LockEdits to True tells Jet to use
        ' pessimistic locking.
        .LockEdits = True
        .FindFirst "[OrderID]=10565"

        ' Try to edit the row. This will cause a lock attempt.
        fEdit = True
        Do While True
            On Error GoTo LockError
            .Edit
            ' If lock fails, allow user to retry.
            If Err = 0 Then
                Exit Do
            End If
        Loop

        ' If row was locked, make changes and post.
        If fEdit Then
            ![ShipName] = "New4 Address"
            .Update
```

```
            Else
                ' Cancel the edit.
                .CancelUpdate
            End If
        End With

EditARecord_Exit:
    rstOrders.Close
    dbsOrdEntry.Close
    Exit Sub

LockError:
    Select Case Err.Number
        ' Data has changed since last read.
        Case 3197
            ' Refresh Recordset for a second try.
            rstOrders.CancelUpdate
            Resume
        Case 3260
            ' Row is locked.
            intLockCount = intLockCount + 1
            'Tried to get the lock twice already.
            If intLockCount > 2 Then
                ' Allow user to choose Cancel/Retry.
                intChoice = MsgBox(Err.Description & " Retry?", _
                    vbYesNo + vbQuestion)
                If intChoice = vbYes Then
                    intLockCount = 1
                Else
                    Resume FailedEdit
                End If
            End If

            ' Yield to Windows.
            DoEvents
            ' Delay a short random interval,
            ' longer each time the lock fails.
            intRndCount = intLockCount ^ 2 * Int(Rnd * 3000 + 1000)
            For intX = 1 To intRndCount: Next intX
            ' Try the edit again.
            Resume
        Case Else
            ' Unanticipated error.
            MsgBox ("Error " & Err.Number & ": " & Err.Description)
            Resume FailedEdit
    End Select
```

```
FailedEdit: ' Begin contingency procedure if edit fails.
    MsgBox "This row could not be edited. Please try again later."
    GoTo EditARecord_Exit
End Sub
```

This code works by moving the program's execution to the LockError section when an error occurs. The code in the LockError section checks the specific error message and tries to correct the problem. It also allows the user the retry or cancel the operation. Note the technique of specifying a random interval for retrying the operation. This is an important technique for making sure two users vying for the same row don't end up in a deadlock situation where code is trying to lock the row at the same time. By introducing a random element into the timing loop, you can minimize the chances of a deadlock.

# Testing a Row for Locking Status

You may want to test a row to check if it's locked without actually locking its page or pages. In Microsoft Jet 3.0, **Recordset** objects have an **EditMode** property. You can use this property in conjunction with the **LockEdits** property to determine if the current row is locked.

The following procedure tests whether the current row in a given **Recordset** is on a locked page:

```
Function fIsRecordLocked(rstCheck As Recordset) As Boolean
    fIsRecordLocked = False

    If rstCheck.LockEdits Then
        If rstCheck.EditMode = dbEditInProgress Then
            fIsRecordLocked = True
        End If
    End If
End Function
```

If you're using Microsoft Jet 2.0, the **EditMode** property is not available. In this situation, you can accomplish the same test by setting the **LockEdits** property of the **Recordset** to **True**, using the **Edit** method to attempt a lock, and then trapping code 3260 if it occurs.

The following procedure tests whether the current row in a given **Recordset** is on a locked page without using the **EditMode** property:

```
Function fIsRecordLocked2(rstCheck As Recordset) As Boolean
    fIsRecordLocked2 = False

    On Error GoTo IsRecordLocked2_Err
    With rstCheck
        .LockEdits = True
        ' Attempt the lock.
        .Edit
```

```
                   ' Cancel the edit.
                   .MoveNext
                   .MovePrevious
             End With
             Exit Function

    IsRecordLocked2_Err:
             fIsRecordLocked2 = True
             Exit Function
    End Function
```

# The Page-Locking Challenge

One of the most common questions raised by developers who are starting their first multiuser Microsoft Jet application is: How do I lock a row? The short answer is: You don't. You have seen that Microsoft Jet reads, writes, and locks data a page at a time, not a row at a time. Depending on the size of the row, the page may contain more than one row. The problem arises that by locking a row, you're locking all the rows on that page. This may cause a problem in high-concurrency applications where unhindered access to specific rows is of paramount concern. You can see how this works in Figure 6.5.

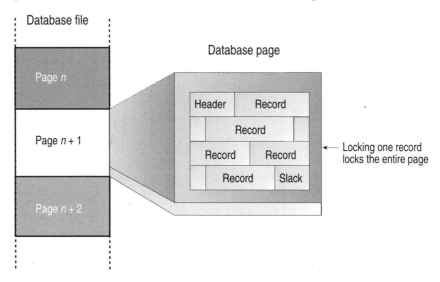

**Figure 6.5    Page locking**

You can use various strategies to work around this design.

The recommended way is to use the SQL DDL CHAR data type, which is a fixed-length data type. With this method, you don't have to pad the column with data as you do with the methods described in the following paragraphs. Therefore, using the CHAR data type is the easiest and only guaranteed way to force this technique. The CHAR data type, however, is not available through the Microsoft Access user interface and can only be used with SQL DDL commands such as ALTER TABLE and CREATE TABLE.

Another strategy is to add columns to the table using the Microsoft Access **Text** data type until the row length is greater than 1024 bytes. Using the **Text** data type is not recommended for this implementation because it's a variable-length data type and you must explicitly pad out the columns with data to achieve a fixed-length format.

Using the Microsoft Access **Format** property is also not recommended to force padding when a row is being added because Microsoft Access only recognizes the **Format** property associated with the table. Other applications that use Microsoft Jet do not recognize the **Format** property and would not properly pad the row.

Using either of these techniques may cause performance degradations because the size of the database will increase due to the fact that every row will occupy 2K of disk space.

For more information on client/server applications, see Chapter 9, "Developing Client/Server Applications."

Another strategy is to use optimistic locking wherever possible. Although optimistic locking does not eliminate page locking, it does minimize the amount of time that a row is locked and therefore minimizes the possibility that an unwanted row will also be locked.

Finally, if neither of these approaches is acceptable, you may want to consider either moving your application to a client/server environment using a server that supports row locking, or implementing your own custom locking scheme as described in the following section.

# Implementing a Custom Locking Scheme

You might encounter situations in your multiuser application where the behavior of page locking is not appropriate, and where the use of optimistic locking is not a suitable workaround. In this case, you may want to consider your own custom locking scheme. Implemented through a set of routines that you write, custom locking completely bypasses Microsoft Jet locking. Your code controls locking by identifying when a row should be locked and unlocked.

The most common approach to this technique is to have a semaphore, or lock table, that identifies when a row is locked. The lock table typically identifies rows by storing the key value of the row, the lock status (locked or unlocked), and the name of the user who has the row locked.

The implementation of a custom locking scheme is not for the faint of heart. It requires a great deal of design, implementation, and testing time, and in many cases, cannot duplicate functionality that is built into Microsoft Jet. For example, even if you implement single-row locking, it would be very difficult to handle data in a **Recordset** that is based on more than one table, because you would have to determine all the tables that contain records that have to be locked. Custom locking schemes are most attractive when they affect only a few tables and are not based on a data model with complex joins and relationships.

# Other Issues in Multiuser Design

Up to this point, the issue of locking has been covered as the main multiuser issue. It is, however, not the only issue. When designing an application for multiuser access, you should keep in mind several additional factors. This section covers these factors.

# Refreshing Data Access Objects Collections

In a single-user system, Data Access Objects always keep track of changes to their collections. As you add objects to collections and delete objects from collections, the engine knows about these changes. However, in a multiuser setting, other users may be modifying collections by adding new tables or queries to the database, or deleting existing objects. In this case, DAO doesn't automatically keep track of changes to collections.

Take the example of the following code, which displays all the **TableDef** objects in the current database:

```
Sub ShowAllTables (dbsTest As Database)
    Dim tblTemp As TableDef

    For Each tblTemp In dbsTest.TableDefs
    Debug.Print tblTemp.Name
    Next tblTemp
End Sub
```

When this code runs, it takes a snapshot of the **TableDefs** collection as it exists at that time. It iterates through each **TableDef** object and displays its name. Assume you have to run this code twice. The first time you run it, ten table names are displayed. But before you can run it again, another user on the network who also has the database open adds a new table. Now you run the code again. It still displays ten table names. This is because DAO doesn't automatically know about changes made to the collections by other users. The solution to this problem is the **Refresh** method. This method forces Microsoft Jet to re-inventory the database and update the collection with the most recent changes.

For more information
on DAO, see Chapter
2, "Introducing Data
Access Objects."

To change the previous code to always display the most current list of TableDefs,
add a **Refresh** method:

```
Sub BetterShowAllTables (dbsTest As Database)
    Dim tblTemp As TableDef

    dbsTest.TableDefs.Refresh
    For Each tblTemp In dbsTest.TableDefs
        Debug.Print tblTemp.Name
    Next tblTemp
End Sub
```

# Requerying Data

If your multiuser application presents data to the user in a visual form, such as in
a window, you may want to update the user's view with the most current data.
While this functionality is automatically available to applications using Microsoft
Access, your application based on Visual Basic or some other language must
explicitly requery data to get the most current view of other users' changes.

To obtain the most current view of data in a **Recordset**, you must first determine
if the **Recordset** supports the **Requery** method. You can do this by checking the
value of the **Restartable** property of the **Recordset**. If the value is **True**, you can
refresh the **Recordset** object's contents by using the **Requery** method. This causes
Microsoft Jet to repopulate the **Recordset** with the most current data.

If the **Recordset** doesn't support the **Requery** method, you must open the
**Recordset** again with the **OpenRecordset** method. The following code illustrates
how to generically requery a **Recordset**. The OpenRecordsetForRequery
procedure opens a dynaset-type **Recordset** on the Orders table. It then tries to
refresh the **Recordset** object's contents by calling fRequeryIfYouCan. If this fails,
it reopens the **Recordset**.

```
Sub OpenRecordsetForRequery()
    Dim dbsOrdEntry As Database
    Dim rstOrders As Recordset

    Set dbsOrdEntry = OpenDatabase _
        ("C:\Samples\Chap06\OrdEntry.mdb", False)
    Set rstOrders = dbsOrdEntry.OpenRecordset _
        ("Orders", dbOpenDynaset)

    If fRequeryIfYouCan(rstOrders) Then
        Debug.Print "Recordset has been refreshed."
    Else
        Set rstOrders = dbsOrdEntry.OpenRecordset _
            ("Orders", dbOpenDynaset)
        Debug.Print "Recordset has been reopened."
    End If
```

```
      rstOrders.Close
      dbsOrdEntry.Close
End Sub

Function fRequeryIfYouCan(rstTest As Recordset)
    If rstTest.Restartable Then
    rstTest.Requery
    fRequeryIfYouCan = True
    Else
    fRequeryIfYouCan = False
    End If
End Function
```

In general, most **Recordset** objects are restartable (or can be requeried). The exceptions are recordsets based on pass-through queries and on crosstab queries without fixed column widths. These types of recordsets cannot be requeried and must be reopened to get the most current state of the data.

# Using Transactions in the Multiuser Environment

You can use Microsoft Jet transactions to group updates in atomic units that can be committed or rolled back as a whole. Because transactions buffer updates to a temporary file instead of real tables, they also have useful effects in multiuser environments. The most common use of transactions in multiuser environments is to make sure users don't see an incomplete view of shared data as it's being changed.

For example, assume your application is running code that is updating data, and another user is simultaneously running a report on that data. If your updates are not wrapped in a transaction, the user running the report could receive inconsistent data with some records updated by your code, some not. By wrapping your updates in a transaction, you make sure the other users' view of the shared data is not affected by your running code until your code is complete.

For more information on transactions, see Chapter 5, "Working with Records and Fields."

Of course, no benefits come without some type of drawback. Be careful of keeping a transaction open too long. All locks that result from your edits with the transaction are kept in place until the transaction is committed or rolled back. This can have harmful effects on the multiuser concurrency of your application.

# Auto-Increment Fields

There are issues with auto-increment fields and locking. Because the value of the next **Counter** number is stored in the table-header page of the database file, Microsoft Jet locks that page when adding a row to a table that has a **Counter** data type. This occurs in Microsoft Jet 2.*x* when inserting a row into another table.

# Identifying Users

In your multiuser application, you may want to programmatically identify the user currently logged on to the system. This is useful for administrative functions such as storing the user's name with edited records to create an audit trail. Several methods are available to achieve this functionality. One involves Microsoft Jet security, another requires you to maintain your own user information, and another requires using utilities included on the CD-ROM.

By implementing a secure database, you force the user to log on to your application with a predefined user name and password. The user name is then available to your application through the **UserName** property of the **Workspace** object. The following procedure writes the user's name and the current date and time to fields:

For more information on users and passwords, see Chapter 10, "Managing Security."

```
Sub WriteAuditTrail(rstCurrent As Recordset)
    ' This example assumes that rstCurrent contains the fields
    ' named UserLastModified and DateLastModified and that
    ' a Move method has positioned the current row.
    rstCurrent.MoveFirst ' Move to first row for this example.
    rstCurrent.Edit
    rstCurrent!UserLastModified = Workspaces(0).UserName
    rstCurrent!DateLastModified = Now
    rstCurrent.Update
End Sub
```

For information on how to use LDBVIEW.EXE and MSLDBUSR.DLL, see "Understanding Jet Locking" on the companion CD-ROM. You can find it in the Papers folder under JETLOCK.DOC.

If you don't want to implement security, but still require user name functionality, you can have your application prompt the user for a name and password at startup and store those values in code variables or a temporary table. This way, you still have access to the user's name, but don't have to implement a secured database.

A new (currently unsupported) way to get this information is to use the graphical 32-bit–only LDBVIEW.EXE or programmatic 32-bit MSLDBUSR.DLL utilities. These are found on the CD-ROM that comes with this guide.

# Optimizing Multiuser Applications

In most scenarios, the very act of implementing a database system in a multiuser environment incurs a substantial performance penalty. Few networks in the world supply "across the wire" performance that approaches local disk access performance. Given this, your biggest tasks in optimizing your multiuser application are minimizing network traffic and identifying and eliminating bottlenecks in your LAN. Most of the following suggestions are based on this supposition that decreasing network traffic has the largest effect on your application's performance.

# Minimizing Network Traffic for Data

Most of the optimizations you perform for data access in a single-user environment create equal, if not greater, improvements in multiuser environments. When you optimize a single-user application, you're concerned only with that application's performance on a local machine. When you optimize a multiuser application, reductions in network traffic help not only the individual user, but all users of the application.

For example, consider the case where your application has to search for a row on a table that has no indexes. In this scenario, Microsoft Jet must perform a *sequential scan* of the entire table to find a match. This means that the entire table must be sent from the server to the workstation's copy of the engine. If the table is large, this can be a quite lengthy operation. The problem is further compounded because the user running the search is waiting a long time for a response, and the high volume of network traffic is in turn slowing down other users. This situation can be alleviated by adding indexes to the table for the columns on which your application searches. However, keep in mind that having indexes may cause increased network traffic and may reduce concurrency and efficient performance.

In another example, assume that your application uses a set of tables containing lookup data that represents zip codes or lists of part numbers and doesn't change often. By moving this type of data to the local workstation, you can eliminate network access that may be made hundreds of times during the application's typical execution.

# Minimizing Network Traffic for Static Objects

As discussed earlier in this chapter, the location of objects in a multiuser application has a direct effect on the application's performance. Consider the following worst-case scenario.

A user has a workstation with 8 MB of RAM and a 200 MB hard disk, of which 100 MB is unused. The software on this machine consists of MS-DOS and the necessary network software to connect to the file server. The user runs your multiuser application completely from the network. This means that he or she has to load Microsoft Windows, Microsoft Jet, and your application from the network. Additionally, every byte of data access, whether it's from a live data table or from a static object such as a query, has to come across the network. Finally, the user is using a temporary swap file mapped to a network drive.

Obviously, this user is not going to be happy with your application's performance. In fact, it would be surprising if the user could even run your application. To understand how to minimize network traffic for static objects, it's useful to work backward from this worst-case scenario and address the individual problems.

You know that the user has the necessary disk space to allow you to move your application to the local level. Start by moving the support software to the user's workstation. This includes installing the operating system, such as Microsoft Windows, on the workstation, setting a permanent swap file on the local drive, and installing the Microsoft Jet components locally. Next, consider whether or not to install the workgroup database for your application at the local level.

Then, install your application on the user's local drive. If your application is based on Microsoft Access, install it locally. If your application is based on VBA or some other language, install the necessary resources such as executable files and dynamic link libraries locally. Figure 6.6 illustrates this optimization technique.

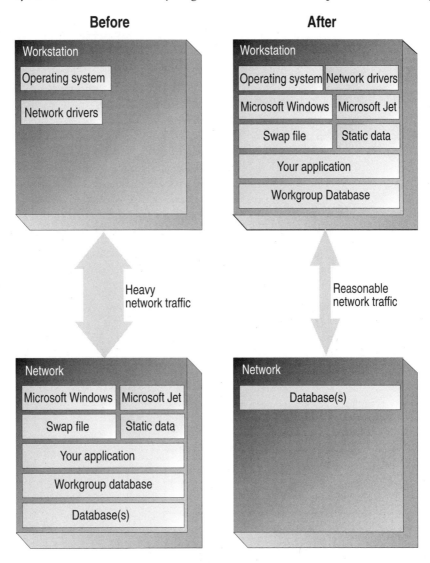

Figure 6.6   Optimizing a workstation

Finally, investigate bottlenecks occurring on your LAN that are due to hardware. You might want to try the following:

- Segment the LAN into subnets. Typically, a server has only one network interface card (NIC) with many nodes connected to it. To reduce this bottleneck, add multiple NICs to the server and spread the nodes across those segments. This is probably the cheapest and biggest performance win because it substantially reduces collisions on the wire and gives each station a larger slice of bandwidth to communicate with the server.

- Add a better NIC to the server. Practically all Pentium systems now come with PCI slots. By using PCI NICs you can experience significantly faster throughput while keeping the CPU utilization lower. Also, many PCI NICs offer a multi-ported design, thus allowing you to do multiple segments from one PCI NIC. An example of this is a server with two PCI slots that uses two four-port PCI NICs. This creates eight segments that go to 36 nodes to reduce collisions on the wire and increase the bandwidth that each node has when communicating with the server. This would allow you to focus on performance issues that are software related instead of hardware related.

  Another option with PCI NICs is the 100 MB Ethernet standard. While the 100 MB hubs required to accompany the 100 MB NICs are expensive, they do provide an alternative to reducing performance issues going over the wire and use existing cabling.

- Add faster disk drives and host adapters to the server. Again, moving to PCI- or EISA-based host adapters can have a significant impact on performance. To eliminate this bottleneck, one approach is to configure the server to use an EISA SCSI RAID controller using eight 1-GB SCSI drives. This increases performance because the EISA card reduces CPU processing by handling some processing itself, and because the RAID configuration allows reads and writes to be spread across the eight disk drives, thus reducing contention issues when trying to access a drive. This is probably the most expensive solution, but it makes a big performance improvement over a one ISA card – one disk solution.

C H A P T E R   7

# Database Replication

*Database replication* is the technology for copying a database so that two or more copies remain synchronized. The original database is converted into a *Design Master* and each subsequent copy of the database is called a *replica*. Together, the Design Master and the replicas comprise the *replica set*. Each member of the replica set contains a common set of replicable objects such as tables, queries, forms, reports, macros, or modules. Each member of the replica set also can contain nonreplicable—or local—objects. Replicas that belong to the same replica set can exchange updates of data or replicable objects. This exchange is called *synchronization*.

If you design your applications for multiple users, database replication can improve the way your users share data. Using database replication, you can reproduce a database so that two or more users can work on their own replica of the database at the same time. Although replicas can be located on different computers or in different offices, they remain synchronized. This chapter discusses how to create and use replicas of your application database.

## Contents

For information on copying the code examples from the companion CD-ROM to your hard disk drive, see "Using the Companion CD-ROM" in the Preface.

### Using CH07.MDB and CHAP07.VBP

If you copied the samples from the companion CD-ROM, you can find the code examples for Microsoft Access in C:\SAMPLES\CHAP07\ ACCESS\CH07.MDB. The corresponding code examples for Visual Basic are in C:\SAMPLES\CHAP07\VB40\CHAP07.VBP.

To run any of the code examples in this chapter, open the .MDB file in Microsoft Access or open the .VBP file in Microsoft Visual Basic 4.0. You can use the examples to help you understand the concepts discussed in the chapter—or you can modify them and use them in your own applications.

# Why Use Database Replication?

The new approach and flexibility that Microsoft Jet database replication offers can be illustrated by the development of a simple application. Imagine that a client has asked you to develop a contact management application that the company's field sales staff can use to monitor sales and orders. Each sales representative has a laptop computer that can be connected to the company's network.

A traditional approach to building this application is to separate the tables from the other objects in the database so that the data can reside on a network server while the queries, forms, reports, macros, and modules reside on the user's computer. When sales representatives want to retrieve or update information in the database, they each log on to the network, open a ContactForm database on the computer, and open the ContactData database from the server.

Database replication enables you to take a new approach to building this application by creating a single database that contains both the data and objects, and then making replicas of the database for each sales representative. Or you can use attached tables and replicate the data database and application database separately. You can make replicas on each user's computer and synchronize each replica with the replica on a network server. Sales representatives update the replicas on their computers during the course of a work session, and you synchronize their replicas with the replica on the server as needed. You can also create a set of local objects such as tables, forms, or reports that are used at only one replica location.

Database replication is well suited to business applications that need to:

- **Share data among offices.**   You can use database replication to create copies of a corporate database to send to each satellite office. Each location enters data into its replica, and all remote replicas are synchronized with the replica at corporate headquarters. An individual replica can maintain local tables that contain information not included in the other replicas in the set.

- **Share data among dispersed users.**   New information that is entered into the database while sales representatives are out of the office can be synchronized any time the sales representatives establish an electronic link with the corporate network. As part of their workday routine, sales representatives can dial into the network, synchronize the replica, and work on the most current version of the database. Because only the incremental changes are transmitted during synchronization, the time and expense of keeping up-to-date are minimized.

- **Make server data more accessible.**   If your application doesn't need to have immediate updates to data, you can use database replication to reduce the network load on your primary server. Introducing a second server with its own copy of the database improves response time. You determine the schedule for synchronizing the replicas and can adjust that schedule to meet the changing needs of your users. Replication requires less centralized administration of the database while offering greater access to centralized data.

- **Distribute application updates.**   When you replicate your application, you automatically replicate not only the data in your tables, but also your application's objects. If you make changes to the design of the database, the changes are transmitted during the next synchronization; you don't have to distribute complete new versions of the software.

- **Back up data.**   At first glance, database replication might appear to be very similar to copying a database. However, while replication initially makes a complete copy of the database, thereafter it simply synchronizes that replica's objects with the original objects at regular intervals. This copy can be used to recover data if the original database is destroyed. Furthermore, users at any replica can continue to access the database during the entire backup process.

Although database replication can solve many of the problems inherent in distributed database processing, it is important to recognize at least two situations in which replication is less than ideal:

- **Large numbers of record updates at multiple replicas**   Applications that require frequent updates of existing records in different replicas are likely to have more record conflicts than applications that simply insert new records into a database. Record conflicts occur when any changes are made to the same record by users at different locations at the same time. Applications with more record conflicts require more administrative time because the conflicts must be resolved manually.

- **Data consistency is critical**   Applications that rely on information being correct at all times, such as funds transfer, airline reservations, and the tracking of package shipments, usually use a transaction method. While transactions can be processed within a replica, there is no support for processing transactions across replicas. The information exchanged between replicas during synchronization is the *result* of the transaction, not the transaction itself.

# The Tools for Implementing Database Replication

You can implement Microsoft Jet database replication with:

- Microsoft Access for Windows 95 running under Windows 95 or Windows NT 3.51

- Briefcase replication in Windows 95 running under Windows 95 only (installed through Microsoft Access for Windows 95)

- Microsoft Replication Manager running under Windows 95 or Windows NT 3.51 (installed through the Microsoft Access Developer's Toolkit)

- DAO programming under Windows 95 or Windows NT 3.51

The first three replication tools provide an easy-to-use visual interface, while the last enables programmers to build replication directly into their applications.

Replication can be used on a variety of computer networks, including Windows 95 peer-to-peer networks, Windows NT 3.51, and Novell NetWare 3.*x* and 4.*x* network servers.

## Microsoft Access Replication

Microsoft Access for Windows 95 provides users with replication commands while they are working in their databases. Users point to Replication on the **Tools** menu and have a choice of:

- Creating a replica

- Synchronizing their replica with another member of the replica set

- Resolving synchronization conflicts

- Recovering the replica set's Design Master, if necessary

**Microsoft Access Users**  If you have a copy of Microsoft Access for Windows 95, one of the easiest ways to become familiar with the concepts and procedures associated with database replication is to experiment with the Microsoft Access replication commands. Open an existing Microsoft Jet database using Microsoft Access, click on the **Tools** menu, point to Replication, and then click **Create Replica** to both convert your database to a Design Master and create a replica. You can then explore the changes made to the design of your database (these are explained in detail in the "Changes to Your Database" section later in this chapter) and the similarities of the replica to the Design Master. Next, make a change to the data in the replica and a change to a table design in the Design Master, and then click Synchronize Now. You can then open the replica and Design Master to confirm that the changes made appear in the other member of the replica set.

# Briefcase Replication

Windows 95 enables users to use replication when they drag a database file into their Briefcase. To use Briefcase replication, simply drag the Microsoft Jet database file from Windows 95 Explorer to the My Briefcase icon on your desktop or portable computer. When you are finished working on the files on the portable computer, reconnect to your main computer and on the **Briefcase** menu click **Update All** to automatically merge the files on your main computer with the modified files in your Briefcase.

Internally, Briefcase works in the following way. When Briefcase replication is installed through the Custom installation option in Microsoft Access for Windows 95, it registers with the Windows 95 Briefcase a special class ID (CLSID) for Microsoft Jet 3.0 .MDB files. When a file with the .MDB extension is dragged into Briefcase, the Briefcase reconciler code is called to convert the database into a replicable form. Before the conversion takes place, however, the reconciler asks if you want to make a backup copy of the original database file. The backup copy has the same file name as the original, except that it has a .BAK file name extension instead of an .MDB file name extension. The copy is kept in the same folder as the original database file.

The reconciler then converts the database into a replicable form, leaves the Design Master at the source, and places a replica in the Briefcase. The reconciler also gives you the option of putting the Design Master into your Briefcase and leaving a replica on the desktop.

You can take your replica with you into the field and then synchronize the changes made on your laptop replica with changes made to the Design Master on the desktop or network. When you click **Update All** or **Update Selection** on the **Briefcase** menu, Briefcase calls the Merge Reconciler, which was also registered at Setup, to merge the changes to the two members of the replica set. Unlike Microsoft Replication Manager, Briefcase replication does not provide you with the ability to set a schedule for synchronizing with other members of the replica set. Synchronization occurs only at the time the **Update** command is clicked and only between the current member and the specified member.

**Note**  If some users of your database need to continue using it in its nonreplicable form, make a copy of your database before converting it to a replicable database.

# Microsoft Replication Manager Utility

You can use Microsoft Replication Manager, which is provided in the Microsoft Access Developer's Toolkit, if you need:

- To manage a large number of replicas.
- To support laptop users who are not always connected to a network. Laptop users can specify a network file location where synchronization information is deposited for later processing.
- To create replicas of more than one database.
- An easy way to set the schedules for synchronizing replicas. Microsoft Replication Manager provides a graphical user interface for scheduling synchronizations between replicas, as well as allowing on-demand synchronization using a single menu command.
- To configure synchronizations to send data, receive data, or send and receive data.
- Additional tools for troubleshooting errors.

Microsoft Replication Manager provides a visual interface for converting databases, making additional replicas, viewing the relationships between replicas, and setting the properties on replicas. One of the most important features of the Microsoft Replication Manager is that you can use it to schedule synchronizations ahead of time so they occur at anticipated times and can be completed unattended. Microsoft Replication Manager gives you the greatest control over the sequence and timetable for synchronization of any Microsoft Jet database engine tool.

Microsoft Replication Manager also runs under Microsoft Windows NT 3.51.

# DAO Programming

Microsoft Jet database replication provides extensions to the DAO programming interface to the Microsoft Jet database engine (available through Microsoft Access for Windows 95 or Microsoft Visual Basic 4.0). These extensions allow programmers and MIS support staff to implement several of the functions of Briefcase replication through DAO coding. You can use the extensions to:

- Convert a database into a replicable database.

- Make additional replicas.

- Synchronize replicas.

- Get and set specific properties of a replicable database.

## Choosing Microsoft Replication Manager or DAO

When you're building your replication-based application, you can use either Microsoft Replication Manager, DAO, or both. Deciding which one is best for your application depends on a few factors.

Microsoft Replication Manager offers the fastest way to create a replication system. You can use its graphical interface to quickly define a replication topology and set replication schedules—without programming. If possible, you should use Microsoft Replication Manager to incorporate replication into your application.

In some cases, DAO may be a better solution than Microsoft Replication Manager. Although DAO requires programming, it gives you the ability to customize your replication system. Generally, DAO should be used under the following circumstances:

- When you need to synchronize replicas on a non-periodic schedule or when certain events occur. For example, you might want to trigger synchronization whenever updated product pricing information is received from headquarters. Because Microsoft Replication Manager does not support event-based replication, you must use DAO to achieve this.

- When you need to distribute your replicated application to users who possess minimal computer expertise. In this case, building a replication application with DAO might be better because you could design a simplified replication interface or make replication completely transparent to users. Although you can distribute Microsoft Replication Manager to your customers on a royalty-free basis, it might not be suitable for users with minimal knowledge of computer concepts.

For more information, see the "Distributing Microsoft Replication Manager with Your Application" section later in this chapter.

## Other Compatible Programs

Microsoft Excel for Windows 95, Visual C++ 4.0, and Visual Basic 4.0 all use Microsoft Jet 3.0 directly or through DAO, and therefore, they can interface with Microsoft Jet database replication.

Microsoft Excel for Windows 95 is not equipped to make a database replicable. However, if Microsoft Excel updates a database that has been made replicable by another Microsoft product, any changes made to the database will correctly synchronize with other replicas.

Because organizations differ in which of the four tools they use to implement database replication, the remainder of this chapter addresses the concepts, planning, implementation, and troubleshooting issues that arise with programmatic control of replication. The next section begins the discussion by introducing concepts that might be new to or different from the way your organization is currently sharing data.

## Microsoft Jet Replication Architecture

The Microsoft Jet replication engine consists of six major components:

- Tracking layer
- Microsoft Replication Manager
- Transporter
- File system transport
- Briefcase reconciler
- Registry entries

The following diagram shows the relationship among these components and between the components and Microsoft Jet.

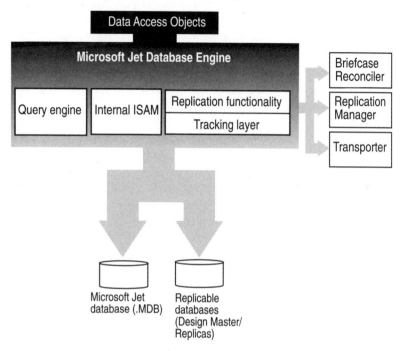

**Figure 7.1   The structure of Microsoft Jet database replication**

This section describes each of these components and identifies the files associated with each component.

# Tracking Layer

The ability to track changes in the database resides within the Microsoft Jet database engine. As its name implies, every action executed by Microsoft Jet at one replica is tracked and recorded in preparation for its transmission to other replicas. Both data and design changes are replicated. The main replication services, including the creation of replicable databases and replica synchronization are included in files MSWNG300.DLL, MSJTRCLR.DLL, and MSJT3032.DLL.

# Microsoft Replication Manager

As described earlier, Microsoft Replication Manager provides the management tools necessary to support replicated applications in dispersed locations. It also can be used to generate reports on the synchronization activity between replicas, which can be used to make sure the distributed application is performing as designed. Microsoft Replication Manager is included in files REPLMAN.EXE and MSJTRMI30.DLL.

# Transporter

For database replication to be useful, it is not enough for there just to be multiple replicas of the same database. The replicas must communicate with one another to remain synchronized. As mentioned earlier, synchronization is the act or process of making the replicas identical, both in terms of the data they contain and how they are designed; changes made to the existing records in one replica are communicated to each of the other replicas that have that same record. Similarly, new records added or old records deleted from one member of the replica set are communicated to each of the other members of the set.

If you use Briefcase or Microsoft Access to synchronize your replicas, Microsoft Jet handles the direct exchange of information between members.

If you use Microsoft Replication Manager, a separate utility called the *Transporter* monitors the changes to a replica and handles the actual exchange of data between replicas. With Microsoft Replication Manager, each replica must have a Transporter assigned to it.

---

**Note** Although you can have more than one Transporter assigned to the same replica, this approach is not recommended because it can cause undesirable side effects.

---

The Transporter performs either *direct* or *indirect* synchronizations between two members of a replica. Direct synchronization occurs when the two members can be opened simultaneously by either the Transporter or the Briefcase reconciler. If both members are on the same computer or are available over a common network, then the Transporter can apply the changes to one member directly to the other member. Indirect synchronization occurs when the target replica set member is not available because it is involved in another synchronization, the member is not in a shared folder, the other computer is temporarily disconnected from the network, the network itself is down, or in any other situation that prevents a direct connection.

When the Transporter is instructed to initiate a synchronization, it first attempts a direct connection with the target member of the replica set. If it can't establish a direct connection, the Transporter for the first member leaves a message for the Transporter of the second member at a shared folder on the network. The shared folder serves as a dropbox location for the target member and stores all the messages sent by all other Transporters in the replica set while the target member is unavailable.

Direct synchronizations are usually processed faster than indirect synchronizations because direct synchronizations allow the first Transporter to bypass the second Transporter completely. In indirect synchronizations, the return message to the first Transporter might take a few minutes, hours, or days, depending upon how often the second member connects to the network. Because a replica set member's availability can change over time, the Transporter might complete a direct synchronization one time and an indirect synchronization the next time. To determine whether a synchronization was direct or indirect, look at the exchange details in the MSysExchangeLog system table.

**Note**  The Transporter can run only on a computer running either Microsoft Windows 95 or Microsoft Windows NT 3.51. If a member of the replica set is stored on a non-Windows server, such as a Novell network, the Transporter must be located on a different computer.

You configure the Transporter through the Microsoft Replication Manager user interface. When Microsoft Replication Manager is first configured on a computer running Microsoft Windows 95 or Microsoft Windows NT 3.51, you are asked for the network folders to be used by the Transporter and whether the Transporter should be started automatically each time the computer is started. If you select automatic startup, a shortcut to the Transporter program is placed in the Windows 95 **Start** menu or the Windows NT Startup group. To change the Transporter startup to manual mode, you should move the Transporter icon to the Microsoft Access folder or program group. The file name for the Transporter is MSJTTR.EXE.

For information about restarting the Transporter if it stops, see Microsoft Replication Manager online Help.

The status of the Transporter is reported through the Microsoft Replication Manager user interface. At the lower-right corner of the map of the replica set, there is an image of two computers with a connection. The connection between the computers changes as the status of the Transporter changes, and a legend explains the status of the Transporter.

# File System Transport

The File System Transport provides messaging services to the Transporter. Later releases might have additional messaging services. The file name for the File System Transport is MSAJETFS.DLL.

# Briefcase Reconciler

The Briefcase reconciler is a special utility that is automatically executed when Windows 95 Briefcase is used. The reconciler ensures a database is replicable, and manages the merging of updates between the Briefcase replica and the Desktop replica. The Briefcase reconciler is implemented by MSJTRCLR.DLL and MSJRCI30.DLL.

# Registry Entries

Parameters for Microsoft Replication Manager, Transporter, and the Briefcase reconciler are stored in the Windows Registry.

The Registry entries for Microsoft Replication Manager under Windows 95 are:

HKEY_LOCAL_MACHINE\Software\Microsoft\Jet\3.0\Replication Manager\3.0

"Path"   c:\Program Files\Common Files\Microsoft Shared\Replication Manager\Replman.exe


The Registry entries for the Transporter under Windows 95 are:

HKEY_LOCAL_MACHINE\Software\Microsoft\Jet\3.0\Transporter

"Path"   c:\Program Files\Common Files\Microsoft Shared\Replication Manager\Msjttr.exe


The Registry entries for Microsoft Replication Manager under Windows NT are:

HKEY_LOCAL_MACHINE\Software\Microsoft\Jet\3.0\Replication Manager\3.0

"Path"   c:\WINNT\MSAPPS\Replication Manager\Replman.exe


The Registry entries for the Transporter under Windows NT are:

HKEY_LOCAL_MACHINE\Software\Microsoft\Jet\3.0\Transporter

"Path"   c:\WINNT\MSAPPS\Replication Manager\msjttr.exe

In addition there are many minor entries for Transporter log file location, last viewed replica, security database, and so on.

The Registry entries for the Briefcase reconciler are:

1.  HKEY_CLASSES_ROOT\CLSID\{ClassID of Access.Database.7}
\Roles\Reconciler =                {C20D7340-5525-101B-8F15-00AA003E4672}

2.  HKEY_CLASSES_ROOT\CLSID\{ClassID of Access.Database.7}
\Roles\NotifyReplica =             {C20D7340-5525-101B-8F15-00AA003E4672}

3.  HKEY_CLASSES_ROOT\CLSID\{C20D7340-5525-101B-8F15-
00AA003E4672}

    \InProcServer32 = "full path of msjtrclr.dll"

    \ResourceDll = "full path of msjrci30.dll"

    \SystemDb = "full path of system.mdw"

    \ThreadingModel = "Apartment"

4.  HKEY_CLASSES_ROOT\CLSID\{C20D7340-5525-101B-8F15-
00AA003E4672}                \SingleChangeHook

# Replica Set Topology

An important part of incorporating replication into your application is planning the appropriate topology for synchronizing data and design changes. A replication topology defines the communication that exists among members of the replica set, along with the logic that determines how synchronization occurs among the various members of the replica set.

If you're using Microsoft Replication Manager to perform replication, all members ultimately update one another using the topology that you create when you graphically link the replicas in the Replication Manager window. When you create a replication topology with Microsoft Replication Manager, the latency in the chaining can be important. If A and B synchronize, then B and C synchronize, and then A and B synchronize again, the time lag between synchronizations can be important. On the other hand, if A and B synchronize, then A and C synchronize, and then B and C synchronize, A is provided with the more current information sooner. The programmer and database administrator must work together to determine the order in which updates are dispersed throughout the database.

If you're using only DAO programming to implement replication, your code must ensure that all members of the replica set are synchronized. This might involve creating a custom replication schedule and synchronizing each member according to the schedule. One way to do this is by storing a list of all replica set members in a table or initialization file.

The following diagram shows alternative topologies that can be created:

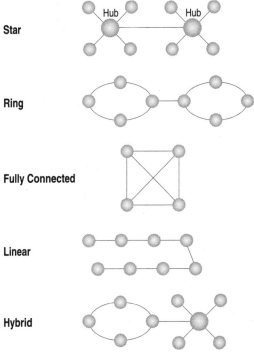

**Figure 7.2    Replica set topologies**

Other types of topologies exist. As the hybrid topology in the diagram suggests, there is an almost limitless variety of combinations and configurations. The type of topology you pick usually depends on your application; however, the star topology is usually the best for most applications.

# Designing Synchronization Control

When designing a replication topology, you'll need to decide how synchronization is initiated and which replica set member initiates it. In simple applications, a single replica might be selected as the member that initiates and controls synchronization. This replica is called the *controlling replica*. For example, in a simple star topology, the replica on the hub workstation might control all synchronization that occurs between members of the replica set. It is possible for a single replica to control all synchronization because the two databases specified in the DAO **Synchronize** method can be *any* two replicable databases in the same replica set.

Having a single controlling replica has the primary advantage of simplicity and ease of programming. It is a suitable design for many applications where the reliability of replication is not a critical element of the application's operation.

In some applications, the reliability of replication is critical. That is, if the controlling replica is corrupted or damaged, or if the controlling replica's computer is unavailable, the consequences might be serious. To increase reliability in these cases, you might want to design your replication topology so that more than one replica can control synchronization. There are several ways to do this. For example, your replication code could run on more than one replica, each of which periodically verifies whether the "default" controlling replica is available. One way to do this is to have a replica use the **OpenDatabase** method to see if the controlling replica and its computer are available. If the default controlling replica is unavailable, one of the other replicas could assume control.

A second way of determining if the controlling replica is available is to have the controlling replica maintain a log of all synchronizations that occur. Periodically, other replicas check the log to verify that a scheduled synchronization has occurred. If a synchronization does not appear in the log, one of the replicas temporarily promotes itself to the status of controlling replica and initiates the synchronization process. For safety, you should replicate the log so you have a backup in case the log at the controlling replica becomes unusable.

Another way to provide redundancy is to always have more than one controlling replica that performs synchronizations. This is the case with the fully connected topology, in which every replica is by definition a controlling replica. Although this can produce significant overhead, it is more reliable.

---

**Note**   Because so many different factors are involved, it is difficult to predict which topology will be the best solution for a specific application. You might want to experiment with a few different topologies in your replication scheme to determine which one produces the best results.

---

## Staggered Synchronization Schedules

If you're implementing your replication topology with more than one controlling replica, consider using staggered schedules at each of the controlling replicas. If two members of the replica set both attempt to synchronize with a third member at approximately the same time, one of the synchronizations will succeed and the other will fail. The member that attempted—but failed—to synchronize continues to attempt to synchronize, thereby generating additional network traffic and overhead. Using a staggered schedule helps make sure that the target member is not "busy" when the synchronization is initiated.

# Star Topology

In the star topology (see Figure 7.2), a single hub periodically synchronizes with each of its satellite replicas. In this topology, all data is shared among replicas through a single, centralized database. The star topology reduces data latency time among members of the replica set because data has to travel at most two "hops" to synchronize with any other member of the set. If the average quantity of data to exchange during synchronization is relatively small, the star topology can be a fast and efficient solution.

One of the potential disadvantages of the star topology, however, is that the first satellite does not receive any new data from the other satellites and the last satellite receives all the new data from all the other satellites. To make sure that all satellites are properly synchronized, you must make two synchronization passes around the star.

A second potential disadvantage of the star is that the hub is involved with every synchronization and therefore must be able to handle a greater load than any of the satellite replicas. As a result, the star topology has a practical limit to the number of satellite replicas it can support because so much activity is centered at the hub. An effective way of handling this is to create additional stars and connect their hubs. Or, you can place the hub on a dedicated high-end computer capable of handling a heavy load. However, if your application exchanges only a small amount of data with each synchronization, the hub might be able to support a relatively large number of workstations.

Another potential disadvantage of the star is that it contains a single point of failure—the hub. If the controlling replica is located at the hub, and the hub fails, synchronization cannot continue among any members of the replica set. This problem can be handled in code by reassigning the controlling replica.

If you use the star topology, consider locating the Design Master at a satellite computer instead of at the hub. This has several advantages. First, you can better protect the Design Master by making it unavailable to users who have permission to modify the design of database objects. Second, you can modify the Design Master and test these modifications offline. This prevents a set of incomplete changes from being replicated to other workstations during synchronization. When you've completed your design modifications, you can synchronize with the hub, which in turn synchronizes with other members of the replica set.

The star topology is a good starting point for many applications. It is reasonably simple to implement and can be designed to be both efficient and reliable. If you're implementing replication for the first time, the star topology is recommended. For more information, see the "Synchronizing the Star Topology" section later in this chapter.

# Ring Topology

In the ring topology, (see Figure 7.2) A synchronizes with B, B synchronizes with C, C synchronizes with D, and D synchronizes with A. The main advantage of the ring is that each computer handles approximately the same load, except when the replica at one computer is used to control synchronization. For more information, see "Synchronizing the Ring Topology" later in this chapter.

Latency times for a ring topology can be greater than latency times for a star topology. This is because data might have to travel multiple "hops" before it disperses to every replica. For a large number of replicas, it might take a while to disperse data throughout the replica set.

Another potential problem with simple ring implementations is that if any of the databases is unavailable, data fails to disperse throughout the application. This can be handled in your code, however, by routing information around the failure point instead of through it.

Ring topologies can be expanded by adding additional rings and connecting two or more of the replicas within each ring.

# Fully Connected Topology

As its name suggests, the fully connected topology involves a replica set in which each replica synchronizes with every other replica. One way of conceptualizing the fully connected topology is as a star topology where every replica acts as a hub.

The fully connected topology has several benefits. One of the most significant benefits is the low latency time for data propagation. Because each replica synchronizes with every other replica, data is sent directly to all replicas without having to indirectly disperse through a series of replicas.

Another benefit of the fully connected topology is its high degree of redundancy and reliability. In the fully connected topology, each replica is a controlling replica that initiates synchronization. As a result, the impact of computer or replica failure on the entire application is minimized.

The fully connected topology can be useful in applications where data is changed frequently in most or all of the replicas and it's important to disperse these changes as quickly as possible.

Despite its benefits, the fully connected topology can be inefficient because it involves many more synchronizations than other topologies and therefore requires more overhead and network traffic. If your application involves frequent synchronization among a large number of replicas, the fully connected topology might generate a prohibitive amount of overhead. In a fully connected scenario with $n$ replicas, the number of synchronizations that occur is $n$ times $n$. For example, 30 replicas would involve 900 separate synchronizations. If you're using a fully connected topology, it might be wise to stagger the replication schedules to reduce the amount of collisions that occur with simultaneous synchronizations.

# Linear Topology

The linear topology is similar to the ring topology, but a loop through all the replicas is not completed. That is, the first and last replicas do not synchronize with each other.

The linear topology is simple to implement, but it is usually not as efficient as some of the other topologies. The main problem with the linear topology is the long latency time for data dispersion.

To illustrate this, consider four replicas, A, B ,C, and D, that are synchronized using a linear scheme, with A as their controlling replica. If a change is made to data in replica D, but to none of the other replicas, it would take six synchronizations, starting at A, before all other replicas have D's changes. These synchronizations are: A-B, B-C, C-D, A-B, B-C, A-B. If this were set up as a ring topology, A and D would be directly connected, so it would take only four synchronizations for D's changes to be fully dispersed: A-B, B-C, C-D, D-A.

When designing a topology for your application, it is a good idea to count the number of synchronizations that must occur in different situations to fully disperse data throughout the replica set. Although the number of synchronizations is not the only measure of a topology's effectiveness, it can tell you something about the efficiency of your replication architecture.

# Making Your Database Replicable

Microsoft Jet databases are not replicable until they are converted into a replicable form. To make your database replicable, first identify the objects in the database you don't want replicated and set their **KeepLocal** property to the string `"T"` (the quotation marks are part of the string). Next, make your database replicable by setting its **Replicable** property to `"T"`. For more information on making additional replicas of your database, see "Making Additional Replicas" later in this chapter.

---

**Important**  The Microsoft Jet database engine does not allow you to protect a replicable database with a database password. Before you begin using replication, remove any database password protection from the database you will be making replicable. Setting user permissions does not interfere with replica synchronization.

---

# Keeping Objects Local

When you convert a nonreplicable database to a replicable form, all of the objects in the database are converted to replicable objects. If you don't want all objects in your database dispersed throughout the replica set, you can append and set the **KeepLocal** property on any objects you don't want replicated. For example, if your database has a table containing confidential salary information, initialization information, or names of users who log on to the database, you might want to keep that information only at your replica. You can set the table's **KeepLocal** property to "T" to keep it local while all other objects are replicated when the database is replicated.

The following code shows how to determine if a specified table already has the **KeepLocal** property appended to it:

```
Public Function IsLocal(strTable As String, strDB As String) As Integer
    Dim intMatch As Integer, tbl As TableDef, targetdb As Database
    Dim intI As Integer, ws As Workspace

    On Error GoTo OnErrIsLocal_Err
    Set targetdb = OpenDatabase(strDB, False)
    Set tbl = targetdb.TableDefs(strTable)

    'Does the local property exist on the table?

    For intI = 0 To tbl.Properties.Count - 1
        If tbl.Properties(intI).Name = "KeepLocal" Then intMatch = True
        Debug.Print tbl.Properties(intI).Name
    Next intI

    If intMatch = True Then
        If tbl.Properties("KeepLocal") = "T" Then
            IsLocal = True
            Exit Function
        End If
    End If

    IsLocal = False
    Exit Function


OnErrIsLocal_Err: '--- Error Handler ---
    Select Case Err
        Case 0
            Exit Function
        Case Else
            MsgBox "ERROR " & Err & ": " & Error
            Exit Function
    End Select

End Function
```

**Important**  If the object on which you are setting the **KeepLocal** property has already inherited that property from another object, the value set by the other object has no effect on the behavior of the object you want to keep local. You must directly set the property for each object.

On **TableDef** and **QueryDef** objects, you create and append the **KeepLocal** property to the object's **Properties** collection. On forms, reports, macros, and modules defined by a host application (such as Microsoft Access for Windows 95), you create and append the **KeepLocal** property to the **Properties** collection of the **Document** object representing the object. For example, the following code appends the **KeepLocal** property to the **Properties** collection of a **Document** object for a module:

```
Sub SetKeepLocal(dbs As Database)
    Dim doc As Document, prp As Property, Cont As Container

    Set doc = dbs.Containers!Modules.Documents![Utility Functions]
    Set prp = doc.CreateProperty("KeepLocal", dbText, "T")

    doc.Properties.Append prp
End Sub
```

If you set the **KeepLocal** property and the property has not already been appended or inherited, you will receive an error. In the following example, the program sets the **KeepLocal** property to "T" and includes an error handler in case Microsoft Jet can't complete the action. If called, the error handler both appends and sets the property.

```
Sub SetKeepLocalEvenIfInherited(objParent As Object)
    Const errPropNotFound = 3270

    On Error GoTo KeepLocalPropHndlr_Err
    objParent.Properties("KeepLocal").Value = "T"
    Exit Sub

KeepLocalPropHndlr_Err: '--- Error Handler ---
    If (Err = errPropNotFound) Then
        objParent.Properties.Append objParent.CreateProperty _
            ("KeepLocal", dbText, "T")
    Else
        ' User-defined error handler
    End If
    Resume Next

End Sub
```

You cannot apply the **KeepLocal** property to objects after they have been converted into a replicable form.

If you have set a relationship between two tables in your database, you must set the **KeepLocal** property the same for both tables—both tables must be local or both must be replicable. If the property is not set the same for both tables, the conversion will fail. However, the **KeepLocal** property cannot be set while the relationship is in effect. Before setting the property, remove the relationship between the tables. After setting the **KeepLocal** property, add the relationship back to the two tables and proceed with converting the database.

# Converting Your Database

When you convert your database into a replicable form, the database you convert becomes the Design Master for the new replica set. You can have only one Design Master in a replica set. Any changes to the design of the database, or to any of the replicable tables, queries, forms, reports, macros, and modules in the database can be made only in the Design Master. This prevents users at multiple replicas from making conflicting changes to the database's design and objects.

You can convert your database from a nonreplicable form to a replicable form in one of four ways:

- Using the **Create Replica** command in Microsoft Access
- Dragging the database file to the My Briefcase icon
- Using the **Convert Database to Design Master** command in Microsoft Replication Manager
- Using DAO code

This section describes how to convert your database using DAO.

## Determining the Replicable Status of Your Database

Before you convert a database, you might want to determine whether the database is already replicable. The following code shows how to determine the replicable status of a database. It returns **True** if the specified database is replicable; otherwise it returns **False**:

```
Public Function IsReplicable(strDB As String) As Integer
    Dim intMatch As Integer, targetdb As Database, intI As Integer

    On Error GoTo OnErrIsReplicable_Err

    Set targetdb = OpenDatabase(strDB, False)

    ' Does the replicable property exist? If not, the database
    ' isn't replicable, so return False.
    For intI = 0 To targetdb.Properties.Count - 1
        If targetdb.Properties(intI).Name = "Replicable" Then
            intMatch = True
        End If
    Next intI
```

```
        If intMatch = True Then
            If targetdb.Properties("Replicable") = "T" Then
                IsReplicable = True
                Exit Function
            End If
        End If

        IsReplicable = False
        Exit Function

OnErrIsReplicable_Err: '--- Error Handler ---
    Select Case Err
        Case 0
            Exit Function
        Case Else
            MsgBox "ERROR " & Err & ": " & Error
            IsReplicable = Err
            Exit Function
    End Select
End Function
```

## Setting the Replicable Property

To make a database replicable, set its **Replicable** property to "T". The following code provides an example of how to do this. If the **Replicable** property doesn't exist, this code creates it and sets it to the specified value.

```
Public Function SetReplicable(strDB As String) As Integer
    Dim prpReplicable As Property, targetdb As Database

    On Error GoTo OnErrSetReplicable_Err

    Set targetdb = OpenDatabase(strDB, True)

    ' If the Replicable property doesn't exist, create it.
    ' Turn off error handling in case the property already exists.
    On Error Resume Next
    Set prpReplicable = targetdb.CreateProperty("Replicable", _
        dbText, "T")
    targetdb.Properties.Append prpReplicable
    targetdb.Properties("Replicable") = "T"
    SetReplicable = True
    Exit Function
```

```
OnErrSetReplicable_Err: '--- Error Handler ---
    Select Case Err
    Case 0
        Exit Function
        Case Else
            MsgBox "ERROR " & Err & ": " & Error
            Exit Function
    End Select
End Function
```

During the conversion process, Microsoft Jet maintains all the property settings of your original database.

## Creating a Single-Master Replica Set

Programmers who are familiar with the use of a single-master database on a server might want to implement the same topology using Microsoft Jet replication. The single-master topology establishes the Design Master as the only member of the replica set that accepts changes to either the design of a database or the contents of the database. All other replicas in the set are read-only.

The only way to create a single-master replica set is to use Microsoft Replication Manager; you cannot implement the topology through DAO programming.

▶  **To create a single-master replica set**

1. Launch Microsoft Replication Manager.

2. On the **File** menu, click **Convert Database to Design Master**.

3. Highlight the database you want to convert and click Open.

4. On the third screen of the Convert Database to Design Master Wizard, click I Want All Replicas To Be Read-Only and Data Changes To Be Made Only At The Design Master.

5. Complete the remainder of the Wizard screens.

# Changes to Your Database

When you convert a nonreplicable database into a replicable database, Microsoft Jet:

- Adds new fields to each existing table in your database.

- Adds new tables to your database.

- Adds new properties to your database.

- Changes the behavior of AutoNumber fields.

- Increases the physical size of your database file as a result of the additional fields and tables.

## New Fields

The conversion process adds several new system fields to each existing table in a database. Among these fields are a unique identifier, a generation indicator, and a lineage indicator.

### Unique Identifier

During the conversion of a database, Microsoft Jet first looks at the existing fields in a table to determine if any field uses both the AutoNumber data type and ReplicationID field size. If no field uses that data type and field size, Microsoft Jet adds the s_Guid field, which stores the ReplicationID AutoNumber that uniquely identifies each record. The ReplicationID AutoNumber for a specific record is identical across all replicas.

The ReplicationID AutoNumber is a 16-byte GUID (Globally Unique Identifier, sometimes referred to as an UUID, or Universally Unique Identifier) that appears in the following format:

{2FAC1234-31F8-11B4-A222-08002B34C003}

The hyphens and braces are used in display only and do not form part of the GUID.

Autogenerated GUID fields are identified by the coltypeGUID and JET_bitColumnAutogenerate, or JET_bitPreventDelete (System field). There can be more than one field in a table with coltypeGUID, but there can be only one autogenerated field of coltypeGUID in a table (regardless of whether it is replicable). If an autogenerated GUID field is added to a table, GUID values are generated for all records in the table. The value of an autogenerated GUID cannot be changed or deleted.

If you are concerned that the GUID is actually not unique and therefore not any better than your own random number scheme, the following description of how the GUID is generated should remove any doubt.

GUIDs are created from the network NodeID, a time value, a clock sequence value, and a version value. For example, the GUID

{2FAC1234-31F8-11B4-A222-08002B34C003}

is created from

<time_low>-<time_mid>-<time_hi_and_version>-<clock_seq_and_reserved>-<clock_seq_low>-<node>

Time, version, and clock sequence, and so on, are described in more detail in the following paragraphs.

### Time

The timestamp is a 60-bit value equivalent to the number of 100ns ticks since Oct. 15, 1582 AD. This means time values are valid until approximately AD 3400. The time_low field is set to the least significant 32 bits of the timestamp. The time_mid is set to bits 32 to 47 of the timestamp.

### Version

GUID generation algorithms are available in different versions. The version field defines which is used. The time_hi_and_version component has the 12 least significant bits set to timestamp bits 48 to 59. The four most significant bits are set to the 4-bit version number of the GUID version being used.

### Clock Sequence

The clock sequence component accounts for loss of monoticity of the clock—for example, when a clock is reset. The clock_seq_low is set to the eight least significant bits of the clock sequence. The clock_seq_hi_and_reserved least significant 6 bits are set to the six most significant bits of the clock sequence. The clock_seq_hi_and_reserved most significant 2 bits are set to 0 and 1.

### Node

The NodeID is constructed in one of two ways depending upon the presence or absence of a network card. If a network card is present, the NodeID is retrieved from NetBIOS. The first 6 bytes are extracted from the synchronous adapter status network control block. This is the IEEE 802 48-bit node address.

If a network card is not installed, a 47-bit random number (plus 1 bit for local), is generated. The random number is composed of:

- The computer name.
- The value of the program counter.
- The system memory status.
- The total bytes and free bytes on the hard drive.
- The stack pointer (value).
- A LUID (Locally Unique ID).
- Whatever random data was in the NodeID buffer at create time.

It is unlikely that this number will be duplicated on this or any other machine.

The NodeID returned is explicitly made into a Multicast IEEE 802 address so that it will not conflict with a real IEEE 802–based node address. The LocalOnly bit contains 1 if the address was made up, 0 if it's a real IEEE 802 address.

### Generation Identifier

During the conversion process, Microsoft Jet also adds a field called s_Generation to each table in the database. The s_Generation field is used to expedite incremental synchronization by allowing the sending replica to avoid sending records that have not been updated since the last synchronization. Whenever a record is modified, its generation is set to 0.

In general, during a synchronization all records with generation 0 are sent, and then the generation for the record is incremented to one more than the last generation, which now becomes the new highest generation. The sending replica knows the last generation sent to that specific receiving replica, and sends only records with generation 0 and generations higher than the previous generations.

The receiving replica does not apply generations received out of sequence. In some cases, Microsoft Jet replication might determine that there are too many records to be sent in a single message.

Generally, there is a single generation field per record. To optimize synchronizations for databases that contain Memo or OLE Object fields (sometimes referred to as a BLOBs, or binary large objects), an extra generation field is associated with each BLOB. If the BLOB is modified, this generation value is set to 0 so that the BLOB is sent during the next synchronization. If a record modifies other fields, but not the BLOB, the BLOB generation is not set to 0 and the BLOB is not sent.

This extra generation field is named Gen_*xxxx*, where *xxxx* is the comment field name (truncated, if necessary). If this name duplicates an existing field name, the prefix is changed, one character at a time, until a unique name is found. A **ColGeneration** property is set on the comment field to identify the added Gen_*xxxx* field. One of these fields is set for each comment field.

### Lineage Identifier

During the conversion process, Microsoft Jet also adds a field named s_Lineage to each table in the database. The s_Lineage field contains a list of nicknames for replicas that have updated the record and the last version created by each of those replicas. The version is an integral field that is incremented when the record is changed. The first pair of values in the lineage reflects the current version and the name of the last member of the replica set to update the record. This is a binary field and is not usually readable by users.

## Replication System Tables

Microsoft Jet adds several system tables to the database during the conversion process. Most of these tables are system tables, which are not normally visible to users and cannot be manipulated by programmers. The following table describes the major tables.

| Name | Description |
|------|-------------|
| MSysRepInfo | Stores information relevant to the entire replica set, including the identity of the Design Master. It contains a single record. This table appears in all members of the replica set. |
| MSysReplicas | Stores information on all replicas in the replica set. This table appears in all members of the replica set. |
| MSysTableGuids | Relates table names to GUIDs. TableGuids are used in tables such as MSysTombstones as a reference to a table name stored in this table. This allows efficient renaming of tables. In addition, this table includes the level number used for ordering tables so that updates can be processed efficiently. This is a local table that is updated by the tracking layer at the Design Master and, as part of the processing of design changes, at all other members of the replica set. |
| MSysSchemaProb | Identifies errors that occurred while synchronizing the design of the replica. This table exists only if a design conflict has occurred between the user's replica and another member of the replica set. |
| MSysErrors | Identifies where and why errors occurred during data synchronization. This table appears in all members of the replica set. |
| MSysExchangeLog | Stores information about synchronizations that have taken place between this member and other members of the replica set. This is a local table. |
| MSysSidetables | Identifies the tables that experienced a conflict and the name of the conflict table that contains the conflicting records. This table exists only if a conflict occurs between the user's replica and another member of the set. |
| MSysSchChange | Stores design changes that have occurred at the Design Master so that they can be dispersed to any member of the replica set. The records in this table are deleted periodically to minimize the size of the table. |
| MSysTombstone | Stores information on deleted records, and allows deletes to be dispersed to other replicas. This table appears in all members of the replica set. |
| MSysTranspAddress | Stores addressing information for Transporters and defines the set of Transporters known to this replica set. This table appears in all members of the replica set. |
| MSysSchedule | Stores information for scheduled synchronization. The Transporter for a local replica set member uses this table to determine when the next synchronization with another Transporter should take place, and how to synchronize data and design changes with the other Transporter. |

| Name | Description (*cont'd*) |
|------|------------------------|
| MSysGenHistory | Stores a history of generations. It contains a record for each generation that a replica knows about. It is used to avoid sending common generations during synchronizations and to resynchronize replicas that are restored from backups. This table appears in all members of the replica set, but it is merged by a process slightly different from that used with normal replicated tables. |
| MSysOthersHistory | Stores a record of generations received from other replicas. It contains one generation from every message seen from other replicas. |

## Replication Properties

Microsoft Jet adds new properties to your database when it becomes replicable: **Replicable**, **ReplicaID**, and **DesignMasterID**. The **Replicable** property is set to "T", indicating the database is now replicable. After the property is set to "T", however, it cannot be changed. Setting the property to "F" (or any value other than "T") returns an error message. The **ReplicaID** is a 16-byte value that provides the Design Master or replica with a unique identification.

The **DesignMasterID** property can be used to make a replica the new Design Master for the replica set. This property should be set only at the current Design Master. Under extreme circumstances—for example, the loss of the original Design Master—you can set the property at the current replica. However, setting this property at a replica, when there is already another Design Master, might partition your replica set into two irreconcilable sets and prevent any further synchronization of data. If you determine that it is necessary to set this property at a replica, first synchronize the replica with all other replicas in the set.

**Warning** Never create a second Design Master in a replica set. The existence of a second Design Master can result in the loss of data.

There are two new properties that you can append and set on the individual tables, queries, forms, reports, macros, and modules in your database: **KeepLocal** and **Replicable**. To prevent an object from being copied to other replicas in a replica set, you can set the **KeepLocal** property of the object to "T" prior to converting the database into a replicable form. After the database is converted, you can set the **Replicable** property to "T" to make a local object replicable. For more information on these two properties, see the "Making Objects Replicable or Local" section later in this chapter.

# Increases in the Physical Size of Your Database

The addition of three new fields during the conversion process imposes two limitations on your tables. First, Microsoft Jet allows a maximum of 2048 bytes (not counting Memo or OLE Object fields) in a record. Replication uses a minimum of 28 bytes to store unique identifiers and information about changes to the record. If the record contains either Memo or OLE Object fields, replication uses an additional 4 bytes for each of those fields. The total number of bytes available in a record in a replicated table can be calculated as follows:

2048 bytes
−28 bytes for replication overhead
−(4 bytes * the number of Memo fields)
−(4 bytes * the number of OLE Object fields)
= the maximum number of bytes available

Second, Microsoft Jet allows a maximum of 255 fields in a table, of which at least three fields are used by replication. The total number of fields available in a replicated table can be calculated as follows:

255 fields
−3 system fields
−the number of Memo and OLE Object fields
= the number of fields available

Few well-designed applications use all the available fields in a table or characters in a record. However, if you have a large number of Memo fields or OLE Object fields in your table, you should be aware of your remaining resources.

In addition to decreasing the available number of characters and fields, Microsoft Jet replication also imposes a limitation on the number of nested transactions allowed. You can have a maximum of seven nested transactions in a nonreplicable database, but a replicated database can have a maximum of six nested transactions.

Just as the addition of three new fields to your tables adds to the size of each record, the addition of new system tables adds to the size of your database. Many of these new tables contain only a few records, but some of the new tables can grow significantly depending upon the frequency of synchronization between replicas.

The size of your database file is significant for three reasons:

- Microsoft Jet supports files up to a maximum of 1 GB in size.

- Many users have limited space available on their hard drives and the creation of a replicable database that is larger than the original file can use up all available disk space.

- If you choose to make a backup copy of the nonreplicable form of your database, you must have sufficient space on your hard drive.

### Changes to the Behavior of AutoNumber Fields

When you convert a nonreplicable database to a replicated database, the AutoNumber fields in your tables change from incremental to random. All existing AutoNumber fields in existing records retain their values, but new values for inserted records are random numbers. Random AutoNumber fields are not meaningful because they aren't in any particular order and the highest value isn't on the record inserted last. When you open a table with a random AutoNumber key, the records appear in the order of ascending random numbers, not in chronological order. With random AutoNumber fields it is possible—although highly unlikely—for records inserted at different replicas to be assigned the same value. If this happens, updates could be made in the wrong records. If you experience such problems, consider using the s_Guid field as the primary key. Because all numbers in the s_Guid field are unique, each record has a different ID.

Before you convert your nonreplicable database into a replicated database, determine if any of your applications or users rely on the order and incremental nature of the AutoNumber field. If so, you can use an additional Date/Time field to provide sequential ordering information.

# Database Security

For more information on database security, see Chapter 10, "Managing Security."

Replicable databases use the same security model as nonreplicable databases: Users' permissions on the database are determined at the time they start Microsoft Access and log on. As a programmer, it's up to you to make sure the same security information is available at each location where a replica is used. You can do this by making the identical system database (the file that stores security information) available to users at each location where a replica is used. The default security system database is called SYSTEM.MDW. The SYSTEM.MDW cannot be replicated, but can be manually copied to each location. Another way to make the same system database available to all your users is to re-create the entries for users and groups at each location in the local system database by entering the same user and group names with their associated PIDs at each location. Modifications to permissions is a design change and can only be made in the Design Master.

Security permissions control certain aspects of database replication. For example, a user must have Administer permission on the database to:

- Convert a nonreplicable database into a replicable database.

- Make a local object replicable, make a replicable object local, or make a replica the new Design Master for the set.

- Designate a replica as the new Design Master. You can perform this action in any replica in the set; however, you should never have more than one Design Master in a set at one time.

By default, Administer permission is granted to the Users group, the Admins group, and the creator of the database. If security is to be maintained, you must restrict this permission to selected users.

Care should be taken to ensure there is always at least one user with the Administer permission on the database. It is possible that a site with a replicable database, which is the Design Master, and its associated SYSTEM.MDW could be destroyed through a hard disk failure. While it is possible to use another replica to retain access to the data, you will need to make one of the replicas the Design Master. This can be done only by a user with Administer permission on the database. Therefore, you must make sure the SYSTEM.MDW at the remote site provides Administer permission on the database to one of the users.

# Making Additional Replicas

Although changes to the design of the database can be made only in the Design Master, additional replicas can be made from any member of the set. In fact, the only way for new copies of the database to be included in the replica set is for them to be created from an existing member. Once created, all new replicas become part of the replica set. All the members of a replica set have a unique identity and can communicate and synchronize with one another. Each replica set is independent from all other replica sets, and replicas in different sets cannot communicate or synchronize with each other.

---

**Important**   Never try to make additional replicas from the original, nonreplicable database. The result would not be an additional replica, but rather a new replicable database and replica set.

---

When you convert your database by setting its **Replicable** property to "T", you have only one member (the Design Master) in the replica set, and you make your first replica from it. You can make your first replica, and subsequent replicas, by using the **MakeReplica** method. For example, to make a replica, you can use the following code:

```
Sub MakeAdditionalReplica(strReplicableDB, strNewReplica)
    Dim dbs As Database

    Set dbs = OpenDatabase(strReplicableDB)

    dbs.MakeReplica strNewReplica, "First Replica of " & _
        strReplicableDB, dbRepMakeReadOnly
    dbs.Close
End Sub
```

If you include the **dbRepMakeReadOnly** constant, the replicable elements of the newly created replica cannot be modified. Otherwise, users are able to make changes to the data in the new replica. As Microsoft Jet creates the new replica, all data definition language property settings of the source replica are included in the new replica. You can make subsequent replicas from either the Design Master or any replica in the set.

When using the **MakeReplica** method, be sure that the objects you are replicating are not locked, or the method will fail. Microsoft Jet locks objects while they are open in design mode or being updated during a synchronization. Programmers might easily overlook this requirement and attempt to make a replica from the database that has locked objects.

---

**Note**  When you make a new replica, you copy all of the replicable objects and properties from the source replica to the new replica. Although you copy all attached tables, the path to an attached table might no longer be accurate because of the new replica's location on the network. Be sure to test the new replica to determine if you need to establish a new path for any of the attached tables.

---

# Controlling Replica Creation

If users have Microsoft Access installed on their computers, they can replicate any database if they have permission to open it. Users can simply use Microsoft Access menu commands to perform the replication. Although this might be acceptable in some applications, other applications might want to control the creation of new replicas.

If you want to control creation of replicas, you can provide a custom user interface designed for that purpose. Providing a custom user interface for creating new replicas enables the application to track new members of the replica set as they are created. If a user creates a replica outside the control of your application, it won't be possible to synchronize with that replica using DAO because your application won't know about the new replica.

To prevent users from creating a replica of a database using Microsoft Access menu commands, you can grant them Open privileges for the database when they start your application and then revoke that privilege when they exit your application. This prevents them from opening the database using Microsoft Access when they are not running your application. Although this is not an infallible system, it discourages the majority of users from creating replicas.

The following code sample grants or revokes the currently logged on user's privileges to open the specified database. This function can be called when the application starts and closes.

```
Function SetDBAccess(dbs As Database, intGrantAccess As Integer) _
    As Integer
    Dim Cont As Container, doc As Document

    On Error GoTo OnErrSetDBAccess_Err
```

```
      Set Cont = dbs.Containers("Databases")

      'Documents(0) is the document representing the entire database
      Set doc = Cont.Documents(0)

      doc.UserName = CurrentUser() 'Get the currently logged on user.
      ' This is supported only in Microsoft Access.

      If intGrantAccess = True Then
          doc.Permissions = dbSecFullAccess  'Grant Open privileges.
      Else
          doc.Permissions = dbSecNoAccess    'Revoke Open privileges.
      End If

      dbs.Containers.Refresh
      Exit Function

OnErrSetDBAccess_Err: '--- Error Handler ---
      SetDBAccess = Err
      Exit Function

End Function
```

# Using Replicas Instead of Backups

With database replication, it is no longer necessary to make a separate backup copy of your database. Each member of the replica set serves as a backup of the replicable portion of the database. In fact, you are strongly advised not to back up and restore members of the replica set as you would ordinary files. If you back up and restore the Design Master, you could lose critical information about changes to the design of the database as well as the ability of the Design Master to synchronize with the other replicas in the set. If the Design Master is corrupted or unusable, do not copy or restore an older version of the Design Master; instead, make another member of the replica set the Design Master. To make a replica the Design Master, use the **DesignMasterID** property as described in the "Moving the Design Master" section later in this chapter.

---

**Important**  A copy of the Design Master created with a backup and restore program might not be able to synchronize with the rest of the replica set.

---

# Synchronizing Replicas

For database replication to be useful, the members of the replica set must communicate with one another to remain up-to-date. Synchronization is the process of making the design and data in all the members identical. Changes made to the existing records in one member are periodically communicated to each of the other members that have that same record. Similarly, new records added or old records deleted from one member are communicated to the other members of the replica set.

You can synchronize one member with another by using either Microsoft Access for Windows 95, Briefcase, Microsoft Replication Manager, or DAO.

You can keep the members of the replica set synchronized using the **Synchronize** method. By specifying the target database file name, you can synchronize one user's replica with another member of the set. You can also perform one-way or two-way exchanges . For example, you might use the following code to perform a two-way exchange between members:

```
Sub synchronizeDBs(strDBName, strSyncTargetDB)
    Dim dbs As Database

    Set dbs = OpenDatabase(strDBName)

    ' Synchronize replicas (bidirectional exchange).
    dbs.Synchronize strSyncTargetDB, dbRepImpExpChanges
    dbs.Close
End Sub
```

If you do not provide an exchange argument, the synchronization is bidirectional (import and export).

When Microsoft Jet synchronizes two members of the replica set, it always synchronizes design changes before it synchronizes changes to data. The design of both members must be at the same version level before data can be synchronized. For example, even if you use **dbRepExportChanges** to specify that data changes flow only from the current members to the designated target, design changes could be made to the current member if it has a lower version number than the target member.

If you want to prevent users from making changes to the design of your database, do not put the Design Master on the network server. Instead, keep the Design Master at a network location that is accessible only to you. As you make changes to your application, you can synchronize with the replica on the server and rely on it to pass these changes on to other replicas in the replica set.

# Synchronizing the Star Topology

As described in the "Replica Set Topology" section earlier in this chapter, you can implement a variety of topologies for synchronizing members of the replica set. The following code examples show how to implement the star and the ring topologies.

The following code provides a simple example of implementing synchronization using a star topology. In this sample, the hub is specified as an input parameter. The list of replica paths is stored in a table whose name is specified in the parameter strReplicas. The table itself is stored in a database whose name is specified in the parameter strDB. The table must have a field named Path that contains the replica paths. The name of the replica acting as the hub is specified in strHub.

```
Function StarSync(strDB As String, strReplicas As String, strHub _
    As String) As Integer
    Dim dbs As Database, dbsHub As Database, dbsPaths As Database
    Dim rstReplicas As Recordset

    On Error GoTo OnErrStarSync_Err

    Set dbsPaths = OpenDatabase(strDB)
    Set rstReplicas = dbsPaths.OpenRecordset _
        (strReplicas, dbOpenSnapshot)

    On Error Resume Next
    Set dbsHub = OpenDatabase(strHub)   ' Open the hub database.
    ' If the hub specified in strHub is unavailable, return an
    ' application-error so the caller can reassign a new hub and
    ' call the function again.

    If Err <> 0 Then
        StarSync = False
        Exit Function
    End If


    ' Synchronize all members of the replica set with the hub.
    ' Since error trapping is turned off, the program continues to
    ' sync with other replicas if the Synchronize method fails for
    ' any replica.

    Err = 0
    Do Until rstReplicas.EOF
        If rstReplicas!Path <> strHub Then ' Hub can't sync with itself.
        Debug.Print rstReplicas!Path
            dbsHub.Synchronize rstReplicas!Path
        End If
```

```
                     ' If an error occurred while synchronizing with the current
                     ' replica, log an error that stores which replica failed to
                     ' synchronize. The procedure LogError is a custom, programmer-
                     ' written procedure for logging errors to a text file.

                     If Err <> 0 Then
                         MsgBox ("Synchronization failure at " & rstReplicas!Path)
                         Err = 0
                     End If
                     rstReplicas.MoveNext
                 Loop

                 dbsHub.Close
                 rstReplicas.Close
                 dbsPaths.Close
                 Exit Function

         OnErrStarSync_Err: ' --- Error Handler ---
                 dbsHub.Close
                 rstReplicas.Close
                 dbsPaths.Close
                 StarSync = Err
                 Exit Function

         End Function
```

# Synchronizing the Ring Topology

The following code provides a simple example of implementing synchronization
using a ring topology. The list of replicas is stored in a table with a name specified
by strReplicas. Each replica listed in the table is synchronized with the replica
specified in the next record of the table. The last replica in the list is synchronized
with the first.

```
Function RingSync(strDB As String, strReplicas As String) As Integer
    Dim dbsSyncSource As Database, dbsPaths As Database
    Dim rstReplicas As Recordset

    On Error GoTo OnErrRingSync_Err
    Set dbsPaths = OpenDatabase(strDB)
    Set rstReplicas = _
        dbsPaths.OpenRecordset(strReplicas,dbOpenSnapshot)

    On Error Resume Next
    Do Until rstReplicas.EOF
        Set dbsSyncSource = OpenDatabase(rstReplicas!Path)
```

```
            ' If an error occurred while opening the database, log an error.
            If Err <> 0 Then
                MsgBox ("Synchronize failure at " & rstReplicas!Path)
                Err = 0
            End If

            rstReplicas.MoveNext
            If rstReplicas.EOF Then Exit Do
            ' If an error occurs during synchronization, keep moving around
            ' the ring.
            On Error Resume Next
            Debug.Print rstReplicas!Path
            dbsSyncSource.Synchronize rstReplicas!Path
            dbsSyncSource.Close
        Loop

        ' Synchronize the last member in the list with the first member to
        ' complete the ring.

        rstReplicas.MoveFirst
        dbsSyncSource.Synchronize rstReplicas!Path
        dbsSyncSource.Close
        rstReplicas.Close
        dbsPaths.Close
        Exit Function

OnErrRingSync_Err: ' --- Error Handler ---
        dbsSyncSource.Close
        rstReplicas.Close
        RingSync = Err
        Exit Function

End Function
```

# Synchronizing Data in Wide Area Networks

The way in which you manage synchronization within your application can depend on your network. Synchronization strategies for computers connected by a single local area network (LAN) are usually quite different from synchronization strategies for computers connected using wide area networks (WANs) and modems. For computers connected through a single LAN, synchronization can occur frequently because telecommunication overhead does not have to be considered.

With WANs, telecommunication overhead can be a major factor because of longer data transmission times and higher transmission rates. In this section, two different WAN topologies are discussed, along with possible ways to handle synchronization.

The following diagram shows a company that has an order entry department in Denver and headquarters in Boston. Each day, customers call an 800 number to order products from the company's catalog, and these orders are entered into a custom Microsoft Jet database application.

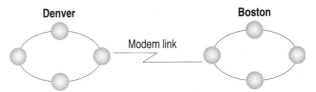

**Figure 7.3    Ring topology synchronization over a WAN**

Once a day, sales transactions entered in Denver must be transferred to headquarters, where managers can run queries against the data to track sales totals, geographic sales distribution, and other statistics. Conversely, updated product information such as new products and discounts on existing products must be sent from headquarters to the sales office as soon as it is available. Computers in the order entry department comprise a single LAN, and computers at headquarters comprise another LAN. The two LANs are connected through a modem.

In this environment, how can replication be configured efficiently to meet the company's requirements? Configuring replication within each LAN is a fairly straightforward task. For example, the databases in Denver could be configured to synchronize data every 30 minutes using a ring topology. In a ring topology, computer A updates computer B, which updates computer C, and so on. This update chain occurs repeatedly at specified intervals and can be set using Microsoft Replication Manager or in code using DAO methods and the Timer event. The databases in Boston can be configured to regularly synchronize data in a similar manner.

The main concern is the bottleneck created by the modem link between Denver and Boston. For a large number of sales transactions, the telecommunications overhead of frequently synchronizing data between the two cities would be high. But because headquarters needs information only once a day, a good strategy would be to wait until night to synchronize one of the computers in Denver with one of the computers in Boston. The computer in Boston and the computer in Denver must be fully synchronized within their respective rings before they synchronize between the two rings. After the information is synchronized between the two computers, the periodic synchronization that occurs between computers in the same city disperses the information to all computers.

Because product information in Boston must be sent to Denver only when new information is available, replication can be configured to occur only when necessary. This might occur once or twice a week. To handle this, a user could click a button on a form to synchronize the databases in Denver and Boston whenever product information changes. A more sophisticated solution would be to set a value in a table each time information in one of the product tables changes. A procedure linked to a Timer event would periodically check this value and invoke the **Synchronize** method whenever the value is set.

---

**Note**   Networks have topologies too, and these should not be confused with replication topologies. For example, a network topology can be a ring, a star, or a straight line. Although the diagram shows a ring (circle), this refers to the replication topology. The underlying network topology is not shown and can be of almost any type.

---

# "Cleaning" Records Before Synchronizing

In some applications, a certain percentage of records are discarded because of bad or missing information. For example, in an application where information on hard copy forms is entered into a database, a certain percentage of these records must be discarded because they are incomplete. In other applications, some data might need "fixing" before it can be used. For example, a field in a table might be designed to hold a string of comma-separated numbers, but might instead contain non-comma separators, letters, or other mistakes.

When data is synchronized, all updated data is dispersed, regardless of whether it is useful to a particular application. Bad data in one database becomes bad data in multiple databases when synchronization occurs. Therefore, when building a replication system for your application, you might want to consider writing procedures that either purge or fix data before it is replicated to other systems.

# Making Objects Replicable or Local

When you convert a nonreplicable database to a replicable form, you convert all of the objects in the database to replicable objects unless you set their **KeepLocal** properties to "T". After you make a database replicable, however, all new objects created in the Design Master, or in any other replicas in the set, are treated as local objects. Local objects remain in the replica in which they're created and are not copied throughout the replica set. Each time you make a new replica in the set, all the replicable objects in the source replica are included in that new replica, but none of the local objects are included.

If you create a new object in a replica and want to change it from local to replicable so that all users can use it, you can either create the object in or import it into the Design Master. Be sure to delete the local object from any replicas; otherwise, you will encounter a design error. After the object is part of the Design Master, set the object's **Replicable** property to "T".

**Important** If the object on which you are setting the **Replicable** property has already inherited that property from another object, the value set by the other object has no effect on the behavior of the object you want to make replicable. You must directly set the property for each object.

On **Database**, **TableDef**, and **QueryDef** objects, you create and append the **Replicable** property to the object's **Properties** collection.

On forms, reports, macros, and modules defined by a host application (such as Microsoft Access for Windows 95), you create and append the **Replicable** property to the **Properties** collection of the **Document** object representing the object. For example, the following code appends the **Replicable** property to the **Properties** collection of a **Document** object for a module:

```
Sub CreateReplicableProperty(dbs As Database)
    Dim doc As Document, prp As Property

    Set doc = dbs.Containers!Modules.Documents![Utility Functions]
    Set prp = doc.CreateProperty("Replicable", dbText, "T")

    doc.Properties.Append prp
End Sub
```

If you set the **Replicable** property and the property has not already been appended or inherited, you will receive an error. In the following example, the program sets the **Replicable** property to "T" and includes an error handler in case Microsoft Jet can't complete the action. If called, the error handler both appends and sets the property.

```
Sub SetReplicableEvenIfInherited(objParent As Object)
    Const errPropNotFound = 3270

    On Error GoTo ReplicablePropHndlr_Err
    objParent.Properties("Replicable").Value = "T"
    Exit Sub

ReplicablePropHndlr_Err: ' --- Error Handler ---
    If (Err = errPropNotFound) Then
        objParent.Properties.Append _
            objParent.CreateProperty("Replicable", dbText, "T")
    Else
        ' user-defined error handlier
    End If
    Resume Next

End Sub
```

The next time you synchronize, the newly replicable object will appear in the other replicas in the set. Similarly, if there is a replicable object that you want to make local, set its **Replicable** property to "F". You can also set the **Replicable** property by selecting or clearing the Replicable check box in the object's property sheet in Microsoft Access.

---

**Warning**   When you change the status of an object from replicable to local by setting the value of the object's **Replicable** property from "T" to "F", the object is deleted from all members of the replica set except the Design Master. Extra care should be taken when you change the replicable status of a table. Even if you temporarily make a replicable table local at the Design Master and then make it replicable again, the table will be deleted and re-created at each replica during the next synchronization. Any data entered in the table at a replica since the last synchronization will be lost unless you synchronize all replicas before making the design change.

---

A database that can have replicas containing both replicable and local objects is much more useful because users can share corporate, division, or workgroup data that is common to all their tasks, while maintaining location-specific data and customized queries and reports.

# Conflicts and Errors

When using database replication, you might occasionally encounter synchronization conflicts, synchronization errors, or design errors. *Synchronization conflicts* occur when the same record is updated at two members of the replica set, and Microsoft Jet attempts to synchronize the two versions. The synchronization succeeds, but the changes at only one of the members are applied to the other. *Synchronization errors* occur when a data change at one replica set member cannot be applied to another member because it would violate a constraint such as a referential integrity rule or uniqueness assertion. The synchronization succeeds, but the content of the database at different members is different. *Design errors* occur when a design change at the Design Master conflicts with a design change at a replica. The synchronization fails and the content of the databases at different members starts to diverge.

Synchronization errors and design errors are much more significant problems than synchronization conflicts because the replica set members no longer share a common design or identical data. This section describes the factors contributing to conflicts and errors, and suggests ways to prevent or resolve them.

# Synchronization Conflicts

Whenever you synchronize two members of a replica set, there is always the possibility of conflict between versions because the same record might have been updated at both locations. During synchronization, if Microsoft Jet detects that the same record was changed at both members, Jet treats it as a synchronization conflict. Even if the changes made at one replica set member were in different fields than the changes made at the other member, Microsoft Jet treats it as a synchronization conflict.

When a synchronization conflict occurs, Microsoft Jet does not attempt to resolve the conflict based on the content of the records or the changes made to the data. Instead, it uses a simple algorithm to select one of the record versions to be the official change and writes the data from the other record version into a conflict table. It is then the responsibility of the programmer, database administrator, user, or a custom resolution program to review each conflict to determine that the correct information was applied to the database.

The algorithm Microsoft Jet uses to select one record version over the other is based on the record's version number, which is stored in the table's s_Lineage field. Each time a change is made to the data in a record, the version number increases by one. For example, a record with no changes has a version number of 0. A change to data updates the version number to 1. A second change to the same data, or a change to different data in the record, changes the version number to 2. If the record at one replica set member has been changed once and the same record at the second member has been changed three times, then the record at the second member has a higher version number than the record at the first member. When Microsoft Jet compares the version numbers for the same record, it assumes that the version that has changed the most is the more correct of the two versions. If both records have the same version number, Microsoft Jet examines the ReplicaID and selects the replica set member with the lowest ReplicaID.

While this algorithm and its underlying assumption might not be the most appropriate in all applications, it allows Microsoft Jet to quickly and consistently complete the synchronization process and preserves all the information from both versions for later review. The data from the record version that Microsoft Jet did not select is stored in a conflict table in the member where the change was made. Conflict tables derive both their names and fields from the underlying tables. Conflict table names are in the form *table*_Conflict, where *table* is the original table name. For example, if the original table name is Customers, the conflict table name is Customers_Conflict. Because conflicts are reported only to the replica set member that originated the losing update, conflict tables are not replicated.

# Resolving Conflicts Using DAO

After synchronizing two replicas, you should review each conflict to determine that the correct information was applied to the database. You can determine if a conflict has occurred for a specific table by using the **ConflictTable** property. This property returns the name of the conflict table containing the database records that conflicted during synchronization. For example, to find the name of the conflict table, examine each record conflict, and take action to resolve each conflict, you can use the following code:

```
Sub Resolve(dbs As Database)
    Dim tdfTest As TableDef, rstConflict As Recordset

    For Each tdfTest In dbs.TableDefs
    If (tdfTest.ConflictTable <> "") Then
            Set rstConflict = dbs.OpenRecordset(tdfTest.ConflictTable)
        ' Process each record.
            rstConflict.MoveFirst
            While Not rstConflict.EOF
                ' Do conflict resolution.
                ' Remove conflicting record when finished.
                rstConflict.Delete
                rstConflict.MoveNext
            Wend
            rstConflict.Close
    End If
    Next tdfTest
End Sub
```

If there is no conflict table, or if the database is nonreplicable, the property returns a zero-length string.

As you review each conflict in the conflict table, you should take the appropriate action. If the record version selected by Microsoft Jet was the correct version and no further action is necessary, you can delete the record from the conflict table. If the record version selected by Microsoft Jet was not the correct version, you might want to:

- Manually enter the data from the conflict table into the database.

- Develop a custom conflict-resolution routine that always assigns a higher priority to changes in one specific replica over another replica.

- Consider whether procedural changes regarding how data is entered or changed in records are necessary.

### Resolving Conflicts Using Microsoft Access

If you handle replication through the Microsoft Access for Windows 95 user interface, Microsoft Access automatically notifies you of a synchronization conflict each time you open a database with conflicts. Microsoft Access ships with a default Conflict Resolver to assist you in displaying a list of all tables that have synchronization conflicts and choosing whether to apply the data from the conflict table after all. You run the default Conflict Resolver by clicking Yes when asked if you want assistance resolving the conflicts. You can also launch the Conflict Resolver at any time by pointing to Replication on the Microsoft Access **Tools** menu and clicking **Resolve Conflicts**.

You can replace the default Conflict Resolver with a custom function for reviewing and processing the records in a conflict table. If you want to use a custom function instead of the default Conflict Resolver, create the **ReplicationConflictFunction** property and set the value to the text string name of the custom function. The custom function must be stored in a module at the Design Master (not as a separate dynamic-link library), and the module must be replicated.

▶ **To replace the Microsoft Access Conflict Resolver**

1. On the Microsoft Access **File** menu, click **Open Database**.

2. Highlight the replicable database you want to have use the custom Conflict Resolver function and click Open.

3. On the **File** menu, click **Database Properties**.

4. Click the Custom tab.

5. In the Name field, type *ReplicationConflictFunction* (do not put spaces between the words).

6. In the Value field, enter the name of the custom function.

7. Click OK to exit the dialog box.

If you want to return to using the default Conflict Resolver after using a custom function, set the property's value to " " (an empty string).

# Synchronization Errors

You need be aware of at least four sources of potential synchronization errors when building your application:

- Table-level validation (TLV) rules
- Duplicate keys
- Referential integrity
- Record Locks

## Table-Level Validation Rules

Microsoft Jet allows you to establish table-level validation (TLV) rules to restrict the value or type of data entered into a table. However, if you implement TLV without determining that any existing data does not violate the validation rule, you might encounter a synchronization error in the future. For example, assume that you apply a TLV rule to a field that already contains data and test to make sure that the existing values meet the rule. There might be new or updated records at other replica set members that do not satisfy the new rule. If you do not test the existing values at the other members and change the values that fail the rule, the next synchronization will fail to correctly update the records. When Microsoft Jet applies the new or updated records from the other member to the member on which you set the TLV rule, Microsoft Jet tests each insertion or update against the rule. If the value fails, the update fails and an error is written to the MSysErrors table at the receiving member. To correct the error, you must correct the invalid values at the sending replica set member. You can avoid the error by synchronizing all members of the replica set before applying a TLV rule.

## Duplicate Keys

Duplicate keys can occur when two users at different replicas either simultaneously insert a new record and use the same primary key for their respective records or change the key on two different records when both happen to use the same value. When the replicas are synchronized, the synchronization succeeds, but Microsoft Jet writes a duplicate key error to the MSysErrors table for each of the records that could not be inserted or updated. To correct a duplicate key error, change the value of one of the keys or delete the duplicate record.

## Referential Integrity

Referential integrity preserves the relationship between tables when adding or deleting records. Enforced referential integrity prevents you from adding or deleting a record to a related table if there is no corresponding record in the primary table. In some situations, enforced referential integrity might result in synchronization errors. For example, if a user at the Design Master deletes a record with a primary key from a table and a user at a replica inserts a record that references that key, the next synchronization of the two members generates two errors. During synchronization, Microsoft Jet attempts to delete the primary key record at the replica but cannot. The reference to a record or records in a related table at the replica prevents the deletion from succeeding. Microsoft Jet also attempts to add the referencing record at the Design Master but cannot. The new record references a primary key that no longer exists at the Design Master. To correct the two errors you must delete from the replica the record that references the deleted primary key.

The outcome of the preceding scenario changes if you enforce cascading deletes in your application. With cascading deletes in effect, Microsoft Jet deletes both the primary key record and all referencing records at the Design Master. When the Design Master is synchronized with the replica, the referencing record fails to synchronize because there is no longer a valid primary key; Microsoft Jet records the error in the MSysErrors table. In this situation, however, the error will correct itself during the next synchronization when the replica is notified that the primary key has been deleted from the record.

## Record Locks

If a record is locked when Microsoft Jet attempts to update it during a synchronization, Microsoft Jet retries the update several times. If the record remains locked after repeated attempts, the synchronization fails and Microsoft Jet records an error in the MSysErrors system table. Although this type of error is exceedingly rare, it might occur in certain multiuser applications. Errors caused by locked records can be ignored because Microsoft Jet will retry updating the records during the next synchronization. Because it is unlikely that the same record will be locked during the next synchronization, the record is updated and the error is removed from the MSysError table.

## Correcting Errors

Synchronization errors are recorded in the MSysErrors table and replicated to all members of the replica set. This table includes information about the:

- Table involved.
- Record that encountered the errors.
- Replica or replicas where the error was detected.
- Replica that last changed the record.
- Type of operation that failed.
- Reason it failed.

Errors must be corrected as soon as possible, because they indicate that the data in different replicas might be diverging. You should be especially careful to correct synchronization errors before moving or renaming your database, because the error is recorded against the ReplicaID at the time the error occurred. If the ReplicaID is changed it will not be possible for Microsoft Jet to automatically remove the error records during a subsequent synchronization. If the error record is not removed, you will continue to receive notification of the error each time you open the database in Microsoft Access even if you have corrected the problem.

In many circumstances, errors are self-correcting during the next synchronization. For example, during an attempted synchronization, an update would be rejected if another user has the record locked. Microsoft Jet records an error and attempts to reapply the update at a later time. If the subsequent update succeeds, the error record is removed. As a general rule, always synchronize all members of the replica set before manually correcting synchronization errors. Due to the nature of bidirectional synchronizations, it might take more than one synchronization to clear the error record from MSysErrors after the error is corrected. However, all corrected errors should be cleared from the MSysErrors table after two bidirectional synchronizations.

### Correcting Errors Using Microsoft Access

Just as Microsoft Access for Windows 95 automatically notifies you of a synchronization conflict each time you open a database with conflicts, it also notifies you of any synchronization errors. The default Conflict Resolver that ships with Microsoft Access first displays a list of all the tables with synchronization errors. After you select a table, the Conflict Resolver displays the following information for each error: the replica set member, path, table name, record ID, attempted operation, and the reason the operation failed. You can review each error individually and take the appropriate action for correcting the error.

# Design Errors

The order in which you make design or data changes to the database has important implications for synchronizing members of the replica set. As you make changes in the design of your database, Microsoft Jet records each change in the MSysSchChange system table. Each change is recorded as a separate record in the table, and each record contains all the information about the design change. When Microsoft Jet synchronizes two members of the replica set, it compares the MSysSchChange table at the initiating member with the MSysSchChange table at the target member. If the two members are not at the same design level, Microsoft Jet applies all the design changes from the most current (highest number of levels) member to the design of the less current member. For example, if the Design Master has been changed six times, each replica must receive all six changes to make its design identical to that of the Design Master. Because of the latency in the synchronization process, one replica might have received only four of the design changes, while another replica might have received all six changes. When the replica having only four changes synchronizes with a replica that has all six changes (or with the Design Master), Microsoft Jet applies the remaining two changes to the design of the less current replica.

When Microsoft Jet applies all the design changes from one replica set member to another, it applies the changes in the exact order that the changes were made in the Design Master, and, consequently, the order in which the changes were recorded as records in the MSysSchChange table. Microsoft Jet does not examine later records in the table to determine if a design change was undone or further modified by a later change. For example, if you add a table to your database and then make the table replicable, Microsoft Jet records the creation of the table as one design change and makes the table replicable as a second design change. If you then delete the replicable table, Microsoft Jet records that as a third design change. At the next synchronization, Jet applies each change in order, even though the table doesn't exist when the synchronization is complete.

Applying design changes to replicas in the exact order the changes were made at the Design Master is a strength of Microsoft Jet database replication that ensures all replicas become identical to the Design Master. However, changes that you or a user make at a replica can cause design errors. For example, if a user at a replica creates a local table and gives it the default name table1, and you create a replicable table at the Design Master and also give it the default name table1, Microsoft Jet will fail when it attempts to synchronize the replica with the Design Master because the replica already has a table with that name. The design error is recorded in the MSysSchemaProb system table and is available for your review.

The MSysSchemaProb table is a local table and is present only when an error occurs when updating the structure of a replica. The table provides details about the cause of the error, including:

- The type of command that failed (**Create Index**, **Create Table**, and so on).
- The text of the error message.
- The design version that encountered the problem.
- Context information such as table names and field names.

The rows in the MSysSchemaProb table are automatically deleted when the corresponding design change is successfully applied during synchronization.

To solve design errors, you should carefully review the MSysSchemaProb table to identify the action that failed and then manually remove the element at the replica that is blocking the change. The blocking element must always be removed at the replica even if the design change at the Design Master was the instigator of the error. For example, to correct the error of the two tables named table1, you must delete the table from the replica even though the table was in existence prior to the creation of the table at the Design Master. Removing the blocking element at the Design Master has no effect on correcting the error because the information about the design change is already stored as a record in the MSysSchChange table. Deleting table1 at the Design Master simply adds a new record to the MSysSchChange table (recording that table1 was deleted) instead of removing the record that created table1 in the first place. Because Microsoft Jet does not allow programmers to change the contents of the MSysSchChange table, you cannot correct the error except by removing the blocking element at the replica.

# Advanced Design Considerations

Although Microsoft Jet makes database replication easy to implement through DAO programming or through Microsoft Access in combination with Microsoft Replication Manager and Briefcase, replication can be complicated by a number of special considerations. These considerations include:

- Moving the Design Master.
- Compacting your database before synchronizing.
- Synchronizing all members of the replica set before making design changes.
- Closing tables before synchronizing.
- Using list boxes tied to replicated tables.
- Distributing Microsoft Replication Manager with your applications.
- Making a database nonreplicable.

This section presents these additional factors that must be included in your planning, design, and implementation of database replication.

## Moving the Design Master

The Design Master is the most important member of a replica set because it is the only member in which you can make changes to the structure of the database. Under certain circumstances, you might have to move the Design Master to a replica. For example, you might have the Design Master on your computer while another member of your development team has a replica on his or her computer. While you are on vacation, you want the other programmer to be able to make changes to the database. You can use the **DesignMasterID** property to accomplish the transfer and synchronize the old and new Design Masters, as shown in the following code:

```
Sub SetNewDesignMaster(stroldDM, strNewDM)
    Dim dbs As Database, newdmdb As Database

    ' Open current Design Master in exclusive mode.
    Set dbs = OpenDatabase(stroldDM, True)

    ' Open database that will become the new Design Master.
    Set newdmdb = OpenDatabase(strNewDM)

    dbs.DesignMasterID = newdmdb.ReplicaID
    dbs.Synchronize strNewDM, dbRepImpExpChanges
    dbs.Close
    newdmdb.Close
End Sub
```

You must have the Design Master open to make another replica the new Design Master. The Design Master is, by definition, read-write. If you make a replica that is designated read-only into the Design Master, the target replica is made read-write; the old Design Master also remains read-write.

If the Design Master is erased or corrupted, you can designate a replica to become the new Design Master. However, remember that you can have only one Design Master at a time.

If you decide to make your own replica the new Design Master for the set, synchronize it with all the replicas in the replica set before setting the **DesignMasterID** property in your replica. You must have your replica open in exclusive mode to make it the Design Master.

## Compacting Your Database Before Synchronizing

Each time you change the design of your replicable database, Microsoft Jet stores information about the change in the MSysSchemaChg system table. If you change the same object more than once before synchronizing, Microsoft Jet continues to store the newest design in preparation for the synchronization. Frequent compacting of the database after you make design changes helps to reduce the overhead required for storing changes and reduces the information sent to the replicas. You might find it most efficient to compact your database daily and again just before synchronization.

## Synchronizing Before Making Design Changes

When two members of a replica set are synchronized, Microsoft Jet applies the design changes to each member before applying the data changes. You can reduce the amount of processing during synchronization and reduce the potential for conflicts if you synchronize all the replicas in the set before making design changes in the database.

## Closing Tables Before Synchronizing

Microsoft Jet must open tables exclusively before design changes are applied to them. If you are using a table in a database at the time you want to synchronize, Microsoft Jet suggests that you first close the table. If you use a "Synchronize Now" button on a form so users can easily click the button whenever they need to synchronize, be sure the button does not have an associated table open—either directly or through a query—in the database that is being synchronized.

## Using List Boxes with Replicated Tables

If you tie list boxes to replicable tables, under certain circumstances the list box might display system fields in addition to your regular data fields. If the option to display system objects is turned on, then the system fields in the replication system tables are also displayed. After they're visible, they might appear in the related list box.

To avoid displaying system tables, either clear the System Objects check box on the View tab of the Microsoft Access Options dialog box (**Tools** menu), or base the list box on a query that selects only the fields you want displayed.

## Distributing Microsoft Replication Manager with Your Application

You can distribute your Microsoft Access database application to others by including Microsoft Replication Manager. Setting up replicated databases with Microsoft Replication Manager is a cooperative effort involving the programmer and the site administrator. To prepare your database for replication and distribution, you need information from the site administrator, and you need to assist the administrator—preferably in person at the customer's site.

The recommended topology for using Microsoft Replication Manager with your application is a star topology, shown in Figure 7.4. You should place the Design Master on a satellite computer along with Microsoft Replication Manager, but you should not have it on a synchronization schedule. (You, or the administrator at the site, can synchronize it with the hub replica when a structural change to the database is needed.) The replica on the hub becomes the synchronization partner for each of the other replicas in the organization. In addition to the Design Master and the hub replica, a base replica is used with the setup program to copy subsequent replicas to users' machines. After a copy is made on a user's computer and it is synchronized with the hub, the copy becomes a true replica with its own unique identification.

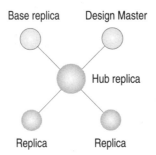

**Figure 7.4   Star topology for distributing your application**

## Making a Database Nonreplicable

After you've converted a database into a replicable database, you can't convert it back to its former status as a nonreplicable database. However, if you no longer want to use replication and want to decrease the size of a replicated database, you can create a new, nonreplicable database that contains all of the objects and data in your replicated database without the additional system fields, tables, and properties associated with replication.

▶ **To make a nonreplicable database from a replicable one using Microsoft Access**

1. Create and open a new database.

2. Import the objects (except tables) that you want in the new database.

3. On the **File** menu in the new database, point to Get External Data, and then click **Import**.

4. Create a query for each table in the replica that takes all the data in the old table and puts it a new table. Do not include the fields s_Generation, s_Guid, s_Lineage, or any other replication system fields in the query unless your application must have them to function correctly.

5. For each table in the new database, create the same index used in the replica table and the relationships that existed for the replica table.

6. Save your new database.

C H A P T E R   8

# Accessing External Data

For information on how to access external data through ODBC, see Chapter 9, "Developing Client/Server Applications."

You can use the Microsoft Jet database engine to access other popular desktop database files, spreadsheets, and textual data stored in tabular format. One way to access external data is through installable ISAM (IISAM) drivers.

Supported desktop database installable ISAM formats include older versions of Microsoft Jet, Microsoft FoxPro, dBASE, and Paradox. Supported spreadsheets include Microsoft Excel and Lotus 1-2-3. Additional support is provided for text files in character-delimited and fixed-length formats.

This chapter discusses general strategies and techniques for accessing external data through installable ISAMs and includes specific examples. In addition, it provides detailed information on managing access to text data.

**Contents**

For information on copying the code examples from the companion CD-ROM to your hard disk drive, see "Using the Companion CD-ROM" in the Preface.

## Using CH08.MDB and CHAP08.VBP

If you copied the samples from the companion CD-ROM, you can find the code examples for Microsoft Access in C:\SAMPLES\CHAP08\ ACCESS\CH08.MDB. The corresponding code examples for Visual Basic are in C:\SAMPLES\CHAP08\VB40\CHAP08.VBP.

In addition to the usual Microsoft Access and Visual Basic files, this chapter uses some files in external data formats. Four of these files, JET_SAMP.MDB, SAMPLE.DBF (a Microsoft FoxPro 3.0 database), WBSAMPLE.XLS (a Microsoft Excel 7.0 workbook file), and WSSAMPLE.XLS (a Microsoft Excel 4.0 worksheet), are found in the C:\SAMPLES\CHAP08 directory. The text file examples are found in separate directories: the comma-delimited text file and its accompanying SCHEMA.INI file are found in C:\SAMPLES\CHAP08\TEXT_CSV; the fixed-length text file and its accompanying SCHEMA.INI file are found in C:\SAMPLES\CHAP08\TEXT_FXD. The example that accompanies the section "Refreshing a Link" is found in the C:\SAMPLES\CHAP08\LOSTLINK directory.

To run any of the code examples in this chapter, open the .MDB file in Microsoft Access or open the .VBP file in Microsoft Visual Basic 4.0. You can use the examples to help you understand the concepts discussed in the chapter—and you can modify them and use them in your own applications.

# Understanding Data Sources and Access Methods

This section discusses the possible database formats you can access through the Microsoft Jet database engine, as well as the differences between data access techniques that you can use. It also discusses the resources you need to connect to external data sources, the objects and methods that you specifically *cannot* use when you are working with external data, and the transaction methods available on supported databases.

## Supported External Data Sources and Versions

Microsoft Jet can use data from any of the following external data sources:

- Microsoft Jet databases such as those created by Microsoft Access, Visual Basic, Visual C++, or Microsoft Excel. (This includes databases created with previous versions of Microsoft Jet.)
- Microsoft FoxPro, versions 2.0, 2.5, 2.6, 3.0, and DBC.

- dBASE III®, dBASE IV®, and dBASE 5.0.
- Paradox, versions 3.*x*, 4.*x*, and 5.*x*.
- Microsoft Excel 3.0, 4.0, 5.0, and 7.0 worksheets.
- Lotus WKS, WK1, WK3, and WK4 spreadsheets.
- ASCII text files in tabular format.

---

**Note**   Before you can access any external data sources, you need to make sure that you have installed the appropriate IISAM drivers. Microsoft Access users can click the **Custom/Complete** button in Microsoft Access Setup and select the **ISAMs** check box in the **Options** list box. Microsoft Visual Basic 4.0 users can click the **Custom** button in Microsoft Visual Basic 4.0 Setup and select the **ODBC and Drivers** check box and the **Installable ISAMs** check box in the **Options** list box.

---

Your Microsoft Jet application can read from and write to (in most cases) external tables, spreadsheets, and text files. You can view and edit external tables with your application without affecting their accessibility from their native applications. If you choose to link an external table, spreadsheet, or text file to a Microsoft Jet database, you can use it just as you would any other table in the database. You can create queries on the data and create forms and reports that use the data. If the external data source permits multiuser read-write access, you can even view and update the data while other users access the external data source through its native application.

# Linking, Opening, and Importing External Tables

You can access external data tables in three ways: by linking the table in a Microsoft Jet database; by opening the table directly; or by importing the data in the table into a Microsoft Jet database table. The answers to the following questions will determine the data access method you choose:

- Do you need to maintain access to the data from another application?

  If you need to maintain access to the data from another application, such as the native application used to create the database, you should link or open the external table rather than import the data. Some of the IISAM drivers provide import or export capabilities, but you shouldn't use the import feature unless you are migrating data from another database system, spreadsheet, or textual data source to a Microsoft Jet database.

- Does the data reside on an ODBC data source?

  If the table you want to access resides on an ODBC data source, for best performance you should always link the table rather than attempt to open it directly. In general, you will not need to import data from an ODBC data source.

- Will you need to establish the connection to the data frequently or just once?

If you need frequent access to the data source, use a link, because linked tables maintain all connection information between sessions. If you only need occasional access to the data source, you can reduce the size of your Microsoft Jet database by opening the external table directly in code rather than storing the connection information in a link. If you need to access the data source only one time to migrate the data to Microsoft Jet format, use the import capabilities of the installable ISAM (if available).

# Differences Between Linked and Opened Tables

If you need to maintain data in its original format (rather than importing it into a Microsoft Jet database), you must choose whether to link the table or open it directly. In most cases, you'll find that linking makes sense with ODBC data sources as it is usually faster; directly opening the table is usually faster for all data sources accessed through IISAM drivers. There are some fundamental differences in the appearance, behavior, and performance of each access method. This section describes these differences.

---

**Important**  You cannot use the **Seek** method with linked tables.

---

## Linking a Table

A linked table appears and behaves just like any other table in your Microsoft Jet database (although there are slight performance differences associated with connecting to and retrieving remote data). All of the information necessary to establish and maintain a connection to the remote data source is stored within the table definition. You can also use the **OpenRecordset** method in Microsoft Access or Visual Basic to open a linked table. The following example demonstrates how to link an external table:

```
Public Sub LinkVisualFoxProTable()
    ' This example links a FoxPro 3.0 table to a Microsoft Jet database.
    Dim dbsCurrent As DATABASE
    Dim tdfSales As TableDef

    Set dbsCurrent = OpenDatabase("C:\Samples\Chap08\Jet_Samp.mdb")
    Set tdfSales = dbsCurrent.CreateTableDef("Western Division Sales")

    tdfSales.Connect = "FoxPro 3.0;DATABASE=C:\Samples\Chap08"
    tdfSales.SourceTableName = "Sample"
    dbsCurrent.TableDefs.Append tdfSales
    dbsCurrent.Close
End Sub
```

For information about updating link information when tables are moved, see the "Maintaining Links" section later in this chapter.

## Opening a Table

In contrast, when you open a table directly, you must supply the connection information at the beginning of each session to establish a connection to the data source. None of the information needed to establish a connection to the remote data source is stored in your Microsoft Jet database. To open a table directly, you must use the **OpenDatabase** method in Microsoft Access or Visual Basic, and you must supply connection information (such as the data source, user name, password, and database name), as in the following example:

```
Public Sub OpenExcel7Workbook()
    ' This example opens the worksheet SampleSheet in a Microsoft Excel
    ' 7.0 workbook from a Jet database.
    Dim dbsCurrent As DATABASE

    Set dbsCurrent = OpenDatabase ("C:\Samples\Chap08\WBSample.xls", _
        False, False, "Excel 5.0;HDR=NO;")
    dbsCurrent.Close
End Sub
```

# External Data Access Requirements

Before you can connect your application to a remote data source, you must make sure that the remote data is accessible to your application's users and that your application is properly designed to handle remote data source security challenges. You must also make sure that your application interacts correctly with case-sensitive data sources and that the installable ISAM is correctly initialized for the data source you want to access. Finally, you must check, especially when converting existing Microsoft Access or Visual Basic code, that your code doesn't use objects or methods that are specific to Microsoft Jet data sources when accessing non-Jet data sources.

## Accessing Data Over a Secured Network

As with any other resource on a network, your application must have access to the server and share where the external data resides. You must determine if your application needs read-only or read-write permissions on the share, and you should establish the permissions according to your needs.

In addition, you must make sure that your application has proper access to the table or spreadsheet through the host application's security. You can provide password information to the host application as part of the connection string.

For database servers accessed as ODBC data sources, you may need to provide authentication information at additional levels (such as at the table or view level as well as at the database level). You should test remote data on ODBC data sources for accessibility by common users of your application rather than by those with system-level or administrative privileges. Your code should also handle requests for additional information from the remote data source (such as user name and password requests).

## Overview of Installable ISAM Windows Registry Settings

For a complete listing of Windows Registry settings and their uses, see Appendix C, "Registry Settings."

Each installable ISAM driver has a corresponding Windows Registry setting that configures the driver upon initialization. During the installation process for the IISAM drivers, the Setup program creates keys in the Windows Registry for the following data sources:

- Microsoft FoxPro, versions 2.0, 2.5, 2.6, 3.0, and DBC
- dBASE III, dBASE IV, and dBASE 5.0
- Paradox, versions 3.*x*, 4.*x*, and 5.*x*
- Microsoft Excel 3.0, 4.0, and 5.0 worksheets
- Lotus WK1, WK3, and WK4 spreadsheets
- ASCII text files in tabular format

During this process, the Microsoft Access or Visual Basic Setup program also assigns a set of default values to each installable ISAM. Your application can alter these values to change the behavior of certain aspects of each driver. For example, you can select a collating sequence for the FoxPro IISAM that changes the case-sensitive behavior of the driver, as discussed in the following section.

---

**Note** The Setup program does not write many of the settings for the Jet 2.*x* and Jet 3.0 installable ISAM drivers, or for the ODBC drivers. If you make any changes to the Windows Registry settings for any IISAM or for ODBC, you must shut down and restart Microsoft Jet so that the new settings can take effect.

---

## Accessing Data on Case-Sensitive Data Sources

Your application must be designed to support operations, such as searching, on external, case-sensitive data sources. Some desktop database products and database servers are case-sensitive by default. These include Microsoft FoxPro, dBASE, and Paradox. In addition, some database servers accessible through ODBC can be configured as case-sensitive.

If you need to search on a case-sensitive data source, you can design your queries using OR clauses to capture all possible combinations (all upper-case, all lower-case, or proper-case). There are, however, three cases where products that are typically case-sensitive are never case-sensitive.

- If you're connecting to an Xbase database, such as Microsoft FoxPro or dBASE, check the CollatingSequence value in the \Jet\3.0\Engines\Xbase key of the Windows Registry. If this value is set to ASCII, all operations are case-sensitive; if it is set to International, all operations are not case-sensitive.

- If you're connecting to a Paradox database, check the CollatingSequence value in the \Jet\3.0\Engines\Paradox key of the Windows Registry. If this value is set to ASCII, all operations are case-sensitive; if it is set to International, Norwegian-Danish, or Swedish-Finnish, all operations are not case-sensitive.

- If you're connecting to a database server through ODBC, case-sensitivity will be determined by the server's configuration. Check with your database server administrator to determine if your server is configured as case-sensitive or not case-sensitive.

---

**Note** If a case-sensitive query is performed across multiple data sources, the collating sequence in effect on the database that hosts the query will determine the query's case-sensitivity.

---

## Unsupported Objects and Methods

Microsoft Jet database applications cannot use Microsoft Jet–specific objects and methods with external data sources. The following are unsupported through the installable ISAM drivers.

| Unsupported object or method | Type |
|---|---|
| CompactDatabase | DAO method |
| Container | Data Access Object |
| CreateDatabase | DAO method |
| CreateField | DAO method (This method is supported on new tables but cannot be used to expand tables with existing fields.) |
| CreateQueryDef | DAO method |
| Document | Data Access Object |
| QueryDef | Data Access Object |
| Relation | Data Access Object |
| RepairDatabase | DAO method |

### Transaction Support

Although some methods and objects aren't supported through installable ISAM drivers, the IISAM drivers *do* support transactions on external databases that support transactions. The following table lists the transaction methods that are available on supported databases.

| DAO transaction method | Description |
| --- | --- |
| BeginTrans | Begins a transaction on the selected data source. |
| CommitTrans | Completes a transaction on the selected data source by saving changes. |
| Rollback | Completes a transaction on the selected data source by losing changes. |

# Establishing Access to External Data

Now that you're familiar with the different methods of accessing data and external data source limitations, you're ready to learn how to establish a connection and link or open external tables. This section illustrates the linking procedure by linking to a FoxPro table, demonstrates the table opening procedure by opening a worksheet in a Microsoft Excel workbook and a Microsoft Excel worksheet, and describes how to link text files through an example that uses a comma-delimited file. In addition, this section describes procedures for updating and deleting links and creating a table in an external data format.

# Establishing a Connection

Before you can establish a connection to an external data source, you must decide whether to link or open the target table. The connection information you supply is essentially the same in either case—but the techniques are slightly different. The following sections explain how to establish connections for linking and opening external tables.

## Supplying Connection Information for Linking an External Table

When you link an external table by creating or modifying a **TableDef** object, you must supply information indicating the type and location of the external database as well as the name of the table you want to link. You can accomplish this by doing one of the following:

- Set the **SourceTableName** and **Connect** properties of the **TableDef** object. This technique has the added advantage of working with existing **TableDef** objects.

- Pass the *source* and *connect* values as arguments in the **CreateTableDef** method.

## Setting Connection Information With the SourceTableName and Connect Properties

The following code fragment sets the connection information with the **Connect** and **SourceTableName** properties and assumes you want to connect to the table Q1Sales in the FoxPro 3.0 database Region1 on the share \\Sales\Regional:

```
Set tdfRegionOne = dbsCurrent.CreateTableDef("First Quarter Sales")
tdfRegionOne.Connect = "FoxPro 3.0;DATABASE=\\Sales\Regional\Region1"
tdfRegionOne.SourceTableName = "Q1Sales"
```

---

**Important**   Use a semicolon (;) to separate parameters specified in the **Connect** property. Don't include any spaces on either side of the semicolon.

---

## Setting Connection Information When You Create the TableDef

The following code fragment sets the connection information when you create the **TableDef** and assumes you want to connect to the table Q1Sales in the FoxPro 3.0 database Region1 on the share \\Sales\Regional:

```
Set tdfRegionOne = dbsCurrent.CreateTableDef("First Quarter Sales", _
    0, "Q1Sales", "FoxPro 3.0;DATABASE=\\Sales\Regional\Region1;")
```

# Supplying Connection Information for Opening an External Table

When you open an external table directly, you must supply a database path and a source database type as arguments in the **OpenDatabase** method. The source database name argument, *dbname*, is described in detail in the next section, "Specifying Database Names."

The following code fragment assumes you want to connect to the FoxPro 3.0 database Region1 on the share \\Sales\Regional:

```
Set dbsCurrent = OpenDatabase("\\Sales\Regional\Region1", _
    False, False, "FoxPro 3.0")
```

In general, you can use the following methods and properties in Visual Basic code to specify connection information:

- **OpenDatabase** method. Use the *source* argument of the **OpenDatabase** method to specify the source database type, and use the *dbname* argument to specify the database name. For ODBC data sources, use the *source* argument of the **OpenDatabase** method to specify the DSN.

- **CreateTableDef** method. Use the *connect* argument of the **CreateTableDef** method to specify the source database type or the database path, and use the *source* argument to specify the source table name.

- **OpenRecordset** method. Use the *source* argument of the **OpenRecordset** method to specify the source table name.

- **Connect** property. Use the **Connect** property to specify the source database type with the database specifier setting and use the database name with the database path setting. For ODBC data sources, use the **Connect** property to specify connection information including the DSN, user ID, password, and database name.

For examples illustrating how to supply connection information for opening an external table, see the "Putting It All Together: Building a Connection String" section later in this chapter.

## Specifying Database Names

When you specify a database name for a database, spreadsheet, or text file supported by an installable ISAM, you must include the fully qualified path to the file. On a local drive, you must include the drive letter, directory path, and file name; on a network drive, you must include the server name, share, directory path, and file name. You can also map a server, share, and directory path to a logical drive and indicate the database name as the drive letter followed by the file name. The following examples illustrate each of these situations.

To specify the FoxPro database Region1 in the \FoxPro3 directory on the local C drive, use the following database name:

```
C:\FoxPro3\Region1
```

To specify the FoxPro database Region1 on the Regional share on the Sales server, use the following database name:

```
\\Sales\Regional\Region1
```

To specify the FoxPro database Region1 on the Regional share on the Sales server where the network path \\Sales\Regional has been assigned to drive G, use the following database name:

```
G:\Region1
```

---

**Note**  ODBC data sources use a different specifier, called a DSN, to indicate the database name. For all ODBC data sources, use the empty string "" as the database name. The ODBC DSN is described in the following section, "Specifying Data Source Names."

---

## Specifying Data Source Names

For more information on creating a DSN through the ODBC Manager application, see the ODBC Manager online Help.

ODBC data sources use a different syntax for specifying database names and connection information. You can add the data source name, or DSN, by using the ODBC Manager application or the **RegisterDatabase** method of the **DBEngine** object. Data source names are stored in the Windows Registry subkey ODBC.INI.

Each entry in the ODBC.INI subkey assigns a logical DSN to a set of attributes that includes: the name of the ODBC database server; the name of the database on the server, if multiple databases are supported; the type of server (for example, SQL Server); a description of network and connection parameters; and additional information, such as character set conversions. Because connections to ODBC data sources rely on this information, your application must make sure users have the appropriate DSN in their Windows Registry before you attempt to access remote data.

## Specifying Source Database Types

Each external ISAM format has an associated database type that must be specified when using the driver. Each installable ISAM driver also has a Windows Registry subkey that configures the behavior of the driver. When you build a connection string, as discussed in "Putting It All Together: Building a Connection String" later in this chapter, you must include a source database type so that Microsoft Jet knows how to handle the external data.

---

**Note**  All ODBC data sources use the source database type ODBC.

---

The following table lists the source database types.

| Data source | Source database types |
| --- | --- |
| dBASE | dBASE III |
| | dBASE IV |
| | dBASE 5.0 |
| Microsoft Excel | Excel 3.0 |
| | Excel 4.0 |
| | Excel 5.0* |
| FoxPro | FoxPro 20 |
| | FoxPro 2.5 |
| | FoxPro 2.6 |
| | FoxPro 3.0 |
| | FoxPro DBC |
| Lotus | Lotus WK1 |
| | Lotus WK3 |
| | Lotus WK4 |

| Data source | Source database types (*cont'd*) |
|---|---|
| ODBC | ODBC |
| Paradox | Paradox 3.*x* |
|  | Paradox 4.*x* |
|  | Paradox 5.*x* |
| Text | Text |

\* The Excel 5.0 source database type string is used to specify Microsoft Excel 5.0 and Microsoft Excel 7.0 workbooks.

**Important**  You must enter the source database type strings exactly as they appear in the table, including spaces and punctuation.

## Specifying a Password

Microsoft Jet honors the security system in all external data sources that support security. Your application must supply a password to the external data source to establish a connection. You can do this by prompting the user for this information and building it into the connection string, or you can "hard code" the password into your application.

**Note**  If you store sensitive data in the external data source, you shouldn't hard code passwords in your Microsoft Jet application.

Use the PWD parameter to pass the password to the external data source, as in the following example. You must follow the password parameter with a semicolon.

```
Set tdfRegionOne = dbsCurrent.CreateTableDef("First Quarter Sales", _
    0, "Q1Sales", _
    "FoxPro 3.0;DATABASE=\\Sales\Regional\Region1;PWD=RollsRoyce;")
```

**Note**  You can use the password parameter to specify database passwords only; you cannot use the password to log on to a network. If your application requires network access, you must establish these connections before attempting to access the external data.

You cannot use the PWD parameter to decrypt Microsoft Excel worksheets or workbooks; you must unprotect and save the worksheet or workbook in Microsoft Excel before you can open it with the Microsoft Excel installable ISAM driver.

### Saving ODBC Passwords Between Sessions

If you don't want to hard code sensitive ODBC database passwords into your application or require your users to enter a password each time they start the application, you can set the **Attributes** property of the **TableDef** object to **dbAttachSavePWD**. This saves the ODBC password as part of the table definition. Each time the user opens the remote table through the **TableDef**, the password information is automatically applied. The following line of code shows how to save a password:

```
RegionOne.Attributes = dbAttachSavePWD
```

For more on the MSysConf table, see Chapter 9, "Developing Client/Server Applications."

If your remote data is particularly sensitive, you may not want to allow users to save their passwords. To change this behavior, you must modify the MSysConf table in your remote database to disallow local storage of login IDs and passwords (by default, local storage is allowed). If your application has already been deployed with password saving enabled, you can still disallow local user ID and password saving with MSysConf; ODBC will automatically prompt users for any missing authentication information when they attempt to open the remote database.

## Putting It All Together: Building a Connection String

A complete connection string includes all information necessary to connect to and open an external data source on a local drive, network, or ODBC-compliant database server. Connection strings consist of a database type followed by a database name or a DSN (ODBC data sources only). If the external data source requires additional information, such as an ODBC database name, a user ID, or a password, you can include these in the connection string as well. You can set a connection string by using the **OpenDatabase** method, the **CreateTableDef** method, or the **Connect** property.

The following code fragment sets the connection string with the **OpenDatabase** method:

```
Set dbsCurrent = OpenDatabase("\\Sales\Regional\Region1", _
    False, False, "FoxPro 3.0")
```

The following code fragment sets the connection string with the **CreateTableDef** method; connection information is supplied as arguments in the method:

```
Set tdfRegionOne = dbsCurrent.CreateTableDef("First Quarter Sales", _
    0, "Q1Sales", "FoxPro 3.0;DATABASE=\\Sales\Regional\Region1"
```

The following code fragment sets the connection string with the **Connect** property, **CreateTableDef** method, and **SourceTableName** property:

```
Set tdfRegionOne = dbsCurrent.CreateTableDef("First Quarter Sales")
tdfRegionOne.Connect = "FoxPro 3.0;DATABASE=\\Sales\Regional\Region1"
tdfRegionOne.SourceTableName = "Q1Sales"
```

# Opening an External Table

You need to perform two steps to open an external table directly:

1. Use the **OpenDatabase** method of the **Workspace** object to open the Microsoft Jet database and provide connection information for the external table. Arguments in the **OpenDatabase** method specify the database name, whether the external data source is opened as exclusive, whether the external data source is opened as read-only, and the source database type.

2. Use the **OpenRecordset** method of the **Database** object to create a new **Recordset** object for the external table. Use the *source* argument of the **OpenRecordset** method to supply the name of the table to open.

---

**Note**  The *dbname* argument of the **OpenDatabase** method is used to specify the database name, and the *source* argument of the **OpenRecordset** method is used to specify the table name for all installable ISAM drivers. For external data sources that store one table per file, the *dbname* argument should contain the full directory or network path to the file, and *source* should contain the data file name with no extension. For external data sources that store multiple tables in a file, *dbname* should contain the full directory or network path to the file including the file name and extension; *source* should contain the table name.

---

For more information about working with **Recordset** objects, see Chapter 5, "Working with Records and Fields."

You can specify a *type* argument for the **OpenRecordset** method if you want more control over the **Recordset** type. By default, Microsoft Jet creates a dynaset-type **Recordset** object. You can also specify a snapshot-type **Recordset** object with the **dbOpenSnapshot** constant or a table-type **Recordset** object with the **dbOpenTable** constant.

---

**Important**  The **dbOpenTable** constant is not a valid argument for ODBC databases.

---

After you've opened the table, you can access the **Recordset** object you created just as you would any other **Recordset** in your Microsoft Jet database. Keep in mind, however, that you must re-establish your connection to the external data source and re-create the **Recordset** object for each session.

The following code examples open a table that is stored in a Microsoft Excel 7.0 workbook and a Microsoft Excel 4.0 worksheet on the companion CD-ROM. The first example opens a single worksheet in a workbook; the second example opens a worksheet that is the only "table" in its file.

The examples are identical except for the **OpenDatabase** and **OpenRecordset** methods. The first example appears in its entirety in the next section; code fragments from the second example that use different parameters also appear here. Both complete examples are on the companion CD-ROM.

## Example: Opening a Table in a Microsoft Excel 7.0 Workbook

The sample database CH08.MDB on the CD-ROM contains the Microsoft Excel 7.0 workbook WBSAMPLE.XLS and code module discussed in this example.

This example steps you through opening a table that is stored in a Microsoft Excel 7.0 workbook on the companion CD-ROM. The example follows the steps outlined in the previous section, "Opening an External Table."

The first step is to open the Microsoft Jet database:

```
Set dbsCurrent = OpenDatabase("C:\Samples\Chap08\WBSample.xls", _
    False, False, "Excel 5.0;HDR=NO;")
```

Notice that the example specifies the Microsoft Excel 7.0 workbook as Excel 5.0 and that it suppresses headers. If you don't suppress headers in this example, the **RecordCount** displayed in the message box will be 49.

The second step is to create a **Recordset** for the external data using code similar to the following:

```
Set rstSales = dbsCurrent.OpenRecordset("SampleSheet$")
```

Notice the dollar sign character following the sheet name. This tells the installable ISAM that you're referencing the entire sheet.

The following is a complete code example that you can find in the Chap08 Microsoft Access database or Visual Basic project on the companion CD-ROM. The example establishes the connection, creates a **Recordset** object, and counts the records in the **Recordset** to make sure that it can be accessed.

```
' This example opens the worksheet SampleSheet in a Microsoft Excel 7.0
' workbook from a Microsoft Jet database and tests the external data
' by computing the number of records in the worksheet.

Public Sub OpenExcel7Workbook()
    Dim dbsCurrent As Database
    Dim rstSales As Recordset
    Dim qdfNumOrders As QueryDef
    Dim intNumRecords As Integer

    ' Open the Microsoft Jet sample database for Chapter 8.
    Set dbsCurrent = OpenDatabase("C:\Samples\Chap08\WBSample.xls", _
        False, False, "Excel 5.0;HDR=NO;")
    ' Create a Recordset for the Microsoft Excel workbook.
    Set rstSales = dbsCurrent.OpenRecordset("SampleSheet$")

    ' Execute a MoveLast and count the records.
    rstSales.MoveLast
    intNumRecords = rstSales.RecordCount
    MsgBox "There are " & intNumRecords & " rows in this worksheet."
    rstSales.Close
    dbsCurrent.Close
End Sub
```

## Example: Opening a Microsoft Excel 4.0 Worksheet

The sample database CH08.MDB on the CD-ROM contains the Microsoft Excel 4.0 worksheet WSSAMPLE.XLS and code module discussed in this example.

This example steps you through opening a Microsoft Excel 4.0 worksheet on the companion CD-ROM. The example follows the steps outlined earlier in this chapter.

The first step is to open the Microsoft Jet database:

```
Set dbsCurrent = OpenDatabase("C:\Samples\Chap08", _
    False, False, "Excel 4.0;HDR=NO;")
```

The next step is to create a **Recordset** for the external data:

```
Set rstSales = dbsCurrent.OpenRecordset("WSSample")
```

You can find the complete code example in the Excel4WorksheetSample module on the companion CD-ROM. The example establishes the connection, creates a **Recordset** object, and counts the records in the **Recordset** to make sure that it can be accessed.

# Creating a Link to an External Table

The following procedure outlines the four steps to creating a link to an external table. (This explanation uses the **CreateTableDef** method and the **Connect** and **SourceTableName** properties.)

▶ **To create a link to an external table**

1. Use the **OpenDatabase** method of the **Workspace** object to open the Microsoft Jet database that will store the linked table definition.

2. Use the **CreateTableDef** method of the **Database** object to create a table definition for the linked table. You can assign a unique, descriptive name to the **TableDef** object, which can be any valid Microsoft Jet table name.

3. Use the **Connect** and **SourceTableName** properties of the **TableDef** object to set the connection information for the linked table. This step establishes the connection and provides authentication services, such as user name and password presentation to the remote data source, if needed.

4. Use the **Append** method of the **TableDefs** collection to append the table definition for the linked table to the **TableDefs** collection.

After you've created the link, you can access the external table as you would any other table in your Microsoft Jet database. The link remains current unless you delete the link or delete or move the external table. You can update the link information to an external table that has been moved by refreshing the link.

For information about removing and refreshing links, see the "Maintaining Links" section later in this chapter.

## Example: Linking a FoxPro Database

The sample database CH08.MDB on the CD-ROM contains the FoxPro database and code module discussed in this example.

The following example steps you through linking a FoxPro database on the companion CD-ROM to a Microsoft Jet database. The example follows the steps outlined in the previous section, "Creating a Link to an External Table."

The first step is to open a Microsoft Jet database:

```
Set dbsCurrent = OpenDatabase("C:\Samples\Chap08\Jet_Samp.mdb")
```

The second step is to create the table definition:

```
Set tdfSales = dbsCurrent.CreateTableDef("Western Division Sales")
```

The third step is to set the connection information:

```
tdfSales.Connect = "FoxPro 3.0;DATABASE=C:\Samples\Chap08"
tdfSales.SourceTableName = "Sample"
```

**Note**  You can use the **Connect** property to specify the database name, and the **SourceTableName** property to specify the table name for all installable ISAM drivers. For external data sources that store one table per file, the **Connect** property should contain the full directory or network path to the file, and the **SourceTableName** property should contain the data file name with no extension. For external data sources that store multiple tables in a file, the **Connect** property should contain the full directory or network path to the file including the file name and extension; the **SourceTableName** property should contain the table name.

The fourth and final step is to append the **TableDef** to the **TableDefs** collection:

```
dbsCurrent.TableDefs.Append tdfSales
```

The following is a complete code example that you can also find in the FoxProSample module. The example establishes the connection, appends the linked table, and tests the data to make sure that it can be accessed.

```
' This example links a FoxPro 3.0 table to a Microsoft Jet database
' and tests the link by computing the sum of the extended prices.

Public Sub LinkVisualFoxProTable()
    Dim dbsCurrent As Database
    Dim tdfSales As TableDef
    Dim qdfNumOrders As QueryDef
    Dim rstTotalSales As Recordset

    ' Open the Microsoft Jet sample database for Chapter 8.
    Set dbsCurrent = OpenDatabase("C:\Samples\Chap08\Jet_Samp.mdb")
    ' Create a table definition for the FoxPro table.
    Set tdfSales = dbsCurrent.CreateTableDef("Western Division Sales")
```

```
' Provide source database type, database name with Connect property.
tdfSales.Connect = "FoxPro 3.0;DATABASE=C:\Samples\Chap08"
' Provide name of FoxPro table with the SourceTableName property.
tdfSales.SourceTableName = "Sample"
' Append TableDef to the TableDefs collection to create the link.
dbsCurrent.TableDefs.Append tdfSales

' Run a simple query to ensure the data is accessible.
Set qdfNumOrders = dbsCurrent.CreateQueryDef("Total Western Sales")
qdfNumOrders.SQL = "SELECT Sum (Ext_price) As Tally FROM " _
    & "[Western Division Sales];"
Set rstTotalSales = qdfNumOrders.OpenRecordset()

MsgBox "Total Sales = $" & rstTotalSales!Tally
rstTotalSales.Close
dbsCurrent.Close
End Sub
```

# Special Considerations for Desktop Databases

The following sections describe special information that will help you understand how Microsoft Jet interacts with Borland dBASE, Microsoft FoxPro, and Borland Paradox databases. Each desktop database is covered separately.

## Working with dBASE Databases

Borland's dBASE product line includes the following versions supported by the Microsoft Jet Xbase installable ISAM driver: dBASE III, dBASE IV, and dBASE 5.0. dBASE databases differ from Microsoft Jet databases in four major areas: data types, handling of deleted records, specification of indexes, and storage of Memo fields. The following sections describe these differences.

### Converting dBASE Data Types to Jet Data Types

Microsoft Jet translates each dBASE data type into the corresponding Microsoft Jet data type when your application reads the data. The following table shows the one-to-one correspondence between data types.

| dBASE data type | Microsoft Jet data type |
| --- | --- |
| Character | Text |
| Numeric, Float | Double |
| Logical | Boolean |
| Date | Date/Time |
| Memo | Memo |
| OLE | OLE Object |

## Handling Deleted Records

When you delete a record from a dBASE table through your application, the record is marked as deleted in the table. The record is not, however, removed from the table because dBASE allows users to recover deleted records until the table is packed. Because you cannot pack a dBASE table through Microsoft Jet, deleted records will continue to appear in your application's data set.

To force Microsoft Jet to filter out deleted records in a dBASE table, you must set a value in the Windows Registry. You can do this by setting the Deleted value in \Jet\3.0\Engines\Xbase to 01 (**True**) and restarting Microsoft Jet to hide deleted records from your application.

## Handling dBASE Indexes

You can speed up Microsoft Jet access to dBASE tables by specifying the dBASE .NDX or .MDX index files to use. Index files are specified in an .INF file, which you can create either by linking your dBASE table through the Microsoft Access user interface or by creating a text file with the same file name as your dBASE database and appending an .INF extension. The following procedure describes how to create an .INF file for the hypothetical dBASE database SALES.DBF.

1. Create the text file SALES.INF.

2. On the first line, add the database type identifier enclosed in square brackets. For example, to specify dBASE III indexes, type the following:

   ```
   [dBASE III]
   ```

3. Assign an index number to the first index for the database. Number the first index NDX1, the second NDX2, and so on. If you want to specify multiple index files (.MDX) for dBASE IV or dBASE 5.0 databases, use index numbers of the form MDX1, MDX2, and so on. You can also specify unique indexes by prepending a "U" to the index number.

4. Follow the index number with an equal sign and the file name of the index you want to specify, including the extension. Don't put any spaces in this entry. For example, to specify the index CUSTNAME.NDX as the first index and the unique index CUSTNO.NDX as the second index, add the following entries:

   ```
   NDX1=CUSTNAME.NDX
   UNDX1=CUSTNO.NDX
   ```

5. Repeat steps 3 and 4 until you've specified all indexes for the database table. Your completed .INF file should look similar to the following:

   ```
   [dBASE III]
   NDX1=CUSTNAME.NDX
   UNDX1=CUSTNO.NDX
   ```

6. Save the .INF file to the directory that contains your dBASE database. Alternatively, you can create a Windows Registry entry to point to the path where the .INF is stored. This is useful if you cannot store the .INF file in the same directory as the database or if you want to keep all .INF files in one shared location for easy maintenance.

If you want to create an INFPath entry in your Windows Registry, you must manually add the Registry value in the Registry Editor as a string value. To add the value, open the \Jet\3.0\Engines\Xbase folder in the Windows Registry, on the **Edit** menu, click **New**, and then click **String Value**. Type **INFPath** as the name, and type the full directory or network path to the .INF file in the data field. Save the Registry changes and restart Microsoft Jet to use this setting.

Keep in mind that Microsoft Jet will need to periodically update your index files as you change data in your dBASE database. If you associate index files with a dBASE database that is linked or opened from a Microsoft Jet database, you need to make sure the indexes are available to your Microsoft Jet database as well.

---

**Important**  Don't delete or move the index files or the .INF file without updating associated references (such as the Windows Registry). If Microsoft Jet doesn't have access to up-to-date index information, it cannot correctly process queries.

---

### Handling Memo Fields

Memo fields for dBASE databases are stored in the file system instead of in the database. If you want to link or open a dBASE database that has Memo fields, make sure the Memo files are stored in the same directory as the database files.

## Working with FoxPro Databases

The Microsoft FoxPro product line includes the following versions supported by the Microsoft Jet Xbase installable ISAM driver: FoxPro 2.0, FoxPro 2.5, FoxPro 2.6, FoxPro 3.0, and FoxPro DBC. FoxPro databases differ from Microsoft Jet databases in four major areas: data types, handling of deleted records, specification of indexes, and storage of Memo fields. The following sections describe these differences.

### Converting FoxPro Data Types to Jet Data Types

Microsoft Jet translates each FoxPro data type into the corresponding Microsoft Jet data type when your application reads the data. The following table shows the one-to-one correspondence between data types.

| FoxPro data type | Microsoft Jet data type |
|---|---|
| Character | Text |
| Numeric, Float | Double |
| Logical | Boolean |
| Date | Date/Time |
| Memo | Memo |
| General | OLE Object |
| Double* | Double |
| Currency* | Currency |
| Integer* | Long |
| DateTime* | Date/Time |

\* Supported in Microsoft FoxPro 3.0 and Microsoft FoxPro DBC only

## Handling Deleted Records

When you delete a record from a FoxPro table through your application, the record is marked as deleted in the table. The record is not, however, removed from the table because FoxPro allows users to recover deleted records until the table is packed. Because you cannot pack a FoxPro table through the Microsoft Jet database engine, deleted records will continue to appear in your application's data set.

To force Microsoft Jet to filter out deleted records in a FoxPro table, you must set a value in the Windows Registry. You can do this by setting the Deleted value in \Jet\3.0\Engines\Xbase to 01 (**True**) and restarting the Microsoft Jet database engine to hide deleted records from your application.

## Handling FoxPro Indexes

You can speed up Microsoft Jet access to FoxPro tables by specifying which FoxPro .IDX or .CDX index files to use. Index files are specified in an .INF file, which you can create by linking your FoxPro table through the Microsoft Access user interface or by creating a text file with the same file name as your FoxPro database and appending an .INF extension. The following procedure describes how to create an .INF file for the hypothetical FoxPro database SALES.DBF.

1. Create the text file SALES.INF.
2. On the first line, add the database type identifier enclosed in square brackets. For example, to specify FoxPro 2.0 indexes, type the following:

```
[FoxPro 2.0]
```

3. Assign an index number to the first index for the database. Number the first index IDX1, the second IDX2, and so on. If you want to specify combined index files (.CDX) for FoxPro databases, use index numbers of the form CDX1, CDX2, and so on. You can also specify unique indexes by prepending a "U" to the index number.

4. Follow the index number with an equal sign and the file name of the index you want to specify, including the extension. Do not put any spaces in this entry. For example, to specify the index CUSTNAME.IDX as the first index and the unique index CUSTNO.IDX as the second index, add the following entries:

```
IDX1=CUSTNAME.IDX
UIDX1=CUSTNO.IDX
```

5. Repeat steps 3 and 4 until you have specified all indexes for the database table. Your completed .INF file should look similar to the following:

```
[FoxPro 2.0]
IDX1=CUSTNAME.IDX
UIDX1=CUSTNO.IDX
```

6. Save the .INF file to the directory that contains your FoxPro database. Alternatively, you can create a Windows Registry entry to point to the path where the .INF is stored. This is useful if you cannot store the .INF file in the same directory as the database or if you want to keep all .INF files in one shared location for easy maintenance.

   If you want to create an INFPath entry in your Windows Registry, you must manually add the Registry value in the Registry Editor as a string value. To add the value, open the \Jet\3.0\Engines\Xbase folder in the Windows Registry, on the **Edit** menu, click **New**, and then click **String Value**. Type INFPath as the name and type the full directory or network path to the .INF file in the data field. Save the Registry changes and restart Microsoft Jet to use this setting.

Keep in mind that Microsoft Jet will need to periodically update your index files as you change data in your FoxPro database. If you associate index files with a FoxPro database that is linked or opened from a Microsoft Jet database, you must make sure the indexes are available to your Jet database as well.

---

**Important** Don't delete or move the index files or the .INF file without updating associated references (such as the Windows Registry). If Microsoft Jet doesn't have access to up-to-date index information, it cannot correctly process queries.

---

### Handling Memo Fields

Memo fields for FoxPro databases are stored in the file system rather than in the database. If you want to link or open a FoxPro database that has Memo fields, make sure the Memo files are stored in the same directory as the database files.

## Working with Paradox Databases

Borland's Paradox product line includes the following versions supported by the Microsoft Jet Paradox installable ISAM driver: Paradox 3.*x*, Paradox 4.*x*, and Paradox 5.*x*. Paradox databases differ from Microsoft Jet databases in three major areas: data types, handling of indexes and keys, and dependency on network resources. The following sections describe these differences.

### Converting Paradox Data Types to Jet Data Types

Microsoft Jet translates each Paradox data type into the corresponding Jet data type when your application reads the data. The following table shows the one-to-one correspondence between data types.

| Paradox data type* | Microsoft Jet data type |
| --- | --- |
| Alphanumeric | Text |
| Number | Double |
| Short number | Integer |
| Currency | Double |
| Date | Date/Time |
| Memo | Memo |
| OLE | OLE Object (Note that the Microsoft Jet database engine recognizes the object but will not let you open it.) |
| Logical (Paradox 5.*x*) | Boolean |
| Integer (Paradox 5.*x*) | Long |
| Timestamp (Paradox 5.*x*) | Date/Time |
| Binary (Paradox 5.*x*) | Byte |
| BCD (Paradox 5.*x*) | Double |
| Time (Paradox 5.*x*) | Date/Time |
| Autoinc (Paradox 5.*x*) | Counter |

* Paradox Graphic, Binary, and Formatted memo types aren't supported and won't appear when you display external Paradox tables.

### Handling Paradox Indexes and Keys

Paradox uses a .PX index file to store primary key information for each table that has a primary key. Microsoft Jet must be able to locate the .PX each time you attempt to use the table. If the .PX is unavailable, Microsoft Jet will be unable to open the Paradox table.

You cannot update data in a Paradox table that has no primary key. Also, you cannot open a Paradox table that has no primary key in shared mode.

### Understanding the ParadoxNetPath, ParadoxUserName, and ParadoxNetStyle Settings

For more information about Paradox-specific settings in the Windows Registry, see the Paradox section of Appendix C, "Registry Settings."

Microsoft Jet uses three settings to control user access to Paradox tables that reside on a file server. You can set each of these values in the Windows Registry.

The first value, ParadoxNetPath, indicates the location of the network control file PARADOX.NET (for Paradox 3.*x* databases) or the file PDOXUSRS.NET (for Paradox 4.*x* databases). This setting must be identical for all users accessing a particular Paradox database.

The second value, ParadoxUserName, is a string value that is displayed in Paradox to an interactive Paradox user when the user attempts to place a lock that is incompatible with the lock held by the Microsoft Jet Paradox installable ISAM driver.

The third value, ParadoxNetStyle, indicates whether users are accessing the Paradox database using the Paradox 3.*x* or Paradox 4.*x* locking method.

For more information on Paradox network dependencies and locking methods, consult the Borland Paradox documentation.

## Special Considerations for Spreadsheets

The following sections describe special information that will help you understand how Microsoft Jet interacts with Lotus 1-2-3 spreadsheets and Microsoft Excel worksheets and workbooks. Both spreadsheet products have one common feature worth mentioning: the HDR parameter in the connection string. Additional considerations for each spreadsheet product are covered separately in the sections that follow.

### Using the HDR Parameter to Suppress Headers

The Windows Registry keys that manage behavior in Lotus 1-2-3 spreadsheets and Microsoft Excel worksheets and workbooks contain a setting that determines whether the installable ISAM should use the data in the cells of the first row of the sheet as column names in the Microsoft Jet database. This setting, FirstRowHasNames, is found in the \Jet\3.0\Engines\Lotus folder for Lotus 1-2-3 and the \Jet\3.0\Engines\Excel folder for Microsoft Excel. When the value of FirstRowHasNames is **True** (the default), *all* sheets of that product family are handled as if the first row contained column name information.

To override this Windows Registry setting on a sheet-by-sheet basis, you must use the HDR parameter in the connection string. Set HDR to **True** (HDR=**Yes**) to instruct the installable ISAM to use the data in the first row of the sheet as column names, regardless of the Registry setting. Set HDR to **False** (HDR=**No**) to instruct the installable ISAM to treat the first row of the sheet as data, regardless of the Registry setting.

The following code example opens a worksheet in a Microsoft Excel 7.0 workbook from the sample database JET_SAMP.MDB and computes the number of records in the worksheet. When the HDR parameter in the connection string is set to **No**, the count is 50 records; when it's set to **Yes**, the count is 49.

```
Public Sub TestHDRConnectParameter()
    Dim dbsCurrent As DATABASE
    Dim rstSales As Recordset
    Dim qdfNumOrders As QueryDef
    Dim rstTotalSales As Recordset
    Dim intNumRecords As Integer

    ' Open the Microsoft Jet sample database for Chapter 8.
    Set dbsCurrent = OpenDatabase("C:\Samples\Chap08\WBSample.xls", _
        False, False, "Excel 5.0;HDR=No;")
    ' Create a Recordset for the Microsoft Excel workbook.
    Set rstSales = dbsCurrent.OpenRecordset("SampleSheet$")
    ' Execute a MoveLast and count the records.
    rstSales.MoveLast
    intNumRecords = rstSales.RecordCount
    MsgBox "There are " & intNumRecords & " rows in this " & _
        "worksheet (HDR=No)."
    ' Close the Recordset and Microsoft Jet sample database.
    rstSales.Close
    dbsCurrent.Close
    MsgBox "Closed the 50-record Recordset and sample database."
    ' Open the Microsoft Jet sample database with HDR set to "Yes".
    Set dbsCurrent = OpenDatabase("C:\Samples\Chap08\WBSample.xls", _
        False, False, "Excel 5.0;HDR=Yes;")
    ' Create another Recordset for the Microsoft Excel workbook.
    Set rstSales = dbsCurrent.OpenRecordset("SampleSheet$")
    ' Execute a MoveLast and check the count.
    rstSales.MoveLast
    intNumRecords = rstSales.RecordCount
    MsgBox "Now there are " & intNumRecords & " rows in this " & _
        "worksheet (HDR=Yes)."
    rstSales.Close
    dbsCurrent.Close
End Sub
```

## Working with Lotus 1-2-3 Worksheets

Lotus Development Corporation's 1-2-3 product line includes the following worksheet versions supported by the Microsoft Jet Lotus installable ISAM driver: Lotus WKS, Lotus WK1, Lotus WK3, and Lotus WK4. Specific versions of Lotus worksheets allow different amounts of access to the data when linked or opened through the Lotus installable ISAM:

- Lotus .WKS and .WK4 files allow read-only access to the data. You cannot add, delete, or modify rows in worksheets created with these versions.

- Lotus .WK1 and .WK3 files allow read and insert access to the data. You can read all rows and add new rows but you cannot delete or modify existing rows in worksheets created with these versions.

### Specifying Sheets and Ranges in Lotus Worksheet Files

You can specify a subset of the available data when you open a Lotus 1-2-3 single- or multi-sheet worksheet file. In single-sheet files, you can open the entire sheet, a named range of cells, or an unnamed range of cells. In a multi-sheet file, you can open a single sheet, a named range anywhere in the multi-sheet file, or an unnamed range in a single sheet. The following table lists the conventions for the DATABASE and *source* arguments you must supply to access each of these objects.

| To access this object | In this Lotus version | Use this syntax |
| --- | --- | --- |
| Entire sheet in a single-sheet file | WKS and WK1 | Specify the fully qualified network or directory path to the worksheet file with the DATABASE parameter; specify the worksheet as **FILENAME#WKS** or **FILENAME#WK1** with the *source* argument, where **FILENAME** is the name of the worksheet. |
| Entire sheet in a multi-sheet file | WK3 and WK4 | Specify the fully qualified network or directory path to the multi-sheet file, including the multi-sheet file name, with the DATABASE parameter; specify the worksheet as **SHEETNAME:** with the *source* argument, where **SHEETNAME** is the name of the worksheet. **Important:** You must follow the worksheet name with a colon (:). |

| To access this object | In this Lotus version | Use this syntax (*cont'd*) |
|---|---|---|
| Named range of cells in a single- or multi-sheet file | WKS, WK1, WK3, and WK4 | Specify the fully qualified network or directory path to the single- or multi-sheet file, including the file name, with the DATABASE parameter; specify the named range as **NamedRange** with the *source* argument, where **NamedRange** is the name you assigned to the range in Lotus 1-2-3. **Important:** You must name the range in Lotus 1-2-3 before attempting to open or link it. |
| Unnamed range of cells in a single-sheet file | WKS and WK1 | Specify the fully qualified network or directory path to the worksheet file, including the worksheet file name, with the DATABASE parameter; specify the range as **A1..Z256** with the *source* argument. Replace **A1..Z256** with range of cells you want to access. |
| Unnamed range of cells in a multi-sheet file | WK3 and WK4 | Specify the fully qualified network or directory path to the multi-sheet file, including the file name, with the DATABASE parameter; specify the sheet you want to link or open as **SHEETNAME:** and the range as **A1..Z256** with the *source* argument. For example, to access cells A1 through Z256 in worksheet SHEETNAME, you would use the following in the *source* argument **SHEETNAME:A1..Z256**. |

**Note**  You cannot specify a value in a range that exceeds the maximum number of rows, columns, or sheets for the worksheet. See your Lotus 1-2-3 documentation for these values.

For examples that illustrate the concepts discussed in this section, see the "Microsoft Excel Sheet and Range Specification Examples" section later in this chapter.

# Working with Microsoft Excel Worksheets and Workbooks

The Microsoft Excel product line includes the following single-sheet worksheet and multi-sheet workbook versions supported by Microsoft Jet installable ISAMs: Excel 3.0 and Excel 4.0 (single-sheet) and Excel 5.0 and Excel 7.0 (multi-sheet workbooks). There are a few operations that you cannot perform on Microsoft Excel worksheets or workbooks through the Microsoft Excel installable ISAM:

- You cannot delete rows from Microsoft Excel worksheets or workbooks.

- You can clear data from individual cells in a worksheet, but you cannot modify or clear cells that contain formulas.

- You cannot create indexes on Microsoft Excel worksheets or workbooks.

- You cannot read encrypted data through the Microsoft Excel installable ISAM. The PWD parameter in the connection string cannot be used to open an encrypted worksheet or workbook, even if you supply the correct password. You must decrypt all Microsoft Excel worksheets or workbooks through the Excel user interface if you plan to link or open them in your Microsoft Jet database.

## Specifying Sheets and Ranges in Microsoft Excel Worksheet and Workbook Files

You can specify a subset of the available data when you open a Microsoft Excel worksheet or workbook. In worksheet files, you can open the entire sheet, a named range of cells, or an unnamed range of cells. In a workbook file, you can open a single worksheet, a named range anywhere in the workbook, or an unnamed range in a single worksheet. The following table lists the conventions for the DATABASE and *source* arguments you must supply to access each of these objects.

| To access this object | In this version of Microsoft Excel | Use this syntax |
|---|---|---|
| Entire sheet in a worksheet file | Microsoft Excel 3.0 and Microsoft Excel 4.0 | Specify the fully qualified network or directory path to the worksheet file with the DATABASE parameter; specify the sheet as **FILENAME#XLS** with the *source* argument, where **FILENAME** is the name of the worksheet. |
| Entire worksheet in a workbook file | Microsoft Excel 5.0 and Microsoft Excel 7.0 | Specify the fully qualified network or directory path to the workbook file, including the workbook file name, with the DATABASE parameter; specify the sheet as **SHEETNAME$** with the *source* argument, where **SHEETNAME** is the name of the worksheet. **Important:** You must follow the worksheet name with a dollar sign ($). |

| To access this object | In this version of Microsoft Excel | Use this syntax (*cont'd*) |
|---|---|---|
| Named range of cells in a worksheet or workbook file | Microsoft Excel 3.0, Microsoft Excel 4.0, Microsoft Excel 5.0, and Microsoft Excel 7.0 | Specify the fully qualified network or directory path to the worksheet or workbook file, including the worksheet or workbook file name, with the DATABASE parameter; specify the named range as **NamedRange** with the *source* argument, where **NamedRange** is the name you assigned to the range in Microsoft Excel. **Important:** You must name the range in Microsoft Excel before attempting to open or link it. |
| Unnamed range of cells in a worksheet file | Microsoft Excel 3.0 and Microsoft Excel 4.0 | Specify the fully qualified network or directory path to the worksheet file, including the worksheet file name, with the DATABASE parameter; specify the range as **A1:Z256** with the *source* argument. Replace **A1:Z256** with range of cells you want to access. |
| Unnamed range of cells in a single worksheet in a workbook file | Microsoft Excel 5.0 and Microsoft Excel 7.0 | Specify the fully qualified network or directory path to the workbook file, including the workbook file name, with the DATABASE parameter; specify the sheet you want to link or open as **SHEETNAME$** and the range as **A1:Z256** with the *source* argument. For example, to access cells A1 through Z256 in worksheet SHEETNAME, you would use the following in the *source* argument **SHEETNAME$A1:Z256**. |

**Note**  You cannot specify a value in a range that exceeds the maximum number of rows, columns, or sheets for the worksheet or workbook. See your Microsoft Excel documentation for these values.

## Microsoft Excel Sheet and Range Specification Examples

The following code examples illustrate how to specify an entire worksheet, a named range, and an unnamed range of cells in a Microsoft Excel 4.0 worksheet and a Microsoft Excel 7.0 workbook.

This first example opens a Microsoft Excel 4.0 worksheet from a Microsoft Jet database three times to demonstrate how to open an entire worksheet, how to open a named range in a worksheet, and how to open an unnamed range in a worksheet. The ranges are tested by counting the number of records that appear in the **Recordset**.

```
Public Sub Excel4SheetAndRangeTest()
    Dim dbsCurrent As DATABASE
    Dim rstSales As Recordset
    Dim qdfNumOrders As QueryDef
    Dim intNumRecords As Integer

    ' Open the Microsoft Jet sample database for Chapter 8.
    Set dbsCurrent = OpenDatabase("C:\Samples\Chap08", _
        False, False, "Excel 4.0;HDR=NO;")
    ' Create a Recordset for the worksheet WSSample.xls.
    Set rstSales = dbsCurrent.OpenRecordset("WSSample#XLS")
    ' Execute a MoveLast and count the records.
    rstSales.MoveLast
    intNumRecords = rstSales.RecordCount
    MsgBox "There are " & intNumRecords & " rows in this worksheet."
    rstSales.Close

    Set dbsCurrent = OpenDatabase("C:\Samples\Chap08\WSSample.xls", _
        False, False, "Excel 4.0;HDR=NO;")
    ' Create a Recordset for the named range "FirstTenRows" in
    ' the worksheet WSSample.xls.
    Set rstSales = dbsCurrent.OpenRecordset("FirstTenRows")
    ' Execute a MoveLast and count the records.
    rstSales.MoveLast
    intNumRecords = rstSales.RecordCount
    MsgBox "There are " & intNumRecords & " rows in this named range."
    rstSales.Close

    Set dbsCurrent = OpenDatabase("C:\Samples\Chap08\WSSample.xls", _
        False, False, "Excel 4.0;HDR=NO;")
    ' Create a Recordset for the range A1 through G5
    ' in the worksheet WSSample.xls.
    Set rstSales = dbsCurrent.OpenRecordset("A1:G5")
    ' Execute a MoveLast and count the records.
    rstSales.MoveLast
    intNumRecords = rstSales.RecordCount
    MsgBox "There are " & intNumRecords & " rows in this range."

    rstSales.Close
    dbsCurrent.Close
End Sub
```

This next example opens a worksheet in a Microsoft Excel 7.0 workbook from a Microsoft Jet database three times to demonstrate how to open a worksheet in a workbook, how to open a named range in a workbook, and how to open an unnamed range in a worksheet in the workbook. The ranges are tested by counting the number of records that appear in the **Recordset**.

```
Public Sub Excel7SheetAndRangeTest()
    Dim dbsCurrent As DATABASE
    Dim rstSales As Recordset
    Dim qdfNumOrders As QueryDef
    Dim intNumRecords As Integer

    ' Open the Jet sample database for Chapter 8.
    Set dbsCurrent = OpenDatabase("C:\Samples\Chap08\WBSample.xls", _
        False, False, "Excel 5.0;HDR=NO;")
    ' Create a Recordset for the worksheet SampleSheet in the
    ' workbook WBSample.xls.
    Set rstSales = dbsCurrent.OpenRecordset("SampleSheet$")
    ' Execute a MoveLast and count the records.
    rstSales.MoveLast
    intNumRecords = rstSales.RecordCount
    MsgBox "There are " & intNumRecords & " rows in this worksheet."
    rstSales.Close

    Set dbsCurrent = OpenDatabase("C:\Samples\Chap08\WBSample.xls", _
        False, False, "Excel 5.0;HDR=NO;")
    ' Create a Recordset for the named range "SecondTenRows" in the
    ' workbook WBSample.xls.
    Set rstSales = dbsCurrent.OpenRecordset("SecondTenRows")
    ' Execute a MoveLast and count the records.
    rstSales.MoveLast
    intNumRecords = rstSales.RecordCount
    MsgBox "There are " & intNumRecords & " rows in this named range."
    rstSales.Close

    Set dbsCurrent = OpenDatabase("C:\Samples\Chap08\WBSample.xls", _
        False, False, "Excel 5.0;HDR=NO;")
    ' Create a Recordset for the range A1 through G5 in the
    ' worksheet SampleSheet in the workbook WBSample.xls.
    Set rstSales = dbsCurrent.OpenRecordset("SampleSheet$A1:G5")
    ' Execute a MoveLast and count the records.
    rstSales.MoveLast
    intNumRecords = rstSales.RecordCount
    MsgBox "There are " & intNumRecords & " rows in this range."

    rstSales.Close
    dbsCurrent.Close
End Sub
```

# Special Considerations for Text Files

You can use the Microsoft Jet Text installable ISAM to link and open character-delimited and fixed-length text files. Commas, tabs, or user-defined delimiters are valid in the source file.

Microsoft Jet recognizes null values in character-delimited files by the presence of two consecutive delimiting characters. Microsoft Jet recognizes null values in fixed-length files by the absence of data (spaces) in the data column.

Microsoft Jet determines the format of the text file by reading the file directly or by using a schema information file. The schema information file, which is always named SCHEMA.INI and is always kept in the same location as the text data source, provides the installable ISAM with information on the general format of the file, the column name and data type information, and a number of other data characteristics. A SCHEMA.INI file is always required for accessing fixed-length data; a SCHEMA.INI file is recommended when your text table contains DateTime, Currency, or Decimal data or any time you want more control over the handling of the data in the table.

---

**Important**  Microsoft Jet doesn't support multiuser access to text files. When you open a text file through Microsoft Jet, you have exclusive access to the file.

---

The following table lists the few limitations to the size of text tables and objects.

| Object | Maximum size per text file |
|---|---|
| Field | 255 |
| Field name | 64 characters |
| Field width | 32,766 characters |
| Rows | 65,000 bytes |

## Understanding SCHEMA.INI Files

SCHEMA.INI files provide schema information about the records in a text file. Each SCHEMA.INI entry specifies one of five characteristics of the table: the text file name; the file format; the field names, widths, and types; the character set; and special data type conversions. The following sections discuss these characteristics.

### Specifying the File Name

The first entry in the SCHEMA.INI is always the name of the text source file enclosed in square brackets. The following example illustrates the entry for file SAMPLE.TXT:

```
[SAMPLE.TXT]
```

## Specifying the File Format

The Format option in the SCHEMA.INI specifies the format of the text file. The text installable ISAM can read the format automatically from most character-delimited files. You can use any single character as a delimiter in the file except the double quotation mark. The Format setting in SCHEMA.INI overrides the setting in the Windows Registry on a file-by-file basis. The following table lists the valid values for the Format option.

| Format specifier | Table format |
| --- | --- |
| TabDelimited | Fields in the file are delimited by tabs. |
| CSVDelimited | Fields in the file are delimited by commas (comma-separated values). |
| Delimited(*) | Fields in the file are delimited by asterisks. You can substitute any character for the asterisk except the double quotation mark. |
| FixedLength | Fields in the file are of a fixed-length. |

For example, to specify a format of comma-delimited, you would add the following line to the SCHEMA.INI:

```
Format=CSVDelimited
```

## Specifying the Fields

You can specify field names in a character-delimited text file in two ways: either include the field names in the first row of the table and set ColNameHeader to **True**; or specify each column by number and designate the column name and data type. You must specify each column by number and designate the column name, data type, and width for fixed-length files.

---

**Note**  The ColNameHeader setting in SCHEMA.INI overrides the FirstRowHasNames setting in the Windows Registry on a file-by-file basis.

---

If you use the ColNameHeader option to specify field names in a character-delimited file, you can also instruct Microsoft Jet to guess the data types of the fields. Use the MaxScanRows option to indicate how many rows Microsoft Jet should scan when guessing the column types. If you set MaxScanRows to zero, Microsoft Jet scans the entire file. The MaxScanRows setting in the SCHEMA.INI overrides the setting in the Windows Registry on a file-by-file basis.

The following example shows how to indicate that Microsoft Jet should use the data in the first row of the table to determine field names and should examine the entire file to determine the data types used:

```
ColNameHeader=True
MaxScanRows=0
```

The next example shows how to designate fields in a table using the column number (Col*n*) option, which is optional for character-delimited files and required for fixed-length files. The example shows the SCHEMA.INI entries for two fields, a 10-character CustomerNumber text field and a 30-character CustomerName text field:

```
Col1=CustomerNumber Text Width 10
Col2=CustomerName Text Width 30
```

The syntax of the Col*n* entry follows:

**Col***n*=*ColumnName type* [**Width #**]

The following table describes each part of the Col*n* entry.

| Parameter | Description |
|---|---|
| *ColumnName* | The text name of the column. If the column name contains embedded spaces, it must be enclosed in double quotation marks. |
| *type* | Value types are: |
| | Microsoft Jet data types |
| |     Bit |
| |     Byte |
| |     Short |
| |     Long |
| |     Currency |
| |     Single |
| |     Double |
| |     DateTime |
| |     Text |
| |     Memo |
| | ODBC data types |
| |     Char (same as Text) |
| |     Float (same as Double) |
| |     Integer (same as Short) |
| |     LongChar (same as Memo) |
| |     Date *date format* |
| *Width* | The literal string value `Width`. Indicates that the following number designates the width of the column (optional for character-delimited files, required for fixed-length files). |
| # | The integer value that designates the width of the column (required if *Width* is specified). |

## Selecting a Character Set

You can select from two character sets: ANSI and OEM. The following example shows the SCHEMA.INI entry for an OEM character set. The CharacterSet setting in the SCHEMA.INI overrides the setting in the Windows Registry on a file-by-file basis. The following example shows the SCHEMA.INI entry that sets the character set to ANSI:

```
CharacterSet=ANSI
```

## Specifying Data Type Formats and Conversions

The SCHEMA.INI file contains a number of options that you can use to specify how data is converted or displayed when read by Microsoft Jet. The following table lists each of these options.

| Option | Description |
|---|---|
| DateTimeFormat | Can be set to a format string indicating dates and times. This entry should be specified if all date/time fields in the import/export are handled with the same format. All of the Microsoft Jet formats except AM and PM are supported. In the absence of a format string, the Windows Control Panel short date picture and time options are used. |
| DecimalSymbol | Can be set to any single character that is used to separate the integer from the fractional part of a number. If this entry is absent, the default value in the Windows Control Panel is used. |
| NumberDigits | Indicates the number of decimal digits in the fractional portion of a number. If this entry is absent, the default value in the Windows Control Panel is used. |
| NumberLeadingZeros | Specifies whether a decimal value less than 1 and greater than $-1$ should contain leading zeros; this value can either be **False** (no leading zeros) or **True**. |
| CurrencySymbol | Indicates the currency symbol to be used for currency values in the text file. Examples include the dollar sign ($) and Dm. If this entry is absent, the default value in the Windows Control Panel is used. |
| CurrencyPosFormat | Can be set to any of the following values:<br><br>0  Currency symbol prefix with no separation ($1)<br>1  Currency symbol suffix with no separation (1$)<br>2  Currency symbol prefix with one character separation ($ 1)<br>3  Currency symbol suffix with one character separation (1 $)<br><br>If this entry is absent, the default value in the Windows Control Panel is used. |

| Option | Description (*cont'd*) |
|---|---|
| CurrencyDigits | Specifies the number of digits used for the fractional part of a currency amount. If this entry is absent, the default value in the Windows Control Panel is used. |
| CurrencyNegFormat | Can be one of the following values: |

| | |
|---|---|
| 0 | ($1) |
| 1 | –$1 |
| 2 | $–1 |
| 3 | $1– |
| 4 | (1$) |
| 5 | –1$ |
| 6 | 1–$ |
| 7 | 1$– |
| 8 | –1 $ |
| 9 | –$ 1 |
| 10 | 1 $– |
| 11 | $ 1– |
| 12 | $ –1 |
| 13 | 1– $ |
| 14 | ($ 1) |
| 15 | (1 $) |

| Option | Description (*cont'd*) |
|---|---|
| | The dollar sign is shown for purposes of this example, but it should be replaced with the appropriate CurrencySymbol value in the actual program. If this entry is absent, the default value in the Windows Control Panel is used. |
| CurrencyThousandSymbol | Indicates the single-character symbol to be used for separating currency values in the text file by thousands. If this entry is absent, the default value in the Windows Control Panel is used. |
| CurrencyDecimalSymbol | Can be set to any single character that is used to separate the whole from the fractional part of a currency amount. If this entry is absent, the default value in the Windows Control Panel is used. |

## Examples of SCHEMA.INI Files

This section shows two examples of SCHEMA.INI files. The first example is the schema information file for a comma-delimited text file, and the second example is for a fixed-length file. These examples work with the comma-delimited and fixed-length example files on the companion CD-ROM.

The first example is the SCHEMA.INI file for the text table Sample.txt in the C:\CHAP08\TEXT_CSV directory on the companion CD-ROM. This file does not contain header information in the first row and is in comma-delimited format. The character set is ANSI and there are seven columns. Each of the columns is designated by name, along with the corresponding data type, but only three columns include a width designator. (Width designators are optional for character-delimited files.)

```
[SAMPLE.TXT]
ColNameHeader=False
Format=CSVDelimited
CharacterSet=ANSI
Col1=Customer char width 4
Col2="Order Number" char width 4
Col3="Product Code" char width 4
Col4=Quantity short
Col5="Extended Price" currency
Col6=Shipped bit
Col7=Billed bit
```

The second example is the SCHEMA.INI file for the text table SAMPLE.ASC in the C:\CHAP08\TEXT_FXD directory on the companion CD-ROM. This file does not contain header information in the first row and is in fixed-length format. The character set is ANSI and there are seven columns. Each of the columns is designated by name, along with the corresponding data type and each includes a width designator, as required.

```
[SAMPLE.ASC]
ColNameHeader=False
Format=FixedLength
CharacterSet=ANSI
Col1=Customer char width 4
Col2="Order Number" char width 5
Col3="Product Code" char width 5
Col4=Quantity short width 3
Col5="Extended Price" currency width 10
Col6=Shipped bit width 2
Col7=Billed bit width 2
```

## Linking a Comma-Delimited Text File

The procedures for linking a comma-delimited file are similar to those for linking other database tables. If you want Microsoft Jet to use the information in the SCHEMA.INI file, however, you must place the data file and the schema initialization file in the same directory. The following example illustrates how to link a comma-delimited text file.

```
' This example links a comma-delimited text file to a Microsoft Jet
' database and tests the link by computing the sum of the extended
' prices.

Public Sub LinkCSVText()
    Dim dbsCurrent As DATABASE
    Dim tdfSales As TableDef
    Dim qdfNumOrders As QueryDef
    Dim rstTotalSales As Recordset

    ' Open the Jet sample database for Chapter 8.
    Set dbsCurrent = OpenDatabase("C:\Samples\Chap08\Jet_Samp.mdb")
    ' Create a table definition for text table.
    Set tdfSales = dbsCurrent.CreateTableDef("Central Division Sales")
    ' Provide source database type, database name with Connect property.
    tdfSales.Connect = "TEXT;DATABASE=C:\Samples\Chap08\text_csv"
    ' Provide name of text table with the SourceTableName property.
    tdfSales.SourceTableName = "Sample.txt"
    ' Append TableDef to the TableDefs collection to create the link.
    dbsCurrent.TableDefs.Append tdfSales

    ' Run a simple query to ensure the data is accessible.
    Set qdfNumOrders = dbsCurrent.CreateQueryDef("Total Central Sales")
    qdfNumOrders.SQL = "SELECT Sum ([Extended Price]) As Tally " _
        & "FROM [Central Division Sales];"
    Set rstTotalSales = qdfNumOrders.OpenRecordset()
    MsgBox "Total Sales = $" & rstTotalSales!Tally
    rstTotalSales.Close
    dbsCurrent.Close
End Sub
```

# Maintaining Links

Links to external tables are convenient because they store all of the connection information you need to access the table in the future. Connection information for linked tables resides in the **TableDef** object for that table in your Microsoft Jet database. If you move or delete the external table, you must update the corresponding **TableDef** object to reflect this change.

# Updating Links to Tables That Have Moved

If you move a table that you previously linked, you need to *refresh* the link before you can access the table again. To refresh a link, you must reset the **Connect** property of the **TableDef** object to point to the table's new location. Then, use the **RefreshLink** method of the **TableDef** object to update the link information.

The following procedure shows how to reset the location for a FoxPro table that has been moved to another directory. The FoxPro table LostLink.dbf was originally linked to JET_SAMP.MDB from the \SAMPLES\CHAP08 directory. The table has since been moved to the \SAMPLES\CHAP08\LOSTLINK directory. When you try to open the linked table, Microsoft Jet reports that it couldn't find the object "LostLink."

1. Try to open the table LostLink.dbf through Microsoft Access. Microsoft Access displays the message `Couldn't find object 'LostLink'`.

2. Run the following code:

```
Public Sub RefreshLostFoxProLink()
    Dim dbsCurrent As DATABASE
    Dim qdfNumOrders As QueryDef
    Dim rstTotalSales As Recordset

    ' Open the Microsoft Jet sample database for Chapter 8.
    Set dbsCurrent = OpenDatabase("C:\Samples\Chap08\Jet_Samp.mdb")
    dbsCurrent!LostLink.Connect = "FoxPro 3.0" & _
        ";DATABASE=C:\Samples\Chap08\LostLink"
    dbsCurrent.TableDefs!LostLink.RefreshLink

    ' Run a simple query to ensure the data is accessible.
    Set qdfNumOrders = dbsCurrent.CreateQueryDef _
        ("Test Access to Refreshed Link")
    qdfNumOrders.SQL = "SELECT Sum (Ext_price) As Tally " _
        & "FROM LostLink;"
    Set rstTotalSales = qdfNumOrders.OpenRecordset()
    MsgBox "Total Sales = $" & rstTotalSales!Tally
    rstTotalSales.Close
    dbsCurrent.Close
End Sub
```

3. Try to open the table LOSTLINK.DBF through Microsoft Access once again. Microsoft Access opens the linked table.

# Deleting Links to External Tables

You can also delete the **TableDef** object associated with an external table. This removes the table's icon from your Microsoft Jet database along with the associated linking information. When you delete a **TableDef** that defines a linked table from your Microsoft Jet database, the external table is unaffected.

# Creating an External Table

You can create a table in an external data format through Microsoft Access by creating a Microsoft Access table with the same structure and exporting the structure to the external data format.

---

**Important**  This example uses the **TransferDatabase** method, which is only available in Microsoft Access; you cannot create a database or database table in an external data format through Visual Basic.

---

▶ **To create an external table**

1. Use the **OpenDatabase** method of the **Workspace** object to open a Microsoft Access database.

2. Use the **CreateTableDef** method of the **Database** object to create a table definition for the Microsoft Access table.

3. Use the **CreateField** method of the **TableDef** object to create one or more fields in the Microsoft Access table.

4. Use the **Append** method of the **Fields** collection to add the new field or fields to the Microsoft Access table.

5. Use the **Append** method of the **TableDefs** collection to create the Microsoft Access table.

6. Use the Microsoft Access **TransferDatabase** method to create the external table in the specified directory.

7. Use the **Delete** method of the **TableDefs** collection to delete the Microsoft Access table definition.

After you've created the table, you can access it from the table's native application or you can link or open it as you would any other external table. The following example demonstrates how to create a structure in a Microsoft Access table and use the structure as the basis for a FoxPro table:

```
Public Sub CreateExternalFoxProTable()
    Dim dbsCurrent As DATABASE
    Dim tdfNewExternalDatabase As TableDef
    Dim tdfTestNewTable As TableDef
    Dim fldContactName As Field, fldPhoneNumber As Field
    Dim qdfInsertRecords As QueryDef
    Dim rstCheckRecordCount As Recordset
    Dim intNumRecords As Integer
```

```
' Create a Database object pointing to the current database.
Set dbsCurrent = CurrentDb
' Create a table definition for the Microsoft Access table that will
' provide the structure information for the FoxPro table.
Set tdfNewExternalDatabase = _
    dbsCurrent.CreateTableDef("AccessTable")
' Create two text fields in the Microsoft Access table.
Set fldContactName = _
    tdfNewExternalDatabase.CreateField("Contact_name", dbText)
fldContactName.Size = 30
Set fldPhoneNumber = _
    tdfNewExternalDatabase.CreateField("Phone_number", dbText)
fldPhoneNumber.Size = 25
' Append the newly created fields to the Microsoft Access table.
tdfNewExternalDatabase.Fields.Append fldContactName
tdfNewExternalDatabase.Fields.Append fldPhoneNumber
' Append the TableDef to the TableDefs collection.
dbsCurrent.TableDefs.Append tdfNewExternalDatabase

' Use the TransferDatabase method to export the Microsoft Access
' table's structure to a FoxPro table; this creates a new FoxPro
' table in the specified directory.
DoCmd.TransferDatabase acExport, "FoxPro 2.6", _
    "C:\Samples\Chap08", acTable, "AccessTable", "FoxTable"
' Delete the TableDef for the Microsoft Access table.
dbsCurrent.TableDefs.Delete "AccessTable"

' Link the new table and test it by inserting a few records.
Set tdfTestNewTable = dbsCurrent.CreateTableDef("FoxTable")
tdfTestNewTable.Connect = _
    "FoxPro 2.6;DATABASE=C:\Samples\Chap08;"
tdfTestNewTable.SourceTableName = "FoxTable"
dbsCurrent.TableDefs.Append tdfTestNewTable
Set qdfInsertRecords = _
    dbsCurrent.CreateQueryDef("Insert Records")
qdfInsertRecords.SQL = _
    "INSERT INTO FoxTable VALUES ('C. J. Date', '555-5050')"
qdfInsertRecords.Execute
qdfInsertRecords.SQL = _
    "INSERT INTO FoxTable VALUES ('Edgar F. Codd', '011-56-8989')"
qdfInsertRecords.Execute
qdfInsertRecords.SQL = _
"INSERT INTO FoxTable VALUES ('Roger Penrose', '333-5050')"
qdfInsertRecords.Execute
qdfInsertRecords.SQL = _
    "INSERT INTO FoxTable VALUES ('John von Neumann', " & _
    "'555-8989')"
qdfInsertRecords.Execute
qdfInsertRecords.SQL = _
    "INSERT INTO FoxTable VALUES ('Alan Turing', '011-56-5050')"
```

```
qdfInsertRecords.Execute
qdfInsertRecords.SQL = _
"INSERT INTO FoxTable VALUES ('Niklaus Wirth', '330-2430')"
qdfInsertRecords.Execute

' Count the records to ensure that six records were added.
Set rstCheckRecordCount = tdfTestNewTable.OpenRecordset()
rstCheckRecordCount.MoveLast
intNumRecords = rstCheckRecordCount.RecordCount
MsgBox "Successfully added " & intNumRecords & " records."
rstCheckRecordCount.Close
dbsCurrent.Close
End Sub
```

# Performance Optimization and Troubleshooting Tips

When you link or open external tables in a Microsoft Jet database, it's easy to forget that you're accessing the data through an additional service layer (the installable ISAM). When you consider the amount of overhead involved in maintaining a connection, transferring and translating data, and maintaining a remote index in a foreign format, you can see why certain Microsoft Jet operations are significantly slower when executed against an external data source. The first part of this section discusses one way to dramatically increase performance when you only need to read data in a single pass. The remainder of the chapter focuses on two common problems: connections and temporary space.

## Using Forward-Only Recordset Objects

For more information about the **dbForwardOnly** option, see Chapter 5, "Working With Records and Fields."

If your application only needs to read through records in an external table in a single pass, you can dramatically increase the performance of your application by using the **Recordset** option **dbForwardOnly**. Although this option limits the direction of travel through the Recordset and restricts the use of a few other methods, it offers perhaps the greatest performance improvement possible when used with very large external tables. The following methods are unavailable when you use the **dbForwardOnly** option. The **Bookmark** property is also unavailable.

**Unavailable methods when dbForwardOnly is used**

| | |
|---|---|
| Clone | FindFirst |
| FindLast | FindNext |
| Move (with any value other than 1) | MoveFirst |
| MoveLast | MovePrevious |
| OpenRecordset | |

# Resolving Connection Problems

If your application cannot connect to the external data source, there are a number of things you can check.

- Make sure you can access the external table through the file system. If the table is stored on a network share, for example, check that you have sufficient privileges to access that share.

- Check that the external table is accessible through its native application. For example, if you're trying to open a Microsoft Excel worksheet, check that you can open the worksheet in Microsoft Excel.

- Check the code that establishes the connection to the external table carefully to make sure that it follows the guidelines in "Establishing a Connection" earlier in this chapter.

- If you were able to connect to the external table through your application before but you cannot now, check that the table is still in its original location. If the table is linked in your Microsoft Jet database and it has been moved, see "Maintaining Links" earlier in this chapter.

- If you receive the message `Unable to find installable ISAM`, check the source database type value in the table in "Specifying Source Database Types," earlier in this chapter. (Remember that Excel 7.0 is not a valid source database type; use Excel 5.0 instead.)

- If the source database type matches one of the values in the table in "Specifying Source Database Types," check that the installable ISAM driver resides in the directory specified in the Windows Registry.

- If you are supplying parameters to a case-sensitive data source, check that the parameters are of the correct form and case.

- Check the system on which the external data source resides for sufficient disk space.

# Understanding Temporary Space Needs

Microsoft Jet creates temporary indexes on your local machine when you query a database. This occurs even when the database is remotely located and in a different file format. These indexes can be as small as a few kilobytes or as large as several megabytes, depending on the data source.

You must make sure users of your application have sufficient resources to accommodate these temporary space needs. All users should have a defined value for the TEMP variable and enough disk space to store the indexes that Microsoft Jet may create.

---

**Important**  If users lack the disk space necessary to store temporary indexes, your application may behave unpredictably.

---

CHAPTER 9

# Developing Client/Server Applications

This chapter introduces you to the concepts of client/server development using the Microsoft Jet database engine. Microsoft Jet contains a number of features that enable you to create client/server applications with any application that can use the Data Access Objects interface, such as Microsoft Access, Microsoft Visual Basic, or Microsoft Excel. Microsoft Jet is tightly integrated with the Open Database Connectivity (ODBC) standard, which enables access to the most popular and widely used SQL database servers.

Most of the other chapters in this guide assume you are already familiar with the basic concepts of database design. As such, they do not include introductory material that explains basic concepts. However, because client/server computing is a new concept to most developers, the first section of this chapter contains introductory material that will help you get up to speed with the general concepts involved, as well as provide you with specific tips to write a good client/server application.

The rest of this chapter discusses optimization techniques for client/server applications, such as optimizing SQL pass-through queries, determining when to use Find methods, caching remote data, configuring your system to use ODBC efficiently, selecting a **Recordset** type, and allocating and maintaining connection resources. In addition, this chapter provides information on how to actually implement your client/server application using Microsoft Jet. You'll learn how the Microsoft Jet components work in a client/server environment, including code examples that work with Microsoft SQL Server. You can easily modify the code examples to also work with other ODBC databases.

### Contents

For information on copying the code examples from the companion CD-ROM to your hard disk drive, see "Using the Companion CD-ROM" in the Preface.

### Using PUBS.VBP

Many of the code examples in this chapter are included in the Visual Basic BookSales sample application PUBS.VBP. If you copied the samples from the companion CD-ROM, you will find two versions of the sample Visual Basic project. You can find a starting version of PUBS.VBP in \SAMPLES\CHAP09\VB40\SHPSTART, and an ending version in \SAMPLES\CHAP09\VB40\SHPEND.

To run the BookSales code examples in this chapter, open the .VBP file in Microsoft Visual Basic 4.0. To use this application, you must reconnect the tables in PUBS.MDB, change the gConnect$ constant to connect to your own SQL Server, and make sure the DSN is registered with ODBC. If you want to use the InsertSale stored procedure called by the BookSales application, you must create this procedure on your server, as described in the ReadMe file in \SAMPLES\CHAP09\VB40.

# Introduction to Client/Server Design

If you have read Chapter 6, "Creating Multiuser Applications," you are already familiar with the way Microsoft Jet supports applications in a file-server environment. You will recall that in a file-server architecture, there is no real intelligence on the server—it merely responds to requests for files. These requests are handled with little or no knowledge on the server's part as to what is actually contained in the files. The performance and simplicity of the file-server architecture make it ideal for prototyping multiuser systems, which allows developers to successfully implement small to moderate-size applications.

However, there are certain applications whose needs exceed the capabilities of file-server systems. For example, once an application exceeds a certain number of concurrent users or becomes mission critical, there are several performance, security, and data integrity issues that arise which no file-server system can accommodate fully.

Fortunately, another technology is available to meet these needs. This technology is the *client/server* architecture, and it requires you to think about your database development efforts in new ways. This introduction will bring you up to speed with the aspects of client/server applications that are important to developers. Microsoft Jet makes it possible to create successful client/server systems by using the Open Database Connectivity (ODBC) standard. Essentially, when you think of client/server applications, Microsoft Jet is on a local machine, which talks to an *ODBC server* at a remote location; this is different from the traditional way of thinking about Microsoft Jet applications, where Microsoft Jet is on a local machine, and then communicates with an .MDB file on a remote server.

To get a first look at how different this new architecture is, consider the simple task of opening a table as illustrated in the following DAO code:

```
Dim dbsCurrent As Database
Dim rstTest As Recordset
Dim strName As String

Set dbsCurrent = OpenDatabase("mydatabase.mdb")
Set rstTest = dbsCurrent.OpenRecordset("mytable")
strName = rstTest!LastName
```

In a file-server system, the following operations are performed:

1. Microsoft Jet opens the file MYDATABASE.MDB, a very inexpensive operation in terms of time and resources.

2. The Microsoft Jet DLL running on your user's workstation looks inside the database file for information about a table named MyTable. This results in several relatively inexpensive disk reads and some memory manipulations on your user's machine.

3. Microsoft Jet loads details about the MyTable table into your user's workstation's memory, such as how many fields it has, what the data types are, which indexes are available, as well as information about exactly where in the database file the first data page can be found.

4. The executing copy of Microsoft Jet on your user's workstation reads the actual data from disk and makes it available to the user's application.

In a client/server system, these operations become:

1. As in steps 1 and 2 in the previous procedure, Microsoft Jet opens the file MYDATABASE.MDB, retrieves some information from it, and then sets up some in-memory structures.

2. When Microsoft Jet loads MyTable, it sees that it's a link to an ODBC database. Accordingly, it tries to create a connection to the ODBC server. This is a relatively expensive operation, which may take anywhere from a half second to several seconds.

3. When the ODBC server receives a connection request, it sets aside memory and other resources and prepares for other requests. It then replies with a connection.

4. With a connection in hand, Microsoft Jet issues a request to the server for the MyTable data.

5. The server returns the requested data to Microsoft Jet and makes it available to the application's user.

If you read these steps carefully, you can see the fundamental difference between file-server and client/server architectures. In a file-server system, the database engine is completely responsible for physically retrieving the data from the database. It knows explicitly where in the file to find the data, and returns it directly to the user.

In a client/server system, the local database engine (the "client" part of client/server) formats a request for a specific set of data and passes this "generic" request to the database server (the "server" part of client/server). The local database engine has no idea of where the data is physically stored, nor does it care. It's up to the database server to process the request and pass the data back to the client.

At this point, you may say "Well, I understand the difference now, but why is client/server better?" With client/server applications, you can request exactly what you want. With file-server applications, you have a much lower degree of granularity; for example, even if you only select one column from one table, Microsoft Jet must read at least a 2K page. Also, by isolating all database files under the control of one database engine (for instance, the server) and one physical machine, the server can provide advanced functionality that can't be furnished with a file-server architecture. Features like online backup via log files, advanced hardware support such as uninterruptable power supplies or hot swappable disk drives, and multiprocessor machines can all be added to the server with no changes to the client machines.

# General Principals in Client/Server Design

As mentioned before, the fundamental differences between file-server and client/server systems mean that you have to design your applications in a fundamentally different way to take full advantage of the client/server architecture. This section outlines the general principals you should follow while on the road to developing a successful client/server application.

## Sets of Records

ODBC servers deal with sets of records. These are almost always the result of a SELECT statement that has been sent to the server, either explicitly by your program, or by Microsoft Jet on your behalf. Once the server has returned these records to the client, it really doesn't want to deal with them again. For example, operations like finding a particular record, or even scrolling backwards to a previous record, are not supported by most servers. Microsoft Jet will make those operations work for you; however, these operations do come with a price attached as you'll see in the following sections.

## Network Traffic and Round Trips

When your client program is working with a server, one of the main bottlenecks is usually the network traffic that gets generated between your client application and the server application. A *round trip* is a conversation with the server where Microsoft Jet asks the server for something and receives an answer. A well written client/server application tries to minimize round trips. Indeed, Microsoft Jet itself does a lot to minimize round trips by caching results locally to avoid asking the server for the same information multiple times. You can help Microsoft Jet minimize round trips by structuring your application in certain ways that are discussed throughout this chapter.

# Tips for Writing a Good Application

If you want to write a good client/server application, how do you start? This section shows how you can make your application run better with your ODBC server database. It uses code in the BookSales sample application, provided on the companion CD-ROM. The following table shows some of the improvements gained by adopting each strategy in the BookSales sample application. Because the sample has a relatively small number of records, most improvements will be greater with more records.

| Strategy | Times faster (approximate)* |
| --- | --- |
| Using **dbSQLPassthrough** on bulk queries (deleting 100 records using bulk operations with SQL pass-through, versus using a dynaset and **Delete** method) | 32 |
| Using linked tables (loading a combo box with 10 records) | 3.75 |
| Limiting data returned (returning only 100 records instead of 1000) | 4.6 |
| Using snapshots where dynasets are not needed | 4.3 |
| Creating SQL statements (versus adding data through a dynaset; 100 record stores) | 4 |
| Using stored procedures (versus using a dynaset) | 2 |
| Recordset caching (using **FillCache** versus walking through the records the first time) | 2 |

\*  Note the numbers in this chapter are approximate and did not come from a performance lab.

The remainder of this section briefly introduces implementing these strategies. For additional optimization techniques, see the "Optimizing Client/Server Applications" section later in this chapter.

## Using dbSQLPassthrough on Bulk Queries

The first lesson to learn when working with ODBC data is that queries work much faster than individual operations. For example, the data loading section of the BookSales sample application (located in the DATALOAD.BAS module) performs several cleanup tasks on the server tables before loading new data. It deletes all the records in the Sales, TitleAuthor, Authors, Titles, and Stores tables. If this application was originally .MDB based, it might delete these records by opening a **Recordset** and stepping through each record using the **Delete** method, but using a "DELETE Stores" query is faster than programmatically stepping through individual records and deleting them.

Once you've modified your code to use SQL statements, you can tell Microsoft Jet to assign more of the processing burden to the servers. By using the **dbSqlPassthrough** option with the **Execute** command, you are telling Microsoft Jet to send the command directly to the server without doing any of its own processing. Thus, your code should look something like:

```
dbPubs.Execute "Delete stores", dbSQLPassThrough
```

The important thing to note about this code fragment is that the **Delete** statement is not valid Microsoft Jet SQL syntax. If you run this query without using the **dbSQLPassThrough** flag, a run-time error will occur. By identifying the query as a pass-through query, you are relying on the syntax of the server, not of Microsoft Jet. You should always be careful that if you use SQL pass-through queries, your SQL statements must be syntactically valid for the server. Microsoft Jet will not translate the query.

For more information about bulk queries, see the "Using SQL Pass-Through Queries" section later in this chapter.

---

**Tip** Bulk operations are generally the best candidates for pass-through queries.

---

## Using Linked Tables

There are two basic ways to work with data stored on a server:

- You can open the database directly using the DAO **OpenDatabase** method, specifying a connect string to identify the server, database, and connection information.

- You can create a permanent link to tables through a Microsoft Jet database file.

Although opening the database directly sounds faster than linking, that is not the case. When you access data through the **OpenDatabase** method, every time the table is accessed, Microsoft Jet must retrieve information about tables, such as field names and types. When you link a table, the engine stores this information permanently in the local Microsoft Jet database. This effectively caches the information, making it quickly accessible each time the table needs to be opened. In effect, you have eliminated a round-trip to the server.

For example, the BookSales sample application computes the time to load the stores combo box, load the Books list box, and then buy a book, and then a message box is displayed each time but only if the correct command-line argument is given. These small recordsets, which are typical of a well written client/server application, show a greater improvement over larger recordsets because the speed improvement you see from linked tables only affects the initial opening of the recordset. To make the change from directly accessing the server to using linked tables, replace the following code:

```
' Note that you must alter the ODBC Connect string, as described in
' README.DOC, if you want this to work with your application.
Set dbPubs = OpenDatabase("", False, False, _
    "ODBC;dsn=server1;uid=usr;pwd=pw;database=Pubs")
```

with:

```
Set dbPubs = OpenDatabase("C:\Samples\Chap09\Pubs")
```

As the results show, linked tables provide a dramatic performance improvement. For more information on linking tables, see the "Linking Remote Tables" section later in this chapter.

## Limiting Returned Data

For more information about limiting returned data, see Chapter 4, "Queries."

Some of the strategies for converting a file-server application to client/server are easy to implement. Others may require rethinking or redesigning the way your application works. The concept of limiting the data returned by the server is one of the strategies that may require some extensive work in your conversion process. However, the performance gains are potentially very large, and the more data you have, the bigger the payoff.

As an example, consider the following code that opens a **Recordset** on the Orders table:

```
Set rstOrders = dbCurrent.OpenRecordset("Orders")
```

In a stand-alone or file-server environment, this command is a perfectly acceptable way of opening a table in a Microsoft Jet database. Because Microsoft Jet reads data at a page level, selecting all columns is no less efficient than selecting a single column.

However, when you ask your ODBC server to open the Orders table, the server starts sending the contents of the Orders table to your machine when you request data. As far as the server is concerned, you have asked for the entire contents of the table. This can be a very slow and resource-intensive task.

If you look closely at what your application really needs, you may find that you rarely need all records from a table, or all fields in each record. This brings up the point of this technique: In a client/server system, you want to return the least data that is absolutely necessary for the currently executing part of your application. One of the most detrimental things you can do in a client/server environment is to request more data from the server than you actually need. The less data you request, the less time is spent getting the data. This being the case, you should always evaluate your application's data needs. In some cases, you may even set limits on what your application can expect. For instance, if you give the user the ability to do searches and then display what data is found, before bringing data over, you may want to first check that the amount of data is not too much. If it's an extremely large amount, you may ask users to limit the search more, or let them know that there may be some delays if they proceed.

The remainder of this section will discuss the two principal ways to limit the amount of returned data:

- By limiting the number of fields you select from the database.
- By limiting the number of records you select from the database.

## Restricting Fields

To limit the amount of data traveling across a network, you can limit the number of fields you select from the database. Although SELECT * is quick and easy to type, it may not be quick and easy for the network to return all the data. For example, consider a table with fifteen fields, one being an integer key value, and the rest being **Memo** and **Text** fields. If you are interested only in the key value, select only that field. Otherwise, your application will be subject to a performance penalty caused by retrieving unnecessary fields.

The BookSales sample application doesn't enjoy a real performance benefit from the technique of limiting fields because almost all the fields in the tables are used. Also, because there are no **Memo** or **OLE Object** fields which could potentially slow down the application, you don't need to exclude such fields. However, if your tables have lots of fields, consider retrieving just the few you need to display. If the user then wishes to see more detailed information, your application can request additional fields using a separate query.

## Restricting Records

You can limit the number of records you select from a database by using a WHERE clause in your query. If the user is supplying the WHERE clause, you can first send a SELECT COUNT(*) with that WHERE clause to find out how many records will be returned, and then decide if you want the WHERE clause to be more limiting.

For example, when the starting version of the BookSales sample application (\SAMPLES\CH09\VB40\SHPSTART\PUBS.VBP) loads books into the Books list box (on the BookList form), it returns all of the books, and then walks through the recordset using **FindFirst** and **FindNext** to find the records that belong in the list box. Changing this to a WHERE clause as shown in the final version (\SAMPLES\CH09\VB40\SHPEND\PUBS.VBP) makes this 4.5 times faster, even on this small set of 100 records.

A sample SELECT statement with a WHERE clause looks like this:

```
SELECT au_id, au_lname, au_fname FROM authors WHERE state = 'WA' ORDER
BY au_lname
```

This is a good way to structure the query if your application needs all three fields that are returned. It also illustrates the concept of limiting the number of returned records by specifying a WHERE clause. Note that the statement also orders the data before returning it by using an ORDER BY clause. Although Microsoft Jet does provide the ability to sort a recordset, for efficiency reasons, it's always better to let the server do the sort.

## Using Snapshots Where Dynasets Are Not Needed

If you read Chapter 5, "Working with Records and Fields," you should be familiar with the different types of **Recordset** objects that Microsoft Jet supports. A dynaset-type **Recordset** offers much more functionality than a snapshot-type **Recordset**. However, in terms of performance, this functionality can be quite expensive to provide. If you don't need to update your data and if the data doesn't contain **Memo** or **OLE Object** fields, snapshot-type **Recordset** objects are generally faster.

If you do not explicitly specify a **Recordset** type in your code, by default Microsoft Jet will use the one with the most functionality. In the case of remote databases, this would be a dynaset-type **Recordset**. This choice may offer the most functionality, but it isn't necessarily the one that offers the best performance.

For example, data retrieval is 4 times faster if you replace the following code:

```
set rstStores = dbsPubs.OpenRecordset(strSelectStatement)
```

with:

```
Set rstStores = dbsPubs.OpenRecordset(strSelectStatement,
dbOpenSnapshot)
```

However, if your table contains **OLE Object** or **Memo** fields, a dynaset-type **Recordset** may be faster.

For more information on using dynasets or snapshots, see the "Choosing a Recordset Type" section later in this chapter.

## Creating SQL INSERT Statements

Using pass-through queries (by specifying the **dbSQLPassthrough** option) on bulk operations almost always results in better performance. An extension of this technique that is sometimes useful is to generate SQL INSERT statements directly rather than to use the programmatic **AddNew** and **Update** methods through DAO code.

However, this usually is not worth the extra coding effort if you are performing large numbers of these operations. For example, in bulk data loading operations, it's usually worth writing the DAO code to loop through records, and attempting to optimize performance within the code.

The BookSales sample application includes a bulk data loader that creates the sample data used by the rest of the application; you can find this code in the DataAlterSales procedure of the DATALOAD.BAS module. Using the **Recordset** approach, the code to add a single record is:

```
Set rstSales = dbsPubs.OpenRecordset("sales", dbOpenDynaset, _
    dbAppendOnly)
rstSales.AddNew
rstSales!stor_id = "6380"    ' All Linked to the first store.
rstSales!ord_num = gSALESID$ & Format$(intRecordLoop&, "0000")
rstSales!ord_Date = Now
rstSales!qty = 5
rstSales!payterms = "Net 60"
rstSales!title_id = "BU2075"
rstSales.Update
rstSales.Close
```

The same code, implemented using a pass-through query, becomes:

```
strInsert$ = "INSERT INTO Sales VALUES('6380', '"
strInsert$ = strInsert$ & gSALESID$ & Format$(intRecordLoop&, "0000")
strInsert$ = strInsert$ & "', '" & Now
strInsert$ = strInsert$ & "', 5, 'NET 60', 'BU2075')"

dbsPubs.Execute strInsert$, dbSQLPassThrough
```

Building an INSERT statement from scratch like this can be tricky if your data has embedded quote (") characters. If you're only doing single updates, the time saved is generally not worth the effort, especially if the update is tied to a form.

For more information, see the "Inserting and Updating Data on a Remote Data Source" section later in this chapter.

## Using Stored Procedures

If you are using an existing client/server database, you'll likely find that the administrator has created many stored procedures that you can use. *Stored procedures* are procedures stored on the server that are used for a wide variety of operations. Their main purpose is to build logic into the processing of SQL statements. For instance, if you want to select data from one of two tables on the server, depending upon a value from a third table, a stored procedure would be an ideal candidate. Pass-through queries allow you to invoke this specialized server-side functionality.

For specialized scenarios, you may find that it's worth creating your own stored procedures. For example, the BookSales sample application contains code that buys a book. Usually you can code this by using DAO code to issue an **Edit** or **AddNew** method along with an **Update** on a dynaset-type **Recordset**. When combined with the **dbAppendOnly** flag on the **Recordset**, this is an efficient and simple technique.

To run this code in PUBS.VBP, you must create a stored procedure named InsertSale on your server.

However, you could create a stored procedure to do the same operation, as shown in the BookSales sample application. The following code in the BuyBook procedure of the BOOK.BAS module shows how the sample application calls the stored procedure, named InsertSale:

```
Set dbsPubs = OpenDatabase(App.Path & "\pubs.mdb")

strStoredProcCall$ = "InsertSale '" & gstrStoreId$ & "', '" _
& gstrOrderNumber$ & "', '"
strStoredProcCall$ = strStoredProcCall$ & Now & "', " & gintQuant% _
& ", '" & gstrPayTerms$
strStoredProcCall$ = strStoredProcCall$ & "', '" _
& gstrTitleArray(lstboxidx%) & "'"

dbsPubs.Execute strStoredProcCall$, dbSQLPassThrough
```

This code inserts the new sale into the Sales table. Notice that the database being opened is a local Microsoft Jet database. This functionality is new in version 3.0 of Microsoft Jet. You can use it to open a native Microsoft Jet database and set the **Database** object's **Connect** property. Any SQL pass-through queries are then made against the server database specified in the **Connect** property.

Stored procedures on the server are faster than dynamic SQL statements, just as stored queries in Microsoft Jet are faster than dynamic SQL. That is, a stored procedure is a precompiled execution plan. No parsing needs to occur, only execution.

When your application is waiting for user input, it isn't worth the added complication of stored procedures to increase the speed, because neither the user nor the server benefits from the increased speed. Stored procedures really become useful when there is a lot of logic required—for example, when satisfying a business rule that a particular book has to be in stock and then checking to see if more books should be ordered on each purchase.

For more information about queries, see the "Using SQL Pass-Through Queries" section later in this chapter.

### Recordset Caching

Dynaset-type **Recordset** objects are generally slower at reading data than snapshot-type **Recordset** objects. However, because they are updatable, your application may need to use them in many common scenarios. One way to scroll through the data faster—especially when the dynaset is being used by a form—is to make use of the **Recordset CacheSize** and **CacheStart** properties, and the **FillCache** method. For example, you might use the following code when you open your form:

```
dsBooks.CacheSize = 20
dsBooks.CacheStart = dsBooks.Bookmark
dsBooks.FillCache
```

This will preload an internal buffer with 20 records worth of data. As the user moves through those records through your application's user interface, they display quickly because they won't have to be retrieved from the server.

For more information, see the "Caching Remote Data" section later in this chapter.

# Optimizing Client/Server Applications

This section discusses optimization techniques to improve the performance of your client/server applications. This section presents techniques for optimizing client/server queries; creating and using SQL pass-through queries; using **Find** methods; caching remote data; configuring your system to use ODBC more efficiently; and choosing a **Recordset** type to use with your application.

# Optimizing Queries in the Client/Server Environment

A common requirement of applications is the ability to build an SQL string based on values that the user provides. This technique is often referred to as using *dynamic SQL*. Dynamic SQL is easy to use, and it enables you to avoid storing queries in the local Microsoft Jet database.

Unfortunately, using dynamic SQL requires that Microsoft Jet perform numerous steps, especially when using ODBC data, as described here:

1. Microsoft Jet parses the SQL string.
2. Microsoft Jet compiles the SQL string, determining which parts go to the ODBC server.
3. Microsoft Jet builds a server-specific query and sends it to the ODBC server.
4. The ODBC server parses and compiles the SQL string.
5. The ODBC server retrieves the results and returns them to Microsoft Jet.
6. DAO looks at the results and builds the appropriate **Recordset** and **Field** objects.

The alternative to using dynamic queries is to save the queries as stored queries in the local Microsoft Jet database. After a query has been saved and compiled once, Microsoft Jet can reduce the number of steps required to execute that query.

In comparison to dynamic queries, the engine performs the same steps, except steps 1 and 2 only need to be done the first time a query is executed. After that, only steps 3–6 need to take place.

You can use a parameterized query and simply re-execute the query to accept new parameter values. This yields substantial savings, especially for client/server applications. If you don't need to update the results and the query only uses server data, an SQL pass-through query might be a better choice.

It's also important to note the difference between dynamic queries and stored queries when your application is used on machines with less than ideal memory configurations. When Microsoft Jet executes a dynamic query, it has to load several different engine modules to parse, optimize, and execute the query. Each of these modules takes up memory. When you create and store a query, Microsoft Jet parses it and stores it in a compiled state. This eliminates the need to load the modules responsible for parsing and optimization, and reduces the memory requirements of Microsoft Jet.

# Using SQL Pass-Through Queries

SQL pass-through queries are SQL statements that are sent directly to the database server without interpretation by the Microsoft Jet database engine. SQL pass-through queries provide your application with the ability to directly manipulate the features of your database server. This section describes the common uses of SQL pass-through queries as well as how to design and integrate them into your application.

# What are SQL pass-through queries?

SQL pass-through query objects are composed of two pieces of information: the SQL statement and the ODBC connection string. The SQL statement is interpreted only by the database server and must follow the server's SQL language guidelines. Furthermore, pass-through SQL statements cannot contain Microsoft Jet–specific elements or Visual Basic commands or functions.

For more information on operations that cannot be performed by your database server, see the "Unsupported Operators and Functions" section later in this chapter, or your database server documentation.

# What can you do with SQL pass-through queries?

You typically use SQL pass-through queries to:

- Perform DDL operations on the server.
- Take advantage of server-specific features such as stored procedures.
- Run an SQL query using the database server's syntax.
- Run an SQL query that returns multiple result sets.
- Maintain user accounts or perform other system administration tasks.
- Run maintenance operations like Microsoft SQL Server's DBCC.
- Execute multiple INSERT or UPDATE statements in a single batch operation.

# How do SQL pass-through queries work?

When your application executes SQL pass-through queries, Microsoft Jet opens a new connection to the database or uses an existing connection. Then, Microsoft Jet passes the SQL statement directly to the ODBC driver, without interpreting it as a Microsoft Jet SQL query (in other words, the SQL statement can contain commands that are unavailable in Microsoft Jet SQL provided they are valid in your database server's SQL language).

The database server interprets the statement and returns the query results (if applicable) and any error or informational messages that arise during query execution. As with other queries, if there are any results to fetch, they are fetched on demand as required by the application; this reduces network traffic and ensures that data is only transferred when needed.

Although SQL pass-through queries bypass the Microsoft Jet query processor, they use the Microsoft Jet **Recordset** processor to create and manage result sets that may be generated by your query. This lets you use foreign-dialect SQL statements to take advantage of your database server's query processing capabilities while maintaining the power and ease-of-use of Microsoft Jet's **Recordset** model after the data has been retrieved.

# How do you create an SQL pass-through query?

You can create and execute an SQL pass-through query by creating a **QueryDef** object or by using the **Execute** method on the **Database** object.

---

**Note**  If your SQL pass-through query returns a result set, the Microsoft Jet database engine creates a snapshot-type **Recordset** for the results.

---

## Using an SQL Pass-Through Query With a Stored QueryDef Object

There are four steps to creating and executing an SQL pass-through query using a **QueryDef** object.

1. Use the **CreateQueryDef** method of the **Database** object to create a new **QueryDef** object. If you plan to use the **QueryDef** object again, save it in the database by assigning a name; if you plan to use the query one time, pass in an empty string for the *name* argument.

2. Set the **Connect** property of the **QueryDef** object to a valid ODBC connection string. This identifies the query as an SQL pass-through query to the Microsoft Jet database engine. Microsoft Jet will not parse the SQL code in the query (which is set in the next step) when you specify an ODBC connection string.

3. Set the **SQL** property of the **QueryDef** object to the SQL statement you want to execute against the remote database. The syntax of the SQL statement may not be a valid Microsoft Jet SQL statement, but it must conform to the syntax of the remote database server. If the remote database server cannot execute the statement, a trappable error occurs.

   If your query returns a set of records, you must also set the **ReturnsRecords** property of the **QueryDef** object to **True**. This instructs Jet to prepare a **Recordset** object to hold the query results. If you don't set the **ReturnsRecords** property to **True** for a query that returns records, a trappable error results.

   ---

   **Note**  You can return multiple result sets from a single query. See the "Processing Multiple Result Sets" section later in this chapter.

   ---

4. Use the **OpenRecordset** method of the **QueryDef** object to open the result set.

This example shows how to create and execute a simple SQL pass-through **QueryDef** called Total Orders.

```
Public Sub SQLPassthroughQueryDef()
    Dim dbsOrders As DATABASE, qdfPassthrough As QueryDef
    Dim rstFromQuery As Recordset, intNumRecords As Integer

    Set dbsOrders = OpenDatabase("C:\Samples\Chap09\Pubs")

    On Error GoTo DisplayErrors
    Set qdfPassthrough = dbsOrders.CreateQueryDef("Total Orders")

    qdfPassthrough.Connect = "ODBC;DATABASE=pubs;UID=sa; _
        PWD=;DSN=Publishers"
    qdfPassthrough.SQL = "SELECT * FROM Sales"
    qdfPassthrough.ReturnsRecords = True

    Set rstFromQuery = qdfPassthrough.OpenRecordset(dbOpenSnapshot)

    rstFromQuery.MoveLast
    intNumRecords = rstFromQuery.RecordCount
    MsgBox intNumRecords & " records were returned by this query."
    dbsOrders.QueryDefs.Delete "Total Orders"
    dbsOrders.Close
    Exit Sub

DisplayErrors:
    VerboseErrorHandler
    dbsOrders.QueryDefs.Delete "Total Orders"
    dbsOrders.Close
End Sub
```

## Executing SQL Pass-Through Queries With the Execute Method

There are three steps to executing SQL pass-through queries by using the **Execute** method:

1. Open the Microsoft Jet database that contains the link to the remote database table you want to access.

2. Set the **Connect** property of the **Database** object to point to the remote database server you want to query.

3. Use the **Execute** method of the **Database** object with the **dbSQLPassThrough** flag to run the query.

This example shows how to execute an SQL pass-through query from code.

```
Public Sub SQLPassthroughInCode()
    Dim dbsOrders As DATABASE
    ' This code sets the "Billed" field values in the OrderDetails
    ' table on the SQL Server database to 0 (False).

    On Error GoTo DisplayErrors

    Set dbsOrders = OpenDatabase("C:\Samples\Chap09\Pubs")

    dbsOrders.Connect = "ODBC;DATABASE=pubs;UID=sa;PWD=;DSN=Publishers"
    dbsOrders.Execute "UPDATE Titles SET Royalty = 33", dbSQLPassThrough
    dbsOrders.Close
    Exit Sub

DisplayErrors:
    VerboseErrorHandler
    dbsOrders.Close

End Sub
```

### Processing Multiple Result Sets

SQL pass-through queries can return more than one result set. When you assign the result set to a **Recordset** or display the results using a Microsoft Visual Basic **Data** control or a Microsoft Access datasheet, form, or report, only the first result set from the query is processed. To remedy this situation, you must use a make-table query to capture the additional result sets into Microsoft Jet tables.

When Microsoft Jet returns the result sets from your query, it writes the results into new tables. The names of these new tables are derived from the table name you specify in the make-table query with ascending integer values following the initial table name. For example, if your query returns two result sets to the table SalesFigures, the first table would be named SalesFigures and the second would be named SalesFigures1.

# Criteria for Using Find Methods

The **Find** methods are useful for moving to a record that meets a specific criteria within a **Recordset**. A common error that developers make when converting code to work with an ODBC database is to try to replace **Seek** method calls with **Find** method calls. As a general rule, this code will be slow.

When trying to find an individual record, the best approach is to create a new **Recordset** with a WHERE clause that contains the **Find** criteria. This will return all records that match the criteria. Because this is a single operation on the server, this approach is much more efficient than using the **Find** methods, especially if the number of records returned is small.

## Using Find With Dynasets

If your program can't be modified to eliminate the use of **Find** methods, then understanding exactly how they work will help you make the best use of them. **Find** is fairly efficient when the search criteria is a match against fields that are indexed on the server.

Microsoft Jet recognizes these cases and executes a query on the server that returns primary keys for all the records that match the search criteria. If matching records are found, it then moves through the keys it has stored for the **Recordset** until it finds a match. If the local **Recordset** is small, this is a relatively quick operation.

One result of this strategy is that unsuccessful **Find** operations will be as fast as the server allows. This isn't something you'll be able to take advantage of in all scenarios, but it may be useful in some.

## Using Find With Snapshots

**Find** methods are also reasonably efficient if the following are both true:

- The **Recordset** is a snapshot-type **Recordset**.
- The number of records in the snapshot-type **Recordset** is small.

In the previous case, the **Find** criteria are resolved by searching the data that has already been downloaded into the snapshot on the local machine. Of course, if the snapshot is not yet fully populated, the time required to fetch the data increases the search time. This means that **Find** operations that fail will be slow if all the records need to be fetched (unlike the previous dynaset case in which no further fetching occurs if the **Find** fails).

## Conditions That Cause Find to Work Slowly

Find methods are usually slow if all of the following are true:

- The **Recordset** is a dynaset-type **Recordset** on an ODBC data source.
- The number of records in the **Recordset** is more than about 100.
- The Find criteria do not match the two requirements outlined in the previous section.

The algorithm used to resolve the criteria in this case is to fetch each record and examine each one until either a match is found or all records have been examined.

# Caching Remote Data

You can use the Microsoft Jet **CacheSize** and **CacheStart** properties to store all or a part of the data contained in a dynaset-type **Recordset** in local memory. Local caching of records dramatically speeds up operations when moving through dynaset records in both directions, and shows significant improvements even when moving in a forward-only direction.

To use caching, you specify the number of records to be stored by the value of **CacheSize** (a long integer) and the beginning record by the bookmark stored as the value of **CacheStart** (a string variable). Applying the **FillCache** method automatically retrieves every value in the cache range and fills the cache with server data; this is more efficient than filling the cache as each record is fetched, so if you know ahead of time that all records in the cache range will be visited, then you should call **FillCache** every time you move **CacheStart**. Fetches within the cache boundary occur locally, speeding display of the cached records in a datasheet or in a continuous form. The allowable range of values for **CacheSize** is between 5 and 1200 records; if the size of the cache exceeds available memory, the excess records spill into a temporary disk file. Typically, you set the value of **CacheSize** to 100. To recover the cache memory, set **CacheSize** = 0.

If you set the **CacheSize** and **CacheStart** properties, as you move through records, the data you fetch will be cached until you move out of the defined range. Once you've hit the end of the range defined by **CacheSize** and **CacheStart**, you need to move the **CacheStart** setting to a new position to stay synchronized with the set of records you're working with. Then, caching will continue with the new range, reusing values appropriately if the new cache range overlaps the old.

Using a cache can provide significant performance benefits over not specifying a cache. If the application requires backward scrolling within the cached region, the performance improvements will be even greater. Depending on your scenario, using a cache may be faster than using a read-only, forward-only snapshot, especially if the snapshot contains memo or long binary fields that are referenced only occasionally. For more information about forward-only snapshots, see the "The Forward-Only Option" section later in this chapter.

The size of the cache you use is determined by the application's needs. For example, if you are displaying these records to the user, then you might use a cache size determined by the number of records permitted on the screen. If the code has no user interaction, then you can make a tradeoff between local memory availability, network traffic, and record size.

**Note** One important distinction with caching ODBC data is that the cached data will include **Memo** fields but not long binary fields (such as **OLE Object** fields). Hence the cache can get large if you have those types of fields in your result set. If it becomes too large, then the cache overflows onto disk. Although more expensive than in-memory cache, this is still usually better then generating more round-trips to the server. If you are using other Microsoft Jet data sources, then only a pointer to the database page containing the **Memo** or long binary field is stored in the cache, and the actual contents are only retrieved if the field itself is retrieved.

# Configuring Your System to Use ODBC More Efficiently

This section describes three techniques you can use to improve the way ODBC works with your application. You'll learn how to administer some remote database functions using the MSysConf table, how to limit the amount of network traffic when you query a remote data source, and how to avoid problems when converting code from local table use to client/server use.

## Using the MSysConf Table

The MSysConf table is a special table that you create in your remote database to control certain Microsoft Jet behavior. MSysConf helps you maintain security on your remote database by disabling the feature that enables users to store the logon ID and password for an attached SQL database in locally linked tables.

You can also use the MSysConf table to set the number of records of data that are retrieved at one time and the number of seconds of delay between each retrieval.

### Creating the MSysConf Table

You create the MSysConf table in each remote database you want to access. When you create the table, give all users of your application permission to use the SELECT statement on this table; the system administrator is the only person who needs INSERT/UPDATE/DELETE permission. If your remote database is case-sensitive, you must type the table name and field names exactly as they appear in the following table.

| Field name | Data type | Allows Null? |
|---|---|---|
| Config | Any valid server data type that corresponds to a 2-byte integer. | No |
| chValue | VARCHAR(255) | Yes |
| nValue | Any valid server data type that corresponds to a 4-byte integer. | Yes |
| Comments | VARCHAR(255) | Yes |

## Specifying Settings in the MSysConf Table

The MSysConf table currently recognizes three configuration settings. These settings are activated by adding a record to the table for each setting. Only two of the four fields in the table are currently used; the rest are reserved for future use and are ignored in this release.

The following table lists the three records you can use in the MSysConf table.

| Config field value | nValue field value | Description |
|---|---|---|
| 101 | 0 or 1 | When this value is set to 0, the system doesn't allow local storage of the logon ID and password in attachments; when the value is set to 1, the system allows local storage of the logon ID and password in attachments. The default value is 1. |
| 102 | *D* | This value, *D*, designates the delay, in seconds, between each retrieval operation performed by background population of a **Recordset** in the Microsoft Access user interface or a Visual Basic **Data** control. Setting a higher delay time decreases network traffic, but increases the amount of time that read-locks are held on data (if the server uses read-locks). The default value is 10 seconds. |
| 103 | *N* | This value, *N*, designates the number of records retrieved during the background population of a **Recordset** in the Microsoft Access user interface or a Visual Basic **Data** control. The default value is 100 records. |

# Requesting Only the Necessary Data

If your application doesn't need all the records and fields of a table to perform an operation, you can save time and resources by requesting fewer of the table's records and fields. Here are a few tips you can use.

- Use restrictive queries to limit the number of records returned.

- Use restrictive queries to limit the fields fetched by your query and exclude fields of long, binary data (such as **OLE Object** or **Memo** data).

- If you need to display **OLE Object** or **Memo** fields but don't need to update them, use a snapshot-type **Recordset**.

- If you rarely need certain fields, open a separate **Recordset** when you need to use those fields.

For more information, see the "Limiting Returned Data" section earlier in this chapter.

## Converting Your Application Code

One strategy for developing and testing client/server applications involves modeling the application on a local machine using local Microsoft Jet tables and converting code before deploying the application in a client/server environment. There are a few things to keep in mind when converting code. The following can have a significant effect on the performance of your application.

- Use SQL pass-through **Update** queries rather than code that loops through a table modifying one record at a time. Although the looping approach works fairly well with local tables, it can be extremely slow (because of increased network traffic and server load) when used with remote tables.

- When you need to insert multiple records into the remote table, use a local table to store the new records, then insert the records into the remote table in one operation.

- When you need to perform multiple updates to remote data, use transactions to ensure data integrity. Transactions can also help you isolate errors in application code.

- Use stored queries (as opposed to dynamic queries) to reduce query compilation and execution time.

# Choosing a Recordset Type

This section discusses the types of **Recordset** objects available through the Microsoft Jet engine and how each type affects the performance and operation of your application. There are three types of recordsets: tables, which are actual database tables; dynasets, which can be updated; and snapshots, which cannot. Since you cannot create a table-type **Recordset** based on a remote data source through ODBC, the remainder of the discussion focuses on dynaset- and snapshot-type **Recordset** objects.

The decision to use a dynaset versus a snapshot is based on resource, speed, and performance considerations in addition to the basic needs of the application (such as the ability to update remote data). For example, if your application doesn't need update capabilities and the **Recordset** you want to use contains fewer than 500 records, a snapshot-type **Recordset** improves the overall data access speed of your application. However, if the **Recordset** you're using is large or contains **Memo** or **OLE Object** fields, using a dynaset may be more efficient. Also, if you only need to move forward through the **Recordset**, by using the **dbForwardOnly** option when opening the **Recordset** you can achieve even better performance.

## Dynaset-Type Recordsets

In its simplest form, a dynaset-type **Recordset** is a collection of *bookmarks* that allow each record in a server database table to be uniquely identified. Each bookmark corresponds to one record on the server. Normally, the value of the bookmark corresponds to the primary key value for that record. For example, if you have an Orders table on the server database that has a primary key on its OrderID field, then internally to Microsoft Jet, the dynaset contains all the OrderID values that correspond to the records that satisfy the query that was issued. Later in this chapter, the "Recordset Population" section discusses exactly how these bookmarks are gathered, and in particular *when* they are gathered.

Note that if you try and examine the contents of the **Bookmark** property of a dynaset, it will *not* contain the value of OrderID. Exactly what it contains varies with the implementation of the recordset, and you should never rely on it. However, it will probably contain the page number in the temporary Microsoft Jet database where the OrderID value is actually stored. The reason the engine does not use key field values as bookmark values is that dynasets can be based on a multi-table join. In such a case, there are actually several primary key values stored by Microsoft Jet—one for each record in each table involved in the join.

When you access the data in dynaset fields, Microsoft Jet uses the bookmark for the record to issue a query in the form "SELECT *field1*, *field2*,... FROM ORDERS WHERE ORDERID=*bookmark*." This statement is then sent to the server. (For performance reasons, Microsoft Jet actually includes up to ten bookmarks in the WHERE clause.) Then, as you request the data, on a field-by-field basis, Microsoft Jet calls the ODBC **SQLGetData** function to return the data from each field.

One of the most important implications of this field-by-field behavior is that data for a field is not retrieved from the server unless that field is explicitly retrieved by your application's code. For example, only if your code contained a line like:

```
strNew = rstOrders!Photo
```

would the Photo field actually be retrieved from the server. This behavior is of particular interest if the table you are accessing has binary or memo fields that contain large amounts of data. If you don't reference those large fields in your code, Microsoft Jet does not have to retrieve them from the server.

Once you have the bookmarks you need, the most time-consuming part of using a dynaset is actually retrieving the data. To speed this up, you can tell a **Recordset** to cache the data that it retrieves and keep it in memory so that if you need it again you can avoid retrieving it from the server again. You can control dynaset caching by using the **FillCache** method and the **CacheStart** and **CacheSize** properties of the **Recordset** object.

For more information, see the "Caching Remote Data" section earlier in this chapter.

## Snapshot-Type Recordsets

When compared with dynasets, snapshots are fairly simple to understand—they are a *complete copy* of all the requested fields in your query. As you move through a snapshot-type **Recordset** for the first time, all data is copied first into memory and then, if need be, into a temporary Microsoft Jet database in the temporary directory on the user's workstation. The resulting set of data is read-only and by default, it can be scrolled forward and backward. Later in this chapter, the "Recordset Population" section discusses exactly when the data is retrieved.

### The Forward-Only Option

By default, when you request a dynaset- or snapshot-type **Recordset**, you can scroll through the records in both directions. Snapshot-type **Recordset** objects have an additional feature that can conserve connection resources by allowing scrolling in only one direction. This kind of snapshot-type **Recordset**, which is helpful when you only need to make a single pass through the **Recordset**, is called a *forward-only snapshot.*

You can specify a forward-only snapshot by calling the **OpenRecordset** method with **dbOpenSnapshot** for the *type* parameter and **dbForwardOnly** as the *option* parameter. This fetches the result set into a non-scrollable buffer, which conserves system memory. (Although you can specify **dbForwardOnly** for a dynaset, it's ignored.) As the name suggests, you cannot use the **MovePrevious** or **MoveFirst** methods, or the **Move** method with a negative parameter. Less obviously, you also cannot use **MoveLast** because it implies having a set of *records*—with **dbForwardOnly**, only *one record* exists at any given time.

A forward-only snapshot does not save any data from previous records that you have retrieved. Thus, you avoid the in-memory copy and temporary database creation operations, often with considerable performance savings.

## Performance Characteristics of Dynasets and Snapshots

Dynaset- and snapshot-type **Recordset** objects differ in the way they retrieve and cache data. They also differ in performance and data accessibility. Frequently, the needs of your application will dictate which **Recordset** type you can use. Ask yourself the following questions about your application and use the answers that follow as a guide to help you choose the right **Recordset** type for your application and to help you understand the tradeoffs between the two types.

### Do you need to update the remote data?

If you need to update the remote data, you must use a dynaset-type **Recordset**. If, however, you don't need to update data or see changes made by other users, use a snapshot-type **Recordset**. Snapshot-type **Recordset** objects are faster to open and scroll through than dynaset-type **Recordset** objects.

### Is your result set large?

If your result set contains a large number of records, a dynaset-type **Recordset** is faster and more efficient than a snapshot-type **Recordset**. The performance difference in large **Recordset** objects occurs because your application must retrieve all records in a snapshot-type **Recordset** when you move from the first record to the last. In a dynaset-type **Recordset**, your application only needs to retrieve the bookmark fields initially. As each record, or group of records, in the dynaset-type **Recordset** is visited, the application fetches the data from the server that corresponds to the bookmarks.

If your result set contains a small number of records, a snapshot-type **Recordset** is faster and more efficient than a dynaset-type **Recordset**. The performance difference in small **Recordset** objects occurs because your application can fetch and hold a few hundred complete records more easily than it can fetch and hold a few hundred bookmarks and subsequently fetch the data from the server that corresponds to the bookmarks at the application's request. This is especially true of scrolling speed: Snapshot-type **Recordset** objects are faster because all the data is cached locally.

### Do you need to retrieve data from all fields in the remote table?

If your application doesn't need all fields in the remote table, you can improve opening and scrolling performance in recordsets by restricting the fields fetched from the server.

### Does your Recordset contain OLE Object or Memo fields?

For dynaset-type **Recordset** objects, if your application fetches records that include **OLE Object** or **Memo** and you don't need to view or update these objects, you can improve performance by ensuring that they aren't fetched. The Microsoft Jet database engine only fetches **OLE Object** and **Memo** records if they are visible through the user interface of your application (a Microsoft Access form or report, for example) when the rest of the record is fetched. You can remove the objects from the form and add a button to expose the **OLE Object** or **Memo** as needed. This will let users of your application retrieve the **OLE Object** or **Memo** at will without the burden of displaying this information when it isn't needed.

It's also important to understand that **Memo** fields are cached in a snapshot-type **Recordset**. **OLE Object** fields are not.

## Recordset Population

Regardless of which type of **Recordset** you use, dynaset or snapshot, both are populated in the same way. What does this mean? When you first call the **OpenRecordset** method, Microsoft Jet returns control to your program as soon as the first record is available. At that stage, no other records have been retrieved. In other words, in the case of a dynaset, only one primary key value has been retrieved from the server, and in the case of a snapshot, only one record of data has been fetched. If you close the **Recordset** at this stage, that is the sum total of all data that is retrieved.

You probably want more than one record, however. Therefore, each time you move the cursor forward (for instance, by using the **MoveNext** method, or the **Move** method with a positive parameter), Microsoft Jet retrieves either key values (dynaset) or record data (snapshot) until it reaches the end of the requested records. Issuing a **MoveLast** forces Microsoft Jet to retrieve all data.

If you are using a Microsoft Access form or the Microsoft Visual Basic **Data** control, then some background retrieval is done for you. For example, while the first record is being displayed on a form, Microsoft Access is retrieving the bookmark (dynaset) or data (snapshot) for subsequent records while checking the keyboard to see if the user has typed anything. The Visual Basic **Data** control does the same thing. You can adjust the size and rate of these retrievals with the MSysConf table described in the "Using the MSysConf Table" section earlier in this chapter. For Visual Basic, you can additionally control the dynaset cache size by setting the **CacheSize** property of the **Recordset** and then assigning the **Recordset** to the **Data** control's **Recordset** property. By default, the **Data** control caches fifty records.

## Effects of Asynchronous Queries

For more information on Registry settings, see Appendix C, "Registry Settings."

If your ODBC driver, database server, and network operating system support asynchronous operations, Microsoft Jet executes ODBC queries asynchronously. This allows your application to cancel a long-running query or to switch to another task while the query runs on the server. Microsoft Jet interrogates the server at the interval specified by the AsyncRetryInterval value in the Windows Registry key \Jet\3.0\Engines\ODBC. By default, this value is set to 500 milliseconds.

If your application cancels an asynchronous query (or closes the query before all results have been fetched), Microsoft Jet calls the ODBC **SQLCancel** function. The **SQLCancel** function discards any pending results and returns control to the application. Some database servers or network operating systems respond quickly to query cancellations; others may require your application to wait several seconds. For more information, see the previous section, "Recordset Population."

In addition, Microsoft Jet cancels a query when the interval specified by the **QueryTimeout** value in the Windows Registry key \Jet\3.0\Engines\ODBC is reached. By default, this value is set to 6000 milliseconds. A timed-out query isn't necessarily an indicator of trouble on the server; it simply means that the query did not return results in the time allotted. If you plan to execute a lengthy query, you can set the query's **ODBCTimeout** property to override the query timeout value in the Windows Registry. For more information on the **ODBCTimeout** value, see the "Setting Connection Timeout" section later in this chapter.

# Managing Connection Resources

Microsoft Jet connections to remote data sources require memory resources on both client and server systems. The process of connecting to a server when you need to retrieve or change data can also take time on both machines. You can minimize the effects of connection delays and conserve system resources by following the guidelines in this section.

## Preconnecting

One of the things that Microsoft Jet hides from your program is the concept of *connections*. Every operation on an ODBC database requires a mechanism for conversing with the database server—connections provide this mechanism. The first time you issue a command that requires access to the server, for instance, when you open a server table, Microsoft Jet opens a connection to the server. When you finish the operation, Microsoft Jet keeps the connection open in anticipation of the next operation. Similarly, if you have a connection open for a long time but aren't doing anything with it, Microsoft Jet will silently close it and then reopen it when you resume working.

In some situations, you may want the connection to be opened at a time you control rather than when the first operation occurs. For example, if your program has a startup or initialization routine already in place, you may wish to establish connections in that routine. This front-loads the execution time of your application, making it easier to avoid delays later in your application. Also, connections to your particular database might take a long time to establish if, for example, the database server is across the country or you're connected via a modem.

One way to minimize delays in opening forms or populating tables is to connect to the database server when your application starts. This technique, called preconnecting, allows you to set up the connection to the database before the user requests data. Preconnecting effectively speeds up the first routine data retrieval operation in your application while causing only a slight delay during application startup.

There are two simple techniques for establishing a connection at application startup. The first technique applies to applications that can use different ODBC data sources; the second technique is used when the ODBC data source name is known and can be hard-coded into the application. Although each technique uses the database's **Close** method, Microsoft Jet does not close the connection to the ODBC data source immediately. It caches the connection for the period of time specified by the ConnectionTimeout setting in the Windows Registry.

For example, the BookSales sample application opens a connection early in the program with the code:

```
' Note that the sample uses gCONNECT$, which has been replaced
' with connection information in this code example.
Set dbPubs = OpenDatabase("", False, False, _
    "ODBC;dsn=server1;uid=usr;pwd=passwd;database=pubs")
dbPubs.Close
```

For more information on Registry settings, see Appendix C, "Registry Settings."

Although it appears that this operation won't do anything, Microsoft Jet caches the connection for a time controlled by the **ConnectionTimeout** setting in the Windows Registry.

## Preconnecting to an Arbitrary ODBC Data Source

When you design an application that uses an ODBC data source, you may not have all the information to establish a connection and authenticate a user. One way to get a user connected to an ODBC data source is to display a dialog box listing all registered ODBC data sources on the user's system. The user can then choose the appropriate data source name from the dialog box and supply user name and password information, if applicable. Your application can store the user's connection information in a string by assigning the database's **Connect** property to a string variable. The following code illustrates this technique:

```
Public Sub PreConnectWithoutODBCParameters()
    Dim dbsLocal As Database, strPreConnect As String
    Set dbsLocal = OpenDatabase("", False, False, "ODBC;")
    strPreConnect = dbsLocal.Connect
    dbsLocal.Close
End Sub
```

## Preconnecting to a Known ODBC Data Source

When you know information about the ODBC data source and can hard-code it into the application, you can preconnect to the data source by including the ODBC DSN and database information as part of your application's code and requiring the user to supply his or her authentication information at run time. Simply construct a form to gather the user name and password and build a connection string containing these values, as in the following example:

```
Public Sub PreConnectWithODBCParameters(strUserName As String, _
    strPassword As String)
    Dim dbsLocal As DATABASE, strConnectionInfo As String

    Set dbsLocal = OpenDatabase("C:\Samples\Chap09\Pubs")
```

```
        strConnectionInfo = "ODBC;database=pubs;dsn=Publishers"
        strConnectionInfo = strConnectionInfo & "uid=" & strUserName & ";"
        strConnectionInfo = strConnectionInfo & "pwd=" & strPassword & ";"

        Set dbsLocal = OpenDatabase("", False, False, strConnectionInfo)
        dbsLocal.Close
End Sub
```

---

**Note**  By default, if there is no explicit user name and password specified at connect time, Microsoft Jet will attempt to connect to an ODBC data source with the same user name and password supplied by the user to initialize the Microsoft Jet engine. To change this default and avoid the additional overhead of a failed logon attempt against ODBC data sources that use different user names or passwords, your application should set the Microsoft JetTryAuth setting in the \Jet\3.0\Engines\ODBC folder of the Windows Registry to 0. This disables the automatic authentication attempt.

---

## Reducing Connection Use

Microsoft Jet can share multiple connections to an ODBC data source when the data source name and database are identical or when the data source names of the connections are identical and no connection uses a dedicated database (that is, none of the connections specifies a value for the DATABASE parameter in the connection string). For example, if you connect two applications to different tables in the same database, Microsoft Jet provides a single, dedicated connection to manage the bookmarks for each of the tables. A third, shared connection can then be used to fetch records from, insert records into, and update records on either of the tables.

Microsoft Jet lets you execute multiple queries and allocates and terminates connections automatically. Depending on the ODBC database server you use, however, you may need to watch the number of queries that remain partially completed at a given time.

For example, an Oracle server can handle multiple, simultaneous partially completed queries; it does so by allocating additional resources at the database server layer. Microsoft SQL Server, however, uses a streamlined connection model that requires fewer resources on the database server. Consequently, each connection to Microsoft SQL Server can service only one query at a time.

If the database server used by your application supports multiple, simultaneous, partially completed queries on a single connection, your application effectively uses only one connection. If your application connects to a database server that services one query at a time, you should try to reduce the number of connections your application requires.

## Reducing Connections by Limiting the Size of Recordsets

If your database server services one query at a time, you can reduce connection usage by limiting the size of dynaset-type recordsets to 100 records. A dynaset-type **Recordset** with 100 or fewer records can be managed through a single connection. If the dynaset-type **Recordset** contains more than 100 records, however, Microsoft Jet must use two connections to manage the **Recordset**: one connection to maintain the key values and a second connection to retrieve the data associated with those keys for all records visible on the application user's screen. Although it's possible for other dynaset-type **Recordset** objects to share the second (data values) connection, they cannot share the first (bookmark) connection, as it's possible that not all key values have been retrieved from the server. You should note however, that as soon as all bookmarks have been fetched, that connection is available for reuse.

## Active Statements and Connections

When the results of a query on a remote data source haven't been completely fetched, the connection to the data source has an "active statement" on the connection. Depending on the type of data source or the behavior of the driver, you may not be able to execute another SQL statement on a connection until the active statement has completed. Furthermore, this type of connection is held open until the last record of the result set has been fetched. In this case, Microsoft Jet may need to allocate additional connections to support other queries or operations (rather than discarding query results that have not been fetched or forcing the application to complete the fetch operation to close the statement).

To determine whether your ODBC data source or driver allows multiple, active statements on a single connection, Microsoft Jet requests the SQL_ACTIVE_STATEMENTS value from the ODBC driver with the **SQLGetInfo** API call. The value returned from the driver can represent a limitation in either the driver or the data source.

If the ODBC driver or data source is further limited by supporting only one statement per connection and only one connection per session (that is, a driver that doesn't allow Microsoft Jet to open a second connection), Microsoft Jet forces linked tables to behave as snapshot-type **Recordset** objects by ignoring any unique indexes on the remote table. This allows Microsoft Jet to provide read-only data access to the remote data source, rather than denying access to the data source due to insufficient connection resources.

## Completing Active Statements

If you need to close connections to conserve connection resources, you can complete the active statement on a connection. Active statements can usually be completed or cleared by fetching the remaining records in the **Recordset** containing the query results. The easiest way to complete a statement that has a pending fetch operation is to execute the **Recordset** object's **MoveLast** method. This will close the active statement and release the connection associated with the statement.

---

**Note**  This technique is not recommended for very large **Recordset** objects.

---

## Setting Connection Timeout

One way to prevent idle connections from being cached is to set the ODBC connection timeout value to a very low number. By default, the ODBC timeout value is set to 60 seconds (or one minute), but you can change this value in one of two ways. If you want to set the value for every instance of the Microsoft Jet engine to another value, simply change the ODBC ConnectionTimeout value in the \Jet\3.0\Engines\ODBC folder of the Windows Registry to the new idle time (in seconds).

Microsoft Jet closes the connection after the specified number of seconds of idle time unless a condition exists, as described in the following section, that prevents the connection from closing. This means that Microsoft Jet closes connections even if forms displaying remote data are still open. Microsoft Jet automatically reconnects when the application requires a connection again.

---

**Note**  A ConnectionTimeout setting of 0 causes the connection to remain open indefinitely (no timeout).

---

## Connections that Microsoft Jet Cannot Close

There are two reasons that Microsoft Jet refuses a request to close a connection even when the idle time has expired. The first is pending query results, as discussed earlier in this chapter. If your application hasn't finished fetching the results of a query against a remote data source, Microsoft Jet will be unable to close the connection until the active statement on the connection has completed. To learn how to complete a statement, see the "Completing Active Statements" section earlier in this chapter.

The second reason that Microsoft Jet might refuse to close a connection is that the connection has a pending transaction. Your application must commit or roll back the transaction before Microsoft Jet can release the connection. Since the decision to commit or roll back is usually based on logic in your application, you must ensure that all branches in your decision tree result in one of these conclusions. If the application does not determine the outcome of the transaction, Microsoft Jet will automatically roll back the transaction when you close the **Workspace** object that initiated the transaction.

## Caching Authentication Information

For more information on security, see Chapter 10, "Managing Security."

As discussed earlier in "Preconnecting," Microsoft Jet tries to use the authentication information supplied to the local Microsoft Jet engine against the remote data source, unless you specify otherwise. You can use this behavior to allow the user to provide one user name and password for all data (local or remote) accessed by your application. In environments where this is not practical or desired, you may want to set the Microsoft JetTryAuth Registry setting to 0.

This also means that each time you attempt to use a linked table that doesn't contain a stored user name and password, you must supply a user name and password to access the remote data. In this case, Microsoft Jet prompts the user for a user name and password through an ODBC driver logon dialog box.

Once the user has logged on to the remote data source, Microsoft Jet stores the authentication information until the application closes. This allows reconnections to the data source to occur "behind the scenes" and without interruption. Cached authentication information can also be applied to other tables on the same data source provided they are in the same database. If your application connects the user to another database server or database, Microsoft Jet again prompts the user for a user name and password through the ODBC driver logon dialog box—if a user name and password are required.

Once the user establishes a connection to a remote database using a specific user name and password, that authentication information does not change throughout the user's session (until the application terminates). This behavior, which is an effect of Microsoft Jet's connection sharing and caching model, prevents the loss of the user's authentication information even if the user opens remote linked tables that have different user names and passwords stored within. If your application design requires different levels of security on a number of remote tables, you should use the data source's security features to ensure that each user has the desired privileges.

# Implementing Client/Server Applications Using Microsoft Jet

Now that you're familiar with some of the basic concepts involved in client/server design, as well as some key optimization techniques, you probably want to see how you can use Microsoft Jet to implement your application. This section provides additional details on how the engine works in client/server architectures.

## Inserting and Updating Data on a Remote Data Source

When you insert records or update data on a remote data source, you must be aware of a few characteristics of the database server that may affect your application's behavior. This section discusses how to perform simple record insertions, how Microsoft Jet handles updates, how to speed up inserts and updates with bulk operations, the effects of changes to primary keys on the engine's ability to effectively manage insert and update operations, and how to refresh the data in your **Recordset** with the latest data from the database server.

### Inserting Records

You can insert new records into a remote database table by opening a linked table and inserting the records as you would with any other Microsoft Jet table. Although this is the simplest method, there are other ways to insert data that are much faster in the client/server environment.

Whenever you insert records using DAO operations, you should use the **dbAppendOnly** option. This causes the engine to optimize its operations for adding data.

## Handling Inserts and Updates to Remote Data

When a user inserts a record into a remote table, Microsoft Jet sends values for every field in the recordset to the remote database. Similarly, when a user updates records in the remote database, the engine sends the values that changed during the update.

You should be aware of three special cases when using Microsoft Jet to insert or update remote data.

- If the remote database server supplies default values on insert, Microsoft Jet honors those defaults. You can override these values if needed. Microsoft Jet uses the server defaults only when no value is specified.

- If the remote database contains a trigger that is set to activate when a user changes data in a specific field, the trigger will not be invoked unless the user has actually changed the data in that field. When Microsoft Jet updates a record, it does not provide values for every field; it only provides values for the records that you have changed.

- Microsoft Jet does not overwrite the data in a field that the ODBC API **SQLSpecialColumns** identifies as a SQL_ROWVER. These values are generated and maintained by the remote database server, and Microsoft Jet does not allow you to modify these fields.

## Speeding up Inserts and Updates With Bulk Operations

You can perform bulk operations, such as multiple-record insert, update, and delete operations, in one of two ways: You can use an SQL pass-through query or you can use the Microsoft Jet query processor. The Microsoft Jet query processor provides additional functionality, but can be somewhat slower than the SQL pass-through method for bulk operations.

The difference between using the Microsoft Jet query processor and an SQL pass-through query is in the way Microsoft Jet prepares for a bulk operation. When executing a bulk operation through its own query processor, Microsoft Jet builds a keyset for all records that will be affected by the operation. Then, the engine executes the operation for each record in the keyset, one record at a time.

The benefits of using the Microsoft Jet query processor are:

- It allows for partially successful bulk queries.

- It allows you to perform some bulk operations that may not be available on the remote database server.

The only drawback is the speed of the operation. You have to determine if the advantages offered by Microsoft Jet's query processor outweigh the possible performance penalties. If you find that performance is your highest goal, consider using pass-through queries. For information on SQL pass-through queries, see the "Using SQL Pass-Through Queries" section earlier in this chapter.

## Maintaining an Updated Picture of Remote Data

Another important consideration when working with remote data is whether your copy of the data is up-to-date. Before you attempt to insert, update, or delete records on the remote database server, you should ensure that your "picture" of the data is current.

Although you can create a new **Recordset** to capture the most recent data, there is a much faster method. Use the **Requery** method of the **Recordset** object to refresh the data. This method works with snapshot- and dynaset-type **Recordset** objects. You can use this method as a first step before an insert or update operation or any time you suspect the remote data may have changed.

You should note that because table-type **Recordset** objects do not support the **Requery** operation, you may want to consider using dynaset- or snapshot-type **Recordset** objects if you need the ability to control refreshing. This decision is made easier by the fact that you cannot open a table-type **Recordset** on ODBC data sources.

# Understanding Client/Server Query Behavior

Query operations in your client/server application are handled either locally or remotely. With local processing, Microsoft Jet handles the query. With remote processing, the remote database server handles the processing.

To successfully implement a client/server application, you should be aware of the differences between these two types of processing. This section discusses some key differences between local and remote query processing and lists operators and functions that may not be supported by the remote database server. This section also explains how to trace SQL operations.

## Remote vs. Local Processing

When you create and execute a query, Microsoft Jet must decide which portion of the query to process locally through its own query processor, and which portion to send to the remote database server for processing. Microsoft Jet always sends the entire query to the server unless it contains items the server cannot process.

Because Microsoft Jet's query processor supports heterogeneous joins, queries based on other queries, arbitrary expressions, and user-defined functions, your query may contain elements that the database server cannot interpret. To maximize the performance of queries in a client/server application, you should familiarize yourself with the capabilities of the server and design queries that use those capabilities. Use standard query optimization techniques for your server and use Microsoft Jet–specific query enhancements only when needed. Your goal should be to make it as easy as possible for Microsoft Jet to send your complete query to the server for processing.

Keep the following conditions in mind when constructing a query for the remote database server:

- If your query joins data from multiple data sources, Microsoft Jet has to perform at least one part of the query locally.
- If your query cannot be expressed in a single SQL statement, Microsoft Jet has to perform part of the query locally.

## Unsupported Operators and Functions

When you construct a query to send to the server, Microsoft Jet determines which parts of the query can be handled by the server and which parts must be handled locally. Microsoft Jet uses the ODBC call **SQLGetInfo** to ask the ODBC driver which operators and functions are available on the server. When Microsoft Jet encounters a statement containing an operator or function that cannot be processed by the server, that statement must be evaluated locally.

The following tables list operators and functions that Microsoft Jet sends to the server in SQL statements if they are supported by your server. See your server documentation for further details.

**General operators**

| | | |
|---|---|---|
| = | - | IS NULL |
| < > | * | IS NOT NULL |
| < | / | LIKE |
| > | & | MOD |
| < = | AND | NOT |
| > = | DIV | OR |
| + | IN | |

**Math functions**

| | | |
|---|---|---|
| ABS | FIX | SGN |
| ATN | INT | SIN |
| COS | LOG | SQR |
| EXP | RND | TAN |

### String functions

| | | |
|---|---|---|
| ASC | LEFT | SPACE |
| CHR | LEN | STR |
| INSTR | MID | STRING |
| LCASE | RTRIM | TRIM |
| LTRIM | RIGHT | UCASE |

### Aggregate functions

| | | |
|---|---|---|
| AVG | MIN | SUM |
| COUNT | MAX | |

### Conversion functions

| | | |
|---|---|---|
| CCur | CLng | CVDate |
| CDbl | CSng | |
| CInt | CStr | |

### Date and Time functions

| | | |
|---|---|---|
| DATE | DATEPART('*ww*') | MONTH |
| DATEPART('*ddd*') | DATEPART('*www*') | NOW |
| DATEPART('*hhh*') | DATEPART('*yyy*') | SECOND |
| DATEPART('*mmm*') | DATEPART('*yyyy*') | TIME |
| DATEPART('*nnn*') | DAY | WEEKDAY |
| DATEPART('*qqq*') | HOUR | YEAR |
| DATEPART('*sss*') | MINUTE | |

In addition, some servers don't support the following features:

- Outer joins
- Expressions, or nonfield references, in the ORDER BY clause
- The LIKE operator when applied to Text, Memo, or binary fields
- Unfamiliar wildcards in LIKE expressions
- Expressions that use a mixture of incompatible operators and functions, such as `A LIKE B * C`

The following features are unsupported on all known ODBC-accessible servers.

- Aggregation of reports constructed in Microsoft Access that contain multiple levels of grouping and totals
- User-defined functions that use variable arguments
- Microsoft Jet–specific SQL extensions, such as TOP or TRANSFORM

## Tracing SQL Operations

For complete information on Microsoft Jet Registry settings, see Appendix C, "Registry Settings."

If you want to get a better picture of the SQL statements that Microsoft Jet sends to the remote database server through ODBC, you can trace the SQL operations. To enable SQL tracing, create a **TraceSQLMode** setting in the \Jet\3.0\Engines\ODBC folder in the Windows Registry and set the value to 1. When you close and restart Microsoft Jet, the engine will log all ODBC calls in the text file SQLOUT.TXT, which is created in the current directory on your hard disk.

Microsoft Jet always appends new SQL statements to the file while **TraceSQLMode** is enabled. If you want to disable SQL logging, set the value of **TraceSQLMode** to 0 and restart Microsoft Jet.

---

**Note**   You must create the ODBC Registry key manually; this key is not created during the setup process.

---

The following table lists the SQL output strings that can appear in the SQLOUT.TXT file.

| Log entry | Description |
|---|---|
| SQLExecDirect:  <SQL-string> | The calling application executed a non-parameterized user query. |
| SQLPrepare:  <SQL-string> | The calling application prepared a parameterized user query. |
| SQLExecute:  (PARAMETERIZED QUERY) | The calling application executed a prepared, parameterized user query. |
| SQLExecute:  (GOTO BOOKMARK) | The calling application fetched a single record based on a bookmark. |
| SQLExecute:  (MULTI-RECORD FETCH) | The calling application fetched ten records based on ten bookmarks. |
| SQLExecute:  (MEMO FETCH) | The calling application fetched a **Memo** for a single record based on a bookmark. |
| SQLExecute:  (GRAPHIC FETCH) | The calling application fetched an **OLE Object** for a single record based on a bookmark. |
| SQLExecute:  (RECORD-FIXUP SEEK) | The calling application fetched a single record based on an index key (not necessarily the bookmark index). |
| SQLExecute:  (UPDATE) | The calling application updated a single record based on a bookmark. |

| Log entry | Description (*cont'd*) |
|---|---|
| SQLExecute: (DELETE) | The calling application deleted a single record based on a bookmark. |
| SQLExecute: (INSERT) | The calling application inserted a single record in dynaset mode. |
| SQLExecute: (SELECT INTO insert) | The calling application inserted a single record in export mode. |

If you are trying to track specific query behavior or diagnose a problem, you may want to archive or delete the **SQLOUT.TXT** file before running the query. After you run the query, scan the file for the first instance of **SQLPrepare** or **SQLExecDirect**, which should correspond to your first query.

# Linking Remote Tables

The easiest way to use remote tables with DAO is to link the tables to your application's Microsoft Jet database. This makes the tables appear as if they were native Microsoft Jet tables in your application's database. Besides convenience, one of the main advantages to linking is that Microsoft Jet caches information about the remote table in the stored link. Each time you open the linked table, information about its location, indexes, and other attributes are quickly accessible to Microsoft Jet, and opening is therefore faster.

Microsoft Jet also supports linking to SQL views on the remote data source, but with some restrictions, as discussed in the "Updating Tables With No Unique Index" section later in this chapter.

## How Microsoft Jet Links Remote Tables

Once you have established a connection to a remote data source, Microsoft Jet calls a series of ODBC API functions to determine the available objects such as tables on the remote data source. First, Microsoft Jet calls the **SQLTables** ODBC function to retrieve a list of all tables, views, synonyms, and similar objects (to ensure that the table you want to link exists).

Next, to get information on the requested table, Microsoft Jet calls ODBC informational functions such as **SQLColumns** (to determine the field names in the table) and **SQLStatistics** (to determine a table's indexes). Finally, Microsoft Jet determines how to best represent the data types in the remote table with Microsoft Jet data types (a process called *data type mapping*, which is discussed later in this chapter in the "Mapping Data Types" section).

## How Microsoft Jet Determines If a Remote Table Can Be Updated

When Microsoft Jet opens a **Recordset**, it attempts to use a dynaset-type **Recordset**, which allows your application to update the data in the remote table. This is only possible if the remote table is uniquely indexed. These unique key values on each record of a remote table allow direct access to the records for all updates. The fields that comprise the unique keys are called *bookmarks*.

When you link a table, Microsoft Jet determines the bookmark field or fields by choosing the first unique index returned by **SQLStatistics** as the primary index (if any unique indexes exist on the table). The **SQLStatistics** function always returns indexes in a specific order: clustered indexes, followed by hashed indexes, followed by "other" indexes. Furthermore, **SQLStatistics** alphabetizes the indexes within each group. Therefore, if you want Microsoft Jet to select a particular index, you can name the index so that it appears first in the alphabetical listing.

---

**Note**   Microsoft Jet does not attempt to determine the optimal set of fields that uniquely identifies a record in the table through the **SQLSpecialColumns** ODBC function call. Furthermore, Microsoft Jet does not attempt to use a database server's native record number identifier as a unique index (due to the potentially ambiguous nature of such identifiers in a multiuser environment).

---

If Microsoft Jet is unable to identify a unique index on the remote table, it must open a snapshot-type **Recordset**, which can't be updated. (Note that Microsoft Jet cannot open a table on an ODBC data source as a table-type **Recordset**.) You can get around this behavior by creating an artificial index, as discussed in the next section.

## Updating Tables With No Unique Index

You can link a server view to your application's database just as you would link a table with no unique index. Microsoft Jet will treat the linked view as a snapshot-type **Recordset**, unless you create an artificial unique index on the link (not on the server view). Therefore, you can think of linking to an SQL view the same as you would linking to any other data source with a non-unique index.

To make a server view or other table with no index updatable, select a group of fields that uniquely identify each record in the view. Then, create a data definition query on the linked table. (Do not use an SQL pass-through query, as you aren't trying to create an index on the server tables or the server view.)

This gives Microsoft Jet enough information to uniquely identify records on the linked view and allows your application to use all operations normally associated with dynaset-type **Recordset** objects (such as INSERT, UPDATE, and DELETE operations).

**Note**  You can't link server-based stored procedures using this technique.

# Using Transactions

For information on Microsoft Jet transactions in non-client/server environments, see Chapter 5, "Working with Records and Fields."

This section describes the behavior of Microsoft Jet transactions in a client/server environment. This section also discusses the limitations of transactions and what you should avoid when using transactions in your application.

## Transaction Behavior

Often, to enforce data integrity, a set of operations must be considered as a single unit. For example, the transfer of funds from one bank account to another consists of two operations: entering a debit in one account and a matching credit in the other account. In practice, either both operations must succeed or neither operation should be processed.

In this situation, the debit and credit operations are a single unit, or a *transaction*. A transaction is a set of operations that are committed (saved) if and only if all of the operations succeed. If any of the operations fail, all of the operations that succeeded are rolled back (canceled), and the data is returned to the state it was in before the transaction began.

DAO supports three transaction methods: one for starting, one for committing, and one for rolling back a transaction:

- The **BeginTrans** method begins a new transaction.
- The **CommitTrans** method commits all changes made to data by the most recent **BeginTrans** method.
- The **Rollback** method rolls back, or cancels, all changes made to data by the most recent **BeginTrans** method.

**BeginTrans**, **CommitTrans**, and **Rollback** are all methods of the **Workspace** object.

On most servers, transactions hold locks that prevent other users from updating or even reading data affected by the transaction until it's committed or rolled back. You should therefore keep your transactions as short as possible and avoid beginning a transaction and then waiting for the user's response before completing it.

This hypothetical example shows a transfer using two common update operations, a withdrawal and a deposit. The transfer occurs in the context of a transaction. If either operation fails, the transaction makes sure that the operation as a whole fails.

```
Sub TransferFunds ()
    Dim wspDefault As Workspace, dbsBanking As Database
    Dim qdfTransferFunds As QueryDef

    On Error GoTo TransferFailed

    Set wspDefault= DBEngine.Workspaces(0)
    Set dbsBanking = wspDefault.OpenDatabase("banking.mdb")

    ' Begin the fund transfer transaction.
    wspDefault.BeginTrans

    ' Create a temporary SQL pass-through query.
    Set qdfTransferFunds = dbsBanking.CreateQueryDef("")
    qdfTransferFunds.Connect = _
        "ODBC;DATABASE=bank;DSN=FirstFederal;UID=dagny;PWD=bandit"
    qdfTransferFunds.ReturnsRecords = False

    qdfTransferFunds.SQL = "UPDATE Accounts SET Balance = " & _
        "Balance - 100 WHERE AccountID = 'DAGNY_SAV'"

    ' Subtract 100 from the savings account.
    qdfTransferFunds.Execute

    qdfTransferFunds.SQL = "UPDATE Accounts SET Balance = " & _
        "Balance + 100 WHERE AccountID = ' DAGNY_CHK'"

    ' Add 100 to the checking account.
    qdfTransferFunds.Execute

    qdfTransferFunds.SQL = "INSERT INTO LogBook " & _
        "(Type, Source, Destination, Amount) VALUES " & _
        "('Transfer', 'DAGNY_SAV', 'DAGNY_CHK', 100)"

    ' Log the transaction.
    qdfTransferFunds.ExecuteWspDefault.CommitTrans
    ' Commit the transaction.
    DbsBanking.Close
Exit Sub
```

```
TransferFailed:
    MsgBox Error$
    ' If one operation fails, roll them all back.
    WspDefault.Rollback
    Exit Sub
End Sub
```

## How Microsoft Jet Uses ODBC Transactions

When your DAO code does not use transaction methods explicitly, Microsoft Jet will use ODBC in *auto-commit* mode. In this mode, each SQL statement sent to the server has an implicit transaction around it; that is, the SQL statement has an immediate effect on the ODBC data and cannot be rolled back. Microsoft Jet stops using auto-commit mode and uses explicit ODBC transactions with:

- SQL statements that modify data (for example, UPDATE, INSERT, or APPEND).

- Explicit DAO transaction methods.

When using so-called "bulk operation" SQL statements such as UPDATE, INSERT, and APPEND, Microsoft Jet places a transaction around the operation so that it can succeed or fail as a single entity. This is necessary because one such Microsoft Jet SQL statement may actually correspond to many individual server statements.

## DAO Transactions

Multiple concurrent transactions on **Recordset** objects against a single server are actually a single transaction because a single connection is being used to service updates for both dynasets. You should structure your transactions so that they do not overlap; transactions are intended to be atomic units.

If the server supports transactions at all, Microsoft Jet assumes only single-level support; that is, no nesting of transactions. Therefore, if your application code nests transactions, only the outermost **BeginTrans**, **CommitTrans**, and **Rollback** methods are actually sent to the server; nested transactions are silently ignored.

These transaction semantics also apply to SQL pass-through queries that modify server data, so explicit transactions within the pass-through queries cannot be used. For more information on SQL pass-through queries, see the "Using SQL Pass-Through Queries" section earlier in this chapter.

## Transaction Limitations

Although transactions can improve the functionality and performance of your client/server applications, they have several limitations, as described in the following sections.

## Transactions Cannot Be Nested

Although Microsoft Jet supports nesting transactions on its own native data sources, ODBC doesn't support nesting transactions. Because of this, Microsoft Jet doesn't support any transaction nesting against ODBC data and will ignore attempts to nest transactions. This is a common code change you need to make when converting code that runs against local data sources to work with ODBC data sources.

## Some Queries Are Not Allowed in Transactions

Some queries may not be allowed within a transaction. For example, SQL Server doesn't allow data-definition, permission, or backup-related statements within transactions. Check your server's documentation to determine these limits.

## Server Transaction Commands Are Not Allowed

Microsoft Jet often conserves connections by sharing them between queries. If you use server-specific transaction commands in pass-through queries, they can confuse the internal tracking of server transactions performed by Microsoft Jet, as well as provide you with unexpected results. For example, on SQL Server, don't use the SQL Server command BEGIN TRAN. Instead, use the **BeginTrans** method. Microsoft Jet translates DAO transaction methods into the equivalent server commands.

## Server Limits on Locks

Locks may be placed on the server for every operation you perform inside a transaction. Be aware of the number of locks you're requesting and make sure your server is configured to handle them.

## Isolating Transactions

For efficiency reasons, remote data used within **Workspace** objects does not have an isolated transaction space. For example, if you use two **Workspace** objects to open a table attached to an ODBC data source, transaction methods on one **Workspace** will affect transactions on the other. Because it's unusual to have two different sets of transactions used concurrently, this isn't likely to affect much code.

If you want to have multiple concurrent transactions on your server, you can force each workspace to have a distinct remote transaction space by setting the **IsolateODBCTrans** property of the **Workspace** object to **True**. This prevents the workspace from sharing connections with other workspaces, which guarantees transaction isolation.

# Dividing Data Efficiently

One of the key elements in successful client/server design is deciding where to put the data. The key to making this decision lies in recognizing and utilizing the strengths of each system. You are really designing two databases and establishing links between them. Although there are many techniques available to increase Microsoft Jet performance against ODBC data sources, the initial design of the data model will have the greatest effect on performance.

## Client-Side Data Considerations

On the client-side of the client/server data model, you can store lookup tables (such as parts lists) and "master" tables. The Microsoft Jet database on each client machine can also store all of the queries needed to access and manipulate remote data.

### Why use local lookup tables?

It's more efficient for order entry personnel to use lookup tables to choose from a list of available products than for them to type in the name or stock number of each item in an order, but why should you store the lookup tables on the local machine? One reason is performance; local lookup tables respond to queries much more quickly.

Another reason is that the values in a lookup table are relatively static; although the items in an organization's product offerings may periodically change, this is usually an infrequent occurrence that can be planned for ahead of time, and the local lookup tables can be updated easily. When it's time to update the lookup table of product offerings, you can post the updated table to the server and have all users run a query to update the local tables.

### Why store master tables on the client?

Master tables are often good candidates for client-side tables. For example, a salesperson might maintain a local table of customers and each customer might have a number of orders. By storing the customer data locally, each salesperson has access to order information for their respective customers; the order information itself remains in the detail table on the server where order entry personnel can update the information, accounting can gather billing information, and shipping can determine which orders need to be filled. Master tables can also be indexed for faster performance.

## Server-Side Data Considerations

You should use the database server primarily for storing centralized, detailed data. Most database servers are very efficient at storing large amounts of data in a secured environment while also providing high-speed concurrent access to multiple users. For example, this makes them perfect candidates for detail tables in order entry systems which provide data for many different groups within an organization (such as salespeople, shipping personnel, and accounting staff).

# Handling Server-Generated Errors

When you receive an ODBC error from Microsoft Jet, the error message does not contain the specific error that occurred on the server. This message is stored in the **Errors** collection. As you will recall from Chapter 2, "Introducing Data Access Objects," the **Errors** collection is a zero-based collection of error messages that starts with the first error that occurs. You can walk through the **Errors** collection to display all messages logged by the system.

This sample function is a simple error handler that exposes errors at each level in the client/server system. The VerboseErrorHandler function handles errors in many of the code examples found throughout this chapter.

```
Public Function VerboseErrorHandler()
    ' Error handling routine ErrorHandler handles
    ' all ODBC errors in the Microsoft Jet layer.
    Dim errX As Error
    Dim intCounter As Integer

    Select Case Err
        Case 3146 To 3299 ' DAO error range
            ' Get a count of errors in the collection.
            MsgBox "There are " & Errors.Count & _
                " errors in the errors collection."
            ' Iterate through the collection, starting
            ' with the innermost error.
            intCounter = 0
            For Each errX In DBEngine.Errors
                MsgBox "SQL Server Error # " & intCounter & _
                    &" " & Errors(intCounter)
                intCounter = intCounter + 1
            Next errX
        Case Else
            ' Returns control to caller.
    End Select
End Function
```

# Mapping Data Types

Most database servers support a rich set of data types, including a number of floating point types of varying scale and precision. The set of data types supported by Microsoft Jet may not exactly match many of the data types on a specific database server. To allow transparent data access, however, Microsoft Jet must select an equivalent data type for each field in a remote table. This section discusses the rules that Microsoft Jet uses to select local data types to represent standard ODBC data types and vice versa.

## A Word About Floating Point Data

Techniques for handling floating point data (any numeric data which does not have a fixed number of digits after the decimal point) vary among database servers. Furthermore, when remote floating point data is coerced into a numeric format acceptable to Microsoft Jet (as in the case of linked tables), minor numeric data accuracy loss may occur. Although these accuracy losses usually occur in very large or very small floating point numbers and have no appreciable effect on common mathematical operations, they can cause a problem when used for exact comparisons. One case that is particularly important is that of floating point data in fields that are part of a unique index.

When fields containing floating point values are used as part of a unique index and any variation (even a very small one) exists between the numeric data on the local and remote data sources, Microsoft Jet may mark the record containing the discrepancy as **#Deleted**. This occurs because Microsoft Jet requests the record from the server by presenting its key value. The server table doesn't contain a record with key values that exactly match (because of the loss of accuracy) the values requested by Microsoft Jet, therefore it appears to Microsoft Jet that another user has deleted the record.

To remedy this situation, you can force Microsoft Jet to select another unique index (if available) that doesn't use any floating point values. Rename the new index (that is, the index that doesn't contain floating point values) so that it appears alphabetically before the original index and re-establish the link to the remote table. Microsoft Jet automatically updates the link with the new index as the primary index on the remote table.

## ODBC to Jet Data Type Mapping

For a complete description of data types recognized by ODBC, as well as a complete explanation of precision and scale in ODBC, see Appendix D of the *Microsoft ODBC 2.0 Programmer's Reference and SDK Guide.*

Microsoft Jet calls the ODBC **SQLColumns** function to gather information on the fields in the remote table. **SQLColumns** returns (among other things) the following information for each field in the table, which determines how the data type of each field will be mapped to a Microsoft Jet data type.

| Argument | Description |
|---|---|
| fSqlType | The fSqlType argument returns the SQL data type of the field. Valid SQL data types include a minimum set, which provides basic ODBC conformance, a core set, which is a superset of the minimum set and adds X/Open and SAG CAE (92)–compliant types, and an extended set, which includes the minimum set, the extended set, and additional data types that support specific database servers. |
| lPrecision | The lPrecision argument returns the maximum number of digits used by the data type represented in the field. |
| wScale | The wScale argument returns the maximum number of digits to the right of the decimal point used by the data type represented in the field. |

Microsoft Jet uses the fSqlType, lPrecision, and wScale values to determine an appropriate local data type, on a field-by-field basis, and uses that data type to represent the remote data in a linked table. Each time Microsoft Jet executes an action or parameterized query against the remote data source, the information stored in the linked table is used to ensure that ODBC calls are made with a valid ODBC data type. The following table lists ODBC data types and the corresponding Microsoft Jet data types.

| ODBC data type | Microsoft Jet data type |
|---|---|
| SQL_BIT | Yes/No |
| SQL_TINYINT SQL_SMALLINT | Number (Integer) |
| SQL_INTEGER | Number (Long Integer) |
| SQL_REAL | Number (Single) |
| SQL_FLOAT SQL_DOUBLE | Number (Double) |
| SQL_TIMESTAMP SQL_DATE | DateTime |
| SQL_TIME | Text |
| SQL_CHAR SQL_VARCHAR | Varies based on the lPrecision value: For data types where the lPrecision is less than or equal to 255, the Microsoft Jet data type is Text and the **FieldSize** is equal to the value of lPrecision; For data types where the lPrecision is greater than 255, the Microsoft Jet data type is Memo. |

| ODBC data type | Microsoft Jet data type (*cont'd*) |
| --- | --- |
| SQL_BINARY<br>SQL_VARBINARY | Varies based on the lPrecision value:<br>For data types where the lPrecision is less than or equal to 255, the Microsoft Jet data type is Binary and the **FieldSize** is equal to the value of lPrecision;<br>For data types where the lPrecision is greater than 255, the Microsoft Jet data type is OLE Object. |
| SQL_LONGVARBINARY | OLE Object |
| SQL_LONGVARCHAR | Memo |
| SQL_DECIMAL<br>SQL_NUMERIC | Varies based on a combination of the lPrecision and wScale values:<br>For data types where the wScale equals 0 and lPrecision is less than or equal to 4, the Microsoft Jet data type is Number (Integer);<br>For data types where the wScale equals 0 and lPrecision is less than or equal to 9, the Microsoft Jet data type is Number (Long Integer);<br>For data types where the wScale is greater than or equal to 0, and lPrecision is less than or equal to 15, the Microsoft Jet data type is Number (Double).<br><br>For data types where the wScale is greater than 0 and less than or equal to 4, lPrecision is less than or equal to 15, the Microsoft Jet data type is Number (Double); and the **FieldSize** is equal to the value of lPrecision; if wScale >4 the Microsoft Jet data type is Double.<br><br>**Special Mappings for Microsoft SQL Server**<br>For data types where the wScale equals 4 and lPrecision equals 19, the Microsoft Jet data type is Currency;<br>for data types where the wScale equals 4 and lPrecision equals 10, the Microsoft Jet data type is Currency. |

## Microsoft Jet to ODBC Data Type Mapping

When you send data from a Microsoft Jet client to a remote data source, the Microsoft Jet engine must find an appropriate ODBC data type to receive the data. This data type mapping can involve rather complex decisions for Microsoft Jet as many database servers implement only a subset of the ODBC data types. Therefore, Microsoft Jet tries a prioritized list of data types and maps the local data to the first data type supported on the remote data source. Note that some Microsoft Jet data types are unsupported on some database servers.

| Microsoft Jet data type | ODBC data type |
| --- | --- |
| Yes/No | SQL_BIT<br>SQL_SMALLINT<br>SQL_INTEGER<br>SQL_VARCHAR(5) |
| Number (Byte) | SQL_SMALLINT<br>SQL_INTEGER<br>SQL_VARCHAR(10) |
| Number (Integer) | SQL_SMALLINT<br>SQL_INTEGER<br>SQL_VARCHAR(10) |
| Number (Long Integer) | SQL_INTEGER<br>SQL_VARCHAR(20) |
| Currency | SQL_DECIMAL(19,4) (Microsoft SQL Server and Sybase SQL Server only)<br>SQL_FLOAT<br>SQL_VARCHAR(30) |
| Number (Single) | SQL_REAL<br>SQL_FLOAT<br>SQL_VARCHAR(30) |
| Number (Double) | SQL_FLOAT<br>SQL_VARCHAR(40) |
| DateTime | SQL_TIMESTAMP<br>SQL_VARCHAR(40) |
| Text (Field Size) | SQL_VARCHAR($n$), where $n$ is the smaller of the Microsoft Jet **FieldSize** and the database server's maximum size for a VARCHAR. |
| Binary (Field Size) | SQL_VARBINARY($n$), where $n$ is the smaller of the Microsoft Jet **FieldSize** and the database server's maximum size for a VARBINARY.<br>If SQL_VARBINARY is not supported on the database server, the query fails. |
| Memo | SQL_LONGVARCHAR if the server supports it.<br>Otherwise, SQL_VARCHAR($n$), where $n$ is the server's maximum size for a VARCHAR if the maximum size is greater than 2000.<br>If neither case is supported on the database server, the query fails. |
| OLE Object | SQL_LONGVARBINARY if the server supports it.<br>Otherwise, SQL_VARBINARY ($n$), where $n$ is the database server's maximum size for a VARBINARY if the maximum size is greater than 2000.<br>If neither case is supported on the database server, the query fails. |

C H A P T E R   1 0

# Managing Security

Implementing security in your application protects sensitive data and intellectual
property such as your application's structure and programming code, and
prevents your application's users from inadvertently changing object designs or
code in a way that would cause your application to stop working. This chapter is
designed to explain the Microsoft Jet security model and show you how to
properly implement its use in your application.

**Contents**

For information on
copying the code
examples from the
companion CD-ROM
to your hard disk
drive, see "Using the
Companion CD-ROM"
in the Preface.

## Using CH10.MDB and CHAP10.VBP

If you copied the samples from the companion CD-ROM, you can find
the code examples for Microsoft Access in C:\SAMPLES\CHAP10\
ACCESS\CH10.MDB. The corresponding code examples for Visual Basic
are in C:\SAMPLES\CHAP10\VB40\CHAP10.VBP.

To run any of the code examples in this chapter, open the .MDB file in
Microsoft Access or open the .VBP file in Microsoft Visual Basic 4.0. You
can use the examples to help you understand the concepts discussed in the
chapter—or you can modify them and use them in your own applications.

# Using Microsoft Access as a Security Tool

If you're building Microsoft Jet applications using a program other than Microsoft Access (such as Visual Basic or Microsoft Excel), you can secure your applications using DAO. This interface gives you much of the same functionality that exists in Microsoft Access. However, to create a secure environment, you must build workgroup databases with the Workgroup Administrator program. Currently, this utility ships only with Microsoft Access. Because of this, you must use Microsoft Access to set up the initial elements of a secured system.

Because Microsoft Access includes Workgroup Administrator, and because it has a full user interface for working with security, many developers using Visual Basic (or a similar programming environment that supports Microsoft Jet) use Microsoft Access to initiate and maintain security. Although you have full programmatic access to existing security through DAO, it's often easier to use Microsoft Access to develop and maintain security in your application.

Additionally, the Security Wizard described in this chapter is included with Microsoft Access. If you want to use its functionality, you must use Microsoft Access.

# The Microsoft Jet Security Model

Microsoft Jet provides a robust and powerful security model that gives you a great deal of control over users' access to your application. Because of the flexibility, the model is somewhat more complicated than those provided by other desktop databases. Indeed, security is one of the more commonly misunderstood aspects of Microsoft Jet and is usually incorrectly implemented by developers who lack a cohesive understanding of its workings. The following section contains detailed information, but it's structured in a way that helps you understand the model before describing how to implement security.

## User-Level and Share-Level Security

Microsoft Jet provides both share-level and user-level security. In share-level security systems, passwords are associated with specific objects, not with users. Any user who knows the password for an object can access that object. Microsoft Jet supports share-level security with a database password. Add a password to your database when all you want to do is prevent unauthorized users from opening your application, and you're not concerned about what they do once they're inside.

If you need more control, however, perhaps because you want to prevent users from modifying the design of your tables and queries, Microsoft Jet also provides user-level security. With user-level security, users are *authenticated* when they open a Microsoft Jet **Workspace**. The process of authentication involves the user logging on to the system with a name and password. After the user is authenticated, the system determines the user's access to an object by comparing the user's identification to a set of object permissions that have been defined by the application's administrator. Different users can have different permissions for the same objects.

Microsoft Jet user-level security functions as follows. Administrators assign specific permissions on **Database** objects to users and groups. When a user starts up a session of the Microsoft Jet database engine in a secure environment, the user logs on, passing in a user name and password. The password's function is to authenticate the user, not to give access to any particular objects. Microsoft Jet then records in an internal structure all the groups to which that user belongs. Every time the user tries to perform an action such as opening a database, browsing a table, or modifying a query, Microsoft Jet first checks to see if the user, *or* any of the groups to which the user belongs, have the necessary permission. If any do, Microsoft Jet performs the action. If no one does, Microsoft Jet returns an error indicating that permission is denied, and the operation fails.

## Advantages of User-Level Security

The advantages of user-level security become obvious after you start working with secure systems. As an example, suppose you have a Salary table and two groups of people who use that table: managers who can update the table and workers who can view but not update the table. In a user-level system such as one created with Microsoft Jet, you can assign update permissions for the Salary table to the managers group and read permissions to the workers group. Then you enlist each user in your system into one of these two groups. The users manage their own passwords, and their passwords are used to verify their identity rather than to identify a permission for an object.

In a share-level system, two passwords would be used to implement this scheme: an update password and a read password, both applied directly to the Salary table. In this scenario, you would have to provide the passwords directly to the appropriate people. This is even more complicated if you have to change a password; you must have administrative mechanisms in place to make sure that all users get their appropriate updated passwords. Also, any time a user is moved from the managers group to the workers group, the password for the managers group must be changed to maintain security.

You can see that even in this simple scenario, the administrative headaches associated with share-level security can be substantial. When you imagine a real application with many tables, users, and groups, you can quickly see that share-level security is a difficult solution.

# Elements of the Model

To implement security, Microsoft Jet uses a set of elements that, taken as a whole, describe the model. The four elements that make up the model are:

- The user of your application. This may be a real person or a process running on a computer.
- The group. A group is a logical collection of users who require the same level of access to a set of objects. Users can belong to more than one group.
- The SystemDB or workgroup database. A Microsoft Jet database that physically stores the definitions of users, groups, and passwords.
- Your database. A database that contains your application's objects, along with the permission settings for each object for each user and group.

Figure 10.1 illustrates how these elements relate.

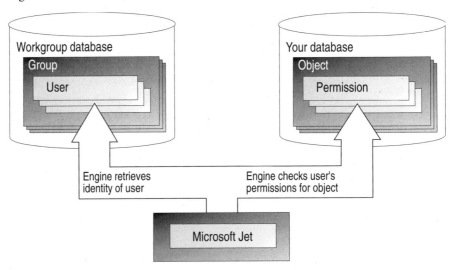

**Figure 10.1    The Microsoft Jet security model**

## Users and Groups

Microsoft Jet defines users of your application in two ways: as individual users or as groups of users.

---

**Note**  User and groups share the same namespace in Microsoft Jet: You can't have a user and group with the same name.

---

If you've never built or administered a user-level security system before, it's important to understand that there is no such thing as a permission on an object that exists by itself. Permissions on objects are always granted to specific users or predefined groups of users. In a Microsoft Jet database, it doesn't make sense to think of a table with a permission on it, because a permission exists only in the dual context of a user or group and the object it applies to.

## The Security Identifier

After a user logs on, Microsoft Jet uses a special number to identify that user. This number, called a security identifier (SID) is a machine-readable value that varies in length and will be 128 bytes at most. It's created by Microsoft Jet when a user or group is created. When user requests access to objects, Microsoft Jet uses the user or group's SID for identification. The user's name and password are not used. Basically, the name and password are used only for authentication—the process of verifying a person's identity. From then on, Microsoft Jet uses the SIDs to determine a user's access to objects.

## The Personal Identifier

In addition to the SID, Microsoft Jet also uses a personal identifier (PID). This value is a variable-length string that you specify when you create a user. The value is then used to help create the encrypted SID for that user. The user name and PID are fed to the encryption program that generates the SID for that account. If you feed the same user name and PID back into the encryption program, you get the same SID. This gives you the ability to re-create user accounts if your system database becomes corrupted or is lost.

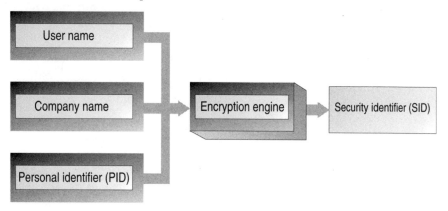

Figure 10.2    Creating security identifiers

## Default Users

Microsoft Jet defines one default user for you: Admin. The Admin user is the default user account. If your application does not have a workgroup database, your users are implicitly logging on as the Admin user. Unfortunately, the Admin user is not very well named, as this user has no particular administrative abilities. Because most users are logged on as Admin without ever knowing it, and because all users by default have permissions to the objects they create, any objects owned by the Admin user or to which the Admin user has explicit permissions are unsecured. Think of the Admin user as the DefaultUser account or, for those familiar with Windows NT, the Everybody account.

Understanding how the SIDs of these default accounts are generated helps you understand how the security model works. The Admin user's SID is identical across all installations of Microsoft Access and Visual Basic. Even if no one in your workgroup is using the Admin account (because you have password-protected it), all objects owned by Admin, or to which Admin has explicit permissions, are still open to anyone using Microsoft Jet. This is one of the most common misunderstandings regarding Microsoft Jet security. Fortunately, once you understand the problem, it's easily prevented: Make sure that Admin has no explicit permissions and owns no objects. The Security Wizard makes this easy.

Microsoft Jet also creates two accounts, Creator and Engine, that are used internally. These accounts are not accessible by users.

## Default Groups

As with users, Microsoft Jet defines default groups for you: the Admins group and the Users group. The Admins group is designed to hold user accounts for people who are the true administrators of the workgroup. They manage user and group membership and have the power to clear users' passwords. Members of the Admins group that was open when you created the database always have permission to grant permissions on any object in that database. For example, if user Bob is a member of the Admins group, he may not have permissions to open a particular table, but he will be able to grant himself permission to open that table, even if he doesn't own the table: The Admins group of other workgroups doesn't have this privilege. At least one member of the Admins group should exist at all times.

**Warning**  Although Microsoft Jet allows you to delete the last member of the Admins group, this is not advised, because only the object's owner has irrevocable permissions for that object. If that owner's account ever becomes corrupted or deleted, and cannot be re-created because you don't have that user's name and PID, there is *no way* to recover the permissions for that object. In other words, there is no member of the Admins group to fall back to.

The SID of the Admins group is unique for each **Workgroup**. It's created by the Workgroup Administrator utility by encrypting three strings that you enter: user name, company name, and workgroup ID. The setup program for Microsoft Access for Windows 95 creates a workgroup database by default. It uses the user name and company name as seeds to the encryption program to generate the Admins group's SID. It does not use a workgroup ID. Because the user name and company name are visible in the Microsoft Access user interface, it's essential that you create a new workgroup (and thus a new SID for your Admins group) using all three strings, including a workgroup ID, to ensure the security of your workgroup.

The Users Group is the default group for new users. By definition, all users of your application should be members of the Users group. Any permissions assigned explicitly to the Users group are available to all users in all installations of Microsoft Jet. By default, the Users group gets full permissions for all newly created objects. This is the main mechanism Microsoft Jet uses to "hide" security for the majority of applications that don't need it. Even though Microsoft Jet security is always "on," if you don't need its functionality and don't want your users to have to log on and worry about permissions, by making all users equal the Users group ensures that you don't have to worry about security.

### Ownership

The concept of ownership is crucial to understanding the Microsoft Jet security model. The user who creates an object *owns* that object. This ownership grants that user special privileges for that object in that he or she can always assign or revoke permissions for that object. This privilege cannot be revoked by any other user, including the Admin user or a member of the Admins group.

To effectively manage security, you may find that you need to change the ownership of an object. You can do this directly through DAO using the **Owner** property, or by logging on to Microsoft Jet through Microsoft Access and using the Import utility or the Change Owner dialog box.

## Workgroup Database

As mentioned earlier, **User** and **Group** objects and their passwords are not stored in your database. They are stored in a Microsoft Jet database known as the *workgroup database*. The default name of this database is SYSTEM.MDW, and it's a standard database in that it can be opened by Microsoft Jet. While it's structurally no different from the databases you create, it does contain several system tables that the engine uses to store security information.

The workgroup database stores records for each user and group in the **Workgroup**: which users belong to which groups, encrypted passwords, and the SID for each user and group. When you use Microsoft Jet commands that affect user or group objects or their passwords, the engine reads and writes to the workgroup database.

**Figure 10.3   The workgroup database**

You can use the same workgroup database for multiple applications. As long as the user, group, and password information remains the same across applications, you can point Microsoft Jet to the same workgroup database. When a user logs on to Microsoft Jet, the engine looks in the workgroup database for the user's name and password to authenticate the user. From then on, Microsoft Jet uses only the SID that it found for that user.

For more information, see Appendix C, "Registry Settings."

In Microsoft Jet versions prior to 3.0, the initialization file, usually MSACCESS.INI or MSACC20.INI, was used to store the path and name of the workgroup database. In version 3.0, the path and name of the workgroup database are stored in the Windows Registry. In all versions, the keyword signifying the workgroup database is SystemDB.

## Startup Command-Line Options

You can start applications that use Microsoft Jet (such as Microsoft Access and Microsoft Visual Basic) with the following command-line options that configure the security environment:

- **/User** *username.* Starts Microsoft Jet using the specified user name.

- **/Pwd** *password.* Starts Microsoft Jet using the specified password.

- **/Profile** *user profile.* Starts Microsoft Jet using the options in the specified user profile instead of the standard Windows Registry settings created when you installed Microsoft Jet. This replaces **/Ini** used in previous versions of Microsoft Jet to specify an initialization file.

- **/Wrkgrp** *path of workgroup information file.* Starts Microsoft Jet using the specified workgroup information file.

## The Secured Database

The final element of Microsoft Jet security is your database. This is where the objects that have to be secure are stored. The actual permissions related to specific objects for specific users and groups are stored in system tables in your database. However, no user, group, or password information is stored here. Such information is stored in the workgroup database.

For example, when a user requests access to an object, Microsoft Jet has already retrieved the user's SID and his group's from the workgroup database at logon. These SIDs are then compared to the SIDs in your database's system tables to verify that the user has sufficient permissions to access the object.

### Permissions

Microsoft Jet defines a set of permissions that give you fine control over a user's access to an object. For example, you can allow one user to read an object's contents, but not change them.

Microsoft Jet supports both *explicit* and *implicit* permissions. Explicit permissions are those you explicitly grant to a user. When an explicit permission is granted to a user, no other users are affected. Implicit permissions, on the other hand, are those granted to a group. Because a group contains users, all users receive the permissions granted to the group. If a user is added to a group, that user automatically gets all the implicit permissions of that group. Microsoft Jet uses a *least restrictive* algorithm when resolving discrepancies in user and group permissions. For example, if a user has explicit read permissions to a table but no write permission, and that user also belongs to a group that has write permission to the table, the user will be able to write to the table because of the implicit write permission.

Microsoft Jet defines permission levels as numeric constants. For convenience (and more readable code), you can use built-in constants when specifying permissions. These built-in constants are available in Microsoft Access, Visual Basic, Microsoft Excel, and Visual C++. For other programming environments, you may want to create the constant definitions yourself.

---

**Note** You should generally used predefined constants instead of hard-coded values. These values may change in future releases of Microsoft Jet, but the constants should always be valid. The description of the following constants apply to both **Container** and **Document** objects.

---

The following set of tables describes the possible permission settings. Later in this chapter you'll learn how to apply permissions to objects using these settings.

The following table shows permissions available for all Microsoft Jet objects.

| Constant | Description |
| --- | --- |
| dbSecNoAccess | No access to the object |
| dbSecFullAccess | Full access to the object |
| dbSecDelete | Can delete the object |
| dbSecReadSec | Can read the object's security-related information |
| dbSecWriteSec | Can alter access permissions |
| dbSecWriteOwner | Can change the **Owner** property |

The following table shows permissions available for the **Tables** container or any **Document** in a **Documents** collection.

| Constant | Description |
| --- | --- |
| dbSecCreate | Can create new documents (valid only with a **Container** object) |
| dbSecReadDef | Can read the object definition, including column and index information |
| dbSecWriteDef | Can modify or delete the object definition, including column and index information |
| dbSecRetrieveData | Can retrieve data from the **Document** |
| dbSecInsertData | Can add records |
| dbSecReplaceData | Can modify records |
| dbSecDeleteData | Can delete records |

The following table shows permissions available for the **Databases** container or any **Document** object in a **Documents** collection.

| Constant | Description |
| --- | --- |
| dbSecDBCreate | Can create new databases (valid only on the databases' **Container** object in the system database [SYSTEM.MDW]) |
| dbSecDBExclusive | Exclusive access |
| dbSecDBOpen | Can open the database |
| dbSecDBAdmin | Defines the right of a user to change the database password |

# Securing Your Database

It's important to realize that Microsoft Jet security is always enabled—every time a user performs any action, Microsoft Jet first checks to make sure the user has sufficient permissions to perform that action. However, most Microsoft Jet users never realize that they are logging on and never see a security-related message. How does this happen? The illusion that security is not enabled is created by granting full permissions, by default, to the Users group for all objects.

This arrangement works well because there are no "back doors" through security. Applications that don't need the engine's security services still use it, even though it's not apparent.

If you're using Microsoft Jet with Visual Basic, you can run your application without a workgroup database.

In this case, users are logged on as the default Admin user. In a nonsecured environment, this account has full permissions. In a secured environment, the default Admin user doesn't have any permissions and is not able to use the Microsoft Jet database. To use security from a Visual Basic application, first set up security using Microsoft Access, then create a Registry entry for your application that points to your workgroup database.

To successfully implement security, you should do some advance planning. This involves setting up a worksheet that lists all of the potential users of your applications, logical groupings of users, and a list of the operations that each group should be able to perform. You then map this information to the Microsoft Jet security model of users, groups, and object permissions.

Securing your database is a multistep process that changes the default behavior of users and groups by replacing the built-in accounts with your own secure version. This section outlines each of these steps.

## Creating the Workgroup Database

As mentioned previously, one of the key aspects of securing your database is the process of creating a SystemDB database. This process can be accomplished only with Workgroup Administrator, which ships with Microsoft Access. Because the Microsoft Jet security model relies on the existence of a workgroup database to store user, group, and password information, your first step is to create a workgroup database unique to your application. The key point of this process is that it creates a unique SID for the Admins group. Using Workgroup Administrator (WRKGADM.EXE), follow these steps:

▶ **To create a workgroup database unique to your application**

1. Start the Workgroup Administrator program (WRKGADM.EXE).

2. Click Create to create a new workgroup.

3. Specify a user name, an organization, and a unique workgroup ID and click OK.

   The workgroup can contain letters and numbers up to 20 characters in length. This value is used by the encryption program, along with the user name and organization name, to create an encrypted value unique to your workgroup.

4. Specify the name and path for the new workgroup database and click OK.

   Workgroup databases by default have an extension of .MDW, but this is not required. You can assign any extension.

5. A confirmation form asks you to confirm the creation of the new workgroup database. It also displays the information you've entered so far. Be sure to write this information down and store it in a safe place. If your new workgroup database ever becomes corrupted or is lost, you will need this information to re-create the workgroup database. Click OK to create the system database.

## Creating a New Admin User

As mentioned earlier, the Admin user is a default user created by Microsoft Jet in every workgroup. Because the Admin user is the same across every default workgroup database created by Microsoft Access, you want to make sure your secure objects are owned and maintained by your Admin user, not the default.

The easiest way to do this is to use Microsoft Access. Of course, you could also write DAO code to programmatically create the user.

▶ **To create a new Admin user through Microsoft Access**

1. On the **Tools** menu, point to Security, and then click User and Group Accounts.

2. Under User, click New.

3. In the New User/Group dialog box, type a Name and Personal ID for the new Admin user, and then click OK.

4. Select the new Admin user, and then under Available Groups, click Admins. Click Add.

   Be sure to assign a password for your new Admin user. Also be sure to write down this new user's password and PID and store it in a safe place. You will need it if you ever have to re-create the account.

▶ **To set a password on the default Admin user account**

1. On the **Tools** menu, point to Security, and then click User and Group Accounts.

2. On the Change Logon Password tab, enter a new password for the default Admin user.

3. Exit and restart Microsoft Access.

## Running the Microsoft Access Security Wizard

The next step does the actual work of securing your application.

▶ **To secure your application with the Microsoft Access Security Wizard**

1. Start Microsoft Access and log on with the name and password of your new Admin user, created in the procedure described in the previous section.

   This step ensures that the Security Wizard treats you as the owner of all objects in the database.

   ---

   **Note**  It is very important to make sure you're using the workgroup database that you created in step one when running the Security Wizard. You can do this by running Workgroup Administrator (WRKGADM.EXE), clicking Join, and selecting your workgroup database. Do not use the default SYSTEM.MDW workgroup database that ships with Microsoft Access.

   ---

2. On the **Tools** menu, point to Security, and then click User Level Security Wizard. Follow the prompts on the screen. This wizard:

   • Creates a new, encrypted database.

   • Exports all objects from the current database to the new database.

   • Revokes all permissions from all users for all objects, except for your Admin user.

Note that the Security Wizard does not change the original database in any way. The new database it creates becomes your secured database.

## Creating Your Own Users and Groups

Now that you have a database containing your secured objects, create the users and groups that your application needs. The easiest way to do so is to use the Microsoft Access User and Group Accounts dialog box, available from the **Security** command on the **Tools** menu.

---

**Note**  It's generally best to create the groups you need and assign permissions to the groups rather than to individual users. This way, administering your workgroup becomes simply a matter of assigning users to the appropriate groups.

---

### Assigning Permissions for Users to the Objects

The final step is to assign the actual permissions to objects for users and groups. This step tells Microsoft Jet which users can access which objects. Again, using Microsoft Access is the quickest way to accomplish this.

Your new database is now secure. The only people who can get into the objects in the database are those for whom you assigned permissions, and anyone who is a member of the Admins group of the workgroup database in place when you ran the Security Wizard.

## Removing Security From a Database

Securing a database is usually a one-way process. After a database is secured, you probably won't have to remove security. However, certain development issues might require you to work with an unsecured copy. You can follow these steps to reverse the process of securing your database.

▶ **To remove security from a database**

1. Start Microsoft Access and log on as a member of the Admins group. This can be the Admin user you created when you secured the database, or any member of the Admins group. Be sure to use your own secure workgroup when starting Microsoft Access.

2. Assign full permissions to the Users group for all objects in the database.

   Because all users are automatically part of the Users group in Microsoft Jet, this step has the effect of rendering security "invisible" again.

3. Clear the password for the Admin user by specifying a blank password.

4. Restart Microsoft Access and log on as Admin.

5. Create a new database and import all objects from the secured database. This is easily accomplished using the **Get External Data** command on the **File** menu.

---

**Note** In versions prior to Microsoft Access for Windows 95, database relationships cannot be imported, either through Microsoft Access, or with the Microsoft Access Import Database add-in. You can write DAO code to programmatically re-create them, or manually re-create them.

---

The new database you created in step five is now an unsecured version of the original. As always, Microsoft Jet security is still active, but transparent.

## Securing Your Database Without Asking Users To Log On

If you want to secure some objects in a database but you don't need to grant various permissions to different groups of users, you might want to consider securing your application without asking users to log on.

1. Follow the steps to secure a database using the Security Wizard in the "Securing Your Database" section earlier in this chapter.

2. While logged on as a member of the Admins group, assign the permissions you want to be generally available to the default Admin user. Don't give the default Admin user the permission to modify the design of tables and queries.

3. Remove the default Admin user from the Admins group. This prevents users who are logged on as Admin from granting themselves further permissions.

4. Clear the default Admin user's password. Users will be able to open your database without logging on and to perform all actions to which you give the default Admin user permissions.

Now you need a way to perform administrative duties such as setting permissions and assigning users to groups. Because you have removed the Admin user from the Admins group, you won't be able to perform these actions when logged on as Admin. And because the Admin user has no password, the log-on dialog box will not be displayed. You'll need to log on a member of the Admins group to perform these duties. You can do this by editing the command-line argument of the Microsoft Access Program Manager icon to include a user name and password using the /User and /Pwd command-line options. (For more information, see the "Startup Command-Line Options" section earlier in this chapter.) When you start Microsoft Access using this icon, even though you don't encounter the log-on dialog box, you will be logged on and able to perform administrative duties.

Of course, if you choose to keep this icon on your computer rather than deleting and re-creating the command-line each time, you'll have to make sure your computer is physically secure, because someone could copy the user name and password arguments from the command line and gain access to your system.

# Using DAO to Program Security

As you learned in Chapter 2, the DAO interface gives you programmatic access to Microsoft Jet. This interface extends to security in that much of the security implementation of your application can be programmed through DAO. The use of DAO is very important in the context of security because it's the only way to programatically manipulate security. Unlike other elements of the database, such as DDL operations on objects, you cannot use Microsoft Jet SQL to view or alter security settings.

# Workspace Interaction with Security

When performing programmatic security operations, you must be logged on as a user with sufficient permissions to do that work. The usual way to do this is to open a **Workspace** object with the user name and password of an Admin user or a member of the Admins group. This is accomplished using the **CreateWorkspace** method of the **DBEngine** object.

For example, assume your workgroup has an Admin user named "TopDog" with a password of "AllPowerful." You would use the following code to open a workspace from which to perform the remainder of your security operations:

```
Dim wrkTemp As Workspace
Set wrkTemp = DBEngine.CreateWorkspace("", "TopDog", "AllPowerful")
```

Workspaces are often thought of as mere transaction spaces—a way to create multiple independent transactions. However, an equally important use is the ability they provide to programmatically log on to a workgroup as another user. An obvious disadvantage of this approach is that the user name and password of a powerful user are hard-coded into the program code. The work-around for this is to programmatically prompt the person running the code for a user name and password.

# Securing Objects

Now that you have seen some specific examples of using DAO to program security, you should have a good idea of what's involved. You might find it helpful to review some of what you learned in Chapter 2, "Introducing Data Access Objects."

All DAO access to users, groups, and permissions happens through the **Container** and **Document** objects. **Containers** and **Documents** are DAO's way of exposing the objects in a database to the database's host, whether that host is you as a programmer using DAO or an application such as Microsoft Access. **Containers** and **Documents** differ from other collections and objects in that they allow Microsoft Jet to store and manage objects that it knows nothing about. For example, in a Microsoft Jet database created by Microsoft Access, there are **Document** objects to store Microsoft Access forms and reports. Even though Microsoft Jet recognizes these objects, it does allow the host (in this case, Microsoft Access) to store these objects and does maintain security on them. By locating programmatic security access at the **Containers** and **Documents** level, Microsoft Jet extends its security services to any application that requires it.

All Microsoft Jet databases contain at least three containers:

- Tables contain a **Document** object for each table and query in the database.
- Relationships contain a **Document** object for each relationship in the database.
- Databases contain a **Document** object for the database itself.

Microsoft Jet defines a set of permissions for the three containers it supports directly. Permissions for other containers must be defined by the application that defines the permissions. Only then can Microsoft Jet maintain security on these foreign objects. For example, Microsoft Access defines a set of permissions for **Form** objects that it stores in the **Forms** container it adds to the database. You can use the Object Browser in Microsoft Access to see these permissions constants.

## Common Permissions

Permissions to objects are handled by working with the **Permissions** property. This property is a long value (also known as a long integer). Different permissions are assigned by setting or resetting specific bits or groups of bits of that long value. Therefore, setting permission values is typically done by combining predeclared constants using the Visual Basic operators **And** and **Or**. The following table describes the security constants and values that are predefined for all Microsoft Jet objects.

| Constant | Value | Description |
|---|---|---|
| dbSecNoAccess<br>dbSecFullAccess | &H0<br>&HFFFFF | If you want to remove all permissions from an object for a user or group, set its **Permissions** property to dbSecNoAccess. You can grant all permissions for a given user or group to an object by setting its **Permissions** property to dbSecFullAccess. |
| dbSecDelete | &H10000 | The permission to delete an object. For example, if a user has the dbSecDelete bit set on a **Table** object, the user can delete that table. Note that although you can set this permission on a **Container** object, it has no effect. Only Microsoft Jet can create and delete containers, and this is done on an internal level. |
| dbSecReadSec | &H200000 | The permission to read an object's permissions settings. An owner of an object implicitly has this permission. If you do not have dbSecReadSec permission to an object and try to use DAO to do anything to the object's **Permission** property, you receive an error. |
| dbSecWriteSec | &H40000 | The permission to alter an object's permission settings. As with dbSecReadSec, the owner of the object implicitly has this permission, so you can't orphan an object by deleting it. |
| dbSecWriteOwner | &H80000 | The permission to change the owner of an object. You do this by setting the **Owner** property of the appropriate **Container** or **Document** object. |

## Permissions for Tables and Queries

Microsoft Jet stores both tables and queries in the **Tables** container. This section uses "tables" to refer to both tables and queries. The following permission constants are defined.

| Constant | Value | Description |
|---|---|---|
| dbSecReadDef | &H4 | The permission to read the definition of a table. |
| dbSecWriteDef | &H8 Or dbSecReadDef Or dbSecDelete | The permission to alter the definition of a table. Note that this permission is a combination of the &H8 value and the Read Definitions and Delete permissions. You have to be able to read the definition of an object in order to change that definition. |
| dbSecRetrieveData | &H10 Or dbSecReadDef | The permission to read data stored in the table. This permission is combined with the Read Definitions permission. Although you could separate the two permissions, most applications that use Microsoft Jet, such as Microsoft Access, require the ability to read the table's definition in order to be able to read the table's data. |
| dbSecInsertData | &H20 | The permission to insert new rows into the table. |
| dbSecDeleteData | &H80 | The permission to delete data rows from a table. Note the subtle distinction between deleting data and replacing all columns in the row with null data, which is controlled by the dbSecReplaceData permission. |
| dbSecReplaceData | &H40 | The permission to modify data that exists in the table. |

These permissions can be combined using the **Or** keyword. For example, to grant a user Modify Data and Insert Data permissions to a table, you use the following:

```
docCurrent.Permissions = dbSecInsertData Or dbSecReplaceData Or _
    dbSecRetrieveData
```

Note that the dbSecRetrieveData permission is included: Most programs require the ability to read data before it can be updated.

**Microsoft Access Users**   Microsoft Access defines a number of permission settings for use with its own objects. These permissions are described in the following table.

| Constant | Value | Description |
|---|---|---|
| acSecFrmRptReadDef | &H4 | Reads the definition of a form or report. |
| acSecFrmRptWriteDef | &H8 Or acSecFormRptReadDef Or dbSecDelete | Alters the definition of a form or report. |
| acSecFrmRptExecute | &H100 | Executes the form or report. |
| acSecMacReadDef | &HA | Reads the definition of a macro. |
| acSecMacWriteDef | &H6 Or acSecMacReadDef | Alters the definition of a macro. |
| acSecMacExecute | &H8 | Executes the macro. |
| acSecModReadDef | &H2 | Reads the definition of a module. |
| acSecModWriteDef | &H4 Or acSecModReadDef Or dbSecDelete | Alters the definition of a module. |

Execute permission defines the ability to "run" the object. For example, execute permission on a form gives you the ability to open the form and browse or print it. For macros, execute permission defines the ability to open the macro and run its contents. You can see that there is no execute permission for modules. Obviously, if Microsoft Access had to check the permission for every function for a given user, performance would be severely degraded.

ReadDef permissions define the ability to open the object in Design mode. Unlike tables and queries, ReadDef permissions are not required for Microsoft Access objects.

WriteDef permissions define the ability to open an object in Design mode and to save any changes made to the object's definition.

## Permissions for Databases

As with other objects, the **Database** object has its own unique permissions. Permissions for the database itself are set by modifying the document in the **Databases** container. While this may seem to be counterintuitive at first, it does make sense when you remember that all permission settings work at the **Containers** and **Documents** level. To work the **Database** object into this scheme, Microsoft Jet defines a database **Container** object called MSysDb. By setting the **Permission** property of this document, you are in effect setting the permissions for the database itself. The following permissions are defined for this document.

| Constant | Value | Description |
|---|---|---|
| dbSecDBOpen | &H2 | Defines the permission to open the database. If a user does not have this permission, the user cannot open the database. This is the most restrictive form of permissions. |
| dbSecDBOpenExclusive | &H4 | Defines the permission to open the database exclusively. This permission is useful in multiuser environments where you want to deny users the permission to open a shared database exclusively. If a user could open a shared database exclusively, your multiuser system would quickly become a single-user system. |
| dbSecDBAdmin | &H8 | Defines users' permission to change a database password and make a database replicable. |

As an example, assume that you don't want user Hannah to have permission to open a database, but you want to allow user Jayne to open it exclusively. The following code accomplishes this:

```
Sub AssignDBPerms ()
    Dim docDatabase As Document
    Dim dbsCurrent As Database

    Set dbsCurrent = OpenDatabase("C:\Samples\Chap10\NwindJet.mdb")
    Set docDatabase = dbsCurrent.Containers!Databases!MSysDB

    ' Remove Hannah's permission to open the database.
    docDatabase.UserName = "Hannah"
    docDatabase.Permissions = docDatabase.Permissions And _
        Not dbSecDBOpen

    ' Give Jayne the ability to open the database exclusively.
    docDatabase.UserName = "Jayne"
    docDatabase.Permissions = docDatabase.Permissions Or _
        dbSecDbExclusive Or dbSecDbOpen
End Sub
```

## A Special Case

You can also use Microsoft Jet to prevent a specific user from creating databases. Because this permission is applied to a specific user and not to a specific database, the permission is stored in the **Databases** container of the SystemDB database. By default, this permission is set for anyone in the Admins group or the Users group. For example, the following code denies the Users group the permission to create databases:

```
Sub RemoveCreatePerms ()
    Dim dbsSystem As Database
    Dim conTemp As Container
```

```
DBEngine.SystemDB = "C:\Samples\Chap10\System.mdw"

    Set dbsSystem = OpenDatabase("C:\Samples\Chap10\System.mdw")
    Set conTemp = dbsSystem.Containers!Databases

    conTemp.UserName = "Users"
    conTemp.Permissions = conTemp.Permissions And Not dbSecDBCreate
End Sub
```

Note that the path to the workgroup database (C:\Samples\Chap10\System.mdw
in this example) will probably be different on your system.

## Database Passwords

In some cases, the only security a developer needs is the ability to prevent
unauthorized users from opening the database; after the user has the database
open, no other security is needed. To meet this need, Microsoft Jet 3.0 enables
you to password protect the database itself.

### Setting the Database Password

The database password can be set either through Microsoft Access, or through
DAO with the **NewPassword** method. The following code opens the Orders
database and assigns a password to it:

```
Sub SetDBPassword ()
    Dim dbsTmp As Database

    Set dbsTmp = OpenDatabase("C:\Samples\Chap10\NwindJet.mdb", True)

    dbsTmp.NewPassword "","topsecret"
    dbsTemp.Close
End Sub
```

### Opening a Password-Protected Database

After a database password has been set, all attempts to open that database fail
unless the correct password is given. To open a password-protected database using
DAO, you specify the password as part of the Connect string argument. For
example, the following code opens the password-protected Orders database:

```
Sub OpenProtectedDB()
    Dim dbsTmp As Database

    Set dbsTmp = OpenDatabase("C:\Samples\Chap10\Orders.mdb", _
        False,False,";pwd=topsecret")
End Sub
```

### Changing the Database Password

To change the database password, you must supply both the existing and new passwords to the **NewPassword** method. The following example changes the password of the Orders database from "topsecret" to "ultrasecret":

```
Sub ChangeDBPassword ()
    Dim dbsTmp As Database

    Set dbsTmp = OpenDatabase("C:\Samples\Chap10\Orders.mdb",True, _
        False,";pwd=topsecret")
    dbsTmp.NewPassword "topsecret","ultrasecret"
    dbsTemp.Close
End Sub
```

It's important to note that this new capability increases the chance that generic OpenDatabase code can stop working. You should always check to see if your attempt to open a database has succeeded. Given that your code may encounter a password-protected database, it should have the flexibility to handle such cases.

---

**Warning** If you lose the password to your database, you can never open the database again! Make sure you have adequate safeguards: Always have hard copies of your database passwords stored in a secure place.

---

The database password is stored in the database header pages of the database itself. Setting a database password has no effect on the workgroup database.

### Preventing Users From Setting a Database Password

In an unsecured environment, any user can set a database password. This can create problems for your application because other users won't be able to open it. You can prevent users from doing this by removing Administer permissions from the **Database** object.

If you're concerned about users maliciously setting a database password, follow the steps to secure a database using the Security Wizard in the "Securing Your Database" section earlier in this chapter. This will prevent all users who aren't members of the Admins group from setting the database password.

If, however, you're just concerned about preventing casual users from setting a database password, you don't need to fully implement security. Simply remove Administer permissions from the **Database** object for the Admin user, the Users group, and the Admins group. All users who try to set the database password will fail and receive a permission denied error: Before they could set the password, they would first have to explicitly grant themselves permission to do so. For many applications, that is security enough.

## Permissions for Containers

You can directly set permissions on **Container** objects to control a user's ability to create new objects of a given type. The **dbSecCreate** permission gives the user the ability to create an object in the container it's associated with. Note that this permission is useful only in the context of **Container** objects. The following code shows you how to check to see if a user has permission to create an object in a given container:

```
Sub CheckCreate ()
    Dim conTemp As Container
    Dim dbsCurrent As Database

    DBEngine.SystemDB = "C:\Samples\Chap10\System.mdw"

    Set dbsCurrent = OpenDatabase("C:\Samples\Chap10\NwindJet.mdb")
    Set conTemp = dbsCurrent.Containers!Tables

    conTemp.UserName = "Laura"
    If conTemp.Permissions And dbSecCreate Then
    Debug.Print "Laura can create tables."
    Else
    Debug.Print "Laura cannot create tables."
    End If
    dbsCurrent.Close
End Sub
```

# Diving Right In

This section shows you how to use DAO to work with permissions on objects. The following initialization procedure is assumed for the examples. Additionally, the dbsCurrent and docTemp object variables are global to all the example procedures.

```
Dim dbsCurrent As Database
Dim docTemp As Document
Dim strUser As String
Dim strObject As String

Sub InitializeExamples ()
    Set dbsCurrent = OpenDatabase("C:\Samples\Chap10\NwindJet.mdb")
End Sub
```

## Granting Read Permission to a User for a Table

This code works by setting an object variable on the **Document** objects for the Changes Log table. It then sets the **UserName** property of the document to the user for whom you want to change permissions. You could also assign a group name to the **UserName** property if you wanted to set that group's permissions. Finally, the code sets the permissions by modifying the **Permissions** property of the **Document** object. Note that instead of explicitly assigning the **Permissions** property to dbSecRetrieveData, the **Or** operator is used to add the permission to any existing permissions. This ensures that this code does not remove other permissions that the user already has assigned.

```
Sub GrantReadPerms
    Dim docTmp As Document

    strUser = "Auditor Jane"
    strObject = "Changes Log"
    Set docTemp = dbsCurrent.Containers!Tables.Documents(strObject)
    docTemp.UserName = strUser
    docTemp.Permissions = docTemp.Permissions Or dbSecRetrieveData
End Sub
```

## Determining If a User Has Read Permission for a Table

```
Sub CheckReadPerms()
    strUser = "Auditor Jane"
    strObject = "Changes Log"
    Set docTemp = dbCurrent.Containers!Tables.Documents(strObject)
    docTemp.UserName = strUser
    If (docTemp.Permissions And dbSecRetrieveData) > 0 Then
        Debug.Print "Auditor Jane has read permissions for table."
    Else
        Debug.Print "Auditor Jane does not have read permissions " _
            & "for table."
    End If
End Sub
```

Like the code in the previous example, a document object variable is set and pointed to a specific user. Then the desired permission is masked to the **Permissions** property of the object with the **And** operator, and checked to see if the resulting value is greater than 0. If it is, the user has the specified permission. In general, you shouldn't check for a specific permission with the equal sign (=) as in the following line:

```
If (docTemp.Permissions = dbSecRetrieveData) Then
```

Rarely does a user have only one permission set. If the user had any other permission set (besides dbSecRetrieveData), this example would fail. To check for a specific permission, you should use **And** with that permission's value and the object's **Permission** property, and check for a resulting value greater than 0.

You should also note that this example checks only for explicit permissions: those assigned to that user for that object. It does not take into account any implicit permissions that exist through group ownership. The following example is more thorough in that it uses the **AllPermissions** property to take into account the user's group permissions:

```
Sub CheckAllReadPerms()
    Dim intCounter As Integer

    strUser = "Auditor Jane"
    strObject = "Changes Log"

    Set docTemp = dbCurrent.Containers!Tables.Documents(strObject)
    docTemp.UserName = strUser

    If (docTemp.AllPermissions And dbSecRetrieveData) > 0 Then
    Debug.Print "Auditor Jane has implicit or explicit read " _
            & "permissions for table."
    Else
    Debug.Print "Auditor Jane has no permissions."
    End If
End Sub
```

## Removing Write Permission From a User for a Table

This example shows how you can remove all write data permissions for a user or group. It works by first creating a long integer value that combines the Insert data, Replace data, and Delete data permissions with an **Or** operation. It then uses the **And Not** operator to reset the appropriate bits in the document's **Permissions** property. This has the effect of removing those permissions. Remember that you're affecting only the user's explicit permissions with this code. The user may have other permissions due to membership in various groups.

```
Sub RemoveWritePerms()
    Dim lngNoWrite As Long

    strUser = "Auditor Jane"
    strObject = "Changes Log"

    Set docTemp = dbsCurrent.Containers!Tables.Documents(strObject)

    docTemp.UserName = strUser
    lngNoWrite = dbSecInsertData Or dbSecReplaceData Or dbSecDeleteData
    docTemp.Permissions = docTemp.Permissions And Not lngNoWrite
End Sub
```

## Granting Modify Design Permission to a Group for a Query

This example works like previous ones except that it sets permissions for a group. It does this by setting the **UserName** property of the document to the name of a group. Because users and groups share the same namespace and as such cannot have identical names, Microsoft Jet knows that you're referring to a group and not a user.

```
Sub GrantExecute()
    Dim strGroup As String
    Dim lngPerms As Long

    strGroup = "Data Entry Group"
    strObject = "qryUpdatePayroll"
    lngPerms = dbSecReadDef And dbSecWriteDef

    Set docTemp = dbCurrent.Containers!Tables.Documents(strObject)
    docTemp.UserName = strGroup
    docTemp.Permissions = docTemp.Permissions Or lngPerms
End Sub
```

## Showing All Permissions for All Objects for All Users and Groups

This example iterates through each **Users** and **Groups** collection. Within those collections it iterates through all the **Containers** and **Documents** collections in the current database and displays the permissions. This approach is useful if you want to see permissions for all the objects in the database, not just the default table and query objects that Microsoft Jet recognizes. For example, this code could be used on a database created with Microsoft Access to show permissions on not only the Microsoft Jet objects, but also the application-specific Microsoft Access objects such as forms, reports, macros, and modules.

```
Sub ShowPermissions()
    Dim wspCurrent As Workspace
    Dim usrTemp As User
    Dim grpTemp As GROUP
    Dim conTemp As Container

    Set wspCurrent = DBEngine.Workspaces(0)

    For Each usrTemp In wspCurrent.Users
        Debug.Print "User: " & usrTemp.Name
        Debug.Print "----------------------"
        For Each conTemp In dbsCurrent.Containers
            Debug.Print "  Container: " & conTemp.Name
            For Each docTemp In conTemp.Documents
                docTemp.UserName = usrTemp.Name
                Debug.Print "    Document: " & docTemp.Name & _
                    " Permissions: " & docTemp.Permissions
```

```
            Next docTemp
        Next conTemp
    Next usrTemp

    For Each grpTemp In wspCurrent.Groups
    Debug.Print "Group: " & grpTemp.Name
        Debug.Print "---------------------"
        For Each conTemp In dbsCurrent.Containers
            Debug.Print " Container: " & conTemp.Name
            For Each docTemp In conTemp.Documents
                docTemp.UserName = grpTemp.Name
                Debug.Print "   Document: " & docTemp.Name & _
                    " Permissions: " & docTemp.Permissions
            Next docTemp
        Next conTemp
    Next grpTemp
End Sub
```

## A Better Solution

The main problem with the ShowPermissions code is that it returns only a numeric permission value for each object. The following three procedures present a much more readable output.

First, the ShowPermissions procedure is modified to call a function to decode the value of an object's **Permissions** property:

```
Sub ShowPermissionsAsText()
    Dim wspCurrent As Workspace
    Dim usrTemp As User
    Dim grpTemp As Group
    Dim conTemp As Container
    Dim intType As Integer

    Set wspCurrent = DBEngine.Workspaces(0)

    For Each usrTemp In wspCurrent.Users
        Debug.Print "User: " & usrTemp.Name
        Debug.Print "---------------------"
        For Each conTemp In dbsCurrent.Containers
            Debug.Print " Container: " & conTemp.Name
            Select Case conTemp.Name
                Case "Tables": intType = 1
                Case "Databases": intType = 2
                Case Else: intType = -1
            End Select
            For Each docTemp In conTemp.Documents
                docTemp.UserName = usrTemp.Name
                Debug.Print "   Document: " & docTemp.Name
                Debug.Print "     Permissions: " & _
                    DecodePerms(intType, docTemp.Permissions)
```

```
                Next docTemp
            Next conTemp
        Next usrTemp

        For Each grpTemp In wspCurrent.Groups
            Debug.Print "Group: " & grpTemp.Name
            Debug.Print "---------------------"
            For Each conTemp In dbsCurrent.Containers
                Select Case conTemp.Name
                    Case "Tables": intType = 1
                    Case "Databases": intType = 2
                    Case Else: intType = -1
                End Select
                Debug.Print "  Container: " & conTemp.Name
                For Each docTemp In conTemp.Documents
                    docTemp.UserName = grpTemp.Name
                    Debug.Print "    Document: " & docTemp.Name
                    Debug.Print "      Permissions: " & _
                        DecodePerms(intType, docTemp.Permissions)
                Next docTemp
            Next conTemp
        Next grpTemp
End Sub
```

Next, two new procedures are added to perform the actual conversion:

```
Function DecodePerms(intType As Integer, lngPerms As Long) As Variant
    Dim varTemp As Variant

    ' Decode the common permissions.
    If (lngPerms And dbSecNoAccess) > 0 Then _
        varTemp = AddString(varTemp, "dbSecNoAccess")

    If (lngPerms And dbSecFullAccess) > 0 Then _
        varTemp = AddString(varTemp, "dbSecFullAccess")

    If (lngPerms And dbSecDelete) > 0 Then _
        varTemp = AddString(varTemp, "dbSecDelete")

    If (lngPerms And dbSecReadSec) > 0 Then _
        varTemp = AddString(varTemp, "dbSecReadSec")

    If (lngPerms And dbSecWriteSec) > 0 Then _
        varTemp = AddString(varTemp, "dbSecWriteSec")

    If (lngPerms And dbSecWriteOwner) > 0 Then _
        varTemp = AddString(varTemp, "dbSecWriteOwner")
```

```
    ' Decode specific permissions.
    Select Case intType
        Case 1
            ' It's a table or query.
            If (lngPerms And dbSecReadDef) > 0 Then _
                varTemp = AddString(varTemp, "dbSecReadDef")

            If (lngPerms And dbSecWriteDef) > 0 Then _
                varTemp = AddString(varTemp, "dbSecWriteDef")

            If (lngPerms And dbSecRetrieveData) > 0 Then _
                varTemp = AddString(varTemp, "dbSecRetrieveData")

            If (lngPerms And dbSecInsertData) > 0 Then _
                varTemp = AddString(varTemp, "dbSecInsertData")

            If (lngPerms And dbSecReplaceData) > 0 Then _
                varTemp = AddString(varTemp, "dbSecReplaceData")

            If (lngPerms And dbSecDeleteData) > 0 Then _
                varTemp = AddString(varTemp, "dbSecDeleteData")

        Case 2
            ' It's a database.
            If (lngPerms And dbSecDBOpen) > 0 Then _
                varTemp = AddString(varTemp, "dbSecDBOpen")

            If (lngPerms And dbSecDBExclusive) > 0 Then _
                varTemp = AddString(varTemp, "dbSecDBExclusive")

            If (lngPerms And dbSecDBAdmin) > 0 Then _
                varTemp = AddString(varTemp, "dbSecDBAdmin")

        Case 3
            ' It's a container.
            If (lngPerms And dbSecWriteOwner) > 0 Then _
                varTemp = AddString(varTemp, "dbSecWriteOwner")

            If (lngPerms And dbSecCreate) > 0 Then _
                varTemp = AddString(varTemp, "dbSecCreate")

        Case Else
            ' Unknown object, pass the perms back.
            varTemp = lngPerms
    End Select

    DecodePerms = varTemp
End Function
```

```
Function AddString(varCurrent As Variant, varIn As Variant) As Variant
    Dim varTemp As Variant

    If varCurrent = "" Then
        varTemp = varIn
    Else
        varTemp = varCurrent & "," & varIn
    End If

    AddString = varTemp
End Function
```

This works as follows:

1. The ShowPermissionsAsText procedure iterates through each object and retrieves the value of the **Permissions** property.

2. This value is sent to DecodePerms, which compares it to the permission constants for that particular object type.

3. The **DecodePerms** function calls the **AddString** function to add the text representation of the permission name to a string, and returns it to **DecodePerms**.

4. The **DecodePerms** function takes the final concatenated string and passes it back to ShowPermissionsAsText for display.

---

**Note**  The **DecodePerms** function decodes permissions only for Microsoft Jet–specific objects. You can modify it to include other application-defined permissions, such as those defined by Microsoft Access for Microsoft Access–specific objects.

---

# Securing Users and Groups

The **Users** collection contains all users currently defined in the workgroup. Similarly, the **Groups** collection contains all groups. By manipulating these collections, you define and control the workgroup that Microsoft Jet uses. The **Groups** and **Users** collections are interesting in that they are self-referencing. You can see from the DAO hierarchy that the **Users** collection contains a **Groups** collection, and the **Groups** collection contains a **Users** collection. Using this structure, you can easily find which users belong to which groups, and which groups contain which users.

## Evaluating Users and Groups

As with other collections, you use the **Count** property to determine the number of members. To find the number of users in the current workgroup, you use:

```
Debug.Print DBEngine.Workspaces(0).Users.Count
```

Similarly, to find the number of groups in the current workgroup, use:

```
Debug.Print DBEngine.Workspaces(0).Groups.Count
```

To determine the number of groups a specific user belongs to, use the **Count** property of that user's **User** object's **Groups** collection:

```
Debug.Print DBEngine.Workspaces(0).Users!Hannah.Groups.Count
```

The following procedure works these concepts into a generic routine that displays the information for a given user:

```
Sub ShowUserGroups (strUser As String)
    Dim usrTemp As User
    Dim grpTemp As Group

    DBEngine.SystemDB = C:\Samples\Chap10\System.mdw"

    Set usrTemp = DBEngine.Workspaces(0).Users(strUser)

    For Each grpTemp In usrTemp.Groups
    Debug.Print grpTemp.Name
    Next grpTemp
End Sub
```

The following procedure reverses this logic to show all the users in a given group:

```
Sub ShowGroupUsers(strGroup As String)
    Dim usrTemp As User
    Dim grpTemp As Group

    DBEngine.SystemDB = C:\Samples\Chap10\System.mdw"

    Set grpTemp = DBEngine.Workspaces(0).Groups(strGroup)

    For Each usrTemp In grpTemp.Users
        Debug.Print usrTemp.Name
    Next usrTemp
End Sub
```

Finally, you can show all users and the groups they belong to with the following code:

```
Sub ShowUsersGroups()
    Dim wspCurrent As Workspace
    Dim usrTemp As User
    Dim grpTemp As GROUP

    DBEngine.SystemDB = C:\Samples\Chap10\System.mdw"

    Set wspCurrent = DBEngine.Workspaces(0)
```

```
      For Each usrTemp In wspCurrent.Users
          Debug.Print "User: " & usrTemp.Name
          For Each grpTemp In usrTemp.Groups
              Debug.Print "  Group: " & grpTemp.Name
          Next grpTemp
      Next usrTemp
  End Sub
```

Keep the following points in mind when working with **User** and **Group** objects:

- If a user or group is deleted from the workgroup, any object that has specific permissions for that user or group retains those permissions. If that user or group is re-created using the same user name and PID, those permissions will become active again. This behavior is evidenced by the fact that the **Owner** property of objects from which the owner has been deleted returns "<Unknown>".

- To determine all the users and groups that have permissions on an object, you should iterate through each user and group name, set the **UserName** property, and check the **Permissions** property. You can also use the **AllPermissions** property. Unlike the **Permissions** property, which returns only the permissions for the given user or group, the **AllPermissions** property returns all permissions of an object for a user, including permissions implied through group membership.

- Not everyone has permissions to view user and group information. Generally, it's best to be logged on as the Admin user, or a user who is a member of the Admins group, before attempting to retrieve this information. This is also true if you want to modify security settings: You should be logged on as user with sufficient rights.

- If you're using a workgroup database that was created with Microsoft Access 1.*x* using Microsoft Jet 1.*x*, you cannot use the **Groups** collection of a **User** object. Instead, write a short program that looks at each of the groups and determines if the user is in that group. Of course, the best way to avoid this problem is to upgrade your workgroup database to the Microsoft Jet 2.0 format.

# User and Group Examples

Now that you understand the conceptual points of working with users and groups, here are some specific examples.

## Removing a User From a Group

This example deletes user Peter from the Admins group. It works by first checking to see if the specified user is actually a member of the specified group. It does this by disabling error handling and assigning a temporary string to the group name the user is theoretically in. If the string is assigned, the user is a member of the group. In this case, the **Delete** method is used on the user's **Groups** collection. If the string is not assigned, this indicates that the user is not a member of the specified group, and the code displays an error message.

```
Sub RemoveUserFromGroup()
    Dim usrTemp As User
    Dim strTemp As String
    Dim strGroup As String

    strUser = "Peter"
    strGroup = "Admins"

    DBEngine.SystemDB = C:\Samples\Chap10\System.mdw"

    Set usrTemp = DBEngine.Workspaces(0).Users(strUser)

    On Error Resume Next
    strTemp = usrTemp(strGroup).Name
    If strTemp = strGroup Then
        usrTemp.Groups.Delete strGroup
    Else
        Debug.Print "User: " & strUser & " does not exist in group " _
            & strGroup
    End If
End Sub
```

## Changing a User's Password

To change a user's password, you use the **NewPassword** method on the user's **User** object. For obvious security reasons, you must supply the user's current password. This example changes user Hannah's password from "tooeasy" to "MuchHarder123."

```
Sub ChangePwd ()
    Dim usrTemp As User
    Dim strUser As String
    Dim strOld As String
    Dim strNew As String

    strUser = "Hannah"
    strOld = "tooeasy"
    strNew = "MuchHarder123"

    Set usrTemp = DBEngine.Workspaces(0).Users(strUser)

    usrTemp.NewPassword strOld, strNew
End Sub
```

## Determining if a User Has a Password

This code works because you can specify blank strings for both arguments to the
**NewPassword** method. This has the effect of not changing the user's password.
The method fails with a trappable error if the user already has a password.

```
Sub fUserHasPassword ()
    Dim usrTemp As User
    Dim strUser As String
    DBEngine.SystemDB = C:\Samples\Chap10\System.mdw"

    strUser = "Hannah"

    Set usrTemp = DBEngine.Workspaces(0).Users(strUser)

    On Error Resume Next
    usrTemp.NewPassword "", ""
    Select Case Err
        Case 0
            Debug.Print "User " & strUser & " has no password!"
        Case 3033
            Debug.Print "User " & strUser & " has a password."
        Case Else
            ' Unexpected error.
            Error Err
    End Select
End Sub
```

## Adding a New User to an Existing Group

This example shows how to create a new user. The important step to note is
adding the new user to the **Users** group. This is not done automatically by
Microsoft Jet: Your code must handle additions to groups for new users. The
code works by first creating a new user with the **CreateUser** method of the
**Workspace** object. It then appends this new user to the **Users** collection to make
it a permanent part of security. Finally, it adds the Users group to the collection
of groups associated with this user.

```
Sub AddUser ()
    Dim wrkTemp As Workspace
    Dim usrNew As User
    Dim strUser As String
    Dim strPID As String
    Dim strInitialPassword As String
```

```
        strUser = "Jayne"
        strPID = "xzy4321"
        strInitialPassword = "OpenSesame"

        DBEngine.SystemDB = C:\Samples\Chap10\System.mdw"

        Set wrkTemp = DBEngine.Workspaces(0)
        Set usrNew = wrkTemp.CreateUser(strUser, strPID, strInitialPassword)

        wrkTemp.Users.Append usrNew
        usrNew.Groups.Append wrkTemp.CreateGroup("Users")
End Sub
```

# Owner Access Queries

Microsoft Jet gives you a powerful method to leverage security when using queries. You can use the optional WITH OWNERACCESS OPTION clause in your queries to give the person running the query the permission levels assigned to the query's owner.

For example, suppose that a user doesn't have permission to view the payroll information in your application. You can create a query that uses the WITH OWNERACCESS OPTION to allow the user to view this information:

```
SELECT LastName,
FirstName, Salary
FROM Employees
ORDER BY LastName
WITH OWNERACCESS OPTION;
```

If a user is otherwise prevented from creating or adding to a table, you can use the WITH OWNERACCESS OPTION to enable the user to run a make-table or append query.

Owner access queries have two restrictions. First, you can't change the owner of an owner access query. If you need to do this, you must remove the WITH OWNERACCESS clause, change the owner, and then change it back to an owner access query. Second, only the owner of an owner access query can save design changes to that query. If you have several developers who need to modify an owner access query, assign those developers to a group, then make the group the owner of the query using the steps previously described.

# Security and Database Replication

For more information on replication, see Chapter 7, "Database Replication."

Replicable databases use the same security model as all Microsoft Jet databases: Users' permissions on database objects are determined at the time they start Microsoft Jet and log on. As a developer, it's up to you to make sure the same security information is available at each location where a replica is used.

You can do this by making the identical workgroup database available to users at each location where a replica is used. Although the workgroup database cannot be replicated, it can be manually copied to each location.

Another way to make the same system database available to all your users is to re-create the entries for users and groups at each location in the local workgroup database by entering the same user and group names with their associated PIDs at each location. Modifications to permissions are considered design changes and can be made only in the Design Master replica.

Some security permissions control certain aspects of database replication. For example, a user must have Administer permission on the database to:

- Convert a nonreplicable database into a replicable database.
- Make a local object replicable, make a replicable object local, or transfer Design Master status to another replica. You can perform these actions only in the Design Master replica.
- Make a replica of the Design Master. You can perform this action in any replica in the set; however, you should never have more than one Design Master replica in a set at a time.

By default, Administer permission is granted to the Users group, the Admins group, and the creator of the database. If security is to be maintained, you must restrict this permission to selected users.

# The Microsoft Access Security Wizard

The source code for the Security Wizard in Microsoft Access for Windows 95 is provided on the companion CD-ROM in \SAMPLES\ CHAP10\ WZSECURE.MDA.

The Microsoft Access Security Wizard is by far the easiest way to secure a database. You can use it to choose the object types to secure and then secure the objects by revoking all permissions for all accounts except that of the user running the wizard.

As of Microsoft Access for Windows 95, the Security Wizard is built into the product.

# Database Encryption

Database encryption is separate from Microsoft Jet security in that it's not part of the security model. Rather, it's a function provided by the engine you can use to encrypt the actual database file at the operating-system level. This procedure prevents someone from using a disk or file editor at the operating-system level to bypass Microsoft Jet and look directly at the database file.

If a database isn't encrypted, it's possible for a person to use a disk editor to view the contents of the file. Even though the representation of your data and object definitions may be hard to read, the data is there. Also, a knowledgeable person could use a disk or file editor to read the SID of the database owner or the SID of the Admins group in use when the database was created. Given that SID, a person could assume ownership of the database and do anything he or she wanted. For these reasons, it is recommended that you encrypt your database if you want to protect against this potential problem.

If you look at pages in an unencrypted database, you would see something similar to this:

```
12··Brewery·LondonWX1·6LTUK{71}·555-2282{71}·555-9199^{nlee_A-_→__¶
|··_COMMIComércio·MineiroPedro·AfonsoSales·AssociateAv.·dos·usiadas,¶
23São·PauloSP05432-043Brazil{11}·555-7647oob\SQH4%_→__·~*S·1_Y···W¶
···p_ÿ_ƒ__†_ÿ_P_µ_0_«_<_"_1_□··_LAMAILa·maison·d'AsieAnnette··let¶
Sales·Manager1·rue·Alsace-LorraineToulo·e31000France61.77.61.¶
1061.77.61.1lrg\VQQI4'_→__Œ··_LACORLa·corne·d'abondanceDaniel·¶
ToniniSales·epresentative67,·avenue·de·EuropeVersailles·
78000France30.59.84.1030.59.85.11□tic^^T>*_→__o··_KOENEKöniglich·
EssenPhilip·esAssociateMaubelstr.··90Brandenburg14776Germany0555-0¶
9876bbXQLLA4%_→__...··_ISLATIsland·TradingHelen·BennettMarketing·
ManagerGarden·HouseCrowther·WayHedge·EndLancashireLA9·PX8UK{24}·555-
8888>okkibX05$_→__...··_HUNGOHungry·Owl·All-Night·GrocersPatricia·
McKennaSales·Associate8·Johnstown·RoadCorkCo.·CorkIreland2967·
5422967·3333xog`'XTD5%__>··_HUNGCHungry·Coyote·Import·StoreYoshi·
LatimerSales·RepresentativeCity·Cen¶
```

You can see that some of the database's contents are visible. However, after you encrypt the database, the same page would look like this:

```
KDòìDTẀ  G..š  F_içë•viⵞ0å⊕³DÚ1Á1'_kÚ˝É˝__Đ,Üi:Ñl`mロ³>#*Ghﬀ»»ìⓐéŠ'˝sù
ì_ᵐᵃ,_½_°R_z˝Î-YⱭF_P_püⵓi•riŠÁÑÙˆ£?Ễ¦××■G¦¦Ü?¦_•ⁱ¶2_Ibò⌐5•
_'t_‡X}Dؽ!ji-v•´_Ẁロ•;†PpˆÚ-Dᛏ Ẁ0ö˝"o;fⱭ_?_⊕•ⱡÔšⓐ[_ⱭxZⱭ*+ⱶ.uⱥᵃⱭÀˋ-
*loẼ_mmẼÑ_aîéロiⱥ_cCf?•b²îÚ;*ÍCÖⓐN‹ロ[_£ⱥⱡö˛L/•ÿ˝_YÜnˆÓ5Ɑⱱⱪ»ÖT⊁ⱥ«˙
H_eAÎ_aⱮ•\BÎ_Hⱷ°Õ‡Ễ_ロ°ⁱ›ẀロSslⱮロÅéè_Ç½ⱪ_à3G_Uà_4˝_-³ⓐ•Ú\H¦Gò²•
sórᵃ×Ö_œⱥûⱸⱮ•ロ_PⱭⱨÖ5⚭ⓐòì_òÔ%´XüTw!Î_}•êⱷⱮÿˆkⱵⱬ•'Q_Ru‡loⱤ½_×_ⱥ´Œ_ⱥB•_•
0,,)0i⌐l•YDï_Í›iä⌐•âlÔ6qⱭ⁏•ⱤⱥⱮⱭhôóµᵃ_%•'_Ɱᵃ•ý›ÎⱤLᵗ•bÎû8DÎⱧ≤ÜÃ³⌐Ɑ_
zrᵃÑqlT(_+LL½¿jÓⱨ¦Ⱨ•ⱥ2˝_áiⱠm- Üⱬµ⥤Sî,X‹n_„_ÿˋᵗÎòiµ›+8*wⱤŠýÿÎôÎⓐ-
ê¦Y*MÎÙ+šロ[•ⁱ¦‡Ɛb_ⁱⱥŠ⌐~h«-ÜⱺⱺⱭˋÜⱭロ¥ⱥÀ°;\Ⱥ_×⅘_6n_hⱼⱪ⚬²Ñ_5ùŒ__ⁱ!i:ˆ•
bbⱠⓐ•·9__?ⁱⱤâ¦•f_Öx{,,„_°±Ɛ-Ⱥ_=«ⱲⱧ.Ⱨ$⚬Ɑ,ロ˝⚬÷Îⱼzⱺ-l•´_ⱠÓYn!Ṽ_•
Ũlⱥ˝⁻ⁱⱬ˝‹Î·ᵐÀ'8•ⁱ8ⱥ⅘˝F‹ⱥÿJ²d˝D•mMJ§M(_%_(Ⱨ‹wóᵗⱺ[ⱭⱿ_-5îH_•
_ⱼ+ûÎ)uⱼⱣ_ⱮⱥⱯÓ÷Á2•òB»éⱮⱮ_"_$•vⱥ_⊕Ⱶ_´Ⱐ¶
```

This version is obviously unreadable: Microsoft Jet has encrypted every byte in the database file.

As you've learned, Microsoft Jet reads and writes data one "page" at a time. These pages, consisting of 2048 bytes of data, are encrypted as units. Given this, you can see that encryption works on the entire database file, not just table data.

Only the owner of the database, or a member of the Admins group of the workgroup database in use when the database was created, can encrypt or decrypt that database. Due to the overhead of encrypting and decrypting, there is a performance degradation of approximately 10% to 15% in encrypted databases. Encrypted files are also essentially uncompressible using compression software such as that included with MS-DOS. This is because compression relies upon repeated patterns in the data, and encryption effectively removes any patterns.

---

**Note** For database encryption, Microsoft Jet uses the RSA Data Security Incorporated RC4 algorithm with a 32-bit key per 2K page.

---

CHAPTER 11

# DAO C++ Classes

This chapter describes how to programmatically access Microsoft Jet using the DAO C++ classes, also known as dbDAO. The dbDAO classes expose the same Data Access Objects and functionality as Visual Basic and use similar syntax. By handling such tasks as managing object instance lifetimes, these classes make programming in C++ as convenient as programming in Visual Basic. The dbDAO classes are available in the DAO Software Development Kit (SDK), which is included in the DAOSDK folder on the companion CD-ROM.

The chapter begins with a discussion of the relationship between the dbDAO classes, the DAO OLE Automation interfaces, and the MFC DAO classes. A simple dbDAO application follows, which serves as an example for coding with the dbDAO classes. The chapter then describes how to install the DAO SDK and ends with discussions on notable dbDAO programming considerations.

**Contents**

# Using Microsoft Visual C++ and Data Access Objects

DAO, the programming interface to Microsoft Jet, was originally designed for use with Visual Basic and Access Basic. With the advent of OLE Automation, it is now possible to write C++ code that uses DAO.

As of Microsoft Jet 3.0, the DAO DLL is an OLE Automation in-process server containing an embedded type library. With the type library, client programs can query the server for descriptions of exposed objects through the OLE **IDispatch** interface. Because this is a time-consuming process, various efforts have been taken to make DAO C++ coding easier. The result is three different types of DAO C++ coding:

- DAO OLE Automation interfaces
- dbDAO classes
- MFC DAO classes

Although this chapter describes how to use the dbDAO classes, other options are mentioned so you can determine if they better meet your needs.

# DAO OLE Automation Interfaces

For information on using OLE Automation, see the Microsoft Press *OLE 2 Programmer's Reference.*

DAO provides a vtable-based implementation of OLE Automation. The DAO SDK provides header files describing the vtable interfaces for DAO, eliminating the need to use **IDispatch**. After the initial creation of an instance of the **DBEngine** object, instances of objects are created through their parent objects, using the same object hierarchy as described in Chapter 2. Otherwise, these objects are typical OLE Component Object Model (COM) objects; therefore, the application programmer is responsible for explicitly releasing the objects.

# dbDAO Classes

For the DAO programmer familiar with Visual Basic, programming with the DAO interfaces requires additional knowledge about the nuts and bolts of OLE COM. The dbDAO classes help the programmer because they:

- Require only a small amount of OLE COM knowledge. The dbDAO classes handle reference counting (**AddRef** and **Release**), support dynamic allocation and deallocation of objects, and provide full collection support. They also use native C++ data types where possible, or standard OLE variants.
- Require only a small amount of C++ knowledge. The syntax of the C++ calls is very similar to Visual Basic.
- Provide support for bulk fetching directly into your data structures.

Like the DAO interfaces, the dbDAO classes expose the full functionality of DAO properties and methods. The dbDAO classes were designed to incur the lowest possible overhead short of programming directly to the OLE Automation object. They are part of the DAO SDK.

# MFC DAO Classes

As of Visual C++ 4.0, DAO functionality is accessible through the Microsoft Foundation Classes (MFC). Based on the **CRecordset** classes that were written for ODBC, the new **CDAORecordset** classes provide similar functionality using a similar design paradigm. For more information on using the MFC DAO classes, see the Visual C++ 4.0 MFC documentation.

# Deciding Which DAO C++ Classes to Use

If you are familiar with OLE COM programming, then the DAO interfaces may be all you need. Even so, programming with these interfaces requires the declaration of many temporary variables in order to work down the DAO hierarchy to the object you want to work with. This creates many lines of code in itself, in addition to the fact that each of these objects must be explicitly released by the programmer, which requires additional tracking.

For the additional overhead of a 150K DLL, the dbDAO classes enable you to write much more concise code, with no need to keep track of object lifetimes. Conveniences like the classes that handle variants (often the required type used by DAO properties and methods) make programming much easier: Rather than filling out the VARIANT structure, the programmer can simply cast the variable to the appropriate class.

The MFC DAO classes are fully integrated with the MFC wizards and the general MFC object structure. If you are already familiar with MFC, or if you're writing simple database applications that you'd like to easily integrate into your existing MFC-based code, then this is the way for you. If you're more experienced with programming DAO from Visual Basic, then getting started with the dbDAO classes will require less time.

# Using the dbDAO Classes

The intent of the dbDAO classes is to make the resulting DAO C++ code as similar to equivalent Visual Basic code as possible. Fundamental DAO concepts such as properties, methods, and collections are supported by the dbDAO classes.

This section begins by showing a simple dbDAO application that serves as a starting point for learning to program with dbDAO. Afterwards, a more generalized explanation of dbDAO syntax spells out the differences between dbDAO and Visual Basic DAO.

## The Employee Application

The Employee application is a simple dbDAO application for displaying and updating table entries. It is located in the \DAOSDK30\SAMPLES\EMPLOYEE folder of your DAO SDK installation.

The application displays a form, shown in Figure 11.1, containing various database fields. You can use toolbar buttons to add records, delete records, move forward, and move backward. You can also choose the same commands from the **Edit** menu.

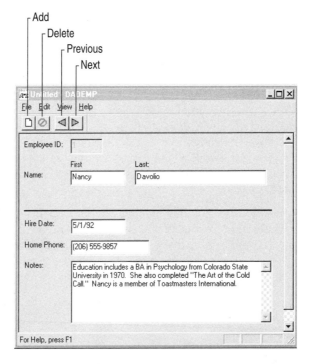

**Figure 11.1    The Employee application**

The Employee application uses the database located in the \DAOSDK30\ SAMPLES\EMPLOYEE folder. This database contains a single table called Employees, which has the following fields.

| Field | Data type |
| --- | --- |
| Employee ID | Counter |
| Last Name | Text |
| First Name | Text |

| Field | Data type (*cont'd*) |
| --- | --- |
| Hire Date | Date/Time |
| Home Phone | Text |
| Notes | Memo |

The following sections discuss the Employee application's features in detail.

## Setting up the Employee Application

Install the DAO SDK by running the Setup program. For more information on installing the DAO SDK, see the "DAO SDK Files" section later in this chapter. From Visual C++, open the EMPLOYEE.MDP project workspace file, which is located in the \SAMPLES\EMPLOYEE folder. This file contains all the settings needed to build the Employee application; just click the **Build** command on the **Build** menu to create EMPLOYEE.EXE.

For more information, see "Installing DAO on Another Machine" in DAO SDK online Help.

**Note**   To run this application, the DAO run-time libraries must be properly installed. By default, the DAO SDK Setup program installs the DAO run-time libraries. Setup can also be modified to install the DAO run-time libraries without installing the other SDK contents (such as header files and import libraries, which only the application developer would require).

DAO SDK Setup adds header, library, and source file directories to your Visual C++ environment. The EMPLOYEE.MDP project workspace file contains the specific settings for building the Employee application.

In addition to the corresponding header files for each source file, the following files are included:

- **DBDAO.H**   Contains the dbDAO class definitions
- **STDAFX.H**   Includes other necessary header files for using Win32, OLE, and MFC

Note that because the dbDAO classes use MFCs (such as **CObject** and **COleVariant**), your application must include these files. Likewise, because the dbDAO classes are built on top of the DAO OLE Automation interfaces, the various OLE header files must be included. STDAFX.H includes all the necessary header files for building your dbDAO application.

For more information on the MFC document/view architecture, see the MFC documentation that comes with Visual C++.

The Employee application uses the MFC document/view architecture. The document portion manipulates the data; therefore, most of the dbDAO code resides here. The view portion contains display code. The Employee application is form-based and derives from the MFC **CFormView** class. The focus of this discussion is the dbDAO code, so this discussion won't go into great detail about using MFC.

The document (DAOEMDOC.CPP) holds the database connection and defines the following member variables:

```
public:
    CdbRecordset      m_cEmpRecordSet;
    BOOL              m_bConnected;
protected:
    CdbDBEngine       m_cDBEngine;
    CdbDatabase       m_cEmpDatabase;
    CdbBookmark       m_cLastGoodRecord;
```

These declarations correspond to the Visual Basic **Dim** statement. Note that dbDAO classes are prefaced by the **Cdb** prefix. The document contains variables for the engine, the database connection, and the recordset that is displayed by the form. The *m_bConnected* member variable is a **Boolean** value that is **True** if the connection to EMPLOYEE.MDB is open; otherwise, it is **False**.

A bookmark called *m_cLastGoodRecord* is defined for use by the various positioning functions to keep track of the last record visited. Note that dbDAO defines the **CdbBookmark** class for bookmarks, whereas bookmarks are typed as **Variants** in Visual Basic.

Because the recordset is used by various code modules, it is given public access. The engine, database, and bookmark member variables are given protected access, so that their values cannot be modified by other code modules.

The OnNewDocument member function is overridden so that the member variables are initialized upon initial creation of the document, and the **DBEngine** object is initialized. For more information on other ways of initializing the engine, see the "Initializing CdbDBEngine" section later in this chapter. OnNewDocument calls ConnectToDatabase, which is described in the following section.

## Connecting to the Employee Database

From the user's perspective, this is the point where the Employee application begins. A dialog box prompts for the location of EMPLOYEE.MDB. The application uses this information to connect to the database and open a table-type recordset on the Employees table. Note that this application is designed to work only with EMPLOYEE.MDB; specifying another database causes an error (unless that database happens to have a table named Employees). The following code describes the ConnectToDatabase function:

```
BOOL CDAOEMPDoc::ConnectToDatabase()
{
    CFileDialog      cOpenFile(  TRUE,
                        _T("MDB"),
                        _T("employee.mdb"),
                        OFN_HIDEREADONLY | OFN_OVERWRITEPROMPT,
                        (_T("Access Files (*.mdb) | *.mdb ||")));
```

```
// Get the location of the database (assume it's the Employee example).
cOpenFile.DoModal();

// Open the database and the recordset.
try
    {
    // NOTE: Use the default collection rather than Workspaces.Items.
    m_cEmpDatabase = m_cDBEngine.OpenDatabase(cOpenFile.m_ofn.lpstrFile);
    m_cEmpRecordSet = m_cEmpDatabase.OpenRecordset(_T("Employees"));
    }

catch (CdbException e)
    {
    CdbLastOLEError exError;
    TCHAR szBuf[256];

    wsprintf(szBuf, _T("Error %d : %s\n"), DBERR(e.m_hr),
            (LPCTSTR) exError.GetDescription());
    AfxMessageBox(szBuf);
    return (FALSE);
    }

    return TRUE;;
}
```

Notice the similarity in the C++ calls to **OpenDatabase** and **OpenRecordset** to the way these functions are called in Visual Basic. The dbDAO variables behave like objects with associated properties and methods. Collections are also supported; for example, the call to **OpenDatabase** could be rewritten using the **Workspaces** collection as follows:

```
m_cEmpDatabase = m_cDBEngine.Workspaces[0L].OpenDatabase(cOpenFile.m_ofn.lpstrFile);
```

Note that the index is cast as LONG; otherwise, the compiler interprets the "0" as NULL. For more information on dbDAO properties, methods, and collections, see the "dbDAO Syntax" section later in this chapter.

To handle exceptions raised by errors, the dbDAO code is nested in a **try-catch** block. For example, if the Employees table is not found in the database, the **OpenRecordset** call throws an exception. Execution immediately switches to the **catch** block, which in this case displays a dialog box containing the offending error. The DBERR macro is used to convert the error from an HRESULT to a Visual Basic error number. For more information on errors, see the "Handling dbDAO Errors" section later in this chapter.

Also note that strings in this function are wrapped in the _T macro. Using this macro allows the code to compile for both ANSI and Unicode™. The dbDAO class run-time libraries are available in both ANSI and Unicode versions. For more information, see the "ANSI and Unicode Strings" section later in this chapter.

## Reading Records from the Employee Database

Reading data and displaying the results on the form occur in the view portion of the code. The view defines the following member variables in DAOEMVW.H:

```
protected:// Declare members for the employee table columns to be used.
    //{{AFX_DATA(CDAOEMPView)
    enum { IDD = IDD_MAINFORM };
    long            m_nEmpNum;
    CString         m_strFirstName;
    CString         m_strHomePhone;
    CString         m_strLastName;
    CString         m_strNotes;
    COleDateTime    m_HireDate;
    //}}AFX_DATA
```

IDD_MAINFORM is the resource ID for the form. The form contains controls associated with each of the six member variables. Each member variable in turn is used to store a field for the current record being read. Note the choice of data types of the corresponding member variables with respect to their Microsoft Jet data types in the Employee table: **long** for **Counter**, **CString** for **Text** and **Memo**, and **COleDateTime** for **Date/Time**.

The **CDAOEMPView** constructor initializes the member variables. The OnInitialUpdate member function performs a one-time initialization of the view. Typically, **CFormView** overrides this function to use Dialog Data Exchange (DDX) to set the initial values of the controls that have been mapped by the member variables. In the Employee application, OnInitialUpdate calls **SetFieldStates**, which checks to see if a database is connected. If the application is not connected to the Employee database, the form is disabled; that is, it isn't displayed on the screen until the connection is made.

After the connection is made, the first record from the Employees table is displayed, which updates the view's appearance. The application also updates the view whenever the position in the recordset is changed in response to one of the four commands available from the toolbar or **Edit** menu. Each command invokes a related function within the document. (Because the recordset contains the data, it is associated with the document and not the view.) For example, clicking **Next** calls OnEditNext:

```
void CDAOEMPDoc::OnEditNext()
{
    if(!OKToMove())
        return;

    m_cEmpRecordSet.MoveNext();

    // Watch for end of the Recordset.
    if(m_cEmpRecordSet.GetEOF())
        {
```

```
                              MessageBeep(0);
                              m_cEmpRecordSet.MovePrevious();
                              }
                       else
                              {
                              UpdateAllViews(NULL);
                              }

               }
```

OnEditNext first calls OKToMove, which checks to see if the record has been updated. (Record updates are discussed in the "Updating Records from the Employee Database" section later in this chapter.) **MoveNext** then positions the recordset to the next record. The end-of-file condition is checked; if it occurs, then the application moves back to the previous record; otherwise, the view is updated. Note that there is no need to update the view if the end of the recordset is reached; the application moves back to the last record displayed.

In terms of actually reading data, when the view is updated, the application calls the OnUpdate member function to update the form view's appearance:

```
void CDAOEMPView::OnUpdate(CView* pSender, LPARAM lHint, CObject* pHint)
{
    CDAOEMPDoc* pDoc = GetDocument();
    ASSERT_VALID(pDoc);
    try
        {
        m_nEmpNum = VTOLONG(pDoc->m_cEmpRecordSet.GetField(EMP_EMPLOYEE_ID));

        // Convert the Variant strings to CStrings.
        VarToCStr(&m_strFirstName, &pDoc->m_cEmpRecordSet.GetField(EMP_FIRST_NAME));
        VarToCStr(&m_strHomePhone, &pDoc->m_cEmpRecordSet.GetField(EMP_HOME_PHONE));
        VarToCStr(&m_strLastName, &pDoc->m_cEmpRecordSet.GetField(EMP_LAST_NAME));
        VarToCStr(&m_strNotes, &pDoc->m_cEmpRecordSet.GetField(EMP_NOTES));

        // COleDateTime
        m_HireDate = pDoc->m_cEmpRecordSet.GetField(EMP_HIRE_DATE);
        }
    catch (CdbException e)
        {
        CdbLastOLEError exError;
        TCHAR szBuf[256];

        wsprintf(szBuf, _T("Error %d : %s\n"), DBERR(e.m_hr),
                (LPCTSTR) exError.GetDescription());
        AfxMessageBox(szBuf);
        }
```

```
UpdateData(FALSE); // Invoke Dialog Data Exchange (copy member data to form controls).

Invalidate(); // Repaint.
}
```

OnUpdate uses the dbDAO **GetField** method, which does not exist in Visual Basic DAO. You use **GetField** to bypass the **Fields** collection, resulting in more readable code and a performance gain.

Data is returned as variants; therefore, you must convert returned values to member variables' data types. DAOEMP.H defines several useful macros for handling data conversion, such as VTOLONG, which converts a variant to a LONG data type:

```
#define VTOLONG(v)    ((v).vt==VT_I4 ? (LONG)(v).iVal:0L)
```

Note that this conversion converts a null value represented by VT_NULL into the long value 0L, which may not always be what you want.

Although not shown in the Employee application, the dbDAO **GetRowsEx** function provides an alternate method of reading data directly as native C data types. Although it involves writing more code, **GetRowsEx** realizes a performance improvement because it bypasses this extra data conversion. For more information on **GetRowsEx**, see the "Performing Bulk Fetches with GetRows and GetRowsEx" section later in this chapter.

The final step is to update the form controls themselves by calling the **UpdateData** member function with an argument of **FALSE**. **UpdateData** uses DDX to maintain mappings between data of the **CDAOEMPView** class and the controls in the dialog template resource for this form view.

## Adding Records to the Employee Database

The OnEditAdd member function adds records to the Employee database:

```
void CDAOEMPDoc::OnEditAdd()
{
    if(!OKToMove())
        return;

    // Remember location before adding in case the user
    // cancels and you need to return.
    m_cLastGoodRecord = m_cEmpRecordSet.GetBookmark();
    m_cEmpRecordSet.AddNew();

    UpdateAllViews(NULL);
}
```

As with any attempt to reposition within the recordset, OkToMove is called first to check whether or not the current record has been edited by the user. Before adding the new record, the current position is saved by using a bookmark. This is done with the **GetBookmark** method as in Visual Basic. The bookmark itself is typed as **CdbBookmark** in dbDAO rather than as a variant, but this is irrelevant; the bookmark is merely used for returning to a row. If the user deletes the new record, the bookmark is used to move back to the previous position.

## Deleting Records from the Employee Database

The OnEditDelete member function deletes records from the Employee database:

```
void CDAOEMPDoc::OnEditDelete()
{
    // Delete method depends on current mode.

    short nEditMode = m_cEmpRecordSet.GetEditMode();

    try
        {
        switch (nEditMode)
            {
            case dbEditNone: // Just delete it.
                {
                m_cEmpRecordSet.Delete();
                m_cEmpRecordSet.MoveFirst();
                break;
                }

            case dbEditInProgress: // Forget changes.
                {
                m_cEmpRecordSet.CancelUpdate();
                m_cEmpRecordSet.Delete();
                m_cEmpRecordSet.MoveFirst();
                break;
                }

            case dbEditAdd: // If new record, go back to last known.
                {
                m_cEmpRecordSet.CancelUpdate();
                m_cEmpRecordSet.SetBookmark(m_cLastGoodRecord);
                }
            }

        UpdateAllViews(NULL);
        }
```

```
catch (CdbException e)
    {
    CdbLastOLEError exError;
    TCHAR szBuf[256];

    wsprintf(szBuf, _T("Error 0x%lx : %s\n"), e.m_hr,
            (LPCTSTR) exError.GetDescription());
    AfxMessageBox(szBuf);
    }
}
```

The behavior of this method depends on whether the current record is new or has been edited. OnEditDelete uses **case** statement logic based on the value returned by **GetEditMode**. Note that dbDAO conveniently defines the same data access constants as Visual Basic DAO, such as **dbEditNone**. Depending on this value, OnEditDelete behaves as follows:

- If the record has not been edited (**dbEditNone**), delete it and move to the first row of the table.
- If the record has been edited (**dbEditInProgress**), first cancel the update, then delete it and move to the first row of the table.
- If the record is a newly added record (**dbEditAdd**), first cancel the update, and then move to the previous record using the saved bookmark. Note that there is no need to call **Delete**, as newly added records are not part of the recordset until **Update** is called.

In all three cases, it is necessary to update the view by calling **UpdateAllViews**.

## Updating Records from the Employee Database

The UpdateEmpRec member function updates records from the Employee database:

```
void CDAOEMPDoc::UpdateEmpRec(long m_nEmpNum, LPCTSTR lpszFirstName,
        LPCTSTR lpszHomePhone, LPCTSTR lpszLastName,
        LPCTSTR lpszNotes, DATE HireDate)
{
    // Convert the date to a dbVariant.
    COleVariant cdbHireDate;
    cdbHireDate.date = HireDate;
    cdbHireDate.vt = VT_DATE;

    try
        {
        // The recordset must be in edit mode.
        if (m_cEmpRecordSet.GetEditMode() == dbEditNone)
            m_cEmpRecordSet.Edit();
```

```
m_cEmpRecordSet.SetField(EMP_FIRST_NAME,
        COleVariant(lpszFirstName, VT_BSTRT));
m_cEmpRecordSet.SetField(EMP_HOME_PHONE,
        COleVariant(lpszHomePhone, VT_BSTRT));
m_cEmpRecordSet.SetField(EMP_LAST_NAME,
        COleVariant(lpszLastName, VT_BSTRT));
m_cEmpRecordSet.SetField(EMP_NOTES,
        COleVariant(lpszNotes, VT_BSTRT));
m_cEmpRecordSet.SetField(EMP_HIRE_DATE, cdbHireDate);

// Commit the changes.
m_cEmpRecordSet.Update();

// Return to the edited record.
CdbBookmark cBookmark = m_cEmpRecordSet.GetLastModified();
m_cEmpRecordSet.SetBookmark(cBookmark);
}

catch (CdbException e)
    {
    CdbLastOLEError exError;
    TCHAR szBuf[256];

    wsprintf(szBuf, _T("Error 0x%lx : %s\n"), e.m_hr,
            (LPCTSTR) exError.GetDescription());
    AfxMessageBox(szBuf);
    }
}
```

Because recordset manipulation functions live in the document, the application must pass the record's field values from the view to UpdateEmpRec. To update the values, the dbDAO classes define an analogous method to **GetField** called **SetField**, which likewise enables you to bypass the **Fields** collection.

Updating values involves the reverse data conversions of reading values: Member variables must be converted to variants. The MFC **COleVariant** class handles most common data type conversions. However, there is no conversion for DATE types, so UpdateEmpRec uses a temporary variable (*cdbHireDate*) to store the resulting variant.

---

**Note** You must make sure that the recordset is in **Edit** mode before attempting an update. This happens by default for an added record, but **Edit** mode must be turned on explicitly for an existing record. This is a result of the document/view split; actions in the view must be mapped to corresponding behavior in the document. Any edits entered into the form are not updated until the user issues a menu or toolbar command, resulting in a position change in the recordset.

---

# dbDAO Syntax

The following comparison of the previous dbDAO code (with lengthy argument names and macro decorations removed), shows how syntactically similar it is to Visual Basic.

| dbDAO | | Visual Basic |
|---|---|---|
| CdbDBEngine | e; | |
| CdbDatabase | d; | Dim d as Database |
| CdbRecordset | r; | Dim r as Recordset |
| | | |
| d = e.OpenDatabase("nwind.mdb"); | | Set d = OpenDatabase("nwind.mdb") |
| r = d.OpenRecordset("Employees"); | | Set r = d.OpenRecordset("Employees") |

One notable difference is that for dbDAO, declaring a variable of class **CdbDBEngine** must be the first DAO call. This declaration calls the constructor function that creates the **CdbDBEngine** object. For more information, see the "Initializing CdbDBEngine" section later in this chapter.

For more information on language differences, see the DAO SDK Help topics for C++, and the corresponding Visual Basic examples.

Other than language differences—regarding how to type variables, for example—there are some general differences in the way DAO properties, methods, and collections appear in code, as detailed in the following sections.

## dbDAO Properties

Properties in the dbDAO classes are defined differently from the way they are defined in Visual Basic. The **PropName** type library property, for example, is exposed as two methods, **GetPropName** and **SetPropName**. If the property is read-only, then only the **Get** method is exposed. If the property is write-only, then only the **Set** method is exposed. The **Get** method takes no arguments and returns the value of the property, using the appropriate C data type where possible. The **Set** method takes a single argument—the new value to which you want to set the property—again using the appropriate C data type where possible.

For example, the **Name** property of an object is mapped to the **GetName** and **SetName** methods. Therefore, its C prototypes are as follows:

```
CString    GetName (VOID);
VOID       SetName (LPCTSTR pstr);
```

### Variants

Some properties return data of various types. The most obvious of these are the **Value** properties of **Field** objects. These have to return variants because the data type of the return value isn't known until run time, because the return value may contain a null value, or for both reasons.

### Default Properties

Visual Basic has default properties. For example, the code

```
a = rs!FirstName
```

is equivalent to

```
a = rs!FirstName.Value
```

Here, **Value** is the default property of the **Field** object. Because C++ has no equivalent syntax, you have to ask for the default property by name:

```
a = rs.Fields["FirstName"].GetValue();
```

---

**Note**   For this particular call, the performance of this code could be improved by using the dbDAO **GetField** method, as follows:

```
a = rs.GetField("FirstName");
```

---

## dbDAO Methods

Visual Basic methods map directly to methods in the dbDAO classes. Visual Basic methods that take optional arguments may also omit any or all optional arguments in these classes. If you omit an optional argument, a default value is supplied for the argument.

Methods take C types as arguments rather than the more common VARIANT data type used in the OLE classes and VBA. For more information, see the individual method prototypes in DBDAO.H.

## dbDAO Collections

The dbDAO classes emulate Visual Basic collections by providing member variables that point to collections. As with default values, there is no automatic lookup syntax, which means you have to use an explicit **Item** method. Overloading of this method allows you to specify either an ordinal or string index in the collection.

Automatic construction and destruction of these references means that statements like

```
d.m_Tabledefs.Item(i).Name
```

are legal and result in the correct allocation of the referenced **Item** (a **TableDef** object in this case), and its deallocation when the reference is complete. Of course, for repeated access, it's better to declare an explicit reference, but for one-time use, this is a convenient way to retrieve collection values.

A convenient shorthand for specifying an item in a collection is to use the [ ] operator. The same statement would then be:

```
d.m_Tabledefs[i].Name
```

---

**Note** If you use reference fields by ordinal, cast the index as LONG to prevent the compiler from interpreting "0" as NULL.

---

## dbDAO Objects

The dbDAO classes have the same object names as in Visual Basic, except that all objects are prepended with **Cdb**. For example, **Recordset** becomes **CdbRecordset**, **DBEngine** becomes **CdbDBEngine,** and so on. New objects defined by the dbDAO classes that don't exist in Visual Basic are **CdbBookmark**, **CdbLastOleError**, and **CdbException,** which are described in the "Other dbDAO Programming Considerations" section later in this chapter.

Other objects used internally in the dbDAO classes are **CdbObject**, **CdbOleObject**, and **CdbGetRowsEx**. Because they are used internally, they exist in the dbDAO header file.

# DAO SDK Files

The dbDAO classes are included in the DAO SDK, which is on the companion CD-ROM.

Visual C++ 4.0 also includes the DAO SDK. The dbDAO classes do not work with earlier versions of Visual C++. The only supported form of DAO for Visual C++ is a 32-bit in-process DLL requiring either Windows 95 or Windows NT; dbDAO does not work with Win32s.

Running the DAO SDK Setup program in \DAOSDK\DISK1 does everything required to start programming with dbDAO, including copying all necessary DLLs, updating the Registry, and setting up a directory structure for the headers, libraries, and sample programs.

The following tables describe the files that are installed by DAO SDK Setup.

### INCLUDE Files

| File | Description |
| --- | --- |
| DBDAO.H | Provides all dbDAO class definitions and helper macros, and includes other necessary header files. DBDAO.H must be included by all applications that use dbDAO. |
| DBDAOERR.H | Defines all the errors that can be returned by DAO. See the "Handling dbDAO Errors" section later in this chapter for more information on how to handle errors in dbDAO. |

| File | Description (*cont'd*) |
|------|------------------------|
| DAOGETRW.H | Required by applications that use the OLE Automation form of **GetRowsEx**. It defines HRESULTs not included in DBDAOERR.H, binding constants for the function, and the DAOCOLUMNBINDING structure. DAOGETRW.H does not have to be included in programs that use dbDAO; it is provided so you can rebuild DBDAO.CPP. For more information about using **GetRowsEx**, see the "Performing Bulk Fetches with GetRows and GetRowsEx" section later in this chapter. |
| _DBDAO.H | Used in the compilation of DBDAO.CPP. _DBDAO.H contains needed definitions and helper macros for the dbDAO source files. _DBDAO.H does not have to be included in programs that use dbDAO; it is provided so you can rebuild DBDAO.CPP. |
| DBDAOINT.H | Defines the underlying DAO OLE Automation (OA) interfaces, their methods, parameters, and so on. Use this file to program directly to the DAO OA interfaces. It is included by DBDAO.H. |
| DBDAOID.H | Defines the interface IDs for the underlying DAO OA objects. It is included by DBDAO.H. |

## SRC Files

| File | Description |
|------|-------------|
| DBDAO.CPP | Source code for the dbDAO class libraries. This code creates a set of C++ classes that "cover" the OLE Automation interfaces that DAO exposes. A compiled version of this code is provided in DBDAO3.DLL, which is installed in your system directory. The source code is provided for ease of debugging and building other versions of the dbDAO DLL. For information on the other versions you can build, see the "Other dbDAO DLL Versions" section later in this chapter. |
| DBDAOUID.CPP | Source code for DBDAOUID.LIB. Useful for programming directly to the DAO OLE Automation interface. |
| DBDAO.MAK | Makefile for dbDAO class libraries. See the "Other dbDAO DLL Versions" section later in this chapter for information on the other versions you can build. |

### LIB Files

| File | Description |
|------|-------------|
| DBDAO.RC | Generated resource file. |
| STDAFX.H | Standard MFC header file. |
| DBDAO3.LIB | Import library for DBDAO3.DLL. |
| DBDAO3U.LIB | Import library for DBDAO3U.DLL (Unicode version of DBDAO3.DLL). |
| DBDAOUID.LIB | Import library that defines the GUIDs for DAO. |
| DEBUG\\*.DLL | Debug versions of the DBDAO3[U]D.DLL files. To use these, copy them to your application directory or system directory. |

### SAMPLES Files

| File | Description |
|------|-------------|
| EMPLOYEE | Based on Employees table in EMPLOYEE.MDB. Allows viewing of data and simple edits. |
| DAOREAD | Demonstrates different methods for reading data and displays fetch time for each method. |
| GETROWS | Demonstrates how to use the **GetRows** and **GetRowsEx** methods. |

### SETUP Files

| File | Description |
|------|-------------|
| DAOMIN.RUL | Template InstallShield setup script. |
| REGADLL | Directory with source files for rebuilding the provided setup support DLL. |
| DAOSETUP.RTF | Detailed instructions on creating your own setup program without using InstallShield. |

# Other dbDAO Programming Considerations

Most of the dbDAO classes correspond to their Visual Basic equivalents, but the classes described in the following sections have no Visual Basic counterparts or have C++-specific extensions. These classes handle variant data type conversion, bookmarks, and errors.

# Initializing CdbDBEngine

The **CdbDBEngine** class initializes the DAO **DBEngine** object. This is different from Visual Basic. There are two constructors, as follows:

- One constructor calls **CoCreateInstance** to create an instance of the **DBEngine** object and obtain a **DAODBEngine** interface pointer (the underlying OA interface as defined in DBDAOINT.H). The same constructor enables you to add an additional reference to an existing instance of the **DBEngine**.

- The other constructor takes five parameters, allowing the user to specify the default user, the default password, the IniPath, whether the **DBEngine** object is private or shared, and whether to start the engine on construction. After the engine is started, these properties cannot be modified.

Each private engine is a new instance of DAO. A shared engine is common across all instances, enabling them to share open workspaces, databases, recordsets, and so on.

If you don't start the engine on construction, you can use a **Start** method to start it.

# Handling dbDAO Errors

The dbDAO classes use exception handling to let you know when errors occur. The **CdbException** class provides an HRESULT member; the **CdbLastOLEError** and **CdbError** classes offer more detailed error handling.

To catch an exception for dbDAO, use the **CdbException** class in your **catch** statement:

```
try
    {
    // Some dbDAO function calls
    }
catch (CdbException e)
    {
    // Handle the exception.
    }
```

In many cases, you'll just want your exception handling code to examine the HRESULT returned. In these cases, you need only the **CdbException** object, whose only member is *m_hr*, the HRESULT. Error constants that can be returned by dbDAO member functions are defined in DBDAOERR.H. To determine exactly what the error was, you can compare the HRESULT in **CdbException** with values defined in DBDAOERR.H. For example:

```
#include <dbdao.h>

void OpenADatabase(CString stDBName)
    {
    CdbDBEngine dben;
    CdbDatabase db;

    try
        {
        db = dben.OpenDatabase(stDBName);
        }
    catch (CdbException e)
        {
        If (e.m_hr == E_DAO_FileNotFound);
        // Inform the user that the file specified doesn't exist.
        // E_DAO_FileNotFound is a constant defined in dbdaoerr.h.
        }
    }
```

DAO returns numeric error values in two forms. One is in the form of an HRESULT. This is the form familiar to OLE programmers. The other is in the form of a Visual Basic error number. This is the form more familiar to Visual Basic programmers who have worked with DAO. To read the HRESULT, examine the *m_hr* member of the **CdbException** object. To read the error as a Visual Basic error number value, wrap the *m_hr* member of **CdbException** in a DBERR macro (defined in DBDAO.H).

For more involved error handling, you may want to use the **CdbError** class. This class is associated with the **CdbDBEngine** object's **CdbErrors** collection. It holds the last DAO error. The members of this class contain:

- The number value associated with the error.

- The DAO description for that error.

- The object on which the error occurred (in the form DAO.*object*; for example, DAO.Database).

- The DAO Help file and Help context for obtaining more information about the error.

The number value stored in the **CdbError** object is in the form of a Visual Basic error number rather than an HRESULT, as in the **CdbException** object. For example:

```
void OpenADatabase(CString stDBName)
    {
    CdbDBEngine dben;
```

```
CdbDatabase db;

try
    {
    db = dben.OpenDatabase(stDBName);
    }
catch (CdbException e)
    {
    int iError, cError;
    CString stError = _T("");

    cError = dben.Errors.GetCount();
    for (iError = 0; iError < cError; iError++)
        {
        stError += dben.Errors[iError].
        stError += _T("\n");
        }
    //Inform the user of the error with stError.
    }
}
```

Also used for more detailed error handling, the **CdbLastOLEError** class is more generic to OLE than to DAO. With **CdbLastOLEError**, you can get extended error information on the last OLE error to occur, including its description. Regardless of whether the last error to occur was a DAO or an OLE error, you can use this class to determine the error. For example:

```
void OpenADatabase(CString stDBName)
    {
    CdbDBEngine dben;
    CdbDatabase db;

    try
        {
        db = dben.OpenDatabase(stDBName);
        }
    catch (CdbException e)
        {
        CdbLastOLEError ex;
        CString stError;

        stError.Format("0x%lx : %s", e.m_hr,
                (LPCTSTR ex.GetDescription()));
        //Inform the user of the error with stError.
        }
    }
```

The **CdbLastOLEError** error always corresponds to the last error stored in the **CdbErrors** collection.

# Performing Bulk Fetches with GetRows and GetRowsEx

The dbDAO classes support the **GetRows** method for fetching multiple rows of data in one call. Like the Visual Basic version, **GetRows** returns the data as variants.

The **GetRowsEx** method is a performance improvement by dbDAO and MFC DAO to avoid the necessity to retrieve all data as variants and then convert to native types. **GetRowsEx** does not exist in Visual Basic DAO.

---

**Important**  The underlying **ICDAORecordset::GetRows** method might not be supported in future versions of DAO; however, the MFC and dbDAO classes that use this method will continue to be supported.

---

## Using the dbDAO GetRows Method

For more information on using safe arrays, see the *OLE 2 Programmer's Reference.*

The **GetRows** method takes one parameter and the number of rows to fetch, and returns the row data as variants. Unlike with Visual Basic, you cannot simply use subscripts to indicate the array field in a variant. Rather, the data is returned as an OLE safe array. The *parray* member of the variant points to an array descriptor. Individual fields are accessed by calling **SafeArrayGetElement**.

The following code from the GetRows sample (found in the \SAMPLES\ GETROWS folder of the DAOSDK installation) shows how to use **GetRows**. Note that the table schema is known *a priori*, allowing the programmer to hard-code the display functions.

```
void CGetRowsDlg::DoGetRows()
{
    COleVariant      cRows;
    COleVariant      varField;
    CString          strLBRow;
    TCHAR            szId[16];
    LONG             lNumRecords;
    LONG             lIndex[2];
    HRESULT          hResult;
    CListBox         *pListBox = (CListBox *)GetDlgItem(IDD_GETROWSLIST);

    // Perform GetRows on Employee table. Retrieve MAX_EMP_REC rows and
    // store results as a variant in cRows.
    cRows = m_cEmpRecordSet.GetRows(MAX_EMP_REC);

    // Find out how many records were actually retrieved.
    // (Safe arrays are 1-based.)
    SafeArrayGetUBound(cRows.parray, 2, &lNumRecords);

    // Clear the list box for displaying the row values.
    pListBox->ResetContent();
```

```
// Step through the returned rows.
for (lIndex[1] = 0; lIndex[1] <= lNumRecords; lIndex[1]++)
    {
    // Clear the string containing the row values.
    strLBRow.Empty();

    // Set array index to EmpID field.
    lIndex[0] = EMP_EMPLOYEE_ID;

    // Use OLE safe array function to access fields.
    hResult = SafeArrayGetElement(cRows.parray, &lIndex[0],
                &varField);

    // Watch out for bad variants.
    if(FAILED(hResult))
        break;

    // EmpID is known to be a long integer value. Store the value in
    // a string. The type check is used because the array may
    // contain empty rows.
    if(varField.vt == VT_I4)
        {
        wsprintf(szId, _T("%d,  "), varField.iVal);
        }
    else    // Empty row           {
        lstrcpy(szId, _T("Unexpected Data Type"));
        }

    strLBRow += (LPCTSTR)szId;

    // Set array index to LastName field.
    lIndex[0] = EMP_LNAME;

    // Use OLE safe array function to access fields.
    SafeArrayGetElement(cRows.parray, &lIndex[0], &varField);

    // Add LastName to the row string.
    strLBRow += (LPCTSTR)varField.bstrVal;

    // Do the same to get first name.
    strLBRow += _T(", ");
    lIndex[0] = EMP_FNAME;
    SafeArrayGetElement(cRows.parray, &lIndex[0], &varField);
    strLBRow += (LPCTSTR)varField.bstrVal;

    // Display string.
    pListBox->AddString(strLBRow);
    }
}
```

## Using the dbDAO GetRowsEx Method

The **GetRowsEx** method retrieves multiple rows and enables you to specify the data types of the fields stored in your application variables. It has the following parameters.

| Parameter | Data type | Description |
|---|---|---|
| *pvBuffer* | LPVOID | Pointer to buffer in which to store returned rows. |
| *cbRow* | LONG | Length of row in bytes. |
| *prb* | LPDAORSETBINDING | Pointer to binding structure (see the following description). |
| *cBinding* | LONG | Number of bindings. |
| *pvVarBuffer* | LPVOID | Pointer to buffer in which to store variable-length data. |
| *cbVarBuffer* | LONG | Length in bytes of *pvVarBuffer*. |
| *lRows* | LONG | Number of rows requested. |

The DAORSETBINDING structure specifies how data is to be copied from the rows to the memory buffer. A separate binding structure must be filled in for each field retrieved. DAORSETBINDING is defined as follows:

```
typedef struct
    {
    DWORD    dwBindIndexType;
    union
        {
        LONG    i;
        LPCTSTR pstr;
        };

    DWORD    dwType;
    DWORD    dwOffset;
    DWORD    cb;

    } DAORSETBINDING, *LPDAORSETBINDING;
```

DAORSETBINDING has the following members.

| Member | Description |
|---|---|
| *dwBindIndexType* | Specifies whether a field is indicated by an index number or by name. Is one of the following values:<br><br>dbBindIndexINT (index)<br>dbBindIndexSTR (name) |
| *dwType* | Specifies the data type. Is one of the following values:<br><br>dbBindI2 (long)<br>dbBindI4 (short)<br>dbBindR4 (float)<br>dbBindR8 (double)<br>dbBindCY (currency)<br>dbBindDATE (DATE)<br>dbBindBOOL (VARIANT_BOOL)<br>dbBindUI1 (unsigned char)<br>dbBindVARIANT (VARIANT)<br>dbBindWCHAR (wchar_t[])<br>dbBindSTRING (same as dbBindWCHAR for Unicode, dbBindUI1 for ANSI)<br>dbBindLPSTR (char_pointer)<br>dbBindLPTSTR (wchar_pointer)<br>dbBindLPSTRING (dbBindLPTSTR for Unicode, dbBindLPSTR for ANSI)<br>dbBindBookmark (CdbBookmark)<br>dbBindBlob (unsigned char pointer) |
| *dwOffset* | Offset in bytes in the row buffer where data is copied. |
| *cb* | Field length in bytes. |

The following code from the GetRows sample shows how to use **GetRowsEx**. Note that the table schema is known *a priori*, allowing the programmer to predefine a structure for the data.

```
// User-defined structure for storing data returned by GetRowsEx.
typedef struct
    {
    LONG    lEmpId;             // Employee ID (long integer)
    TCHAR   *strLastName;       // Last name (variable-length string)
    TCHAR   strFirstName[20];   // First name (20-character string)
    } EMP, *LPEMP ;
```

```
// Employee table binding. This structure can be kept in a header file and modified as
// needed (for example, when you update the table definition). Filling in the structure
// statically allows you to define bindings once, rather than each time you read data.
DAORSETBINDING  Bindings[] =
{
// Index Type      Column      Type           Offset                      Size
{dbBindIndexINT, EMP_ID,    dbBindI4,      offsetof(EMP,lEmpId),       sizeof(LONG)},
{dbBindIndexINT, EMP_LNAME, dbBindLPSTRING, offsetof(EMP,strLastName),  sizeof(TCHAR *)},
{dbBindIndexINT, EMP_FNAME, dbBindSTRING,  offsetof(EMP,strFirstName), sizeof(TCHAR) * 20}
};

// Perform dbDAO GetRowsEx against the Employee table.
void CGetRowsDlg::DoGetRowsEx()
{
    LPEMP           pEmpRows = new EMP[MAX_EMP_REC];
    CListBox        *pListBox = (CListBox *)GetDlgItem(IDD_GETROWSLISTEX);
    CString         strLBRow;
    TCHAR           szId[16];
    LONG            lNumRecords;
    LONG            lCount;
    TCHAR           pBuf[MAX_EMP_REC * 15];      // Allow average of 15 chars/name.

    // Call GetRowsEx to fetch rows.
    lNumRecords = m_cEmpRecordSet.GetRowsEx(
            pEmpRows,                                 // Pointer to data buffer
            sizeof(EMP),                              // Length of row in bytes
            &Bindings[0],                             // Pointer to binding structures
            sizeof(Bindings) / sizeof(DAORSETBINDING), // Number of bindings
            pBuf,                                     // Variable-length data buffer
            sizeof(pBuf),                             // Length of variable-length data
            MAX_EMP_REC);                             // Get MAX_EMP_REC rows

    // Step through the returned rows and display results.
    for (lCount = 0; lCount < lNumRecords; lCount++)
        {
        strLBRow.Empty();        // Clear the string containing the row values.
        wsprintf(szId, _T("%d,  "), pEmpRows[lCount].lEmpId);
        strLBRow += szId;
        strLBRow += pEmpRows[lCount].strLastName;
        strLBRow += _T(", ");
        strLBRow += (LPCTSTR)pEmpRows[lCount].strFirstName;
        pListBox->AddString(strLBRow);
        }

    delete [] pEmpRows;          // Free memory.
}
```

# ANSI and Unicode Strings

All 16-bit applications use ANSI strings. 32-bit applications can use either ANSI or Unicode strings. ANSI applications store strings as **unsigned char**, each byte containing a different character. Unicode applications store strings as **unsigned short**, each short integer value containing a different character.

To specify ANSI, declare the following in your project settings:

```
#define _MBCS
```

To specify Unicode, declare the following in your project settings:

```
#define _UNICODE
```

The advantage of using Unicode in your applications is that it enables you to easily localize your application into languages such as Chinese, where 2 bytes are required to store characters. ANSI applications require special Double Byte Character Set (DBCS) functions to be localized into such languages.

The advantage of using ANSI strings is that, in Windows 95, some Windows system calls take only ANSI strings; therefore, you must convert Unicode strings to ANSI before calling into these functions.

You can compile your application in ANSI or Unicode by using the _T macro. _T is defined by Visual C++ and is used to wrap all string literals. In ANSI, this macro does nothing. In Unicode, it appends the L keyword to inform the compiler that the literal is to be read in as Unicode. For example:

```
void OpenADatabase()
    {
    CdbDBEngine dben;
    CdbDatabase db;

    db = dben.OpenDatabase(_T("MyDB.MDB"));
    }
```

This code compiles for both ANSI and Unicode applications.

# Using dbDAO in a DLL

Although many people use DAO from an executable, you may want to create DLLs for distribution so that others can use them in their applications. If so, then you are responsible for starting DAO from inside the DLL. Various restrictions on DLLs prevent this from being done automatically as the DLL loads, and the dbDAO classes do not handle it for you. Instead, you must explicitly force the load.

For example, the following code works fine inside an executable, but the same code does not work as a DLL:

```
class CMyObj
```

```
    {
public:
    CMyObj();
    ~CMyObj();
private:
    CdbDBEngine m_cDBEng;
    };

CMyObj::CMyObj()
    {
    }

CMyObj::~CMyObj()
    {
    delete m_cDBEng;
    }

// Globally instantiated object - the cause of the DLL problem.
CMyObj myObj;

#ifdef MAKE_AS_DLL
// Exported function that is called by some console app.
// This case hangs.
__declspec(dllexport) void hello()
    {
    }

#else
// When this is built as a console app, it works fine.
void main()
    {
    return;
    }
#endif // MAKE_AS_DLL
```

The line causing the problem is the declaration:

```
CMyObj myObj;
```

When the DLL is loaded and the myObj object is instantiated, a failed attempt to create an instance of the **DBEngine** object is made. To work around this problem, you must create an entry point in your routine that explicitly creates DAO, and have your DLL users call that entry point. You could do this as part of another initialization, for example. In other words, if you declare the global variable as a pointer to **CdbDBEngine**, then construct the class in your initialization function.

# Other dbDAO DLL Versions

Other versions of the dbDAO DLL can be built that vary with respect to the following capabilities:

- Use of ANSI or Unicode strings
- Built-in debugging functionality
- Use of shared or static MFC DLLs

The makefile that is installed with the DAO SDK (DBDAO.MAK) provides you with two pre-built dbDAO DLLs and subprojects to build them, plus six others. The two pre-built DLLs are:

- RELEASE\DBDAO3.DLL (dbDAO – Win32 Release)

  This is the ANSI version of the dbDAO classes. It dynamically links with the MFC DLL, making DBDAO3.DLL smaller and allowing it to share the MFC DLLs on a user's system with other applications that also use MFC 4.0. Developers writing applications with this DLL must make sure their setup program distributes the MFC DLLs. The DAO SDK Setup program installs this file into your system directory.

- RELEASEU\DBDAO3U.DLL (dbDAO – Win32 Release Unicode)

  This is the Unicode version of the dbDAO classes. It is otherwise identical to DBDAO3.DLL. The DAO SDK Setup program installs this file into your system directory.

The other six subprojects defined in the dbDAO makefile are:

- DEBUG\DBDAO3D.DLL (dbDAO – Win32 Debug)

  This is the debug ANSI version of DBDAO3.DLL. It is intended for developers who have to debug into the dbDAO source code. Developers should not ship this version, as it is slower and has debug functionality that users will not want.

- DEBUGU\DBDAO3UD.DLL (dbDAO – Win32 Debug Unicode)

  This is the debug Unicode version of DBDAO3U.DLL. It is intended for developers who have to debug into the dbDAO source code. Developers should not ship this version, as it is slower and has debug functionality that users will not want.

- RELEASES\DBDAO3S.DLL (dbDAO – Win32 Release Static MFC)

  This file is for ANSI applications that are statically linked to the MFC library. It has the MFC class library built into it.

- RELEASEUS\DBDAO3US.DLL (dbDAO–Win32 Release Unicode Static MFC)

   This file is for Unicode applications that are statically linked to the MFC library. It has the MFC library built into it.

- DEBUGS\DBDAO3DS.DLL (dbDAO–Win32 Debug Static MFC)

   This is the debug version for ANSI applications that are statically linked to the MFC library. Developers should not ship this version, as it is slower and has debug functionality that users will not want.

- DEBUGUS\DBDAO3UDS.DLL (dbDAO–Win32 Debug Unicode Static MFC)

   This is the debug version for Unicode applications that are statically linked to the MFC library. Developers should not ship this version, as it is slower and has debug functionality that users will not want.

CHAPTER 12

# ODBC Desktop Database Drivers

This chapter discusses the Microsoft Open Database Connectivity (ODBC) Desktop Database Drivers, which use the Microsoft Jet database engine to provide ODBC-enabled applications with access to six different database formats. This chapter discusses the architecture of the drivers, Microsoft Jet features that the drivers expose, and implementation details. Enhancements that improve driver performance are also discussed.

This chapter assumes you're familiar with the ODBC Application Programming Interface (API). For information about ODBC, refer to the *Microsoft ODBC 2.0 Programmer's Reference and SDK Guide* published by Microsoft Press.

**Contents**

# Introduction

ODBC is an API that uses SQL as the database access language. A wide variety of database management systems (DBMSs) can be accessed with the same ODBC source code that is directly incorporated into an application's source code. With the Microsoft ODBC Desktop Database Drivers, a user of an ODBC-enabled application can open, query, and update a desktop database through the ODBC interface.

ODBC architecture consists of a Driver Manager and a set of ODBC drivers. *ODBC drivers* are database-specific modules that accept function calls from the Driver Manager and translate them into function calls that can operate directly upon databases or database files. The use of these drivers isolates applications from database-specific calls, much the same way printer drivers enable an application to communicate with a variety of printers. Drivers are loaded at run time, so that a user only has to add a new driver to access a new DBMS.

Access to Lotus 1-2-3 is enabled by the Jet Lotus installable ISAM driver. For more information, see Chapter 8, "Accessing External Data."

The Microsoft ODBC Desktop Database Drivers are a Microsoft Jet–based set of ODBC drivers. Whereas Microsoft ODBC Desktop Database Drivers 2.0 included both 16- and 32-bit drivers, version 3.0 includes only 32-bit drivers that work on Microsoft Windows 95 or later, or Microsoft Windows NT 3.51 or later. These drivers provide access to the following types of data sources:

- Microsoft Access
- dBASE
- Microsoft Excel
- Microsoft FoxPro
- Paradox
- Text

The Desktop Database Drivers were created to provide access to the desktop data sources listed (which are among the most widely used in the industry), to satisfy the need of Microsoft applications for this data, and to provide ODBC drivers whose architecture is compatible with Microsoft products. Using the Microsoft Jet database engine to access data has helped the Desktop Database Drivers achieve both of these goals. Because a primary design goal of the drivers has been to expose as much Microsoft Jet functionality as possible in an ODBC context, the drivers provide users with a powerful extension of the Microsoft Jet engine.

# History

The following sections briefly describe the versions of the Desktop Database Drivers.

## Version 1.0

ODBC Desktop Database Drivers 1.0 was released in August of 1993. These drivers used the SIMBA query processor produced by PageAhead Software. SIMBA received ODBC calls and SQL statements, processed them into Microsoft Jet installable ISAM calls, then called the Jet ISAM dispatch layer to load and call the appropriate installable ISAM driver.

## Version 2.0

ODBC Desktop Database Drivers 2.0 was released in December of 1994. These drivers were released for use with ODBC 2.0, which significantly expanded ODBC functionality. The major change in version 2.0 was that the SIMBA query processor was replaced by the Microsoft Jet database engine. There were many advantages to this:

- With the Microsoft Jet database engine, the Desktop Database Drivers are much more tightly integrated with the Microsoft Jet installable ISAM drivers and Microsoft Access technology.

- The Microsoft Jet cursor model offers significant improvements over the SIMBA model, which used the ODBC Cursor Library to provide scrollable cursors. Microsoft Jet provides native support for scrollable cursors.

- Microsoft Jet provides native support for outer joins, updatable and heterogeneous joins, and transactions.

- The Microsoft Jet query optimizer, with enhancements such as Rushmore technology, dramatically increases driver performance.

- Microsoft Jet provides 32-bit versions of the drivers for Microsoft Windows NT.

## Version 3.0

ODBC Desktop Database Drivers 3.0 was released in October of 1995. The primary motivation for this release was support for Microsoft Windows 95 and Microsoft Windows NT 3.51. Only 32-bit drivers are included in this release; the 16-bit drivers supporting Microsoft Windows 3.1 were removed.

# Architecture

The Desktop Database Drivers are two-tier drivers. In a two-tier configuration, the driver does not perform the process of parsing, validating, optimizing, and executing the query. Instead, Microsoft Jet performs these tasks. It processes ODBC API calls and acts as an SQL engine. Microsoft Jet has become an integral, inseparable part of the drivers: It is shipped with the drivers and resides with the drivers, even if no other application on the machine uses it.

The Desktop Database Drivers consist of six different drivers—or, more precisely, one driver file (ODBCJT32.DLL) that is used in six different ways. The DRIVERID flag in the registry entry for a data source determines which driver in ODBCJT32.DLL is being used. This flag is passed in the connection string included in a call to **SQLDriverConnect**. By default, the flag is the ID of the Microsoft Access driver. When this is the case, data and function translation code for Microsoft Access is used, and the data storage inherent in the Microsoft Jet engine is used. When the flag is changed to another driver, data and function code for the selected driver is used, and data is stored using the applicable installable ISAM format.

The DRIVERID flag is changed at setup time by the driver setup file. All drivers except the Microsoft Access driver have an associated setup DLL. When the Setup button in the ODBC Administrator is clicked for a data source, the ODBC installer DLL (ODBCINST.DLL) loads the setup DLL. The setup DLL exports the ODBC installer function **SQLConfigDataSource**. If a window handle is passed to **SQLConfigDataSource**, this function displays a setup window and changes the DRIVERID flag according to the driver selected from the user interface.

When creating a file programmatically, a NULL window handle is passed to **SQLConfigDataSource**, and the function creates a data source dynamically, changing the DRIVERID flag according to the *lpszDriver* argument in the function call. For more information, see the "Creating .MDB Files Programmatically" section later in this chapter.

ODBCJT32.DLL implements ODBC functions on top of the Microsoft Jet API. There is no direct mapping between ODBC and Microsoft Jet functions, however. Many factors, such as the cursor models and SQL mapping, prevent a direct correlation of the functions.

The ODBC driver resides between the Microsoft Jet engine and the ODBC Driver Manager. Some ODBC functions called by an application are handled by the Driver Manager and not passed to the driver. For these functions, Microsoft Jet never sees the function call: It does not have a direct connection to the Driver Manager.

The following figure illustrates the Desktop Database Drivers architecture.

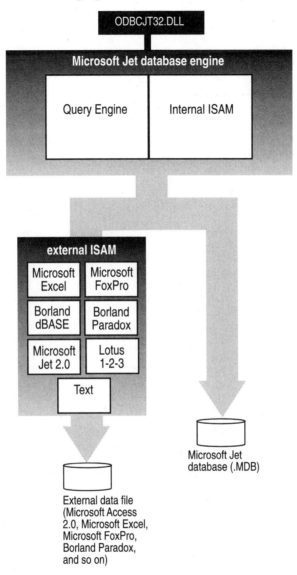

**Figure 12.1   Desktop Database Driver architecture**

# Files

## Driver Files

The following driver files are used by each Desktop Database Driver.

| File | Description |
|------|-------------|
| ODBCJI32.DLL | Separate library containing localized strings for the Desktop Database Drivers. |
| ODBCJT32.DLL | The Desktop Database Drivers file. For more information, see the "Architecture" section earlier in this chapter. |
| ODBCTL32.DLL | File containing generic conversion functions for parsing SQL strings passed in ODBC escape sequences. For more information, see the "Data Conversion" section later in this chapter. |

## Microsoft Jet Files

For more information on how the installable ISAM drivers work, see Chapter 8, "Accessing External Data."

The following Microsoft Jet files, discussed in Chapter 1, "An Overview of Microsoft Jet," are used by each Desktop Database Driver.

| File | Description |
|------|-------------|
| MSJINT32.DLL | Contains all localized Microsoft Jet strings. |
| MSJT3032.DLL | Contains the main engine functionality. |
| MSJTER32.DLL | Contains Microsoft Jet error service. |
| VBAJET32.DLL | Initializes the VBA expression service for Microsoft Jet. |
| VBAR2232.DLL | A run-time version of the VBA expression services. |
| VEN2232.OLB | International resources and localized strings for the VBA components (English language version). |

### Installable ISAM Driver Files

Each of the Desktop Database Drivers has its own IISAM driver, except for the Microsoft Access 3.0 driver. This is because the ISAM for the native Microsoft Access format is built directly into Microsoft Jet. (Note that the MSRD2X32.DLL IISAM is required for access to Microsoft Access 1.*x* and 2.*x* data.) All other database formats require an IISAM that provides data access between Microsoft Jet and the other DBMS.

IISAM and setup files for each of the Desktop Database Drivers are listed in the following table.

| Driver | IISAM file | Setup file |
| --- | --- | --- |
| Microsoft Access | MSRD2X32.DLL | None |
| dBASE | MSXB3032.DLL | ODDBSE32.DLL |
| Microsoft Excel | MSXL3032.DLL | ODEXL32.DLL |
| Microsoft FoxPro | MSXB3032.DLL | ODFOX32.DLL |
| Paradox | MSPX3032.DLL | ODPDX32.DLL |
| Text | MSTX3032.DLL | ODTEXT32.DLL |

MSRD2X32.DLL provides backward compatibility for Microsoft Access 1.*x* and 2.*x* files. No IISAM is needed for Microsoft Access for Windows 95 or later, because the IISAM for that data is part of the stand-alone Microsoft Jet engine.

The same IISAM files are used for the dBASE and Microsoft FoxPro drivers, but the setup files are different. The Microsoft FoxPro driver uses a generic dBASE engine that ensures compatibility with dBASE data sources.

# ODBC Files

The Desktop Database Drivers include the ODBC Core components.

| File | Description |
| --- | --- |
| ODBC32.DLL | ODBC Driver Manager |
| ODBCAD32.EXE | ODBC Administrator |
| ODBCCP32.DLL<br>ODBCCP32.CPL | ODBC Administrator Control Panel |
| ODBCCR32.DLL | ODBC Cursor Library. Because the Desktop Drivers use the native scrollable cursors provided by Microsoft Jet, the Cursor Library is usually not needed. An application can, however, force use of the Cursor Library. |
| ODBCINT.DLL | ODBC Core localized strings |
| ODBC16GT.DLL<br>ODBC32GT.DLL | Thunking files for the Driver Manager |

# Implementation Details

The following sections describe how certain ODBC and SQL features are implemented by the Desktop Database Drivers.

# Conformance Levels

## ODBC API Conformance Level

The Desktop Database Drivers are Level 1 conformant, and support the following Level 2 ODBC functions:

- SQLDrivers
- SQLExtendedFetch
- SQLMoreResults
- SQLNativeSQL
- SQLNumParams
- SQLProcedureColumns
- SQLSetPos

## SQL Conformance Level

The Desktop Database Drivers conform to the Minimum SQL Grammar level, with the following Core and Extended enhancements. For more information on the SQL support provided by the Desktop Database Drivers, see the "SQL Support" section later in this chapter.

- Approximate numeric literals (Core)
- ALTER TABLE statement (Core)
- Binary literals (Extended)
- BETWEEN predicate (Core)
- Correlation names (Core)
- EXISTS predicate (Core)
- IN (*valuelist*) (Core)
- Procedure Invocation (Extended)
- SELECT statement including GROUP BY, HAVING, and UNION clauses (Extended)
- Subqueries (SUBSELECTs) (Core)

### Integrity Enhancement Facility Conformance

The Desktop Database Drivers support the same optional Integrity Enhancement Facility (IEF) features (as contained in the X/Open and SAG SQL CAE specification) that Microsoft Jet exposes. The Desktop Database Drivers do not support the IEF syntax described in Appendix C of the *Microsoft ODBC 2.0 Programmer's Reference and SDK Guide*. This is why a call to **SQLGetInfo** with an *fInfoType* of SQL_ODBC_SQL_OPT_IEF returns an "N," indicating that the drivers do not support IEF. However, the Microsoft Access driver supports the IEF features supported by Microsoft Jet, using Jet syntax. For instance, the Microsoft Access driver supports the same syntax for creating a primary key that Microsoft Jet does.

## Scrollable Cursor Support

Desktop Database Drivers 1.0 supports scrollable cursors through the use of the ODBC Cursor Library. The Cursor Library implements the ODBC function **SQLExtendedFetch** by repeatedly calling **SQLFetch** to populate the Cursor Library cache one row at a time. Scrolling is emulated when the application calls **SQLExtendedFetch** to reposition the cursor on data in the cache. Data is refetched from the driver only when necessary. Because the Cursor Library supports only static cursors, it cannot detect changes in the underlying data source.

With version 2.0 and later drivers, the Cursor Library is no longer necessary. The Desktop Drivers directly support **SQLExtendedFetch** and **SQLSetPos** through the use of native Microsoft Jet cursors. Native Microsoft Jet cursors are much more efficient than the Cursor Library. While the Cursor Library can still be used, its use is discouraged. The Cursor Library incurs a lot of overhead in parsing the SELECT statement it uses to generate the data in its cache, performing a catalog lookup to update data, and creating a searched UPDATE statement with a WHERE clause to update the base table based on data in the temporary file. Microsoft Jet cursors perform direct updates, operating on the base table, that are much faster. For more information, see the "Insert, Delete, and Update Performance" section later in this chapter.

### Supported Cursor Types

The Desktop Database Drivers support forward-only, static, and keyset-driven cursors. Updates are supported on keyset-driven cursors only. Mixed and dynamic cursors are not supported; the driver creates a keyset-driven cursor if a dynamic cursor is requested.

## Cursor Positioning and Positioned Operations

In ODBC, updates and deletes that require cursor positioning can normally be performed by executing a positioned UPDATE or DELETE SQL statement (with the WHERE CURRENT OF clause), or by calling the **SQLSetPos** function with an *fOption* of SQL_POS_UPDATE or SQL_POS_DELETE. The Desktop Database Drivers do not support positioned UPDATE or DELETE SQL statements. They do, however, support the **SQLSetPos** function.

In addition to SQL_POS_UPDATE and SQL_POS_DELETE, **SQLSetPos** can also be called with the SQL_POS_ADD, SQL_POS_POSITION, and SQL_POS_REFRESH *fOptions*. The Microsoft Excel and Text drivers support only SQL_POS_POSITION and SQL_POS_REFRESH, because the files are read-only.

## Cursor Concurrency and Locking

For more information on page-level locking, see Chapter 10, "Managing Security."

When the **SQLSetPos** function is called to add, update, or delete a row, the Desktop Database Drivers can make sure that a row will stay in the same locked or unlocked state as it was before **SQLSetPos** was called. To do this, **SQLSetPos** is called with an *fLock* option of SQL_LOCK_NO_CHANGE. This uses the locking enforced by Microsoft Jet. To guarantee locking by Microsoft Jet, an application should create a keyset-driven cursor and specify SQL_CONCUR_LOCK for the SQL_CONCURRENCY *fOption* in **SQLSetStmtOption**.

Exclusive or explicit row-level locking is not supported by Microsoft Jet. Therefore, the Desktop Database Drivers cannot lock the row specifically, using the SQL_LOCK_EXCLUSIVE *fLock* argument in **SQLSetPos**, then later unlock the row using the SQL_LOCK_UNLOCK argument. If a transaction is used (auto-commit mode off), setting the cursor-concurrency statement option to SQL_CONCUR_LOCK guarantees that the page-level locking supported by Microsoft Jet will be enforced for the duration of the transaction.

For static or forward-only cursors, the concurrency can be set to either read-only (a SQL_CONCURRENCY of SQL_CONCUR_READ_ONLY), or optimistic concurrency in which row versions are compared (SQL_CONCUR_ROWVER). Optimistic concurrency in which row values are compared (SQL_CONCUR_VALUES) is not supported.

# Support for Transactions

Only the Microsoft Access driver supports the use of transactions. The default transaction mechanism is auto-commit, in which each statement that can be contained in a transaction is, in effect, in its own transaction. A transaction is implicitly started when such an SQL statement is executed; upon completion of the statement, it's committed automatically.

When a transaction is explicitly started (by calling **SQLSetConnectOption** with the SQL_AUTOCOMMIT *fOption* set to SQL_AUTOCOMMIT_OFF), the **SQLTransact** function is called to commit or roll back the transaction. The Microsoft Access driver supports multiple active statement handles on a single connection, so when **SQLTransact** is called, all statements on the connection are either committed or rolled back.

All open cursors on all *hstmts* associated with the *hdbc* are closed when the transaction is committed or rolled back. **SQLTransact** leaves any *hstmt* present in a prepared state, if the statement was prepared, or an allocated state, if it was executed directly. Closing all cursors can have unforeseen consequences. For example, say an application has two active statements within an explicit transaction: one statement in which an UPDATE statement was executed, and another statement in which a SELECT statement was executed and then **SQLExtendedFetch** called to return a rowset. If **SQLTransact** is called to commit the update, all the operations performed by the UPDATE statement on the first statement handle are committed (as expected), but in addition, the rowset generated by **SQLExtendedFetch** is deleted, because the cursor on the second statement handle is closed.

The Microsoft Access driver supports multiple active transactions. Because transactions are associated with a connection in ODBC, each transaction must be on a different connection (*hdbc*). Because nested transactions, which are supported natively by the Microsoft Jet engine, are not supported in ODBC, they are not available through the Desktop Database Drivers.

The driver supports only the read-committed transaction isolation level. Transactions can contain DDL statements and DML statements in any order.

# Error Handling

For a list of Microsoft Jet error codes, see Appendix D, "Error Reference."

The Desktop Database Drivers can return both ODBC and Microsoft Jet errors. A call to **SQLError** returns an ODBC SQLSTATE value, a Microsoft Jet error code (if applicable), and an error message. The error message can include an ODBC component identifier, a data-source identifier from Microsoft Jet, a text message from ODBC, and data-source-supplied text from Microsoft Jet.

The native Microsoft Jet error codes can be an important indicator of the nature of a problem. This is especially true when SQLSTATE S1000 (General error) is returned, because the ODBC error text for this SQLSTATE does not convey any information about the problem. An application must rely on the Microsoft Jet error code in this case, and possibly the error message. Some Microsoft Jet error codes are returned for more than one type of error, in which case the error message must be used to determine the error that occurred.

The Desktop Drivers handle most ODBC errors, but the Driver Manager handles state transition errors, invalid arguments, connection option errors, and errors in calls to the driver. The component that returns an error is indicated by the ODBC component identifier in the error message text.

# SQL Support

## Desktop Driver ODBC SQL vs. Microsoft Jet SQL

The ODBC SQL supported by the Desktop Database Drivers is very nearly the same as the SQL supported by Microsoft Jet, with only two major differences:

- Strings passed by an application in ODBC escape syntax, such as date literals, procedure calls, scalar functions, and outer join calls, are translated into strings that are compatible with Microsoft Jet. This translation is performed by ODBCTL32.DLL. When the Microsoft Access driver is used, only ANSI string constants (with single quotation marks) are supported.

- The pattern-matching characters are different for the Desktop Drivers and Microsoft Jet. The search character for a single character is an underscore in ODBC and a question mark in Microsoft Jet; the search character for a sequence of zero or more characters is a percent sign in ODBC and an asterisk in Microsoft Jet. Applications should use the ODBC characters. The translations are made by ODBCJT32.DLL. Microsoft Jet also translates wildcards embedded in dynamic parameter values in parameterized queries.

## ANSI SQL-89 Compliance

Microsoft Jet and the Desktop Drivers do not support all ANSI SQL-89 features, but they do support some features that are not supported by ANSI. The following are the major differences between the two:

- Microsoft Jet SQL permits expressions in GROUP BY and ORDER BY lists, while ANSI SQL allows only columns.

- Microsoft Jet SQL supports more powerful expressions than those specified by ANSI-89.

- Different wildcard characters are used with the LIKE predicate. Note that ODBC SQL supports the ANSI characters, while Microsoft Jet SQL does not.

- Different rules apply to the BETWEEN predicate.

- Microsoft Jet SQL and ANSI SQL support different keywords.

The following ANSI SQL features are not supported by Microsoft Jet SQL:

- Security statements, such as GRANT and LOCK

- DISTINCT aggregate function references

- The LIMIT TO *nn* ROWS clause cannot be used to limit a query's scope in ANSI SQL. Only the WHERE clause can be used to limit the number of rows returned by a query.

The following Microsoft Jet SQL features are enhancements not specified by ANSI SQL-89:

- The TRANSFORM statement providing support for crosstab queries
- Additional aggregate functions (**StDev** and **VarP**)
- The PARAMETERS declaration for defining parameter queries

# SQL Implementation Specifics

This section describes how the Desktop Database Drivers implement SQL statements and clauses through Microsoft Jet, particularly when they are not ANSI compliant or there are limitations to their use.

## Aggregate Functions

An aggregate function and a non-aggregate column reference cannot both be used in the clauses of a single SQL statement.

## BETWEEN Predicate

ODBC SQL supports the same BETWEEN predicate syntax as ANSI, as follows:

*expression1* **BETWEEN** *expression2* **AND** *expression3*

The semantics of this syntax are different for the Desktop Database Drivers and Microsoft Jet SQL. When the Desktop Drivers are used, this statement returns TRUE only if *expression1* is greater than or equal to *expression2*, and *expression1* is less than or equal to *expression3*. This is different from Microsoft Jet SQL, in which *expression2* can be greater than *expression3*, so that the statement would return TRUE only if *expression1* is greater than or equal to *expression3*, and *expression1* is less than or equal to *expression2*.

## Data Conversion

Each driver performs conversion of the C data types used by ODBC applications to the SQL data types used in Microsoft Jet, and vice versa. This conversion is performed in two steps: First, the C data types are converted to an SQL data type that is common to all drivers, and then the common SQL data types are converted to the driver-specific SQL data type used by Microsoft Jet (or vice versa). The first process is performed by a generic conversion function in ODBCTL32.DLL; all drivers use the same function. The second process is performed separately by each driver's code within ODBCJT32.DLL.

ODBCTL32.DLL also contains a generic conversion function for parsing SQL strings that are passed in ODBC escape sequences, such as date literals, procedure calls, scalar functions, and outer join calls. Like data conversion, this is a two-step process, in which the generic conversion process performs parsing that is common to all drivers, and each driver performs its own additional parsing as required.

### Date/Time Values

For maximum interoperability, applications should pass date literals using the ODBC escape-clause syntax: {d *'value'*}, where *value* is of the form "*yyyy-mm-dd.*"

Neither the SQL_DATE nor the SQL_TIMESTAMP data type can be converted to another data type (or itself) by the **CONVERT** function in escape-clause syntax.

The Desktop Database Drivers support adding or subtracting an integer from an SQL_DATE column. The integer specifies the number of days to add or subtract. Date arithmetic is not supported for adding (or subtracting) an SQL_DATE data type to (or from) another SQL_DATE data type.

### DISTINCT Predicate

The DISTINCT predicate is not supported for binary data, Long Text fields in Microsoft Access, or Memo fields in dBASE or Microsoft FoxPro. The DISTINCT predicate is not supported in the set functions (AVG, MAX, MIN, and SUM).

### Identifier Quote Character

The identifier quote character allows strings or characters that would normally be invalid to be used in identifiers. For the Desktop Database Drivers, a valid identifier is a string of no more than 64 characters. The first character of a valid identifier cannot be a space. Valid identifiers cannot include control characters or special characters (`|#*?[].!$\`), or the reserved words listed in Appendix C of the *Microsoft ODBC 2.0 Programmer's Reference and SDK Guide.* If an identifier (column or table name) violates any of these rules, the identifier can be used only if it's enclosed in the identifier quote character. For the Desktop Drivers, this character is a back quote (`). Note that for many other SQL processors, the identifier quote character is a forward quote character.

### LIKE Predicate

The Desktop Database Drivers support the LIKE predicate, but use of an escape clause in a LIKE predicate is not supported. A LIKE predicate used in a procedure is supported only with literals. If data in a Memo column is longer than 255 characters, the LIKE comparison will be based only on the first 255 characters.

### Multiple SQL Statements

Microsoft Jet can perform neither ad-hoc nor stored queries consisting of multiple SQL statements. Only single SQL statements are supported.

## NULL/NOT NULL

The Desktop Database Drivers do not support the NOT NULL constraint in a CREATE TABLE statement. A Microsoft Access application can create a column that does not allow NULLs by creating an index on a column with the Disallow Null option. However, an application using the Desktop Database Drivers is unable to detect whether a column is nullable or not, because **SQLColumns** returns SQL_NULLABLE in the NULLABLE column of its result set for all columns (even if NULLs are disallowed by virtue of an index), or for a table that has a column for which the **Required** property has been set to **Yes**.

## ORDER BY Clause

The columns in the ORDER BY clause do not have to be in the SELECT list. Expressions can be used in the ORDER BY clause. If a SELECT statement contains a GROUP BY clause and an ORDER BY clause, the ORDER BY clause can contain only a column in the result set or an expression that also appears in the GROUP BY clause.

## OUTER JOIN Clauses

The syntax of join statements in Microsoft Jet is shown in Appendix B, "SQL Reference."

The Desktop Database Drivers support left and right outer joins, as well as inner joins. The right table in a left outer join, or the left table in a right outer join, can be used in an inner join. Full and nested outer joins are not supported.

A SELECT statement can contain a list of OUTER JOIN clauses. The column names in the ON clause of the outer join do not have to be in the same order as their respective table names in the OUTER JOIN clause. The comparison operator in the ON clause can be any of the ODBC comparison operators.

An outer join is performed by executing an ODBC OUTER JOIN statement in the ODBC escape clause, or by using Microsoft Jet syntax. The ODBC OUTER JOIN syntax is as follows:

{**oj** *tablename1* [**LEFT** or **RIGHT**] **OUTER JOIN** *tablename2* **ON** *tablename1.column=tablename2.column*}

## Procedure Invocation

You can invoke procedures using the Microsoft Access driver by calling the **SQLExecDirect** or **SQLPrepare** function with the following escape-clause syntax:

{**CALL** *procedure-name* [(*parameter*[,*parameter*]...)]}

where *procedure-name* specifies the name of a procedure stored on the data source and *parameter* specifies a procedure parameter. This escape clause acts as an indicator to the driver that the statement within it, which is ODBC standard syntax, must be translated by the driver to DBMS-specific syntax.

A parameterized query can be used with the same syntax, by passing markers ("?") for parameters in the CALL statement and using **SQLBindParameter** to bind the parameter markers. Expressions and constants are not supported as parameters to a called procedure. An input parameter must be a parameter marker; only bound parameters are supported. If a procedure name includes a dash, it must be delimited by the identifier quote character, a back quote (`).

## Scalar Functions

This section describes the string functions, numeric functions, time and date functions, and data type conversion functions supported by the Desktop Database Drivers. System scalar functions are not supported. The Desktop Drivers do not support user-defined functions.

For more information on the scalar functions that Microsoft Jet supports, see Microsoft Access online Help.

The Desktop Drivers support the following string functions:

| | |
|---|---|
| ASCII | LTRIM |
| CHAR | RIGHT |
| CONCAT | RTRIM |
| LCASE | SPACE |
| LEFT | SUBSTRING |
| LENGTH | UCASE |
| LOCATE | |

The Desktop Drivers support the following numeric functions:

| | |
|---|---|
| ABS | MOD |
| ATAN | POWER |
| CEILING | RAND |
| COS | SIGN |
| EXP | SIN |
| FLOOR | SQRT |
| LOG | TAN |

The Desktop Drivers support the following time and date functions:

| | |
|---|---|
| DAYOFMONTH | MINUTE |
| DAYOFWEEK | SECOND |
| DAYOFYEAR | WEEK |
| HOUR | YEAR |

The Microsoft Access, Microsoft Excel, and Text drivers support the following additional time and date functions:

| | |
|---|---|
| CURDATE | NOW |
| CURTIME | |

Explicit data-type conversions, using the **CONVERT** function in an ODBC escape sequence, can be performed on the following data types:

| | |
|---|---|
| SQL_BINARY | SQL_NUMERIC |
| SQL_CHAR | SQL_REAL |
| SQL_DATE | SQL_SMALLINT |
| SQL_DOUBLE | SQL_TIME |
| SQL_FLOAT | SQL_TIMESTAMP |
| SQL_INTEGER | SQL_TINYINT |
| SQL_LONGVARBINARY | SQL_VARBINARY |
| SQL_LONGVARCHAR | SQL_VARCHAR |

Explicit data-type conversions cannot be performed on the following data types:

SQL_BIGINT
SQL_BIT
SQL_DECIMAL

### Search Conditions

The maximum number of columns in a WHERE clause is 40. The maximum number of search conditions in a HAVING clause is 40.

# Microsoft Jet Feature Support

The following paragraphs describe Microsoft Jet features that are exposed through the Desktop Database Drivers.

# Heterogeneous Joins and Linked Tables Support

A table in a different data source can be linked to a Microsoft Access database. The table cannot be linked programmatically through the Microsoft Access Desktop Database Driver, however. It must be linked from within Microsoft Access or through DAO.

After a table has been linked, its data can be accessed through the Microsoft Access driver. The linked table can be used in a join with other tables, including other linked tables, in the Microsoft Access database. So it's possible, for example, to join a table in a Microsoft Access database with another table in a Microsoft FoxPro database. Such a join between tables created in different DBMSs is called a heterogeneous join. It's also possible to create a heterogeneous join in a stored query using the Microsoft Access user interface. Such a stored query can be accessed as a view in a SELECT statement. Microsoft Jet provides transparent access to the linked database, regardless of the data's location or format. As a result, a linked table, or a heterogeneous join, looks just like any other Microsoft Access table.

# Updatable Query Support

For more information
on queries, see
Chapter 4, "Queries."

Queries can be called as views using a FROM clause in a SELECT statement. The restrictions on updating views depend on the query on which the view is based. If a query is updatable by using **SQLSetPos**, the view that is based on the query is also updatable. Updatability is not affected by how the SQL query is executed. For example, it does not matter whether the SQL query is executed by an SQL string included in a call to the **SQLExecDirect** function, or by executing a stored query.

Queries based on a single table and queries based on tables with a one-to-one relationship are updatable. Queries based on tables with a one-to-many relationship are usually updatable. The following queries are not updatable:

- Aggregation queries (for example, SUM or COUNT)
- UNION queries
- **UniqueValues** properties set to YES
- Queries that include an attached ODBC table with no unique index or a Paradox table without a primary key
- Queries (or underlying tables) for which update or delete permission isn't granted
- Queries that include more than one table or query, where the tables or queries are not joined by a join line in Design view
- Queries that include a calculated field
- Queries that include a read-only field
- Queries that include a field in a record that has been deleted or locked by another user

# Updatable Join Support

The Desktop Database Drivers support updatable joins, in which updates made to the table created by the join are reflected in the base table, and updates made to the base table are also reflected in the table created by the join. However, if a cursor is opened on a query that is based on a one-to-many relationship, you may not be able to update its underlying tables by using **SQLSetPos**. The following types of fields may not be modifiable:

- New records, if the "many" side join field does not appear in the SELECT list. The addition of new records can be enabled by adding the join field from the "many" side to your query.
- The join field from the "many" side, after data on the "one" side has been updated. If the record is saved, changes can be made to the "many" side join field.
- A blank field in the many-only table of an OUTER JOIN if the joined "one" side is also empty.

- A blank field on the "one" side of an OUTER JOIN. This can be done only on the many-only table.

- New records, if the entire unique key of an attached ODBC table is not output. Select all primary key fields of the tables to allow inserts.

# Creating .MDB Files Programmatically

The **SQLConfigDataSource** function is used to add, modify, or delete a data source dynamically. If **SQLConfigDataSource** is called with a window handle, data source setup is performed interactively through the Setup dialog box. If the function is called with a NULL window handle, the data source is set up using keywords that are contained in the *lpszAttributes* argument.

**SQLConfigDataSource** takes as arguments the type of request (add, configure, or remove), the name of the driver, and a list of keyword-value pairs. The following keyword-value pairs are used to add, modify, or delete a file.

| Keyword | Meaning |
| --- | --- |
| DBQ | The name of the database file |
| DEFAULTDIR | The path to the database file for Microsoft Access, or the directory for the other drivers |
| DRIVER | The path specification for the driver |
| DRIVERID | An integer ID for the driver |
| JETINIPATH | The path to the Microsoft Jet initialization file |
| PWD | A password |
| SYSTEMDB | The path to the system database file |
| UID | The user ID name used for logging on |

For a complete specification of the keywords, see Microsoft ODBC Desktop Database Drivers online Help (ODBCJET.HLP).

The following operations can be performed on a Microsoft Access database file by including the appropriate keyword in the call to **SQLConfigDataSource**.

| Keyword | Meaning |
| --- | --- |
| COMPACT_DB | Compacts data. See the "Database Compaction" section later in this chapter. |
| CREATE_DB | Creates a Microsoft Access database file. |
| REPAIR_DB | Repairs a file damaged during commit. See the "Database Repair" section later in this chapter. |
| EXCLUSIVE | Opens the database so it can be accessed by only one user at a time (EXCLUSIVE=TRUE), or by more than one user at a time (EXCLUSIVE=FALSE). |

All of the previously listed values are used for Microsoft Jet files, but this is not a complete list of the keywords that can be used in a call to **SQLConfigDataSource**. Other keywords can be used for other drivers.

# Database Compaction

To programmatically perform data compaction on a database file, include "COMPACT_DB=*source db*; *dest db*; *sort order*" in the list of attributes (*lpszAttributes*) of the **SQLConfigDataSource** function. In this function, *source db* is the full path to the Microsoft Access database to be compacted and *dest db* is the full path for the compacted Microsoft Access database. When compacting a password-protected file, a password and user ID must be entered in the list of attributes for **SQLConfigDataSource**.

This operation runs the standard Microsoft Access compaction process on the database. The same process can be performed through the Setup dialog box for a Microsoft Access data source, which is available from the 32-bit ODBC Control Panel.

# Database Repair

When the Microsoft Access driver is used, if a client failure occurs during the commit process (after **SQLTransact** has been issued, but before the function returns), the affected database may need to be repaired. Repair can be performed either through the Setup dialog box for a Microsoft Access data source, or programmatically by using the **SQLConfigDataSource** function. When repairing a password-protected file, a password and a user ID must be entered in the Set Advanced Options dialog box displayed from the ODBC Setup dialog box (or in the list of attributes for **SQLConfigDataSource**, if repairing programmatically).

These operations run the standard Microsoft Jet repair process on the database. Data in Microsoft Access databases could be affected by this operation.

To repair the database programmatically, include "REPAIR_DB=*pathname*" in the list of attributes (*lpszAttributes*) of the **SQLConfigDataSource** function. In this function, *pathname* is the full path to the Microsoft Access database.

# Unsupported Microsoft Jet Features

The Desktop Database Drivers expose as much Microsoft Jet functionality as possible, but they cannot expose some Microsoft Access features and Jet functionality. As a desktop database, Microsoft Access has many features, particularly user-interface features, that cannot be exposed through the ODBC interface. The following are not supported:

- Microsoft Access forms and reports
- Access Basic or DAO functions. The drivers have no way to call these functions. Queries cannot contain Access Basic functions.
- Microsoft Access macros

For more information on ODBC grammar, see Appendix C of the *Microsoft ODBC 2.0 Programmer's Reference and SDK Guide.*

- Creation of referential integrity. The Desktop Database Drivers do not support the Integrity Enhancement Facility (IEF) syntax necessary for referential integrity.

- Creation of secure Microsoft Access databases with the GRANT statement. The Desktop Database Drivers can use the security if it's set up, but security cannot be set up through the drivers.

- Administration of replication.

# Performance Considerations

This section discusses ways to enhance the performance of the Desktop Database Drivers. It discusses both ODBC API issues and MFC Database programming considerations for improving the speed of an application that uses one of the Desktop Database Drivers.

The Desktop Database Drivers are feature-rich, high-performance ODBC drivers. They offer multiple ways to perform inserts, deletes, and updates. Carefully designing applications to use the optimal methods whenever possible will help maximize the performance of an ODBC application.

## Insert, Delete, and Update Performance

Several options are available for performing inserts, deletes, and updates. Each can be performed by executing an SQL statement or calling **SQLSetPos**. If they're using an SQL statement, they can be performed by calling **SQLExecDirect**, or by preparing the statement and calling **SQLExecute**. Multiple statements can be included in a transaction. This section describes the relative performance of these methods.

### Prepared Execution

Queries can be executed in one of two ways:

- Calling **SQLExecDirect** with the SQL statement
- Calling **SQLPrepare** to prepare the query, and then calling **SQLExecute** to execute the prepared query

**SQLExecDirect** is a better choice if the query will be executed only once. If the query will be executed multiple times, however, (or if a parameterized query will be run multiple times), preparing it with **SQLPrepare**, then executing it with **SQLExecute**, is considerably faster. Every time a query is executed with **SQLExecDirect**, Microsoft Jet parses the query, generates an execution plan, and then executes the query. When **SQLPrepare** is used, the query is parsed just once. Over the course of multiple queries, this can significantly enhance performance.

## SQLSetPos

Using the **SQLSetPos** function to perform an insert, delete, or update operation is much faster than doing the same operation using an SQL statement. This is because there is no need to look into the catalog. Because there is no SQL statement, there is nothing to parse.

Static updatable cursors can also be provided by the Cursor Library. The Cursor Library was required for scrollable cursor support with Desktop Database Drivers 1.0, but later drivers use the native scrollable cursors in Microsoft Jet. Using the Cursor Library to do a positioned update is much slower than using **SQLSetPos** with an *fOption* of SQL_UPDATE. The Cursor Library incurs a lot of overhead. The SELECT statement it uses to generate the data in its cache must be parsed, whereas Microsoft Jet stores parsed strings. To update the data, a catalog lookup has to be performed to open the table that is being updated, and the Cursor Library must create a searched UPDATE statement with a WHERE clause that may have to search through all the data in the temporary file. Even then, the appropriate data might not be found, because the buffered data represents a rowset produced by a fetch, which might not accurately represent the base table. Microsoft Jet cursors perform direct updates on the base table, which are much faster.

## Transactions

When executing multiple insert, delete, or update operations, performance can be enhanced by using transactions. This is performed by turning auto-commit mode off by calling **SQLSetConnectOption** on the connection handle (*hdbc*) with SQL_AUTOCOMMIT set to SQL_AUTOCOMMIT_OFF. When the driver uses auto-commit mode and SQL statements, it must make sure that each individual INSERT, DELETE, or UPDATE statement is flushed to the safe store (usually to disk). If the statements are grouped in a transaction, the driver can delay the writes to disk, then perform only one write during commit time. Because disk I/O takes a relatively long time, turning auto-commit mode off enhances performance.

## Query Performance

The relative performances of the different query methods discussed are shown in the following table. To make the comparison more concrete, 100 inserts were performed using each of these methods to insert into a Microsoft Access 2.0 table that had five columns of text data. Note that these are not exhaustive benchmarking results. They are provided to illustrate the relative merits of these methods. The methods are listed in order of increasing performance.

| Method | Time |
|---|---|
| 100 **SQLExecDirect** inserts in auto-commit mode | 5457 ms |
| 100 **SQLExecDirect** inserts in a single transaction | 4756 ms |
| 100 inserts performed by calling **SQLPrepare/SQLExecute** in auto-commit mode | 3515 ms |
| 100 inserts performed by calling **SQLPrepare/SQLExecute** in a single transaction | 2994 ms |
| 100 **SQLSetPos**/SQL_ADD inserts in auto-commit mode | 831 ms |
| 100 **SQLSetPos**/SQL_ADD inserts in a single transaction | 721 ms |

Adding data by calling **SQLSetPos** in a transaction results in 139 inserts per second. Executing an INSERT SQL statement by calling **SQLExecDirect** in auto-commit mode results in 18 inserts per second. Although the results specifically apply to inserts, the concepts apply equally well to deletes and updates.

# Using Stored Queries

The Microsoft Access Desktop Database Driver supports using stored queries in a Microsoft Access database. Stored queries cannot be created using the Microsoft Access driver; they must be created using Microsoft Access or Visual Basic. Stored queries can be used in the following ways using the Desktop Database Drivers:

- Stored queries can be treated as views, so that you can perform a SELECT statement on the query just as you would from a table. This method has the advantage of being easy-to-use and intuitive. This is not, however, the best method as far as performance is concerned, because the SELECT statement used to invoke the query incurs the overhead of syntax checking and parsing.

- Stored queries can be treated as stored procedures. The {CALL *query-name...*} syntax can then be used to call the stored query (see the "Procedure Invocation" section earlier in this chapter). This is faster than treating the stored query as a view because syntax checking for the SELECT statement is bypassed and the stored query is directly invoked. This method can also be used to execute parameterized queries, by using parameter markers. Parameter markers cannot be used when a stored query is treated as a view.

# Using Microsoft Foundation Classes

For more information, see the documentation for **SQLGetInfo** and the SQL_CURSOR_ COMMIT_ BEHAVIOR and SQL_CURSOR_ ROLLBACK_ BEHAVIOR parameters in the *Microsoft ODBC 2.0 Programmer's Reference and SDK Guide.*

The **CRecordset** C++ class provided with the Microsoft Foundation Classes prepares queries before execution using the **SQLPrepare** function. The **CRecordset::Requery** function can be used to re-execute the query for the **CRecordset** without requiring the ODBC driver to re-parse the SQL statement, because the statement has already been prepared.

By default, MFC library classes load the Cursor Library. The Cursor Library permits updatable snapshots. To get updatable recordsets, but not use the Cursor Library, the dynaset **CRecordset** can be used. This is specified by passing **CRecordset::dynaset** for the first argument of **CRecordset::Open**. With the 32-bit MFC library database classes, it's not enough to pass **CRecordset::dynaset** to **CRecordset::Open**. You must pass FALSE for the last argument of **CDatabase::Open**. This prevents the Cursor Library from loading. The code looks like this:

```
CDatabase db;
db.Open("DataSourceName",FALSE,FALSE,"ODBC;",FALSE);
CYourRecordset rs(&db);
rs.Open(CRecordset::dynaset);
```

By using dynasets, the DYNSET.EXE code, or 32-bit classes, the **SQLSetPos** functionality of the Microsoft Access Desktop Database Driver is used when performing updates, deletes, or inserts. As mentioned earlier, this greatly increases the speed of an application.

The Microsoft Access Desktop Database Driver does not support MFC transactions, but comes close. The MFCs require ODBC drivers to support **Recordset** cursor preservation across rollbacks and commits of transactions.

The Microsoft Access Desktop Database Driver does not guarantee this cursor preservation; however, transactions can be used by requerying after any transaction so that the cursor is restored to the first record in the **Recordset**. The m_bTransactions member variable of the **Database** object must also be forced to TRUE before using **BeginTrans**. The code could look like this:

```
class CTransactDatabase: public CDatabase
{
    public:
    void SetTransactions(){ m_bTransactions=TRUE;}
};
.
.
.
CTransactDatabase db;
db.Open("SomeDataSourceName",FALSE,FALSE,"ODBC;",FALSE);
db.SetTransactions();
db.BeginTrans();
CRecordSet rs(&db);
rs.Open(CRecordset::dynaset);
```

```
      .
      // Manipulate data.
      .

      db.CommitTrans(); // or db.Rollback()
      ::SQLFreeStmt(rs.m_hstmt, SQL_CLOSE);
      db.BeginTrans();
      rs.Requery();
      .
      // Manipulate data.
      .

      db.CommitTrans() // or db.Rollback()
      rs.Close();
      db.Close();
      .
```

CHAPTER 13

# Performance

Microsoft Jet provides a variety of administrative services designed keep your database running smoothly. This chapter explains the engine functionality in the areas of configuration and database compaction. It also covers performance enhancements in Microsoft Jet 3.0 and unsupported tuning functions.

## Contents

For information on copying the code examples from the companion CD-ROM to your hard disk drive, see "Using the Companion CD-ROM" in the Preface.

### Using CH13.MDB and CHAP13.VBP

If you copied the samples from the companion CD-ROM, you can find the code examples for Microsoft Access in C:\SAMPLES\CHAP13\ACCESS\CH13.MDB. The corresponding code examples for Visual Basic are in C:\SAMPLES\CHAP13\VB40\CHAP13.VBP.

To run any of the code examples in this chapter, open the .MDB file in Microsoft Access or open the .VBP file in Microsoft Visual Basic 4.0. You can use the examples to help you understand the concepts discussed in the chapter—or you can modify them and use them in your own applications.

# Configuration Using the Registry

For more information on the Registry, see Appendix C, "Registry Settings."

As you learned in Chapter 1, "An Overview of Microsoft Jet," a variety of settings control the engine's behavior. As of Microsoft Jet 3.0, these settings are stored in the Windows 95 or Windows NT Registry. The Registry is an operating system file that stores configuration information used by Windows and the applications it runs.

> ### Configuring Earlier Versions of Microsoft Jet
>
> Prior to version 3.0, Microsoft Jet used the Windows 3.1 convention of text initialization files called .INI files. Unlike other applications that often have their own .INI files, Microsoft Jet relied on its host application to make sure that the .INI file was created and maintained. For example, when used by Microsoft Access, Microsoft Jet would use the settings in the Microsoft Access .INI file (MSACCESS.INI or MSACC20.INI depending on the version). For Visual Basic 3.0, application developers were expected to manually create an .INI file for their applications.

You can use the Registry Editor program (REGEDIT.EXE under Microsoft Windows 95 and REGEDT32.EXE under Microsoft Windows NT) to view and change Registry settings.

---

**Note**  You should change Registry settings only if you have an advanced understanding of them. What appears to be a simple change may have unwanted effects in your application. Also, it's always a good idea to make a backup copy of your Registry contents before making modifications. You can do this with the **Export Registry File...** command in the Registry Editor program in Windows 95, or the **Unload Hive** command in Windows NT.

---

# The Microsoft Jet Registry

When Microsoft Jet is installed on your system, it's typically done through a host's installation program, such as the Microsoft Access Setup program. Microsoft Jet automatically adds default settings to the Registry when requested to do so by its host installation program. These default settings are used whenever the program calling Microsoft Jet doesn't supply explicit settings.

For information on new Registry value names for Microsoft Jet 3.0, see Appendix C, "Registry Settings."

---

**Note**  Unlike Microsoft Jet 2.x, which adds engine-specific default value names in the .INI file, Microsoft Jet 3.0 does not add engine-specific default value names such as MaxBufferSize and LockRetry to the Registry.

---

Unlike previous versions, Microsoft Jet 3.0 can apply different settings for each instance of the engine.

Microsoft Jet stores its settings in the HKEY_LOCAL_MACHINE tree shown in the path illustrated in Figure 13.1:

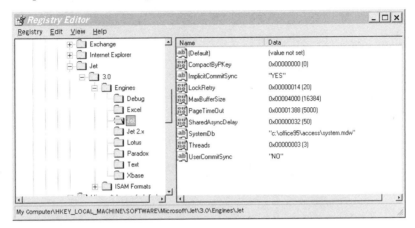

**Figure 13.1    The Microsoft Jet Registry tree with sample data**

The ISAM Formats tree is provided so that clients of Microsoft Jet can view the list of data formats available. The Engines tree contains the settings for Microsoft Jet. These settings are discussed later in this chapter and in Appendix C.

# Repairing Databases

Accidents happen. Users reboot workstations, power goes out, and disk drives go bad. Any one of these occurrences can lead to a corrupt Microsoft Jet database. Fortunately, there is a repair operation.

You can repair a database using the **RepairDatabase** method of the **DBEngine** object. The syntax is:

**DBEngine.RepairDatabase** *databasename*

where *databasename* is the name and path of the database to be repaired.

The following code attempts to open a database and repair it:

```
Sub RepairAndOpen()
    Dim dbsTmp As Database
    Dim errTmp As Error

    Const errDatabaseCorrupt = 1000
```

```
                    ' Disable VBA error handling.
                    On Error Resume Next
                    Set dbsTmp = _
                        OpenDatabase("C:\Samples\Chap13\Corrupt.mdb")
                    If DBEngine.Errors.Count > 0 Then
                        ' If it's a corrupt error, then attempt to repair it.
                        If Err = errDatabaseCorrupt Then
                            Debug.Print "Database is corrupt. " _
                                & "Attempting repair..."
                            DBEngine.RepairDatabase _
                                "C:\Samples\Chap13\Corrupt.mdb"
                        Else
                            For Each errTmp In DBEngine.Errors
                                Debug.Print errTmp.Description
                            Next
                        End If
                    End If
                End Sub
```

# Compacting Databases

For more information on compaction features new to Microsoft Jet 3.0, see the "Compaction" section later in this chapter.

With use, the internal structure of a database can become fragmented, leading to wasted disk space—and to poor performance if the fragmentation is excessive.

Compacting a database:

- Reorganizes a table's pages so they reside in adjacent database pages. This improves performance because the table is no longer fragmented across the database.

- Reclaims unused space created by object and record deletions. When objects or rows are deleted from the database, the space they occupied is potentially marked as available. However, the size of the database never shrinks unless the database is compacted.

- Resets Counter fields so the next value allocated will be one more than the last undeleted Counter record.

- Regenerates the table statistics used in the query optimization process. These statistics can become out of date over time, typically due to transactions that were rolled back or when the database was not properly closed.

- Flags all queries so that they will be recompiled the next time the query is executed. This is important because database statistics can change and a previously compiled query may have an inaccurate query plan.

To compact a database, the following conditions must be met:

- The user logged on to Microsoft Jet must have Modify Design or Administer permission for all tables in the database.

- Sufficient disk space must exist for both the original and compacted versions of the database, even if the database is being compacted through the Microsoft Access user interface using the same file name; the compacted database is renamed as the original database only when compaction is successful.

- Other users must not have the database open. When a database is compacted, it has to be opened exclusively to prevent any users from accessing and modifying the database.

---

**Note**   If an object in a Microsoft Access version 1.*x* database includes the backquote character (`) in its name, you won't be able to compact the database. Use Microsoft Access version 1.*x* to rename the object, and then change any references to it in your queries, forms, reports, macros, and code.

---

You can compact a Microsoft Jet database using the **CompactDatabase** method of the **DBEngine** object. Although the primary use of this method is to compact a database, it supports a variety of other operations with the *options* argument. The general syntax is:

**DBEngine.CompactDatabase** *oldname, newname* [*,locale* [*,options*]]

Where:

- *oldname* is the name of the database you want to compact.

- *newname* is the name of the compacted database you want to create.

- *locale* is a string expression used to specify collating order for *newname*.

- *options* is an integer that specifies one or more options.

You can't use the *newname* argument to specify the same database file as the *oldname* argument.

---

**Microsoft Access Users**   If a Microsoft Jet 2.*x* database contains any Microsoft Access objects, it's mandatory that you use the Microsoft Access **Convert Database** command if you want to open the database through Microsoft Access for Windows 95 using Microsoft Jet 3.0. If a Microsoft Jet 2.*x* database only has data and stored queries, then performing **DBEngine.CompactDatabase** through Visual Basic 4.0 on a Microsoft Jet 3.0 database will enable users of Microsoft Access for Windows 95 to open the Microsoft Jet 3.0 database.

---

## Setting Collating Order

Collating orders, specified by the *locale* argument of the **CompactDatabase** method, enable you to define how a database sorts data. You can specify a collating order when you create the database, or when you compact it. If you do not want to change the database's collating order during the compacting process, leave the *locale* argument blank. The following table lists the supported collating orders.

| Constant | Collating order |
| --- | --- |
| dbLangGeneral | English, German, French, Portuguese, Italian, and Modern Spanish |
| dbLangArabic | Arabic |
| dbLangCzech | Czech |
| dbLangCyrillic | Russian |
| dbLangDutch | Dutch |
| dbLangGreek | Greek |
| dbLangHebrew | Hebrew |
| dbLangHungarian | Hungarian |
| dbLangIcelandic | Icelandic |
| dbLangNordic | Nordic languages (Microsoft Jet 1.0 only) |
| dbLangNorwdan | Norwegian and Danish |
| dbLangPolish | Polish |
| dbLangSwedfin | Swedish and Finnish |
| dbLangSpanish | Traditional Spanish |
| dbLangTurkish | Turkish |

## Setting Options

You use the *options* argument of the **CompactDatabase** method to specify various operations for Microsoft Jet to perform as part of the compact process. Using the *options* argument, you can encrypt and decrypt database files and specify the version of the database file. You cannot use the **CompactDatabase** method to convert a database to a previous version.

The following table describes the available options.

| Constant | Description |
|---|---|
| **dbEncrypt** | Encrypts the database while compacting. |
| **dbDecrypt** | Decrypts the database while compacting. |
| **dbVersion10** | Creates a database that uses Microsoft Jet 1.0 while compacting. |
| **dbVersion11** | Creates a database that uses Microsoft Jet 1.1 while compacting. |
| **dbVersion20** | Creates a database that uses Microsoft Jet 2.0 while compacting. |
| **dbVersion30** | Creates a database that uses Microsoft Jet 3.0 while compacting. |

For more information on database encryption and descriptions, see Chapter 10, "Managing Security."

If you omit an encryption constant or include both **dbDecrypt** and **dbEncrypt**, the new database will have the same encryption as the old database. Also, when you use the *options* argument to convert between versions, only the version of the data format is changed. Application-defined objects such as Microsoft Access forms and reports are not changed.

The following code compacts a database called Customer.mdb into a new database called New.mdb, and in the process, encrypts it and converts it to Microsoft Jet 2.0 format:

```
Sub CompactAndConvert()
    DBEngine.CompactDatabase "C:\Samples\Chap13\Customer.mdb", _
        "New.mdb", , dbEncrypt And dbVersion20
End Sub
```

**Tip**  If your hard disk is badly fragmented, it's a good idea to defragment it before compacting the database. This allows for the data to be written not only sequentially in the database, but also sequentially on disk should space allow.

# Performance Enhancements in Microsoft Jet 3.0

The main goal for Microsoft Jet 3.0 was to significantly increase performance. Particular attention has been given to analyzing the bottlenecks present in version 2.*x* and to benchmarks of Microsoft Jet against other databases. Here's a summary of the changes discussed in the following sections:

- Configurable performance settings:
  - Multithreading
  - Dynamic memory usage
  - Improved buffer refreshing
  - Asynchronous writes

- Key internal performance enhancements:
  - 32-bit architecture
  - Common buffering code
  - LRU buffer replacement
  - Simplified index structure
  - Key compression in indexes
  - Efficient space management
  - Compaction
  - Reduced read locks
  - Improved conflict detection
  - Reduced concurrency conflicts for **Memo** and **OLE Object** data types

# Configurable Performance Settings

Various changes to configurable settings provide better control over performance in Microsoft Jet 3.0.

## Multithreading

Microsoft Jet 3.0 employs threads internally to enhance performance and provide background services such as:

- Read-ahead.
- Write-behind (commit).
- Cache maintenance.
- Quiescent database detection to determine if changes have been made to the database in shared mode.

By default, Microsoft Jet uses a maximum of three threads. You can increase this number by modifying a Registry setting. A typical situation in which you would want to increase the number of threads is when there is a large amount of activity in your database. By default, Microsoft Jet 3.0 doesn't add Registry values to the Registry but simply uses default values. If you want to change the default threading or any other setting discussed in this section, you first need to create the key:

```
HKEY_LOCAL_MACHINE\SOFTWARE\MICROSOFT\JET\3.0\ENGINES\JET
```

in the Windows Registry and add a value called Threads with a data type of DWORD.

## Dynamic Memory Usage

Microsoft Jet 2.x preallocated a default of 512K for its buffer with an upper limit (MaxBufferSize) of 4 MB RAM. Version 3.0 allocates memory on an as-needed basis up to an internally calculated high water mark (a modified behavior for MaxBufferSize). This enables efficient use of memory in large RAM systems without the need to adjust Registry settings.

The high water mark is calculated by the following formula:

```
((Total RAM in Mb - 12)/4 + 512 KB)
```

For a system with 32 MB RAM, Microsoft Jet 3.0 uses a calculated MaxBufferSize of 5632K. You can override the default behavior by setting the MaxBufferSize value in the Windows Registry.

The minimum value that Microsoft Jet 3.0 uses by default is 512K, but the minimum value the user can set is 128K.

Unlike version 2.x, Microsoft Jet 3.0 can exceed the MaxBufferSize. When this happens, the engine starts up a background thread to start flushing pages to bring the buffer pool down to the designated MaxBufferSize.

Microsoft Jet 3.0 reads as many as 32 pages (64K) in one read. It also performs buffer coalescing, which involves writing several consecutive modified pages to disk from the buffer with a single write request.

## Improved Buffer Refreshing

Microsoft Jet 3.0 alters the interpretation of the page time-out argument. In version 2.x, if you set the PageTimeOut argument to 2 seconds, a shared buffer is kept at least 2 seconds, and probably longer. In version 3.0, the buffer is kept no more than 2 seconds,  providing more precise control over the currency of the data returned. The default value for version 2.x is five tenths of a second and the default value for version 3.0 is 5000 milliseconds.

In addition, Microsoft Jet 3.0 recognizes when shared databases are not being updated, and suppresses buffer refreshing. In this way, performance on shared databases that are infrequently changed may approach the performance of databases opened exclusively.

## Asynchronous Writes

Microsoft Jet 3.0 writes changes to the database either synchronously or asynchronously.

In synchronous mode, the changes are written to the database before control returns to the application code. If transactions are used, the changes are written when the transaction commits; if transactions are not used, the changes are written at every recordset **Update** or DML statement. Synchronous mode is the only mode present in Microsoft Jet 2.x.

In asynchronous mode, changes are stored in memory so they can be written to the database in another thread. The changes are written when one of two things occur: A specified period of time (SharedAsyncDelay or ExclusiveAsyncDelay) passes after the first stored change or after the buffer pool becomes full (MaxBufferSize is exceeded).

Asynchronous (or background) writes can improve performance in several ways:

- Effective overlap of I/O and CPU is enabled.
- Control of the CPU is returned to the program executing the code much sooner.
- I/O is reduced. Multiple changes can be merged into a single change. For instance, updating every record on a page may require only a single write of the page when done.
- Locking is reduced. A request to lock a page may discover that the page is queued for writing, and that it already has a lock.

If you're a Microsoft Jet 2.*x* developer who has faithfully used transactions to achieve performance (as recommended for non-DML SQL statements), you should immediately recognize the utility of asynchronous writes in Microsoft Jet 3.0. You can now remove transactions used solely for performance, and allow Microsoft Jet to write changes as needed. In fact, you may see a significant performance improvement by removing explicit transactions when dealing with DAO code and large sets of data. This is due to the fact that modified pages in an explicit transaction spill to a temporary database if the cache defined by MaxBufferSize is exceeded. In version 3.0, this situation is eliminated when you're not using explicit transactions or non-DML statements because Microsoft Jet never flushes the modified pages to the temporary database, significantly reducing the number of writes to disk. While users may experience performance improvements with asynchronous processing, certain behavioral changes may cause the application to function differently, especially in a multiuser environment.

Four Registry values can be modified to change the default behavior of Microsoft Jet writes: UserCommitSync, ImplicitCommitSync, ExclusiveAsyncDelay, and SharedAsyncDelay.

---

**Note** Microsoft Jet 3.0 incorrectly reverses the Boolean sense of the ImplicitCommitSync and UserCommitSync keys when these values are specified in the Registry so that a setting of **No** would be interpreted as **Yes**. They are discussed here in their nonreversed (normal) sense.

UserCommitSync governs how changes made as part of an explicit (user) transaction are written to the database. The default setting is **Yes**. If you use the DAOSQLUpdateTrans example shown at the end of this section with the default setting of UserCommitSync, control doesn't return from the workspace **CommitTrans** statement until the transaction's changes are written to the database.

ImplicitCommitSync governs how changes made outside of a transaction are written to the database. The default setting is **No**. In the DAOUpdate example, a series of recordset **Update** statements may accumulate in memory and be written out together. Likewise, control returns from the database **Execute** statement immediately, and the changes are written asynchronously to the database. Note that Microsoft Jet 3.0 behavior regarding changes made outside of a transaction is different from Microsoft Jet 2.x behavior. If it's important to maintain the synchronous behavior of Microsoft Jet 2.x for SQL DML statements or DAO code in Microsoft Jet 3.0, you have two options: Place the DML statement in an explicit transaction so that it's governed by UserCommitSync, or change the setting of ImplicitCommitSync to **Yes**.

ExclusiveAsyncDelay defaults to 2000 milliseconds and is the maximum time that will elapse before asynchronous changes are written to the database when it's opened in exclusive mode. In the DAOUpdate example, the change caused by the recordset **Update** statement is written to the database within two seconds of the execution of the first recordset **Update** statement.

SharedAsyncDelay defaults to 50 milliseconds and is the maximum time that elapses before asynchronous changes are written to the database when it's opened in shared mode. Note that this effectively produces a corresponding small delay in seeing changes from other users because the changes are not yet in the database. As a rule, increasing this value may enhance performance because there may be fewer disk writes, but may reduce overall concurrency because locks may be held on queued pages.

The following examples illustrate the behavioral changes that occur in Microsoft Jet with corresponding changes to the Registry:

```
Public Sub DAOUpdate()
    Dim dbs As Database
    Dim rst As Recordset
    Dim strAddress As String

    Set dbs = OpenDatabase("C:\Samples\Chap13\NwindJet.mdb", _
        True, False)
    Set rst = dbs.OpenRecordset("SELECT * FROM Customers", _
        dbOpenDynaset)
```

```
        While Not rst.EOF
            rst.Edit
            strAddress = rst!Address
            rst!Address = strAddress
            rst.Update
            rst.MoveNext
        Wend
        dbs.Close
    End Sub

    Public Sub DAOSQLUpdate()
        Dim dbs As Database

        Set dbs = OpenDatabase("C:\Samples\Chap13\NwindJet.mdb", _
            False, False)

        dbs.Execute "UPDATE Customers SET Address = Address", dbFailOnError
        dbs.Close
    End Sub

    Sub DAOSQLUpdateTrans()
        Dim dbs As Database
        Dim wsp As Workspace

        Set wsp = Workspaces(0)
        Set dbs = OpenDatabase("C:\Samples\Chap13\NwindJet.mdb", _
            False, False)

        wsp.BeginTrans
        dbs.Execute "UPDATE Customers SET Address = Address", _
            dbFailOnError
        wsp.CommitTrans
    End Sub
```

# Key Internal Performance Enhancements

## 32-Bit Architecture

Microsoft Jet 3.0 is now a 32-bit–only engine that works efficiently with
Microsoft Windows NT and Microsoft Windows 95.

## Common Buffering Code

All database access—whether for user databases or for the temporary database—
is handled through common buffering code. This eliminates situations in which
pages are needlessly written to disk. It also enables all databases to benefit from
performance enhancements in the core code, including heuristic multipage I/O,
usage-sensitive replacement, and asynchronous I/O.

The fixed size read-ahead buffer that Microsoft Jet 2.*x* allocated for each open database is eliminated as well.

## LRU Buffer Replacement

Microsoft Jet 2.*x* has a first-in, first-out buffer replacement policy. This means that a page might be discarded from memory even though it's being referenced frequently. Version 3.0 implements a least recently used replacement policy: Pages that are being used frequently by the user or the application remain in memory.

## Simplified Index Structure

Microsoft Jet 2.*x* uses three separate index structures—and their associated support routines—for unique keys, short record lists, and long record lists. Microsoft Jet 3.0 uses a single, common index structure throughout.

The largest benefit of this common index structure is that version 3.0 is much more efficient when building indexes.

## Key Compression in Indexes

Microsoft Jet 3.0 indexes support leading key compression. Any bytes that are common to all key pairs in the node are recorded only once. This is done in a way that still allows a node to be searched in a binary fashion. Compression allows duplicate keys to be stored in the same manner as unique keys, and achieves greater densities than possible in version 2.*x*.

When the Microsoft Jet performance team converted a 139 MB Microsoft Jet 2.*x* database that had many referential integrity constraints and contained only data to a version 3.0 database, the resulting file was 116 MB—a 23 MB savings.

---

**Note**  Your databases may not see the reductions in size if you're using Microsoft Access for Windows 95. If your database file contains forms, reports, or modules, you may actually see the size of your database grow when you convert it from Microsoft Access 2.0. This is because VBA, the programming language used in Microsoft Access 95, might require up to four times as much storage space as the equivalent code in Microsoft Access 2.0.

---

## Efficient Space Management

Microsoft Jet 2.*x* uses several mechanisms to monitor free and used space inside the database. Version 3.0 introduces an entirely new mechanism for managing space in the database that allows for the following performance improvements.

## Clustering

It's now possible to grow tables in contiguous chunks of pages, avoiding most of the fragmentation problems in Microsoft Jet 2.x. It's now more likely that scanning a table will be accomplished by visiting the pages in increasing order of page number, avoiding the "bouncing around" problem in version 2.x, and by capitalizing upon the sequential heuristics of many of today's disk controllers. In addition, multipage read ahead is more likely to hit pages related to the table being scanned. This differs from version 2.x, where multipage reads are done by guessing, and may return pages for a number of different tables.

## Concurrent Inserts

Each table now can track pages that are candidates to receive additional records. When an insert is done, Microsoft Jet makes one attempt to lock these pages in succession until a lock is obtained. If none of the candidates can be locked—or if there is insufficient room on the locked page—another page can be allocated to the table.

Version 2.x required that the Table Header Page and last data page both be locked in order to add a new page to a table. This prevented multiple users from inserting rows into the same table at the same time. Microsoft Jet 3.0 no longer imposes this limitation and allows many users to insert rows into the same table at the same time. However, if indexes are present on a table, especially a unique index, then locking conflicts can occur on the index page that needs to be maintained.

## Faster Deletion of Table Contents

Microsoft Jet 2.x maintains data pages by having them doubly linked to each other. Therefore, the deletion of rows requires Microsoft Jet 2.x to traverse through every page in the table. Version 3.0 no longer maintains doubly linked data pages, allowing for extremely fast deletions because not every data page has to be visited. Substantial performance increases are seen when the table doesn't contain a referenced primary key and the table is dropped using a DDL DROP TABLE statement or rows are deleted using a DML DELETE statement that doesn't have a predicate.

## Page Reuse

In Microsoft Jet 2.x, freed index pages were available for immediate reuse. For instance, a table with indexes that has all of its records deleted can be freed and then allocated as a data page.

Microsoft Jet 3.0 defers page reuse until the last user closes the database. This is a key element to version 3.0 performance as this greatly reduces the amount of read locks, thus increasing concurrency and reducing network traffic.

## Compaction

The **DBEngine** object's **CompactDatabase** method copies tables differently in Microsoft Jet 3.0. Microsoft Jet 2.*x* copies in physical order; version 3.0 copies in primary key order (if present). This effectively provides the equivalent of unmaintained clustered indexes, making read-ahead more efficient. However, it's important to note that Microsoft Jet doesn't maintain a clustered index, and that a true clustered index format is achieved only after performing **CompactDatabase**. By compacting the database frequently, you ensure optimal performance for your application and resolve any page corruptions due to hardware problems, and so on.

In the case where compaction is being used to upgrade a database from Microsoft Jet 2.*x* format to version 3.0 format, rows are copied in physical order. This solves an upgrade problem for Microsoft Access for Windows 95, which currently doesn't differentiate between physical order and insertion order. After the database is in a Microsoft Jet 3.0 format, compaction begins to copy rows in primary key order.

To use this feature, you must add a key to the Registry called CompactByPKey with a DWORD value of zero.

## Reduced Read Locks

Microsoft Jet 3.0 greatly reduces the number of read locks compared with version 2.*x* because they are now placed only on long value (**Memo** and **OLE Object**) data types and on index pages being utilized to enforce referential integrity. This greatly reduces the amount of network traffic and the concurrency issues present in version 2.*x*. In Microsoft Jet 2.*x*, read locks were not persistent and they could time out or need to be cleared with **FreeLocks** or **DBEngine.Idle dbFreeLocks**. Version 3.0 read locks are persistent, making **FreeLocks** or **DBEngine.Idle dbFreeLocks** statements obsolete.

## Improved Conflict Detection

Microsoft Jet 2.*x* determines which users have locks using a locking algorithm that walks through a byte range in a manner that frequently hits bytes that are already locked. The user locking the page is determined when version 2.*x* can successfully place a lock. The process of trying to place a lock and failing proved to be a very costly operation in Microsoft Jet 2.*x*.

Microsoft Jet 3.0 modifies this process by reversing the locking order and determining the user locking that page when a lock attempt fails.

### Reduced Concurrency Conflicts for Memo and OLE Data Types

Microsoft Jet 2.*x* stored all of its long value data (**Memo** and **OLE Object** data types) in a special hidden system table. The hidden system table had the sometimes causes concurrency problems. A concurrency problem could occur when users receive locking conflicts when one user is adding a row with a long value data type to a table while another user is doing the same to a different table. Microsoft Jet 3.0 eliminates this concurrency issue by creating individual sets of pages for each long value column.

# Sample Benchmark Timings

During the course of Microsoft Jet 3.0 development, a large effort was organized to implement a suite of benchmarks to gauge the performance of version 3.0. Following are the results from some of those tests.

The tests were conducted on 36 identically configured P560 machines with 32 MB RAM that was, in most instances, configured down to 5 MB RAM, 540 MB IDE and 1.2GB EIDE hard drives with PCI Network Interface Cards. The tests were run using only DAO SQL commands on either Windows NT 3.51 or Windows 95. When run in a network environment, the Network OS was Netware 4.1 on a Dell XPE PowerEdge P90 with four 1GB RAID drives running off a dedicated EISA RAID SCSI host adapter, two four-port PCI full-duplexed Ethernet NICs and 32 MB RAM.

# Load Times for ASCII Files

The following test loads one million rows from a 227 MB ASCII delimited file based on the Set Query benchmark established by Patrick E. O'Neil (University of Massachusetts at Boston). All the reported Set Query benchmarks were run with 16 MB RAM on Windows 95. The following commands create this benchmark with the database opened in shared mode:

```
CREATE TABLE Bench (KSeq LONG, K500K LONG, K250K LONG, K100K LONG, K40K
LONG, K10K SMALL INT, K1K SMALL INT, K100 BYTE, K25 BYTE, K10 BYTE, K5
BYTE, K4 BYTE, K2 BYTE, S1 CHAR (8), S2 CHAR (20), S3 CHAR (20), S4 CHAR
(20), S5 CHAR (20), S6 CHAR (20), S7 CHAR (20), S8 CHAR (20))
```

The number values off of the columns starting with K represent the cardinality of the data. KSeq represents a primary key and K2 represents two unique values.

```
INSERT INTO Bench SELECT * FROM [SetQuery.DAT] IN ''[TEXT; Database=e:\]
```

| Jet 2.*x* sec. | Jet 3.0 sec. | Difference sec. | Times faster |
| --- | --- | --- | --- |
| 5980 | 1569 | 4411 | 3.81 |

# Index Times

The following tests are based on the load times for ASCII files.

`CREATE INDEX KSeq ON Bench (KSeq) WITH PRIMARY`

| Jet 2.x sec. | Jet 3.0 sec. | Difference sec. | Times faster |
|---|---|---|---|
| 339 | 242 | 96 | 1.4 |

`CREATE INDEX K500K ON Bench (K500K)`

| Jet 2.x sec. | Jet 3.0 sec. | Difference sec. | Times faster |
|---|---|---|---|
| 346 | 256 | 89 | 1.35 |

`CREATE INDEX K1K ON Bench (K1K)`

| Jet 2.x sec. | Jet 3.0 sec. | Difference sec. | Times faster |
|---|---|---|---|
| 335 | 242 | 93 | 1.38 |

`CREATE INDEX K25 ON Bench (K25)`

| Jet 2.x sec. | Jet 3.0 sec. | Difference sec. | Times faster |
|---|---|---|---|
| 393.37 | 240 | 153 | 1.64 |

`CREATE INDEX K2 ON Bench (K2)`

| Jet 2.x sec. | Jet 3.0 sec. | Difference sec. | Times faster |
|---|---|---|---|
| 4179 | 234 | 3944 | 17.79 |

# Delete Times

Using the Set Query benchmark, these times show improvement in deleting data without predicates.

`DELETE * FROM Bench`

| Jet 2.x sec. | Jet 3.0 sec. | Difference sec. | Times faster |
|---|---|---|---|
| 383 | 33 | 350 | 11.52 |

# Insert Times

Using the Set Query benchmark, these times show improvements in moving data within a Microsoft Jet database.

```
SELECT * INTO Temp FROM Bench
```

| Jet 2.x sec. | Jet 3.0 sec. | Difference sec. | Times faster |
|---|---|---|---|
| 8451 | 626 | 7824 | 13.48 |

# Read Times

Using the Set Query benchmark, these times show improvement over Microsoft Jet 2.x.

```
SELECT COUNT(*) AS Q2B INTO Q2B FROM Bench WHERE K2 = 2 AND K100 <> 3
```

| Jet 2.x sec. | Jet 3.0 sec. | Difference sec. | Times faster |
|---|---|---|---|
| 271 | 185 | 82 | 1.45 |

# Rushmore Times

Using the Set Query benchmark, these times show version 3.0 improvements to the way that Rushmore algorithms retrieve bookmarks or pointers to actual data.

```
SELECT KSeq, K500K INTO Q4B FROM Bench WHERE K100 > 80 AND K10K BETWEEN
2000 AND 3000 AND K5 = 3 AND (K25 = 11 OR K25 = 19) AND K4 = 3
```

| Jet 2.x sec. | Jet 3.0 sec. | Difference sec. | Times faster |
|---|---|---|---|
| 11 | 4 | 7 | 2.79 |

# Update Times

Using the Set Query benchmark, these times show performance improvement without explicit transactions.

```
Set rs = db.OpenRecordset("Bench", dbOpenTable)

While Not RS.EOF
    RS.Edit
    RS!S8 = "1234567890987654321"
    RS.Update
    RS.MoveNext
Wend
```

| Jet 2.x sec. | Jet 3.0 sec. | Difference sec. | Times faster |
|---|---|---|---|
| 2419 | 1151 | 1268 | 2.1 |

# Unsupported Tuning Functions

## The ISAMStats Function

Inside the DAO object model is a function that the Microsoft Jet performance team used to help them analyze and tune performance. Called **ISAMStats**, this function returns information about the raw disk reads, writes, locks, and caching.

---

**Caution**  These functions are *not* supported as an official part of DAO: You use **ISAMStats** and **ShowPlan** entirely at your own risk. They have not undergone the same quality testing as the supported components of Microsoft Jet. While the functions currently work in Microsoft Jet 3.0, they may not be supported in future releases. Also, the results returned may vary. There is no support available for these functions.

---

If you want to get every last bit of performance out of your database, you may find the following functionality useful when trying to substantiate timing results based on various ways of manipulating data in the database. Note that these apply only to native Microsoft Jet database files. Similar functions do not exist for the other database formats.

The following syntax is used for the **ISAMStats** function:

**ISAMStats(** (*StatNum* **as Long** [, *Reset* **as Boolean**]) **as Long**

This method returns the value of a given engine statistic as defined by *StatNum*, which is defined in the following table. If the optional *Reset* argument is supplied, then the statistic defined by *StatNum* is reset and no value is returned. A *Reset* value of **False** is equivalent to not supplying the argument. The statistics returned apply to the whole engine, regardless of how many databases or sessions are active, including temporary databases.

| StatNum | Description |
|---------|-------------|
| 0 | Number of disk reads |
| 1 | Number of disk writes |
| 2 | Number of reads from cache |
| 3 | Number of reads from read-ahead cache |
| 4 | Number of locks placed |
| 5 | Number of release lock calls |

The following code illustrates a sample use of the **ISAMStats** function:

```
Private Sub cmdTestStats_Click()
    Dim dbs As Database
    Dim strSQL As String
    Dim lngVersion As Long
    Dim lngDiskRead As Long
    Dim lngDiskWrite As Long
    Dim lngCacheRead As Long
    Dim lngCacheReadAheadCache As Long
    Dim lngLocksPlaced As Long
    Dim lngLocksRelease As Long

    ' If you are using Visual Basic, make sure that the database
    ' is open or that the engine is initialized before issuing
    ' any ISAMStatus calls.  DBEngine.Version is used
    ' to satisfy the purpose in this example.

    lngVersion = DBEngine.Version

    ' Explicitly set the counters to zero.
    lngDiskRead = DBEngine.ISAMStats(0, True)
    lngDiskWrite = DBEngine.ISAMStats(1, True)
    lngCacheRead = DBEngine.ISAMStats(2, True)
    lngCacheReadAheadCache = DBEngine.ISAMStats(3, True)
    lngLocksPlaced = DBEngine.ISAMStats(4, True)
    lngLocksRelease = DBEngine.ISAMStats(5, True)

    Set dbs = OpenDatabase("C:\Samples\Chap13\NwindJet.mdb", _
        False, False)

    strSQL = InputBox("Enter a SQL string", "SQL Box", _
        "UPDATE Customers SET ContactName = ContactName")

    dbs.Execute strSQL, dbFailOnError

    ' The following ISAMStats calls will retrieve the latest
    ' values.  The values will accumulate until they are reset.
    lngDiskRead = DBEngine.ISAMStats(0)
    lngDiskWrite = DBEngine.ISAMStats(1)
    lngCacheRead = DBEngine.ISAMStats(2)
    lngCacheReadAheadCache = DBEngine.ISAMStats(3)
    lngLocksPlaced = DBEngine.ISAMStats(4)
    lngLocksRelease = DBEngine.ISAMStats(5)
End Sub
```

The following may help you interpret these statistics.

- The number of disk reads and writes includes all reads and writes in all circumstances, including background read-ahead in separate threads. One read or write doesn't necessarily equal one page: One read or write could represent many pages that were read or written simultaneously. An example of this is commands wrapped in a transaction.

- There are two types of cached reads returned. The regular cache is a set of pages. For example, after executing the SQL DML statement, it's likely that the pages read would remain in cache. The read-ahead cache statistic shows reads that occurred so that they would be available if needed. For example, in certain scenarios, Microsoft Jet 3.0 issues a read request for more pages than it actually needs. In this way, pages can be utilized without actually going to disk again. The number of cache reads doesn't include read-each cache reads.

- The number of locks placed and released may not balance. A single call to release a lock may result in the release of many locks.

A typical scenario in which you might use this function is when you're trying to tune a query and you're not sure how to reduce network traffic. Another scenario might be when you're looking at the effect of placing explicit transactions versus letting Microsoft Jet use its internal transactions. You can also adjust the Registry settings and see how they affect the number of reads and writes to the database. These new statistics can help you validate timings, which may vary due to external circumstances that Microsoft Jet does not control such as varying traffic on the LAN, different processes running on the machine, and disk fragmentation. Therefore, while elapsed time for a computer may vary, the number of reads or writes generally stays the same.

# The ShowPlan Function

The Microsoft Jet query engine implements a cost-based query optimizer. When a query is compiled, the query engine creates a plan of execution. This plan is used internally to find the quickest way to execute a query. This information is not exposed to the user of Microsoft Jet. You can, however, using the ShowPlan key in the Registry, cause the engine to create a text file containing query execution plans.

## Activating ShowPlan

To activate ShowPlan, add the following key to the Registry:

```
\\HKEY_LOCAL_MACHINE\SOFTWARE\MICROSOFT\Jet\3.0\Engines\Debug
```

Under this key, add a string data type called **JETSHOWPLAN** (Make sure you use all capital letters). To turn on ShowPlan, set the value of the new data type to ON. To turn it off, set the value to OFF.

## Using ShowPlan

When ShowPlan is turned on, Microsoft Jet appends text to a file called
SHOWPLAN.OUT every time a query is compiled. This text contains the plan
that the query optimizer has generated for that query.

For example, the following text show the query plan for the Invoices query stored
in the NORTHWIND.MDB database that ships with Microsoft Access for
Windows 95:

```
--- Invoices ---

01) Sort table 'Orders'
02) Inner Join table 'Shippers' to result of '01)'
        using temporary index
        join expression "Shippers.ShipperID=Orders.ShipVia"
03) Sort table 'Employees'
04) Inner Join result of '02)' to result of '03)'
        using temporary index
        join expression "Orders.EmployeeID=Employees.EmployeeID"
05) Inner Join result of '04)' to table 'Customers'
        using index 'Customers!PrimaryKey'
        join expression "Orders.CustomerID=Customers.CustomerID"
06) Inner Join result of '05)' to table 'Order Details'
        using index 'Order Details!OrdersOrder Details'
        join expression "Orders.OrderID=[Order Details].OrderID"
07) Sort table 'Products'
08) Inner Join result of '06)' to result of '07)'
        using temporary index
        join expression "[Order Details].ProductID=Products.ProductID"
```

Note that if you have ShowPlan turned on, Microsoft Jet will append query plans
to the SHOWPLAN.OUT text file every time a query is compiled. As such, the
file can grow quite large. You should only turn this feature on during your
development and debugging process. Never leave it on for production databases.

APPENDIX A

# Specifications

## Database Specifications

| Attribute | Maximum |
|---|---|
| Database (.MDB) file size | 1 gigabyte. Because your database can include linked tables in other files, its total size is limited only by available storage capacity. |
| Number of characters in an object name | 64 |
| Number of characters in a user password | 14 |
| Number of characters in a database password | 20 |
| Number of characters in a user name or group name | 20 |
| Number of concurrent users | 255 |

## Table Specifications

| Attribute | Maximum |
|---|---|
| Number of characters in a table name | 64 |
| Number of characters in a field name | 64 |
| Number of fields in a table | 255 |
| Table size | 1 gigabyte |
| Number of characters in a Text field | 255 |
| Number of characters in a Long Text (Memo) field | 1 gigabyte |
| Size of an OLE Object field | 1 gigabyte |
| Number of indexes in a table | 32 |
| Number of fields in an index | 10 (An index can't contain more than 255 characters.) |

| Attribute | Maximum (*cont'd*) |
|---|---|
| Number of characters in a validation message | 255 |
| Number of characters in a validation rule | 2048 |
| Number of characters in a table or field description | 255 |
| Number of characters in a record (excluding Memo and OLE Object fields) | 2000 |
| Number of characters in a field property setting | 255 |

## Query Specifications

| Attribute | Maximum |
|---|---|
| Number of tables in a query | 32 |
| Number of fields in a recordset | 255 |
| Number of fields in an ORDER BY clause | 10 |
| Number of levels of nested queries | 50 |
| Number of characters in a parameter name | 255 |
| Number of ANDs in an expression | 40 |
| Number of characters in an SQL statement | Approximately 64,000 |

Microsoft Jet stores data using the set of data types shown in the following table. However, keep in mind that each tool you use to view or manipulate data stored in Microsoft Jet might call the data type by a different name. For example, a Boolean field in Microsoft Jet is called a Yes/No field in the Table Design screen in Microsoft Access. In SQL, the same field can be referred to several different ways: BIT, LOGICAL, LOGICAL1, YESNO, or BOOLEAN.

| Data type | Field size | Range of values |
|---|---|---|
| Boolean | 1 byte | 0 or –1 |
| Byte | 1 byte | 0 through 255 |
| Integer | 2 bytes | –32,768 through 32,767 |
| Long Integer | 4 bytes | –2,147,483,648 through 2,147,483,647 |
| Currency | 8 bytes | –922,337,203,685,477.5808 through 922,337,203,685,477.5807 |
| Single | 4 bytes | $-3.4E{-}38$ through $3.4E{+}38$ |
| Double | 8 bytes | $-1.8E{-}308$ through $1.8E{+}308$ |

| Data type | Field size | Range of values (*cont'd*) |
|---|---|---|
| DateTime | 8 bytes | Date and time values between the years 100 and 9999.  Stored as a floating-point value. The integer portion represents the number of days since December 30, 1899. The fractional portion represents the number of seconds since midnight. |
| Text | *n* bytes | 1 through 255 characters, stored variable length |
| LongText (Memo) | 12+ bytes | 12 bytes in the record, plus the actual data length (14 bytes in versions prior to 3.0) |
| LongBinary (OLE Object) | 12+ bytes | 12 bytes in the record, plus the actual data length (14 bytes in versions prior to 3.0) |
| Binary | *n* bytes | 1 through 255 characters of binary data. |
| GUID | 16 bytes | System-generated number that is guaranteed to be unique. Users should never write to this field. |

Microsoft Access has four different contexts, each with its own set of data types, that you can use to access data from Microsoft Jet:

- **Type** property settings available in a table's Design view
- Query Parameters dialog box in the query tool
- SQL window of the query tool
- Visual Basic

See online Help in Microsoft Access for more information on these contexts and their functionality. The following table compares the Microsoft Jet data types to the data types used in the four contexts in Microsoft Access.

| Microsoft Jet data type | Type property settings in table design view | Query parameter data types | Synonyms for Microsoft Jet SQL data types | Visual Basic data types |
|---|---|---|---|---|
| Boolean | Yes/No | Yes/No | Boolean, Bit, Logical, Logical1, YesNo | Boolean |
| Byte | Number, Size=Byte | Byte | Byte, Integer1 | Byte |
| Integer | Number, Size=Integer | Integer | Short, Integer2, Smallint | Integer |
| Long Integer | Number, Size=Long Integer and AutoNumber, Size=Long Integer | Long Integer | Counter, Integer, AutoIncrement | Long |
| Currency | Currency | Currency | Currency, Money | Currency |

| Microsoft Jet data type | Type property settings in table design view | Query parameter data types | Synonyms for Microsoft Jet SQL data types | Visual Basic data types (*cont'd*) |
|---|---|---|---|---|
| Single | Number, Size=Single | Single | Single, Float4, IEEESingle, Real | Single |
| Double | Number, Size=Double | Double | Float, Float8, IEEEDouble, Number, Numeric | Double |
| DateTime | Date/Time | Date/Time | DateTime, Date, Time, TimeStamp | Date |
| Text | Text | Text | Text, Alphanumeric, Char, Character, String, Varchar | String |
| LongText | Memo | Memo | Memo, LongText, LongChar, Note | String |
| Binary | <Not exposed in the Access UI> | Binary | Binary, VarBinary | String |
| LongBinary | OLE Object | Binary, OLE Object | OLEObject, LongBinary, General | String |
| GUID | Number, Size=Replication ID Autonumber, Size =Replication ID (See Note 1) | Replication ID | GUID | N/A |

Keep in mind the following points about data types:

- The only difference between Number and AutoNumber is whether Microsoft Access automatically generates a value for you or whether you need to set the value manually.

- The Query Parameter list has an entry called **Value,** which is a variant data type supported by Microsoft Access and Visual Basic, but not by Microsoft Jet. Data is always strongly typed before it's stored in Microsoft Jet. However, in Microsoft Access or SQL queries, **Value** can be considered a valid synonym for the Visual Basic **Variant** data type.

- The **Integer** data type in Microsoft Jet SQL doesn't correspond to the **Integer** data type for table fields, query parameters, or Visual Basic. Instead, in Microsoft Jet SQL, **Integer** corresponds to a Long Integer for table fields and query parameters and to a **Long** data type in Visual Basic.

# Estimating Microsoft Jet Table Sizes

The following information describes how to determine the approximate size of an .MDB file. However, this approximation cannot be determined with any real accuracy for the following reasons:

- System tables sizes vary greatly.

- The approximation doesn't account for the space taken up by indexes in your database.

- For simplicity, the approximation also assumes contiguous record storage. Microsoft Jet stores records on 2K pages and doesn't split records across pages. Therefore, you might have unused space on individual data pages, generally less than the size of an average record.

- Text can be stored variable length. For example, suppose you have a column that is defined to be variable text with a size of 25 characters, and you store the character Y in this column. The actual storage consumed will be 2 bytes: 1 for the character and 1 for the overhead. This is 23 bytes fewer than you might use to estimate the storage space for a table.

Consider the following when you estimate the size of your database:

- Records in Microsoft Jet versions 1.0 through 2.5 databases have an overhead of 7 bytes per record, and records in version 3.0 databases have an overhead of 6 bytes per record.

- Columns have an overhead of 1 byte, plus 1 byte for every 256 bytes of record storage.

- Fixed columns for Yes/No, Byte, Integer, Long Integer, Single, Double, and Date/Time data types have an overhead of 1 byte per column, rounded to the next higher byte.

- Zero-length text strings occupy 1 byte in the record (plus the overhead).

- For Microsoft Jet versions 1.0 through 2.x , the minimum size of a database is 65,536. These databases always grow in 32K chunks (32,768 bytes). Version 3.0 databases have a minimum size of 40,960 and grow in multiples of 2K.

- A new database created from Microsoft Access for Windows 95 is 83,968 bytes because of additional system tables added by Microsoft Access.

**Example 1: A Table in a Microsoft Jet 3.0 database with 10,000 Records**

| Column | Data type | Size in bytes | Overhead bytes |
|---|---|---|---|
| 1 | Text | 25 | 1 |
| 2 | Text | 25 | 1 |
| 3 | Number/Double | 8 | 1 |
| 4 | Date/Time | 8 | 1 |
| | Record Overhead | NA | 6 |
| | Totals | 66 | 10 |

The total length of the table is 66 + 10, or 76, bytes per record. Because the table has 10,000 records, the total length of the table is 760,000 bytes (76 x 10,000).

This is only an approximation, because this example takes into account the maximum size of the text fields. The actual length of the values in the text fields will determine the table's actual size.

**Example 2: Customers Table from the Sample Microsoft Jet 3.0 Database NORTHWIND.MDB**

| Column | Data type | Size | Overhead bytes |
|---|---|---|---|
| Customer ID | Text | 5 | 1 |
| Company Name | Text | 40 | 1 |
| Contact Name | Text | 30 | 1 |
| Contact Title | Text | 30 | 1 |
| Address | Text | 60 | 1 |
| City | Text | 15 | 1 |
| Region | Text | 15 | 1 |
| Postal Code | Text | 10 | 1 |
| Country | Text | 15 | 1 |
| Phone | Text | 24 | 1 |
| Fax | Text | 24 | 1 |
| <Record Overhead> | NA | 6 | |
| <Overhead for >256 bytes of text> | NA | 1 | |
| Totals | | 267 | 19 |

The total length of the table is 267 + 19, or 286, bytes per record. Because the table has 91 records, the total length of the table is 26,126 bytes (286 x 91).

Again, because the actual lengths of the text field values aren't known, this is only an approximation.

APPENDIX  B

# SQL Reference

The following SQL statements define the Microsoft Jet SQL grammar, using the Backus-Naur Form (BNF).

This BNF follows the notation standards used by the American National Standards Institute (ANSI) in defining standard X.135-1992 (ANSI-SQL 92).

| Symbol | Meaning |
|---|---|
| <> | Angle brackets delimit character strings that are the names of syntactic elements. |
| ::= | Definition operator. Used in a production rule to separate the elements defined by the rule from its definition. <defined_element> ::= <definition> |
| {} | Grouping delimiter. The portion of the formula within the braces is explicitly specified. |
| [] | Optional elements delimiter. The portion of the formula within the brackets can be explicitly specified or it can be deleted. |
| \| | Alternative operator. The vertical bar indicates that the portion of the formula following the bar is an alternative to the portion preceding the bar. If the vertical bar appears at a position where it is not enclosed in braces or square brackets, it specifies a complete alternative for the element defined by the production rule. If the vertical bar appears in a portion of a formula enclosed in braces or square brackets, it specifies alternatives for the contents of the innermost pair of braces or brackets. |
| ... | Repeat indicator. The ellipsis indicates that the element to which it applies in a formula can be repeated any number of times. |
| !! | English text. Defines a syntactic element without the benefit of BNF notation. |

```
<SQL-language-character> ::=
      <SQL-alpha-numeric-character>
    | <SQL-special-characters>

<SQL-alpha-numeric-character> ::=
      <lower-case-letter>
    | <upper-case-letter>
    | <digit>

<lower-case-letter> ::= [a | b | c | d | e | f | g | h | i | j | k | l | m | n | o | p | q
| r | s | t | u | v | w | x | y | z]

<upper-case-letter> ::= [A | B | C | D | E | F | G | H | I | J | K | L | M | N | O | P | Q
| R | S | T | U | V | W | X | Y | Z]

<digit> ::= [0 | 1 | 2 | 3 | 4 | 5 | 6 | 7 | 8 | 9]

<SQL-special-characters> ::=
      <space>
    | <tab>
    | <newline>
    | <carraige-return>
    | <form-feed>
    | <double-quote>
    | <percent>
    | <ampersand>
    | <quote>
    | <asterisk>
    | <plus-sign>
    | <minus-sign>
    | <back-slash>
    | <solidus>
    | <colon>
    | <semicolon>
    | <less-than-character>
    | <equals-character>
    | <greater-than-character>
    | <question-mark>
    | <underscore>
    | <number-sign>

<space> ::= !! space character

<tab> ::= !! tab character

<newline>  ::= !! newline character

<carraige-return> ::= !! carraige-return character

<form-feed> ::= !! form-feed character
```

```
<double-quote> ::= "

<back-quote> ::= `

<percent> ::= %

<ampersand> ::= &

<quote> ::= '

<left-paren> ::= (

<right-paren> ::= )

<asterisk> ::= *

<plus-sign> ::= +

<comma> ::= ,

<minus sign> ::= -

<period> ::= .

<back-slash> ::= \

<solidus> ::= /

<colon> ::= :

<semicolon> ::= ;

<less-than-character> ::= <

<equals-character> ::= =

<greater-than-character> ::= >

<question-mark> ::= ?

<underscore> ::= _

<vertical-bar> ::= |

<left-bracket> ::= [

<right-bracket> ::= ]

<number-sign> ::= #
```

```
<whitespace> ::=
    <space>
  | <tab>
  | <newline>
  | <carraige-return>
  | <form-feed>

<key-word> ::=
    ALL | ANY | AS | ASC | AUTOINCREMENT | AVG
  | BETWEEN | BINARY | BOOLEAN | BY | BYTE
  | CHAR[ACTER] | COUNT | COUNTER | CURRENCY
  | DATABASE | DATABASENAME | DATE | DATETIME | DELETE | DESC | DISTINCT | DISTINCTROW
  | DOUBLE
  | EXISTS
  | FIRST | FLOAT | FROM
  | GROUP
  | HAVING
  | IN | INNER | INSERT | INT | INTEGER | INTO
  | JOIN
  | LAST | LEFT | LEVEL | LIKE | LONG | LONGBINARY | LONGTEXT
  | MAX | MIN
  | NOT | NULL
  | OLEOBJECT | ON | OPTION | ORDER | OUTER | OWNERACCESS
  | PARAMETERS | PERCENT | PIVOT | PROCEDURE
  | REAL | RIGHT
  | SELECT | SET | SHORT | SINGLE | SMALLINT | SOME | STDEV | STDEVP | SUM
  | TABLEID | TIMESTAMP | TEXT | TOP | TRANSFORM
  | UPDATE
  | VALUES | VAR | VARBINARY | VARCHAR | VARP
  | WHERE | WITH
  | YESNO

<token> ::=
    <literal>
  | <comparison-operator>
  | <special-symbol>
  | <identifier>
  | <key-word>

<special-symbol> ::=
    <left-paren>
  | <right-paren>
  | <comma>
  | <period>
  | <colon>
  | <semicolon>
  | <equals-operator>
  | <asterisk>
  | <left-bracket>
  | <right-bracket>
```

```
<identifier> ::=
  <SQL-alpha-numeric-character> [<SQL-language-character>...]
  !! Note: Can include up to 64 characters.

<identifier-delimiter> ::=
    <left-id-delim>
  | <right-id-delim>

<left-id-delim> ::= !! Left identifier delimiter
    <back-quote>
  | <left-bracket>

<right-id-delim> ::= !! Right identifier delimiter
    <back-quote>
  | <right-bracket>

<scalar-expression> ::=
    <numeric-scalar-expression>
  | <character-string-literal>

<numeric-scalar-expression> ::=
    <term>
  | <numeric-scalar-expression> [<plus-operator> | <minus-operator>] <term>

<term> ::=
    <factor>
  | <term> [<multiplication-operator> | <divides-operator>] <factor>

<factor> ::= [<plus-operator> | <minus-operator>]<primary>

<primary> ::=
    <atom>
  | <column-reference>
  | <function-reference>
  | <left-paren><scalar-expression><right-paren>

<atom> ::=
    <literal>
  | <parameter-name>

<literal> ::=
    <character-string-literal>
  | <numeric-literal>
  | <boolean-literal>
  | <datetime-literal>
  | NULL

<character-string-literal> ::= {<single-quote> | <double-quote>} <char-list> {<single-
quote> | <double-quote>}  !! Note that the leading and trailing delimiter must be the same.
Embedded delimiters must be doubled as in Visual Basic.
```

```
<numeric-literal> ::=
    <exact-numeric-literal>
  | <approximate-numeric-literal>

<exact-numeric-literal> ::=
    <signed-integer>[<period><unsigned-integer>]
  |<period><unsigned-integer>

<approximate-numeric-literal> ::=
  <exact-numeric-literal>{E|e}<signed-integer>

<signed-integer> ::=
  [<plus-sign> | <minus-sign>]<unsigned-integer>

<unsigned-integer> ::= <digit> ...

<boolean-literal> ::= {TRUE | FALSE | YES | NO | ON | OFF}

<datetime-literal> ::= <number-sign><date-time-text><number-sign>

<date-time-text> ::= !! any literal that can be parsed as a valid date/time by the
expression service

<table-name> ::=
    <base-table-name>
  | <query-name>
  | <link-name>

<base-table-name> ::= <identifier>

<query-name> ::= <identifier>

<link-name> ::= <identifier>

<qualified-table-name> ::= [[ <connect-string> <period> ] <database-name> <period>]
  <table-name>

<connect-string> ::= <identifier> !!<connect-string> specifies the data source to look for
the given <database-name> in.  If the connect string starts with the name of a Microsoft
Jet data provider followed by a semicolon, then the given database is opened using that
data provider.  If the data provider is missing, or if it is "ODBC", then the rest of the
connect string is interpreted as an ODBC connect string.  In this case, a DSN field is
added to the connect string containing the <database-name>.  If a DSN field had previously
existed, it is replaced with this new DSN field.

<column-reference> ::= <identifier>

<column-reference-list> ::= <column-reference> [<comma> <column-reference> ...]

<constraint-name> ::= <identifier>
```

```
<index-name> ::= <identifier>

<database-name> ::= <identifier>

<manipulation-statement> ::=   [<parameter-declaration> <semicolon>] <data-manipulation-
language-statement> <semicolon>
```
!! Note: Microsoft Jet SQL data manipulation statements consist of an optional <parameter-
declaration> followed by a single <data-manipulation-language-statement>.  Manipulation
statements define stored or temporary query objects in Microsoft Jet.  Note that subqueries
are not supported and similar functionality may be used by using one query as the input to
another.

```
<parameter-declaration> ::= PARAMETERS <parameter-definition-list>

<parameter-definition-list> ::= <parameter-definition> [{<comma> <parameter-definition>}
...]

<parameter-definition> ::= <parameter-name> <parameter-datatype>

<parameter-name> ::= <identifier>

<parameter-datatype> ::=
    <Jet-parameter-datatype-name>
  | <ANSI-SQL-parameter-datatype-name>

<Jet-parameter-datatype-name> ::=
    BOOLEAN
  | BYTE <left-paren> <length> <right-paren>
  | SHORT
  | LONG
  | CURRENCY
  | SINGLE
  | DOUBLE
  | DATETIME
  | TEXT <left-paren> <length> <right-paren>
  | BINARY
  | LONGTEXT <left-paren> <length> <right-paren>
  | LONGBINARY
  | DATABASE
  | TABLEID
  | OLEOBJECT
  | YESNO

<ANSI-SQL-parameter-datatype-name> ::=
    SMALLINT
  | INT[EGER]
  | REAL
  | FLOAT
  | CHAR[ACTER] <left-paren> <length> <right-paren>
  | VARCHAR <left-paren> <length> <right-paren>
```

```
<data-definition-language-statement> ::=
    <table-definition>
  | <alter-table-statement>
  | <drop-table-statement>
  | <index-definition>
  | <drop-index-statement>

<alter-table-statement>  ::=
  ALTER TABLE <base-table-name>
  {ADD
    {COLUMN <column-reference>> <parameter-datatype>[CONSTRAINT <field-constraint>]
  | CONSTRAINT <table-constraint> }
  | DROP {COLUMN <column-reference> | CONSTRAINT <constraint-name> }}

<index-definition>  ::=
  CREATE  [ UNIQUE ] INDEX <index-name>
  ON <base-table-name> <left-paren> <column-reference>
  [ASC|DESC][{<comma> <column-reference> [ASC|DESC]} ...] <right-paren>
  [WITH { PRIMARY | DISALLOW NULL | IGNORE NULL }]

<table-definition>  :==
  CREATE TABLE <base-table-name>
  <left-paren> {<column-reference> <parameter-datatype>
   [CONSTRAINT <field-constraint>]}
  [{<comma> <column-reference> <parameter-datatype>
   [CONSTRAINT <field-constraint>]}...]]]<right-paren>

<drop-table-statement>  ::=
  DROP TABLE <base-table-name>

<drop-index-statement>  ::=
  DROP  INDEX <index-name> ON <base-table-name>

<column-constraint-definition> ::= <constraint-name-definition>
  <column-constraint>

<column-constraint> ::= <unique-specification> |
  <references-specification>

<constraint-name-definition> ::= CONSTRAINT <constraint-name>

<table-constraint-definition> ::= <constraint-name-definition>
  <table-constraint>

<table-constraint> ::=
    <unique-constraint-definition>
  | <referential-constraint-definition>

<unique-constraint-definition> ::=
  <unique-specification> <left-paren> <column-reference-list> <right-paren>
```

```
<unique-specification> ::= UNIQUE | PRIMARY KEY

<referential-constraint-definition> ::=
  FOREIGN KEY <left-paren> <referencing-columns> <right-paren>
  <references-specification>

<references-specification> ::=
  REFERENCES <referenced-table-and-columns>

<referencing-columns> ::= <column-reference-list>

<referenced-table-and-columns> ::= <table-name>
  <left-paren> <reference-column-list> <right-paren>

<reference-column-list> ::= <column-reference-list>

<data-manipulation-language-statement>  :==
  <delete-statement>
  | <insert-statement>
  | <select-statement>
  | <select-into-statement>
  | <transform-statement>
  | <update-statement>

<insert-statement> ::=
  INSERT INTO <table-name> [IN external-database] <insert-columns-and-source>

<insert-columns-and-source> ::=
  {<left-paren> <column-reference-list> <right-paren>}  {SELECT <column-reference-list>
  FROM <table-expression>
  | VALUES <left-paren><scalar-expression-list><right-paren>}

<select-statement> ::=
  SELECT <set-quantifier> <select list> <table expression>

<table-expression> ::=   <from-clause>
  [<where-clause>]
  [<group-by-clause>]
  [<having-clause>]
  [<order-by-clause>]
  [<with-owneraccess-clause]

<select-list> ::=
    <asterisk>
  | <select-sublist> [{<comma> <select-sublist>}...]

<select-sublist> ::=
    <column-qualifier><period><asterisk>
  | <scalar-expression> [AS <column-reference>]
```

```
<from-clause> ::= FROM <table-reference-list>

<table-reference-list> ::=
  <table-reference> [{<comma> <table-reference>}...] [<in-clause>]

<table-reference> ::=
  {<from-table-name> [AS <correlation-name>]} | <joined-table>

<from-table-name> ::=
    <table-name>
  | <tableid-parameter>

<tableid-parameter> ::= <parameter> <identifier> of type TABLEID

<in-clause> ::=
  IN
    <filename-path>        !! For local, Jet-native databases
  | {<left-id-delim><filename-path><right-id-delim> <left-id-delim><database-name><right-
id-delim>}

<filname-path> ::= !! as defined by operating system

<joined-table> ::=
  <table-reference> [ <join-type> ] JOIN <table-reference> ON <search-condition>

<join-type> ::=
    INNER
  | LEFT
  | RIGHT

<where-clause> ::= WHERE <search-condition>

<search-condition> ::=
    <boolean-term>
  | <search-condition> OR <boolean-term>

<boolean-term> ::=
    <boolean-factor>
  | <boolean-term> AND <boolean-factor>

<boolean-factor> ::= [ NOT ] <boolean-primary>

<boolean-primary> ::=
    <predicate>
  | <left-paren><search-condition><right-paren>
```

```
<predicate> ::=
    <comparison-predicate>
  | <between-predicate>
  | <in-predicate>
  | <like-predicate>
  | <null-predicate>

<comparison-predicate> ::=
  <scalar-expression><comparison-operator><scalar-expression>

<between-predicate> ::=
  <scalar-expression> [NOT] BETWEEN <scalar-expression> AND <scalar-expression>
  !! The BETWEEN predicate y BETWEEN x AND z is semantically equivalent to (x <= y AND y <=
z) OR (z <= y AND y <= x).

<in-predicate> ::=
  <scalar-expression> [NOT] IN <left-parn> <scalar-expression-list> <right-paren>

<scalar-expression-list> ::= <scalar-expression> [{<comma> <scalar-expression>}...]

<like-predicate> ::= <scalar-expression> [NOT] LIKE
    <scalar-expression>
  | <pattern>

<pattern> ::=
    <left-bracket> <char-list> <right-bracket>
    !! matches any single character in <char-list>
  | <left-bracket> <bang> <char-list> <right-bracket>
    !! matches any single character not in <char-list>
  | <left-bracket> <char-range> <right-bracket>
    !! matches any single character in <char-range>
  | <left-bracket> <bang> <char-range> <right-bracket>
    !! matches any single character not in <char-range>

<pattern-matching-character> ::=
    <question-mark>  !! matches any single <SQL-alphabetic-character>
  | <pound-sign>  !! matches any single <digit>
  | <asterisk>  !! matches any sequence of zero or more <SQL-alphabetic characters>

<dash> ::= -

<escape-character> ::= ^

<bang> ::= !
<char-list> ::=
    <SQL-alpha-numeric-character>
  | {<escape-character> <special-symbol>}
    [[<SQL-alpha-numeric-character>
  | {<escape-character> <special-symbol>}] ...]
```

```
<char-range> ::=
  <SQL-alpha-numeric-character> <dash> <SQL-alpha-numeric-character>
  !! Where the first <SQL-alpha-numeric-character> has lower ordinal value that the second <SQL-
  !! alpha-numeric-character>

<null-predicate> ::= <scalar-expression> IS [NOT] NULL

<group-by-clause> ::= GROUP BY <grouping-specification-list>

<grouping-specification-list> ::= <grouping-specification>[{<comma> <grouping-
specification>}...]

<grouping-specification> ::=
    <column-reference>
  | <scalar-expression>

<having-clause> ::= HAVING <search-condition>

<order-by-clause> ::= ORDER BY <sort-specification-list>

<sort-specification-list> ::=
  <sort-specification> [{<comma> <sort-specification>}...]

<sort-specification> ::=
  <scalar-expression> [ASC | DESC]

<select-into-statement>  ::=
  SELECT <set-quantifier> <reference-column-list>INTO <base-table-name> [in-clause]
   <table-expression>

<transform-statement> ::=
  TRANSFORM <aggregate-function> <select-statement> PIVOT <pivot-field>
  [IN <left-paren> <scalar-expression> [{<comma> <scalar-expression>}...]<right-paren>]

<union-clause> ::=
  <tabular-data> UNION [ALL] <tabular-data> [{UNION [ ALL ] <tabular-data>}  ...]

<update-statement> ::=
  UPDATE <table-reference-list> SET <set-clause-list> [<where-clause>]

<set-clause-list> ::= <set-clause> [{<comma> <set-clause>}...]

<set-clause> ::=
  <column-reference> <equals-operator>
    {<scalar-expression>
  | NULL}
```

```
<aggregate-reference>::=
     {Avg
   | Count
   | First
   | Last
   | Min
   | Max
   | StDev
   | StDevP
   | Sum
   | Var
   | VarP} <left-paren><scalar-expression><right-paren>

<comparison-operator> ::=
     <equals-operator>
   | <greater-than-operator>
   | <less-than-operator>
   | <greater-than-or-equals-to-operator>
   | <less-than-or-equals-to-operator>
   | <not-equals-operator>

<less-than-operator> ::= <less-than-character>

<greater-than-operator> ::= <greater-than-character>

<equals-operator> ::= <equals-character>

<greater-than-or-equals-to-operator> :== <greater-than-operator> <equals-operator>

<less-than-or-equals-to-operator> ::= <less-than-operator> <equals-operator>

<not-equals-operator> ::= <bang> <equals-operator>

<plus-operator> ::= <plus-sign>

<minus-operator> ::= <minus-sign>

<database-type> ::=
     {dBASE III
   | dBASE IV
   | Paradox 3.x
   | Paradox 4.x
   | Btrieve
   | FoxPro 2.5
   | Excel 3.0
   | Excel 4.0
   | Excel 5.0
   | ODBC
   }<semicolon>
```

```
<pivot-field> ::= <identifier>

<set-quantifier> ::=
    ALL
  | DISTINCT
  | {TOP <unsigned-integer> [PERCENT]}

<tabular-data> ::=
    <select-statement>
  | <stored-query>
  | TABLE <base_table_name>
```

A P P E N D I X   C

# Registry Settings

This appendix describes each of the settings that Microsoft Jet 3.0 installs into the Windows Registry. These settings configure Microsoft Jet and control how external data formats are handled.

## ISAM Formats

The ISAM Formats section is used by client applications to enumerate the available data formats and to find the corresponding engine that supports that format. It contains an entry for each data format supported.

**Tree: \HKEY_LOCALMACHINE\Software\Microsoft\Jet\3.0\ISAM Formats**

| Key name | Description | Example |
|---|---|---|
| Engine | Provides the name of the engine. | "Paradox", "Xbase" |
| ExportFilter | Provides a filter string that is passed to the common open dialog boxes used for exporting files. | "Paradox (*.db)" |
| ImportFilter | Provides a filter string that is passed to common open dialog boxes for importing files. | "Paradox (*.db)" |
| CanLink | **True** if Microsoft Jet supports linking to this format. | **True, False** |
| IsamType | Specifies the transfer macro this ISAM applies to (used by Microsoft Access) where 0 = database, 1 = spreadsheet, and 2 = text. | 0,1,2 |
| OneTablePerFile | Specifies whether the ISAM has one table per file and is required by client applications that need to prompt for file names. | **True, False** |

| Key name | Description | Example (*cont'd*) |
|---|---|---|
| IndexDialog | Specifies whether the ISAM requires a separate dialog for index files. If this value is set to **True**, then the IndexFilter setting must also be provided. | **True, False** |
| IndexFilter | This setting has the same format as the Filter setting, but is used to prompt for index file names. | "FoxPro Index (*.idx; *.cdx)" |
| CreateDbOnExport | If set to Yes, the file name specified for export need not exist for the export to function. | Yes, No |
| ResultTextImport | The common dialog result string for import. | "Import data and objects from the external database into the current database." |
| ResultTextLink | The common dialog result string for linking. | "Create tables in the current database that are linked to tables in the external file." |
| ResultTextExport | The common dialog result string for exporting. | "Export data from the current database into an Excel spreadsheet." |

### Tree: ...\Jet\3.0\ISAM Formats\Jet 2.*x*

The following table details the entries that Microsoft Jet installs for the Jet format.

| Key | Value |
|---|---|
| Engine | Jet 2.*x* |
| IsamType | No |
| OneTablePerFile | No |
| IndexDialog | No |
| CreateDBOnExport | No |

### Tree: ...\Jet\3.0\ISAM  Formats\Paradox...

The following tables detail the entries that Microsoft Jet installs for the Paradox installable ISAMs.

### Paradox 3.x

| Key | Value |
| --- | --- |
| Engine | Paradox |
| ExportFilter | Paradox 3 (*.db) |
| ImportFilter | Paradox (*.db) |
| CanLink | Yes |
| OneTablePerFile | Yes |
| IsamType | 0 |
| IndexDialog | No |
| CreateDBOnExport | No |
| ResultTextImport | Import data from the external file into the current database. Changing data in the current database will not change data in the external file. |
| ResultTextLink | Create a table in the current database that is linked to the external file. Changing data in the current database will change data in the external file. |
| ResultTextExport | Export data from the current database into a Paradox 3.0 file. This process will overwrite the data if exported to an existing file. |

### Paradox 4.x

| Key | Value |
| --- | --- |
| Engine | Paradox |
| ExportFilter | Paradox 4 (*.db) |
| CanLink | Yes |
| OneTablePerFile | Yes |
| IsamType | 0 |
| IndexDialog | No |
| CreateDBOnExport | No |
| ResultTextExport | Export data from the current database into a Paradox 4.0 file. This process will overwrite the data if exported to an existing file. |

### Paradox 5.*x*

| Key | Value |
| --- | --- |
| Engine | Paradox |
| ExportFilter | Paradox 5 (*.db) |
| CanLink | Yes |
| OneTablePerFile | Yes |
| IsamType | 0 |
| IndexDialog | No |
| CreateDBOnExport | No |
| ResultTextExport | Export data from the current database into a Paradox 5.0 file. This process will overwrite the data if exported to an existing file. |

## Tree: ...\Jet\3.0\ISAM Formats\dBASE...

The following tables detail the entries that Microsoft Jet installs for the Borland dBASE formats.

### dBASE III

| Key | Value |
| --- | --- |
| Engine | Xbase |
| ExportFilter | dBASE III (*.dbf) |
| ImportFilter | dBASE III (*.dbf) |
| CanLink | Yes |
| OneTablePerFile | Yes |
| IsamType | 0 |
| IndexDialog | Yes |
| IndexFilter | dBASE Index (*.ndx) |
| CreateDBOnExport | No |
| ResultTextImport | Import data from the external file into the current database. Changing data in the current database will not change data in the external file. |
| ResultTextLink | Create a table in the current database that is linked to the external file. Changing data in the current database will change data in the external file. |
| ResultTextExport | Export data from the current database into a dBASE III file. This process will overwrite the data if exported to an existing file. |

## dBASE IV

| Key | Value |
| --- | --- |
| Engine | Xbase |
| ExportFilter | dBASE IV (*.dbf) |
| ImportFilter | dBASE IV (*.dbf) |
| CanLink | Yes |
| OneTablePerFile | Yes |
| IsamType | 0 |
| IndexDialog | Yes |
| IndexFilter | dBASE Index (*.ndx, *.mdx) |
| CreateDBOnExport | No |
| ResultTextImport | Import data from the external file into the current database. Changing data in the current database will not change data in the external file. |
| ResultTextLink | Create a table in the current database that is linked to the external file. Changing data in the current database will change data in the external file. |
| ResultTextExport | Export data from the current database into a dBASE IV file. This process will overwrite the data if exported to an existing file. |

## dBASE 5.0

| Key | Value |
| --- | --- |
| Engine | Xbase |
| ExportFilter | dBASE 5 (*.dbf) |
| ImportFilter | dBASE 5 (*.dbf) |
| CanLink | Yes |
| OneTablePerFile | Yes |
| IsamType | 0 |
| IndexDialog | Yes |
| IndexFilter | dBASE Index (*.ndx, *.mdx) |
| CreateDBOnExport | No |

| Key | Value (*cont'd*) |
|---|---|
| ResultTextImport | Import data from the external file into the current database. Changing data in the current database will not change data in the external file. |
| ResultTextLink | Create a table in the current database that is linked to the external file. Changing data in the current database will change data in the external file. |
| ResultTextExport | Export data from the current database into a dBASE 5.0 file. This process will overwrite the data if exported to an existing file. |

## Tree: ...\Jet\3.0\ISAM Formats\FoxPro...

The following tables detail the entries that Microsoft Jet installs for the Microsoft FoxPro formats.

### Microsoft FoxPro 2.0

| Key | Value |
|---|---|
| Engine | Xbase |
| ExportFilter | Microsoft FoxPro 2.0 (*.dbf) |
| ImportFilter | Microsoft FoxPro (*.dbf) |
| CanLink | Yes |
| OneTablePerFile | Yes |
| IsamType | 0 |
| IndexDialog | Yes |
| IndexFilter | FoxPro Index (*.idx; *.cdx) |
| CreateDBOnExport | No |
| ResultTextImport | Import data from the external file into the current database. Changing data in the current database will not change data in the external file. |
| ResultTextLink | Create a table in the current database that is linked to the external file. Changing data in the current database will change data in the external file. |
| ResultTextExport | Export data from the current database into a FoxPro 2.0 file. This process will overwrite the data if exported to an existing file. |

## Microsoft FoxPro 2.5

| Key | Value |
|---|---|
| Engine | Xbase |
| ExportFilter | Microsoft FoxPro 2.5 (*.dbf) |
| CanLink | Yes |
| OneTablePerFile | Yes |
| IsamType | 0 |
| IndexDialog | Yes |
| IndexFilter | FoxPro Index (*.idx; *.cdx) |
| CreateDBOnExport | No |
| ResultTextExport | Export data from the current database into a FoxPro 2.5 file. This process will overwrite the data if exported to an existing file. |

## Microsoft FoxPro 2.6

| Key | Value |
|---|---|
| Engine | Xbase |
| ExportFilter | Microsoft FoxPro 2.6 (*.dbf) |
| CanLink | Yes |
| OneTablePerFile | Yes |
| IsamType | 0 |
| IndexDialog | Yes |
| IndexFilter | FoxPro Index (*.idx; *.cdx) |
| CreateDBOnExport | No |
| ResultTextExport | Export data from the current database into a FoxPro 2.6 file. This process will overwrite the data if exported to an existing file. |

## Microsoft FoxPro 3.0

| Key | Value |
|---|---|
| Engine | Xbase |
| ExportFilter | Microsoft FoxPro 3.0 (*.dbf) |
| CanLink | No |
| OneTablePerFile | Yes |
| IsamType | 0 |
| IndexDialog | Yes |

| Key | Value (*cont'd*) |
| --- | --- |
| IndexFilter | FoxPro Index (*.idx; *.cdx) |
| CreateDBOnExport | No |
| ResultTextExport | Export data from the current database into a FoxPro 3.0 file. This process will overwrite the data if exported to an existing file. |

### Microsoft FoxPro DBC

| Key | Value |
| --- | --- |
| Engine | Xbase |
| ImportFilter | Microsoft FoxPro 3.0 (*.dbc) |
| CanLink | No |
| OneTablePerFile | No |
| IsamType | 0 |
| IndexDialog | No |
| CreateDBOnExport | No |
| ResultTextImport | Import data from the external file into the current database. Changing data in the current database will not change data in the external file. |

## Tree: ...\Jet\3.0\ISAM Formats\Text

The following table details the entries that Microsoft Jet installs for the text formats.

| Key | Value |
| --- | --- |
| Engine | Text |
| ExportFilter | Text files (*.txt; *.csv; *.tab; *.asc) |
| ImportFilter | Text files (*.txt; *.csv; *.tab; *.asc) |
| CanLink | Yes |
| OneTablePerFile | Yes |
| IsamType | 2 |
| IndexDialog | No |
| CreateDBOnExport | No |
| FormatFunction | txt,SOA_RptToAscii,1,MS-DOS Text (*.txt) |
|  | Note: This key is added by Microsoft Access. |

| Key | Value (*cont'd*) |
|---|---|
| WizardProject | wzlib70.mda |
| | Note: This key is added by Microsoft Access. |
| ImportWizardFunction | mx_entry |
| | Note: This key is added by Microsoft Access. |
| ExportWizardFunction | mx_entry |
| | Note: This key is added by Microsoft Access. |
| ResultTextImport | Import data from the external file into the current database. Changing data in the current database will not change data in the external file. |
| ResultTextLink | Create a table in the current database that is linked to the external file. Changing data in the current database will change data in the external file. |
| ResultTextExport | Export data from the current database into a text file. This process will overwrite data if exported to an existing file. |

## Tree: ...\Jet\3.0\ISAM Formats\Excel...

The following tables detail the entries that Microsoft Jet installs for the Microsoft Excel formats.

### Microsoft Excel 3.0

| Key | Value |
|---|---|
| Engine | Excel |
| ExportFilter | Microsoft Excel 3 (*.xls) |
| CanLink | Yes |
| OneTablePerFile | No |
| IsamType | 1 |
| IndexDialog | No |
| CreateDBOnExport | Yes |
| WizardProject | wzlib70.mda |
| | Note: This key is added by Microsoft Access. |
| ImportWizardFunction | mx_entry |
| | Note: This key is added by Microsoft Access. |
| ResultTextExport | Export data from the current database into a Microsoft Excel 3.0 file. This process will overwrite data if exported to an existing file. |

### Microsoft Excel 4.0

| Key | Value |
| --- | --- |
| Engine | Excel |
| ExportFilter | Microsoft Excel 4 (*.xls) |
| CanLink | Yes |
| OneTablePerFile | No |
| IsamType | 1 |
| IndexDialog | No |
| CreateDBOnExport | Yes |
| WizardProject | wzlib70.mda |
|  | Note: This key is added by Microsoft Access. |
| ImportWizardFunction | mx_entry |
|  | Note: This key is added by Microsoft Access. |
| ResultTextExport | Export data from the current database into a Microsoft Excel 4.0 file. This process will overwrite data if exported to an existing file. |

### Microsoft Excel 5.0

| Key | Value |
| --- | --- |
| Engine | Excel |
| ExportFilter | Microsoft Excel 5-7 (*.xls) |
| ImportFilter | Microsoft Excel (*.xls) |
| CanLink | Yes |
| OneTablePerFile | No |
| IsamType | 1 |
| IndexDialog | No |
| CreateDBOnExport | Yes |
| FormatFunction | SOA_RptToBIFF, Biff5, soa300.DLL, 8 |
|  | Note: This key is added by Microsoft Access. |
| WizardProject | wzlib70.mda |
|  | Note: This key is added by Microsoft Access. |
| ImportWizardFunction | mx_entry |
|  | Note: This key is added by Microsoft Access. |

| Key | Value (*cont'd*) |
|-----|-----------------|
| ResultTextImport | Import data from the external file into the current database. Changing data in the current database will not change data in the external file. |
| ResultTextLink | Create a table in the current database that is linked to the external file. Changing data in the current database will change data in the external file. Only one user at a time can change data in the file. |
| ResultTextExport | Export data from the current database into a Microsoft Excel 5.0 file. |

## Tree: ...\Jet\3.0\ISAM Formats\Lotus...

The following tables detail the entries that Microsoft Jet installs for the Lotus 1-2-3 formats.

### Lotus WK1

| Key | Value |
|-----|-------|
| Engine | Lotus |
| ExportFilter | Lotus 1-2-3 WK1 (*.wk1) |
| ImportFilter | Lotus 1-2-3 (*.wk*) |
| CanLink | No |
| OneTablePerFile | No |
| IsamType | 1 |
| IndexDialog | No |
| FormatFunction | SOA_RptToBIFF, Biff5, soa300.DLL, 8 |
| | Note: This key is added by Microsoft Access. |
| WizardProject | wzlib70.mda |
| | Note: This key is added by Microsoft Access. |
| CreateDBOnExport | Yes |
| ResultTextImport | Import data from the external file into the current database. Changing data in the current database will not change data in the external file. |
| ResultTextExport | Export data from the current database into Lotus 1-2-3 version 2.0 file. This process will overwrite data if exported to an existing file. |

### Lotus WK3

| Key | Value |
| --- | --- |
| Engine | Lotus |
| ExportFilter | Lotus 1-2-3 WK3 (*.wk3) |
| CanLink | No |
| OneTablePerFile | No |
| IsamType | 1 |
| IndexDialog | No |
| CreateDBOnExport | Yes |
| WizardProject | wzlib70.mda |
| | Note: This key is added by Microsoft Access. |
| ImportWizardFunction | mx_entry |
| | Note: This key is added by Microsoft Access. |
| ResultTextExport | Export data from the current database into Lotus 1-2-3 version 3.0 file. |

### Lotus WK4

| Key | Value |
| --- | --- |
| Engine | Lotus |
| CanLink | No |
| OneTablePerFile | No |
| IsamType | 1 |
| IndexDialog | No |
| CreateDBOnExport | Yes |
| WizardProject | wzlib70.mda |
| | Note: This key is added by Microsoft Access. |
| WizardImportFunction | mx_entry |
| | Note: This key is added by Microsoft Access. |

# Engine Settings

This section describes the keys that all engines must provide in the Engines section of the Registry. Each engine can also provide key values that are specific to their engine. Common keys provided by engines are as follows.

### Tree: ...\Engines\*enginename*

| Key | Type | Default | Required? | Description |
|---|---|---|---|---|
| win32 | String | | Y | The path and name of the DLL that supplies the engine services. |

When Microsoft Jet is installed on your workstation, only the required key (Win32) is created. The keys described in the following tables are all optional. If you want to change the value of one of these keys, you need to create the key and set it to the value you want.

### Tree: ...\Engines\Jet 2.x\ISAM

The following settings apply to Microsoft Jet version 1.*x* and 2.*x* databases. This tree is used by Microsoft Jet when a version 1.*x* or 2.*x* database is accessed.

| Key | Type | Default | Description |
|---|---|---|---|
| PageTimeout | Integer | 5 | The length of time between when data that is not read-locked is placed in an internal cache and when it is invalidated, expressed in tenths of a second. |
| LockedPageTimeout | Integer | 5 | The length of time between when data that is read-locked is placed in an internal cache and when it is invalidated, expressed in tenths of a second. |
| LockRetry | Integer | 20 | The number of times to repeat attempts to access a locked page. (Note that LockRetry is related to CommitLockRetry, described in next table entry.) |
| CommitLockRetry | Integer | 20 | The number of times Microsoft Jet attempts to get a lock on data to commit changes to that data. If it fails to get a commit lock, updates to the data will be unsuccessful. The number of attempts Microsoft Jet makes to get a commit lock is directly related the LockRetry entry. For each attempt made at getting a commit lock, it will try LockRetry the same number of times to get a lock. For example, if CommitLockRetry is 20 and LockRetry is 20, Microsoft Jet will attempt to get a commit lock as many as 20 times; and for each of those times, it can try to get a lock as many as 20 times for a total of 400 attempts at locking. |

| Key | Type | Default | Description (*cont'd*) |
|---|---|---|---|
| Cursor Timeout | Integer | 5 | This value is applicable only to version 1.*x* of Microsoft Jet. CursorTimeout controls the amount of time a reference to a page (a cursor) will remain on that page. If a cursor times out, the internal reference to the page it was referring to is removed. A page can be freed only if all cursors have timed out. The cursor timeout value is measured in 1/10ths of a second and can have a value from 0 to approximately 65,000. |
| IdleFrequency | Integer | 10 | Number of internal operations before causing an Idle call internally. |
| ForceOSFlush | Integer | 0 | Any setting other than 0 means a commit or a write will force flushing the OS cache to disk. A setting of 0 means no force flush occurs. |
| MaxBufferSize | Integer | 512 | The size of the Microsoft Jet internal cache, measured in kilobytes (K). MaxBufferSize must be between 9 and 4096, inclusive. The default is 512. |
| ReadAheadPages | Integer | 8 | Number of pages Microsoft Jet attempts to read ahead for long value objects. Measured in kilobytes (K), the default is 8, which corresponds to four data pages. |

### Tree: ...\Engines\Jet

The table below controls access to Microsoft Jet 3.*x* data. None of these keys are automatically created.

| Key | Type | Default | Description |
|---|---|---|---|
| PageTimeout | Integer | 5000 | The length of time between when data is placed in an internal cache and when it is checked to be potentially invalidated, expressed in milliseconds. |
| LockRetry | Integer | 20 | The number of times to repeat attempts to access a locked page. |
| MaxBufferSize | Integer | calculated | The size of the Microsoft Jet internal memory cache, measured in kilobytes (K). MaxBufferSize can be a minimum of 128 or the maximum that is limited by available memory. MaxBufferSize should never be set to a value larger than half the total memory. The default is calculated by the following formula: ((Total RAM in MB - 12)/4 + 512 KB). |
| SystemDB | String | "system.mdb" | The path and name of the workgroup database (also known as the SystemDB database) to use. If no path is specified, the current directory is used. |

| Key | Type | Default | Description (*cont'd*) |
|---|---|---|---|
| Threads | Integer | 3 | Number of background threads for the engine to use. |
| UserCommitSync | String | Yes | Yes signifies that Microsoft Jet will wait for commits to finish. Any other value means that Microsoft Jet will perform commits asynchronously. See Chapter 13, "Performance" for more information on how this and other Registry settings affect transactions and performance. |
|  |  |  | Note: The correct behavior is documented here. In Microsoft Jet 3.0, the behavior is opposite of what is described here. This will be fixed in the next release of Microsoft Jet. |
| ImplicitCommitSync | String | No | Yes signifies that Microsoft Jet will wait for commits to finish. A value other than Yes means that Microsoft Jet will perform commits asynchronously. |
|  |  |  | Note: The correct behavior is documented here. In Microsoft Jet 3.0, the behavior is opposite of what is described here. This will be fixed in the next release of Microsoft Jet. |
| SharedAsyncDelay | Integer | 50 | Maximum time before asynchronous changes will be written when the database is opened shared. |
| CompactByPKey | Integer | 1 | Disables or enables compacting by primary keys. When this is **True** and the user compacts a database, records will be sorted in primary key order. This creates a pseudo-clustered index effect that Microsoft Jet doesn't maintain during normal use of the database. A value of 0 disables this feature. ExclusiveAsyncDelay is available with any version of Microsoft Jet beyond and including 3.000.2120. At present, this version of Microsoft Jet has shipped only with Microsoft Access for Windows 95. |
| ExclusiveAsyncDelay | Integer | 2000 | Maximum time before asynchronous changes will be written when the database is opened exclusively. The default is 2000. |

# ODBC Settings

The following Registry keys are not installed by any Microsoft ODBC client applications. Like many of the Microsoft Jet keys, if the user wants to change the default behavior, he or she will have to create the appropriate folders and keys and set them accordingly.

**Tree: ...\Engines\ODBC**

| Key | Type | Default | Description |
|---|---|---|---|
| LoginTimeout | Integer | 20 | Number of seconds to wait for a login attempt to succeed. |
| QueryTimeout | Integer | 60 | Number of seconds to wait for a query to execute before failing. |
| ConnectionTimeout | Integer | 600 | Number of seconds to wait before closing an idle connection. |
| AsyncRetryInterval | Integer | 500 | Number of milliseconds to wait between retries on an asynchronous connection. |
| AttachCaseSensitive | Boolean | F | If **False**, will attach to the first name matching the specified string in a match that isn't case-sensitive. If **True**, requires a case-sensitive match of the name. |
| AttachableObjects | String | TABLE | The list of objects that Microsoft Jet will allow attachments to (TABLE, NEW, SYSTEMTABLE, ALIAS, SYNONYM). Values are of type REG_SZ. |
| SnapshotOnly | Boolean | F | If **False**, you will get index information on attachment to allow dynasets if possible. If **True**, Microsoft Jet will ignore index information and thereby force snapshots on all attachments. |
| TraceSQLMode | Boolean | F | Initiates sending a trace of SQL statements sent to an ODBC data source to the file SQLOUT.TXT. Values are 0 (No) and 1 (Yes). The default is 0 (values are of type REG_DWORD). This entry is interchangeable with **SQLTracemode**. |
| TraceODBCAPI | Boolean | F | Initiates sending a trace of ODBC API calls to the file ODBCAPI.TXT. Values are 0 (No) and 1 (Yes). The default is 0 (values are of type REG_DWORD). |
| DisableAsync | Boolean | F | Forces synchronous query execution. Values are 0 (use asynchronous query execution if possible) and 1 (force synchronous query execution). The default is 0 (values are of type REG_DWORD). |
| JetTryAuth | Boolean | T | Uses the Microsoft Access user name and password to log on to the server before prompting. Values are 0 (No) and 1 (Yes). The default is 0 (values are of type REG_DWORD). |

| Key | Type | Default | Description (*cont'd*) |
|---|---|---|---|
| PreparedInsert | Boolean | F | Uses a prepared INSERT statement that inserts data in all columns. Values are 0 (use a custom INSERT statement that inserts only non-**Null** values) and 1 (use a prepared INSERT statement). The default is 0 (values are of type REG_DWORD). |
| | | | Using prepared INSERT statements can cause **Nulls** to overwrite server defaults and can cause triggers to execute on columns that weren't inserted explicitly. |
| PreparedUpdate | Boolean | F | Uses a prepared UPDATE statement that updates data in all columns. Values are 0 (use a custom UPDATE statement that sets only columns that have changed) and 1 (use a prepared UPDATE statement). The default is 0 (values are of type REG_DWORD). |
| | | | Using prepared UPDATE statements can cause triggers to execute on columns that weren't changed explicitly. |
| FastRequery | Boolean | F | Uses a prepared SELECT statement for parameterized queries. Values are 0 (No) and 1 (Yes). The default is 0 (values are of type REG_DWORD). |

# Xbase Settings

The following table details the entries that are installed for the Xbase engine.

**Tree: ...\Engines\Xbase**

| Key | Type | Default | Required? | Description |
|---|---|---|---|---|
| NetworkAccess | Boolean | T | N | A Boolean indicator for file locking preference. If NetworkAccess is Off, tables are opened without any file locks, and records are added and edited without any record locks. This is appropriate only for single-user access. Not setting and clearing of file locks can improve performance. |
| PageTimeout | Integer | 600 | N | The length of time between when data is placed in an internal cache and when it's invalidated. The value is specified in 100 millisecond units. |
| INFPath | String | | N | The full path to the .INF file directory. Microsoft Jet first looks for an .INF file in the directory containing the table. If the .INF file isn't in the database directory, it looks in the INFPath. If no .INF file is found, the ISAM uses the production index file (.CDX or .MDX) for the table. This entry is not written by default. |

| Key | Type | Default | Required? | Description (*cont'd*) |
|---|---|---|---|---|
| CollatingSequence | String | ASCII | N | The collating sequence for all dBASE tables created or opened using Microsoft Access. Possible values are ASCII and International. |
| DataCodePage | String | OEM | N | The character set in which string and memo values are stored. Possible values are OEM and ANSI. If this parameter is set to OEM, string values passed to SetColumn are passed through ANSItoOEM prior to storing in the XBase table. In the same manner, data retrieved from XBase tables are passed through OEMtoANSI before being returned from RetrieveColumn. |
| Deleted | Boolean | T | N | An On or Off indicator that determines how records marked for deletion are handled by Microsoft Jet. On corresponds to the dBASE command SET DELETED ON and indicates never to retrieve or position on a deleted record. Off corresponds to the dBASE command SET DELETED OFF and indicates to treat a deleted record like any other record. |
| Century | Boolean | F | N | An On or Off indicator for formatting the century component of dates in cases where date-to-string functions are used in index expressions. On corresponds to the dBASE command SET CENTURY ON, and Off corresponds to the dBASE command SET CENTURY OFF. |
| Date | String | MDY | N | The date formatting style to use in cases where date-to-string functions are used in index expressions. The possible settings for this entry, which correspond to the dBASE SET DATE command, are American, ANSI, British, French, DMY, German, Italian, Japan, MDY, USA, and YMD. |
| Mark | Integer | 0 | N | The decimal value of the ASCII character used to separate date parts. |
| Exact | Boolean | F | N | An On or Off indicator for date comparisons. On corresponds to the dBASE command SET EXACT ON. Off corresponds to the dBASE command SET EXACT OFF. |
| KanjiStr | Boolean | 00 | N | 00 means to treat strings as simple byte arrays. 01 means to treat strings as DBCS character strings. The KanjiStr entry is equivalent to the dBASE command SET KANJISTRING = ON. It affects the operation of the LEFT(), RIGHT(), SUBSTR(), AT(), REPLICATE(), and STUFF() functions inside the dBASE engine. A setting of 01 is recommended for DBCS countries. |

# Paradox Settings

The following table details the entries that are installed for the Paradox engine.

**Tree: ...\Engines\Paradox**

| Key | Type | Default | Required? | Description |
|---|---|---|---|---|
| PageTimeout | Integer | 600 | N | The length of time between when data is placed in an internal cache and when it's invalidated. The value is specified in 100 millisecond units. The default is 600 (60 seconds). |
| ParadoxUserName | String | Microsoft Access | N | The name to be displayed by Paradox if a table is locked by the Paradox ISAM, and an interactive user accessing the data from Paradox (rather than the ISAM) attempts to place an incompatible lock. This entry isn't added if the computer isn't on a network. The Setup program sets this to the Microsoft Access user name. |
| ParadoxNetPath | String | C:\MS Office\Access | N | The full path to the directory containing the PARADOX.NET file (for Paradox 3.*x*) or the PDOXUSRS.NET file (for Paradox 4.*x*). This entry isn't added unless the computer is on a network. Usually, you need to change the initial setting (added by the Setup program), which is a best guess at where the file might be. The full ParadoxNetPath (including the drive letter) must be consistent for all users sharing a particular database (directory). If you indicate a ParadoxNetPath, you must also specify a ParadoxUserName and a ParadoxNetStyle, or you'll receive an error when trying to access external Paradox data. |
| ParadoxNetStyle | String | 4.*x* | N | The network access style to use when accessing Paradox data. Possible values are 3.*x* and 4.*x* (Note that Paradox 3.*x* users can't set this to 4.*x* or the ISAM will use the wrong locking method.) This entry isn't added unless the computer is on a network. This entry should correspond to whatever version of Paradox users in the group are using. It must be consistent for all users sharing a particular database (directory). |

| Key | Type | Default | Required? | Description (*cont'd*) |
|---|---|---|---|---|
| CollatingSequence | String | ASCII | N | The collating sequence for all Paradox tables created or opened using Microsoft Jet. Possible values are ASCII, International, Norwegian-Danish, Japanese and Swedish-Finnish. Note that the CollatingSequence entry must match the collating sequence used when the Paradox table was built, or the ISAM returns an error with the TableOpen API is used. |
| DataCodePage | String | OEM | N | The character set in which string and memo values are stored. Possible values are OEM and ANSI. If this parameter is set to OEM, string values passed to SetColumn are passed through ANSItoOEM prior to storing in the Paradox table. In the same manner, data retrieved from Paradox tables are passed through OEMtoANSI before being returned from RetrieveColumn. |

# Microsoft Excel Settings

The following table details the entries that are installed for the Microsoft Excel engine.

**Tree: ...\Engines\Excel**

| Key | Type | Default | Required? | Description |
|---|---|---|---|---|
| TypeGuessRows | Integer | 8 | N | The number of rows in the worksheet range to scan to determine column types. If set to zero, then all rows in the range are checked. |
| ImportMixedTypes | String | Text | N | If a column contains more than one type of data (during the scan of TypeGuessRows rows), the type of the column is determined to be JET_coltypText if this parameter is set to Text. If this parameter is set to Majority Type, the most common type in the column determines the column type. |
| AppendBlankRows | Integer | 1 | N | For single worksheet formats (Microsoft Excel 3.0, Microsoft Excel 4.0, Lotus WK1), when exports are performed the new table is added after any existing data on the sheet plus *n* rows, where *n* is given by this parameter. For example, if the worksheet dimensions are A1..B50 prior to the export, and AppendBlankRows is set to 4, new data is stored starting at row 55. This parameter can have values between 0 and 16. |
| FirstRowHasNames | Boolean | T | N | **True** if the cells of the first row of the range contain the column names for the table. |

# Lotus Settings

The Lotus settings are stored in ...\Engines\Lotus. The parameter names, types, and defaults are the same for the Microsoft Excel type.

# Text Settings

The following table details the entries that are installed for the text engine.

**Tree: ...\Engines\Text**

| Key | Type | Default | Required? | Description |
|---|---|---|---|---|
| MaxScanRows | Integer | 25 | N | The number of rows in the file to scan to determine column types. If set to zero, then all rows in the file are checked. |
| FirstRowHasNames | Boolean | Yes | N | **True** if the first row of the file contains the column names for the table. |
| CharacterSet | String | OEM | N | The character set in which string and memo values are stored. Possible values are OEM and ANSI. If this parameter is set to OEM, string values passed to SetColumn are passed through ANSItoOEM prior to storing in the file. In the same manner, data retrieved from the file is passed through OEMtoANSI before being returned from RetrieveColumn. |
| Format | String | CSV Delimited | N | The default format for files read or written by the text IISAM. The format can be overridden by import and export specifications for specific files (through the text wizard) but this value is the default in the absence of a specific file specification. |
| Extensions | String | txt, csv, tab, asc | N | A list of file name extensions to use when determining the list of files to return from the GetObjectInfo API (Infolevel JET_ObjInfoList). Each extension in this list must be from 1 to 3 characters or the string "None". |
| ExportCurrencySymbols | Boolean | T | N | When set to **True**, values in columns of type JET_coltypCurrency are written to the file with the currency symbol. For example, "$1.12". Storing the currency symbols in the file allows the data to be reimported as a currency type. When set to **False**, the previous value would be written as "1.12". |

APPENDIX D

# Error Reference

This appendix presents the complete list of error numbers and error messages returned by the Microsoft Jet database engine. In addition to the error number and message, the following table indicates the class to which the error belongs.

| Class | Description |
| --- | --- |
| BTRIEVE | Btrieve installable ISAM-specific errors (Microsoft Jet version 2.5 and earlier) |
| DAO | DAO-specific errors |
| DBASE | dBASE installable ISAM-specific errors |
| DDL | Data Definition Language-specific errors |
| EXCEL | Microsoft Excel installable ISAM-specific errors |
| IMEX | Generic import/export errors |
| INST ISAM | Generic installable ISAM errors |
| ISAM | Generic Microsoft Jet ISAM errors |
| JPM | Microsoft Jet errors related to property management |
| EXTENDED | Errors that could have extended error information |
| MISC | Microsoft Jet errors not fitting into another category |
| PARADOX | Paradox installable ISAM-specific errors |
| QUERY | Microsoft Jet errors related to queries |
| REF INTEGRITY | Microsoft Jet errors related to referential integrity |
| REMOTE | Microsoft Jet errors specific to ODBC |
| REPLICATOR | Microsoft Jet errors related to replication |
| SECURITY | Microsoft Jet errors related to security |
| TEXT | Text installable ISAM-specific errors |
| UNUSED | Microsoft Jet errors that are no longer used or that have special meaning. Errors that have special meaning are usually translations from other errors and are not generated in the Microsoft Jet code. |

For additional information about these errors, see the Jet Error Message Reference in the DAO SDK online Helpfile on the companion CD-ROM. The Jet Error Message Reference contains the Microsoft Jet error number, error message, and Help topic for each error listed in the following table.

An asterisk (*) means that there is no Jet error message text for a particular error message. An '|' represents a placeholder for a value that is given when the error message is displayed.

| Error number | Microsoft Jet error message | Class |
|---|---|---|
| 3000 | Reserved error ('|'); there is no message for this error. | UNUSED |
| 3001 | Invalid argument. | MISC |
| 3002 | Couldn't start session. | ISAM |
| 3003 | Couldn't start transaction; too many transactions already nested. | ISAM |
| 3004 | Couldn't find database '|'. | REPLICATOR |
| 3005 | '|' isn't a valid database name. | ISAM |
| 3006 | Database '|' is exclusively locked. | ISAM |
| 3007 | Can't open library database '|'. | ISAM |
| 3008 | Table '|' is exclusively locked. | ISAM |
| 3009 | Couldn't lock table '|'; currently in use. | ISAM |
| 3010 | Table '|' already exists. | MISC |
| 3011 | Couldn't find object '|'. | MISC |
| 3012 | Object '|' already exists. | ISAM |
| 3013 | Couldn't rename installable ISAM file. | ISAM |
| 3014 | Can't open any more tables. | ISAM |
| 3015 | '|' isn't an index in this table. | ISAM |
| 3016 | Field won't fit in record. | ISAM |
| 3017 | The size of a field is too long. | MISC |
| 3018 | Couldn't find field '|'. | MISC |
| 3019 | Operation invalid without a current index. | ISAM |
| 3020 | Update or CancelUpdate without AddNew or Edit. | MISC |
| 3021 | No current record. | MISC |
| 3022 | Duplicate value in index, primary key, or relationship. Changes were unsuccessful. | ISAM |
| 3023 | AddNew or Edit already used. | QUERY |
| 3024 | Couldn't find file '|'. | MISC |
| 3025 | Can't open any more files. | ISAM |

| Error number | Microsoft Jet error message | Class (*cont'd*) |
| --- | --- | --- |
| 3026 | Not enough space on disk. | ISAM |
| 3027 | Can't update. Database or object is read-only. | MISC |
| 3028 | Can't start your application. The system database is missing or opened exclusively by another user. | ISAM |
| 3029 | Not a valid account name or password. | SECURITY |
| 3030 | '\|' isn't a valid account name. | SECURITY |
| 3031 | Not a valid password. | SECURITY |
| 3032 | Can't perform this operation. | SECURITY |
| 3033 | No permission for '\|'. | MISC |
| 3034 | Commit or Rollback without BeginTrans. | ISAM |
| 3035 | * | MISC |
| 3036 | Database has reached maximum size. | ISAM |
| 3037 | Can't open any more tables or queries. | MISC |
| 3038 | * | ISAM |
| 3039 | Couldn't create index; too many indexes already defined. | ISAM |
| 3040 | Disk I/O error during read. | ISAM |
| 3041 | Can't open a database created with a previous version of your application. | ISAM |
| 3042 | Out of MS-DOS file handles. | ISAM |
| 3043 | Disk or network error. | UNUSED |
| 3044 | '\|' isn't a valid path. | ISAM |
| 3045 | Couldn't use '\|'; file already in use. | ISAM |
| 3046 | Couldn't save; currently locked by another user. | ISAM |
| 3047 | Record is too large. | ISAM |
| 3048 | Can't open any more databases. | ISAM |
| 3049 | Can't open database '\|'. It may not be a database that your application recognizes, or the file may be corrupt. | MISC |
| 3050 | Couldn't lock file. | ISAM |
| 3051 | Couldn't open file '\|'. | MISC |
| 3052 | MS-DOS file sharing lock count exceeded. You need to increase the number of locks installed with SHARE.EXE. | ISAM |
| 3053 | Too many client tasks. | MISC |
| 3054 | Too many Memo or OLE object fields. | UNUSED |
| 3055 | Not a valid file name. | MISC |
| 3056 | Couldn't repair this database. | MISC |

| Error number | Microsoft Jet error message | Class (*cont'd*) |
| --- | --- | --- |
| 3057 | Operation not supported on attached, or linked, tables. | MISC |
| 3058 | Index or primary key can't contain a null value. | ISAM |
| 3059 | Operation canceled by user. | MISC |
| 3060 | Wrong data type for parameter '|'. | QUERY |
| 3061 | Too few parameters. Expected '|'. | EXTENDED |
| 3062 | Duplicate output alias '|'. | EXTENDED |
| 3063 | Duplicate output destination '|'. | EXTENDED |
| 3064 | Can't open action query '|'. | QUERY |
| 3065 | Can't execute a non-action query. | QUERY |
| 3066 | Query or table must contain at least one output field. | EXTENDED |
| 3067 | Query input must contain at least one table or query. | EXTENDED |
| 3068 | Not a valid alias name. | QUERY |
| 3069 | The action query '|' cannot be used as a row source. | EXTENDED |
| 3070 | Can't bind name '|'. | QUERY |
| 3071 | Can't evaluate expression. | QUERY |
| 3072 | '|' | EXTENDED |
| 3073 | Operation must use an updatable query. | QUERY |
| 3074 | Can't repeat table name '|' in FROM clause. | EXTENDED |
| 3075 | '|1' in query expression '|2'. | EXTENDED |
| 3076 | '|' in criteria expression. | EXTENDED |
| 3077 | '|' in expression. | EXTENDED |
| 3078 | Couldn't find input table or query '|'. | EXTENDED |
| 3079 | Ambiguous field reference '|'. | EXTENDED |
| 3080 | Joined table '|' not listed in FROM clause. | EXTENDED |
| 3081 | Can't join more than one table with the same name ('|'). | EXTENDED |
| 3082 | JOIN operation '|' refers to a non-joined table. | EXTENDED |
| 3083 | Can't use internal report query. | QUERY |
| 3084 | Can't insert data with action query. | QUERY |
| 3085 | Undefined function '|' in expression. | EXTENDED |
| 3086 | Couldn't delete from specified tables. | QUERY |
| 3087 | Too many expressions in GROUP BY clause. | QUERY |
| 3088 | Too many expressions in ORDER BY clause. | QUERY |

| Error number | Microsoft Jet error message | Class (*cont'd*) |
|---|---|---|
| 3089 | Too many expressions in DISTINCT output. | QUERY |
| 3090 | Resultant table not allowed to have more than one Counter or Autonumber field. | ISAM |
| 3091 | HAVING clause ('|') without grouping or aggregation. | UNUSED |
| 3092 | Can't use HAVING clause in TRANSFORM statement. | EXTENDED |
| 3093 | ORDER BY clause ('|') conflicts with DISTINCT. | EXTENDED |
| 3094 | ORDER BY clause ('|') conflicts with GROUP BY clause. | EXTENDED |
| 3095 | Can't have aggregate function in expression ('|'). | EXTENDED |
| 3096 | Can't have aggregate function in WHERE clause ('|'). | EXTENDED |
| 3097 | Can't have aggregate function in ORDER BY clause ('|'). | EXTENDED |
| 3098 | Can't have aggregate function in GROUP BY clause ('|'). | EXTENDED |
| 3099 | Can't have aggregate function in JOIN operation ('|'). | EXTENDED |
| 3100 | Can't set field '|' in join key to Null. | EXTENDED |
| 3101 | There is no record in table '|2' with key matching field(s) '|1'. | EXTENDED |
| 3102 | Circular reference caused by '|'. | EXTENDED |
| 3103 | Circular reference caused by alias '|' in query definition's SELECT list. | EXTENDED |
| 3104 | Can't specify Fixed Column Heading '|' in a crosstab query more than once. | EXTENDED |
| 3105 | Missing destination field name in SELECT INTO statement ('|'). | EXTENDED |
| 3106 | Missing destination field name in UPDATE statement ('|'). | EXTENDED |
| 3107 | Record(s) can't be added; no Insert Data permission on '|'. | EXTENDED |
| 3108 | Record(s) can't be edited; no Update Data permission on '|'. | EXTENDED |
| 3109 | Record(s) can't be deleted; no Delete Data permission on '|'. | EXTENDED |
| 3110 | Couldn't read definitions; no Read Design permission for table or query '|'. | EXTENDED |
| 3111 | Couldn't create; no Create permission for table or query '|'. | EXTENDED |
| 3112 | Record(s) can't be read; no Read Data permission on '|'. | EXTENDED |
| 3113 | Can't update '|'; field not updatable. | UNUSED |
| 3114 | Can't include Memo or OLE object when you select unique values ('|'). | EXTENDED |
| 3115 | Can't have Memo or OLE object in aggregate argument ('|'). | EXTENDED |
| 3116 | Can't have Memo or OLE object in criteria ('|') for aggregate function. | EXTENDED |
| 3117 | Can't sort on Memo or OLE object ('|'). | EXTENDED |
| 3118 | Can't join on Memo or OLE object ('|'). | EXTENDED |
| 3119 | Can't group on Memo or OLE object ('|'). | EXTENDED |
| 3120 | Can't group on fields selected with '*' ('|'). | EXTENDED |

| Error number | Microsoft Jet error message | Class (*cont'd*) |
|---|---|---|
| 3121 | Can't group on fields selected with '*'. | EXTENDED |
| 3122 | '\|' not part of aggregate function or grouping. | EXTENDED |
| 3123 | Can't use '*' in crosstab query. | EXTENDED |
| 3124 | Can't input from internal report query ('\|'). | QUERY |
| 3125 | '\|' isn't a valid name. | MISC |
| 3126 | Invalid bracketing of name '\|'. | EXTENDED |
| 3127 | INSERT INTO statement contains unknown field name '\|'. | EXTENDED |
| 3128 | Must specify tables to delete from. | QUERY |
| 3129 | Invalid SQL statement; expected DELETE, INSERT, PROCEDURE, SELECT, or UPDATE. | QUERY |
| 3130 | Syntax error in DELETE statement. | QUERY |
| 3131 | Syntax error in FROM clause. | QUERY |
| 3132 | Syntax error in GROUP BY clause. | QUERY |
| 3133 | Syntax error in HAVING clause. | QUERY |
| 3134 | Syntax error in INSERT statement. | QUERY |
| 3135 | Syntax error in JOIN operation. | QUERY |
| 3136 | Syntax error in LEVEL clause. | QUERY |
| 3137 | Missing semicolon (;) at end of SQL statement. | QUERY |
| 3138 | Syntax error in ORDER BY clause. | QUERY |
| 3139 | Syntax error in PARAMETER clause. | QUERY |
| 3140 | Syntax error in PROCEDURE clause. | QUERY |
| 3141 | Syntax error in SELECT statement. | QUERY |
| 3142 | Characters found after end of SQL statement. | QUERY |
| 3143 | Syntax error in TRANSFORM statement. | QUERY |
| 3144 | Syntax error in UPDATE statement. | QUERY |
| 3145 | Syntax error in WHERE clause. | QUERY |
| 3146 | ODBC—call failed. | UNUSED |
| 3147 | * | UNUSED |
| 3148 | * | UNUSED |
| 3149 | * | UNUSED |
| 3150 | * | UNUSED |
| 3151 | ODBC—connection to '\|' failed. | EXTENDED |
| 3152 | * | UNUSED |

| Error number | Microsoft Jet error message | Class (*cont'd*) |
|---|---|---|
| 3153 | * | UNUSED |
| 3154 | ODBC—couldn't find DLL '|'. | REMOTE |
| 3155 | ODBC—insert failed on attached (linked) table '|'. | EXTENDED |
| 3156 | ODBC—delete failed on attached (linked) table '|'. | EXTENDED |
| 3157 | ODBC—update failed on attached (linked) table '|'. | EXTENDED |
| 3158 | Couldn't save record; currently locked by another user. | INST ISAM |
| 3159 | Not a valid bookmark. | MISC |
| 3160 | Table isn't open. | INST ISAM |
| 3161 | Couldn't decrypt file. | INST ISAM |
| 3162 | Null is invalid. | MISC |
| 3163 | Couldn't perform operation; data too long for field. | MISC |
| 3164 | Field can't be updated. | MISC |
| 3165 | Couldn't open .INF file. | DBASE |
| 3166 | Missing memo file. | DBASE |
| 3167 | Record is deleted. | MISC |
| 3168 | Invalid .INF file. | DBASE |
| 3169 | Illegal type in expression. | QUERY |
| 3170 | Couldn't find installable ISAM. | UNUSED |
| 3171 | Couldn't find net path or user name. | PARADOX |
| 3172 | Couldn't open PARADOX.NET. | UNUSED |
| 3173 | Couldn't open table 'MSysAccounts' in the system database file. | SECURITY |
| 3174 | Couldn't open table 'MSysGroups' in the system database file. | SECURITY |
| 3175 | Date is out of range or is in an invalid format. | INST ISAM |
| 3176 | Couldn't open file '|'. | IMEX |
| 3177 | Not a valid table name. | IMEX |
| 3178 | * | IMEX |
| 3179 | Encountered unexpected end of file. | IMEX |
| 3180 | Couldn't write to file '|'. | IMEX |
| 3181 | Invalid range. | IMEX |
| 3182 | Invalid file format. | IMEX |
| 3183 | Not enough space on temporary disk. | ISAM |
| 3184 | Couldn't execute query; couldn't find attached, or linked, table. | EXTENDED |
| 3185 | SELECT INTO remote database tried to produce too many fields. | EXTENDED |

| Error number | Microsoft Jet error message | Class (*cont'd*) |
| --- | --- | --- |
| 3186 | Couldn't save; currently locked by user '\|2' on machine '\|1'. | EXTENDED |
| 3187 | Couldn't read; currently locked by user '\|2' on machine '\|1'. | EXTENDED |
| 3188 | Couldn't update; currently locked by another session on this machine. | ISAM |
| 3189 | Table '\|1' is exclusively locked by user '\|3' on machine '\|2'. | UNUSED |
| 3190 | Too many fields defined. | ISAM |
| 3191 | Can't define field more than once. | ISAM |
| 3192 | Couldn't find output table '\|'. | EXTENDED |
| 3193 | (unknown) | UNUSED |
| 3194 | (unknown) | UNUSED |
| 3195 | (expression) | UNUSED |
| 3196 | Couldn't use '\|'; database already in use. | ISAM |
| 3197 | Data has changed; operation stopped. | MISC |
| 3198 | Couldn't start session. Too many sessions already active. | ISAM |
| 3199 | Couldn't find reference. | REF INTEGRITY |
| 3200 | Can't delete or change record. Since related records exist in table '\|', referential integrity rules would be violated. | EXTENDED |
| 3201 | Can't add or change record. Referential integrity rules require a related record in table '\|'. | EXTENDED |
| 3202 | Couldn't save; currently locked by another user. | ISAM |
| 3203 | Can't specify subquery in expression ('\|'). | EXTENDED |
| 3204 | Database already exists. | ISAM |
| 3205 | Too many crosstab column headers ('\|'). | EXTENDED |
| 3206 | Can't create a relationship between a field and itself. | REF INTEGRITY |
| 3207 | Operation not supported on Paradox table with no primary key. | PARADOX |
| 3208 | Invalid Deleted entry in the Xbase section of initialization setting. | DBASE |
| 3209 | Invalid Stats entry in the Xbase section of initialization setting. | DBASE |
| 3210 | Connection string too long. | QUERY |
| 3211 | Couldn't lock table '\|'; currently in use. | EXTENDED |
| 3212 | Couldn't lock table '\|1'; currently in use by user '\|3' on machine '\|2'. | UNUSED |
| 3213 | Invalid Date entry in the Xbase section of initialization setting. | DBASE |
| 3214 | Invalid Mark entry in the Xbase section of initialization setting. | DBASE |
| 3215 | Too many Btrieve tasks. | BTRIEVE |

| Error number | Microsoft Jet error message | Class (*cont'd*) |
|---|---|---|
| 3216 | Parameter '|' specified where a table name is required. | EXTENDED |
| 3217 | Parameter '|' specified where a database name is required. | EXTENDED |
| 3218 | Couldn't update; currently locked. | ISAM |
| 3219 | Invalid operation. | MISC |
| 3220 | Incorrect collating sequence. | PARADOX |
| 3221 | Invalid entries in the Btrieve section of initialization setting. | BTRIEVE |
| 3222 | Query can't contain a Database parameter. | QUERY |
| 3223 | '|' isn't a valid parameter name. | EXTENDED |
| 3224 | Can't read Btrieve data dictionary. | BTRIEVE |
| 3225 | Encountered record locking deadlock while performing Btrieve operation. | BTRIEVE |
| 3226 | Errors encountered while using the Btrieve DLL. | BTRIEVE |
| 3227 | Invalid Century entry in the Xbase section of initialization setting. | DBASE |
| 3228 | Invalid Collating Sequence. | PARADOX |
| 3229 | Btrieve—can't change field. | BTRIEVE |
| 3230 | Out-of-date Paradox lock file. | PARADOX |
| 3231 | ODBC—field would be too long; data truncated. | REMOTE |
| 3232 | ODBC—couldn't create table. | REMOTE |
| 3233 | * | UNUSED |
| 3234 | ODBC—remote query timeout expired. | REMOTE |
| 3235 | ODBC—data type not supported on server. | REMOTE |
| 3236 | * | UNUSED |
| 3237 | * | UNUSED |
| 3238 | ODBC—data out of range. | REMOTE |
| 3239 | Too many active users. | ISAM |
| 3240 | Btrieve—missing Btrieve engine. | BTRIEVE |
| 3241 | Btrieve—out of resources. | BTRIEVE |
| 3242 | Invalid reference in SELECT statement. | EXTENDED |
| 3243 | None of the import field names match fields in the appended table. | IMEX |
| 3244 | Can't import password-protected spreadsheet. | IMEX |
| 3245 | Couldn't parse field names from first row of import table. | IMEX |
| 3246 | Operation not supported in transactions. | MISC |
| 3247 | ODBC—linked table definition has changed. | REMOTE |
| 3248 | Invalid NetworkAccess entry in initialization setting. | INST ISAM |

| Error number | Microsoft Jet error message | Class (*cont'd*) |
|---|---|---|
| 3249 | Invalid PageTimeout entry in initialization setting. | INST ISAM |
| 3250 | Couldn't build key. | ISAM |
| 3251 | Operation is not supported for this type of object. | MISC |
| 3252 | Can't open form whose underlying query contains a user-defined function that attempts to set or get the form's RecordsetClone property. | MISC |
| 3253 | * | UNUSED |
| 3254 | ODBC—Can't lock all records. | REMOTE |
| 3255 | * | UNUSED |
| 3256 | Index file not found. | DBASE |
| 3257 | Syntax error in WITH OWNERACCESS OPTION declaration. | QUERY |
| 3258 | Query contains ambiguous outer joins. | QUERY |
| 3259 | Invalid field data type. | MISC |
| 3260 | Couldn't update; currently locked by user '|2' on machine '|1'. | EXTENDED |
| 3261 | '|' | EXTENDED |
| 3262 | '|' | EXTENDED |
| 3263 | Invalid database object. | MISC |
| 3264 | No fields defined—cannot append Tabledef or Index. | DAO |
| 3265 | Item not found in this collection. | DAO |
| 3266 | Can't append. Field is part of a TableDefs collection. | DAO |
| 3267 | Property can be set only when the field is part of a Recordset object's Fields collection. | DAO |
| 3268 | Can't set this property once the object is part of a collection. | DAO |
| 3269 | Can't append. Index is part of a TableDefs collection. | DAO |
| 3270 | Property not found. | DAO |
| 3271 | Invalid property value. | DAO |
| 3272 | Object isn't a collection. | DAO |
| 3273 | Method not applicable for this object. | DAO |
| 3274 | External table isn't in the expected format. | INST ISAM |
| 3275 | Unexpected error from external database driver ('|'). | INST ISAM |
| 3276 | Invalid database ID. | MISC |
| 3277 | Can't have more than 10 fields in an index. | ISAM |
| 3278 | Database engine hasn't been initialized. | MISC |
| 3279 | Database engine has already been initialized. | MISC |

| Error number | Microsoft Jet error message | Class (*cont'd*) |
|---|---|---|
| 3280 | Can't delete a field that is part of an index or is needed by the system. | ISAM |
| 3281 | Can't delete this index. It is either the current index or is used in a relationship. | ISAM |
| 3282 | Can't create field or index in a table that is already defined. | ISAM |
| 3283 | Primary key already exists. | ISAM |
| 3284 | Index already exists. | ISAM |
| 3285 | Invalid index definition. | ISAM |
| 3286 | Format of memo file doesn't match specified external database format. | INST ISAM |
| 3287 | Can't create index on the given field. | ISAM |
| 3288 | Paradox index is not primary. | PARADOX |
| 3289 | Syntax error in CONSTRAINT clause. | DDL |
| 3290 | Syntax error in CREATE TABLE statement. | DDL |
| 3291 | Syntax error in CREATE INDEX statement. | DDL |
| 3292 | Syntax error in field definition. | DDL |
| 3293 | Syntax error in ALTER TABLE statement. | DDL |
| 3294 | Syntax error in DROP INDEX statement. | DDL |
| 3295 | Syntax error in DROP TABLE or DROP INDEX. | DDL |
| 3296 | Join expression not supported. | MISC |
| 3297 | Couldn't import table or query. No records found, or all records contain errors. | IMEX |
| 3298 | There are several tables with that name. Please specify owner in the format owner.table. | REMOTE |
| 3299 | ODBC Specification Conformance Error ('|'). This error should be reported to the ODBC driver vendor. | UNUSED |
| 3300 | Can't create a relationship. | REF INTEGRITY |
| 3301 | Can't perform this operation; features in this version are not available in databases with older formats. | MISC |
| 3302 | Can't change a rule while the rules for this table are in use. | TLV |
| 3303 | Can't delete this field. It's part of one or more relationships. | REF INTEGRITY |
| 3304 | You must enter a personal identifier (PID) consisting of at least four and no more than 20 characters and digits. | SECURITY |
| 3305 | Invalid connection string in pass-through query. | REMOTE |

| Error number | Microsoft Jet error message | Class (*cont'd*) |
|---|---|---|
| 3306 | At most one field can be returned from a subquery that doesn't use the EXISTS keyword. | QUERY |
| 3307 | The number of columns in the two selected tables or queries of a union query don't match. | QUERY |
| 3308 | Invalid TOP argument in select query. | EXTENDED |
| 3309 | Property setting can't be larger than 2 KB. | JPM |
| 3310 | This property isn't supported for external data sources or for databases created in a previous version. | JPM |
| 3311 | Property specified already exists. | JPM |
| 3312 | Validation rules and default values can't be placed on system or attached (linked) tables. | TLV |
| 3313 | Can't place this validation expression on this field. | TLV |
| 3314 | Field '\|' can't contain a null value. | EXTENDED |
| 3315 | Field '\|' can't be a zero-length string. | EXTENDED |
| 3316 | '\|' | EXTENDED |
| 3317 | One or more values entered is prohibited by the validation rule '\|2' set for '\|1'. | UNUSED |
| 3318 | Top not allowed in delete queries. | EXTENDED |
| 3319 | Syntax error in union query. | QUERY |
| 3320 | '\|' in table-level validation expression. | EXTENDED |
| 3321 | No database specified in connection string or IN clause. | REMOTE |
| 3322 | Crosstab query contains one or more invalid fixed column headings. | EXTENDED |
| 3323 | The query cannot be used as a row source. | QUERY |
| 3324 | This query is a DDL query and cannot be used as a row source. | QUERY |
| 3325 | Pass-through query with ReturnsRecords property set to True did not return any records. | REMOTE |
| 3326 | This Recordset is not updatable. | EXTENDED |
| 3327 | Field '\|' is based on an expression and can't be edited. | EXTENDED |
| 3328 | Table '\|2' is read-only. | EXTENDED |
| 3329 | Record in table '\|' was deleted by another user. | EXTENDED |
| 3330 | Record in table '\|' is locked by another user. | EXTENDED |
| 3331 | To make changes to this field, first save the record. | EXTENDED |
| 3332 | Can't enter value into blank field on "one" side of outer join. | EXTENDED |
| 3333 | Records in table '\|' would have no record on the "one" side. | EXTENDED |
| 3334 | Can be present only in version 1.0 format. | ISAM |
| 3335 | DeleteOnly called with non-zero cbData. | JPM |

| Error number | Microsoft Jet error message | Class (*cont'd*) |
|---|---|---|
| 3336 | Btrieve: Invalid IndexDDF option in initialization setting. | BTRIEVE |
| 3337 | Invalid DataCodePage option in initialization setting. | BTRIEVE |
| 3338 | Btrieve: Xtrieve options aren't correct in initialization setting. | BTRIEVE |
| 3339 | Btrieve: Invalid IndexDeleteRenumber option in initialization setting. | BTRIEVE |
| 3340 | Query '\|' is corrupt. | EXTENDED |
| 3341 | Current field must match join key '\|' on "one" side of one-to-many relationship because it has been updated. | EXTENDED |
| 3342 | Invalid Memo or OLE object in subquery '\|'. | EXTENDED |
| 3343 | Unrecognized database format '\|'. | EXTENDED |
| 3344 | Unknown or invalid reference '\|1' in validation expression or default value in table '\|2'. | EXTENDED |
| 3345 | Unknown or invalid field reference '\|'. | EXTENDED |
| 3346 | Number of query values and destination fields aren't the same. | QUERY |
| 3347 | Can't add record(s); primary key for table '\|' not in recordset. | EXTENDED |
| 3348 | Can't add record(s); join key of table '\|' not in recordset. | EXTENDED |
| 3349 | Numeric field overflow. | INST ISAM |
| 3350 | Object is invalid for operation. | ISAM |
| 3351 | ORDER BY expression ('\|') uses non-output fields. | EXTENDED |
| 3352 | No destination field name in INSERT INTO statement ('\|'). | EXTENDED |
| 3353 | Btrieve: Can't find file FIELD.DDF. | BTRIEVE |
| 3354 | At most one record can be returned by this subquery. | QUERY |
| 3355 | Syntax error in default value. | TLV |
| 3356 | The database is opened by user '\|2' on machine '\|1'. | EXTENDED |
| 3357 | This query is not a properly formed data-definition query. | QUERY |
| 3358 | Can't open Microsoft Jet engine system database. | MISC |
| 3359 | Pass-through query must contain at least one character. | QUERY |
| 3360 | Query is too complex. | QUERY |
| 3361 | Unions not allowed in a subquery. | QUERY |
| 3362 | Single-row update/delete affected more than one row of an attached (linked) table. Unique index contains duplicate values. | REMOTE |
| 3363 | Record(s) can't be added; no corresponding record on the "one" side. | EXTENDED |
| 3364 | Can't use Memo or OLE object field '\|' in SELECT clause of a union query. | EXTENDED |
| 3365 | Property value not valid for REMOTE objects. | DAO |
| 3366 | Can't append a relation with no fields defined. | DAO |

| Error number | Microsoft Jet error message | Class (*cont'd*) |
| --- | --- | --- |
| 3367 | Can't append. Object already in collection. | DAO |
| 3368 | Relationship must be on the same number of fields with the same data types. | DDL |
| 3369 | Can't find field in index definition. | DDL |
| 3370 | Can't modify the design of table '\|'. It's in a read-only database. | EXTENDED |
| 3371 | Can't find table or constraint. | EXTENDED |
| 3372 | No such index '\|2' on table '\|1'. | EXTENDED |
| 3373 | Can't create relationship. Referenced table '\|' doesn't have a primary key. | EXTENDED |
| 3374 | The specified fields are not uniquely indexed in table '\|'. | EXTENDED |
| 3375 | Table '\|1' already has an index named '\|2'. | EXTENDED |
| 3376 | Table '\|' doesn't exist. | EXTENDED |
| 3377 | No such relationship '\|2' on table '\|1'. | EXTENDED |
| 3378 | There is already a relationship named '\|' in the current database. | EXTENDED |
| 3379 | Can't create relationships to enforce referential integrity. Existing data in table '\|2' violates referential integrity rules with related table '\|1'. | EXTENDED |
| 3380 | Field '\|2' already exists in table '\|1'. | EXTENDED |
| 3381 | There is no field named '\|2' in table '\|1'. | EXTENDED |
| 3382 | The size of field '\|' is too long. | EXTENDED |
| 3383 | Can't delete field '\|'. It's part of one or more relationships. | EXTENDED |
| 3384 | Can't delete a built-in property. | DAO |
| 3385 | User-defined properties don't support a Null value. | DAO |
| 3386 | Property '\|' must be set before using this method. | DAO |
| 3387 | Can't find TEMP directory. | UNUSED |
| 3388 | Unknown function '\|2' in validation expression or default value on '\|1'. | EXTENDED |
| 3389 | Query support unavailable. | MISC |
| 3390 | Account name already exists. | SECURITY |
| 3391 | An error has occurred. Properties were not saved. | JPM |
| 3392 | There is no primary key in table '\|'. | EXTENDED |
| 3393 | Can't perform join, group, sort, or indexed restriction. A value being searched or sorted on is too long. | QUERY |
| 3394 | Can't save property; property is a schema property. | JPM |
| 3395 | Invalid referential integrity constraint. | REF INTEGRITY |
| 3396 | Can't perform cascading operation. Since related records exist in table '\|', referential integrity rules would be violated. | EXTENDED |

| Error number | Microsoft Jet error message | Class (*cont'd*) |
|---|---|---|
| 3397 | Can't perform cascading operation. There must be a related record in table '|'. | EXTENDED |
| 3398 | Can't perform cascading operation. It would result in a null key in table '|'. | EXTENDED |
| 3399 | Can't perform cascading operation. It would result in a duplicate key in table '|'. | EXTENDED |
| 3400 | Can't perform cascading operation. It would result in two updates on field '|2' in table '|1'. | EXTENDED |
| 3401 | Can't perform cascading operation. It would cause field '|' to become null, which is not allowed. | EXTENDED |
| 3402 | Can't perform cascading operation. It would cause field '|' to become a zero-length string, which is not allowed. | EXTENDED |
| 3403 | Can't perform cascading operation: '|'. | EXTENDED |
| 3404 | Can't perform cascading operation. The value entered is prohibited by the validation rule '|2' set for '|1'. | UNUSED |
| 3405 | Error '|' in validation rule. | UNUSED |
| 3406 | Error '|' in default value. | UNUSED |
| 3407 | The server's MSysConf table exists, but is in an incorrect format. Contact your system administrator. | REMOTE |
| 3408 | Too many FastFind Sessions were invoked. | MISC |
| 3409 | Invalid field name '|' in definition of index or relationship. | EXTENDED |
| 3410 | * | UNUSED |
| 3411 | Invalid entry. Can't perform cascading operation specified in table '|1' because value entered is too big for field '|2'. | EXTENDED |
| 3412 | '|' | EXTENDED |
| 3413 | Can't perform cascading update on table '|1' because it is currently in use by user '|3' on machine '|2'. | EXTENDED |
| 3414 | Can't perform cascading update on table '|' because it is currently in use. | EXTENDED |
| 3415 | Zero-length string is valid only in a text or Memo field. | MISC |
| 3416 | '|' | UNUSED |
| 3417 | An action query cannot be used as a row source. | QUERY |
| 3418 | Can't open '|'. Another user has the table open using a different network control file or locking style. | PARADOX |
| 3419 | Can't open this Paradox 4.*x* or Paradox 5.*x* table because ParadoxNetStyle is set to 3.*x* in the initialization setting. | PARADOX |
| 3420 | Object is invalid or not set. | DAO |
| 3421 | Data type conversion error. | UNUSED |

| Error number | Microsoft Jet error message | Class (*cont'd*) |
|---|---|---|
| 3422 | Can't modify table structure. Another user has the table open. | ISAM |
| 3423 | You cannot use ODBC to import from, export to, or link an external Microsoft Access or ISAM database table to your database. | REMOTE |
| 3424 | Can't create database; Invalid locale. | ISAM |
| 3425 | This method or property is not currently available on this Recordset. | UNUSED |
| 3426 | The action was canceled by an associated object. | UNUSED |
| 3427 | Error in DAO automation. | UNUSED |
| 3428 | The Jet database engine has encountered a problem in your database. To correct the problem, you must repair and compact the database. | ISAM |
| 3429 | Incompatible installable ISAM version. | ISAM |
| 3430 | While loading the Excel installable ISAM, OLE was unable to initialize. | EXCEL |
| 3431 | This is not an Excel 5 file. | EXCEL |
| 3432 | Error opening an Excel 5 file. | EXCEL |
| 3433 | Invalid parameter in ISAM Engines section of the initialization setting. | INST ISAM |
| 3434 | Can't expand named range. | EXCEL |
| 3435 | Cannot delete spreadsheet cells. | EXCEL |
| 3436 | Failure creating file. | EXCEL |
| 3437 | Spreadsheet is full. | EXCEL |
| 3438 | The data being exported does not match the format described in the SCHEMA.INI file. | TEXT |
| 3439 | You attempted to attach or import a Microsoft Word mail merge file. Although you can export such files, you cannot attach or import them. | TEXT |
| 3440 | An attempt was made to import or attach to an empty text file. To import or attach a text file, the file must contain data. | TEXT |
| 3441 | Text file specification field separator matches decimal separator or text delimiter. | TEXT |
| 3442 | In the text file specification '\|1', the '\|2' option is invalid. | EXTENDED |
| 3443 | The fixed width specification '\|1', contains no column widths. | EXTENDED |
| 3444 | In the fixed width specification '\|1', column '\|2' does not specify a width. | EXTENDED |
| 3445 | An incorrect version of the Jet DLL file (MSAJT200.DLL for 16-bit versions, or MSJT2032 for 32-bit versions) was found. The version must be 2.5 or later. Try reinstalling the application that returned the error. | DAO |

| Error number | Microsoft Jet error message | Class (*cont'd*) |
|---|---|---|
| 3446 | The Jet VBA file (VBAJET.DLL for 16-bit versions, or VBAJET32.DLL for 32-bit versions) is missing. Try reinstalling the application that returned the error. | DAO |
| 3447 | The Jet VBA file (VBAJET.DLL for 16-bit versions, or VBAJET32.DLL for 32-bit versions) failed to initialize when called. Try reinstalling the application that returned the error. | DAO |
| 3448 | A call to an OLE system function was not successful. Try reinstalling the application that returned the error. | DAO |
| 3449 | No country code was found in the connect string for an attached table. | ISAM |
| 3450 | Syntax error in query. Incomplete query clause. | EXTENDED |
| 3451 | Illegal reference in query. | EXTENDED |
| 3452 | You cannot make changes to the design of the database at this replica. | REPLICATOR |
| 3453 | You can't establish or maintain a relationship between a replicated table and local table. | REPLICATOR |
| 3454 | * | UNUSED |
| 3455 | Cannot make the database replicable. | REPLICATOR |
| 3456 | Cannot make the '\|2' object in '\|1' container replicable. | REPLICATOR |
| 3457 | You cannot set the KeepLocal Property for an object that is already replicable. | REPLICATOR |
| 3458 | The KeepLocal Property cannot be set on a database; it can be set only on the objects in a database. | REPLICATOR |
| 3459 | Once a database has been made replicable, it cannot be made unreplicable. | REPLICATOR |
| 3460 | The operation you attempted conflicts with an existing operation involving the replica. | REPLICATOR |
| 3461 | The replication property you are attempting to set or delete is read-only and cannot be changed. | REPLICATOR |
| 3462 | Failure to load a transport .DLL. | REPLICATOR |
| 3463 | Cannot find the .DLL '\|2'. | EXTENDED |
| 3464 | Data type mismatch in criteria expression. | EXTENDED |
| 3465 | The disk drive you are attempting to access is unreadable. | EXTENDED |
| 3466 | * | EXTENDED |
| 3467 | * | EXTENDED |
| 3468 | Access was denied while accessing dropbox '\|2'. | EXTENDED |
| 3469 | The disk for dropbox '\|2' is full. | EXTENDED |
| 3470 | Disk failure accessing dropbox '\|2'. | EXTENDED |
| 3471 | Failure to write to the Transporter log file. | ISAM |
| 3472 | Disk full for path '\|1'. | EXTENDED |

| Error number | Microsoft Jet error message | Class (*cont'd*) |
| --- | --- | --- |
| 3473 | Disk failure while accessing log file '\|1'. | EXTENDED |
| 3474 | Can't open the log file '\|1' for writing. | EXTENDED |
| 3475 | Sharing violation while attempting to open log file '\|1' in deny write mode. | EXTENDED |
| 3476 | Invalid dropbox path '\|2'. | EXTENDED |
| 3477 | Dropbox address '\|2' is syntactically invalid. | EXTENDED |
| 3478 | The replica is not a partial replica. | REPLICATOR |
| 3479 | Cannot make a partial replica the Design Master for the replica set. | REPLICATOR |
| 3480 | The relationship '\|' in the partial filter expression is invalid. | EXTENDED |
| 3481 | The table name '\|' in the partial filter expression is invalid. | EXTENDED |
| 3482 | The filter expression for the partial replica is invalid. | REPLICATOR |
| 3483 | The password supplied for the dropbox '\|2' is invalid. | EXTENDED |
| 3484 | The password used by the Transporter to write to a destination dropbox is invalid. | REPLICATOR |
| 3485 | The object cannot be made replicable because the database is not replicable. | REPLICATOR |
| 3486 | You cannot add a second ReplicationID Autonumber field to a table. | REPLICATOR |
| 3487 | The database you are attempting to make replicable cannot be converted. | REPLICATOR |
| 3488 | The value specified is not a ReplicaID for any replica in the replica set. | REPLICATOR |
| 3489 | The object specified is not replicable because it is missing a necessary resource. | REPLICATOR |
| 3490 | Cannot make a new replica because the '\|2' object in '\|1' container could not be made replicable. | REPLICATOR |
| 3491 | The database must be opened in exclusive mode before it can be made replicable. | REPLICATOR |
| 3492 | The synchronization failed because a design change could not be applied to one of the replicas. | REPLICATOR |
| 3493 | Can't set the specified Registry parameter for the Transporter. | REPLICATOR |
| 3494 | Unable to retrieve the specified Registry parameter for the Transporter. | REPLICATOR |
| 3495 | There are no scheduled exchanges between the two Transporters. | REPLICATOR |
| 3496 | The Replication Manager cannot find the ExchangeID in the MSysExchangeLog table. | REPLICATOR |
| 3497 | Unable to set a schedule for the Transporter. | REPLICATOR |
| 3498 | * | UNUSED |
| 3499 | Can't retrieve the full path information for a replica. | REPLICATOR |
| 3500 | Setting an exchange with the same Transporter is not allowed. | REPLICATOR |
| 3501 | * | UNUSED |
| 3502 | The replica is not being managed by a transporter. | REPLICATOR |

| Error number | Microsoft Jet error message | Class (*cont'd*) |
|---|---|---|
| 3503 | The Transporter's system registry has no value set for the key you queried. | REPLICATOR |
| 3504 | The Transporter ID does not match an existing ID in the MSysTranspAddress table. | REPLICATOR |
| 3505 | You attempted to delete or get information about a partial filter that does not exist in MSysFilters. | REPLICATOR |
| 3506 | The Transporter is unable to open the transporter log. | REPLICATOR |
| 3507 | Failure writing to the Transporter log. | REPLICATOR |
| 3508 | There is no active transport for the Transporter. | REPLICATOR |
| 3509 | Could not find a valid transport for this Transporter. | REPLICATOR |
| 3510 | The replica you are attempting to exchange with is currently being used in another exchange. | REPLICATOR |
| 3511 | * | UNUSED |
| 3512 | Failure to read the transport dropbox. | REPLICATOR |
| 3513 | Transport failed to write to a dropbox. | REPLICATOR |
| 3514 | Transporter could not find any scheduled or on-demand exchanges to process. | REPLICATOR |
| 3515 | The Jet database engine could not find the system clock on your computer. | REPLICATOR |
| 3516 | Could not find transport address. | REPLICATOR |
| 3517 | Transporter could not find any messages to process. | REPLICATOR |
| 3518 | Could not find Transporter in the MSysTranspAddress table. | REPLICATOR |
| 3519 | Transport failed to send a message. | REPLICATOR |
| 3520 | The replica name or ID does not match a currently managed replica. | REPLICATOR |
| 3521 | The two replicas cannot be synchronized because there is no common point to start the synchronization. | REPLICATOR |
| 3522 | The Transporter cannot find the record of a specific exchange in the MSysExchangeLog table. | REPLICATOR |
| 3523 | The Transporter cannot find a specific version number in the MSysSchChange table. | REPLICATOR |
| 3524 | The history of design changes in the replica does not match the history in the design-master replica. | REPLICATOR |
| 3525 | Transporter could not access the message database. | REPLICATOR |
| 3526 | The name selected for the system object is already in use. | REPLICATOR |
| 3527 | The Transporter or Replication Manager could not find the system object. | REPLICATOR |
| 3528 | There is no new data in shared memory for the Transporter or Replication Manager to read. | REPLICATOR |
| 3529 | The Transporter or Replication Manager found previous data in the shared memory. The existing data will be overwritten. | REPLICATOR |

| Error number | Microsoft Jet error message | Class (*cont'd*) |
|---|---|---|
| 3530 | The Transporter is already serving a client. | REPLICATOR |
| 3531 | The wait period for an event has timed-out. | REPLICATOR |
| 3532 | Transport could not be initialized. | REPLICATOR |
| 3533 | The system object used by a process still exists after the process has stopped. | REPLICATOR |
| 3534 | Transporter looked for system event but did not find one to report to client. | REPLICATOR |
| 3535 | Client has asked the Transporter to terminate operation. | REPLICATOR |
| 3536 | Transporter received an invalid message for a replica it manages. | REPLICATOR |
| 3537 | The Transporter's client is no longer present and cannot be notified. | REPLICATOR |
| 3538 | Cannot initialize Transporter because there are too many applications running. | REPLICATOR |
| 3539 | A system error has occurred in the disk I/O for a system drive or your page file has reached its limit. | REPLICATOR |
| 3540 | Your page file has reached its limit or is corrupted. | REPLICATOR |
| 3541 | The Transporter could not be shut down properly and is still active. | REPLICATOR |
| 3542 | Process aborted when attempting to terminate Transporter client. | REPLICATOR |
| 3543 | Transporter has not been set up. | REPLICATOR |
| 3544 | The Transporter is already running. | REPLICATOR |
| 3545 | The two replicas you are attempting to synchronize are from different replica sets. | REPLICATOR |
| 3546 | The type of exchange you are attempting is not valid. | REPLICATOR |
| 3547 | The Transporter could not find a replica from the correct set to complete the exchange. | REPLICATOR |
| 3548 | GUIDs do not match or the requested GUID could not be found. | REPLICATOR |
| 3549 | The file name you provided is too long. | REPLICATOR |
| 3550 | There is no index on the Guid column. | REPLICATOR |
| 3551 | Unable to delete the specified registry parameter for the Transporter. | REPLICATOR |
| 3552 | The size of the registry parameter exceeds the maximum allowed. | REPLICATOR |
| 3553 | The GUID could not be created. | REPLICATOR |
| 3554 | * | UNUSED |
| 3555 | All valid nicknames for replicas are already in use. | REPLICATOR |
| 3556 | Invalid path for destination dropbox. | REPLICATOR |
| 3557 | Invalid address for destination dropbox. | REPLICATOR |
| 3558 | Disk I/O error at destination dropbox. | REPLICATOR |
| 3559 | Failure to write because destination disk is full. | REPLICATOR |

| Error number | Microsoft Jet error message | Class (*cont'd*) |
|---|---|---|
| 3560 | The two replicas you are attempting to synchronize have the same ReplicaID. | REPLICATOR |
| 3561 | The two replicas you are attempting to synchronize both have design-master status. | REPLICATOR |
| 3562 | Access denied at destination dropbox. | REPLICATOR |
| 3563 | Fatal error accessing a local dropbox. | REPLICATOR |
| 3564 | Transporter cannot find the source file for messages. | REPLICATOR |
| 3565 | There is a sharing violation in the source dropbox because the message database is open in another application. | REPLICATOR |
| 3566 | Network I/O error. | REPLICATOR |
| 3567 | Message in dropbox belongs to the wrong Transporter. | REPLICATOR |
| 3568 | Transporter could not delete a file. | REPLICATOR |
| 3569 | The replica has been logically removed from the replica set and is no longer available. | REPLICATOR |
| 3570 | The filters defining a partial replica are out of synch with each other. | REPLICATOR |
| 3571 | The attempt to set a column in a partial replica violated a rule governing partial replicas. | REPLICATOR |
| 3572 | A disk I/O error occurred while reading or writing to the TEMP directory. | REPLICATOR |
| 3573 | The directory you queried for a list of replicas is not a managed directory. | REPLICATOR |
| 3574 | The ReplicaID for this replica was reassigned during a move or copy procedure. | REPLICATOR |
| 3575 | The disk drive you are attempting to write to is full. | EXTENDED |
| 3576 | The database you are attempting to open is already in use by another application. | EXTENDED |
| 3577 | Can't update replication system column. | EXTENDED |
| 3578 | Failure to replicate database; can't determine whether database is open in exclusive mode. | EXTENDED |
| 3579 | Could not create replication system tables needed to make the database replicable. | EXTENDED |
| 3580 | Could not add rows needed to make the database replicable. | EXTENDED |
| 3581 | Can't open replication system table '|' because the table is already in use. | EXTENDED |
| 3582 | Cannot make a new replica because the '|2' object in '|1' container could not be made replicable. | EXTENDED |
| 3583 | Cannot make the '|2' object in '|1' container replicable. | EXTENDED |
| 3584 | Insufficient memory to complete operation. | EXTENDED |
| 3585 | Can't replicate the table; the number of columns exceeds the maximum allowed. | EXTENDED |

| Error number | Microsoft Jet error message | Class (*cont'd*) |
|---|---|---|
| 3586 | Syntax error in partial filter expression. | EXTENDED |
| 3587 | Unknown token in partial filter expression. | EXTENDED |
| 3588 | Error when evaluating the partial filter expression. | EXTENDED |
| 3589 | The partial filter expression contains an unknown function. | EXTENDED |
| 3590 | Violates the rules for partial replicas. | EXTENDED |
| 3591 | Log file path '|1' is invalid. | EXTENDED |
| 3592 | You cannot make a password-protected database replicable or set password protection on a replicable database. | REPLICATOR |
| 3593 | Can't change a replicable database from allowing multiple data masters to allowing only a single data master. | REPLICATOR |
| 3594 | Can't change a replicable database from allowing only a single data master to allowing multiple data masters. | REPLICATOR |
| 3595 | The system tables in your replica are no longer reliable and the replica should not be used. | REPLICATOR |
| 3596 | * | UNUSED |
| 3597 | * | UNUSED |
| 3598 | * | UNUSED |
| 3599 | * | UNUSED |
| 3600 | Aggregation expressions cannot use GUIDs. | QUERY |
| 3601 | * | UNUSED |
| 3602 | * | UNUSED |
| 3603 | * | UNUSED |
| 3604 | * | UNUSED |
| 3605 | Synchronizing a replicated database with a non-replicated database is not allowed. The '|' database is not replicable. | EXTENDED |
| 3606 | * | REPLICATOR |
| 3607 | The replication property you are attempting to delete is read-only and cannot be removed. | REPLICATOR |
| 3608 | Record length too long for an indexed Paradox table. | ISAM |
| 3609 | No unique index found for referenced field of primary table. | REF INTEGRITY |
| 3610 | Same table ('|') referenced as both source and destination in make table query. | EXTENDED |
| 3611 | Can't execute data definition statements on attached data sources. | QUERY |
| 3612 | Multi-level GROUP BY clause not allowed in a subquery. | QUERY |
| 3613 | Can't create a relationship on attached (or linked) SQL tables. | MISC |

| Error number | Microsoft Jet error message | Class (*cont'd*) |
| --- | --- | --- |
| 3614 | GUID not allowed in Find method criteria expression. | MISC |
| 3615 | Type mismatch in JOIN Expression. | QUERY |
| 3616 | Updating data in an attached (or linked) table not supported by this ISAM. | INST ISAM |
| 3617 | Deleting data in an attached (or linked) table not supported by this ISAM. | INST ISAM |
| 3618 | Exceptions table could not be created on import/export. | MISC |
| 3619 | Records could not be added to Exceptions table. | MISC |
| 3620 | The connection to Excel for viewing your attached worksheet has been lost. Possible cause was that Excel has terminated. | EXCEL |
| 3621 | Can't change password on a shared open database. | ISAM |
| 3622 | You must use the dbSeeChanges option with OpenDatabase when accessing a SQLServer table which has an IDENTITY column. | QUERY |
| 3623 | Cannot access the FoxPro 3.0 bound DBF file '\|'. | EXTENDED |
| 3624 | Couldn't read; currently locked by another session on this machine. | ISAM |
| 3625 | The text file specification '\|' does not exist. You can't import, export, or attach using the specification. | EXTENDED |

# Index

## Special Characters

# O

# Q

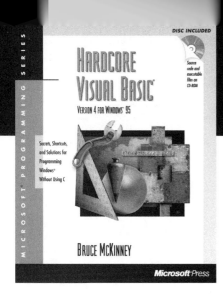

**Unleash the power of Microsoft® Visual Basic® with** HARDCORE VISUAL BASIC!

*Valuable Information Included on CD!*

- Thousands of lines of code that illustrate advanced programming techniques with the Windows API and the new object-oriented features of Visual Basic 4
- The Windows API type library and other useful tools such as Property Shop, Bug Wizard, Time It, and the VBUTIL dynamic-link library

Visual Basic wizard Bruce McKinney shows how to blast through the so-called limits of Visual Basic and reach the powerful object-oriented development tool that lurks within. The result: applications with better performance and more functionality.

HARDCORE VISUAL BASIC provides developers and programmers with detailed coverage of such topics as:

- Exploring the Spirit of Basic — Language purification, the Basic Hungarian naming convention, efficient code versus correct code, and Basic wrappers for un-Basic hacks
- Taking Control of Windows — Calling the Windows® API, understanding C in Basic, and mastering messages and processes
- Programming Objects, Basic Style — Classes and objects, the form class, collecting objects, and creating new controls by delegating to classes
- Painting Pictures — The Basic way of drawing, painting, and animating
- Reusing Code — Modular packages for sorting, shuffling, searching, and parsing; reusable Search, Replace, About, and Color Select forms; classes for editing, animating, managing the keyboard, handling menus, and sharing memory between programs
- Programming in Different Environments — Code for MS-DOS®, Windows 3.1, Windows 95, Windows NT™, and OLE

If you want to push Visual Basic to the max, HARDCORE VISUAL BASIC is your guide— it's essential for any serious Visual Basic programmer's library.

*"HARDCORE VISUAL BASIC is a book for people who like Basic but don't like limits. It's for people who won't take no for an answer. If you're willing to go the extra mile for better performance and more functionality, you'll have fun with this book."*

—*Bruce McKinney*

Microsoft Press® books are available wherever quality books are sold and through CompuServe's Electronic Mall—GO MSP. Call 1-800-MSPRESS for more information or to place a credit card order.* Please refer to BBK when placing your order. Prices subject to change.

*In Canada, contact Macmillan Canada, Attn: Microsoft Press Dept., 164 Commander Blvd., Agincourt, Ontario, Canada M1S 3C7, or call 1-800-667-1115. Outside the U.S. and Canada, write to International Coordinator, Microsoft Press, One Microsoft Way, Redmond, WA 98052-6399, or fax +1-206-936-7329.

ISBN 1-55615-667-7
664 pages, one CD-ROM
$39.95 ($53.95 Canada)

**Microsoft**®Press

# TOUGH DECISIONS
## TO MAKE?
## TURN TO MICROSOFT® TECHNET.

Microsoft TechNet is designed for technical professionals who evaluate and decide on new technology directions, integrate products and platforms, administer enterprise applications and networks, support and train users. Microsoft TechNet is the leading resource for fast, complete answers to technical questions on Microsoft desktop and system products.

Updated monthly, TechNet provides the most complete collection of technical information on Microsoft products anywhere. In one place, you get everything from crucial data on client-server and workgroup computing, systems platforms, and database products to the latest applications support for Microsoft® Windows® and the Macintosh®. Benefits include:

- Twelve monthly Microsoft TechNet CDs containing the complete Microsoft Knowledge Base, product resource kits, datasheets and whitepapers, customer case studies and other valuable technical and strategic information.

- Twelve monthly Microsoft TechNet Supplemental (Drivers and Patches) CDs containing the complete Microsoft Software Library, with drivers for the entire line of Microsoft software products, code samples and patches for many Microsoft products.
- A dedicated Microsoft TechNet CompuServe® forum (GO TECHNET).
- 20% discount on Microsoft Press® books.

Microsoft TechNet is $299 annually for a single-user license, and $699 annually for a single server-unlimited users license. To order Microsoft TechNet, call (800) 344-2121 dept. 3092. Outside of the US and Canada, contact your Microsoft subsidiary, or call (303) 684-0914.

097-000-680

# Register Today!

Return this
*Microsoft® Jet Database Engine
Programmer's Guide*
registration card for a Microsoft Press® catalog

U.S. and Canada addresses only. Fill in information below and mail postage-free. Please mail only the bottom half of this page.

1-55615-877-7A    *Microsoft Jet Database Engine Programmer's Guide*    *Owner Registration Card*

_____
NAME

_____
INSTITUTION OR COMPANY NAME

_____
ADDRESS

_____

_____
CITY                                    STATE          ZIP

# *Microsoft* Press
## *Quality Computer Books*

For a free catalog of
Microsoft Press® products, call
## 1-800-MSPRESS